M000159794

CLINICIAN'S GUIDE TO PSYCHOLOGICAL ASSESSMENT AND TESTING

John M. Spores, PhD, JD, is an associate professor of psychology at Purdue University North Central at Westville, Indiana, and practicing psychologist in the State of Indiana. He is also licensed as an attorney at law. Dr. Spores specializes primarily in the area of psychological assessment and testing. In 1990, he received his PhD in clinical psychology, including a minor in developmental psychology, from Purdue University at West Lafayette, Indiana. He earned his JD degree from Valparaiso University School of Law at Valparaiso, Indiana, which was conferred in 1998.

Spores and his family are Orthodox Christians and members of Saints Constantine and Helen Greek Orthodox Cathedral in Merrillville, Indiana, Father Theodore Poteres, Priest. The Eastern Orthodox Faith plays a fundamental role in his and his family's life.

CLINICIAN'S GUIDE TO PSYCHOLOGICAL ASSESSMENT AND TESTING

WITH FORMS AND TEMPLATES FOR EFFECTIVE PRACTICE

JOHN M. SPORES, PhD, JD

SPRINGER PUBLISHING COMPANY

NEW YORK

Copyright © 2013 Springer Publishing Company, LLC

All rights reserved.

No part of this publication may be reproduced, stored in a retrieval system, or transmitted in any form or by any means, electronic, mechanical, photocopying, recording, or otherwise, without the prior permission of Springer Publishing Company, LLC, or authorization through payment of the appropriate fees to the Copyright Clearance Center, Inc., 222 Rosewood Drive, Danvers, MA 01923, 978–750-8400, fax 978–646-8600, info@copyright.com or on the Web at www.copyright.com.

Springer Publishing Company, LLC
11 West 42nd Street
New York, NY 10036
www.springerpub.com

Acquisitions Editor: Nancy S. Hale
Composition: Newgen Imaging

ISBN: 978-0-8261-9986-7
E-book ISBN: 978-0-8261-9987-4
Digital forms: 978-0-8261-9945-4
Digital versions of the forms found in this book can be obtained at www.springerpub.com/spores

12 13 14 15/ 5 4 3 2 1

The author and the publisher of this Work have made every effort to use sources believed to be reliable to provide information that is accurate and compatible with the standards generally accepted at the time of publication. The author and publisher shall not be liable for any special, consequential, or exemplary damages resulting, in whole or in part, from the readers' use of, or reliance on, the information contained in this book. The publisher has no responsibility for the persistence or accuracy of URLs for external or third-party Internet websites referred to in this publication and does not guarantee that any content on such websites is, or will remain, accurate or appropriate.

Library of Congress Cataloging-in-Publication Data

Spores, John M.
 Clinician's guide to psychological assessment and testing : with forms and templates for effective practice / John M. Spores.
   p. cm.
 Includes index.
 ISBN 978-0-8261-9986-7—ISBN 978-0-8261-9987-4 (ebk)
 1. Psychological tests. 2. Mental illness—Diagnosis. 3. Psychiatric rating scales. I. Title.
 RC473.P79S66 2012
 616.8'0475—dc23

2012026000

Special discounts on bulk quantities of our books are available to corporations, professional associations, pharmaceutical companies, health care organizations, and other qualifying groups.

If you are interested in a custom book, including chapters from more than one of our titles, we can provide that service as well.

For details, please contact:
Special Sales Department, Springer Publishing Company, LLC
11 West 42nd Street, 15th Floor, New York, NY 10036–8002s
Phone: 877–687-7476 or 212–431-4370; Fax: 212–941-7842
Email: sales@springerpub.com

Printed in the United States by Gasch Printing.

*To Jesus Christ, Lord and Savior of me and
my loving family Billie, Andrew, and Demetra Spores,
along with our two loyal dogs Max and Moe Spores.*

Contents

SECTION II. STANDARDIZED PSYCHOLOGICAL TESTS: RESULTS AND INTERPRETATION TABLES

Forms, Figures, and Boxes

Preface

Psychological assessment and testing in mental health has changed significantly from the time I began practicing at a master's degree level in 1982. Although most insurance companies value psychological testing for purposes of accurate diagnosis, and consequently more efficacious treatment, they are simultaneously reluctant to approve more than three to five testing hours due to cost control. Additional criteria for test approval include the following: (a) documented presence of diagnostic ambiguity subsequent to diagnostic interview and clinical observations, (b) lack of response to previous intervention, and (c) demonstrated evidence of medical necessity. The latter renders contemporary psychological testing in mental health essentially focused on resolving differential diagnostic issues as defined by the *Diagnostic and Statistical Manual of Mental Disorders, Fourth Edition, Text Revision* (*DSM-IV-TR*) (American Psychiatric Association, 2000), although supplementary referral questions may also be addressed (e.g., the nature and extent of neuropsychological impairment subsequent to traumatic brain injury).

This means that contemporary psychological testing must be sufficiently justified, brief, and well targeted. Tests that comprise the battery must measure clearly defined and validated constructs, including, for example, the various Axis I and II *DSM-IV-TR* diagnoses, intelligence, and adaptive behavior. The included tests must also be remarkably selective, in their most recently published editions, sufficiently standardized and age appropriate, rapidly scored and interpreted, and the essential results reduced to writing in the most effective and efficient manner.

Graduate training in clinical assessment and testing emphasizes the proper administration, scoring, and interpretation of the most frequently used individual cognitive and personality tests, with some training in data integration and report-writing. However, there is a paucity of coverage regarding critical issues necessary for effective testing practice within the mental health field, including, but not limited to, the following: (a) communication with referral sources as to appropriate testing referral questions, (b) judicious selection of tests as determined by diagnostic and referral questions and carefully gleaned diagnostic interview information, (c) type of information to include in the initial psychological assessment report so as to maximize the probability of insurance authorization for a reasonable number of testing hours, (d) determination of the order of test administration, and (e) organization of the final psychological evaluation report. The latter includes structuring the order and format of essential test results and associated interpretations, effectively presenting the final *DSM-IV-TR* diagnoses, answering supplementary referral questions, and deriving logically inferred and succinct treatment recommendations.

Based upon the completion of more than 2,500 psychological and neuropsychological evaluations which have involved formal standardized testing, including cases ranging in age from approximately 2 to 92 years, I have developed: (a) a standard process of assessment, testing, report-writing, and feedback to patients; and (b) a cohesive test inventory that effectively addresses most *DSM-IV-TR* diagnostic dilemmas and a broad range of related referral questions for the aforementioned age range. The former includes hard copy and electronic versions of referral and related forms, and initial psychological assessment reports for child and adult cases, including critical areas of coverage for purposes of obtaining insurance approval of testing hours. The latter includes hard copy and electronic templates of results and interpretation tables for all tests included in the aforementioned inventory for purposes of rapid and efficient integration into the final psychological evaluation report.

My principal goal in writing this book is to provide psychologists with the practical tools needed for the effective and efficient practice of psychological assessment and testing within contemporary mental health. The corollary is to improve the quality and accuracy of psychodiagnosis, and to adequately address associated referral questions, for the ultimate purpose of more effectively guiding treatment intervention and reducing human suffering.

This book is primarily written for currently practicing clinical and counseling psychologists with a desire to practice assessment and testing either full- or part-time within the mental health field. It is also appropriate for graduate students who are in the advanced stages of training within these specialty areas. The principles and information presented in this book, however, may be generalized to other areas of assessment and testing practice (e.g., school psychology).

REFERENCE

American Psychiatric Association. (2000). *Diagnostic and statistical manual of mental disorders (4th ed., text rev.).* Washington, DC: Author.

Acknowledgments

First and foremost, I would like to thank Beth Stauffer, my office manager, whose invaluable and assiduous work has assisted me in implementing the psychological testing process (see Chapters 1–3) presented in this book. Additional thanks go to Jean Hickman, RN, who for years advised me regarding the proper and effective manner of obtaining insurance authorization for psychological testing cases. Her sage advice is well represented in this book and has endured over the years. I would also like to express appreciation to my colleague Kimberly L. Brunt, PhD, who reviewed my manuscript on several occasions, and provided constructive commentary and encouragement.

Lastly, I express my sincere appreciation to all of the staff at Springer Publishing Company who assisted in this project, including most especially Nancy S. Hale, Editorial Director, Social Sciences, along with Kathryn Corasaniti, Associate Editor and Lindsay Claire, Managing Editor.

Introduction

THE NECESSITY OF STANDARDIZED TESTING FOR ACCURATE ASSESSMENT AND DIAGNOSIS

The *clinical method* of psychological assessment typically employs a semi-structured interview to gather detailed information regarding a patient's presenting symptoms, current mental status, and developmental history. The clinician relies on experience and expert judgment in arriving at diagnostic impressions and treatment recommendations. In the field of mental health, psychiatrists, clinical social workers, psychiatric nurse practitioners, master's- level mental health clinicians, and many doctoral-level psychologists who do not utilize standardized testing all rely primarily on the clinical method.

However, the accuracy and precision of the clinical method is deleteriously affected by numerous factors. Some of these include the clinician's reliance on base rates (e.g., when in doubt diagnose Schizophrenia or Bipolar Disorder on an inpatient unit or Borderline Personality in an outpatient setting), overestimating the accuracy of clinical judgment, being vulnerable to the *hypothesis confirmation bias* in which only that information that corroborates the suspected diagnosis is gathered (Meehl, 1954; Miller, McIntire, & Lovler, 2011), and significant symptom overlap among the various diagnostic categories of the *Diagnostic and Statistical Manual of Mental Disorders, Fourth Edition, Text Revision* (*DSM-IV-TR*) (see e.g., Barlow & Durand, 2012). Response bias on the part of respondents (e.g., acquiescence) and lack of introspection (e.g., see Larsen & Buss, 2010), also contribute to imprecision. Using testing parlance, these factors potentially contribute to a considerable degree of error variance in psychodiagnosis.

Regarding *DSM-IV-TR* diagnoses, a major epidemiological survey indicated that 46.4 % of Americans meet the criteria for a *DSM-IV-TR* disorder at some point in their lifetime (Kessler, Berglund, Demler, Jin, & Walters, 2005). Furthermore, 27.7 % of these manifest comorbidity (Kessler, Berglund, Demler, Jin, & Walters, 2005). The presence of comorbidity and remarkable symptom overlap among the *DSM-IV-TR* diagnostic categories renders accurate diagnosis a daunting challenge when relying solely on the clinical method (Krueger & Markon, 2006).

In particular, many disorders may be masked and remain undiagnosed when employing the clinical method. For example, a child diagnosed with Dysthymic Disorder, Early Onset who is manifesting chronic impairments in attention and concentration, may have comorbid Attention-Deficit/Hyperactivity Disorder, Predominantly Inattentive Type (ADHD–I). Using another example, an adult may have an Axis II Borderline Personality Disorder that is obscured by the more apparent mood cycling of an Axis I Bipolar I Disorder, Mixed Episode.

Moving to a related issue, it is remarkably difficult to discriminate precisely between comparable *DSM-IV-TR* diagnoses using the clinical method, which of course would significantly and negatively impact treatment outcome. Anecdotal evidence of this is reflected within the seemingly innumerable referral questions I have received from my mental health clinical colleagues. Some examples include differentiating the following: (a) Bipolar I Disorder with Psychosis versus Schizophrenia; (b) Cyclothymic Disorder versus Borderline Personality Disorder; (c) Major Depressive Disorder versus Mood Disorder Due to Traumatic Brain Injury; and (d) Major Depressive Disorder with irritability versus Bipolar I Disorder with irritability.

Of final note, the median age of onset for *DSM-IV-TR* disorders is 14 years, with the majority of psychological disorders first manifesting in adolescence and young adulthood (Kessler, Berglund, Demler, Jin, & Walters, 2005). Most experienced clinicians will testify to the observation that many psychological symptoms are generally difficult for people to describe accurately within the context of a clinical interview. After all, many symptoms represent abstractions (i.e., psychological constructs) that must be logically inferred from historical behavior and subjective experience. It is thus reasonable to conclude that such difficulty would be magnified for younger patients including both children and adolescents. Taken together, psychological disorders are common, likely to be comorbid, appear relatively early in life, and are remarkably difficult to accurately diagnose by the exclusive use of the clinical method.

In contrast, the use of standardized psychological testing or the *statistical method* has proven significantly superior in terms of providing reliable and valid diagnoses (Dawes & Corrigan, 1974; Goldberg, 1970; Meehl, 1954; Wiggins, 1973). Furthermore, some diagnoses by definition necessitate standardized testing, including Mental Retardation and Learning Disorders. Similarly, many legitimate referral questions are impossible to address without standardized testing, including for example, identifying the nature and extent of brain damage subsequent to traumatic brain injury (TBI), and the extent of neuropsychological decline in a case of progressive Dementia.

Standardized testing also contends more effectively with issues of response bias on the part of patients and pertinent observers (e.g., parent ratings, self-report ratings). This includes measuring the degree of situational defensiveness, symptom exaggeration or malingering, and inconsistency in responding. Finally, the dimensional nature of psychological disorders is being increasingly recognized (e.g., see Kearney & Trull, 2012). In particular, standardized psychological testing is capable of measuring the degree or severity of *DSM-IV-TR* disorders more precisely than the clinical method. For example, more precise feedback can be afforded to parents regarding cases of mild or high functioning Autistic Disorder, or subclinical levels of Depressive Disorder (i.e., Depressive Disorder Not Otherwise Specified [NOS] or Minor Depressive Disorder).

In practice, the clinical method versus statistical method dichotomy is, to a recognizable extent, artificial (Sawyer, 1966). Diagnoses are arrived at most accurately under the following conditions: (a) the diagnostic interview information gleaned via the clinical method is initially employed to determine a well-targeted and efficient test battery; (b) the ensuing statistical method is employed for objective analysis of reliable and valid trends within the test data; and (c) any alternative interpretations noted within the test data are effectively resolved by reference to the aforementioned diagnostic interview information that provides meaningful diagnostic context (Sawyer, 1966).

Thus, the thesis of this book is that standardized psychological testing or the statistical method, supplemented by the clinical interview method, is requisite for arriving at the most reliable and valid *DSM-IV-TR* diagnoses, for effectively addressing related referral questions, and ultimately for effective treatment planning and intervention. Insurance companies recognize this as evidenced by their relatively consistent approval of a *circumscribed* number of testing hours, which is the product of an effective clinical interview used to justify the requested testing. Such companies reason that the cost of such targeted testing will be offset by more brief and effective treatment.

In my experience, insurance companies will most frequently approve between three and five testing hours, assuming the following have been demonstrated: (a) the presence of diagnostic ambiguity subsequent to clinical interview and observations; (b) the presence of *medical necessity* (i.e., differential *DSM-IV-TR* diagnosis); and, finally, (c) the documented lack of treatment progress (i.e., for cases in which treatment is already in progress). The second criterion, medical necessity, is based upon the medical model. It fundamentally includes the need for accurate *DSM-IV-TR* diagnoses, which will ultimately lead to one or more of the following: (a) symptom alleviation; (b) improvement in overall functioning; (c) prevention of deterioration; and/or (d) restoration of an expected level of development in children (Essential Learning, 2011). Taken together, this pragmatically means that psychological testing must be medically justified, targeted, and exceptionally efficient in terms of test administration, scoring, interpretation, and report writing.

REASONS MENTAL HEALTH PRACTITIONERS DO NOT UTILIZE STANDARDIZED PSYCHOLOGICAL TESTING

Perhaps the most frequent reason mental health clinicians do not employ standardized testing is that they lack such training. Psychiatrists, clinical social workers, and nurse practitioners are simply not trained in psychometrics and standardized testing. Licensed mental health clinicians (LMHC) with master's-level training in clinical or counseling psychology are in most cases precluded by third-party payors from providing standardized testing. Therefore, all of these mental health clinicians employ the clinical method of gathering information, conceptualizing a case in terms of one or more theories of psychopathology (e.g., biological, psychodynamic, cognitive-behavioral, family systems, eclectic), arriving at *DSM-IV-TR* diagnoses using clinical experience and expertise, and providing treatment accordingly.

On the other hand, many practicing clinical and counseling psychologists who are adequately trained in the statistical method provide little or no testing services. Instead, they prefer the clinical method for assessment and treatment. I believe there are several unfortunate yet compelling reasons for this eventuality.

First, graduate training in psychological assessment and testing does not adequately address issues of efficiency. Instead, students are typically trained to administer, score, interpret, and integrate all aspects of various common individual tests, including detailed and comprehensive analyses of examinees' strengths and weaknesses. I believe there is an insufficient amount of training that addresses the process of selecting an efficient test battery contingent on well-specified diagnostic issues, and in determining which test scores are most critical to report and interpret in a particular case. Furthermore, there does not exist a standard format or uniform style for writing psychological evaluation reports comparable to that of journal articles in psychology (see e.g., American Psychological Association, 2010). Reports tend to include ponderous and protracted narrative interpretations that are unnecessarily redundant, tend not to refer directly to standardized scores, are excessively tentative (e.g., "…which may suggest the possibility of or a potential for depression"), are consequently diagnostically ambiguous and obscure, and most pertinently, require excessive time.

Second, psychologists continue to practice standardized testing consistent with their graduate training. Insufficient training in brief and targeted testing contributes to the following: (a) selecting an excessive, overly inclusive, and redundant test battery and (b) requesting an excessive number of testing hours (e.g., 8 or 10 hours for a single case). Insurance companies are correctly cynical of such requests and may even perceive them as an abuse of the mental health care system (i.e., as a means of artificially enhancing billable hours). This increases the likelihood of either an outright denial of testing, or the approval of significantly reduced testing hours (e.g., 1 or 2 hours). This also has a deleterious effect on testing approval for future cases. Thus, psychologists must choose between providing significantly more service hours versus hours reimbursed, or simply not completing the planned test battery. Neither alternative is palatable or reinforcing and a consequential resort to the clinical method is the corollary.

Compounding matters is the paucity of available training resources in psychological assessment and testing that address practical issues of efficiency. The majority of professional books and continuing education seminars are clinical-method oriented and treatment focused for various disorders, symptoms, and problem behaviors. Those that do address testing emphasize the proper administration, scoring, and interpretation of individual tests (see e.g., McCann, 1999).

PURPOSES, INTENDED AUDIENCE, AND ORGANIZATION OF THIS BOOK

This book is essentially a clinical guide in psychological assessment and efficient standardized testing in the field of mental health for purposes of (a) making the most reliable and valid *DSM-IV-TR* differential diagnoses, (b) effectively addressing related and proper referral questions, and (c) making pertinent and succinct treatment recommendations. This book is intended for practicing clinical and counseling psychologists who possess a desire to provide full- or part-time testing services. It is also directly applicable to advanced graduate students in these specialty areas as a supplement to their training in administering, scoring, interpreting, and reporting the results of individual tests. Finally, portions of the book (e.g., the process of testing, organization of the initial and final reports) may be of assistance to school psychologists who conduct testing within the educational system, and psychologists who administer standardized tests in industrial and organizational settings. I assume that the reader is sufficiently trained in diagnostic interviewing, psychometrics, and administering and scoring the various standardized tests presented and discussed in this book.

Section I comprises the first three chapters and is devoted to discussing the *process* of assessment and standardized testing from initiation to completion. More specifically, Chapter 1 outlines this process and provides a step-by-step flowchart. Chapter 2 describes the referral for testing process and completion of the initial psychological assessment report. It is supplemented by various forms and report templates. Chapter 3 describes test administration, scoring, simultaneous interpretation and report writing, and communication of the results. Modifications to the initial report are outlined and discussed, with an emphasis on the manner in which the scoring and interpretation tables for all tests presented throughout Section II of the book are to be incorporated into the final report. The espoused strategy is to maximize the scientific presentation of standardized test scores and their diagnostic meaning, while minimizing report writing time. It also provides a uniform system for composing the final report.

Section II discusses all of the standardized tests covered in this book. Each individual chapter covers a separate classification of tests and provides the following: (a) definitions of pertinent psychological constructs and their measurement; (b) diagnostic reasons for inclusion within a test battery; (c) administration, scoring, and interpretation strategies to maximize the efficiency and accuracy of diagnosis and addressing referral questions; and (d) tabular templates for presenting scores and their interpretations within the final report.

The classification of tests by chapter includes the following: Intelligence Tests (Chapter 4); Achievement Tests (Chapter 5); Neuropsychological Tests (Chapter 6); Symptom Rating Scales (Chapter 7); Self-Report Clinical and Personality Inventories (Chapter 8); Personality Tests (Chapter 9); and Adaptive Behavior Tests (Chapter 10). Note that this taxonomy is based upon an integration of test type and format. Tests comprising my selected inventory were intentionally chosen for purposes of maximizing efficiency and minimizing costs, while addressing the broadest range of *DSM-IV-TR* diagnostic issues and frequently related referral questions.

Section III presents a sampling of cases classified by chronological age including children (Chapter 11), adolescents (Chapter 12), and adults (Chapter 13). These cases are discussed from the point of referral to the completion of the final report. Their purpose is to demonstrate the manner in which this assessment and testing system is intended to be applied in actual practice. A concluding Chapter 14 covers a special forensic report template and case example for conducting competence to stand trial criminal examinations. I believe that standardized psychological testing is of unique assistance to courts in resolving this legal issue. In particular, such testing is capable of presenting critical scientific data in these cases with greater precision as compared to psychiatric examinations that are based largely upon the clinical method.

Lastly, all of the forms, report templates, and test results and interpretation templates presented throughout this book in hard copy are available in modifiable electronic form on the Springer Publishing Company website at www.springerpub.com/spores. However, a formatting note is in order here. While the hard copy and electronic versions are identical in substance, there exist some page formatting differences. First, you will note some differences in font, indents, headers, and punctuation. Second, and more apparent, the electronic test results and interpretation tables include horizontal and vertical lines in order to clearly demarcate the row indices, scales, subscales, and variables from the column test scores and summary score and variable descriptions. The latter were inserted because the electronic versions are intended to be practice-oriented and more easily read by practitioners and laypersons who are not accustomed to reading and interpreting large data sets. I believe these internal lines, while not being strictly APA style format (American Psychological Association, 2010), are more reader-friendly to the majority of individuals who will ultimately read the testing reports. Of course, testing psychologists using these electronic forms may simply delete these internal lines at their discretion.

REFERENCES

American Psychiatric Association. (2000). *Diagnostic and statistical manual of mental disorders (4th ed., text rev.).* Washington, DC: Author.

American Psychological Association. (2010). *Publication manual of the American Psychological Association* (6th ed.). Washington, DC: Author.

Barlow, D. H., & Durand, M. V. (2012). *Abnormal psychology: An integrative approach* (6th ed.). Belmont, CA: Wadsworth, Cengage Learning.

Dawes, R. M., & Corrigan, B. (1974). Linear models in decision making. *Psychological Bulletin, 81,* 95–106.

Essential Learning. (2011). Service delivery and documentation training. Author. Retrieved from http://www.essentiallearning.net

Kearney, C. A., & Trull, T. J. (2012). *Abnormal psychology and life: A dimensional approach.* Belmont, CA: Wadsworth, Cengage Learning.

Kessler, R. C., Berglund, P., Demler, O., Jin, R., & Walters, E. E. (2005). Lifetime prevalence and age-of-onset distributions of DSM–IV disorders in the national Comorbidity Survey Replication. *Archives of General Psychiatry, 62,* 593–602.

Krueger, R. F., & Markon, K. E. (2006). Reinterpreting comorbidity: A model-based approach to understanding and classifying psychopathology. *Annual Review of Clinical Psychology, 2,* 111–133.

Larsen, R. J., & Buss, D. M. (2010). *Personality psychology: Domains of knowledge about human nature* (4th ed.). New York, NY: McGraw-Hill.

McCann, J. T. (1999). *Assessing adolescents with the MACI; Using the Millon Adolescent Clinical Inventory.* New York, NY: John Wiley & Sons, Inc.

Meehl, P. E. (1954). *Clinical versus statistical prediction: A theoretical analysis and review of the evidence.* Minneapolis, MN: University of Minnesota Press.

Miller, L. A., McIntire, S. A., & Lovler, R. L. (2011). *Foundations of psychological testing* (3rd ed.). Thousand Oaks, CA: SAGE Publications, Inc.

Sawyer, J. (1966). Measurement and prediction, clinical and statistical. *Psychological Bulletin, 66,* 178–200.

Wiggins, J. S. (1973). *Personality and prediction: Principles of personality assessment.* Reading, MA: Addison-Wesley.

Overview of the Assessment and Testing Process

1

THE TESTING PROCESS ANALOGOUS TO SCIENTIFIC RESEARCH IN PSYCHOLOGY

The testing process may be efficaciously analogized to steps followed in conducting scientific research in psychology. The latter is initiated by developing a testable research question or questions, and ends with communication of the results by oral presentation and/or formal written report (see e.g., Graziano & Raulin, 2010). Comparably, the testing process begins with a testable referral question or questions and is completed upon communicating the results in written, and frequently, oral formats. Figure 1.1 presents a flowchart of the major sequential steps in the psychological assessment and testing process. Each step comprises specific actions required, along with the pertinent forms and templates I have prepared. These are enumerated vis-à-vis each step in Figure 1.1 and are further introduced below.

OUTLINE OF THE PSYCHOLOGICAL ASSESSMENT AND TESTING PROCESS

Referral for Testing

The initial referral inaugurates the testing process. Referral sources can be classified as either external to your practice or agency (e.g., pediatrician, school, family member, self) or internal in the event you work within a group practice. In the latter case, the referral source is most probably a mental health clinician and colleague who does not provide psychological testing services (see the Introduction). Essential information in the initial referral step includes (a) clearly specified and appropriate diagnostic and related referral questions and (b) tenable reasons as to why testing is necessitated. I have prepared a succinct single-page referral form for this purpose (see Chapter 2).

Initial Psychological Assessment Report

The primary objective of the ensuing step is to complete an initial psychological assessment report by means of a clinical interview, including mental status examination and behavioral observations. Thus, the clinical method is employed to narrow the differential diagnostic focus, guided by the referral source's diagnostic and referral question(s). This facilitates the selection of a well-targeted test battery and the requesting of a circumscribed number of testing hours for maximum efficiency and effectiveness. I have prepared child and adult templates of the initial report (see Chapter 2) such that it may be completed during the interview process. These templates provide a format for semistructured interviewing and ensure that critical information will be gleaned and documented.

I have prepared a single-page test listing form that enumerates the names, abbreviations, and age ranges (by years:months) of each test in my recommended inventory (see Chapter 2). The tests are catalogued by either psychological construct or test format,

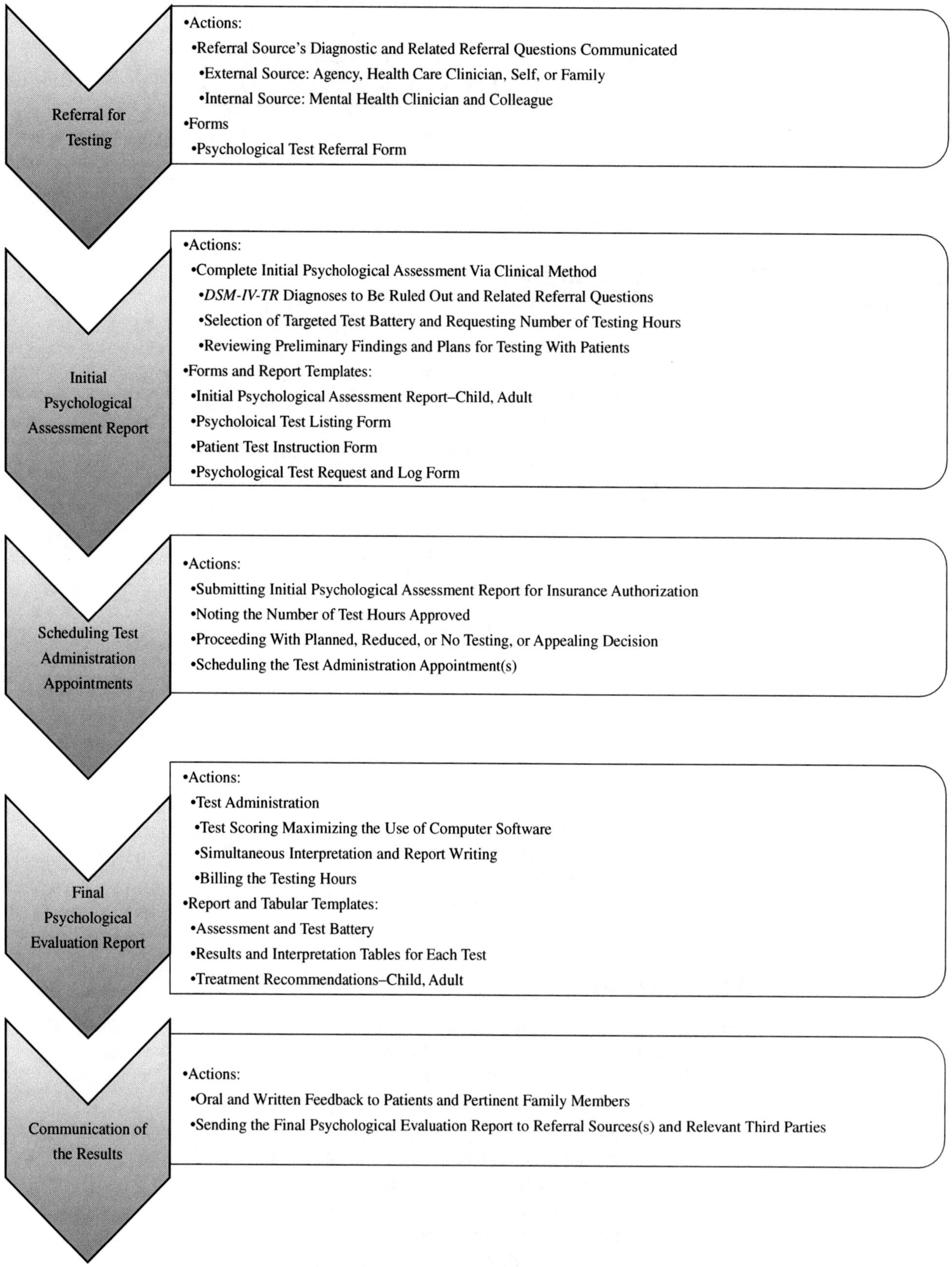

Referral for Testing

- Actions:
  - Referral Source's Diagnostic and Related Referral Questions Communicated
    - External Source: Agency, Health Care Clinician, Self, or Family
    - Internal Source: Mental Health Clinician and Colleague
- Forms
  - Psychological Test Referral Form

Initial Psychological Assessment Report

- Actions:
  - Complete Initial Psychological Assessment Via Clinical Method
    - *DSM-IV-TR* Diagnoses to Be Ruled Out and Related Referral Questions
    - Selection of Targeted Test Battery and Requesting Number of Testing Hours
    - Reviewing Preliminary Findings and Plans for Testing With Patients
- Forms and Report Templates:
  - Initial Psychological Assessment Report–Child, Adult
  - Psycholoical Test Listing Form
  - Patient Test Instruction Form
  - Psychological Test Request and Log Form

Scheduling Test Administration Appointments

- Actions:
  - Submitting Initial Psychological Assessment Report for Insurance Authorization
  - Noting the Number of Test Hours Approved
  - Proceeding With Planned, Reduced, or No Testing, or Appealing Decision
  - Scheduling the Test Administration Appointment(s)

Final Psychological Evaluation Report

- Actions:
  - Test Administration
  - Test Scoring Maximizing the Use of Computer Software
  - Simultaneous Interpretation and Report Writing
  - Billing the Testing Hours
- Report and Tabular Templates:
  - Assessment and Test Battery
  - Results and Interpretation Tables for Each Test
  - Treatment Recommendations–Child, Adult

Communication of the Results

- Actions:
  - Oral and Written Feedback to Patients and Pertinent Family Members
  - Sending the Final Psychological Evaluation Report to Referral Sources(s) and Relevant Third Parties

FIGURE 1.1 ■ **FLOWCHART OF THE ASSESSMENT AND TESTING PROCESS**

selected by whichever identifies them most readily. In addition, patients and pertinent family members should be afforded specific written test instructions such that they remain adequately informed throughout the remaining steps in the process. I have prepared a test instruction form for this purpose (see Chapter 2). Finally, I have prepared a form that is designed to assist the testing psychologist in tracking case progress (see Chapter 2).

Scheduling Test Administration Appointments

The logical next step is obtaining insurance authorization for the requested hours for purposes of scheduling test administration appointments. This is facilitated by immediately submitting the completed initial report. Assuming the request has not exceeded a range of 3 to 5 hours, with the exception of relatively more thorough neuropsychological test batteries (see Chapter 6), third-party payors will routinely approve all or the majority of these hours. In this event, proceeding with the test battery as planned is viable.

Approval of only 1 or 2 hours precipitates more complicated decision making, including proceeding as planned, reducing the test battery, not proceeding with testing, or appealing the decision. Finally, the number and duration of test administration appointments must be scheduled. If proceeding with the planned test battery, this information will already have been determined and communicated to the patient and pertinent family members. Simply scheduling these appointments is all that is required.

Final Psychological Evaluation Report

This step is analogous to running a psychological experiment as designed, ensued by statistical analyses of the results, and finally preparing the manuscript for publication (see e.g., Graziano & Raulin, 2010). Again, with the exception of administering a more in-depth neuropsychological test battery (see Chapter 6), test administration can usually be completed within a single 2-hour session. To maximize efficiency and reduce error variability due to inadvertent mistakes in manual scoring, use of computer-assisted scoring software is essential.

The celerity of the testing process is further enhanced by a method I have designed using simultaneous test interpretation and report writing. First, minor modifications to the initial report are made, including a new final report title, along with the insertion of a template listing the assessment procedures and tests comprising the battery with affixed parenthetical dates of completion (see Chapter 3). One such template is prepared for child cases and one for adult cases.

The body of the final report includes all of the test scores and their succinct interpretations. To complete this most vital section, I have prepared separate tabular templates for each test in my recommended inventory. In general, they include the following components: (a) an initial column listing the most essential indices, scales, subscales, and variables for a test; (b) an ensuing sequence of columns for standard scores; (c) a results column; and (d) a final column defining the measured psychological construct or cluster of symptoms. The majority of tables include pertinent tabular notes identifying standard score means, standard deviations, base rates, and necessary idiosyncratic information for particular variables. The tables are largely accordant with American Psychological Association manuscript style (American Psychological Association, 2010), and are presented and discussed in detail in Section II. Interpretive summaries may be composed by the psychologist and placed strategically between tables to maximize efficiency and minimize writing time.

Finally, I have prepared two templates that include a list of the most frequently applied treatment recommendations for child and adult cases (see Chapter 3). This section is inserted at the end of the final report.

Billing the test hours concludes this penultimate step. Test scoring, interpretation, and report writing should ideally all occur immediately subsequent to the final test administration session. As indicated prior, in most cases only one test administration session will be needed. This permits the billing of all utilized testing hours on this single date of face-to-face service. As an additional advantage, the case data will be fresh in the testing psychologist's memory and thus readily available. In consequence, less time will be needed for reviewing pertinent information.

Communication of the Results

Scheduling a test feedback appointment with the patient and pertinent family members is advisable, although not mandatory. This permits a thorough presentation of the results within a therapeutic context, which is facilitated by immediate reference to the final written report. A copy of the final report should be released to the referral source(s) once it is completed to expedite treatment intervention. Any release form used for this purpose should be HIPPA compliant (Health Insurance Portability and Accountability Act of 1996, 2000; Missouri Bar, 2006). The testing case may be considered complete once communication has been achieved and noted on the case progress form.

SUMMARY

Chapter 1 presented an overview of the psychological testing process from initiation to conclusion. It was intended as a prelude to Chapters 2 and 3, which together explicate the aforementioned steps in significantly more detail, including direct references to the particular forms and report templates alluded to here. Chapter 2 covers the first three steps, from the initial referral to the scheduling of testing appointment(s). Chapter 3 covers test administration through communication of the results.

REFERENCES

American Psychological Association. (2010). *Publication manual of the American Psychological Association* (6th ed.). Washington, DC: Author.

Graziano, A. M., & Raulin, M. L. (2010). *Research methods: A process of inquiry* (7th ed.). Boston, MA: Allyn & Bacon.

Health Insurance Portability and Accountability Act of 1996 (HIPAA), 45 C.F.R. Parts 160 & 164. (2000). Retrieved from http://ecfr.gpoaccess.gov/cgi/t/text/text-idx?c=ecfr&rgn= div5&view=text&node=45: 1.0.1.3.72&idno=45

Missouri Bar. (2006). *HIPAA privacy authorization form.* Jefferson City, MO: Author. Retrieved from http://members.mobar.org/pdfs/publications/public/hipaa.pdf

Referral for Testing, Initial Psychological Assessment Report, and Scheduling Test Administration Appointments

This chapter covers in detail the first three steps outlined in Figure 1.1, including the requisite steps in completing the initial report, and scheduling the test administration appointments. The process begins with properly managing the referral for testing.

REFERRAL FOR TESTING

Assuming you work within a group practice, referral sources may be classified as either external or internal. Common external referral sources include parents, educational institutions and staff, family physicians, pediatricians, neurologists, welfare departments, family services departments, and mental health clinicians in the community who do not provide assessment and testing services.

Internal referral sources largely include mental health clinicians who do not provide psychological testing, including psychiatrists (MD, DO), licensed clinical social workers (MSW, LCSW), nontesting psychologists (PhD, PsyD), licensed mental health clinicians (MA, LMHC), and nurse practitioners (RN). Of course, testing psychologists in individual practice rely exclusively on external referral sources.

In this incipient stage of the testing process, the essential goal is to unequivocally define the referral source's diagnostic and related referral questions. This information focuses and guides the completion of the initial report. Furthermore, the diagnostic and related referral questions must be capable of being empirically addressed by psychological testing.

I have prepared a document titled "Psychological Test Referral Form" (Form 2.1), which facilitates this process. I advise that you review this form with all potential referral sources such that they are completed fully and properly. They can be delivered to you through the patient or pertinent family members, via fax, or U.S. mail. Next, I review the main elements of this form.

Psychological Test Referral Form

This form is designed to be a succinct guide for referral sources to organize their diagnostic questions regarding a case and to avert improper referrals. I assume that all health practitioners have limited time such that a protracted form would discourage referrals. Therefore, this form attempts to achieve a viable balance between obtaining essential referral information and minimizing time to complete the form.

The first portion of the form is devoted to obtaining necessary patient and referral source information. Date of birth is essential to classify the case as child (younger than 18 years) or adult (18 years and older). The referring clinician information is needed for communication of the results, including having a record of that office's case file number for cross-referencing purposes (e.g., citation in a cover letter accompanying the final report).

The middle section presents key selections within a structured checklist format. They permit referring clinicians to quickly indicate (a) whether general psychological testing or more specialized neuropsychological testing is being requested and (b) pertinent reasons for the testing referral. The latter options contain key words and phrases that third-party payors generally consider as acceptable and justifiable for purposes of authorizing test hours. As will become apparent, I have incorporated this same language into the initial report templates for child and adult cases.

The date of the initial behavioral health evaluation (billing code 90801) is primarily needed for internal referrals from mental health clinicians. Many insurance companies will limit the number of initial behavioral health evaluations completed within the same agency or practice to one per annum. The rationale is that the referral for testing is a continuation of the same treatment plan. Thus, in instances of an internal referral, if an initial behavioral health evaluation was indeed completed within a year of the initial psychological assessment session, it should be billed as an individual session (billing code 90806) and considered a continuation of the same treatment plan within the same group practice or agency. This evokes a service coding issue that is in need of further explication.

It is vital that the testing psychologist's service activities remain accordant with their billing codes. It is a well-established precept that the processes of assessment and treatment intervention are inextricably intertwined (see e.g., Corey, 2013; Spiegler & Guevremont, 2010). For instance, the interventions of empathy, and reflection of feeling and content, are frequently employed during an assessment so as to begin the establishment of trust and rapport necessary for both accurate psychodiagnosis and initiating the process of positive behavior change (see e.g., Evans, Hearn, Uhlemann, & Ivey, 2008). Therefore, when using the individual session billing code 90806 to initiate the diagnostic psychological testing process, it is critical to place sufficient documentation of the interventions employed as a continuation of that patient's treatment within the mental health progress note for that session. Some examples include, but are certainly not limited to, the following: (a) *processed issues of concern*, (b) *provided empathy and support*, (c) *employed reframing of negative cognitions*, (d) *provided psychoeducation*, and (e) *provided redirection*. These are all bona fide interventions that also facilitate the assessment process. Diligent and adequately detailed documentation of such interventions along with the patient's responses within the progress note associated with this billing code accomplishes the following: (a) it establishes reasonable agreement between the actual mental health services provided and the 90806 individual billing code and (b) it maximizes the likelihood of reimbursement by third-party payors.

Occasionally, however, some insurance companies will authorize a second initial behavioral health evaluation within the same practice and year, and thus the effort can still be made for such authorization. External referrals do not present such issues, as the initial psychological assessment would be the first session for that autonomous practice or agency and thus properly coded and billed as 90801.

The two subsequent sections of the referral form are in fill-in format. They ask for the referring clinician's current diagnostic impressions or working diagnoses, ensued by diagnoses that the clinician suspects and for which testing is desired (i.e., diagnoses needed to be ruled out). The open-ended format allows flexibility and may be stated concisely or with some elaboration.

A cautionary note immediately follows. It admonishes referring clinicians of testing requests which are routinely denied by third-party payors regarding mental health services, including (a) educational testing for Learning Disorders (see Chapters 4 and 5), (b) vocational testing within the context of career counseling, and (c) psychological testing that is ordered by a court of law (see Chapter 14). The general rationale for denial of these testing requests is lack of *medical necessity* (see the Introduction for a working definition). Regarding the former, testing for Learning Disorders is typically considered to be within the purview of the educational system and to be conducted by school psychologists.

The form ends with an optional open-ended fill-in section permitting the addition of any related referral questions to be addressed by testing. These include, but are not limited to, the following: (a) measurement of a patient's memory abilities, (b) measurement of intellectual functioning, (c) estimating risk for future violence or suicide, and (d) measuring response to treatment intervention in terms of symptom remission (e.g., symptoms of Attention-Deficit/Hyperactivity Disorder [ADHD]).

INITIAL PSYCHOLOGICAL ASSESSMENT REPORT

Information on the "Psychological Test Referral Form" will effectively guide the initial clinical interview and should be referred to during the assessment process.[1] The goal is to complete an initial report that does the following: (a) states provisional diagnoses, (b) confirms those diagnoses to be ruled out by standardized testing, (c) phrases any related referral questions in measurable terms, and (d) requests the most efficacious test battery which will answer the diagnostic and referral questions using the minimum number of testing hours.

To facilitate the process, I have prepared separate initial report templates for child and adult cases, respectively, identified as "Initial Psychological Assessment Report–Child" (Form 2.2) and "Initial Psychological Assessment Report–Adult" (Form 2.3). The available electronic versions can be used to complete the report during the assessment interview. Although they are similar in format, the child version emphasizes and prioritizes presenting symptoms, disorders within the *Diagnostic and Statistical Manual of Mental Disorders, Fourth Edition, Text Revision* (*DSM-IV-TR*) (American Psychiatric Association, 2000), and standardized tests most pertinent to cases younger than age 18 years, along with more developmentally oriented language and inclusion of a separate "Developmental" section. The adult version is better adapted in these areas for those 18 years and older. These report templates are reviewed simultaneously by section. Key differences are noted where appropriate.

Patient Identifying Information

This first section is intentionally succinct and includes name, chronological age in years and months, and date of birth. This information can be obtained from the "Test Referral Form" or directly from the patient and family members.

Referral Information

This section begins with identifying the referral source and reasons for the referral, both of which are provided on the "Test Referral Form." The latter incorporates verbatim language from the form's checklist format. Simply retain those that were selected by the referring clinician and delete those that remained unmarked.

Next, list the *DSM-IV-TR* diagnoses that need to be ruled out, along with the referring clinician's current working diagnosis. Also, note any additional referral questions recorded by the referring clinician and list them in order of priority. You may have to modify these questions somewhat without changing their substance to render them amenable to standardized testing. This information may not be available in cases of self-referral. In this event, delete this portion of the referral information section and proceed directly to the presenting symptoms.

Presenting symptoms are enumerated in order of diagnostic classification, with priority assigned on the basis of both frequency and similarity of symptoms. Note the divergence in ordering between the child and adult "Initial Psychological Assessment Report" templates. The child template presents the following order of headings with their common symptoms: ADHD, ODD/CD, PDD, Mood, Anxiety, PTSD, Psychosis, Neuropsychological,

[1] I assume that your group or individual practice has a consent-to-treat form as part of the intake or admissions process. This form is standard for clinical mental health practice and is not unique to assessment and testing. Thus, I do not include such forms in the interest of reducing the length and scope of this book. Similarly, I do not include a release of information form, as it is also not particular to psychological testing.

and Personality.[2] The order for the adult template is as follows: Mood, Anxiety, PTSD, Psychosis, Neuropsychological, Personality, and ADHD.

Based upon my experience using the clinical method, the selected symptoms are the ones most commonly reported by patients and family members that are most suggestive of each class of disorder. They have been carefully paraphrased in narrative terms based upon more formal *DSM-IV-TR* enumerated criteria (American Psychiatric Association, 2000) so as to indicate the possible presence of these various disorders. The purpose is to enhance the probability of justifying the subsequent testing and to provide some degree of structure to the interview process. Use of the "Test Referral Form" information will permit you to prioritize and adapt the listing for a particular case, and hence reduce valuable interview and writing time. You can easily amend the templates according to your particular referrals and testing cases. Lastly, note that the listing of disorders and their associated symptoms are intentionally phrased in summary terms so as to prevent the interview process from becoming ponderous. Additional symptoms and their disorders may be added as necessary.

The presenting symptoms portion ends with an *onset* course specifier critical for accurately interpreting test data. It should be inquired and recorded for each diagnostic grouping for purposes of reliable and valid diagnosis (e.g., documenting ADHD-type symptoms prior to 7 years of age and identifying premorbid conditions).

Clinical Psychologist

This small section identifies the testing clinician, including name, degree(s), and licensing credentials and numbers. In the State of Indiana wherein I practice, Health Service Provider in Psychology (HSPP) indicates an autonomously functioning psychologist without the need of formal peer supervision. This status, or one equivalent in your state, is a critical credential to list. In the absence of such credential, a supervising psychologist needs to be added to the report.

Mental Status Examination (and Behavioral Observations)

Mental status information covered in both child and adult templates includes the following: (a) affect; (b) mood; (c) thought process and content; (d) short- and long-term memory functioning; (e) sensorium; (f) estimated intellectual functioning based upon verbal skills and reasoning ability; (g) psychotic symptoms; (h) suicidal thoughts, intentions, and plans; and (i) current evidence of self-mutilation and self-harm. The last two assist in assessing imminent danger to self.[3]

Homicidal thoughts may be assessed and added when presenting symptoms include conduct-disordered behaviors, antisocial traits, or a history of violence. However, I do not include them in the report templates as they are less typical and, in my opinion, appear awkward and displaced when reported as being absent without a remarkable history of violent or aggressive behavior.

The remaining mental status examination information is somewhat divergent between the child and adult templates. The child template adds behavioral observations, including activity level for suspected ADHD, and social skills for suspected PDD. Regarding the adult version, I have prepared three extended mental status examination templates that incorporate as many versions of the Mini-Mental State Examination, Second Edition (Folstein, Folstein, White, & Messer, 2010), in the form of results and interpretation tables. The Mini-Mental State Examination, Second Edition (MMSE–2) is normed on individuals aged 18 years 0 months to 100 years 11 months. I most commonly use them for adult neuropsychological test referrals as an effective screening for *DSM-IV-TR* Cognitive Disorders, and disorders due to brain trauma and resulting neuropsychological dysfunction (e.g., Personality Change Due to Head Trauma). Each version may supplant the standard mental status examination section of the adult template. Next, I review these extended mental status examination templates in more detail.

Mental Status Examination Including the Mini-Mental State Examination, Second Edition

The extended templates cover all of the standard mental status examination information reviewed prior, in addition to a results and interpretation table that has been strategically inserted suitable to each version of the MMSE–2. The table is placed immediately subsequent to information regarding affect, mood, and thought, and prior to memory, sensorium, intelligence, and danger to self.

For all three versions, the MMSE–2 is administered and hand-scored simultaneously. It is published in equivalent blue and red forms for purposes of test–retest comparisons. I utilize the blue form when testing a case for the first time, then substitute the red form upon retesting. Hence, the templates identify the blue form because I use it most frequently in practice. The "Level of Consciousness" qualitative item on both forms may be incorporated into the narrative of the mental status examination if deemed clinically useful.

Also, regarding all MMSE–2 versions, I advise using a cutoff score that maximizes detection of a true positive (i.e., sensitivity). To determine such a cutoff, I scrutinized the reported MMSE–2 scores for individuals with documented Dementia for all three versions (Folstein, Folstein, White, & Messer, 2010). The raw score I chose and reported in each tabular template provides 97% confidence that a true case of neuropsychological disorder is recommended for further testing. For convenience, each tabular template reports the raw score cutoff used and the 97% confidence such threshold affords.

Succinctly, the rationale for employing such high confidence is that a patient is typically referred for neuropsychological testing due to prior observations of rather severe symptoms. It is thus in the best interests of the patient to minimize the chances of a false-negative screen due to the dire consequences of precluding or delaying needed treatment.

MMSE–2 Brief Version

The MMSE–2 version assesses the first four cognitive functions in the original MMSE (Folstein, Folstein, & Fanjiang, 2001) with updated norms including registration (i.e., immediate repetition of three unrelated words), orientation to time and place, and recall (i.e., repeating the same recall words with delay and interference of rehearsal; see Form 2.4). Administration time is minimal and hence its primary advantage over the two longer versions. Of a total possible 16 points, the cutoff for screen positive begins at 14 and lower.

A caveat is that the brief version comprises items that are easy to pass, which offsets to some degree the aforementioned high-detection threshold and risks a ceiling effect. Also, administration of fewer items is less reliable as compared to more items (see e.g., Miller, McIntire, & Lovler, 2011). Thus, I advise that you administer the brief version only in cases where limited time precludes administration of one of the longer versions.

MMSE–2 Standard Version

The MMSE–2 Standard Version assesses all of the cognitive functions included in the original MMSE (Folstein, Folstein, & Fanjiang, 2001), with updated norms and some revised items for greater reliability and validity (see Form 2.5). Thus, it adds attention and calculation (i.e., serial sevens), naming objects, repetition of a phrase, comprehending and reproducing three commands in sequence, reading a sentence and reproducing its instruction, writing a sentence, and copying a two-dimensional figure.

Administration time is 5 to 10 minutes with a total possible raw score of 30. The cutoff for the 97% true positive criterion is 27 and lower. While the standard version is more accurate than the brief version, ceiling effects continue to be possible especially if the patient has a satisfactory educational history. Thus, to maximize the chances of a true positive screening decision and substantiate the ordering of a full neuropsychological test battery, I advise administering the MMSE–2 Expanded Version.

MMSE–2 Expanded Version

The MMSE–2 Expanded Version contains two newly developed items added to the standard version, including *Story Memory*, which measures both verbal explicit learning and verbal free immediate recall, and *Symbol–Digit Coding*, which measures both perceptual-motor speed and incidental learning (Folstein et al., 2010; see Form 2.6). Although it adds 10 minutes administration time (totaling about 15 to 20 minutes for the entire expanded version), these items are difficult to perform adequately in the presence of true neuropsychological dysfunction irrespective of education (Folstein et al., 2010).

The total possible raw score is 90 with a positive screen cutoff of 50 and lower. These final two items add a considerable amount of performance points and a commensurate increase in reliability and validity. I advise prioritizing the MMSE–2 Expanded Version in testing referrals involving prominent cognitive presenting symptoms and in all adult neuropsychological testing referrals. Of course, you do have the flexibility of administering the MMSE–2 Standard Version, and should results provide empirical evidence of a positive screening, defer the final two items in the interests of time.

Psychiatric/Medical/Psychological

This section begins with documentation of whether or not an initial mental health assessment (billing code 90801) was completed within the past year. As indicated prior, it is relevant to internal referrals from mental health clinicians and such information is provided by a properly completed "Psychological Test Referral Form" (see Form 2.1). Additional areas covered in this section regard individual and family psychiatric histories (including a selected listing of common disorders), medical functioning, current medications, brain trauma, seizure disorder, major surgeries, vision and hearing, psychotherapy services, and if any past testing has been done. If the last is affirmative, a brief discussion of the type of testing and basic results is indicated, especially if completed within the past several years. Highlighting such information will ultimately facilitate interpretation of the more current testing.

Developmental

This section is included in the child template only, primarily because the information contained therein is most relevant to individuals in their formative years. However, it can be inserted into the adult template if such information is deemed diagnostically important, especially for young adult cases. Areas of coverage include possible prenatal, perinatal, and postnatal complications, neonatal risk factors, and early developmental milestones. Many of the statements are phrased in normal terms, which can be quickly amended upon the gleaning of more aberrant developmental information.

Family

As a rule, the information in this section should be restricted to the following: (a) objective facts regarding the patient's current living situation, including with whom the person lives (e.g., spouse, parents, number of siblings) and (b) diagnostically pertinent, although potentially disputatious, historical or recent stressors impinging on the patient or family system. The latter are important to note when stress-related disorders are being considered in differential diagnosis (e.g., Adjustment Disorders, PTSD, and Acute Stress Disorder).

A caveat here is that such stressors should be phrased prudently using nonspecific terms and invariably preceded by the qualifying word *reported*, such as "There is a *reported* history of child neglect" or "There is currently some *reported* unresolved conflict within the parental dyad." This qualifying word communicates to readers that you are basing your assessment on interviewees' statements or archival records for the purpose of facilitating diagnosis, not as an offer of proof or of objective fact. This tenet applies wherever you decide to place such information, whether it be in this "Family" section or among the presenting symptoms. Following this rule will effectively attenuate the odds that your report will be used to inflame family and legal disputes, while retaining its diagnostic value.

Interpersonal

This section focuses on significant nonfamily relationships. Regardless of whether it is a child or adult case, you essentially want to document whether or not such relationships have been satisfactory in terms of quality or intimacy, and secondarily in terms of quantity. In case of poor quality and quantity, some comments regarding the suspected reason(s) are indicated, including ineffectual social skills, chronic mistrust, fear of rejection, excessive dependency, or simply being associated with the presenting symptoms. If you effectively document remarkable interpersonal trends, this section may be both pithy and diagnostically efficacious.

Educational

The information covered in this section varies somewhat in emphasis between the child and adult templates. The former highlights the current grade level, differentiates academic and behavioral performance, grade retention, and special education services and classification (i.e., learning disability [LD], emotional handicap [EH]). The latter prioritizes total years of formal education (critical for determining proper neuropsychological testing norms), date of high school graduation, academic performance, grade retention, and special education services and classification.

Vocational

The default on the child template is "None," because this will be accurate in the majority of child cases. If an adolescent is employed, his or her work history will not be extensive and the information may be entered in succinct fashion. The adult form presents the most common alternatives, including current or past occupation, job status (i.e., unemployed, retired), and the general course of work history (e.g., consistent, sparse, erratic).

Substance Abuse

The default for both child and adult forms is "Unremarkable." The reason is that the majority of testing referrals, especially those from mental health clinicians, have already addressed whether or not a substance-related disorder exists and do not reference this as a diagnostic question. This is due to the fact that the clinical method is useful for diagnosing substance-related disorders, including the discernment of normal use, abuse, and dependence (Barlow & Durand, 2012). The most frequent differential diagnostic testing referral questions regarding substance abuse include ruling out the following: (a) Substance-Induced Persisting Dementia and Amnestic Disorder and (b) risk for later development of substance abuse and dependence based upon current Axis I and II psychopathology (including family history). If remarkable, this information can usually be summarized from the information recorded by the referring clinician on the "Psychological Test Referral Form" under "Current working diagnosis(es)."

Legal

If you practice in general mental health, the most frequent entry for both child and adult cases regarding legal criminal history will most likely be "Unremarkable." Thus, I have recorded this as the default wording. In the event you regularly receive testing cases that ask you to rule out Conduct Disorder and Antisocial Personality Disorder, I recommend that you create a custom-designed template for this section of the report to reduce typing time.

Initial Assessment Summary

This penultimate section of the "Initial Psychological Assessment Report" first incorporates the final section by reference, which enumerates the current provisional working *DSM-IV-TR* diagnosis(es), ensued by those that need to be *ruled out* (i.e., tested for whether or not they exist). It then provides a rationale for requesting standardized testing, beginning with the need to rule out the stated *DSM-IV-TR* disorders, addressing any related referral questions noted in the "Referral Information" section, and, particularly concerning neuropsychological testing referrals, empirically measuring the nature and extent of neuropsychological deficits for purposes of treatment planning. The latter recognizes the dimensional facet of Cognitive Disorders in terms of differentiating mild, moderate, and severe cases critical for treatment planning and resolving placement decisions (e.g., independent living, assisted living, nursing home care).

Immediately subsequent is an enumeration of all the standardized tests contained in my recommended inventory, differentiated on the basis of child (18 years and younger) and adult (18 years and older). Specific test information includes test name, abbreviation, form, type of subtest battery, if applicable (e.g., full battery, screening battery), and *maximum* estimated hours per test. I advise not exceeding these estimates, and reducing them as frequently as is feasible in order to remain within a 3- to 5-hour range. Although the proper age range for some of the child tests may be determined by the form's name, this information is generally not available on the "Initial Psychological Assessment Report" templates as it would become ponderous.

However, the age range for which each test has been standardized is available on the "Psychological Test Listing Form" (see Form 2.7) and should be readily available to the psychologist during the initial psychological assessment process if needed to facilitate the proper selection of tests. The tests are classified by either psychological construct or test format, whichever way they are most readily identified and are enumerated in the same order as presented in Section II of this book. Specific information recorded on this form includes test name, abbreviation, and age range in years and months.

Although a request for one additional test hour for purposes of data integration and report composition is also listed, I am currently using this infrequently if not at all because it is not likely to be approved. It is probable that I will eventually remove this option from the templates as it simply affords insurance companies an opportunity to reduce your request by 1 hour. Therefore, I believe this time is more effectively incorporated into the time estimate for each individual test or combination of tests, which should be coded as either neuro-psychological testing (billing code 96118) or standard psychological testing (billing code 96101). An issue for which there currently does not exist uniform guidelines regards the most accurate means of assigning these dichotomous billing codes to the number of testing hours requested. Thus, I shall next enumerate several billing code assignment strategies.

In my experience, there are four viable strategies for assigning the two billing codes to the requested testing hours. Succinctly, they include the following: (a) If any test in the battery is neuropsychological, code all requested testing hours as neuropsychological (i.e., billing code 96118), otherwise code them all as standard psychological testing (i.e., billing code 96101). (b) Differentiate the requested testing hours by their fundamental design using the "Psychological Test Listing Form" (Form 2.7) as your guide. (c) Code all testing hours according to the prevailing diagnostic issues and any related questions. (d) Code all testing hours according to the type of tests and testing hours that comprise the vast majority within the particular battery. I shall expound on each of these strategies in this sequence, then conclude with some general suggestions on when and how they may be most effectively implemented.

First, as a rule of efficiency, if the test battery in whole or in part includes a neuro-psychological test or test battery, I simply total the number of requested hours and code it as such (i.e., billing code 96118). Otherwise, I classify the total as standard psychological testing (i.e., billing code 96101). The primary reasons include the following: (a) this distinction is becoming increasingly nebulous, commensurate with mounting evidence of neuropsychological dysfunction being associated with many Axis I *DSM-IV-TR* psychological disorders (Barlow & Durand, 2012); (b) the differential billing is cumbersome and thus can potentially become paradoxically more imprecise; (c) the charge per testing hour is identical (i.e., at least where I practice), rendering the distinction meaningless from a strict pecuniary perspective; and (d) the specific tests and hours being requested are explicitly listed in the "Initial Psychological Assessment Report" for scrutiny by the insurance company. I have rarely encountered insurance coverage difficulties by employing this parsimonious bill coding strategy. In the event the insurance company diverges in opinion, simple coding adjustments can be readily made.

Second, a viable alternative is to differentiate the billing hours according to type of test, psychological and neuropsychological, as I have indicated on the "Psychological Test Listing Form" (Form 2.7). When using this strategy, it is important to incorporate any time necessary for data integration and report writing into that estimated for the individual tests, a practice I endorse irrespective of bill coding strategy. For example, if I order the Rorschach Inkblot Test, Comprehensive System, RIAP, Fifth Edition, and the NEPSY–II Social Perception Subtests, the requested test hours would be 2 hours psychological testing (i.e., billing code 96101) and 1-hour neuropsychological testing (i.e., billing code 96118), respectively, and billed as such assuming approval. However, this method is more unwieldy because you are requesting two separate psychological services within the same testing case, which requires enhanced fastidiousness regarding the documentation and ultimate accuracy of your billing.

The third option is to request the type of testing service according to the principal diagnostic issues and any related questions. Thus, for example, if Personality Change Due to Brain Trauma is being ruled out, all requested testing hours would be coded neuropsychological (i.e., billing code 96118), irrespective of the fact that a standard psychological test may have been added as ancillary to the neuropsychological test battery in order to determine the nature and extent of maladaptive personality traits. The problem with this strategy arises when referrals include the need to rule out both cognitive disorders and more typical psychological disorders, especially those with increasing evidence of underlying neurocognitive dysfunction (e.g., PDD, ADHD).

The fourth and final strategy is to request the one billing code that is the best representative of the entire test battery; that is, whether it is more dominated by neuropsychological or standard psychological tests. For example, if the test battery largely consists of neuropsychological tests, all requested testing hours would be coded 96118 and vice versa.

My general advice is to routinely employ the fourth option, which shall be frequently accordant with option three, although be prepared to supplant this with the most viable alternative that best matches the unique nature of the testing case or insurance company standards. Again, occasional inconsistencies with the criteria of a particular insurance company are typically not fatal, and simple and rapid modifications are more than feasible. Furthermore, with experience you shall become increasingly familiar with the various standards of independent insurance companies and will learn to employ the most conducive strategy. Perhaps the billing code distinction between neuropsychological and psychological testing shall eventually be dropped as obsolete and antiquated, analogous to the now defunct Organic versus Inorganic Mental Disorders distinction espoused by the *Diagnostic and Statistical Manual of Mental Disorders, Third Edition, Revised (DSM-III-R)* (American Psychiatric Association, 1987). Until then, however, the above options can be useful practice billing code guidelines.

Finally, the initial assessment summary section concludes with an attestation that the requested test or tests are (a) standardized properly for the patient's age and (b) are in their most recently published editions. Both are critical for test approval and are consistent with the ethical principles for psychologists (American Psychological Association, 2003).

Pretest *DSM-IV-TR* Diagnoses

With its reliance on the clinical method, one of the essential goals of the initial assessment is to efficaciously narrow the scope of *DSM-IV-TR* disorders to those most likely to be present. This permits focus and precision for the planned follow-up standardized testing. The most logical place to record such information is in the ultimate section of the report employing the familiar *DSM-IV-TR* multiaxial system (American Psychiatric Association, 2000).

The Axis I pretest provisional working diagnoses listed in the templates emphasize the most general Not Otherwise Specified (NOS) disorders, followed by stress-induced Adjustment Disorders, and, regarding the child template, occasionally relevant "995" maltreatment victim-focused codes. This is accordant with my thesis that the clinical method has limited utility in resolving more particularly defined differential diagnostic questions. The provisional working diagnoses are ensued by a more comprehensive (although not exhaustive) listing of the most frequent specific *DSM-IV-TR* disorders, which are the focus of standardized testing.

The child and adult Axis I listings are prioritized somewhat differently, consistent with the different prevalence rates and types of disorders in these age groupings. Axes II, III, and IV are analogously prioritized. The Axis V Global Assessment of Functioning (GAF) default is set at moderate to severe (about 45 to 55) as the most frequently occurring range, although if psychotic symptoms are evident in the presenting symptoms and/or mental status examination, 35 and lower is most appropriate. Standardized psychological testing will probably not be approved for higher ratings as being neither necessary nor cost-effective. Finally, a deferral on prognosis is made due to the provisional status of pretest working diagnoses.

REVIEWING THE PRELIMINARY FINDINGS AND PLANS FOR TESTING WITH PATIENTS

Use of the "Initial Psychological Assessment Report" provides structure and focus to the clinical interview process. It can be completed well within the standard 50-minute clinical hour.[4] Patients, pertinent family members, and guardians should be informed of the

[4] Once the initial report is completed, I save it on an external USB flash drive in a folder titled "INITIAL PSYCHOLOGICAL ASSESSMENTS." I save the patient's particular report beginning with "I" for initial, followed by an underline mark "_", last name, first name, and office file number; for example, I_Smith, Mary 233878. The initial reports will be saved by most computer software alphabetically for ease of location. In cases where I conduct a second initial evaluation, for example, a referral for retesting at a later date, I use "II"; for example, II_Smith, Mary 233878. Of course, I back up all saved files on a second USB flash drive.

following: (a) provisional *DSM-IV-TR* diagnoses, (b) all suspected *DSM-IV-TR* diagnoses in need of being ruled out and related referral questions to be answered, (c) the planned standardized test battery, and (d) estimated number of testing hours.[5] The tests in the planned battery should logically follow from the rule out diagnoses and questions reviewed prior. Section II of this book details the capabilities of each test in the "Psychological Test Listing Form" for purposes of differential diagnosis, supplemented by their respective scoring and interpretation tabular templates.

Finally, information outlining the remaining steps in the testing process should be provided such that patients and their significant relationships are sufficiently cognizant of what to expect. To expedite affording such information, I have prepared a written "Patient Test Instruction Form," discussed immediately subsequent (see Form 2.8).

Patient Test Instruction Form

Item 1 informs patients that the standardized testing must be preauthorized by their insurance carrier using the initial report. Item 2 explicitly states the maximum number of testing hours being requested. Of crucial importance, it also educates patients and their families regarding the core tasks that contribute to the testing hours. Item 2 information will obviate later misunderstandings, as some laypeople possess a misconception that charges should be limited to face-to-face administration time. This partly may be due to a confusion between individual psychotherapy services (i.e., billing code 90806), which are based strictly upon direct service time (e.g., the 50-minute hour), and psychological testing services, which require a significant number of billing activities without the patient being present. The purpose of item 3 is to inform patients of the number and duration of testing appointments, assuming that all or the majority of requested testing hours are approved. It requires the testing psychologist to enter this information in writing; for example "One 2-hour appointment." I advise not exceeding a duration of 2 hours for a single testing session, irrespective of age due to potentially confounding fatigue effects. As should become increasingly apparent as you proceed through this book, with the exception of administering complete neuropsychological test batteries, the majority of test administrations can and should be completed within a single 2-hour appointment.

Item 4 is to ensure that any symptom rating scales that are part of the planned test battery (see Form 2.7, section "Symptom Rating Scales"), which are submitted to patients and accompanying family members at the conclusion of the initial report, are properly completed and returned to the testing psychologist. The language contained therein reinforces their central role in the testing process. If this item does not apply, simply cross it out and place *N/A* adjacent to it. It may be of assistance to explain orally to patients that this item is not applicable in their case and for them to simply ignore it.

Item 5 addresses any self-report inventories which may be included in the test battery (see Form 2.7, section "Self-Report Personality Inventories"), which for standardized test security reasons must be completed on site. The item instructs patients to complete the inventory upon being informed that testing has been authorized. I recommend purchasing computer-administered versions of these tests for immediate automated scoring (see Chapter 8).

Patients should be encouraged to complete such inventories on a day prior to any scheduled test administration appointments for purposes of expediency and to mitigate confounding fatigue effects. If the inventories are loaded upon a single computer, it is prudent to have them call your office in advance to determine availability. Again, if this item does not apply, simply cross it out, place N/A adjacent to it, and reinforce this orally to patients and family members.

Item 6 elucidates the type of services and considerable amount of work completed subsequent to the test administration process, including scoring, interpretation, and report writing. This disabuses patients of the notion that completion of test administration is synonymous with concluding the assessment and testing process. Furthermore, it corroborates the number

[5] *Again, I assume that your group or individual practice has a standard treatment plan form upon which the clinician records the plan for testing and/or intervention, including signature lines for patients, pertinent family members, guardians, and clinicians indicating their mutual agreement and approval. This form is also standard for clinical mental health practice and is not unique to assessment and testing. Thus, I again do not include such forms in the interest of saving space.*

of testing hours requested when reviewing the initial assessment results with patients, and elucidates the reason why patients are ultimately charged for testing hours in excess of face-to-face contact. Finally, item 6 reminds patients and pertinent family members of the recommended feedback session to be conducted subsequent to completion of the final report.

Item 7 concludes the instruction form. It specifically pertains to obtaining the necessary release of information in order to properly communicate the results to referring clinicians and other relevant third parties. Many mental health offices have release of information forms that are HIPPA compliant, and are specifically designed for their services and within their jurisdictions. For this reason, I advise you use the release form that has been approved within your practice and jurisdiction (see e.g., Missouri Bar, 2006).

Obtaining Insurance Precertification

The completed "Initial Psychological Assessment Report" may be submitted for insurance authorization immediately after the conclusion of the clinical interview. I advise not scheduling test administration appointments or self-report clinical and personality inventories prior to insurance authorization. This is due to uncertainty as to which tests and quantity of test hours will be ultimately approved. For expediency, I do recommend submitting any symptom rating scales to patients and family for completion prior to authorization, ideally in proximity to reviewing the tests in the requested battery.

Noting the Number of Test Hours Approved

In my experience, either all or the vast majority of requested test hours are routinely approved under the following two conditions: (a) fastidious use of the "Initial Psychological Assessment Report" templates and (b) judicious adherence to remaining within the advised three to five test hour request range (again with the limited exception of full neuropsychological test batteries). However, occasionally testing hours may be denied outright or circumscribed (e.g., 1–2 hours versus 3–5 requested). In these cases, I recommend administering the entire planned battery for the following reasons: (a) these decisions are infrequent and are offset by the greater number of successful authorizations for testing, (b) this bolsters a salutary professional reputation for providing high-quality services, (c) the time elapsed with an insurance company appealing a case for more hours is cost ineffective, and (d) this ultimately assists in reducing human suffering (which I assume is an essential goal of people entering the helping professions, such as psychology).

Another option is to negotiate a reduced out-of-pocket fee with the patient or authorized family members. This alternative is much less desirable as it requires the agreement be reduced to writing, and necessitates further decisions, including whether you require advanced payment to be placed into trust until service is completed. Finally, I advise against proceeding with a reduced test battery for the following three reasons: (a) the insurance company's authorization will be based upon your recommended test battery, (b) such reduction increases your liability for malpractice, and (c) the difficulty encountered when attempting to rationalize such reduction with the patient and pertinent family members.

In the event testing is denied, I suggest discovering the reasons therefore and attempting to amend the "Initial Psychological Assessment Report" with the additional required information prior to resubmission. The remaining alternatives are (a) negotiating an out-of-pocket fee arrangement as described prior, (b) not proceeding with standardized testing, (c) completing the testing case pro bono due to hardship, or (d) referring to a psychologist or agency who will complete such testing for a reduced fee or pro bono. To effectively record the progress of a testing case, I have prepared a form titled "Psychological Test Request and Log Form" that is discussed next (see Form 2.9).

Psychological Test Request and Log Form

This form represents a rapid reference sheet that tracks a testing case from completion of the initial report to case termination or discharge. It is effective for both the testing psychologist and support staff so as to contact a case as needed, schedule appointments properly, and accurately note case progress.

The form logically begins with patient identification and contact information. The ensuing section notes the requested number and duration of test administration appointments, which should be accordant with that recorded on the "Patient Test Instruction Form." Analogously, the next section includes any self-report clinical and personality inventories that may have been ordered as part of the battery such that the patient may be reminded to complete this upon test authorization. If this does not apply, simply enter N/A as on the "Patient Test Instruction Form."

Subsequent essential information includes the following: (a) type of testing (i.e., psychological or neuropsychological) and number of hours *requested*, (b) type of testing (i.e., psychological or neuropsychological) and number of hours *approved*, and (c) whether or not insurance authorization for testing is required and dates of approval, or alternatively, for those without insurance coverage, a selection for self-pay and the negotiated fee. Insurance authorized dates of approval permits the testing psychologist to prioritize the scheduling of administration appointments such that the testing process does not exceed the duration.

SUMMARY

This chapter delineated the initial phases of the psychological testing process from the initial referral to the scheduling of test administration appointments. They are considered critical in that, if mismanaged, the remaining phases are consequently hindered or precluded. Chapter 3 discusses the final two phases, including (a) completion of the final psychological evaluation report and (b) communication of the assessment and test results (see Figure 1.1).

REFERENCES

American Psychiatric Association. (1987). *Diagnostic and statistical manual of mental disorders* (3rd ed. rev.). Washington, DC: Author.

American Psychiatric Association. (2000). *Diagnostic and statistical manual of mental disorders* (4th ed., text rev.). Washington, DC: Author.

American Psychological Association. (2003). *Ethical principles of psychologists and code of conduct.* Washington, DC: Author.

Barlow, David H., & Durand, Mark V. (2012). *Abnormal psychology: An integrative approach* (6th ed.). Belmont, CA: Wadsworth, Cengage Learning.

Corey, G. (2013). *Theory and practice of counseling and psychotherapy* (9th ed.). Belmont, CA: Brooks/Cole, Cengage Learning.

Evans, D. R., Hearn, M. T., Uhlemann, M. R., & Ivey, A. E. (2008). *Essential interviewing: A programmed approach to effective communication* (7th ed.). Belmont, CA: Brooks/Cole, Cengage Learning.

Folstein, M. F., Folstein, S. E., & Fanjiang, G. (2001). *Mini–Mental State Examination: Clinical guide.* Lutz, FL: Psychological Assessment Resources.

Folstein, M. F., Folstein, S. E., White, T., & Messer, M. A. (2010). *Mini–Mental State Examination, 2nd edition: Users manual.* Lutz, FL: Psychological Assessment Resources.

Miller, L. A., McIntire, S. A., & Lovler, R. L. (2011). *Foundations of psychological testing* (3rd ed.). Thousand Oaks, CA: Sage Publications.

Missouri Bar. (2006). *HIPAA privacy authorization form.* Jefferson City, MO: Author. Retrieved from http://members.mobar.org/pdfs/publications/public/hipaa.pdf

Spiegler, M. D., & Guevremont, D. C. (2010). *Contemporary behavior therapy* (5th ed.). Belmont, CA: Wadsworth, Cengage Learning.

FORM 2.1

NAME OF PRACTICE
PSYCHOLOGICAL TEST REFERRAL FORM

Patient Name: _____   *Patient DOB:* _____

                    (Last)   *(First)*

Account or Patient File #: _____   *Referral date:* _____

Referring Clinician Information: _____

                           Individual, Agency   *Street Address*

_____

City   *State*   *Zip Code*   *Office Phone*   *Office Fax*

Mark one: [ ] Psychological Testing; [ ] Neuropsychological Testing
(needs physician consultation and approval).

The testing referral is needed because (mark all that apply):

[ ] Diagnosis remains ambiguous subsequent to clinical interview, examination, and ongoing observation.

[ ] There has been poor or no response to treatment intervention for undetermined reasons.

[ ] Objective standardized testing will significantly impact treatment planning and outcome.

Behavioral Health Evaluation Date (i.e., 90801) (Mental Health Clinicians Only): _____

Current working diagnosis(es):_____

_____

Diagnosis(es) to be ruled out:_____

Note: As a general practice, health insurance will not authorize the following: (a) educational or vocational testing, and (b) court-ordered psychological testing.

Additional referral question(s) (if any):_____

_____

_____

FORM 2.2

NAME OF PRACTICE
OFFICE TYPE—OUTPATIENT DEPARTMENT
INITIAL PSYCHOLOGICAL ASSESSMENT REPORT—CHILD

Patient Name: _____

        (Last)   **(First)**

Account Number: _____

Date: _____

Patient Identifying Information:

Chronological age is years months. Gender is female. DOB: --/--/----.

Referral Information:

The referral source is MD DO PhD, HSPP PsyD, HSPP MA, LMHC, MSW, LCSW, who indicated that the diagnosis remains ambiguous subsequent clinical interview, examination, and ongoing observation, there has been poor or no response to treatment intervention for unknown reasons, and objective standardized testing will significantly impact treatment planning and outcome.

The stated *DSM-IV-TR* diagnoses needed to be ruled out include Attention-Deficit/Hyperactivity Disorder (ADHD), _____.

Additional referral questions included:
1. _____
2. _____

Presenting symptoms included:

ADHD: difficulty sustaining attention, becoming easily distracted, being continuously forgetful, difficulty listening to others, disorganization, mind-wandering, failing to complete tasks, acting without considering consequences, fidgeting, difficulty remaining seated, and overactivity. These symptoms have an early onset prior to the age of 7 years, have been chronic, and associated with low academic achievement and work productivity.

ODD/CD: frequent loss of temper, being argumentative, repeatedly defying or refusing to follow rules, intentionally annoying others, frequently blaming others, irritable temperament, repeatedly violating the fundamental rights of others, repeatedly violating major societal rules and laws, including stealing, verbal and physical aggression, lack of remorse, and repeated school suspensions and expulsions for rule-breaking behavior.

PDD: chronic deficits in the ability to bond emotionally to others, lack of interest in forming relationships with others, ineffectual interpersonal skills, lack of eye contact and reciprocity, lack of empathy, isolative play and esoteric interests, social isolation, repetitive behaviors, and impaired ability to communicate effectively with others.

Mood: dysphoria, irritability, sad mood, fatigue, agitation, lack of interest, social withdrawal, flat affect, blunted affect, excessive guilt, low self-worth, periodic suicidal thoughts, severe mood swings vacillating from euphoria to dysphoria, affective instability, sleep and appetite problems, racing thoughts, grandiosity, impulsive and risky behaviors, distractibility, and diminished attention and concentration.

Anxiety: chronic apprehension, irritability, muscle tension, restlessness, becoming easily fatigued, sleep problems, periods of intense panic, trembling, difficulty breathing, racing heart, sweating, dizziness, feelings that things and people are not real, feeling detached, nausea, and feelings of terror and dread.

PTSD: exposure to severe trauma with subsequent response of intense fear and horror, repeated nightmares of the trauma, repeated memories of the trauma while awake, behaving as if the trauma was occurring, hypervigilance to anticipated danger, observed startle response, irritability, and anger outbursts.

Psychosis: auditory disturbances including hearing voices without knowing their source, visual disturbances including seeing things that are not actually present, tangential, disorganized, and fragmented speech, flat affect, inappropriate affect, ideas of persecution and grandeur, lack of volition, lost interest, poverty of speech, social withdrawal, and disorganized behavior.

Neuropsychological: reduced awareness of the environment, reduced ability to focus, shift, and sustain attention, disorientation, periods of mental confusion, impairments in immediate and intermediate memory, difficulties retrieving words when speaking to others, using words inappropriately, reduced ability to comprehend the spoken language of others, difficulties recognizing and naming objects, increasing motor dysfunction including loss of balance, motor incoordination, becoming lost and disoriented when navigating familiar routes, and a noticeable decline in forethought, organizing, and logical abstract reasoning abilities.

Personality: chronic difficulties establishing and maintaining interpersonal relationships of adequate intimacy, instability of interpersonal relationships, unstable self-image and sense of self, affective instability including intense episodic dysphoria lasting hours to days, inappropriate intense anger, episodes of self-mutilation in the form of cutting when experiencing dysphoria with dissociation of pain, repeated suicidal behavior, feelings of emptiness, intense fear of abandonment, impulsivity, failing to follow to social norms, chronic lying, frequently disregarding the basic rights of others, aggressiveness, irresponsibility, lack of guilt or remorse, low self-worth, lack of self-confidence, fear of embarrassment and humiliation, excessive dependency on others, need to be the center of attention, and shallow and dramatic emotional expression.

Onset was estimated to be: _____.

Clinical Psychologist:
Psychologist Name, PhD, PsyD, HSPP _____
Psychologist – State License #_____

Mental Status Examination and Behavioral Observations:
Affect was _____. Mood was _____. Thought process was logical, sequential, relevant, and coherent. Thought content was reality-based and normal. Short-term memory functioning was _____. Long-term memory functioning was normal and intact, as evidenced by _____'s ability to provide age-appropriate historical information. _____ was oriented to time, place, and person. Activity

level was normal. Social skills were normal including effective eye contact and reciprocity. Estimated intellectual function based on verbal skills and reasoning abilities is average. Psychotic symptoms were not evident. There was no evidence of suicidal thoughts, intentions, or plans. There was no evidence of self-mutilation or self-harm.

Psychiatric/Medical/Psychological:

The referring clinician completed a Behavioral Health Evaluation (i.e., 90801) in or about _____. No Behavioral Health Evaluation (i.e., 90801) has been done within the past year. Psychiatric history includes outpatient treatment by _____. Family psychiatric history is negative positive for ADHD, Bipolar Disorder, Depressive Disorder, Schizophrenia, Dementia, and Learning Disorder. Medical functioning is unremarkable remarkable for. _____ is not taking any current medications. Current medications include _____. There is a negative history of severe head injuries, seizure disorder, and major surgeries. Vision is normal. Hearing is normal. _____ has been in psychosocial therapy for _____. Previous neuropsychological testing has not been done.

Developmental:

There were no pre-, peri-, or post-natal complications reported. Gestation was full-term. Birth weight was _____ pounds _____ ounces. Birth length was _____ inches. Developmental milestones were reported as falling within the normal range.

Family:

_____ lives with _____.

Interpersonal:

Interpersonal relationships were described as satisfactory in both quality and quantity. Social skills were described as ineffectual with deficits in friendships of adequate intimacy.

Educational:

_____ is in Grade _____. Academic performance has typically been _____. Behavioral grades have typically been _____. There has been no grade retention. _____ was retained in Grade _____, is receiving general special education instruction, has a continuing IEP, and is classified as _____.

Vocational:

None.

Substance Abuse:

Unremarkable.

Legal:

Unremarkable.

Initial Assessment Summary:

Based upon the initial psychological assessment evidence, pre-test working diagnosis and disorders needed to be ruled out are listed below in the ensuing *Pretest DSM-IV-TR Diagnosis* section. The test data shall also provide answers to the additional referral questions listed above in the *Referral Information* section of this report. The test data shall also empirically measure the extent and severity of any neuropsychological deficits for purposes of treatment planning.

The following tests and estimated hours are requested:

1. NEPSY–II, Form Ages 5 to 16, Attention and Executive Functioning, Memory and Learning Subtests (2 hours)
2. Conners' Continuous Performance Test, Second Edition, Version 5 (CPT–II) (1 hour)
3. Conners Comprehensive Behavior Rating Scales (Conners CBRS), Parent and Teacher Forms (1 hour)
4. Conners Comprehensive Behavior Rating Scales (Conners CBRS), Parent and Self-Report Forms (1 hour)
5. Conners Comprehensive Behavior Rating Scales (Conners CBRS), Parent, Teacher, and Self-Report Forms (2 hours)
6. Conners Comprehensive Behavior Rating Scales (Conners CBRS), Self-Report Form (1 hour)
7. NEPSY–II, Form Ages 3 to 4, Attention and Executive Functioning, Memory and Learning Subtests (2 hours)
8. Conners' Kiddie Continuous Performance Test, Version 5 (K–CPT) (1 hour)
9. Conners Early Childhood (Conners EC), Parent and Teacher/Childcare Forms (1 hour)
10. NEPSY–II, Form Ages 3 to 4, Full Battery (6 hours)
11. NEPSY–II, Form Ages 5 to 16, Full Battery (8 hours)
12. NEPSY–II, Form Ages 3 to 4, General Battery (3 hours)
13. NEPSY–II, Form Ages 5 to 16, General Battery (4 hours)
14. NEPSY–II, Form Ages 3 to 4, Social Perception Subtests (1 hour)
15. NEPSY–II, Form Ages 5 to 16, Social Perception Subtests (1 hour)
16. NEPSY–II, Form Ages 3 to 4, Attention and Executive Functioning, Memory and Learning, Social Perception Subtests (3 hours)
17. NEPSY–II, Form Ages 5 to 16, Attention and Executive Functioning, Memory and Learning, Social Perception Subtests (3 hours)
18. Gilliam Autism Rating Scale, Second Edition (GARS–2) (1 hour)
19. Gilliam Asperger's Disorder Scale (GADS) (1 hour)
20. Millon Pre-Adolescent Clinical Inventory (M–PACI) (1 hour)
21. Millon Adolescent Clinical Inventory (MACI) (1 hour)
22. Minnesota Multiphasic Personality Inventory–Adolescent (MMPI–A) (1 hour)
23. Rorschach Inkblot Test, Comprehensive System, RIAP Fifth Edition (Rorschach–CS) (2 hours)
24. Roberts–2 (2 hours)
25. Vineland Adaptive Behavior Scales, Second Edition (Vineland–II) (2 hours)
26. Wechsler Intelligence Scale for Children, Fourth Edition (WISC–IV) (3 hours)
27. Wechsler Preschool and Primary Scale of Intelligence, Third Edition, Form Ages 2:6 to 3:11 (WPPSI–III, Form Ages 2:6 to 3:11) (2 hours)
28. Wechsler Preschool and Primary Scale of Intelligence, Third Edition, Form Ages 4:0 to 7:3 (WPPSI–III, Form Ages 4:0 to 7:3) (3 hours)
29. Wechsler Adult Intelligence Scale, Fourth Edition (WAIS–IV) (3 hours)
30. Wechsler Individual Achievement Test, Third Edition, Pre-Kindergarten (WIAT–III, PK) (2 hours)
31. Wechsler Individual Achievement Test, Third Edition, K–12 (WIAT–III, K–12) (3 hours)
32. Ability–Achievement Discrepancy Analysis (1 hour)
33. Wechsler Memory Scale, Fourth Edition (WMS–IV), Form Ages 16 to 69 (3 hours)
34. Ability, Memory Discrepancy Analysis (1 hour)

One (1) additional hour is requested for data integration and report composition.

Total requested neuropsychological testing hours is (Billing Code 96118). Psychological testing hours is (Billing Code 96101).

Finally, one (1) individual hour (Billing Code 90806) is requested for follow-up test feed-back session and treatment planning.

All of the above-enumerated tests have sufficient empirically derived reliability and validity, and are age-appropriate. Furthermore, these tests are the most recently published editions.

The above-enumerated test has sufficient empirically derived reliability and validity, and is age-appropriate. Furthermore, this test is in its most recently published edition.

Pretest *DSM-IV-TR* Diagnoses:

Axis I:
- ❒ 312.9 Disruptive Behavior Disorder NOS
- ❒ 296.90 Mood Disorder NOS
- ❒ 311 Depressive Disorder NOS
- ❒ 296.80 Bipolar Disorder NOS
- ❒ 300.00 Anxiety Disorder NOS
- ❒ 298.9 Psychotic Disorder NOS
- ❒ 294.9 Cognitive Disorder NOS
- ❒ 309.0 Adjustment Disorder With Depressed Mood
- ❒ 309.24 Adjustment Disorder With Anxiety
- ❒ 309.28 Adjustment Disorder With Mixed Anxiety and Depressed Mood
- ❒ 309.3 Adjustment Disorder With Disturbance of Conduct
- ❒ 309.4 Adjustment Disorder With Mixed Disturbance of Emotions and Conduct
- ❒ 309.9 Adjustment Disorder, Unspecified
- ❒ 995.54 Physical Abuse of Child
- ❒ 995.53 Sexual Abuse of Child
- ❒ 995.52 Neglect of Child

Provisional, Rule Out:
- ❒ 314.01 Attention-Deficit/Hyperactivity Disorder, Combined Type
- ❒ 314.01 Attention-Deficit/Hyperactivity Disorder, Predominantly Hyperactive-Impulsive Type
- ❒ 314.00 Attention-Deficit/Hyperactivity Disorder, Predominantly Inattentive Type
- ❒ 313.81 Oppositional Defiant Disorder
- ❒ 312.81 Conduct Disorder, Childhood-Onset Type
- ❒ 312.82 Conduct Disorder, Adolescent-Onset Type
- ❒ 312.89 Conduct Disorder, Unspecified Onset
- ❒ 299.00 Autistic Disorder
- ❒ 299.80 Asperger's Disorder
- ❒ 299.80 Pervasive Developmental Disorder NOS (Atypical Autistic Disorder)
- ❒ 313.89 Reactive Attachment Disorder, Inhibited Type and Disinhibited Type
- ❒ 300.4 Dysthymic Disorder, Early Onset
- ❒ 296.22 Major Depressive Disorder, Single Episode, Moderate
- ❒ 296.32 Major Depressive Disorder, Recurrent, Moderate
- ❒ 301.13 Cyclothymic Disorder, Early Onset
- ❒ 296.62 Bipolar I Disorder, Mixed, Moderate
- ❒ 296.89 Bipolar II Disorder

❏ 300.02 Generalized Anxiety Disorder
❏ 309.81 Posttraumatic Stress Disorder, Chronic
❏ 300.3 Obsessive-Compulsive Disorder
❏ 295.20 Schizophrenia, Undifferentiated Type, Childhood Onset
❏ 294.9 Mild/Moderate/Severe Neurocognitive Disorder (Cognitive Disorder NOS)
❏ 293.83 Mood Disorder Due to a General Medical Condition
❏ 310.1 Personality Change Due to a General Medical Condition
❏ 315.00 Reading Disorder
❏ 315.01 Mathematics Disorder
❏ 315.2 Disorder of Written Expression
❏ 315.9 Learning Disorder NOS
❏ 315.39 Phonological Disorder
❏ 315.31 Expressive Language Disorder
❏ 315.32 Mixed Receptive-Expressive Language Disorder
❏ 315.4 Developmental Coordination Disorder
❏ 307.0 Stuttering
❏ 307.6 Enuresis (Not Due to a General Medical Condition), Nocturnal/Diurnal
❏ 787.6 Encopresis With Constipation and Overflow Incontinence
❏ 307.7 Encopresis Without Constipation and Overflow Incontinence

Axis II:
❏ V71.09 No Diagnosis
❏ 799.9 Diagnosis Deferred

Rule Out:
❏ 317 Mild Mental Retardation
❏ 318.0 Moderate Mental Retardation
❏ 301.83 Borderline Personality Disorder
❏ 301.81 Narcissistic Personality Disorder

Axis III:
❏ No Contributory or Pertinent Medical Disorders Noted
❏ History of Traumatic Brain Injury (TBI)
❏ Preterm Birth with Low Birth Weight
❏ History of Meningitis
❏ Prenatal Exposure to Teratogens
❏ History of Lead Poisoning
❏ 250.00 Diabetes Mellitus, Type II
❏ 850.9 Concussion
❏ 345.10 Epilepsy, Grand Mal

Axis IV:
❏ Psychosocial Stressors – Social, Educational, Medical

Axis V:
❏ Global Assessment of Functioning (GAF): 45 Serious Moderate symptoms
❏ Prognosis: Deferred pending neuropsychological assessment and test results

_____
Psychologist Name, PhD, PsyD, HSPP
Psychologist – State License #_____

FORM 2.3

NAME OF PRACTICE
OFFICE TYPE—OUTPATIENT DEPARTMENT
INITIAL PSYCHOLOGICAL ASSESSMENT REPORT—ADULT

Patient Name: _____
              (Last)   *(First)*

Account Number: _____

Date: _____

Patient Identifying Information:

Chronological age is years months. Gender is female. DOB: --/--/----.

Referral Information:

The referral source is MD DO PhD, HSPP PsyD, HSPP MA, LMHC, MSW, LCSW, who indicated that the diagnosis remains ambiguous subsequent clinical interview, examination, and ongoing observation, there has been poor or no response to treatment intervention for unknown reasons, and objective standardized testing will significantly impact treatment planning and outcome.

The stated *DSM-IV-TR* diagnoses needed to be ruled out include _____.

Additional referral questions included:
  1. _____
  2. _____

Presenting symptoms included:

Mood: dysphoria, irritability, sad mood, fatigue, agitation, lack of interest, social withdrawal, flat affect, blunted affect, excessive guilt, low self-worth, periodic suicidal thoughts, severe mood swings vacillating from euphoria to dysphoria, affective instability, sleep and appetite problems, racing thoughts, grandiosity, impulsive and risky behaviors, distractibility, and diminished attention and concentration.

Anxiety: chronic apprehension, irritability, muscle tension, restlessness, becoming easily fatigued, sleep problems, periods of intense panic, trembling, difficulty breathing, racing heart, sweating, dizziness, feelings that things and people are not real, feeling detached, nausea, and feelings of terror and dread.

PTSD: exposure to severe trauma with subsequent response of intense fear and horror, repeated nightmares of the trauma, repeated memories of the trauma while awake, behaving as if the trauma was occurring, hypervigilance to anticipated danger, observed startle response, irritability, and anger outbursts.

Psychosis: auditory disturbances including hearing voices without knowing their source, visual disturbances including seeing things that are not actually present, tangential, disorganized, and fragmented speech, flat affect, inappropriate affect, ideas of persecution and grandeur, lack of volition, lost interest, poverty of speech, social withdrawal, and disorganized behavior.

Neuropsychological: reduced awareness of the environment, reduced ability to focus, shift, and sustain attention, disorientation, periods of mental confusion, impairments in immediate and intermediate memory, difficulties retrieving words when speaking to others, using words inappropriately, reduced ability to comprehend the spoken language of others, difficulties recognizing and naming objects, increasing motor dysfunction including loss of balance, motor incoordination, becoming lost and disoriented when navigating familiar routes, and a noticeable decline in forethought, organizing, and logical abstract reasoning abilities.

Personality: chronic difficulties establishing and maintaining interpersonal relationships of adequate intimacy, instability of interpersonal relationships, unstable self-image and sense of self, affective instability including intense episodic dysphoria lasting hours to days, inappropriate intense anger, episodes of self-mutilation in the form of cutting when experiencing dysphoria with dissociation of pain, repeated suicidal behavior, feelings of emptiness, intense fear of abandonment, impulsivity, failing to follow to social norms, chronic lying, frequently disregarding the basic rights of others, aggressiveness, irresponsibility, lack of guilt or remorse, low self-worth, lack of self-confidence, fear of embarrassment and humiliation, excessive dependency on others, need to be the center of attention, and shallow and dramatic emotional expression.

ADHD: difficulty sustaining attention, becoming easily distracted, being continuously forgetful, difficulty listening to others, disorganization, mind-wandering, failing to complete tasks, acting without considering consequences, fidgeting, difficulty remaining seated, and overactivity. These symptoms have an early onset prior to the age of 7 years, have been chronic, and associated with low academic achievement and work productivity.

Onset was estimated to be: _____.

Clinical Psychologist:
Psychologist Name, PhD, PsyD, HSPP _____
Psychologist – State License #_____

Mental Status Examination:
Affect was _____. Mood was _____. Thought process was logical, sequential, relevant, and coherent. Thought content was reality-based and normal. Short-term memory functioning was _____. Long-term memory functioning was normal and intact, as evidenced by _____'s ability to provide a coherent developmental history with key historical dates. Was oriented to time, place, and person. Estimated intellectual function based on verbal skills, fund of general knowledge, and abstract reasoning abilities is average. Psychotic symptoms were not evident. There was no evidence of suicidal thoughts, intentions, or plans. There was no evidence of self-mutilation or self-harm.

Psychiatric/Medical/Psychological:
The referring clinician completed a Behavioral Health Evaluation (i.e., 90801) in or about _____. No Behavioral Health Evaluation (i.e., 90801) has been previously done within the past year. Inpatient psychiatric history is _____. Family psychiatric history is negative positive for ADHD, Bipolar Disorder, Depressive Disorder, Schizophrenia, Dementia, and Learning Disorder. Medical functioning is unremarkable remarkable for _____. Current medications include _____. _____ is not taking any current medications. There is a negative history of severe head injuries, seizure disorder, and major surgeries. Vision is normal. Hearing is normal. _____ has been in psychosocial therapy for _____. Previous neuropsychological testing has not been done.

Family:

_____ lives with _____.

Interpersonal:

Interpersonal relationships were described as satisfactory in both quality and quantity. _____ has manifested chronic difficulties establishing and maintaining interpersonal relationships of adequate intimacy.

Educational:

_____ has completed years of formal education. High school graduation was in or about. Academic performance was typically _____. There was no grade retention. _____ received special education instruction and was classified as _____.

Vocational:

_____ is employed as a _____. _____ is a retired _____. _____ is unemployed. _____ has largely worked as a _____. Work history is _____.

Substance Abuse:

Unremarkable.

Legal:

Unremarkable.

Initial Assessment Summary:

Based upon the initial psychological assessment evidence, pre-test working diagnosis and disorders needed to be ruled out are listed below in the ensuing Pretest *DSM-IV-TR* Diagnosis section. The test data shall also provide answers to the additional referral questions listed above in the "Referral Information" section of this report. The test data shall also empirically measure the extent and severity of any neuropsychological deficits for purposes of treatment planning.

The following tests and estimated hours are requested:

1. Neuropsychological Assessment Battery, Form 1 (NAB) (7 hours)
2. Neuropsychological Assessment Screening Battery (NASB), Form 1 (2 hours)
3. Millon Clinical Multiaxial Inventory–III (MCMI–III) (1 hour)
4. Minnesota Multiphasic Personality Inventory–2–Restructured Form (MMPI–2–RF) (1 hour)
5. Minnesota Multiphasic Personality Inventory–2 (MMPI–2) (1 hour)
6. Rorschach Inkblot Test, Comprehensive System, RIAP Fifth Edition (Rorschach–CS) (2 hours)
7. Neuropsychological Assessment Battery (NAB), Attention Module Subtests, Form 2 (2 hours)
8. Conners' Continuous Performance Test, Second Edition, Version 5 (CPT–II) (1 hour)
9. Conners' Adult ADHD Rating Scales (CAARS –L), Self-Report and Observer Forms (1 hour)
10. Wechsler Adult Intelligence Scale, Fourth Edition (WAIS–IV) (3 hours)
11. Wechsler Memory Scale, Fourth Edition (WMS–IV), Form Ages 16 to 69 (3 hours)
12. Wechsler Memory Scale, Fourth Edition (WMS–IV), Form Ages 65 to 90 (3 hours)
13. Ability–Memory Discrepancy Analysis (1 hour)
14. Wechsler Individual Achievement Test, Third Edition, K–12 (WIAT–III, K–12) (3 hours)

15. Ability–Achievement Discrepancy Analysis (1 hour)
16. Vineland Adaptive Behavior Scales, Second Edition (Vineland–II) (2 hours)

One (1) additional hour is requested for data integration and report composition. Total requested neuropsychological testing hours is (Billing Code 96118). Psychological testing hours is (Billing Code 96101).

Finally, one (1) individual hour (Billing Code 90806) is requested for a follow-up test feedback session and treatment planning.

All of the above-enumerated tests have sufficient empirically derived reliability and validity, and are age-appropriate. Furthermore, these tests are the most recently published editions.

The above-enumerated test has sufficient empirically derived reliability and validity, and is age-appropriate. Furthermore, this test is in its most recently published edition.

Pretest *DSM-IV-TR* Diagnoses:

Axis I:
❏ 296.90 Mood Disorder NOS
❏ 311 Depressive Disorder NOS
❏ 296.80 Bipolar Disorder NOS
❏ 300.00 Anxiety Disorder NOS
❏ 298.9 Psychotic Disorder NOS
❏ 294.9 Cognitive Disorder NOS
❏ 309.0 Adjustment Disorder With Depressed Mood
❏ 309.24 Adjustment Disorder With Anxiety
❏ 309.28 Adjustment Disorder With Mixed Anxiety and Depressed Mood
❏ 309.3 Adjustment Disorder With Disturbance of Conduct
❏ 309.4 Adjustment Disorder With Mixed Disturbance of Emotions and Conduct
❏ 309.9 Adjustment Disorder, Unspecified

Provisional, Rule Out:
❏ 300.4 Dysthymic Disorder, Early/Late Onset
❏ 296.22 Major Depressive Disorder, Single Episode, Moderate
❏ 296.32 Major Depressive Disorder, Recurrent, Moderate
❏ 296.34 Major Depressive Disorder, Recurrent, Severe With Psychotic Features
❏ 301.13 Cyclothymic Disorder
❏ 296.64 Bipolar I Disorder, Mixed, Severe With Psychotic Features
❏ 296.62 Bipolar I Disorder, Mixed, Moderate
❏ 296.89 Bipolar II Disorder
❏ 300.02 Generalized Anxiety Disorder
❏ 309.81 Posttraumatic Stress Disorder, Chronic
❏ 300.3 Obsessive-Compulsive Disorder
❏ 295.30 Schizophrenia, Paranoid Type
❏ 295.10 Schizophrenia, Disorganized Type
❏ 295.20 Schizophrenia, Undifferentiated Type
❏ 295.70 Schizoaffective Disorder, Bipolar Type/Depressive Type
❏ 293.81 Psychotic Disorder Due to a General Medical Condition, With Delusions
❏ 293.82 Psychotic Disorder Due to a General Medical Condition, With Hallucinations
❏ 290.40 Vascular Dementia, Uncomplicated, With Behavioral Disturbance
❏ 290.41 Vascular Dementia, With Delirium
❏ 290.42 Vascular Dementia, With Delusions

❏ 290.43 Vascular Dementia, With Depressed Mood
❏ 294.10 Dementia Due to Head Trauma, Without Behavioral Disturbance
❏ 294.11 Dementia Due to Head Trauma, With Behavioral Disturbance
❏ 294.10 Dementia of the Alzheimer's Type, With Late Early Onset, Without Behavioral Disturbance
❏ 294.11 Dementia of the Alzheimer's Type, With Late Early Onset, With Behavioral Disturbance
❏ 294.10 Dementia Due to... [A General Medical Condition, Parkinson's Disease, Huntington's Disease, Multiple Etiologies], Without Behavioral Disturbance
❏ 294.11 Dementia Due to... [A General Medical Condition, Parkinson's Disease, Huntington's Disease, Multiple Etiologies], With Behavioral Disturbance
❏ 294.8 Dementia Due to Unknown Etiology
❏ 294.10 Substance-Induced Persisting Dementia, Without Behavioral Disturbance
❏ 294.11 Substance-Induced Persisting Dementia, With Behavioral Disturbance
❏ 291.2 Alcohol-Induced Persisting Dementia
❏ 293.83 Mood Disorder Due to Alzheimer's Disease, With Depressive Features
❏ 294.0 Amnestic Disorder Due to..., Transient/Chronic
❏ 292.83 Substance-Induced Persisting Amnestic Disorder
❏ 294.9 Mild/Moderate Neurocognitive Disorder (Cognitive Disorder NOS)
❏ 293.83 Mood Disorder Due to a General Medical Condition
❏ 310.1 Personality Change Due to a General Medical Condition
❏ 314.01 Attention-Deficit/Hyperactivity Disorder, Combined Type
❏ 314.01 Attention-Deficit/Hyperactivity Disorder, Predominantly Hyperactive-Impulsive Type
❏ 314.00 Attention-Deficit/Hyperactivity Disorder, Predominantly Inattentive Type
❏ 299.00 Autistic Disorder
❏ 299.80 Asperger's Disorder
❏ 299.80 Pervasive Developmental Disorder NOS (Atypical Autistic Disorder)
❏ 315.00 Reading Disorder
❏ 315.01 Mathematics Disorder
❏ 315.2 Disorder of Written Expression

Axis II:
❏ V71.09 No Diagnosis
❏ 799.9 Diagnosis Deferred

Rule Out:
❏ 301.83 Borderline Personality Disorder
❏ 301.81 Narcissistic Personality Disorder
❏ 301.7 Antisocial Personality Disorder
❏ 301.50 Histrionic Personality Disorder
❏ 301.82 Avoidant Personality Disorder
❏ 301.6 Dependent Personality Disorder
❏ 301.4 Obsessive-Compulsive Personality Disorder
❏ 301.20 Schizoid Personality Disorder
❏ 301.22 Schizotypal Personality Disorder
❏ 301.0 Paranoid Personality Disorder
❏ 317 Mild Mental Retardation
❏ 318.0 Moderate Mental Retardation

Axis III:

☐ No Contributory or Pertinent Medical Disorders Noted
☐ History of Traumatic Brain Injury (TBI)
☐ 435.9 Ischemic Attack, Transient (TIA)
☐ 436 Stroke (Cerebrovascular Accident)
☐ 332.0 Parkinson's Disease, Primary
☐ 331.0 Alzheimer's Disease
☐ 401.9 Hypertension, Essential
☐ 250.00 Diabetes Mellitus, Type II
☐ 850.9 Concussion
☐ 345.10 Epilepsy, Grand Mal
☐ 345.00 Epilepsy, Petit Mal
☐ 428.0 Failure, Congestive Heart
☐ 070.51 Hepatitis, Viral C

Axis IV:

☐ Psychosocial Stressors – Social, Occupational, Medical, Primary Support Group, Educational

Axis V:

☐ Global Assessment of Functioning (GAF): 45 Serious Moderate symptoms
☐ Prognosis: Deferred pending neuropsychological assessment and test results

---

Psychologist Name, PhD, PsyD, HSPP
Psychologist – State License #_____

FORM 2.4

MMSE–2 BRIEF VERSION TABULAR TEMPLATE WITH STANDARD MENTAL STATUS INFORMATION

Mental Status Examination Including the Mini-Mental State Examination, Second Edition, Brief Version, Blue Form (MMSE–2–BV–BF): Affect was _____. Mood was _____. Thought process was logical, sequential, relevant, and coherent. Thought content was reality-based and normal. The MMSE–2–BV–BF results were as follows:

TABLE 1 ■ **MMSE–2–BV–BF RESULTS**

Cognitive function	Patient's raw score	Maximum possible raw score
Registration	3	3
Orientation to Time	5	5
Orientation to Place	5	5
Recall	3	3
Total Raw Score[a]	**16**	**16**

Note: Lower raw scores indicate greater neurocognitive dysfunction. Overall neurocognitive function data are in boldface.

[a]Raw scores of 14 or less indicate the need for more comprehensive neuropsychological testing.[b]

[b]Using this cutoff, there is 97% confidence that a true case of neuropsychological disorder is recommended for further testing.

Screening result: Negative–positive for neuropsychological disorder.

Immediate, intermediate, and long-term memory functions were normal and intact. _____ was oriented to time, place, and person. Estimated intellectual function based on verbal skills, fund of general knowledge, and abstract reasoning abilities is average. Psychotic symptoms were not evident. There was no evidence of suicidal thoughts, intentions, or plans. There was no evidence of self-mutilation or self-harm.

FORM 2.5

MMSE–2 STANDARD VERSION TABULAR TEMPLATE WITH STANDARD MENTAL STATUS INFORMATION

Mental Status Examination Including the Mini-Mental State Examination, Second Edition, Standard Version, Blue Form (MMSE–2–SV–BF): Affect was _____. Mood was _____. Thought process was logical, sequential, relevant, and coherent. Thought content was reality-based and normal. The MMSE–2–SV–BF results were as follows:

TABLE 1 ■ **MMSE–2–SV–BF RESULTS**

Cognitive function	Patient's raw score	Maximum possible raw score
Registration	3	3
Orientation to Time	5	5
Orientation to Place	5	5
Recall	3	3
Attention and Calculation	5	5
Naming	2	2
Repetition	1	1
Comprehension	3	3
Reading	1	1
Writing	1	1
Drawing	1	1
Total Raw Score[a]	**30**	**30**

Note: Lower raw scores indicate greater neurocognitive dysfunction. Overall neurocognitive function data are in boldface.

[a]Raw scores of 27 or less indicate the need for more comprehensive neuropsychological testing.[b]

[b]Using this cutoff, there is 97% confidence that a true case of neuropsychological disorder is recommended for further testing.

Screening result: Negative–positive for neuropsychological disorder.

Immediate, intermediate, and long-term memory functions were normal and intact. _____ was oriented to time, place, and person. Estimated intellectual function based on verbal skills, fund of general knowledge, and abstract reasoning abilities is average. Psychotic symptoms were not evident. There was no evidence of suicidal thoughts, intentions, or plans. There was no evidence of self-mutilation or self-harm.

FORM 2.6

MMSE–2 EXPANDED VERSION TABULAR TEMPLATE WITH STANDARD MENTAL STATUS INFORMATION

Mental Status Examination Including the Mini-Mental State Examination, Second Edition, Expanded Version, Blue Form (MMSE–2–EV–BF): Affect was. Mood was. Thought process was logical, sequential, relevant, and coherent. Thought content was reality-based and normal. The MMSE–2–EV–BF results were as follows:

TABLE 1 ■ **MMSE–2–EV–BF RESULTS**

Cognitive function	Patient's raw score	Maximum possible raw score
Registration	3	3
Orientation to Time	5	5
Orientation to Place	5	5
Recall	3	3
Attention and Calculation	5	5
Naming	2	2
Repetition	1	1
Comprehension	3	3
Reading	1	1
Writing	1	1
Drawing	1	1
Story Memory	25	25
Processing Speed	35	35
Total Raw Score[a]	**90**	**90**

Note: Lower raw scores indicate greater neurocognitive dysfunction. Overall neurocognitive function data are in boldface.

[a]Raw scores of 50 or less indicate the need for more comprehensive neuropsychological testing.[b]

[b]Using this cutoff, there is 97% confidence that a true case of neuropsychological disorder is recommended for further testing.

Screening result: Negative–positive for neuropsychological disorder.

Immediate, intermediate, and long-term memory functions were normal and intact. _____ was oriented to time, place, and person. Estimated intellectual function based on verbal skills, fund of general knowledge, and abstract reasoning abilities is average. Psychotic symptoms were not evident. There was no evidence of suicidal thoughts, intentions, or plans. There was no evidence of self-mutilation or self-harm.

FORM 2.7

NAME OF PRACTICE
PSYCHOLOGICAL TEST LISTING FORM

Intelligence Tests

Wechsler Preschool and Primary Scale of Intelligence, Third Edition (WPPSI–III)
(ages 2:6 to 7:3)
Wechsler Intelligence Scale for Children, Fourth Edition (WISC–IV) (ages 6:0 to 16:11)
Wechsler Adult Intelligence Scale, Fourth Edition (WAIS–IV) (ages 16:0 to 90:11)

Achievement Tests

Wechsler Individual Achievement Test, Third Edition (WIAT–III) (ages 4:0 to 50:11)

Neuropsychological Tests

NEPSY–II, Form Ages 3 to 4 (ages 3:0 to 4:11)
NEPSY–II, Form Ages 5 to 16 (ages 5:0 to 16:11)
Neuropsychological Assessment Battery (NAB), Form 1 or 2 (ages 18:0 to 97:11)
Neuropsychological Assessment Screening Battery (NASB), Form 1 or 2 (ages 18:0 to 97:11)
Wechsler Memory Scale, Fourth Edition (WMS–IV) (ages 16:0 to 90:11)
Conners' Kiddie Continuous Performance Test, Version 5 (K–CPT) (ages 4:0 to 5:11)
Conners' Continuous Performance Test, Second Edition, Version 5 (CPT–II)
(ages 6:0 to 55:0 and older)

Symptom Rating Scales

Conners Early Childhood (Conners EC), Parent and Teacher/Childcare Forms
(ages 2:0 to 5:11)
Conners Comprehensive Behavior Rating Scales (Conners CBRS), Parent and Teacher
Forms (ages 6:0 to 18:11), and Self-Report Form (ages 8:0 to 18:11)
Gilliam Autism Rating Scale, Second Edition (GARS–2) (ages 3:0 to 22:11)
Gilliam Asperger's Disorder Scale (GADS) (ages 3:0 to 22:11)
Conners' Adult ADHD Rating Scales, Long Version (CAARS–L), Self-Report and
Observer Forms (ages 18:0 to 50:0 and older)

Self-Report Clinical and Personality Inventories

Millon Pre-Adolescent Clinical Inventory (M–PACI) (ages 9:0 to 12:11)
Millon Adolescent Clinical Inventory (MACI) (ages 13:0 to 19:11)
Millon Clinical Multiaxial Inventory–III (MCMI–III) (ages 18:0 to 88:11)
Minnesota Multiphasic Personality Inventory– Adolescent (MMPI–A) (ages 14:0 to 18:11)
Minnesota Multiphasic Personality Inventory–2–Restructured Form (MMPI–2–RF)
(ages 18:0 to 89:11)

Examiner Administered Personality Tests

Rorschach Inkblot Test, Comprehensive System, RIAP Fifth Edition (Rorschach–CS)
(ages 5:0 to 86:0)
Roberts–2 (ages 6:0 to 18:11)

Adaptive Behavior Tests

Vineland Adaptive Behavior Scales, Second Edition (Vineland–II) (ages 0:1 to 90:11)

FORM 2.8

NAME OF PRACTICE
PATIENT TEST INSTRUCTION FORM

Patient Name: _____

Account Number: _____

1. This completed initial psychological assessment will be submitted to your health insurance company for precertification of the ordered tests reviewed with you by the psychologist.
2. A maximum of _____ test hours are being requested, including administration, scoring, interpreting, and integrating the data, and composing the final comprehensive report.
3. Once precertification has been obtained, we shall contact you to schedule the following appointment(s) with the psychologist for purposes of test administration: _____
   _____.
4. Prior to, or at the time of the scheduled test administration appointment(s), please return any symptom rating scales given to you by the psychologist at the time of the initial psychological assessment. They may be returned in person or by mail to:
   Name of Psychologist, PhD, HSPP
   Name of Practice: _____
   Street Address: _____
   City, State: _____
   Please ensure that these rating scales are fully and properly completed, and that they are carefully secured by you until the time you submit them to the psychologist. They are critical for purposes of accurate diagnosis and properly addressing any related referral questions.
5. Once we notify you of test approval, you may come to the office any time during regular business hours (9:00 a.m. – 4:00 p.m.) to complete the following self-administered computer tests: _____
   _____.
   We suggest that you call our office first to determine availability of the testing computer. Upon your arrival, submit this form to the front desk staff for assistance.
6. Upon completion of the test administration process, the tests will be scored, interpreted, and presented within a final Psychological Evaluation Report including diagnoses, answers to any related referral questions, and treatment recommendations. A final appointment with the psychologist is advised for purposes of reviewing the test results and addressing any questions.
7. Reports may be released to the referral source(s) or relevant third parties by completing an "Authorization for Disclosure of Protected Health Information" form. Front desk staff will assist you in this regard.

FORM 2.9

NAME OF PRACTICE
PSYCHOLOGICAL TEST REQUEST AND LOG FORM

Identifying Information:

Patient Name
Last: _____   First: _____

Account Number: _____

Contact

Name: _____   Relationship to Patient: _____

Phone Number: _____

Test administration appointments to be scheduled with psychologist (number and duration): _____

Remind patient to independently complete the following self-administered test(s):
_____

	Date	Psychological Service
Hours Requested:		
Psychological Test Hours: _____	_____	_____
Neuropsychological Test Hours: _____	_____	_____
Hours Approved:		
Psychological Test Hours: _____	_____	_____
Neuropsychological Test Hours: _____	_____	_____

Insurance Authorization: (mark one)
_____ Required – From: _____   To: _____; _____ Not Required
_____ Self-Pay – Negotiated Fee: _____

Additional Information: _____
_____

Final Psychological Evaluation Report and Communication of the Results

This chapter covers the requisite steps in completing the final report and the manner in which such results can be most effectively communicated. Specific topics include (a) test administration, (b) test scoring, (c) simultaneous interpretation and report writing, (d) billing the testing hours, and, finally (e) communication of the results.

TEST ADMINISTRATION

Two important issues regarding test administration include (a) the number and duration of appointments and (b) the order of test administration.

Number and Duration of Appointments

The majority of test administrations should be completed within a 2-hour appointment. The two major exceptions to this tenet include the following: (a) administering a complete neuropsychological test battery for the purpose of ruling out one or more Cognitive Disorders as defined by the *Diagnostic and Statistical Manual of Mental Disorders, Fourth Edition, Text Revision* (*DSM-IV-TR*), which characteristically exceeds 2 hours of administration time; and (b) testing for Learning Disorders, which requires administration of both an intelligence test and achievement test for the purpose of computing a discrepancy analysis. Furthermore, in order to minimize diagnostically confounding fatigue and motivational effects, the duration of any test administration session should not exceed 2 hours. Therefore, the aforementioned neuropsychological and Learning Disorder evaluations can typically be completed within a couple of 2-hour appointments. Date, duration of appointment, and the specific tests and subtests administered should be noted on the "Psychological Test Request and Log Form" (see Form 2.9).

Order of Test Administration

Determining the most efficacious order in which to administer the particular tests is also a key issue. Following are some guidelines that are meant to maximize test reliability and validity. First, highest priority should typically be given to tests that are performance-based and require a good deal of cognitive effort and perseverance on the part of the examinee. This guideline most frequently pertains to measures of cognitive ability and includes intelligence, achievement, and neuropsychological tests (see Form 2.7). Second, although somewhat less obvious, increasing fatigue and flagging motivation on the part of the examinee also risks a diminution in the number and quality of responses ultimately produced on examiner-administered personality tests (see Form 2.7). Therefore, such tests should commonly be afforded a moderate or intermediate degree of priority superseded most frequently by the aforementioned cognitive ability tests.

Third, lowest priority should ordinarily be given to self-report and observer-report instruments that are symptom or behaviorally focused. This is because they are relatively less reliant on performance and ability as compared to the previously mentioned cognitive and personality tests. In particular, these measures include (a) self-report clinical and personality inventories (see Form 2.7) and (b) structured interviews such as the Vineland Adaptive Behavior Scales, Second Edition (Vineland–II) (Sparrow, Cicchetti, & Balla, 2005). Furthermore, the self-report clinical and personality inventories may be completed on an alternate day prior to any scheduled test administration sessions and without scheduling an appointment with the testing psychologist. Structured interviews are usually completed with a family member or third party well within the advised 2-hour criterion. Thus, fatigue here is not typically an issue.

Again, these are only meant as initial guidelines and should be modified according to the particular circumstances of a case. For example, a testing psychologist may use a personality test to initiate administration due to significant test anxiety elicited by an intelligence test in an examinee, wherein the need to provide *correct* answers and the presence of *timing* are both more explicit and potentially daunting.

TEST SCORING

Computerized scoring is readily available for the majority of frequently used standardized psychological tests. It is indispensible for both the efficiency and accuracy of determining standard scores. With the exception of the Conners' Adult ADHD Rating Scales, Long Version (CAARS–L) (Conners, Erhardt, & Sparrow, 1999) and Gilliam Asperger's Disorder Scale (GADS) (Gilliam, 2001), all of the tests in my recommended inventory possess computer-scoring capability (see Form 2.7). Irrespective of price, I recommend you purchase any available computer-scoring software for standardized testing as it is remarkably cost effective. Immediately subsequent to entering the data (usually raw scores), simply print the results needed for test interpretation and report writing.

In contrast, I advise against purchasing interpretation and report-writing software. Test interpretation is an interactive logical process that, for maximum accuracy, requires contextual information to be obtained during the initial psychological assessment and test observations. The scoring and interpretation tables I have prepared for each standardized test in the recommended inventory (see Section II) will facilitate the testing psychologist's thought process in this regard. Furthermore, computer interpretations can be quite inaccurate and misleading if they are printed in written form and become part of the mental health record. Although scoring software may include qualitative descriptions associated with standard scores (e.g., "low average"), these may be easily qualified by accurate test interpretation.

SIMULTANEOUS INTERPRETATION AND REPORT WRITING

The "Initial Psychological Assessment Report" serves as a framework for the "Final Psychological Evaluation Report" (see Form 3.1). Form 3.1 highlights the amendments and additions to the initial report with commentary outlined sections and are reviewed subsequently.

Modifications to the Initial Report

First, the title and heading are amended to read as "Psychological Evaluation Report" or, alternatively, "Neuropsychological Evaluation Report." The particular title is contingent upon the testing request and purpose, along with the type of billing code approved by insurance (see Chapter 2).

Second, the date should be changed to correspond with the date the report was written. Ideally, this should be the same date as the final face-to-face test administration session. This guideline contributes to more rapid and accurate test results as the data and case information are more readily available in the psychologist's short-term or working memory.

Referral information and presenting symptoms should be reviewed to reinforce this information in memory and for proofreading. This is ensued by a new section, "Assessment and Test Battery," which enumerates all of the assessment methods and tests, along with their corresponding date(s) of administration. The listing should reflect the order in which the tests are presented and discussed in the "Test Results and Interpretation" section. If self-report inventories and/or self-report and observer-report symptom rating scales were included, the dates should coincide with the times the instruments were completed. If those dates are not available, then the time of simultaneous test interpretation and report writing should be used. Related to the change of date, updating the age may be necessary, especially if the testing process was protracted longer than 1 month from the initial assessment.

To facilitate the composing of this section, I have prepared separate assessment and test battery templates for child and adult cases that are identified as "Assessment and Test Battery—Child" (Box 3.1) and "Assessment and Test Battery—Adult" (Box 3.2), respectively. Note that these listings include the same tests for child and adult cases found in the "Initial Psychological Assessment Report" templates (see section on "Initial Assessment Summary"), although with the addition of parentheticals for recording date(s) of administration and a modified order to reflect the most frequent test battery sequences.

The mental status examination section can be amended if additional diagnostically useful information was gleaned during the test administration process. This includes, although is not limited to, temporal vacillations in mental status, performance anxiety, and spontaneous commentary providing further evidence as to disturbances in thought content and process. In this case, add subsequent dates of completion within the parentheses adjacent to the mental status examination section.

If completed properly during the initial assessment, the following sections should typically need to be reviewed only for purposes of proofing and to facilitate test interpretation: Psychiatric/Medical/Psychological, Developmental (child cases only), Family, Interpersonal, Educational, Vocational, Substance Abuse, and Legal.

The "Test Results and Interpretation" section replaces the "Initial Assessment Summary" section of the initial report. This is the most vital and lengthy new section. In particular, it comprises a data-driven sequential presentation of the results of each test, including a succinct description of each score measured in terms of psychological constructs, abilities, and/or psychological symptoms. The tabular templates for each test have been fastidiously prepared to permit the simultaneous reporting of scores and interpreting their diagnostic meaning. In essence, this system integrates test interpretation and report writing to enhance the internal consistency and accuracy of both.

Section II of this book is devoted to the presentation of each test in the recommended inventory, along with its respective scoring and interpretation tabular templates to be inserted into the final report. The tables allow succinct interpretations of the results to minimize typing time. I present guidelines regarding the ordering of tests in the ensuing section. Prior to this, I want to finish discussing modifications to the initial report.

The "Pretest *DSM-IV-TR* Diagnoses" is amended to read "Posttest *DSM-IV-TR* Diagnoses." Prior to beginning the "Test Results and Interpretation" section, I routinely review this section along with any referral questions in the "Referral Information" section. Being cognizant of the "rule out" diagnoses and related referral questions allows you to focus on exactly which standard scores from each test are in need of reporting and interpreting.

The posttest diagnoses should logically follow the majority and weight of the evidence, and be a coherent and expected outcome to the reader. Those diagnoses not supported by the data can be effectively noted as having insufficient evidence; for example, "Noted:

Insufficient evidence for Attention-Deficit/Hyperactivity Disorder." This reminds the reader as to what was tested for and subsequently ruled out by the test data.

Other explanatory notations may provide the following: (a) pithy answers to any related referral questions and (b) particular neuropsychological, cognitive, and personality impairments, deficits, and/or strengths. For example, a diagnosis of Dementia may be supplemented with a brief explanatory notation on Axis I enumerating specific measured impairments in memory and language (i.e., aphasia), thus informing the reader which specific criteria for a Dementia have been met. Another example would include noting a measured ability for introspection on Axis II personality functioning, and associating this with a more favorable prognosis. Of course, the prognosis (and, if applicable, the Axis V *Global Assessment of Functioning* [GAF]) should be amended to be commensurate with the posttest diagnoses.

Finally, the "Psychological Evaluation Report" culminates with an enumeration of treatment recommendations. To facilitate the composing of this ultimate section, I have prepared separate treatment recommendation templates for child and adult cases that are identified as "Treatment Recommendations—Child" (Box 3.3) and "Treatment Recommendations—Adult" (Box 3.4), respectively. With the exception of the first and last items, which address psychiatric and substance abuse interventions, respectively, the child and adult listings are differentially worded to cover the most frequently indicated recommendations for that population.

For example, the child listing includes recommendations for improving more fundamental psychological abilities, including emotion regulation, executive functioning, and emotional intelligence. It also consists of recommendations for communicating the psychological test results with a child's or adolescent's school, and for child case management services.

In contrast, the adult listing includes treatment for Axis II maladaptive personality traits, communicating test results with vocational rehabilitation services, and adult day treatment services. Of course, these recommendations can be revised, elaborated, or replaced with more applicable recommendations. This includes, but is not limited to, recommending supplementary psychological testing should any diagnoses remain in question and amenable to clarification with the addition of one or two tests.[1]

Test Results and Interpretation: Principles for Test Order

Here, I discuss rules for ordering the test results and interpretation section. They are offered to facilitate the simultaneous reporting and interpretation of scores, along with enhancing the clarity and readability of the report. First, I discuss principles to follow for the initial ordering of tests. Next, I discuss contingency rules for modifying the initial test order, depending on what the psychologist discovers during the process of test interpretation.

The Initial Ordering of Tests

Cognitive ability tests that directly measure major psychological constructs should typically receive first priority. As stated prior, these include intelligence, achievement, and neuropsychological tests. Second priority should ordinarily be assigned to self-report clinical and personality inventories and symptom rating scales, which most closely parallel the *DSM-IV-TR* diagnostic categories, principally because they are of most direct assistance in differential diagnosis. Within this grouping, tests that more thoroughly measure the existence of a specific *DSM-IV-TR* disorder of relevance to a particular case should receive greater priority, for example, the Gilliam Autism Rating Scale, Second Edition (GARS–2) (Gilliam, 2006). For testing cases attempting to rule out Mental Retardation, this includes the Vineland–II (Sparrow et al., 2005), which should immediately ensue

[1] Once the final "Psychological Evaluation Report" is completed, I save it on the same external USB flash drive as the "Initial Psychological Assessment Report," although within a separate folder entitled "TESTING REPORTS." In this case, I save the patient's final report beginning with "R" for report, followed by an underline mark "__," last name, first name, and office file number; for example, R_Smith, Mary 233878. Again, the final reports will typically be saved alphabetically by computer software for easy location. In cases in which I conduct some additional psychological testing, which is the direct consequence of the original testing report, for example, to rule out Attention-Deficit/Hyperactivity Disorder suggested by neuropsychological test results, I use "S" (e.g., S_Smith, Mary 233878) and save it within a third folder on the same USB flash drive entitled, "SUPPLEMENTARY TESTING REPORTS." Again, I back up all saved files on a second USB flash drive.

any intelligence test results. This is because measured impairments in adaptive behavior are integral for such diagnosis (American Psychiatric Association, 2000).

Finally, examiner-administered personality tests that provide only indirect corroborating evidence regarding *DSM-IV-TR* diagnostic categories should typically be reported last, for example, the Rorschach Inkblot Test, Comprehensive System (Rorschach–CS) Depression Index (Exner, 2003). However, their importance here should not be minimized by such placement. In general, their implicit nature and low face validity renders these tests remarkably resistant to intentional efforts on the part of examinees to distort or manipulate the results (see Chapter 9). In this sense, they can be an invaluable part of a particular test battery. Furthermore, the data from these tests provide important evidence regarding etiology and potential targets for treatment intervention; for example, morbid responses (MOR) on the Rorschach–CS empirically demonstrate the presence of pessimism (Exner, 2003), thus indicating the need to modify a negative cognitive style as a viable treatment objective.

Next, I discuss rules for changing the initial test order contingent upon particular patterns of test results and their associated interpretations. It is certainly not intended as an exhaustive list and includes the most frequently occurring in practice.

Principles for Modifying the Initial Test Order
The principles for modifying the initial test order address the following: (a) response styles affecting test validity, (b) completely invalid test results, (c) test data that contradicts the vast majority of evidence, and (d) making explicit the logical thought process of the testing psychologist.

The first principle regards a distinct test-taking response pattern by the respondent, which deleteriously or otherwise compromises validity. The majority of tests involving self-report and observer-report data, at least within the recommended test inventory (see Form 2.7), include validity scales or test-taking response scales. When a respondent reveals a remarkable pattern that adversely affects validity for that particular test, and suggests a likely similar pattern on another test of the same format that does not include such validity scales, the former should be reported first.

For example, if a parent's ratings on the Conners Comprehensive Behavior Rating Scales (Conners, 2008) indicate a negative response style and likely magnification of symptoms, this test should be interpreted prior to the Gilliam Autism Rating Scale—Second Edition (Gilliam, 2006), which does not include validity scales. This is because the parent likely manifested a similar negative response style on the latter, which is more easily interpreted if such was revealed and discussed beforehand.

The second principle regards invalid test results. In instances where data is per se invalid and meaningful interpretation is precluded, such test should be given last priority. This most frequently includes either (a) insufficient data though negligence or flagrant test defensiveness or (b) pervasive and markedly excessive symptom exaggeration. The former may support a diagnosis of Noncompliance (*DSM-IV-TR* Code V15.81), while the latter may be useful in diagnosing either Malingering (*DSM-IV-TR* Code V65.2) or Factitious Disorder (*DSM-IV-TR* Codes 300.16 and 300.19). In any case, such data is best saved for last to supplement or qualify the diagnosis of more treatment-oriented *DSM-IV-TR Clinical and Personality Disorders.*

The third principle addresses test data that contradicts the vast majority of valid and reliable results in the battery. For example, a series of neuropsychological attention and memory subtests, along with symptom rating scales, can unequivocally show evidence of Attention-Deficit/Hyperactivity Disorder, Combined Type, yet a 20-minute continuous performance test is completely normal. I refer to the latter as a *false negative result*, as it inexplicably contradicts the vast weight of the evidence. Both false positive and false negative test results are most effectively reported and interpreted last, as it would otherwise unnecessarily disrupt the logical flow of the report.

The final principle is most aptly characterized as a general guideline. The test reporting and interpreting sequence should reflect the psychologist's logical thought process. As such, the ultimate test order should most clearly communicate this process.

BILLING THE TESTING HOURS

Immediately after the completing and signing of the final report, I enter all remaining activity on the "Psychological Test Request and Log Form." I then bill all of the used testing hours (not to exceed the number approved) on that date of service, which should usually coincide with the final date of face-to-face contact. In cases where more than one test administration appointment was necessitated, I place within my billing note all dates of contact and the particular test or subtests completed. Finally, in cases of test batteries involving exclusively self-report clinical and personality inventories, I bill all used testing hours on the date of simultaneous test interpretation and report writing. In this manner, nothing is billed prior to completion of the final report. Furthermore, the billing process is more efficient and minimizes billing errors.

COMMUNICATION OF THE RESULTS

The final goal in the testing process is to effectively communicate the results. This includes patients and any pertinent family members, referring clinicians in the event the case was not simply a self-referral, and any third parties deemed significant to the ongoing care of the patient.

Patients and Pertinent Family Members

Oral feedback to patients, along with any pertinent family members who are responsible for their care, should be mandatory in cases of self-referrals. Self-referrals include those initiated by patients or family members who are in some manner responsible for their welfare. All information and data within the report should be readily accessible to adults responsible for their own or their dependent's care. That is, full and complete disclosure of the entire report should be the prevailing rule. This is based on the premise that the final report comprises only that information and data deemed immediately relevant to diagnosis and sufficiently addressing any associated referral questions.

Every attempt should be made to utilize the feedback process therapeutically, including an integration of logical reasoning and the judicious employment of various treatment techniques and interventions (e.g., psychoeducation, reframing, processing issues of concern, providing support and empathy). As discussed in Chapter 2, if the 90806 individual billing code is being used for the test feedback session, diligent documentation of such interventions within the associated progress note is vital so as to maintain consistency between such code and the actual services provided. For additional and valuable guidance of how to integrate treatment interventions with psychological test data and feedback, I refer the reader to Finn (2007) who discusses in detail the concept and techniques of *therapeutic assessment* in which test results are effectively used to promote positive psychological change. The final "Psychological Evaluation Report" is the vehicle that organizes this feedback process. I personally give the patient and family members a hard copy of the final report, while I review the report with them in electronic form.

For the majority of cases, especially involving individuals with a 12th grade education or above, reviewing test results in the reported sequence is effective, culminating in a discussion of the posttest *DSM-IV-TR* diagnoses, answers to referral questions, and finally, recommendations for intervention. The review parallels the logical flow of the written report. For those with lesser degrees of formal education, consider reporting the posttest *DSM-IV-TR* diagnoses, answers to referral questions, and treatment recommendations first, such that the essential results do not become nebulous and/or obfuscated as the more detailed quantitative scores are reviewed.

Copies of the report may be released to the patient and family for their records, and to subsequent treating clinicians when follow-up treatment is initiated and the providers are adequately identified. Releasing the report to the patient and family permits them to present the report to treating clinicians from whom they seek follow-up consultation and treatment, and to any relevant third party for purposes of continuity of care.

Referring Clinicians

If the case was referred by another clinician, the final report should be released to that professional immediately subsequent to its completion. This may be accomplished prior to providing oral feedback to patients and any family members, as it is integral to more rapid and effective treatment intervention. As such, I advise the patient or responsible family members to complete a proper release of information form sometime prior to finishing the test administration process, unless, for some particular reason, they desire to know the results prior to release.

Although many referring clinicians are not well versed in psychometrics, the vast majority are sufficiently cognizant of *DSM-IV-TR* diagnoses to comprehend the essential results. Furthermore, the data-driven results and interpretation tables are readily available in the body of the report, which facilitates a more in-depth understanding of the results, along with the manner in which the diagnoses and answers to related referral questions were derived. Finally, referring clinicians should be encouraged to contact the testing psychologist directly with any follow-up questions.

Pertinent Third Parties

Pertinent third parties who should also receive a copy of the final report are most frequently identified during or following the oral feedback process. In this case, additional release forms may be completed for each third party, or the patient and family can release their copy if they indeed requested one.

SUMMARY

This chapter addressed the final two phases of the psychological assessment and testing process, including (a) completion of the final "Psychological Evaluation Report" and (b) communication of the results (see Figure 1.1). More specific topics included strategies for test administration, test scoring, simultaneous interpretation and report writing, billing the testing hours, and communication of the results.

This completes Section I of this book, the process of psychological assessment and standardized testing. Note that Section I largely emphasized *process* issues and variables. In contrast, Section II presents results and interpretation tables for all of the standardized tests in the same order listed in my recommended inventory (see Form 2.7). Therefore, Section II emphasizes more of the *content* of psychological testing.

REFERENCES

American Psychiatric Association. (2000). *Diagnostic and statistical manual of mental disorders* (4th ed., text rev.). Washington, DC: Author.

Conners, C. K. (2008). *Conners Comprehensive Behavior Rating Scales (Conners CBRS): Manual and interpretive update*. North Tonawanda, NY: Multi-Health Systems.

Conners, C. K., Erhardt, D., & Sparrow, E. (1999). *Conners' Adult ADHD Rating Scales (CAARS): Technical manual*. North Tonawanda, NY: Multi-Health Systems.

Exner, J. E. (2003). *The Rorschach a comprehensive system: Basic foundations and principles of interpretation* (4th ed., Vol. 1). Hoboken, NJ: John Wiley.

Finn, S. E. (2007). *In our client's shoes: Theory and techniques of therapeutic assessment*. New York, NY: Routledge.

Gilliam, J. E. (2001). *Gilliam Asperger's Disorder Scale examiner's manual (GADS)*. Austin, TX: PRO–ED.

Gilliam, J. E. (2006). *Gilliam Autism Rating Scale (GARS-2) examiner's manual* (2nd ed.). Austin, TX: PRO–ED.

Sparrow, S. S., Cicchetti, D. V., & Balla, D. A. (2005). *Vineland Adaptive Behavior Scales, 2nd edition (Vineland–II): Survey forms manual*. Minneapolis, MN: Pearson.

FORM 3.1

FINAL PSYCHOLOGICAL EVALUATION REPORT

Name of Practice:

Office Type: Outpatient Department

PSYCHOLOGICAL[1] EVALUATION REPORT

[1] *Or use "Neuropsychological" in the alternative.*

Patient Name: Last, First: _____

Account Number: _____

Date[2]: _____

[2] *Insert the date the "Psychological Evaluation Report" was completed. Ideally, this should be the date of the last face-to-face test administration session.*

Patient Identifying Information:

Chronological age is years months. Gender is female. DOB: (––/––/––––).

Referral Information:

The referral source is MD DO PhD, HSPP PsyD, HSPP MA, LMHC, MSW, LCSW, who indicated that the diagnosis remains ambiguous subsequent to clinical interview, examination, and ongoing observation, there has been poor or no response to treatment intervention for unknown reasons, and objective standardized testing will significantly impact treatment planning and outcome.

The stated *DSM-IV-TR* diagnoses needed to be ruled out include Attention-Deficit/Hyperactivity Disorder (ADHD).

Additional referral questions included:
1. _____
2. _____

Presenting symptoms included:

ADHD: difficulty sustaining attention, becoming easily distracted, being continuously forgetful, difficulty listening to others, disorganization, mind-wandering, failing to complete tasks, acting without considering consequences, fidgeting, difficulty remaining seated, and overactivity. These symptoms have an early onset prior to the age of 7 years, have been chronic, and associated with low academic achievement and work productivity.

ODD/CD: frequent loss of temper, being argumentative, repeatedly defying or refusing to follow rules, intentionally annoying others, frequently blaming others, irritable temperament, repeatedly violating the fundamental rights of others, repeatedly violating major societal rules and laws, including stealing, verbal and physical aggression, lack of remorse, and repeated school suspensions and expulsions for rule-breaking behavior.

PDD: chronic deficits in the ability to bond emotionally to others, lack of interest in forming relationships with others, ineffectual interpersonal skills, lack of eye contact and reciprocity, lack of empathy, isolative play and esoteric interests, social isolation, repetitive behaviors, and impaired ability to communicate effectively with others.

Mood: dysphoria, irritability, sad mood, fatigue, agitation, lack of interest, social withdrawal, flat affect, blunted affect, excessive guilt, low self-worth, periodic suicidal thoughts, severe mood swings vacillating from euphoria to dysphoria, affective instability, sleep and appetite problems, racing thoughts, grandiosity, impulsive and risky behaviors, distractibility, and diminished attention and concentration.

Anxiety: chronic apprehension, irritability, muscle tension, restlessness, becoming easily fatigued, sleep problems, periods of intense panic, trembling, difficulty breathing, racing heart, sweating, dizziness, feelings that things and people are not real, feeling detached, nausea, and feelings of terror and dread.

PTSD: exposure to severe trauma with subsequent response of intense fear and horror, repeated nightmares of the trauma, repeated memories of the trauma while awake, behaving as if the trauma was occurring, hypervigilance to anticipated danger, observed startle response, irritability, and anger outbursts.

Psychosis: auditory disturbances including hearing voices without knowing their source, visual disturbances including seeing things that are not actually present, tangential, disorganized, and fragmented speech, flat affect, inappropriate affect, ideas of persecution and grandeur, lack of volition, lost interest, poverty of speech, social withdrawal, and disorganized behavior.

Neuropsychological: reduced awareness of the environment, reduced ability to focus, shift, and sustain attention, disorientation, periods of mental confusion, impairments in immediate and intermediate memory, difficulties retrieving words when speaking to others, using words inappropriately, reduced ability to comprehend the spoken language of others, difficulties recognizing and naming objects, increasing motor dysfunction including loss of balance, motor incoordination, becoming lost and disoriented when navigating familiar routes, and a noticeable decline in forethought, organizing, and logical abstract reasoning abilities.

Personality: chronic difficulties establishing and maintaining interpersonal relationships of adequate intimacy, instability of interpersonal relationships, unstable self-image and sense of self, affective instability including intense episodic dysphoria lasting hours to days, inappropriate intense anger, episodes of self-mutilation in the form of cutting when experiencing dysphoria with dissociation of pain, repeated suicidal behavior, feelings of emptiness, intense fear of abandonment, impulsivity, failing to follow to social norms, chronic lying, frequently disregarding the basic rights of others, aggressiveness, irresponsibility, lack of guilt or remorse, low self-worth, lack of self-confidence, fear of embarrassment and humiliation, excessive dependency on others, need to be the center of attention, and shallow and dramatic emotional expression.

Onset was estimated to be: _____

Assessment and Test Battery[3,4]:

[3] *Add "Assessment and Test Battery" listing here in the order in which they will be reported in the "Test Results and Interpretation" section below. Also include pertinent dates of completion in adjacent parentheses.*

[4] *See "Assessment and Test Battery" Child and Adult templates.*

1. Diagnostic Interview (--/--/----): _____
   _____

2. Mental Status Examination and Behavioral Observations (--/--/----): _____

3. Conners Continuous Performance Test, Second Edition, Version 5 (CPT–II)
   (--/--/----): _____

4. _____

5. _____

Clinical Psychologist:
Psychologist Name, PhD, PsyD, HSPP _____
Psychologist – State License #_____

Mental Status Examination and Behavioral Observations:
Affect was _____. Mood was _____. Thought process was logical, sequential, relevant, and coherent. Thought content was reality-based and normal. Short-term memory functioning was _____. Long-term memory functioning was normal and intact, as evidenced by _____'s ability to provide age-appropriate historical information. _____ was oriented to time, place, and person. Activity level was normal. Social skills were normal including effective eye contact and reciprocity. Estimated intellectual function based on verbal skills and reasoning abilities is average. Psychotic symptoms were not evident. There was no evidence of suicidal thoughts, intentions, or plans. There was no evidence of self-mutilation or self-harm.

Psychiatric/Medical/Psychological:
The referring clinician completed a Behavioral Health Evaluation (i.e., 90801) in or about _____. No Behavioral Health Evaluation (i.e., 90801) has been done within the past year. Psychiatric history includes outpatient treatment by _____. Family psychiatric history is negative positive for ADHD, Bipolar Disorder, Depressive Disorder, Schizophrenia, Dementia, and Learning Disorder. Medical functioning is unremarkable remarkable for _____ is not taking any current medications. Current medications include _____. There is a negative history of severe head injuries, seizure disorder, and major surgeries. Vision is normal. Hearing is normal. _____ has been in psychosocial therapy for _____. Previous neuropsychological testing has not been done.

Developmental:
There were no pre-, peri-, or post-natal complications reported. Gestation was full-term. Birth weight was _____ pounds _____ ounces. Birth length was _____ inches. Developmental milestones were reported as falling within the normal range.

Family:
_____ lives with _____.

Interpersonal:
Interpersonal relationships were described as satisfactory in both quality and quantity. Social skills were described as ineffectual with deficits in friendships of adequate intimacy.

Educational:
_____is in grade _____. Academic performance has typically been _____. Behavioral grades have typically been _____. There has been no grade retention. _____ was retained in grade _____, is receiving general special education instruction, has a continuing IEP, and is classified as _____.

Vocational:
None.

Substance Abuse:
Unremarkable.

Legal:
Unremarkable.

Test Results and Interpretation[5]:

CPT–II[6,7] _____

MACI[8] _____

_____

_____

Posttest *DSM-IV-TR* Diagnoses[9]:

Axis I:

❑ 312.9 Disruptive Behavior Disorder NOS
❑ 296.90 Mood Disorder NOS
❑ 311 Depressive Disorder NOS
❑ 296.80 Bipolar Disorder NOS
❑ 300.00 Anxiety Disorder NOS
❑ 298.9 Psychotic Disorder NOS
❑ 294.9 Cognitive Disorder NOS
❑ 309.0 Adjustment Disorder With Depressed Mood
❑ 309.24 Adjustment Disorder With Anxiety
❑ 309.28 Adjustment Disorder With Mixed Anxiety and Depressed Mood
❑ 309.3 Adjustment Disorder With Disturbance of Conduct
❑ 309.4 Adjustment Disorder With Mixed Disturbance of Emotions and Conduct
❑ 309.9 Adjustment Disorder, Unspecified
❑ 995.54 Physical Abuse of Child
❑ 995.53 Sexual Abuse of Child
❑ 995.52 Neglect of Child
Provisional, Rule Out:

❑ 314.01 Attention-Deficit/Hyperactivity Disorder, Combined Type
❑ 314.01 Attention-Deficit/Hyperactivity Disorder, Predominantly Hyperactive-Impulsive Type
❑ 314.00 Attention-Deficit/Hyperactivity Disorder, Predominantly Inattentive Type
❑ 313.81 Oppositional Defiant Disorder
❑ 312.81 Conduct Disorder, Childhood-Onset Type
❑ 312.82 Conduct Disorder, Adolescent-Onset Type
❑ 312.89 Conduct Disorder, Unspecified Onset
❑ 299.00 Autistic Disorder
❑ 299.80 Asperger's Disorder
❑ 299.80 Pervasive Developmental Disorder NOS (Atypical Autistic Disorder)
❑ 313.89 Reactive Attachment Disorder, Inhibited Type and Disinhibited Type
❑ 300.4 Dysthymic Disorder, Early Onset
❑ 296.22 Major Depressive Disorder, Single Episode, Moderate
❑ 296.32 Major Depressive Disorder, Recurrent, Moderate
❑ 301.13 Cyclothymic Disorder, Early Onset
❑ 296.62 Bipolar I Disorder, Mixed, Moderate
❑ 296.89 Bipolar II Disorder
❑ 300.02 Generalized Anxiety Disorder
❑ 309.81 Posttraumatic Stress Disorder, Chronic
❑ 300.3 Obsessive-Compulsive Disorder

---

[5] Delete entire section "Initial Assessment Summary" and replace with new "Test Results and Interpretation" section.

[6] Insert tabular templates for each test in the battery. Enter pertinent scores and results for selected indices, scales, subscales, and/or variables for each test.

[7] See tabular templates for each test in the recommended inventory (Section II).

[8] Insert succinct narrative interpretations of the data at strategic points between tables.

[9] Replace "Pretest" with "Posttest," then modify the Posttest DSM-IV-TR Diagnoses according to the test results and interpretations. Add elaborative diagnostic notations and succinct answers to any related referral questions where pertinent.

❏ 295.20 Schizophrenia, Undifferentiated Type, Childhood Onset
❏ 294.9 Mild/Moderate/Severe Neurocognitive Disorder (Cognitive Disorder NOS)
❏ 293.83 Mood Disorder Due to a General Medical Condition
❏ 310.1 Personality Change Due to a General Medical Condition
❏ 315.00 Reading Disorder
❏ 315.01 Mathematics Disorder
❏ 315.2 Disorder of Written Expression
❏ 315.9 Learning Disorder NOS
❏ 315.39 Phonological Disorder
❏ 315.31 Expressive Language Disorder
❏ 315.32 Mixed Receptive-Expressive Language Disorder
❏ 315.4 Developmental Coordination Disorder
❏ 307.0 Stuttering
❏ 307.6 Enuresis (Not Due to a General Medical Condition), Nocturnal/Diurnal
❏ 787.6 Encopresis With Constipation and Overflow Incontinence
❏ 307.7 Encopresis Without Constipation and Overflow Incontinence

Axis II:

❏ V71.09 No Diagnosis
❏ 799.9 Diagnosis Deferred

Rule Out:

❏ 317 Mild Mental Retardation
❏ 318.0 Moderate Mental Retardation
❏ 301.83 Borderline Personality Disorder
❏ 301.81 Narcissistic Personality Disorder

Axis III:

❏ No contributory medical disorders noted
❏ History of Traumatic Brain Injury (TBI)
❏ Preterm birth with low birth weight
❏ History of Meningitis
❏ Prenatal exposure to teratogens
❏ History of lead poisoning
❏ 250.00 Diabetes Mellitus, Type II
❏ 850.9 Concussion
❏ 345.10 Epilepsy, Grand Mal

Axis IV:

❏ Psychosocial Stressors – Social, Educational, Medical

Axis V:

❏ Global Assessment of Functioning (GAF): 45 Serious Moderate symptoms
❏ Prognosis: Deferred pending neuropsychological assessment and test results[10]

Treatment Recommendations[11, 12]:

1. Psychiatric biological intervention for the above-listed Axis I *DSM-IV-TR* diagnoses, and palliative for the above listed Axis II *DSM-IV-TR* diagnoses.
2. Psychotherapy to improve executive functioning skills, emotional self-regulation, mood stability, self-esteem, emotional intelligence, social and interpersonal skills, assertiveness skills, and for symptom reduction.

[10] *Modify the prognosis consistent with the test results, interpretations, and final diagnoses.*

[11] *Add "Treatment Recommendations" here.*

[12] *See "Treatment Recommendations" Child and Adult templates.*

3. Child case management services are advised for more comprehensive behavioral intervention.
4. It is advised that these test and assessment results be shared with the school for coordination of mental health treatment intervention with academic intervention, for continuity of care, and to assist in determining eligibility for special services.
5. Substance abuse intervention.

_____

Psychologist Name, PhD, PsyD, HSPP
Psychologist – State License #_____

Box 3.1 Assessment and Test Battery—Child **51**

BOX 3.1

ASSESSMENT AND TEST BATTERY—CHILD

Assessment and Test Battery

1. Diagnostic Interview (--/--/----)

2. Mental Status Examination and Behavioral Observations (--/--/----)

3. Conners' Continuous Performance Test, Second Edition, Version 5 (CPT–II) (--/--/----)

4. Conners' Kiddie Continuous Performance Test, Version 5 (K–CPT) (--/--/----)

5. Conners Comprehensive Behavior Rating Scales (Conners CBRS), Parent and Teacher Forms (--/--/----)

6. Conners Comprehensive Behavior Rating Scales (Conners CBRS), Parent and Self-Report Forms (--/--/----)

7. Conners Comprehensive Behavior Rating Scales (Conners CBRS), Self-Report Form (--/--/----)

8. Conners Early Childhood (Conners EC), Parent and Teacher/Childcare Forms (--/--/----)

9. NEPSY–II, Full Battery, Form Ages 3 to 4 (--/--/----)

10. NEPSY–II, Full Battery, Form Ages 5 to 16 (--/--/----)

11. NEPSY–II, General Battery, Form Ages 3 to 4 (--/--/----)

12. NEPSY–II, General Battery, Form Ages 5 to 16 (--/--/----)

13. NEPSY–II, Form Ages 3 to 4, Social Perception Subtests (--/--/----)

14. NEPSY–II, Form Ages 5 to 16, Social Perception Subtests (--/--/----)

15. NEPSY–II, Form Ages 3 to 4, Attention and Executive Functioning, Memory and Learning Subtests (--/--/----)

16. NEPSY–II, Form Ages 5 to 16, Attention and Executive Functioning, Memory and Learning Subtests (--/--/----)

17. NEPSY–II, Form Ages 3 to 4, Attention and Executive Functioning, Memory and Learning, Social Perception Subtests (--/--/----)

18. NEPSY–II, Form Ages 5 to 16, Attention and Executive Functioning, Memory and Learning, Social Perception Subtests (--/--/----)

19. Gilliam Autism Rating Scale, Second Edition (GARS–2) (--/--/----)

20. Gilliam Asperger's Disorder Scale (GADS) (--/--/----)

21. Millon Pre-Adolescent Clinical Inventory (M–PACI) (--/--/----)

22. Millon Adolescent Clinical Inventory (MACI) (--/--/----)

(Cont.)

BOX 3.1

ASSESSMENT AND TEST BATTERY—CHILD (*Cont.*)

23. Minnesota Multiphasic Personality Inventory–Adolescent (MMPI–A) (––/––/––––)

24. Rorschach Inkblot Test, Comprehensive System, RIAP, Fifth Edition, Ages 5 to 17 (Rorschach–CS, Ages 5 to 17) (––/––/––––)

25. Roberts–2 (––/––/––––)

26. Vineland Adaptive Behavior Scales, Second Edition (Vineland–II) (––/––/––––)

27. Wechsler Intelligence Scale for Children, Fourth Edition (WISC–IV) (––/––/––––)

28. Wechsler Preschool and Primary Scale of Intelligence, Third Edition, Form Ages 2:6 to 3:11 (WPPSI–III, Form Ages 2:6 to 3:11) (––/––/––––)

29. Wechsler Preschool and Primary Scale of Intelligence, Third Edition, Form Ages 4:0 to 7:3 (WPPSI–III, Form Ages 4:0 to 7:3 (––/––/––––)

30. Wechsler Adult Intelligence Scale, Fourth Edition (WAIS–IV) (––/––/––––)

31. Wechsler Individual Achievement Test, Third Edition, Pre-Kindergarten (WIAT–III, PK) (––/––/––––)

32. Wechsler Individual Achievement Test, Third Edition, K–12 (WIAT–III, K–12) (––/––/––––)

33. Ability–Achievement Discrepancy Analysis (––/––/––––)

34. Wechsler Memory Scale, Fourth Edition (WMS–IV), Form Ages 16 to 69 (––/––/––––)

35. Ability–Memory Discrepancy Analysis (––/––/––––)

Box 3.2 Assessment and Test Battery—Adult **53**

BOX 3.2

ASSESSMENT AND TEST BATTERY—ADULT

Assessment and Test Battery

1. Diagnostic Interview (--/--/----)

2. Mental Status Examination (--/--/----)

3. Mental Status Examination Including the Mini-Mental State Examination, Second Edition, Expanded Version, Blue Form (MMSE–2–EV–BF) (--/--/----)

4. Mental Status Examination Including the Mini-Mental State Examination, Second Edition, Standard Version, Blue Form (MMSE–2–SV–BF) (--/--/----)

5. Mental Status Examination including the Mini-Mental State Examination, Second Edition, Brief Version, Blue Form (MMSE–2–BV–BF) (--/--/----)

6. Mental Status Examination including the Mini-Mental State Examination (MMSE) (--/--/----)

7. Wechsler Adult Intelligence Scale, Fourth Edition (WAIS–IV) (--/--/----)

8. Wechsler Memory Scale, Fourth Edition (WMS–IV), Form Ages 65 to 90 (--/--/----)

9. Wechsler Memory Scale, Fourth Edition (WMS–IV), Form Ages 16 to 69 (--/--/----)

10. Ability–Memory Discrepancy Analysis (--/--/----)

11. Wechsler Individual Achievement Test, Third Edition, K–12 (WIAT–III, K–12) (--/--/----)

12. Ability–Achievement Discrepancy Analysis (--/--/----)

13. Neuropsychological Assessment Battery (NAB), Form 1 (//;//)

14. Neuropsychological Assessment Battery (NAB), Attention Module, Form 2 (--/--/----)

15. Neuropsychological Assessment Screening Battery (NASB), Form 1 (--/--/----)

16. Neuropsychological Assessment Battery (NAB), ## and ## Modules, Form 1 (--/--/----)

17. Millon Clinical Multiaxial Inventory–III (MCMI–III) (--/--/----)

18. Minnesota Multiphasic Personality Inventory–2–Restructured Form (MMPI–2–RF) (--/--/----)

19. Minnesota Multiphasic Personality Inventory–2 (MMPI–2) (--/--/----)

20. Rorschach Inkblot Test, Comprehensive System, RIAP Fifth Edition, Ages 18 to 86 (Rorschach–CS, Ages 18 to 86) (--/--/----)

21. Conners' Continuous Performance Test, Second Edition, Version 5 (CPT–II) (--/--/----)

22. Conners' Adult ADHD Rating Scales (CAARS–L), Self-Report and Observer Forms (--/--/----)

23. Vineland Adaptive Behavior Scales, Second Edition (Vineland–II) (--/--/----)

24. Legal System Questionnaire (LSQ) (--/--/----)

BOX 3.3

TREATMENT RECOMMENDATIONS—CHILD

Treatment Recommendations

1. Psychiatric biological intervention for the above-listed Axis I *DSM-IV-TR* diagnoses, and palliative for the above-listed Axis II *DSM-IV-TR* diagnoses.

2. Psychotherapy to improve executive functioning skills, emotional self-regulation, mood stability, self-esteem, emotional intelligence, social and interpersonal skills, assertiveness skills, and for symptom reduction.

3. Child case management services are advised for more comprehensive behavioral intervention.

4. It is advised that these assessment and test results be shared with _____'s school for coordination of mental health treatment intervention with academic intervention, for continuity of care, and to assist in determining eligibility for special services.

5. Substance abuse intervention.

Box 3.4 Treatment Recommendations—Adult **55**

BOX 3.4

TREATMENT RECOMMENDATIONS—ADULT

Treatment Recommendations

1. Psychiatric biological intervention for the above-listed Axis I *DSM-IV-TR* diagnoses, and palliative for the above-listed Axis II *DSM-IV-TR* diagnoses.

2. Psychotherapy to modify Axis II maladaptive personality traits, and for the above-listed Axis I *DSM-IV-TR* diagnoses.

3. EMDR psychotherapy for PTSD.

4. Adult case management services are advised for more comprehensive behavioral intervention.

5. Adult day treatment services are advised to improve (a) basic coping and daily living skills, (b) adaptive behavioral skills, and (c) psychological stability.

6. It is advised that these test and assessment results be shared with _____'s academic institution to assist in determining eligibility for special services.

7. It is advised that these assessment and test results be shared with vocational rehabilitation for coordination of mental health treatment intervention with vocational intervention and for continuity of care.

8. Substance abuse intervention.

Intelligence Tests 4

THE CONSTRUCT OF INTELLIGENCE AND ITS MEASUREMENT

The psychological construct of *intelligence* has been defined as the ability to learn from experience, acquire knowledge, and use resources effectively in adapting to new situations or solving problems (Ciccarelli & White, 2012; Wechsler, 1975). This definition espouses the *aptitude view of intelligence* or the ability to learn, in contrast to the *achievement view* which is more associated with educational attainment (Larsen & Buss, 2010). Therefore, it is proposed that intelligence tests measure a complex cognitive ability trait, referred to as a general factor *g* or *intelligence quotient* (IQ), which represents an integration of several more specific types of advanced formal reasoning or *s* factors (Spearman, 1927), and thus cortical functioning. This is in contrast to measuring more rudimentary neuropsychological brain–behavior relationships (see Chapter 6).

Construct validity for tests that measure *g* or IQ has been most consistently provided by robust and reliable predictions of academic performance spanning over 100 years (Binet, 1903; Elshout & Veenman, 1992; Gagne & St. Pere, 2001; Sternberg & Kaufman, 1998; Terman, 1916; Willingham, 1974). Additional corroborating and cogent evidence of the adaptive nature of intelligence is provided by a wealth of predictive positive correlations between IQ and occupational performance (Hunter, 1983; Hunter & Hunter, 1984), health and longevity (Deary, Whalley, & Starr, 2003; Gottfredson, 2004; Gottfredson & Deary, 2004), and, as least in part, social mobility (Capron & Duyme, 1989; Mackintosh, 1998). In fact, there are indications that intellectual ability or IQ may have commensurate or greater impact on many real-life outcomes as opposed to stylistic noncognitive personality traits (e.g., see Gottfredson, 2004).

Therefore, I believe we can be confident in the construct of intelligence as defined here. I am also convinced that (a) measuring intellectual ability plays a vital role in mental health practice, and (b) it can be reliably and validly measured by means of adequately developed standardized IQ tests.

DIAGNOSTIC REASONS FOR INCLUSION WITHIN A TEST BATTERY

Intelligence tests are integral to ruling out Borderline Intellectual Functioning, Mental Retardation, and Learning Disorders. The last two require additional standardized tests of adaptive behavior and achievement (see Chapters 10 and 5, respectively). They are also useful as part of a neuropsychological battery in which the focus of testing is on memory ability, wherein an ability–memory discrepancy analysis is diagnostically desired (see Chapter 6). Finally, they may be employed independently as a screening tool for a Learning Disorder; for example, by noting any measured discrepancies between verbal and perceptual reasoning abilities.

The most likely related referral questions include (a) estimating the likely success of an individual matriculating through a training or educational program, (b) suggesting the level and types of training indicated by the results, (c) addressing issues of mental competence, and (d) recommendations for adjusting psychological interventions based on measured intelligence. As such, the most likely referral sources include (a) welfare programs to assist in determining eligibility for disability benefits, (b) vocational rehabilitation programs to assist in career development, (c) court referrals to determine issues of competency and insanity, (d) mental health professionals such that they may adjust treatment intervention accordingly, and (e) adults or parents whose child is experiencing significant difficulties with academic performance.

INSURANCE COVERAGE ISSUES

Referrals for intelligence testing from welfare and vocational rehabilitation programs do not present coverage difficulties. These programs routinely remunerate for such testing as part of their services. Referrals from mental health professionals requesting intelligence testing may be denied for want of medical necessity. Thus, meticulous documentation of how such testing will improve treatment outcome is necessitated. Finally, self and parental referrals are likely to be denied due to lack of medical necessity per se and, regarding largely minors, within the purview of the educational system.

In the latter case, the probability of approval can be somewhat enhanced under the following two conditions: (a) advising the parents to obtain documentation of the school's refusal to complete testing despite remarkable academic underachievement, associating the child's academic problems with an emerging psychological disorder (e.g., escalating depressive symptoms), and explicitly incorporating these facts within the initial report; and (b) documenting how psychological treatment for a valid psychological disorder will be better adapted and, hence, more effective, with an accurate measure of intellectual ability. For example, reasoning that the patient's self-monitoring of negative cognitions associated with Dysthymic Disorder may be precluded due to suspected extremely low or borderline verbal ability.

THE WECHSLER TESTS

I have selected use of the three Wechsler intelligence tests because of their diagnostically useful factor structure. Furthermore, they are conveniently conormed companions to the Wechsler tests of achievement and memory. This permits quantitative ability–achievement and ability–memory discrepancy analyses (see Chapters 5 and 6, respectively).

The Wechsler Preschool and Primary Scale of Intelligence, Third Edition (WPPSI–III) is normed on children aged 2 years 6 months to 7 years 3 months (Wechsler, 2002a, 2002b). There exist two forms based upon the following age ranges: (a) 2 years 6 months to 3 years 11 months and (b) 4 years 0 months to 7 years 3 months. The Wechsler Intelligence Scale for Children, Fourth Edition (WISC–IV) is normed on children aged 6 years 0 months to 16 years 11 months (Wechsler, 2003a, 2003b). Finally, the Wechsler Adult Intelligence Scale, Fourth Edition (WAIS–IV) is normed on individuals 16 years 0 months to 90 years 11 months (Wechsler, 2008a, 2008b). Together, the three versions comprise an impressive age range so as to effectively apply to the majority of referred testing cases within mental health practice.

All of the Wechsler tests are published by the Psychological Corporation (PsychCorp), which is an affiliate of Pearson, Incorporated. CD-ROM scoring software is available for all three versions and includes (a) the WPPSI–III Scoring Assistant (2002), (b) the WISC–IV Scoring Assistant (2003), and (c) the WAIS–IV Scoring Assistant (2008). Next, I review the results and interpretation tables in detail, along with the manner in which they are intended to be employed.

RESULTS AND INTERPRETATION TABLES

Form 4.1 contains the results and interpretation tables of the WPPSI–III, Form Ages 2:6 to 3:11, while Form 4.2 contains the results and interpretation tables to the WPPSI–III, Form Ages 4:0 to 7:3. Form 4.3 contains the results and interpretation tables to the WISC–IV. Finally, Form 4.4 contains the WAIS–IV scoring and interpretation tables. Because of the comparable factor structure among the three tests, their respective tables are similarly organized. This resemblance also facilitates their use by the testing psychologist. Unless otherwise indicated, my comments apply to all three Wechsler results and interpretation tables.

Composite Score Summary

Table 1 begins the analysis by presenting a summary of the composite scores. These are the principal data for considering diagnoses based upon criteria listed in the *Diagnostic and Statistical Manual of Mental Disorders, Fourth Edition, Text Revision* (*DSM-IV-TR*) (American Psychiatric Association, 2000). Because of its usual prominent diagnostic role, the Full Scale contains a number of distinctive features including bold text, association with the construct definition of intelligence, and full APA-formatted references of such construct definition located within the Table 1 notes.

Among the composites that contribute to the Full Scale, there currently exists discrepancy among the Wechsler tests. This is due to both age-related differences in specific types of intelligence measured and differences in test construction. First, the WAIS–IV and the WISC–IV have moved exclusively to the factor-analyzed *indices*; whereas, the WPPSI–III retains the theoretical *IQs*.[1] Second, note the lack of a Working Memory Index on the WPPSI–III and the addition of a useful General Language Composite, which can effectively screen for a Learning Disorder. Although the latter is optional, in that it does not contribute to the Full Scale, I invariably administer it as being diagnostically useful and cost-effective. Also note that in all the Wechsler results and interpretation tables, scales that are either optional and/or do not contribute to the Full Scale are listed last.

In order from left to right, the columns present the scale name, composite score, percentile rank, 90% confidence interval, qualitative description, and the measured abilities associated with a particular scale. These columns are in need of further explication.

First, the standard scores are afforded priority by virtue of their being coterminous with the scale names. This is because they are linear transformations, which preserve the individual's score position when compared to the norm reference group mean and standard deviation. Percentile ranks are included as they tend to be more easily comprehended by lay individuals. Note that they are area transformations, which exaggerate deviation changes near the mean and minimize such changes in the extremes. The adjacent confidence intervals duly report and acknowledge the margins of error in test measurement.

Next, the qualitative descriptions used are the most recently published (Wechsler, 2008b). For convenience, Box 4.1 represents a succinct guide for inserting the appropriate qualitative descriptions into the results and interpretation tables for all Wechsler tests.[2] The table in Box 4.1 is adapted from three tables in the WAIS-IV technical manual that provide the standard scores, corresponding standard deviations from the mean, and descriptive classifications (Wechsler, 2008b, Tables 6.1, 6.2, & 6.3, pp. 124–125). Note that the subtest scale scores are not associated with descriptive classifications within the manual. Therefore, for interpretative convenience, I applied the descriptive classifications to the subtest scaled score ranges that corresponded to the same standard deviation ranges of the composite scores.

[1] *The WPPSI–IV will undoubtedly undergo transition to the quantitatively derived indices, as did the WISC–IV and WAIS–IV before it.*

[2] *The WPPSI–III Scoring Assistant, WISC–IV Scoring Assistant, and WAIS–IV Scoring Assistant all provide the proper qualitative descriptions. Therefore if you purchase this software, use of Box 4.1 is not necessary for the composite score summary tables.*

Lastly, immediately flanking the qualitative descriptions are interpretive summary descriptions of the abilities measured by each composite score. For accuracy, these descriptions were carefully composed and worded based upon my review of the subtest factor loadings and more elaborate narrative descriptions of the various indices and quotients provided within the respective technical and interpretive manuals (Wechsler, 2002b, 2003b, 2008b). Their inclusion is a key component for expediting the interpretation process, while enhancing both precision and clarity. Furthermore, they facilitate comprehension of the results to readers and the feedback process with patients and family members. For this reason, you will find such scale, subtest, and variable interpretive descriptions for virtually all of the results and interpretation tables I have devised throughout Section II.

Table 1 is accompanied by notes that further clarify in succinct style the meaning of the scores. The composite score mean and standard deviation are first provided. This is ensued by a clarification of the directional significance of the scores. One of the most frequent questions asked by patients and family members during feedback is, "What do high scores and low scores mean?" As a general principle, I have chosen to emphasize the problematic direction in the table notes. I believe this interpretive approach is more consistent with the primary purpose of psychological testing in mental health, which is to detect any disorder or problems in need of rectification. The remaining notes clarify abbreviations used in the table body and provide references to the defined construct of intelligence.

In general, the Table 1 composite score summary is designed to provide maximum information concerning scores and their meaning regarding the measured construct of intelligence. A succinct narrative interpretation of the data should routinely address three issues: (a) reporting critical, statistically significant composite score differences ($p < .05$), (b) highlighting the diagnostic significance of the data, and (c) addressing any related referral questions.

Regarding the former, the principal WPPSI–III comparison is that between the Verbal and Performance Intelligence Quotients. For both the WAIS–IV and the WISC–IV, the analogous comparison is between the Verbal and Perceptual Reasoning Indices. Statistical significance should be noted and the interpretation of the Full Scale properly qualified for diagnostic purposes. Regarding the WAIS–IV, comparison of the Processing Speed and Working Memory Indices to that of the Full Scale ($p < .05$) is germane, as statistical significance may convince the testing psychologist to supplant the Full Scale with the General Ability Index for purposes of more accurate interpretation and diagnosis. Any other comparisons reported should be diagnostically pertinent, otherwise not addressed in the interests of brevity.[3]

Subtest Score Summary

Subtest score summary tables follow the composite score summary. They are intended to be supplementary and reported *only* when not doing so renders the *DSM-IV-TR* diagnosis misleading or fails to adequately address any related referral questions. For example, consider the following results: Full Scale = 57 and Verbal and Perceptual Reasoning are statistically equivalent ($p > .05$). If the diagnostic issue is to simply rule out Mild Mental Retardation with no accompanying referral questions, the subtest score summary tables need not be reported. The report should move immediately to standardized data regarding adaptive behavior functioning; for example, the Vineland Adaptive Behavior Scales, Second Edition (Sparrow, Cicchetti, & Balla, 2005; also see Chapter 10).

[3] *Note that here and throughout the book, the motif I wish to convey is brevity and pertinence of the report. Many psychologists are trained to compose comprehensive psychological evaluation reports. Although remarkably thorough, such reports are also ponderous. Two risks are that the most imperative results will become obfuscated and/or the reader will simply stop reading. The approach I am advocating is designed to minimize such risks, while maximizing accuracy.*

The subtest score summary tables are similarly designed to that of the composite score summary table with two exceptions. First, there is no confidence interval column in order to obviate the reporting of excessive data. Furthermore, the confidence intervals reported in the composite score summary adequately convey to the reader the fact that there exists some degree of inevitable measurement error.

Second, I added a comparable qualitative description column so as permit narrative interpretation of the tables to be as succinct as possible. As indicated prior, for convenience I inserted a subtest score column into Box 4.1. Note that the subtest scores are associated with the identical standard deviation ranges as the composite scores. This will allow the testing psychologist to insert consistent, and therefore comparable, qualitative descriptions into the subtest score results and interpretation tables.[4] Once again, the measured abilities inserted for each subtest were based upon my scrutiny of the subtest descriptions, along with the results of cited empirical research of the specific cognitive abilities measured by each subtest available within the respective technical and interpretive manuals (Wechsler, 2002b, 2003b, 2008b).

Finally, the subtest score table notes provide much of the same information as the composite score summary table with one necessary addition. Subtests that are optional are explicitly identified and defined as such. This is essentially to inform the reader that core test data were not neglected in the evaluation.

[4] *The WPPSI-III Scoring Assistant, WISC-IV Scoring Assistant, and WAIS-IV Scoring Assistant do not report qualitative descriptions for the subtest scores. Therefore, you will need Box 4.1 to insert such information into the tables.*

SUMMARY

This chapter discussed the testing of intelligence and its application to addressing *DSM-IV-TR* differential diagnoses and related referral questions. First, the construct of intelligence and its measurement was defined. Next, diagnostic reasons justifying the inclusion of such tests within a particular battery were discussed, ensued by insurance coverage issues. The Wechsler tests of intelligence were then cited as those recommended and hence included within my test inventory. The chapter concluded with an extended presentation of the Wechsler results and interpretation tables I have prepared, along with how they are intended to be employed.

The next chapter addresses the formal testing of achievement. As such, coverage will begin with the measurement of academic learning. However, the more frequent and diagnostically relevant testing for *DSM-IV-TR* Learning Disorders, which requires the inclusion of an intelligence test as discussed prior, shall be the major emphasis of Chapter 5.

REFERENCES

American Psychological Association. (2010). *Publication manual of the American Psychological Association* (6th ed.). Washington, DC: Author.

Binet, A. (1903). *Experimental study of intelligence.* Paris: Schleicher.

Capron, C., & Duyme, M. (1989). Assessment of the effects of socioeconomic status on IQ in a full cross-fostering design. *Nature, 340,* 552–553.

Ciccarelli, S. K., & White, J. N. (2012). *Psychology* (3rd ed.). Upper Saddle River, NJ: Pearson Education.

Deary, I. J., Whalley, L. J., & Starr, J. M. (2003). IQ at age 11 and longevity: Results from a follow-up of the Scottish Mental Survey 1932. In C. E. Finch, J. M. Robine, & Y. Christen (Eds.), *Brain and longevity: Perspectives in longevity* (pp. 153–164). Berlin: Springer.

Elshout, J., & Veenman, M. (1992). Relation between intellectual ability and working method as predictors of learning. *Journal of Educational Research, 85,* 134–143.

Gagne, F., & St. Pere, F. (2001). When IQ is controlled, does motivation still predict achievement? *Intelligence, 30,* 71–100.

Gottfredson, L. S. (2004). Intelligence: Is it the epidemiologists' elusive "fundamental cause" of social class inequalities in health? *Journal of Personality and Social Psychology, 86,* 174–199.

Gottfredson, L. S., & Deary, I. J. (2004). Intelligence predicts health and longevity, but why? *Current Directions in Psychological Science, 13*, 1.

Hunter, J. E. (1983). *Test validation for 12,000 jobs: An application of job classification and validity generalization analysis to the General Aptitude Test Battery (GATB).* Test Research report No. 45. Washington, DC: US Employment Service, US Department of Labor.

Hunter, J. E., & Hunter, R. F. (1984). Validity and utility of alternate predictors of job performance. *Psychological Bulletin, 96*, 72–98.

Larsen, R. J., & Buss, D. M. (2010). *Personality psychology: Domains of knowledge about human nature* (4th ed.). New York, NY: McGraw-Hill.

Mackintosh, N. J. (1998). *IQ and human intelligence.* Oxford, UK: Oxford University Press.

Sparrow, S. S., Cicchetti, D. V., & Balla, D. A. (2005). *Vineland Adaptive Behavior Scales, Second Edition (Vineland–II): Survey forms manual.* Minneapolis, MN: Pearson.

Spearman, C. E. (1927). *The abilities of man: Their nature and measurement.* New York, NY: Macmillan.

Sternberg, R. J., & Kaufman, J. (1998). Human abilities. *Annual Review of Psychology, 49*, 479–502.

Terman, L. M. (1916). *The measurement of intelligence: An explanation of and a complete guide for the use of the Stanford revision and extension of the Binet-Simon Intelligence Scale.* Boston, MA: Houghton Mifflin.

WAIS–IV Scoring Assistant. (2008). [CD-ROM Computer Software]. San Antonio, TX: PsychCorp Center–II, Pearson.

Wechsler, D. (1975). *The collected papers of David Wechsler.* New York, NY: Academic Press.

Wechsler, D. (2002a). *Wechsler Preschool and Primary Scale of Intelligence, Third Edition (WPPSI–III): Administration and scoring manual.* San Antonio, TX: The Psychological Corporation-Pearson.

Wechsler, D. (2002b). *Wechsler Preschool and Primary Scale of Intelligence, Third Edition (WPPSI–III): Technical and interpretive manual.* San Antonio, TX: The Psychological Corporation-Pearson.

Wechsler, D. (2003a). *Wechsler Intelligence Scale for Children, Fourth Edition (WISC–IV): Administration and scoring manual.* San Antonio, TX: The Psychological Corporation-Pearson.

Wechsler, D. (2003b). *Wechsler Intelligence Scale for Children, Fourth Edition (WISC–IV): Technical and interpretive manual.* San Antonio, TX: The Psychological Corporation-Pearson.

Wechsler, D. (2008a). *Wechsler Adult Intelligence Scale, Fourth Edition (WAIS–IV): Administration and scoring manual.* San Antonio, TX: The Psychological Corporation-Pearson.

Wechsler, D. (2008b). *Wechsler Adult Intelligence Scale, Fourth Edition (WAIS–IV): Technical and interpretive manual.* San Antonio, TX: The Psychological Corporation-Pearson.

Willingham, W. W. (1974). Predicting success in graduate education. *Science, 183*, 273–278.

WISC–IV Scoring Assistant. (2003). [CD-ROM Computer Software]. San Antonio, TX: PsychCorp Center–I, Pearson.

WPPSI–III Scoring Assistant. (2002). [CD-ROM Computer Software]. San Antonio, TX: PsychCorp Center–I, Pearson.

Box 4.1 Wechsler Intelligence Tests Qualitative Description Guide **63**

BOX 4.1

WECHSLER INTELLIGENCE TESTS QUALITATIVE DESCRIPTION GUIDE

Composite scores	Subtest scores	Standard deviations from mean	Qualitative description
130 and above	16 to 19	+2 to +3	Very superior
120 to 129	14 to 15	+1⅓ to +1⅔	Superior
110 to 119	12 to 13	+⅔ to +1	High average
90 to 109	8 to 11	−⅔ to +⅓	Average
80 to 89	6 to 7	−1⅓ to −1	Low average
70 to 79	4 to 5	−2 to −1⅔	Borderline
69 and below	1 to 3	−3 to −2⅓	Extremely low

Source: Adapted from Wechsler, D. (2008). *Wechsler Adult Intelligence Scale, Fourth Edition (WAIS-IV): Technical and interpretive manual.* San Antonio, TX: The Psychological Corporation-Pearson, Tables 6.1–6.3, pp. 124–126.

FORM 4.1

WPPSI–III, FORM AGES 2:6 TO 3:11 RESULTS AND INTERPRETATION TABLES

WPPSI–III, Form Ages 2:6 to 3:11

TABLE 1 ■ COMPOSITE SCORE SUMMARY

Scale	Composite score	PR	90% CI	Qualitative description	Measured abilities
Verbal Intelligence Quotient (VIQ)	--	--	[000, 000]	Very superior	Verbal reasoning, comprehension, and conceptualization
Performance Intelligence Quotient (PIQ)	--	--	[000, 000]	Superior	Visual–spatial (nonverbal) reasoning, organization, and conceptualization
Full Scale Intelligence Quotient (FSIQ)[a]	**000**	**0.00**	**[000, 000]**	**Low average**	**General intelligence: ability to learn from experience, acquire knowledge, and use resources effectively in adapting or solving problems[b]**
General Language Composite (GLC)[c]	--	--	[000, 000]	Average Borderline	Receptive and expressive language; word-retrieval from memory; association of visual stimuli with language

Note: Composite score mean = 100, standard deviation = 15. Lower scores indicate greater intellectual impairment. PR, percentile rank; CI, confidence interval. -- denotes not administered, or score type not available or computed. General intellectual ability data are in boldface.

[a]The Full Scale Intelligence Quotient includes the Verbal and Performance Intelligence Quotient composite scores.

[b]Ciccarelli, S. K., & White, J. N. (2012). *Psychology* (3rd ed.). Upper Saddle River, NJ: Pearson Education; Wechsler, D. (1975). *The collected papers of David Wechsler*. New York, NY: Academic Press.

[c]Optional composite not included in the Full Scale Intelligence Quotient.

TABLE 2 ■ VERBAL INTELLIGENCE SUBTEST SCORE SUMMARY

Subtest	Scaled score	PR	Qualitative description	Measured abilities
Receptive Vocabulary	00	0.00	High average	Receptive language; auditory and visual discrimination; integration of visual perception and auditory input
Information	--	--	Low average	Range of factual knowledge
Picture Naming	--	--	Superior	Expressive language; word-retrieval from long-term memory; association of visual stimuli with language

Note: Scale score mean = 10, standard deviation = 3. Lower scores indicate greater intellectual impairment. PR, percentile rank. -- denotes not administered, or score type not available or computed.

TABLE 3 ■ PERFORMANCE INTELLIGENCE SUBTEST SCORE SUMMARY

Subtest	Scaled score	PR	Qualitative description	Measured abilities
Block Design	00	0.00	Very superior	Analysis and synthesis of abstract visual stimuli; nonverbal concept formation and reasoning
Object Assembly	--	--	Low average	Analysis and synthesis of abstract visual stimuli; nonverbal concept formation

Note: Scale score mean = 10, standard deviation = 3. Lower scores indicate greater intellectual impairment. PR, percentile rank. -- denotes not administered, or score type not available or computed.

(Cont.)

FORM 4.1

WPPSI–III, FORM AGES 2:6 TO 3:11 RESULTS AND INTERPRETATION TABLES (*Cont.*)

TABLE 4 ■ **GENERAL LANGUAGE SUBTEST SCORE SUMMARY**

Subtest	Scaled score	PR	Qualitative description	Measured abilities
Receptive Vocabulary	00	0.00	Average	Receptive language; auditory and visual discrimination; integration of visual perception and auditory input
Picture Naming	--	--	Superior	Expressive language; word-retrieval from long-term memory; association of visual stimuli with language

Note: Scale score mean = 10, standard deviation = 3. Lower scores indicate greater intellectual impairment. PR, percentile rank. -- denotes not administered, or score type not available or computed.

FORM 4.2

WPPSI–III, FORM AGES 4:0 TO 7:3 RESULTS AND INTERPRETATION TABLES

WPPSI–III, Form Ages 4:0 to 7:3

TABLE 1 ■ **COMPOSITE SCORE SUMMARY**

Scale	Composite score	PR	90% CI	Qualitative description	Measured abilities
Verbal Intelligence Quotient (VIQ)	--	--	[000, 000]	Very superior	Verbal reasoning, comprehension, and conceptualization
Performance Intelligence Quotient (PIQ)	--	--	[000, 000]	Superior	Visual–spatial (nonverbal) reasoning, organization, and conceptualization
Processing Speed Quotient (PSQ)	--	--	[000, 000]	High average	Mental processing speed; graphomotor processing; attention and concentration
Full Scale Intelligence Quotient (FSIQ)[a]	**000**	**0.00**	**[000, 000]**	**Low average**	**General intelligence: ability to learn from experience, acquire knowledge, and use resources effectively in adapting or solving problems[b]**
General Language Composite (GLC)[c]	--	--	[000, 000]	Average Borderline	Receptive and expressive language; word-retrieval from memory; association of visual stimuli with language

Note: Composite score mean = 100, standard deviation = 15. Lower scores indicate greater intellectual impairment. PR, percentile rank; CI, confidence interval. -- denotes not administered, or score type not available or computed. General intellectual ability data are in boldface.

[a]The Full Scale Intelligence Quotient includes the Verbal and Performance Intelligence Quotient composite scores, and the Processing Speed Coding subtest score.

[b]Ciccarelli, S. K., & White, J. N. (2012) *Psychology* (3rd ed.). Upper Saddle River, NJ: Pearson Education; Wechsler, D. (1975). *The collected papers of David Wechsler*. New York, NY: Academic Press.

[c]Optional composite not included in the Full Scale Intelligence Quotient.

TABLE 2 ■ **VERBAL INTELLIGENCE SUBTEST SCORE SUMMARY**

Subtest	Scaled score	PR	Qualitative description	Measured abilities
Information	00	0.00	High average Low average	Range of factual knowledge
Vocabulary	--	--	Superior Borderline	Word knowledge; degree of language development; verbal concept formation; long-term memory
Word Reasoning	--	--	Average	Verbal comprehension; verbal and analogical reasoning; verbal abstraction
Comprehension*	--	--	--	Practical knowledge and judgment; knowledge of conventional standards of behavior
Similarities*	--	--	--	Degree of abstract reasoning; associative and categorical reasoning; verbal concept formation

Note: Scale score mean = 10, standard deviation = 3. Lower scores indicate greater intellectual impairment. PR, percentile rank.
*denotes supplemental or optional subtest. -- denotes not administered, or score type not available or computed.

(Cont.)

FORM 4.2

WPPSI–III, FORM AGES 4:0 TO 7:3 RESULTS AND INTERPRETATION TABLES (*Cont.*)

TABLE 3 ■ PERFORMANCE INTELLIGENCE SUBTEST SCORE SUMMARY

Subtest	Scaled score	PR	Qualitative description	Measured abilities
Block Design	00	0.00	Very superior	Analysis and synthesis of abstract visual stimuli; nonverbal concept formation and reasoning
Matrix Reasoning	--	--	Superior High average	Knowledge of part-whole relationships; broad visual intelligence; classification and spatial ability
Picture Concepts	--	--	Extremely low	Abstract categorical reasoning
Picture Completion*	--	--	Borderline	Visual perception and organization; concentration; visual recognition of object's essential details
Object Assembly*	--	--	Low average	Analysis and synthesis of abstract visual stimuli; nonverbal concept formation

Note: Scale score mean = 10, standard deviation = 3. Lower scores indicate greater intellectual impairment. PR, percentile rank. *denotes supplemental or optional subtest. -- denotes not administered, or score type not available or computed.

TABLE 4 ■ PROCESSING SPEED SUBTEST SCORE SUMMARY

Subtest	Scaled score	PR	Qualitative description	Measured abilities
Coding	00	0.00	Average	Visual–motor coordination; visual perception; psychomotor speed; attention and concentration; learning
Symbol Search[a]	--	--	Superior	Speed of visual search; attention and concentration

Note: Scale score mean = 10, standard deviation = 3. Lower scores indicate greater intellectual impairment. PR, percentile rank. -- denotes not administered, or score type not available or computed.

[a]Not included in the Full Scale Intelligence Quotient.

TABLE 5 ■ GENERAL LANGUAGE SUBTEST SCORE SUMMARY

Subtest[a]	Scaled score	PR	Qualitative description	Measured abilities
Receptive Vocabulary	00	0.00	Average	Receptive language; auditory and visual discrimination; integration of visual perception and auditory input
Picture Naming	--	--	Superior	Expressive language; word-retrieval from long-term memory; association of visual stimuli with language

Note: Scale score mean = 10, standard deviation = 3. Lower scores indicate greater intellectual impairment. PR, percentile rank. -- denotes not administered, or score type not available or computed.

[a]These subtests are not included in the Full Scale Intelligence Quotient.

FORM 4.3

WISC–IV RESULTS AND INTERPRETATION TABLES

WISC–IV

TABLE 1 ■ **COMPOSITE SCORE SUMMARY**

Index/scale	Composite score	PR	90% CI	Qualitative description	Measured abilities
Verbal Comprehension Index (VCI)	--	--	[000, 000]	Very superior	Verbal reasoning, comprehension, and conceptualization
Perceptual Reasoning Index (PRI)	--	--	[000, 000]	Superior	Visual–spatial (nonverbal) reasoning, organization, and conceptualization
Working Memory Index (WMI)	--	--	[000, 000]	High average	Attention and concentration; holding immediate memory traces while executing cognitive tasks
Processing Speed Index (PSI)	--	--	[000, 000]	Average Borderline	Mental processing speed; graphomotor processing
Full Scale[a]	**000**	**0.00**	**[000, 000]**	**Low average**	**General intelligence: the ability to learn from experience, acquire knowledge, and use resources effectively in adapting to new situations or solving problems**[b]

Note: Composite score mean = 100, standard deviation = 15. Lower scores indicate greater intellectual impairment. PR, percentile rank; CI, confidence interval. -- denotes not administered, or score type not available or computed. General intellectual ability data are in boldface.

[a]The Full Scale includes Verbal Comprehension, Perceptual Reasoning, Working Memory, and Processing Speed Composite scores.

[b]Ciccarelli, S. K., & White, J. N. (2012). *Psychology* (3rd ed.). Upper Saddle River, NJ: Pearson Education; Wechsler, D. (1975). *The collected papers of David Wechsler.* New York, NY: Academic Press.

TABLE 2 ■ **VERBAL COMPREHENSION SUBTEST SCORE SUMMARY**

Subtest	Scaled score	PR	Qualitative description	Measured abilities
Similarities	00	0.00	Very Superior	Degree of abstract reasoning; associative and categorical reasoning; verbal concept formation
Vocabulary	--	--	Superior Borderline	Word knowledge; degree of language development; verbal concept formation; long-term memory
Comprehension	--	--	Extremely low	Practical knowledge and judgment; knowledge of conventional standards of behavior
Information*	--	--	--	Range of factual knowledge
Word reasoning*	--	--	--	Verbal comprehension; verbal and analogical reasoning; verbal abstraction

Note: Scale score mean = 10, standard deviation = 3. Lower scores indicate greater intellectual impairment. PR, percentile rank.
*denotes supplemental or optional subtest. -- denotes not administered, or score type not available or computed.

(Cont.)

FORM 4.3

WISC–IV RESULTS AND INTERPRETATION TABLES (*Cont.*)

TABLE 3 ■ PERCEPTUAL REASONING SUBTEST SCORE SUMMARY

Subtest	Scaled score	PR	Qualitative description	Measured abilities
Block Design	00	0.00	Very superior	Analysis and synthesis of abstract visual stimuli; nonverbal concept formation and reasoning
Picture Concepts	--	--	Extremely low	Abstract categorical reasoning
Matrix Reasoning	--	--	Superior High average	Knowledge of part-whole relationships; broad visual intelligence; classification and spatial ability
Picture Completion*	--	--	--	Visual perception and organization; concentration; visual recognition of object's essential details

Note: Scale score mean = 10, standard deviation = 3. Lower scores indicate greater intellectual impairment. PR, percentile rank.
*denotes supplemental or optional subtest. -- denotes not administered, or score type not available or computed.

TABLE 4 ■ WORKING MEMORY SUBTEST SCORE SUMMARY

Subtest	Scaled score	PR	Qualitative description	Measured abilities
Digit Span	00	0.00	Superior	Rote learning and memory; attention; auditory sequential processing; mental manipulation; visuospatial imaging
Letter–Number Sequencing	--	--	Extremely low	Attention and concentration; mental manipulation; memory span; short-term auditory memory
Arithmetic*	--	--	--	Attention and concentration; mental alertness; short-term memory; numerical reasoning; long-term memory

Note: Scale score mean = 10, standard deviation = 3. Lower scores indicate greater intellectual impairment. PR, percentile rank.
*denotes supplemental or optional subtest. -- denotes not administered, or score type not available or computed.

TABLE 5 ■ PROCESSING SPEED SUBTEST SCORE SUMMARY

Subtest	Scaled score	PR	Qualitative description	Measured abilities
Coding	00	0.00	Average	Visual–motor coordination; visual perception; psychomotor speed; attention and concentration; learning
Symbol Search	--	--	Superior	Speed of visual search; attention and concentration
Cancellation*	--	--	--	Speed of visual search; attention and concentration

Note: Scale score mean = 10, standard deviation = 3. Lower scores indicate greater intellectual impairment. PR, percentile rank.
*denotes supplemental or optional subtest. -- denotes not administered, or score type not available or computed.

FORM 4.4

WAIS–IV RESULTS AND INTERPRETATION TABLES

WAIS–IV

TABLE 1 ■ **COMPOSITE SCORE SUMMARY**

Index/scale	Composite score	PR	90% CI	Qualitative description	Measured abilities
Verbal Comprehension Index (VCI)	--	--	[00, 00]	Very superior	Verbal reasoning, comprehension, and conceptualization
Perceptual Reasoning Index (PRI)	--	--	[00, 00]	Superior	Visual–spatial (nonverbal) reasoning, organization, and conceptualization
Working Memory Index (WMI)	--	--	[00, 00]	High average	Attention and concentration; holding immediate memory traces, while executing cognitive tasks
Processing Speed Index (PSI)	--	--	[00, 00]	Average Borderline	Mental processing speed; graphomotor processing
Full Scale[a]	**000**	**0.00**	**[000, 000]**	**Low average**	**General intelligence: the ability to learn from experience, acquire knowledge, and use resources effectively in adapting to new situations or solving problems[b]**
General Ability Index (GAI)[c]	--	--	[00, 00]	Extremely low	General intellectual ability minimizing the effects of working memory and processing speed

Note: Composite score mean = 100, standard deviation = 15. Lower scores indicate greater intellectual impairment. PR, percentile rank; CI, confidence interval. -- denotes not administered, or score type not available or computed. Full Scale data are in boldface.

[a]The Full Scale includes Verbal Comprehension, Perceptual Reasoning, Working Memory, and Processing Speed Composite scores.

[b]Ciccarelli, S. K., & White, J. N. (2012). *Psychology* (3rd ed.). Upper Saddle River, NJ: Pearson Education; Wechsler, D. (1975). *The collected papers of David Wechsler*. New York, NY: Academic Press.

[c]The General Ability Index includes only the Verbal Comprehension and Perceptual Reasoning composite scores.

TABLE 2 ■ **VERBAL COMPREHENSION SUBTEST SCORE SUMMARY**

Subtest	Scaled score	PR	Qualitative description	Measured abilities
Similarities	00	0.00	Very superior	Degree of abstract reasoning; associative and categorical reasoning; verbal concept formation
Vocabulary	--	--	Superior Borderline	Word knowledge; degree of language development; verbal concept formation; long-term memory
Information	--	--	High average Low average	Range of factual knowledge
Comprehension*	--	--	--	Practical knowledge and judgment; knowledge of conventional standards of behavior

Note: Scale score mean = 10, standard deviation = 3. Lower scores indicate greater intellectual impairment. PR, percentile rank.
*denotes supplemental or optional subtest. -- denotes not administered, or score type not available or computed.

(Cont.)

FORM 4.4

WAIS–IV RESULTS AND INTERPRETATION TABLES (*Cont.*)

TABLE 3 ■ PERCEPTUAL REASONING SUBTEST SCORE SUMMARY

Subtest	Scaled score	PR	Qualitative description	Measured abilities
Block Design	00	0.00	Very superior	Analysis and synthesis of abstract visual stimuli; nonverbal concept formation and reasoning
Matrix Reasoning	--	--	Superior High average	Knowledge of part-whole relationships; broad visual intelligence; classification and spatial ability
Visual Puzzles	--	--	Average Low average	Analysis and synthesis of abstract visual stimuli; broad visual intelligence; nonverbal reasoning
Picture Completion*	--	--	--	Visual perception and organization; concentration; visual recognition of object's essential details
Figure Weights*	--	--	--	Analogical reasoning; inductive and deductive logic; quantitative reasoning

Note: Scale score mean = 10, standard deviation = 3. Lower scores indicate greater intellectual impairment. PR, percentile rank.
*denotes supplemental or optional subtest. -- denotes not administered, or score type not available or computed.

TABLE 4 ■ WORKING MEMORY SUBTEST SCORE SUMMARY

Subtest	Scaled score	PR	Qualitative description	Measured abilities
Digit Span	00	0.00	Superior	Rote learning and memory; attention; auditory sequential processing; mental manipulation; visuospatial imaging
Arithmetic	--	--	High average	Attention and concentration; mental alertness; short-term memory; numerical reasoning; long-term memory
Letter–Number Sequencing*	--	--	--	Attention and concentration; mental manipulation; memory span; short-term auditory memory

Note: Scale score mean = 10, standard deviation = 3. Lower scores indicate greater intellectual impairment. PR, percentile rank.
*denotes supplemental or optional subtest. -- denotes not administered, or score type not available or computed.

TABLE 5 ■ PROCESSING SPEED SUBTEST SCORE SUMMARY

Subtest	Scaled score	PR	Qualitative description	Measured abilities
Symbol Search	00	0.00	Superior	Speed of visual search; attention and concentration
Coding	--	--	Average	Visual–motor coordination; visual perception; psychomotor speed; attention and concentration; learning
Cancellation*	--	--	--	Speed of visual search; attention and concentration

Note: Scale score mean = 10, standard deviation = 3. Lower scores indicate greater intellectual impairment. PR, percentile rank.
*denotes supplemental or optional subtest. -- denotes not administered, or score type not available or computed.

Achievement Tests

5

THE CONSTRUCT OF ACHIEVEMENT AND ITS MEASUREMENT

The psychological construct of *achievement* is generally defined as the degree of previous learning or accomplishment in various types of subject matter or specific academic areas (Gregory, 2011; Miller, McIntire, & Lovler, 2011). Achievement tests employed in psychological practice typically measure an individual's mastery within fundamental academic subjects, including oral language, reading, writing, and mathematics. This is contrasted with intelligence tests, which measure aptitude or the ability to learn (Larsen & Buss, 2010; see also Chapter 5).

Achievement tests are frequently used to determine (a) academic needs, (b) educational placement, (c) eligibility for special educational instruction, and (d) need for special testing accommodations. It is reasonable to assume that when academic skills are accurately measured and educational needs identified, the likelihood of proper instruction and satisfactory grades are maximized. Because academic success is, in turn, predictive of career advancement (Roth, Bevier, Switzer, & Schippmann, 1996) and ultimately psychological adjustment (Kaplan, Damphous, & Kaplan, 1994), achievement testing is relevant to mental health.

DIAGNOSTIC REASONS FOR INCLUSION WITHIN A TEST BATTERY

In mental health practice, the principal reason for requesting an achievement test is to rule out one or more Learning or Communication Disorders as defined by the *Diagnostic and Statistical Manual of Mental Disorders, Fourth Edition, Text Revision* (*DSM-IV-TR*) (American Psychiatric Association, 2000), including (a) Reading Disorder, (b) Mathematics Disorder, (c) Disorder of Written Expression, (d) Learning Disorder Not Otherwise Specified (NOS), (e) Phonological Disorder, (f) Expressive Language Disorder, and (g) Mixed Receptive-Expressive Language Disorder. This means that a test battery employing an achievement test will almost invariably coexist with a conormed intelligence test, which provides the diagnostically requisite ability–achievement discrepancy analysis (American Psychiatric Association, 2000). I am cognizant of psychologists who utilize selected achievement tests and subtests to assist in ruling out Attention-Deficit/Hyperactivity Disorder (ADHD). However, I believe that selected neuropsychological subtests that measure the more fundamental and diagnostically relevant abilities of attention, executive functioning, memory, and learning are far superior in directly and more accurately detecting the existence of ADHD symptoms (see Chapter 6).

Although infrequent in practice, a potential use of an achievement test is to address any referral questions that simply request a measure of an individual's mastery of identified fundamental academic subjects. However, as discussed, subsequent insurance coverage for such purposes is precarious at best.

The most likely referral sources include (a) vocational rehabilitation programs to assist in determining educational needs and to foster career development, (b) mental health professionals such that they may adjust treatment intervention accordingly, (c) university student support services departments to test for one or more suspected Learning Disorders regarding one of their students; and (d) adults or parents who believe that they or their child may have an undiagnosed Learning Disorder.

INSURANCE COVERAGE ISSUES

Insurance authorization issues for achievement testing closely mirror those discussed concerning intelligence testing. First, vocational rehabilitation programs fund achievement testing because determining educational needs and furthering training is an integral part of their services. Referrals from mental health professionals requesting achievement testing risk denial of authorization due to want of medical necessity. Thus, once again, fastidious documentation of how achievement testing will modify treatment so as to improve outcome is essential.

Self, parental, and university referrals are unlikely to be covered for the same reason as intelligence testing. Strategies for improving the probability of authorized intelligence testing apply to the requesting of achievement testing (see Chapter 4). In these cases, I advise that you inform the patient and/or family of the likely odds of denial and that such testing will likely be self-pay.

THE WECHSLER TEST

I have selected the Wechsler Individual Achievement Test, Third Edition (WIAT–III), which is normed on individuals aged 4 years 0 months to 50 years 11 months (Pearson [PsychCorp], 2009a, 2009b). The test's academic coverage is from preschool (i.e., Pre-Kindergarten [PK]) through Grade 12.

The WIAT–III is conormed on the Wechsler Preschool and Primary Scale of Intelligence, Third Edition (WPPSI–III), Wechsler Intelligence Scale for Children, Fourth Edition (WISC–IV), and Wechsler Adult Intelligence Scale, Fourth Edition (WAIS–IV) for purposes of ability–achievement discrepancy analyses as a requisite for diagnosing Learning and Communication Disorders. I do not perform such intensive testing and intricate comparisons using the WIAT–III and WPPSI–III. This is due to the lack of demand for Learning Disorders testing in the mental health field for children under age 6 to years 0 months. The WIAT–III Scoring Assistant (2009) provides rapid and efficient computer scoring, including all relevant statistical ability–achievement discrepancy comparisons.

Next, I discuss the results and interpretation tables that involve the WIAT–III. I initially review the reporting and interpreting of the achievement test results independently, so as to familiarize readers with this instrument. However, the subsequent emphasis is on the application of the WIAT–III within the context of an ability–achievement discrepancy analysis, consistent with its most frequent use in ruling out Learning and Communication Disorders among school-age children and older.

RESULTS AND INTERPRETATION TABLES

WIAT–III

The WIAT–III composite factor structure and subtests are admittedly complex because they vary depending upon grade level. I have dichotomized the results and interpretation tables into PK (Form 5.1) and Grades K through 12 (K–12; Form 5.2). Because they are similarly designed and organized, I discuss them simultaneously as was done with the Wechsler intelligence tests. Important variances between the two shall be made explicit.

Composite Score Summary

Forms 5.1 and 5.2 contain the results and interpretation tables of the WIAT–III, PK and WIAT–III, K–12, respectively. As with the intelligence tests, Table 1 of Forms 5.1 and 5.2 presents the composite score data. Table 1 of Form 5.1 is limited to two composites due to the more circumscribed academic abilities measured. Oral Language in Form 5.1 is abbreviated such that Table 2 subtests, which load on this composite, can be quickly cross-referenced. Table 1 of Form 5.2 includes the full complement of composites, with notations identifying the somewhat varying applicable grade ranges. Thus, both the testing psychologist and reader can easily identify which academic areas apply in a given case.

The Total Achievement composite information appears in boldface. Ensuing the composite score names are the composite score, percentile rank, 90% confidence interval, qualitative description, and measured abilities associated with a particular composite. The WIAT–III composite standard scores are transformed as on the Wechsler intelligence tests. Therefore, the identical standard score ranges and similar qualitative descriptions are employed. The examiner's manual provides a succinct qualitative description guide to facilitate the entering of proper labels into this column (Pearson [PsychCorp], 2009a, Table 4.1, p. 81).[1] Note that the K–12 (Form 5.2), Written Expression measured abilities are further denoted by more particular grade ranges.

In this instance, the measured abilities listed are largely the subtest names (with some occasional parenthetical embellishments), which load on that particular composite. The specific wording was based upon my review of the test's factor structure and subtests described at length in both the examiner's manual and technical manual (Pearson [PsychCorp], 2009a, 2009b). In the case of measuring more general areas of achievement, I considered the subtest names, with occasional supplemental wording, to be satisfactory summary descriptors for purposes of accurate interpretation.

Finally, Table 1 is accompanied by notes indicating the composite score mean and standard deviation, directional significance of the scores, and abbreviation definitions. Included in the last is the meaning of "--", which indicates that the composite score was not available or computed. Although you will find this notation in many of the results and interpretation tables, they are particularly important regarding the WIAT–III, K–12. This is because a score may not be available due to it not falling within the grade level of the examinee.

The K–12 Table 1 composite score summary is designed to provide maximum information concerning scores and their meaning as applied to the measured construct of achievement. A narrative summary of Table 1 should routinely address four issues: (a) noting overall achievement, (b) analyzing an examinee's strengths and weaknesses by reporting statistically significant composite score differences ($p < .05$), (c) highlighting the diagnostic significance of the data, and (d) addressing any related referral questions.

In contrast, the PK Table 1 composite score summary provides much less information such that the testing psychologist should focus the analysis on Table 2 subtest performance. I placed it first to be consistent with (a) the principle of analyzing test results from general to more specific (i.e., deductive reasoning) and (b) other Wechsler results and interpretation tables. For any particular case, table order may be easily reversed at the testing psychologist's discretion.

Subtest Score Summary

Subtest score summary tables (Table 2) follow the composite score tables in Forms 5.1 and 5.2, so as to analyze more specific strengths and weaknesses. Although the PK and K–12 subtest tabular columns are the same, they present quite different subtest content, which shall be first addressed.

The WIAT–III PK has a single subtest Table 2 due to the entire battery comprising only five subtests, two of which load on the Oral Language composite initially listed in

[1] *The WIAT-III Scoring Assistant automatically inserts the proper qualitative descriptions. Therefore, if you purchase this software, repeated reference to the qualitative description guide included in the examiner's manual is circumvented.*

Table 1. Thus, the complete subtest profile is presented within one succinct table. On the other hand, the WIAT–III, K–12 measures and presents significantly more achievement composites, which require a sequence of subtest results and interpretation tables. The subtest tables are organized by the composite upon which they load, and in the order by which the composites appear in Table 1. Such order may be modified to prioritize certain results.

Column information is the same as that provided in Table 1, including subtest score name, standard score, percentile rank, 90% confidence interval, qualitative description, and measured abilities. The subtest name is associated with varying applicable grade ranges as was done in the composite score Table 1. It is to be noted that the WIAT–III subtest scores are transformed identical to the composite scores (*M* = 100, *SD* = 15), hence differing from current and past Wechsler intelligence tests, previous editions of the WIAT, and general testing tradition. Thus, the same guide provided in the examiner's manual may be used in determining the proper qualitative description for each subtest standard score (Pearson [PsychCorp], 2009a, Table 4.1, p. 81). You will note that such descriptions differ somewhat from those of the Wechsler intelligence tests.

Finally, the measured abilities listed for each subtest were once again based upon my perusal of the rather elaborate subtest descriptions provided in both the examiner's manual and technical manual (Pearson [PsychCorp], 2009a, 2009b). The specific terms I selected were those I believed captured the essence of each test regarding academic abilities. Note that I occasionally incorporated test administration time descriptors, which I believe are critical to defining some academic abilities; that is, power versus speed abilities (see e.g., Goh, 2004).

When the WIAT–III is administered without a companion intelligence test, most commonly with preschoolers and children younger than 6 years 0 months, its purpose will typically be to answer referral questions regarding preacademic/academic abilities. Thus, I recommend reporting all of the subtest results that sufficiently answer such questions. Usually, this will require reporting all of the subtest results, with pithy narrative summaries following each table in terms of analyzing more specific strengths and weaknesses.

Ability–Achievement Discrepancy Analyses

As I stated prior, the most frequent use of an achievement test within mental health practice would be to rule out *DSM-IV-TR* Learning and Communication Disorders among school-aged individuals, with an emphasis on the former. The *DSM-IV-TR* defines a Learning Disorder as a measured area of achievement that is significantly lower than expected based upon age, education, and *measured intelligence*, and which is associated with dysfunction (American Psychiatric Association, 2000). I therefore administer the WIAT–III most frequently with either the conormed WISC–IV or WAIS–IV, which permits the diagnostically requisite ability–achievement discrepancy analysis.

Again, I do not perform such analysis using the WIAT–III PK and WPPSI–III because (a) there tends not to be a demand for such intricate testing among this young age range and (b) formal academic instruction has not yet begun in earnest. The latter, in my opinion, technically precludes Learning Disorder diagnoses pursuant to the *DSM-IV-TR* dysfunction standard. Of course, these instruments can be used to effectively identify preschool children who are at risk for Learning and Communication Disorders, thus permitting early intervention and prevention.

The following four results and interpretation tables are reviewed here in detail: (a) WISC–IV/WIAT–III Ability–Achievement Discrepancy Analysis Simple Difference Method (Form 5.3), (b) WISC–IV/WIAT–III Ability–Achievement Discrepancy Analysis Predicted Difference Method (Form 5.4), (c) WAIS–IV/WIAT–III Ability–Achievement

Discrepancy Analysis Simple Difference Method (Form 5.5), and (d) WAIS–IV/WIAT–III Ability–Achievement Discrepancy Analysis Predicted Difference Method (Form 5.6). Again, because they are organized similarly, I will discuss them simultaneously while inserting comments on germane differences when warranted.

Some prelusory comments are in order. Note that all of these results and interpretation tables include the entire complement of tests, composites, and subtests necessary to indicate whether or not a Learning or Communication Disorder exists. This obviates the need to search for and insert the necessary tables from separate report templates. The testing psychologist may delete some of the auxiliary data for purposes of brevity. I shall identify such data in the subsequent detailed discussion. Also, succinct narrative interpretations of the table results should be inserted by the testing psychologist where appropriate.

Wechsler Intelligence Test Composite Score Summary

The analysis begins by selecting the intelligence test composite score which most accurately measures an examinee's cognitive competence. This score is used to quantitatively compute an examinee's expected level of achievement across the academic abilities measured. The Full Scale is the most frequently utilized for this purpose. However, a statistically significant difference of atypical magnitude or effect size between the Verbal Comprehension Index (VCI) and the Perceptual Reasoning Index (PRI) may obfuscate the meaning of the Full Scale. In such cases, the testing psychologist may desire to choose either the VCI or PRI as the most reliable and valid measure of intellectual competence.

Therefore, Table 1 is designed to begin such preliminary analysis of the intelligence test data. It is virtually identical to Table 1 presented within the separate WISC–IV and WAIS–IV results and interpretation tables (see Forms 4.3 and 4.4, respectively), with the exception of the Working Memory, Processing Speed, and General Ability (WAIS–IV only) Indices being deleted. This is explicated in the Table 1 notes.

VCI–PRI Index Level Discrepancy Comparison

Table 2 completes the analysis by reporting the VCI–PRI index level discrepancy comparison results. In order of presentation, Table 2 reports the VCI, PRI, VCI–PRI difference, the critical value at the .05 alpha level, an accompanying asterisk if statistically significant ($p < .05$), Cohen's d effect size computation, effect size result, and finally, the percentage of the normative sample who obtained the listed VCI–PRI difference (i.e., base rate). The effect size or magnitude is rapidly computed by the absolute VCI–PRI difference, divided by the composite standard deviation of 15 (Warner, 2008). The base rate is effective in clarifying on a more pragmatic basis the degree to which the discrepancy is typical or aberrant. Table 2 notes define the meaning of statistical significance, the manner in which effect size is computed and the result determined (Warner, 2008), and defines base rate. These notes are designed to facilitate feedback.

Immediately subsequent to Table 2 notes, I have inserted several of the most common narrative interpretations of the VCI–PRI index level discrepancy comparison results. In order of presentation, they include (a) selection of the Full Scale as an acceptable measure of general intelligence, (b) selection of the VCI and accompanying rationale, and (c) selection of the lower of the VCI and PRI and accompanying rationale. Testing psychologists may use any one of these narrative interpretations in whole or in part, amend them, or insert their own established criteria and accompanying narrative interpretations.

From this point and hereinafter, you shall find similar common narrative interpretations of tabular results and/or definitions of principal psychological constructs immediately following the tabular notes. These are inserted so as to structure and expedite the test interpretation and report-writing process. In all cases, testing psychologists may employ them at their discretion and simply delete narrative commentary that does not apply or is not indicated.

WIAT–III Composite and Subtest Score Summaries

Table 3 reports the WIAT–III composite score results, while Tables 4 through 7 report the WIAT–III subtest score results classified by composite and maintaining the order by which they are enumerated in Table 3. Note that they are virtually identical to the results and interpretation tables when reporting the achievement test results alone for K–12 (Form 5.2).

Tables 4 through 7 address the dysfunction element of the *DSM-IV-TR* criteria for a learning disorder. That is, in the event an examinee's achievement scores are within average limits or above, the diagnostic criteria are not met irrespective of the ability–achievement discrepancy results due to want of impairment in functioning. In the interests of brevity, the testing psychologist may administer, score, report, and interpret only those composites and subtests that are pertinent to differential diagnosis.

Ability–Achievement Discrepancy Methods

The WIAT-III employs two statistical methods in computing the ability–achievement discrepancy analyses: (a) simple difference (Forms 5.3 and 5.5) and (b) predicted difference (Forms 5.4 and 5.6). Next, I discuss each method in this respective order.

Simple difference method. Simple difference discrepancies are obtained by subtracting the selected intelligence test composite score from each *actual* or obtained WIAT–III standard score. Because it is a more straightforward analysis, it is most easily comprehended by those unfamiliar with psychometrics and statistical analyses.

Tables 8 and 9 together comprise the simple difference ability–achievement discrepancy analyses and are thus mandatory (Forms 5.3 and 5.5). The tables are preceded by notations indicating which ability score was selected according to results of Tables 1 and 2, with the Full Scale as the default, ensued by the actual standard ability score obtained by the examinee. If either the VCI or PRI supplants the Full Scale, appropriate amendments must be made at this point, and within the body and notes of both Tables 8 and 9.

Table 8 begins by presenting a list of the composite score names with abbreviations, such that they may be associated with subtests in Table 9, which load on each composite. Their order is preserved with that of Table 3, which initially reports the WIAT–III composite results in more detail. This facilitates the process of cross-referencing. The first column is followed by (a) WIAT–III standard score, (b) ability standard score, (c) achievement score minus ability score difference, (d) statistical significance result, and (e) base rate of the measured difference found in the norm-reference group.

The difference is computed in this manner so that minus values indicate achievement is lower than ability, whereas zero difference and positive values immediately show no evidence of a Learning or Communication Disorder. Thus, in the event that the WIAT–III achievement score is equal to or exceeds the ability score, a simple *N/A* notation is placed within the statistical results and base rate columns for that composite as such data are unnecessary. This renders the table both more manageable and comprehensible. The testing psychologist by discretion may choose to insert these data, although statistical significance in the opposing direction (i.e., achievement above ability) must be clearly delineated to avoid confusion.

Regarding statistical significance, the more conservative $p < .01$ alpha level is the default. I chose this because of the accrued error rates of the ability test separately, achievement test separately, and their statistical comparisons, in addition to the accumulated error rate of repeated hypotheses tests. The latter is analogous to *experimentwise error rate* in psychological research, which increases the chances of a Type I error or concluding that an effect is present when in fact it is not (see e.g., Gravetter & Wallnau, 2013). The testing psychologist may easily insert the more common $p < .05$ if failing to detect a disorder that actually exists would be severely detrimental in a particular case (i.e., a Type II error).

Table 8 notes define the meaning of statistical significance, the N/A notation, the manner in which the difference score was computed, and the meaning of base rate. Again, this is to buttress the feedback process.

Table 9 presents the ability standard score and WIAT–III subtest score discrepancy results in the same manner as Table 8. The subtest score names are enumerated in the approximate order as the composites in Table 8, and associated with composite abbreviations for cross-referencing. Note that some subtests contribute to more than one composite, hence the approximation of order. Finally, Table 9 notes are identical to those of Table 8.

Predicted difference method. Predicted difference discrepancies are computed by subtracting each WIAT–III standard score *predicted* by the selected intelligence test composite score from the *actual* WIAT–III standard score. Clinicians well versed in psychological testing and psychometrics may be more accustomed to, and appreciative of, the additionally complex prediction-oriented method. Therefore, the predicted difference method may be more compelling for these types of clinicians. In terms of objective accuracy, the two methods are comparable and should not lead to contradictory results and interpretations (Pearson [PsychCorp], 2009a, 2009b).

Tables 8 and 9 comprise the predicted difference ability–achievement discrepancy analyses and are again mandatory (Forms 5.4 and 5.6). Once again, Table 8 is immediately preceded by notations indicating which ability score was selected according to the results of Tables 1 and 2, with the Full Scale as the default, ensued by the actual standard ability score obtained by the examinee.

Tables 8 and 9 for the predicted difference method are analogous to the same numbered tables regarding the simple difference method, with the exception of columns 2 and 3. Thus, I will circumscribe the discussion to these two most fundamental variances, while illustrating some consequential notational differences. Column 2 presents the examinee's *actual* or obtained WIAT–III standard score, while the adjacent column 3 presents the WIAT–III standard score *predicted* by the chosen intelligence test composite score. The subtraction is analogously made such that negative scores show potential disorder, and zero differences or positive scores are not in need of further analyses (i.e., N/A). Lastly, the only amendment in the predicted difference notes in Tables 8 and 9 is the alternative manner in which the difference scores were calculated.

SUMMARY

This chapter discussed the testing of achievement and its measurement with special emphasis on testing for *DSM-IV-TR* Learning and Communication Disorders among school-aged individuals. The chapter began by defining the construct of achievement both in general and more specific to clinical testing practice. This was ensued by discussions of the most common reasons to include them within a test battery, along with related insurance authorization issues. The WIAT–III was then introduced as the selected achievement test and its characteristics reviewed. Results and interpretation tables were then presented beginning with those measuring achievement only, followed by the more intricate, complex, and frequent type of testing to determine the presence of one or more Learning and/or Communication Disorders. Lastly, regarding the latter, two ability–achievement methods were presented and contrasted, including simple difference and predicted difference.

Chapter 6 covers neuropsychological testing, the final area of cognitive assessment and testing relevant to mental health practice. The differential focus shall be on the measurement of more fundamental brain–behavior relationships, which assists in the diagnosis of *DSM-IV-TR* disorders, which involve brain damage or dysfunction as a principal etiological component (e.g., Dementia, Attention-Deficit/Hyperactivity Disorder).

REFERENCES

American Psychiatric Association. (2000). *Diagnostic and statistical manual of mental disorders* (4th ed., text rev.). Washington, DC: Author.

Goh, D. S. (2004). *Assessment accommodations for diverse learners.* Boston, MA: Pearson, pp. 25–27.

Gravetter, F. J., & Wallnau, L. B. (2013). *Statistics for the behavioral sciences* (9th ed.). Belmont, CA: Wadsworth, Cengage Learning.

Gregory, R. J. (2011). *Psychological testing: History, principles, applications.* Boston, MA: Pearson Education.

Kaplan, D. S., Damphous, K. R., & Kaplan, H. B. (1994). Mental health implications of not graduating from high school. *Journal of Experimental Education, 62,* 105–123.

Larsen, R. J., & Buss, D. M. (2010). *Personality psychology: Domains of knowledge about human nature* (4th ed.). New York, NY: McGraw-Hill.

Miller, L. A., McIntire, S. A., & Lovler, R. L. (2011). *Foundations of psychological testing* (3rd ed.). Thousand Oaks, CA: Sage Publications.

Pearson (PsychCorp). (2009a). *Wechsler Individual Achievement Test–Third edition (WIAT–III): Examiner's manual.* San Antonio, TX: Author.

Pearson (PsychCorp). (2009b). *Wechsler Individual Achievement Test–Third edition (WIAT–III): Technical manual (on CD-ROM).* San Antonio, TX: Author.

Roth, P. L., Bevier, C. A., Switzer, F. S., & Schippmann, J. S. (1996). Meta-analyzing the relationship between grades and job performance. *Journal of Applied Psychology, 81,* 548–556.

Warner, R. M. (2008). *Applied statistics.* Thousand Oaks, CA: Sage Publications.

WIAT–III Scoring Assistant. (2009). [CD-ROM computer Software]. San Antonio, TX: PsychCorp Center–II, Pearson.

FORM 5.1

WIAT–III, PRE-KINDERGARTEN (PK) RESULTS AND INTERPRETATION TABLES

WIAT–III, PK

TABLE 1 ■ PK COMPOSITE ACHIEVEMENT SCORE SUMMARY

Composite	Standard score	PR	90% CI	Qualitative description	Measured abilities
Oral Language (OL)	000	00.0	[000, 000]	Very superior average	Listening comprehension (receptive vocabulary, oral discourse comprehension); oral expression (expressive vocabulary, oral word fluency, sentence repetition)
Total Achievement	**000**	**0.00**	**[000, 000]**	**Very low**	**General proficiency in basic PK academic subjects, including oral language, early reading, alphabet writing, and math problem solving**

Note: Standard score mean = 100, standard deviation = 15. Lower scores indicate greater impairment in achievement. PK, pre-kindergarten; PR, percentile rank; CI, confidence interval. Total achievement data are in boldface.

TABLE 2 ■ PK ACHIEVEMENT SUBTEST SCORE SUMMARY

Subtest (relevant composite initials)	Standard score	PR	90% CI	Qualitative description	Measured abilities
Listening Comprehension (OL)	000	00.0	[000, 000]	Very superior Superior	Listening vocabulary; inferring and remembering details from oral sentences and discourse
Oral Expression (OL)	000	00.0	[000, 000]	Above average Average	Speaking vocabulary; word retrieval; word retrieval efficiency; flexibility of thought process; syntactic knowledge
Early Reading Skills	000	0.00	[000, 000]	Below average	Naming letters; letter-sound correspondence (alphabetic principle); phonological awareness; word reading comprehension
Alphabet Writing Fluency	000	0.00	[000, 000]	Low	Writing all the letters of the alphabet accurately (upper or lower case; print or cursive) within a 30-second time limit
Math Problem Solving	000	00.0	[000, 000]	Very low	Basic math concepts; everyday math applications; geometry; algebra (unlimited time)

Note: Standard score mean = 100, standard deviation = 15. Lower scores indicate greater impairment in achievement. PK, pre-kindergarten; PR, percentile rank; CI, confidence interval; OL, oral language composite.

FORM 5.2

WIAT–III, K–12 RESULTS AND INTERPRETATION TABLES

WIAT–III, K–12

TABLE 1 ■ COMPOSITE ACHIEVEMENT SCORE SUMMARY

Composite	Standard score	PR	90% CI	Qualitative description	Measured abilities
Oral Language (Grades K–12)	--	--	[000, 000]	Very superior	Listening comprehension (receptive vocabulary, oral discourse comprehension); oral expression (expressive vocabulary, oral word fluency, sentence repetition)
Total Reading (Grades 1–12)	--	--	[000, 000]	Superior	Word reading; pseudoword decoding (phonics); reading comprehension; oral reading fluency
Basic Reading (Grades 1–12)	--	--	[000, 000]	Above average	Word reading; pseudoword decoding (phonics)
Reading Comprehension and Fluency (Grades 2–12)	--	--	[000, 000]	Average	Reading comprehension; oral reading fluency
Written Expression (Grades K–12)	--	--	[000, 000]	Below average	Alphabet writing fluency (Grades K–3); spelling; sentence composition (sentence combining and building; Grades 1–12); essay composition (content and organization, grammar and mechanics) (Grades 3–12)
Mathematics (Grades K–12)	--	--	[000, 000]	Low	Math problem solving; numerical operations
Total Achievement (Grades K–12)	**000**	**0.00**	**[000, 000]**	**Very low**	**General degree of knowledge and proficiency in basic academic subjects, including oral language, reading, written expression, and mathematics**

Note: Standard score mean = 100, standard deviation = 15. Lower scores indicate greater impairment in achievement. PR, percentile rank; CI, confidence interval; K, kindergarten. -- denotes not administered, or score type not available or computed. Total achievement data are in boldface.

TABLE 2 ■ ORAL LANGUAGE ACHIEVEMENT SUBTEST SCORE SUMMARY

Subtest	Standard score	PR	90% CI	Qualitative description	Measured abilities
Listening Comprehension (Grades K–12)	000	00.0	[000, 000]	Very superior Superior	Listening vocabulary; inferring and remembering details from oral sentences and discourse
Oral Expression (Grades K–12)	--	--	[000, 000]	Above average Low	Speaking vocabulary; word retrieval; word retrieval efficiency; flexibility of thought process; syntactic knowledge
Oral Reading Fluency (Grades 1–12)	--	--	[000, 000]	Very low	Speed, accuracy, fluency, and prosody (i.e., rhythm) of contextualized oral reading

Note: Standard score mean = 100, standard deviation = 15. Lower scores indicate greater impairment in achievement. PR, percentile rank; CI, confidence interval; K, kindergarten. -- denotes not administered, or score type not available or computed.

(Cont.)

FORM 5.2

WIAT–III, K–12 RESULTS AND
INTERPRETATION TABLES (*Cont.*)

TABLE 3 ■ READING ACHIEVEMENT SUBTEST SCORE SUMMARY

Subtest	Standard score	PR	90% CI	Qualitative description	Measured abilities
Early Reading Skills (Grades K–3)	000	0.00	[000, 000]	Very superior	Naming letters; letter-sound correspondence (alphabetic principle); phonological awareness; word reading comprehension
Word Reading (Grades 1–12)	--	--	[000, 000]	Superior Above average	Speed and accuracy of decontextualized word recognition; reading aloud a list of words of increasing difficulty
Pseudoword Decoding (Grades 1–12)	--	--	[000, 000]	Average Below average	Ability to decode nonsense words that include common syllables; reading aloud a list of nonsense words accurately; phonics
Reading Comprehension (Grades 1–12)	--	--	[000, 000]	Low	Understanding types of written passages after reading them (fictional stories; informational text; advertisements; how-to passages)
Oral Reading Fluency (Grades 1–12)	--	--	[000, 000]	Very low	Speed, accuracy, and prosody (i.e., rhythm) of contextualized oral reasoning; reading passages aloud and answering comprehension problems

Note: Standard score mean = 100, standard deviation = 15. Lower scores indicate greater impairment in achievement. PR, percentile rank; CI, confidence interval; K, kindergarten. -- denotes not administered, or score type not available or computed.

TABLE 4 ■ WRITTEN EXPRESSION ACHIEVEMENT SUBTEST SCORE SUMMARY

Subtest	Standard score	PR	90% CI	Qualitative description	Measured abilities
Alphabet Writing Fluency (Grades K–3)	000	0.00	[000, 000]	Very superior	Writing all the letters of the alphabet accurately (upper or lower case; print or cursive) within a 30-second time limit
Spelling (Grades K–12)	--	--	[000, 000]	Above average	Written spelling of letter sounds and single words
Sentence Composition (Grades 1–12)	--	--	[000, 000]	Average Below average	Sentence formulation and written syntactic ability (sentence combining and building)
Essay Composition (Grades 3–12)	--	--	[000, 000]	Low Very low	Spontaneous compositional writing (10-minute duration)

Note: Standard score mean = 100, standard deviation = 15. Lower scores indicate greater impairment in achievement. PR, percentile rank; CI, confidence interval; K, kindergarten. -- denotes not administered, or score type not available or computed.

TABLE 5 ■ MATHEMATICS ACHIEVEMENT SUBTEST SCORE SUMMARY

Subtest	Standard score	PR	90% CI	Qualitative description	Measured abilities
Math Problem Solving (Grades K–12)	000	00.0	[000, 000]	Very superior Average	Basic math concepts; everyday math applications; geometry; algebra (unlimited time)
Numerical Operations (Grades K–12)	--	--	[000, 000]	Below average Very low	Written math computations in basic skills, basic operations with integers, geometry, algebra, and calculus

Note: Standard score mean = 100, standard deviation = 15. Lower scores indicate greater impairment in achievement. PR, percentile rank; CI, confidence interval; K, kindergarten. -- denotes not administered, or score type not available or computed.

FORM 5.3

WISC–IV/WIAT–III ABILITY–ACHIEVEMENT DISCREPANCY ANALYSIS SIMPLE DIFFERENCE METHOD RESULTS AND INTERPRETATION TABLES
WISC–IV

TABLE 1 ■ COMPOSITE SCORE SUMMARY

Index/Scale	Composite score	PR	90% CI	Qualitative description	Measured abilities
Verbal Comprehension Index (VCI)	000	00	[00, 00]	Very superior	Verbal reasoning, comprehension, and conceptualization
Perceptual Reasoning Index (PRI)	--	--	[00, 00]	Superior	Visual–spatial (nonverbal) reasoning, organization, and conceptualization
Full Scale[a]	**000**	**0.00**	**[000, 000]**	**Low average**	**General intelligence: the ability to learn from experience, acquire knowledge, and use resources effectively in adapting to new situations or solving problems[b]**

Note: Composite score mean = 100, standard deviation = 15. Lower scores indicate greater intellectual impairment. PR, percentile rank; CI, confidence interval. -- denotes not administered, or score type not available or computed. Full Scale data are in boldface.

[a]The Full Scale includes Verbal Comprehension, Perceptual Reasoning, Working Memory, and Processing Speed Composite scores; the latter two are not reported as they are peripheral to the primary analyses.

[b]Ciccarelli, S. K., & White, J. N. (2012). *Psychology* (3rd ed.). Upper Saddle River, NJ: Pearson Education; Wechsler, D. (1975). The collected papers of David Wechsler. New York, NY: Academic Press.

TABLE 2 ■ VCI–PRI INDEX LEVEL DISCREPANCY COMPARISON

VCI composite score	PRI composite score	Difference	Critical value .05*	Cohen's *d* effect size[a]	Effect size results[b]	Base rate[c]
000	000	±00	0.00	0.0	Large medium	00.0%

Note: *denotes that the VCI–PRI difference occurs by chance less than 5 times in 100 and is therefore statistically significant.
[a]Computed as the absolute value of VCI–PRI/standard deviation (15).

[b]Effect size score ranges: 0.0 to 0.2 (small effect); 0.3 to 0.7 (medium effect); 0.8 and higher (large effect).

[c]Percentage of the normative sample who obtained the listed VCI–PRI difference.

The VCI–PRI difference was not statistically significant, manifested a small effect size, and yielded an acceptably high base rate in the normative sample. Thus, the Full Scale was deemed an acceptable measure of general intelligence and was used in the ability–achievement discrepancy analysis.

The VCI–PRI difference was statistically significant and favored the former/latter. The difference also yielded both a large effect size and remarkably low base rate in the normative sample. Thus, the Full Scale was deemed an unacceptable measure of general intelligence and was dropped from further analysis. The ensuing ability–achievement discrepancy analysis was completed using the VCI for the following reasons: (a) to determine if any measured achievement deficits exist beyond the impact of language ability and (b) evidence that the VCI tends to yield higher correlations with general intelligence as compared to other WISC–IV indices. The ensuing ability–achievement discrepancy analysis was completed using the lower VCI/PRI to minimize false positive results.

(Cont.)

FORM 5.3

WISC–IV/WIAT–III ABILITY–ACHIEVEMENT DISCREPANCY ANALYSIS SIMPLE DIFFERENCE METHOD RESULTS AND INTERPRETATION TABLES (*Cont.*)

WIAT–III, K–12

TABLE 3 ■ COMPOSITE ACHIEVEMENT SCORE SUMMARY

Composite	Standard score	PR	90% CI	Qualitative description	Measured abilities
Oral Language (Grades K–12)	--	--	[000, 000]	Very superior	Listening comprehension (receptive vocabulary, oral discourse comprehension); oral expression (expressive vocabulary, oral word fluency, sentence repetition)
Total Reading (Grades 1–12)	--	--	[000, 000]	Superior	Word reading; pseudoword decoding (phonics); reading comprehension; oral reading fluency
Basic Reading (Grades 1–12)	--	--	[000, 000]	Above average	Word reading; pseudoword decoding (phonics)
Reading Comprehension and Fluency (Grades 2–12)	--	--	[000, 000]	Average	Reading comprehension; oral reading fluency
Written Expression (Grades K–12)	--	--	[000, 000]	Below average	Alphabet writing fluency (Grades K–3); spelling; sentence composition (sentence combining and building) (Grades 1–12); essay composition (content and organization, grammar and mechanics) (Grades 3–12)
Mathematics (Grades K–12)	--	--	[000, 000]	Low	Math problem solving; numerical operations
Total Achievement (Grades K–12)	**000**	**0.00**	**[000, 000]**	**Very low**	**General degree of knowledge and proficiency in basic academic subjects, including oral language, reading, written expression, and mathematics**

Note: Standard score mean = 100, standard deviation = 15. Lower scores indicate greater impairment in achievement. PR, percentile rank; CI, confidence interval; K, kindergarten. -- denotes not administered, or score type not available or computed. Total achievement data are in boldface.

TABLE 4 ■ ORAL LANGUAGE ACHIEVEMENT SUBTEST SCORE SUMMARY

Subtest	Standard score	PR	90% CI	Qualitative description	Measured abilities
Listening Comprehension (Grades K–12)	000	00.0	[000, 000]	Very superior Superior	Listening vocabulary; inferring and remembering details from oral sentences and discourse
Oral Expression (Grades K–12)	--	--	[000, 000]	Above average Average	Speaking vocabulary; word retrieval; word retrieval efficiency; flexibility of thought process; syntactic knowledge
Oral Reading Fluency (Grades 1–12)	--	--	[000, 000]	Very low	Speed, accuracy, fluency, and prosody (i.e., rhythm) of contextualized oral reading

Note: Standard score mean = 100, standard deviation = 15. Lower scores indicate greater impairment in achievement. PR, percentile rank; CI, confidence interval; K, kindergarten. -- denotes not administered, or score type not available or computed.

(*Cont.*)

FORM 5.3

WISC–IV/WIAT–III ABILITY–ACHIEVEMENT DISCREPANCY ANALYSIS SIMPLE DIFFERENCE METHOD RESULTS AND INTERPRETATION TABLES (*Cont.*)

TABLE 5 ■ READING ACHIEVEMENT SUBTEST SCORE SUMMARY

Subtest	Standard score	PR	90% CI	Qualitative description	Measured abilities
Early Reading Skills (Grades K–3)	000	0.00	[000, 000]	Very superior	Naming letters; letter-sound correspondence (alphabetic principle); phonological awareness; word reading comprehension
Word Reading (Grades 1–12)	--	--	[000, 000]	Superior Above average	Speed and accuracy of decontextualized word recognition; reading aloud a list of words of increasing difficulty
Pseudoword Decoding (Grades 1–12)	--	--	[000, 000]	Average Below average	Ability to decode nonsense words, which include common syllables; reading aloud a list of nonsense words accurately; phonics
Reading Comprehension (Grades 1–12)	--	--	[000, 000]	Low	Understanding types of written passages after reading them (fictional stories; informational text; advertisements; how-to passages)
Oral Reading Fluency (Grades 1–12)	--	--	[000, 000]	Very low	Speed, accuracy, and prosody (i.e., rhythm) of contextualized oral reasoning; reading passages aloud and answering comprehension problems

Note: Standard score mean = 100, standard deviation = 15. Lower scores indicate greater impairment in achievement. PR, percentile rank; CI, confidence interval; K, kindergarten. -- denotes not administered, or score type not available or computed.

TABLE 6 ■ WRITTEN EXPRESSION ACHIEVEMENT SUBTEST SCORE SUMMARY

Subtest	Standard score	PR	90% CI	Qualitative description	Measured abilities
Alphabet Writing Fluency (Grades K–3)	000	0.00	[000, 000]	Very superior	Writing all the letters of the alphabet accurately (upper or lower case; print or cursive) within a 30-second time limit
Spelling (Grades K–12)	--	--	[000, 000]	Above average	Written spelling of letter sounds and single words
Sentence Composition (Grades 1–12)	--	--	[000, 000]	Average Below average	Sentence formulation and written syntactic ability (sentence combining and building)
Essay Composition (Grades 3–12)	--	--	[000, 000]	Low Very low	Spontaneous compositional writing (10-minutes duration)

Note: Standard score mean = 100, standard deviation = 15. Lower scores indicate greater impairment in achievement. PR, percentile rank; CI, confidence interval; K, kindergarten. -- denotes not administered, or score type not available or computed.

TABLE 7 ■ MATHEMATICS ACHIEVEMENT SUBTEST SCORE SUMMARY

Subtest	Standard score	PR	90% CI	Qualitative description	Measured abilities
Math Problem Solving (Grades K–12)	000	00.0	[000, 000]	Very superior Average	Basic math concepts; everyday math applications; geometry; algebra (unlimited time)
Numerical Operations (Grades K–12)	--	--	[000, 000]	Low Very low	Written math computations in basic skills, basic operations with integers, geometry, algebra, and calculus

Note: Standard score mean = 100, standard deviation = 15. Lower scores indicate greater impairment in achievement. PR, percentile rank; CI, confidence interval; K, kindergarten. -- denotes not administered, or score type not available or computed.

(*Cont.*)

FORM 5.3

WISC–IV/WIAT–III ABILITY–ACHIEVEMENT DISCREPANCY ANALYSIS SIMPLE DIFFERENCE METHOD RESULTS AND INTERPRETATION TABLES (*Cont.*)

ABILITY–ACHIEVEMENT DISCREPANCY ANALYSIS

ABILITY SCORE TYPE: WISC–IV FULL SCALE

ABILITY SCORE: 000

TABLE 8 ■ **WIAT–III COMPOSITE: SIMPLE DIFFERENCE METHOD[a]**

Composite	WIAT–III standard score	WISC–IV Full Scale	Difference	Critical value .01*	Base rate[b]
Oral Language (OL)	000	000	±00	0.00	00.0%
Total Reading (TR)	000	000	±00	0.00	00.0%
Basic Reading (BR)	000	000	±00	N/A	N/A
Reading Comprehension and Fluency (RC)	000	000	±00	0.00	00.0%
Written Expression (WE)	000	000	±00	0.00	00.0%
Mathematics (MA)	000	000	±00	0.00	00.0%
Total Achievement	000	000	±00	0.00	00.0%

Note: * denotes that the WIAT–III – WISC–IV Full Scale standard score difference occurs by chance less than 1 time in 100 and is therefore statistically significant. N/A, not applicable; the WIAT–III standard score was equal to or exceeded the WISC–IV Full Scale.

[a]The differences are obtained by subtracting the employed WISC–IV composite score from each WIAT–III standard score.

[b]Percentage of the normative sample who obtained the listed WIAT–III – WISC–IV Full Scale standard score difference.

TABLE 9 ■ **WIAT–III SUBTEST: SIMPLE DIFFERENCE METHOD[a]**

Subtest (relevant composite initials)	WIAT–III standard score	WISC–IV Full Scale	Difference	Critical value .01*	Base rate[b]
Listening Comprehension (OL)	000	000	±00	0.00	00.0%
Oral Expression (OL)	000	000	±00	0.00	00.0%
Early Reading Skills	000	000	±00	N/A	N/A
Word Reading (TR) (BR)	000	000	±00	0.00	00.0%
Pseudoword Decoding (TR) (BR)	000	000	±00	0.00	00.0%
Reading Comprehension (TR) (RC)	000	000	±00	0.00	00.0%
Oral Reading Fluency (TR) (RC)	000	000	±00	N/A	N/A
Spelling (WE)	000	000	±00	0.00	00.0%
Sentence Composition (WE)	000	000	±00	0.00	00.0%
Essay Composition (WE)	000	000	±00	0.00	00.0%
Math Problem Solving (MA)	000	000	±00	0.00	00.0%
Numerical Operations (MA)	000	000	±00	0.00	00.0%

Note: * denotes that the WIAT–III – WISC–IV Full Scale standard score difference occurs by chance less than 1 time in 100 and is therefore statistically significant. N/A, not applicable; the WIAT–III standard score was equal to or exceeded the WISC–IV Full Scale.

[a]The differences are obtained by subtracting the employed WISC–IV composite score from each WIAT–III standard score.

[b]Percentage of the normative sample who obtained the listed WIAT–III – WISC–IV Full Scale standard score difference.

FORM 5.4

WISC–IV/WIAT–III ABILITY–ACHIEVEMENT DISCREPANCY ANALYSIS PREDICTED DIFFERENCE METHOD RESULTS AND INTERPRETATION TABLES

WISC–IV

TABLE 1 ■ COMPOSITE SCORE SUMMARY

Index/Scale	Composite score	PR	90% CI	Qualitative description	Measured abilities
Verbal Comprehension Index (VCI)	000	00	[00, 00]	Very superior	Verbal reasoning, comprehension, and conceptualization
Perceptual Reasoning Index (PRI)	--	--	[00, 00]	Superior	Visual-spatial (nonverbal) reasoning, organization, and conceptualization
Full Scale[a]	**000**	**0.00**	**[000, 000]**	**Low average**	**General intelligence: the ability to learn from experience, acquire knowledge, and use resources effectively in adapting to new situations or solving problems[b]**

Note: Composite score mean = 100, standard deviation = 15. Lower scores indicate greater intellectual impairment. PR, percentile rank; CI, confidence interval. -- denotes not administered, or score type not available or computed. Full Scale data are in boldface.

[a]The Full Scale includes Verbal Comprehension, Perceptual Reasoning, Working Memory, and Processing Speed Composite scores; the latter two are not reported as they are peripheral to the primary analyses.

[b]Ciccarelli, S. K., & White, J. N. (2012). *Psychology* (3rd ed.). Upper Saddle River, NJ: Pearson Education; Wechsler, D. (1975). The collected papers of David Wechsler. New York, NY: Academic Press.

TABLE 2 ■ VCI–PRI INDEX LEVEL DISCREPANCY COMPARISON

VCI composite score	PRI composite score	Difference	Critical value .05*	Cohen's d effect size[a]	Effect size results[b]	Base rate[c]
000	000	±00	0.00	0.0	Large medium	00.0%

Note: *denotes that the VCI–PRI difference occurs by chance less than 5 times in 100 and is therefore statistically significant.

[a]Computed as the absolute value of VCI–PRI/standard deviation (15).

[b]Effect size score ranges: 0.0 to 0.2 (small effect); 0.3 to 0.7 (medium effect); 0.8 and higher (large effect).

[c]Percentage of the normative sample who obtained the listed VCI–PRI difference.

The VCI–PRI difference was not statistically significant, manifested a small effect size, and yielded an acceptably high base rate in the normative sample. Thus, the Full Scale was deemed an acceptable measure of general intelligence and was used in the ability–achievement discrepancy analysis.

The VCI–PRI difference was statistically significant and favored the former/latter. The difference also yielded both a large effect size and remarkably low base rate in the normative sample. Thus, the Full Scale was deemed an unacceptable measure of general intelligence and was dropped from further analysis. The ensuing ability–achievement discrepancy analysis was completed using the VCI for the following reasons: (a) to determine if any measured achievement deficits exist beyond the impact of language ability and (b) evidence that the VCI tends to yield higher correlations with general intelligence as compared to other WISC–IV indices. The ensuing ability–achievement discrepancy analysis was completed using the lower VCI/PRI to minimize false positive results.

(Cont.)

FORM 5.4

WISC–IV/WIAT–III ABILITY–ACHIEVEMENT DISCREPANCY ANALYSIS PREDICTED DIFFERENCE METHOD RESULTS AND INTERPRETATION TABLES (*Cont.*)

WIAT–III, K–12

TABLE 3 ■ COMPOSITE ACHIEVEMENT SCORE SUMMARY

Composite	Standard score	PR	90% CI	Qualitative description	Measured abilities
Oral Language (Grades K–12)	--	--	[000, 000]	Very superior	Listening comprehension (receptive vocabulary, oral discourse comprehension); oral expression (expressive vocabulary, oral word fluency, sentence repetition)
Total Reading (Grades 1–12)	--	--	[000, 000]	Superior	Word reading; pseudoword decoding (phonics); reading comprehension; oral reading fluency
Basic Reading (Grades 1–12)	--	--	[000, 000]	Above average	Word reading; pseudoword decoding (phonics)
Reading Comprehension and Fluency (Grades 2–12)	--	--	[000, 000]	Average	Reading comprehension; oral reading fluency
Written Expression (Grades K–12)	--	--	[000, 000]	Below average	Alphabet writing fluency (Grades K–3); spelling; sentence composition (sentence combining and building) (Grades 1–12); essay composition (content and organization, grammar and mechanics) (Grades 3–12)
Mathematics (Grades K–12)	--	--	[000, 000]	Low	Math problem solving; numerical operations
Total Achievement (Grades K–12)	**000**	**0.00**	**[000, 000]**	**Very low**	**General degree of knowledge and proficiency in basic academic subjects, including oral language, reading, written expression, and mathematics**

Note: Standard score mean = 100, standard deviation = 15. Lower scores indicate greater impairment in achievement. PR, percentile rank; CI, confidence interval; K, kindergarten. -- denotes not administered, or score type not available or computed. Total achievement data are in boldface.

TABLE 4 ■ ORAL LANGUAGE ACHIEVEMENT SUBTEST SCORE SUMMARY

Subtest	Standard score	PR	90% CI	Qualitative description	Measured abilities
Listening Comprehension (Grades K–12)	000	00.0	[000, 000]	Very superior Superior	Listening vocabulary; inferring and remembering details from oral sentences and discourse
Oral Expression (Grades K–12)	--	--	[000, 000]	Above average Low	Speaking vocabulary; word retrieval; word retrieval efficiency; flexibility of thought process; syntactic knowledge
Oral Reading Fluency (Grades 1–12)	--	--	[000, 000]	Very low	Speed, accuracy, fluency, and prosody (i.e., rhythm) of contextualized oral reading

Note: Standard score mean = 100, standard deviation = 15. Lower scores indicate greater impairment in achievement. PR, percentile rank; CI, confidence interval; K, kindergarten. -- denotes not administered, or score type not available or computed.

(*Cont.*)

FORM 5.4

WISC–IV/WIAT–III ABILITY–ACHIEVEMENT DISCREPANCY ANALYSIS PREDICTED DIFFERENCE METHOD RESULTS AND INTERPRETATION TABLES (*Cont.*)

TABLE 5 ■ **READING ACHIEVEMENT SUBTEST SCORE SUMMARY**

Subtest	Standard score	PR	90% CI	Qualitative description	Measured abilities
Early Reading Skills (Grades K–3)	000	0.00	[000, 000]	Very superior	Naming letters; letter-sound correspondence (alphabetic principle); phonological awareness; word reading comprehension
Word Reading (Grades 1–12)	--	--	[000, 000]	Superior Above average	Speed and accuracy of decontextualized word recognition; reading aloud a list of words of increasing difficulty
Pseudoword Decoding (Grades 1–12)	--	--	[000, 000]	Average Below average	Ability to decode nonsense words, which include common syllables; reading aloud a list of nonsense words accurately; phonics
Reading Comprehension (Grades 1–12)	--	--	[000, 000]	Low	Understanding types of written passages after reading them (fictional stories; informational text; advertisements; how-to passages)
Oral Reading Fluency (Grades 1–12)	--	--	[000, 000]	Very low	Speed, accuracy, and prosody (i.e., rhythm) of contextualized oral reasoning; reading passages aloud and answering comprehension problems

Note: Standard score mean = 100, standard deviation = 15. Lower scores indicate greater impairment in achievement. PR, percentile rank; CI, confidence interval; K, kindergarten. -- denotes not administered, or score type not available or computed.

TABLE 6 ■ **WRITTEN EXPRESSION ACHIEVEMENT SUBTEST SCORE SUMMARY**

Subtest	Standard score	PR	90% CI	Qualitative description	Measured abilities
Alphabet Writing Fluency (Grades K–3)	000	0.00	[000, 000]	Very superior	Writing all the letters of the alphabet accurately (upper or lower case; print or cursive) within a 30-second time limit
Spelling (Grades K–12)	--	--	[000, 000]	Above average	Written spelling of letter sounds and single words
Sentence Composition (Grades 1–12)	--	--	[000, 000]	Average Below average	Sentence formulation and written syntactic ability (sentence combining and building)
Essay Composition (Grades 3–12)	--	--	[000, 000]	Low Very low	Spontaneous compositional writing (10-minute duration)

Note: Standard score mean = 100, standard deviation = 15. Lower scores indicate greater impairment in achievement. PR, percentile rank; CI, confidence interval; K, kindergarten. -- denotes not administered, or score type not available or computed.

TABLE 7 ■ **MATHEMATICS ACHIEVEMENT SUBTEST SCORE SUMMARY**

Subtest	Standard score	PR	90% CI	Qualitative description	Measured abilities
Math Problem Solving (Grades K–12)	000	00.0	[000, 000]	Very superior Average	Basic math concepts; everyday math applications; geometry; algebra (unlimited time)
Numerical Operations (Grades K–12)	--	--	[000, 000]	Low Very low	Written math computations in basic skills, basic operations with integers, geometry, algebra, and calculus

Note: Standard score mean = 100, standard deviation = 15. Lower scores indicate greater impairment in achievement. PR, percentile rank; CI, confidence interval; K, kindergarten. -- denotes not administered, or score type not available or computed.

(Cont.)

FORM 5.4

WISC–IV/WIAT–III ABILITY–ACHIEVEMENT DISCREPANCY ANALYSIS PREDICTED DIFFERENCE METHOD RESULTS AND INTERPRETATION TABLES (*Cont.*)

ABILITY–ACHIEVEMENT DISCREPANCY ANALYSIS

ABILITY SCORE TYPE: WISC–IV FULL SCALE

ABILITY SCORE: 000

TABLE 8 ■ **WIAT–III COMPOSITE: PREDICTED DIFFERENCE METHOD**[a]

Composite	Actual WIAT–III standard score	Predicted WIAT–III standard score	Difference	Critical value .01*	Base rate[b]
Oral Language (OL)	000	000	±00	0.00	00.0%
Total Reading (TR)	000	000	±00	0.00	00.0%
Basic Reading (BR)	000	000	±00	N/A	N/A
Reading Comprehension and Fluency (RC)	000	000	±00	0.00	00.0%
Written Expression (WE)	000	000	±00	0.00	00.0%
Mathematics (MA)	000	000	±00	0.00	00.0%
Total Achievement	000	000	±00	0.00	00.0%

Note: *denotes that the actual WIAT–III standard score – predicted WIAT–III standard score difference occurs by chance less than 1 time in 100 and is therefore statistically significant. N/A, not applicable; the actual WIAT–III standard score was equal to or exceeded the predicted WIAT–III standard score.

[a]The differences are obtained by subtracting each WIAT–III standard score predicted by the employed WISC–IV composite score from the actual WIAT–III standard score.

[b]Percentage of the normative sample who obtained the listed actual WIAT–III standard score – predicted WIAT–III standard score difference.

TABLE 9 ■ WIAT–III SUBTEST: PREDICTED DIFFERENCE METHOD[a]

Subtest (relevant composite initials)	Actual WIAT–III standard score	Predicted WIAT–III standard score	Difference	Critical value .01*	Base rate[b]
Listening Comprehension (OL)	000	000	±00	0.00	00.0%
Oral Expression (OL)	000	000	±00	0.00	00.0%
Early Reading skills	000	000	±00	N/A	N/A
Word Reading (TR) (BR)	000	000	±00	0.00	00.0%
Pseudoword Decoding (TR) (BR)	000	000	±00	0.00	00.0%
Reading Comprehension (TR) (RC)	000	000	±00	0.00	00.0%
Oral Reading Fluency (TR) (RC)	000	000	±00	N/A	N/A
Spelling (WE)	000	000	±00	0.00	00.0%
Sentence Composition (WE)	000	000	±00	0.00	00.0%
Essay Composition (WE)	000	000	±00	0.00	00.0%
Math Problem Solving (MA)	000	000	±00	0.00	00.0%
Numerical Operations (MA)	000	000	±00	0.00	00.0%

Note: *denotes that the actual WIAT–III standard score – predicted WIAT–III standard score difference occurs by chance less than 1 time in 100 and is therefore statistically significant. N/A, not applicable; the actual WIAT–III standard score was equal to or exceeded the predicted WIAT–III standard score.

[a]The differences are obtained by subtracting each WIAT–III standard score predicted by the employed WISC–IV composite score from the actual WIAT–III standard score.

[b]Percentage of the normative sample who obtained the listed actual WIAT–III standard score – predicted WIAT–III standard score difference.

FORM 5.5

WAIS–IV/WIAT–III ABILITY–ACHIEVEMENT DISCREPANCY ANALYSIS SIMPLE DIFFERENCE METHOD RESULTS AND INTERPRETATION TABLES

WAIS–IV

TABLE 1 ■ COMPOSITE SCORE SUMMARY

Index/Scale	Composite score	PR	90% CI	Qualitative description	Measured abilities
Verbal Comprehension Index (VCI)	000	00	[00, 00]	Very superior	Verbal reasoning, comprehension, and conceptualization
Perceptual Reasoning Index (PRI)	--	--	[00, 00]	Superior	Visual-spatial (nonverbal) reasoning, organization, and conceptualization
Full Scale[a]	**000**	**0.00**	**[000, 000]**	**Low average**	**General intelligence: the ability to learn from experience, acquire knowledge, and use resources effectively in adapting to new situations or solving problems[b]**

Note: Composite score mean = 100, standard deviation = 15. Lower scores indicate greater intellectual impairment. PR, percentile rank; CI, confidence interval. -- denotes not administered, or score type not available or computed. Full Scale data are in boldface.

[a]The Full Scale includes Verbal Comprehension, Perceptual Reasoning, Working Memory, and Processing Speed Composite scores; the latter two are not reported as they are peripheral to the primary analyses.

[b]Ciccarelli, S. K., & White, J. N. (2012). *Psychology* (3rd ed.). Upper Saddle River, NJ: Pearson Education; Wechsler, D. (1975). The collected papers of David Wechsler. New York, NY: Academic Press.

TABLE 2 ■ VCI–PRI INDEX LEVEL DISCREPANCY COMPARISON

VCI composite score	PRI composite score	Difference	Critical value .05*	Cohen's d effect size[a]	Effect size results[b]	Base rate[c]
000	000	±00	0.00	0.0	Large medium	00.0%

Note: *denotes that the VCI–PRI difference occurs by chance less than 5 times in 100 and is therefore statistically significant.

[a]Computed as the absolute value of VCI–PRI/standard deviation (15).

[b]Effect size score ranges: 0.0 to 0.2 (small effect); 0.3 to 0.7 (medium effect); 0.8 and higher (large effect).

[c]Percentage of the normative sample who obtained the listed VCI–PRI difference.

The VCI–PRI difference was not statistically significant, manifested a small effect size, and yielded an acceptably high base rate in the normative sample. Thus, the Full Scale was deemed an acceptable measure of general intelligence and was used in the ability–achievement discrepancy analysis.

The VCI–PRI difference was statistically significant and favored the former/latter. The difference also yielded both a large effect size and remarkably low base rate in the normative sample. Thus, the Full Scale was deemed an unacceptable measure of general intelligence and was dropped from further analysis. The ensuing ability–achievement discrepancy analysis was completed using the VCI for the following reasons: (a) to determine if any measured achievement deficits exist beyond the impact of language ability and (b) evidence that the VCI tends to yield higher correlations with general intelligence as compared to other WAIS–IV indices. The ensuing ability–achievement discrepancy analysis was completed using the lower VCI–PRI to minimize false positive results.

(Cont.)

FORM 5.5

WAIS–IV/WIAT–III ABILITY–ACHIEVEMENT DISCREPANCY ANALYSIS SIMPLE DIFFERENCE METHOD RESULTS AND INTERPRETATION TABLES (*Cont.*)

WIAT–III, K–12

TABLE 3 ■ **COMPOSITE ACHIEVEMENT SCORE SUMMARY**

Composite	Standard score	PR	90% CI	Qualitative description	Measured abilities
Oral Language (Grades K–12)	--	--	[000, 000]	Very superior	Listening comprehension (receptive vocabulary, oral discourse comprehension); oral expression (expressive vocabulary, oral word fluency, sentence repetition)
Total Reading (Grades 1–12)	--	--	[000, 000]	Superior	Word reading; pseudoword decoding (phonics); reading comprehension; oral reading fluency
Basic Reading (Grades 1–12)	--	--	[000, 000]	Above average	Word reading; pseudoword decoding (phonics)
Reading Comprehension and Fluency (Grades 2–12)	--	--	[000, 000]	Average	Reading comprehension; oral reading fluency
Written Expression (Grades K–12)	--	--	[000, 000]	Below average	Alphabet writing fluency (Grades K–3); spelling; sentence composition (sentence combining and building) (Grades 1–12); essay composition (content and organization, grammar and mechanics) (Grades 3–12)
Mathematics (Grades K–12)	--	--	[000, 000]	Low	Math problem solving; numerical operations
Total achievement (Grades K–12)	**000**	**0.00**	**[000, 000]**	**Very low**	**General degree of knowledge and proficiency in basic academic subjects, including oral language, reading, written expression, and mathematics**

Note: Standard score mean = 100, standard deviation = 15. Lower scores indicate greater impairment in achievement. PR, percentile rank; CI, confidence interval; K, kindergarten. -- denotes not administered, or score type not available or computed. Total achievement data are in boldface.

TABLE 4 ■ **ORAL LANGUAGE ACHIEVEMENT SUBTEST SCORE SUMMARY**

Subtest	Standard score	PR	90% CI	Qualitative description	Measured abilities
Listening Comprehension (Grades K–12)	000	00.0	[000, 000]	Very superior Superior	Listening vocabulary; inferring and remembering details from oral sentences and discourse
Oral Expression (Grades K–12)	--	--	[000, 000]	Above average Low	Speaking vocabulary; word retrieval; word retrieval efficiency; flexibility of thought process; syntactic knowledge
Oral Reading Fluency (Grades 1–12)	--	--	[000, 000]	Very low	Speed, accuracy, fluency, and prosody (i.e., rhythm) of contextualized oral reading

Note: Standard score mean = 100, standard deviation = 15. Lower scores indicate greater impairment in achievement. PR, percentile rank; CI, confidence interval; K, kindergarten. -- denotes not administered, or score type not available or computed.

(Cont.)

FORM 5.5

WAIS–IV/WIAT–III ABILITY–ACHIEVEMENT DISCREPANCY ANALYSIS SIMPLE DIFFERENCE METHOD RESULTS AND INTERPRETATION TABLES (*Cont.*)

TABLE 5 ■ **READING ACHIEVEMENT SUBTEST SCORE SUMMARY**

Subtest	Standard score	PR	90% CI	Qualitative description	Measured abilities
Word Reading (Grades 1–12)	--	--	[000, 000]	Superior Above average	Speed and accuracy of decontextualized word recognition; reading aloud a list of words of increasing difficulty
Pseudoword Decoding (Grades 1–12)	--	--	[000, 000]	Average Below average	Ability to decode nonsense words, which include common syllables; reading aloud a list of nonsense words accurately; phonics
Reading Comprehension (Grades 1–12)	--	--	[000, 000]	Low	Understanding types of written passages after reading them (fictional stories; informational text; advertisements; how-to passages)
Oral Reading Fluency (Grades 1–12)	--	--	[000, 000]	Very low	Speed, accuracy, and prosody (i.e., rhythm) of contextualized oral reasoning; reading passages aloud and answering comprehension problems

Note: Standard score mean = 100, standard deviation = 15. Lower scores indicate greater impairment in achievement. PR, percentile rank; CI, confidence interval. -- denotes not administered, or score type not available or computed.

TABLE 6 ■ **WRITTEN EXPRESSION ACHIEVEMENT SUBTEST SCORE SUMMARY**

Subtest	Standard score	PR	90% CI	Qualitative description	Measured abilities
Spelling (Grades K–12)	--	--	[000, 000]	Above average	Written spelling of letter sounds and single words
Sentence Composition (Grades 1–12)	--	--	[000, 000]	Average Below average	Sentence formulation and written syntactic ability (sentence combining and building)
Essay Composition (Grades 3–12)	--	--	[000, 000]	Low Very low	Spontaneous compositional writing (10-minute duration)

Note: Standard score mean = 100, standard deviation = 15. Lower scores indicate greater impairment in achievement. PR, percentile rank; CI, confidence interval; K, kindergarten. -- denotes not administered, or score type not available or computed.

TABLE 7 ■ **MATHEMATICS ACHIEVEMENT SUBTEST SCORE SUMMARY**

Subtest	Standard score	PR	90% CI	Qualitative description	Measured abilities
Math Problem Solving (Grades K–12)	000	00.0	[000, 000]	Very superior Average	Basic math concepts; everyday math applications; geometry; algebra (unlimited time)
Numerical Operations (Grades K–12)	--	--	[000, 000]	Low Very low	Written math computations in basic skills, basic operations with integers, geometry, algebra, and calculus

Note: Standard score mean = 100, standard deviation = 15. Lower scores indicate greater impairment in achievement. PR, percentile rank; CI, confidence interval; K, kindergarten. -- denotes not administered, or score type not available or computed.

(*Cont.*)

FORM 5.5

WAIS–IV/WIAT–III ABILITY–ACHIEVEMENT DISCREPANCY ANALYSIS SIMPLE DIFFERENCE METHOD RESULTS AND INTERPRETATION TABLES (*Cont.*)

ABILITY–ACHIEVEMENT DISCREPANCY ANALYSIS

ABILITY SCORE TYPE: WAIS–IV FULL SCALE

ABILITY SCORE: 000

TABLE 8 ■ **WIAT–III COMPOSITE: SIMPLE DIFFERENCE METHOD**[a]

Composite	WIAT–III standard score	WAIS–IV Full Scale	Difference	Critical value .01*	Base rate[b]
Oral Language (OL)	000	000	±00	0.00	00.0%
Total Reading (TR)	000	000	±00	0.00	00.0%
Basic Reading (BR)	000	000	±00	N/A	N/A
Reading Comprehension and Fluency (RC)	000	000	±00	0.00	00.0%
Written Expression (WE)	000	000	±00	0.00	00.0%
Mathematics (MA)	000	000	±00	0.00	00.0%
Total Achievement	000	000	±00	0.00	00.0%

Note: *denotes that the WIAT–III – WAIS–IV Full Scale standard score difference occurs by chance less than 1 time in 100 and is therefore statistically significant. N/A, not applicable; the WIAT–III standard score was equal to or exceeded the WAIS–IV Full Scale.

[a]The differences are obtained by subtracting the employed WAIS–IV composite score from each WIAT–III standard score.

[b]Percentage of the normative sample who obtained the listed WIAT–III – WAIS–IV Full Scale standard score difference.

TABLE 9 ■ **WIAT–III SUBTEST: SIMPLE DIFFERENCE METHOD**[a]

Subtest (relevant composite initials)	WIAT–III standard score	WAIS–IV Full Scale	Difference	Critical value .01*	Base rate[b]
Listening Comprehension (OL)	000	000	±00	0.00	00.0%
Oral Expression (OL)	000	000	±00	0.00	00.0%
Word Reading (TR) (BR)	000	000	±00	0.00	00.0%
Pseudoword Decoding (TR) (BR)	000	000	±00	0.00	00.0%
Reading Comprehension (TR) (RC)	000	000	±00	0.00	00.0%
Oral Reading Fluency (TR) (RC)	000	000	±00	N/A	N/A
Spelling (WE)	000	000	±00	0.00	00.0%
Sentence Composition (WE)	000	000	±00	0.00	00.0%
Essay Composition (WE)	000	000	±00	0.00	00.0%
Math Problem Solving (MA)	000	000	±00	0.00	00.0%
Numerical Operations (MA)	000	000	±00	0.00	00.0%

Note: *denotes that the WIAT–III – WAIS–IV Full Scale standard score difference occurs by chance less than 1 time in 100 and is therefore statistically significant. N/A, not applicable; the WIAT–III standard score was equal to or exceeded the WAIS–IV Full Scale.

[a]The differences are obtained by subtracting the employed WAIS–IV composite score from each WIAT–III standard score.

[b]Percentage of the normative sample who obtained the listed WIAT–III – WAIS–IV Full Scale standard score difference.

FORM 5.6

WAIS–IV/WIAT–III ABILITY–ACHIEVEMENT DISCREPANCY ANALYSIS PREDICTED DIFFERENCE METHOD RESULTS AND INTERPRETATION TABLES

WAIS–IV

TABLE 1 ■ COMPOSITE SCORE SUMMARY

Index/Scale	Composite score	PR	90% CI	Qualitative description	Measured abilities
Verbal Comprehension Index (VCI)	000	00	[00, 00]	Very superior	Verbal reasoning, comprehension, and conceptualization
Perceptual Reasoning Index (PRI)	--	--	[00, 00]	Superior	Visual-spatial (nonverbal) reasoning, organization, and conceptualization
Full Scale[a]	**000**	**0.00**	**[000, 000]**	**Low average**	**General intelligence: the ability to learn from experience, acquire knowledge, and use resources effectively in adapting to new situations or solving problems[b]**

Note: Composite score mean = 100, standard deviation = 15. Lower scores indicate greater intellectual impairment. PR, percentile rank; CI, confidence interval. -- denotes not administered, or score type not available or computed. Full Scale data are in boldface.

[a]The Full Scale includes Verbal Comprehension, Perceptual Reasoning, Working Memory, and Processing Speed Composite scores; the latter two are not reported as they are peripheral to the primary analyses.

[b]Ciccarelli, S. K., & White, J. N. (2012). *Psychology* (3rd ed.). Upper Saddle River, NJ: Pearson Education; Wechsler, D. (1975). The collected papers of David Wechsler. New York, NY: Academic Press.

TABLE 2 ■ VCI–PRI INDEX LEVEL DISCREPANCY COMPARISON

VCI composite score	PRI composite score	Difference	Critical value .05*	Cohen's *d* effect size[a]	Effect size results[b]	Base rate[c]
000	000	±00	0.00	0.0	Large medium	00.0%

Note: *denotes that the VCI–PRI difference occurs by chance less than 5 times in 100 and is therefore statistically significant.

[a]Computed as the absolute value of VCI–PRI/standard deviation (15).

[b]Effect size score ranges: 0.0 to 0.2 (small effect); 0.3 to 0.7 (medium effect); 0.8 and higher (large effect).

[c]Percentage of the normative sample who obtained the listed VCI–PRI difference.

The VCI–PRI difference was not statistically significant, manifested a small effect size, and yielded an acceptably high base rate in the normative sample. Thus, the Full Scale was deemed an acceptable measure of general intelligence and was used in the ability–achievement discrepancy analysis.

The VCI–PRI difference was statistically significant and favored the former/latter. The difference also yielded both a large effect size and remarkably low base rate in the normative sample. Thus, the Full Scale was deemed an unacceptable measure of general intelligence and was dropped from further analysis. The ensuing ability–achievement discrepancy analysis was completed using the VCI for the following reasons: (a) to determine if any measured achievement deficits exist beyond the impact of language ability and (b) evidence that the VCI tends to yield higher correlations with general intelligence as compared to other WAIS–IV indices. The ensuing ability–achievement discrepancy analysis was completed using the lower VCI–PRI to minimize false positive results.

(Cont.)

FORM 5.6

WAIS–IV/WIAT–III ABILITY–ACHIEVEMENT DISCREPANCY ANALYSIS PREDICTED DIFFERENCE METHOD RESULTS AND INTERPRETATION TABLES (*Cont.*)

WIAT–III, K–12

TABLE 3 ■ **COMPOSITE ACHIEVEMENT SCORE SUMMARY**

Composite	Standard score	PR	90% CI	Qualitative description	Measured abilities
Oral Language (Grades K–12)	--	--	[000, 000]	Very superior	Listening comprehension (receptive vocabulary, oral discourse comprehension); oral expression (expressive vocabulary, oral word fluency, sentence repetition)
Total Reading (Grades 1–12)	--	--	[000, 000]	Superior	Word reading; pseudoword decoding (phonics); reading comprehension; oral reading fluency
Basic Reading (Grades 1–12)	--	--	[000, 000]	Above average	Word reading; pseudoword decoding (phonics)
Reading Comprehension and Fluency (Grades 2–12)	--	--	[000, 000]	Average	Reading comprehension; oral reading fluency
Written Expression (Grades K–12)	--	--	[000, 000]	Below average	Alphabet writing fluency (Grades K–3); spelling; sentence composition (sentence combining and building) (Grades 1–12); essay composition (content and organization, grammar and mechanics) (Grades 3–12)
Mathematics (Grades K–12)	--	--	[000, 000]	Low	Math problem solving; numerical operations
Total Achievement (Grades K–12)	**000**	**0.00**	**[000, 000]**	**Very low**	**General degree of knowledge and proficiency in basic academic subjects, including oral language, reading, written expression, and mathematics**

Note: Standard score mean = 100, standard deviation = 15. Lower scores indicate greater impairment in achievement. PR, percentile rank; CI, confidence interval; K, kindergarten. -- denotes not administered, or score type not available or computed. Total achievement data are in boldface.

TABLE 4 ■ **ORAL LANGUAGE ACHIEVEMENT SUBTEST SCORE SUMMARY**

Subtest	Standard score	PR	90% CI	Qualitative description	Measured abilities
Listening Comprehension (Grades K–12)	000	00.0	[000, 000]	Very superior Superior	Listening vocabulary; inferring and remembering details from oral sentences and discourse
Oral Expression (Grades K–12)	--	--	[000, 000]	Above average Low	Speaking vocabulary; word retrieval; word retrieval efficiency; flexibility of thought process; syntactic knowledge
Oral Reading Fluency (Grades 1–12)	--	--	[000, 000]	Very low	Speed, accuracy, fluency, and prosody (i.e., rhythm) of contextualized oral reading

Note: Standard score mean = 100, standard deviation = 15. Lower scores indicate greater impairment in achievement. PR, percentile rank; CI, confidence interval; K, kindergarten. -- denotes not administered, or score type not available or computed.

(Cont.)

FORM 5.6

WAIS–IV/WIAT–III ABILITY–ACHIEVEMENT DISCREPANCY ANALYSIS PREDICTED DIFFERENCE METHOD RESULTS AND INTERPRETATION TABLES (*Cont.*)

TABLE 5 ■ READING ACHIEVEMENT SUBTEST SCORE SUMMARY

Subtest	Standard score	PR	90% CI	Qualitative description	Measured abilities
Word Reading (Grades 1–12)	--	--	[000, 000]	Superior Above average	Speed and accuracy of decontextualized word recognition; reading aloud a list of words of increasing difficulty
Pseudoword Decoding (Grades 1–12)	--	--	[000, 000]	Average Below average	Ability to decode nonsense words, which include common syllables; reading aloud a list of nonsense words accurately; phonics
Reading Comprehension (Grades 1–12)	--	--	[000, 000]	Low	Understanding types of written passages after reading them (fictional stories; informational text; advertisements; how-to passages)
Oral Reading Fluency (Grades 1–12)	--	--	[000, 000]	Very low	Speed, accuracy, and prosody (i.e., rhythm) of contextualized oral reasoning; reading passages aloud and answering comprehension problems

Note: Standard score mean = 100, standard deviation = 15. Lower scores indicate greater impairment in achievement. PR, percentile rank; CI, confidence interval. -- denotes not administered, or score type not available or computed.

TABLE 6 ■ WRITTEN EXPRESSION ACHIEVEMENT SUBTEST SCORE SUMMARY

Subtest	Standard score	PR	90% CI	Qualitative description	Measured abilities
Spelling (Grades K–12)	--	--	[000, 000]	Above average	Written spelling of letter sounds and single words
Sentence Composition (Grades 1–12)	--	--	[000, 000]	Average Below average	Sentence formulation and written syntactic ability (sentence combining and building)
Essay Composition (Grades 3–12)	--	--	[000, 000]	Low Very low	Spontaneous compositional writing (10-minutes duration)

Note: Standard score mean = 100, standard deviation = 15. Lower scores indicate greater impairment in achievement. PR, percentile rank; CI, confidence interval; K, kindergarten. -- denotes not administered, or score type not available or computed.

TABLE 7 ■ MATHEMATICS ACHIEVEMENT SUBTEST SCORE SUMMARY

Subtest	Standard score	PR	90% CI	Qualitative description	Measured abilities
Math Problem Solving (Grades K–12)	000	00.0	[000, 000]	Very superior Average	Basic math concepts; everyday math applications; geometry; algebra (unlimited time)
Numerical Operations (Grades K–12)	--	--	[000, 000]	Low Very low	Written math computations in basic skills, basic operations with integers, geometry, algebra, and calculus

Note: Standard score mean = 100, standard deviation = 15. Lower scores indicate greater impairment in achievement. PR, percentile rank; CI, confidence interval; K, kindergarten. -- denotes not administered, or score type not available or computed.

(*Cont.*)

FORM 5.6

WAIS–IV/WIAT–III ABILITY–ACHIEVEMENT DISCREPANCY ANALYSIS PREDICTED DIFFERENCE METHOD RESULTS AND INTERPRETATION TABLES (*Cont.*)

ABILITY–ACHIEVEMENT DISCREPANCY ANALYSIS

ABILITY SCORE TYPE: WAIS–IV FULL SCALE

ABILITY SCORE: 000

TABLE 8 ■ WIAT–III COMPOSITE: PREDICTED DIFFERENCE METHOD[a]

Composite	Actual WIAT–III standard score	Predicted WIAT–III standard score	Difference	Critical value .01*	Base rate[b]
Oral Language (OL)	000	000	±00	0.00	00.0%
Total Reading (TR)	000	000	±00	0.00	00.0%
Basic Reading (BR)	000	000	±00	N/A	N/A
Reading Comprehension and Fluency (RC)	000	000	±00	0.00	00.0%
Written Expression (WE)	000	000	±00	0.00	00.0%
Mathematics (MA)	000	000	±00	0.00	00.0%
Total Achievement	000	000	±00	0.00	00.0%

Note: *denotes that the actual WIAT–III standard score – predicted WIAT–III standard score difference occurs by chance less than 1 time in 100 and is therefore statistically significant. N/A, not applicable; the actual WIAT–III standard score was equal to or exceeded the predicted WIAT–III standard score.

[a]The differences are obtained by subtracting each WIAT–III standard score predicted by the employed WAIS–IV composite score from the actual WIAT–III standard score.

[b]Percentage of the normative sample who obtained the listed actual WIAT–III standard score – predicted WIAT–III standard score difference.

TABLE 9 ■ WIAT–III SUBTEST: PREDICTED DIFFERENCE METHOD[a]

Subtest (relevant composite initials)	Actual WIAT–III standard score	Predicted WIAT–III standard score	Difference	Critical value .01*	Base rate[b]
Listening Comprehension (OL)	000	000	±00	0.00	00.0%
Oral Expression (OL)	000	000	±00	0.00	00.0%
Word Reading (TR) (BR)	000	000	±00	0.00	00.0%
Pseudoword Decoding (TR) (BR)	000	000	±00	0.00	00.0%
Reading Comprehension (TR) (RC)	000	000	±00	0.00	00.0%
Oral Reading Fluency (TR) (RC)	000	000	±00	N/A	N/A
Spelling (WE)	000	000	±00	0.00	00.0%
Sentence Composition (WE)	000	000	±00	0.00	00.0%
Essay Composition (WE)	000	000	±00	0.00	00.0%
Math Problem Solving (MA)	000	000	±00	0.00	00.0%
Numerical Operations (MA)	000	000	±00	0.00	00.0%

Note: *denotes that the actual WIAT–III standard score – predicted WIAT–III standard score difference occurs by chance less than 1 time in 100 and is therefore statistically significant. N/A, not applicable; the actual WIAT–III standard score was equal to or exceeded the predicted WIAT–III standard score.

[a]The differences are obtained by subtracting each WIAT–III standard score predicted by the employed WAIS–IV composite score from the actual WIAT–III standard score.

[b]Percentage of the normative sample who obtained the listed actual WIAT–III standard score – predicted WIAT–III standard score difference.

Neuropsychological Tests

THE CONSTRUCT OF NEUROPSYCHOLOGICAL FUNCTIONING AND TESTING

Neuropsychology constitutes the study of brain–behavior relationships (Gregory, 2011). As such, the construct of *neuropsychological functioning* (also known as neurocognitive functioning) may be defined as performance on mental and behavioral tasks, which are direct indicators of neurological or organic brain functioning (Barlow & Durand, 2012; Gregory, 2011).

Neuropsychological tests and test batteries vary considerably regarding the specific tasks and abilities measured. However, Bennet's (1988) model of brain–behavior relationships effectively organizes the categories of abilities measured by the majority of available neuropsychological test batteries, including the ones appearing in my recommended test battery (see Form 2.7 section on Neuropsychological Tests) and presented in detail later in this chapter. In successive order of brain processing, they include (a) sensory input, (b) attention and concentration, (c) memory and learning, (d) language and sequential processing (i.e., left hemisphere functions) occurring contemporaneously with spatial processing and manipulatory ability (i.e., right hemisphere functions), (e) executive functioning (i.e., logical analysis, concept formation, reasoning, planning, flexibility of thinking), and (f) motor output (Bennet, 1988).

DIAGNOSTIC REASONS FOR INCLUSION WITHIN A TEST BATTERY

Neuropsychological testing is principally ordered to rule out, establish a baseline, or measure the progression of one or more Cognitive Disorders as delineated by the *Diagnostic and Statistical Manual of Mental Disorders, Fourth Edition, Text Revision* (*DSM-IV-TR*) (American Psychiatric Association, 2000) including most especially Dementia. Irrespective of etiology, Dementia includes the essential symptom of memory impairment (i.e., inability to learn new or recall previous information), along with a minimum of one or more of the following: (a) language dysfunction (i.e., aphasia), (b) motor disability in the presence of intact motor function (i.e., apraxia), (c) failure to interpret objects accurately despite normal sensory function (i.e., agnosia), and (d) impaired executive functioning (American Psychiatric Association, 2000). Neuropsychological testing is also effective for diagnosing the presence of Amnestic Disorder, which includes similarly defined memory impairment as its primary symptom irrespective of etiology (American psychiatric Association, 2000).[1]

By listing the above diagnoses under the label *Cognitive Disorders*, the *DSM-IV-TR* acknowledges the proliferation of evidence indicating the presence of neuropsychological dysfunction in many previously conceptualized *nonorganic mental disorders* (American Psychiatric Association, 1987). Because it is currently viable to measure such dysfunction directly, it is incumbent upon psychologists to increasingly reflect this in their test batteries in order to effectuate reliable and valid diagnoses.

In particular, I believe two previously conceptualized nonorganic *DSM-IV-TR* disorders now necessitate neuropsychological testing as part of an effective battery. They include

[1] *Delirium is the third major DSM-IV-TR Cognitive Disorder, which involves an acute onset of remarkably impairing symptoms, including disturbance in consciousness (e.g., inability to focus), and a rapid and patent decline in cognition (e.g., disorientation) (American Psychiatric Association, 2000). As such, it is most effectively and efficiently diagnosed by administration of an empirically based standardized mental status examination: e.g., the Mini-Mental State Examination, 2nd Edition (Folstein, Folstein, White, & Messer, 2010). Extended Version; Wechsler Memory Scale, Fourth Edition, Brief Cognitive Status Exam (Wechsler, 2009a).*

(a) Attention-Deficit/Hyperactivity Disorder (ADHD) and (b) Pervasive Developmental Disorder (PDD), the latter including Autistic Disorder, Asperger's Disorder, and PDD Not Otherwise Specified (NOS) or Atypical Autistic Disorder. First, with respect to ADHD, research using neuroimaging techniques convincingly shows evidence of neuropsychological dysfunction in brain regions responsible for regulating executive functions, attention, and inhibitory control, particularly within the prefrontal cortex (Peterson et al., 2009; Shaw et al., 2009).

Second, Autistic Spectrum Disorders have been linked to the malfunctioning of *mirror neuron systems*, thus accounting for deficits in *theory of mind*, social perception, empathy, and language (Oberman & Ramachandran, 2007). Succinctly, mirror neurons permit our comprehension of others' thoughts and feelings by reacting to them as if they were our own (Mcintosh, Reichmann-Decker, Winkielman, & Wilbarger, 2006). Theory of mind is the ability to understand that people possess internal mental states, including feelings, desires, beliefs, and intentions, which direct and explain their behavior (Sigelman & Rider, 2012). Therefore, measured deficits in theory of mind, in particular, and in social perception, in general, are diagnostic of both neuron dysfunction and the presence of PDD.

Neuropsychological subtests that measure social perception and theory of mind in children and adolescents are now available (see the NEPSY–II) and increase the veracity of PDD diagnoses, along with indicating valuable targets for treatment intervention.

Neuropsychological tests also are useful in answering a referring clinician's more general question of whether or not there exists neurocognitive dysfunction in a particular case, which may be considered a distinct comorbid disorder, thus complicating treatment intervention. In these cases, I order an age-appropriate neuropsychological test battery to rule out a *DSM-IV-TR* Neurocognitive Disorder (i.e., Cognitive Disorder NOS), and more particularly attempt to (a) quantify its severity (i.e., mild, moderate, severe) and (b) qualitatively identify any particular deficits for purposes of treatment planning.

Additionally, neuropsychological testing is indicated when there exists a need to rule out a psychiatric disorder due to head trauma or brain damage. Applicable *DSM-IV-TR* disorders include, but are not limited to, the following: (a) Personality Change Due to Head Trauma; (b) Mood Disorder Due to Head Trauma; (c) Psychotic Disorder Due to Head Trauma, With Delusions; and (d) Psychotic Disorder Due to Head Trauma, With Hallucinations. For these cases, a symptom-relevant personality or adaptive behavior test should accompany the neuropsychological test battery. The latter measures whether or not the head trauma has resulted in significant brain damage, while the former assists in measuring the presence of the psychological symptom or behavioral impairment component.

Occasionally, referring clinicians will directly request a standardized measurement of a particular neuropsychological ability (see Bennet's 1988 model above). The most likely requested ability includes memory, and its facilitator, learning. Lastly, selected neuropsychological language subtests are useful in screening for possible Reading Disorder, and one of the following Communication Disorders: (a) Phonological Disorder, (b) Expressive Language Disorder, and (c) Mixed Receptive–Expressive Language Disorder.

The most likely referral sources for neuropsychological testing purposes include (a) physicians (i.e., psychiatrists, neurologists, pediatricians, family practitioners), (b) nonmedical mental health professionals, and (c) attorneys (e.g., tort law, probate law, disability). Referrals from family members are possible when there exists a history of Dementia in immediate or extended family relatives and they are sophisticated regarding the usefulness of neuropsychological testing.

INSURANCE COVERAGE ISSUES

Referrals from medical practitioners (MD, DO) for neuropsychological testing are almost invariably approved as meeting the criterion of medical necessity, especially if there is a stated need to rule out, establish a baseline, or measure the progression of one of the above mentioned *DSM-IV-TR* Cognitive Disorders. This also includes psychological testing referrals to rule out ADHD and PDD in which neuropsychological subtests, such as attention, executive functioning, memory, learning, and social perception, are requested by the psychologist as part of the battery. The key is to diligently document the referral source information, including medical credentials, specialty of practice, *DSM-IV-TR* diagnoses to be ruled out, and related referral questions, consistent with the format of the initial report (see Forms 2.2 and 2.3).

In contrast, referrals for neuropsychological testing from nonmedical mental health professionals, attorneys, and family members are more tenuous as not possessing sufficient medical necessity. Insurance companies are significantly more amenable to authorization subsequent to medical consultation and the documented concurrence that neuropsychological testing is indeed indicated. It is also effective, responsible, and ethical practice. This is the essential reason why the parenthetical statement, "needs physician consultation and approval," follows the neuropsychological testing selection on the "Psychological Test Referral Form" (see Form 2.1).

Such consultation may be conducted between the referring clinician and supervising medical practitioner if within a group practice, or in the alternative, between the patient and medical practitioner by direct examination and subsequent referral for neuropsychological testing. Although the latter is more circuitous, it is more likely to result in authorization.

THE NEUROPSYCHOLOGICAL TESTS

I have classified the following as neuropsychological tests and selected them for my practice: (a) NEPSY–II (Korkman, Kirk, & Kemp, 2007a, 2007b), (b) Neuropsychological Assessment Battery (NAB; Stern & White, 2003a, 2003b), (c) Wechsler Memory Scale, Fourth Edition (Wechsler, 2009a, 2009b), (d) Conners' Kiddie Continuous Performance Test (K–CPT), Version 5 (Conners, 2001), and (e) Conners' Continuous Performance Test, Second Edition, Version 5 (CPT–II) (Conners, 2004). I will discuss each test independently in this sequence using an organization similar to those of Chapters 4 and 5, including the particular test and its essential characteristics, followed by the associated results and interpretation tables and the manner in which they are to be employed.

NEPSY–II

NEPSY is an abbreviation for *neuropsychological* rather than a true acronym. It is a comprehensive neuropsychological test battery normed on children and adolescents from 3 years 0 months to 16 years 11 months. It is a flexible battery which principally yields subtest scores for various specific neuropsychological abilities, as opposed to composite or index scores. The complete battery of subtests are classified conceptually by the general neuropsychological ability or domain they have in common, including the following: (a) attention and executive functioning, (b) language, (c) memory and learning, (d) sensorimotor, (e) social perception, and (e) visuospatial processing. It is a theoretically based internal structure which is supported empirically by predicted patterns of intercorrelations among the various subtests (Korkman et al., 2007b).

The selection of subtests to be administered is determined predominantly by the following two factors: (a) the differential diagnostic issues and related referral questions and (b) the chronological age of the examinee. The latter is due to the fact that the array of NEPSY–II subtests applies to varying age ranges. Note that this is analogous to the subtests of the Wechsler Individual Achievement Test, Third Edition (WIAT–III) (Pearson [PsychCorp], 2009) (see Chapter 5). I have organized the NEPSY–II results and interpretation tables according to these two factors (see below Forms 6.1 through 6.4).

Although the test battery yields an assortment of quantitative data, in practice I find the standard scores, referred to as *primary scores*, to be the most useful for determining various *DSM-IV-TR* diagnoses and for addressing associated referral questions. The two primary scores I report and interpret include (a) scale scores ($M = 10$, $SD = 3$) and (b) percentile ranks. Percentile ranks are the only type of score available for a number of NEPSY–II subtests, which manifest remarkably skewed distributions or restricted ranges. As a general rule, such aberrant distributions are more probable when more fundamental or rudimentary neurocognitive abilities are measured (see e.g., Stern & White, 2003a, 2003b).

The NEPSY–II Scoring Assistant and Assessment Planner (2007) provides rapid and efficient computer scoring. Furthermore, a NEPSY–II training CD is available for new users (2007). The former is essential for utilizing this complex yet flexible test battery in an efficient manner.

Results and Interpretation Tables

I have designed and created four NESPY–II results and interpretation tables based upon two variables: (a) form of the test (viz., Ages 3 to 4 and Ages 5 to 16) and (b) type of test battery (viz., Full and General). The tables regarding test form are similar in organization and thus I discuss them together, again noting differences when indicated. Alternatively, the Full Battery and General Battery are selected for significantly different diagnostic reasons and purposes. Thus, I discuss them separately beginning with the former as it is the more inclusive.

NEPSY–II Full Battery. The NEPSY–II Full Battery Results and Interpretation Tables are dichotomized into Form Ages 3 to 4 (Form 6.1) and Form Ages 5 to 16 (Form 6.2). This coincides with the two record forms and accompanying response booklets published with this test. The Full Battery tables are to be used when a complete neuropsychological workup is necessitated (e.g., when the history is positive for brain trauma and testing is ordered to determine the full nature and extent of neuropsychological deficits). The Full Battery results and interpretation tables are also useful as providing an overview of all the available subtests in order to determine a more circumscribed and targeted type of neuropsychological testing. The latter is driven by the diagnostic and referral questions presented, and thereafter accomplished through a careful process of subtest selection.

There are six tables in all. Each table represents one of the general neuropsychological abilities or domains enumerated prior with their associated subtests. Both forms begin with a column identifying the subtest score name. Regarding Form Ages 5 to 16 only, the second column lists the age range for each subtest. This assists the psychologist in selecting a proper test battery for a particular case and estimating administration time. The accompanying administrative manual provides the average estimated administration time for each subtest to facilitate this process (Korkman et al., 2007a). Age range information is unnecessary for Form Ages 3 to 4 because all subtests apply to this more narrowly defined age grouping.

The ensuing two columns provide two of the available primary scores, including the scaled score and percentile rank, respectively. The next column reports the classification indicated by these two primary scores. Table 6.2 in the NEPSY–II clinical and interpretative manual provides a succinct and pragmatic guide showing the scaled score and percentile rank ranges adjacent to their corresponding classifications (Korkman et al., 2007b, p. 136). Reference to this single table will permit the rapid determination of the proper interpretative classifications to be inserted into the NEPSY–II results and interpretation tables.[2]

The final column in the NEPSY–II tables provides succinct descriptions of the neuropsychological abilities measured by each of the corresponding subtests. The exact wording was based upon my diligent and detailed review of the rather elaborate subtest descriptions and abilities available within the NEPSY–II clinical and interpretive manual (Korkman et al., 2007b). This vital feature speeds interpretation and facilitates communication and feedback.

Tabular notes provide the following information: (a) scaled score mean and standard deviation, (b) meaning of lower scores, (c) age-range units representing years (Form Ages 5 to 16 only), (d) notation of PR as percentile rank, and (e) "--" as denoting that the subtest was either not administered, or that the score type was not available or computed. Again, the latter may occur due to the examinee not falling within the proper age range, or the primary score is not available due to skewness or restricted range present within the score distribution. In order to truncate the report, I advise simply deleting subtests that were not administered due to reasons of either age or subtest selection. However, the "--" notation provides the testing psychologist with discretion in reporting and is required for unavailable scores. Finally, there are some specific table notes that clarify what exactly is being measured; for example, noting that Narrative Memory Total includes both free recall (i.e., no hints given) and cued recall (i.e., hints given).

Because many professionals and laypeople are unfamiliar with the more esoteric neuropsychological constructs measured by the NEPSY–II, I have inserted definitions of each immediately ensuing the tabular notes. These definitions are paraphrased in more readable fashion from those provided in the NESPY–II manuals (Korkman et al.,2007a, 2007b). This minimizes report-writing time while facilitating communication and feedback.

The results of each table should be summarized in narrative form. The most effective approach is to outline the overall pattern of results for each table, such as "The majority of language subtests were measured within normal limits, and thus there is no evidence of language dysfunction or aphasia." This strategy focuses the reader on the results profile and avoids redundancy. It is also consistent with the American Psychological Association publication style principle of not restating specific results that are provided in the table (American Psychological Association, 2010).

NEPSY–II General Battery. The NEPSY–II General Battery provides an abbreviated measure of overall neuropsychological functioning. The remarkably fewer number of preselected subtests provides an abridged and efficient measure of all domains except social perception. These subtests were selected because they are the most sensitive to the presence of brain dysfunction for their corresponding domains (Korkman et al., 2007a). Thus, the General Battery is optimally used when approved testing hours are limited, and/or a brief measure of neuropsychological functioning is being requested.

The NEPSY–II General Battery results and interpretation tables are similarly dichotomized into Form Ages 3 to 4 (Form 6.3) and Form Ages 5 to 16 (Form 6.4). Note the identical information presented, although with a significantly reduced number of subtests. As indicated by the test authors, this condensed battery may be strategically expanded in areas indicated by a particular case, as further testament to the flexibility of the NEPSY–II. Similarly, the test provides an array of supplemental scores and data analyses that the psychologist may want to add within the narrative summaries of the tabular results in order to highlight diagnostically useful or intervention-related issues; for example, contrast scores compare discrepancies in performance within and between subtests.

[2] *The NEPSY–II Scoring Assistant and Assessment Planner automatically inserts the proper classifications.*

Neuropsychological Assessment Battery

The NAB is a comprehensive yet efficient and flexible neuropsychological test battery, with all of the subtests conormed on individuals aged 18 years through 97 years. It affords the testing psychologist with both a fixed and flexible battery approach.

More specifically, the full battery comprises five main modules, each of which measures a general neuropsychological ability or domain consistent with both Bennet's 1988 model, and the criteria established for the *DSM-IV-TR* Cognitive Disorders of Dementia and Amnestic Disorder (American Psychiatric Association, 2000). They may be administered in whole or in part contingent upon the diagnostic and referral questions. In order of administration, the main modules include Attention, Language, Memory, Spatial, and Executive functions. Note the similarity in content to the NEPSY–II. In addition, the NAB yields both subtest *T*-scores (*M* = 50, *SD* = 10), referred to as *primary scores*, along with module index scores (*M* = 100, *SD* = 15), thus analogous to the familiar Wechsler standard score transformations. Although there exists an array of available scores (e.g., secondary and descriptive scores), the subtest *T*-scores and module index scores are of most relevance to differential diagnosis, and therefore form the basis of the reporting and interpretation strategy.

Other unique and advantageous features of the NAB include the following: (a) availability of equivalent Forms A and B, (b) choice between demographically corrected norms (White & Stern, 2003a) and U.S. census-matched norms (White & Stern, 2003b), (c) optional neuropsychological test screening, and (d) inclusion of pragmatic daily living subtests within each module. Some brief comments on each of these features are in order.

Equivalent Forms A and B permit a more accurate measure of symptom progression because they reduce practice effects. Demographically corrected norms compare the examinee's performance to neurologically healthy individuals of the same age, sex, and education, and are recommended for clinical diagnostic purposes (Stern & White, 2003b). In the alternative, if for some utilitarian reason the testing psychologist prefers comparing the examinee's performance to the U.S. population, the U.S. census-matched norms may be employed (Stern & White, 2003b). This sample more closely represents key U.S. demographic characteristics, including geographic region by age group, education, sex, and ethnicity.

The Neuropsychological Assessment Screening Battery (NASB) is an abbreviated measure of an examinee's functioning in each of the domains or modules. This provides empirical data to determine whether or not follow-up testing with the respective complete modules are necessitated. The measurement of practical daily living skills enhances (a) ecological validity (Stern & White, 2003b), (b) generalizability of the results, and (c) meaningful feedback to referring clinicians, patients, and family members regarding the nature and extent of dysfunction.

The Neuropsychological Assessment Battery Software Portfolio (NAB–SP) (2008) provides rapid and efficient computer scoring. In addition, this neuropsychological test is accompanied by the most detailed, comprehensive, and laudable video training program I have yet encountered. More specifically, the NAB administrative training program comprises six disks, the first introducing the test and reviewing the NAB Screening Module (2004a), and the remaining disks each devoted to an entire module, including NAB Attention (2004b), NAB Language (2004c), NAB Memory (2004d), NAB Spatial (2004e), and NAB Executive Functions (2004f).

Results and Interpretation Tables

I have prepared three NAB results and interpretation tables. They are designed to accomplish the three most frequent clinical applications for which I have used this test instrument, including the Full Battery, Screening Battery, and Attention Module. The last is designed for the particular purpose of ruling out ADHD in adults. I present and discuss them separately in this order, again proceeding from the more to less inclusive as done with the NEPSY–II above. Furthermore, I most frequently administer the Full Battery because administration time is typically only about 3½ hours (Stern & White, 2003b).

NAB Full Battery. The NAB Full Battery results and interpretation tables are presented in Form 6.5. The boldfaced and underlined title is default set at Form 1 because I administer Form 2 only when otherwise indicated by retesting or for more narrowly defined diagnostic purposes (e.g., testing to rule out ADHD). Note that the title does not specifically indicate that this is the Full Battery as evident in Table 1.

Table 1 of Form 6.5 presents the most essential, diagnostically pertinent results, analogous to the Wechsler intelligence test Table 1 composite score results. In columnar order of presentation, tabular information includes (a) module name, (b) index standard score, (c) percentile rank, (d) 90% confidence interval, (e) interpretive category, and (f) measured abilities associated with each index score. As with the Wechsler tests, the Total NAB data are in boldface so as to highlight overall neuropsychological functioning. The index scores are listed in their respective administrative order.

Box 6.1 presents one succinct interpretative guide for both the NAB index scores and subtest *T*-scores. This table is a significant adaptation based upon an integration of the most essential data provided in the tables of the interpretive manual (Stern & White, 2003b, Tables 6.8 and 6.9, pp. 124 and 128, respectively). It is specifically designed to enhance the ease and precision of entering labels into the interpretive category column.[3] Regarding the index scores, note the 10 interpretive categories, including five unimpaired and five impaired, which are remarkably useful in making finer level-of-functioning discriminations. That is, if impairment is demonstrated in a particular case, diagnostically supplemental comments concerning level of severity are made possible (e.g., Vascular Dementia, Mild Severity). Irrespective of the *DSM-IV-TR* not including severity specifiers for the Cognitive Disorders (American Psychiatric Association, 2000), clinicians find such qualifiers extremely useful both in planning intervention and tracking progression.

As for previous tests, the measured abilities appearing in the final column are based upon the following: (a) analysis of the NAB factor structure, (b) description of the subtests loading on each factor, (c) general description of each module, and (d) validity evidence provided in the psychometric and technical manual (Stern & White, 2003a, pp. 141–255). Such extensive scrutiny was necessitated due to the complex nature of the neurocognitive abilities and constructs measured by this test.

Table 1 general notes provide the following information: (a) index score mean and standard deviation, (b) type and definition of norms used in the analysis, with the default being the more frequently employed demographically corrected norms, (c) directional meaning of lower scores, (d) abbreviated meaning of PR as percentile rank and CI as confidence interval, and (e) "--" as denoting that the score is for various reasons not available. Additional specific notes provide key definitions of crucial constructs not defined within the table (e.g., working memory), along with commentary on test format or task type (e.g., forced-choice item format) when such further information elucidates the particular abilities being measured. The construct definitions were devised in the same manner as the measured abilities. I will review Table 2 prior to making suggestions concerning the manner in which the two tables can be most effectively summarized in the narrative report.

Table 2 presents the results of the pragmatic NAB Daily Living Skills subtests, which are most relevant to a patient's ability to function in some vital everyday tasks. The design of Table 2 matches that of Table 1 with the single exception of not listing confidence intervals. Scrutiny of the subtests and their measured skills as defined by this test (Stern & White, 2003b) evinces their pragmatism and significance in planning effective intervention. Each subtest represents a practical measure within each of the neuropsychological

[3] *The Neuropsychological Assessment Battery Software Portfolio (NAB–SP) computer scoring software automatically provides the proper interpretive categories for both the index scores and primary T-scores. Therefore, if you purchase this software, use of Box 6.1 is not necessary.*

domains measured in Table 1. Respectively, the subtests and their domains are as follows: (a) Driving Scenes–Attention, (b) Bill Payment–Language, (c) Memory, Immediate and Delayed–Memory, (d) Map Reading–Spatial, and (e) Judgment–Executive Functions. Again, reference to Box 6.1 assists in inserting the proper interpretive categories for the measured subtest *T*-scores. Lastly, Table 2 notes are comparable to those of Table 1.

The NAB is a remarkably sophisticated instrument, including voluminous quantitative statistical analyses regarding module index and subtest scores, secondary and descriptive scores, between-score comparisons, and finally, qualitative features analyses (e.g., recording perseverations, neglect, omissions). Yet, I am here advising that the core analysis be circumscribed to the above two quantitative tables. Although the tenor of this psychological testing book espouses relevance and efficiency, I believe some additional detailed commentary as to how this tenet applies to this intricate test is warranted.

Referring clinicians, patients, and patients' families, especially regarding neuropsychological questions, are interested in the essential results. For example, "Do the results support a diagnosis of Dementia? If so, what are the *primary deficits* and what is the *degree of severity*? Does the patient need assisted living, or can he or she at this point live independently?" Including a myriad of subtest and supplementary scores and analyses will certainly inundate the reader, in addition to creating an unwieldy report. The principal purpose of the report (i.e., communication) can easily become lost within a labyrinth of data. Using prudence, any relevant supplementary results may be effectively inserted into the narrative summaries of Tables 1 and 2, which I discuss next.

I advise that separate interpretive summaries ensue each NAB table because they serve significantly varying, although complementary, purposes. The narrative summary of Table 1 should deductively proceed from general to specific and minimally address the following in respective order: (a) overall neuropsychological functioning, including evidence and degree of unimpaired or impaired functioning; (b) module domain index results addressing presence and degree of impairment (if any); and (c) whether or not the aforementioned results are indicative of a formal *DSM-IV-TR* Cognitive Disorder by matching results to criteria. The following represents an example:

> Results indicate the presence of moderately impaired overall neuropsychological functioning. Memory, and the related neurocognitive ability of attention, both show mild-to-moderate impairment, while language shows moderate impairment and thus aphasia. The remaining indices are measured to be within normal limits. Hence, the minimum criteria for Dementia are met, with overall impairment estimated to be within the mild-to-moderate range.

Note that the sample narrative succinctly interprets the diagnostic meaning of Table 1 results without unnecessary redundancy. It also demonstrates the simultaneous nature of the psychological test interpretation and report-writing process espoused by this book.

Because the Table 2 Daily Living Skills subtests represent a pragmatic representative sample of the Table 1 domains, it is an effective complement. Frequently, Table 2 results mirror those of Table 1, and such association may be briefly summarized within the related narrative interpretation. Such narrative should address the following: (a) daily living skills showing impairment (if any) and to what degree, (b) any association with Table 1 domains that are similarly impaired, (c) nonimpaired skills, and (d) implications for intervention, including living arrangements. The following represents an example:

> Results indicate that immediate and delayed memory for medication instructions, and for people's identifying information, are moderately-to-severely impaired. The ability to read maps and pay bills also show moderate degrees of impairment. These results are consistent with Table 1 results, and indicate that Mr. Jones will need assistance in these pragmatic skills.

Note the pithy and complementary nature of this narrative interpretation of Table 2. Lastly, the measured domain and daily living skills deficits may be enumerated within the posttest *DSM-IV-TR* diagnoses portion of the final report. For example:

Axis I: 294.8 Dementia Due to Unknown Etiology, Mild-to-Moderate Severity.

Noted Impairments: Memory, Attention, Language (aphasia).

The daily living skills impairments may be addressed under treatment recommendations.

NAB Screening Battery. The NASB results and interpretation tables are presented in Form 6.6. There are three tables (Table 1 to Table 3). Together, they represent the maximum data needed to report an examinee's overall and domain neuropsychological functioning. Daily Living Skills subtests are not reported simply because a negative screening domain score obviates their subsequent administration. The versatility of this test instrument shall become apparent as these tables and their uses are reviewed.

As stated prior, because medical necessity is normally not an issue regarding neuropsychological testing, and because the NAB full battery administration is routinely under 4 hours, use of the NASB is less frequent. However, the NASB is advantageous when (a) insurance authorization is unexpectedly limited (e.g., 2 hours), (b) the patient is uninsured and therefore self-pay, (c) the patient's degree of impairment hinders tolerance for full test battery administration, and (d) the referring clinician is directly requesting a neuropsychological screen.

Table 1 presents the NASB screening domain score results. As such, this table shall be invariably required for inclusion within the final report. It is essentially the companion to Table 1 of the NAB Full Battery (Form 6.5, Table 1), and therefore is similarly organized. In the interests of brevity, I will highlight three principal differences.

First, the second column is titled "Standard score." This is because, although it is transformed as is the complete domain module score ($M = 100$, $SD = 15$), it is not truly an index score. Second, this column contains a potential asterisk general table symbol (*). This is to be attached immediately adjacent to a reported standard score if it falls within the range indicating that follow-up administration of the respective complete NAB module is necessitated for reliable and valid interpretation of functioning within that domain. A general tabular note is added that defines the asterisk's diagnostic and administrative implications.

The selected ranges maximize a true positive hit rate or sensitivity and minimize false negatives. More specifically, by employing the recommended ranges, 95% of examinees expected to require administration of the full module shall be so recommended (Stern & White, 2003b). Although this increases the likelihood of administering the full battery, it effectively minimizes missing a true Cognitive Disorder. This criterion is in accord with the cutoff score I employ for all MMSE–2 versions regarding a screen positive result for neuropsychological disorder (see Chapter 2).

The NASB predicts performance on the complete domain modules at both ends of the functioning dimension. In particular, a sufficiently high screening standard score efficaciously indicates nonimpaired functioning to such a degree that administration of the full module will provide little additional diagnostic information. Analogously, a sufficiently low score predicts impaired functioning to such a degree that administration of the full module is obviated. Finally, a middle range, or what may be conceptualized as a *borderline* or *transitional* score, requires additional testing with the complete module for more precise quantification of ability level.

I have prepared a pithy NASB decision guide pursuant to test guidelines in Box 6.2. In particular, this table is the product of a succinct integration of five more detailed independent tables available within the interpretation manual (Stern & White, 2003b, Tables

[4] *The Neuropsychological Assessment Battery Software Portfolio (NAB–SP) computer scoring software automatically flags borderline screening scores by the designation "Administer," and those sufficiently high and low as "Do not administer." Therefore, if you purchase this software, use of Box 6.2 is not necessary.*

[5] *The Neuropsychological Assessment Battery Software Portfolio (NAB–SP) computer scoring software automatically provides the proper interpretive categories for the screening domain standard scores.*

6.3–6.7, pp. 120–124).[4] It is significantly adapted in order to speed the interpretation process. Note that the impaired, borderline, and nonimpaired ranges vary somewhat among the screening domains. Thus, the Table 1 interpretive category will be contingent upon whether or not a definitively high or low score, or borderline score, is obtained for that particular screening module.

Table 6.1 in the NAB interpretation manual provides screening domain score ranges with their corresponding interpretative categories (Stern & White, 2003b, Table 6.1, p. 120).[5] Note that these are the same score ranges and interpretive categories as reported for the module index scores (see Box 6.1). I recommend inserting the associated interpretive category for sufficiently high and low standard scores that do not require further testing. In contrast, I advise that you insert "Not yet determined" for borderline or transitional scores as indicated in Box 6.2. This means that for sufficiently high and low scores, Box 6.2 must be either cross-referenced with Table 6.1 in the NAB interpretive manual, or with the adapted Box 6.1 in this book due to the standards being identical for the screening index and full index scores. The "Not yet determined" entry does not apply to the Total Screening Index.

The third and final modification in NASB Table 1 is the repetitive qualification "Marker of …" in describing the measured abilities. This is due to the screening nature of these domain scores. Once again, the wording of the screening-measured abilities was predicated upon descriptions and validity evidence provided by the particular psychometrics and technical manual (Stern & White, 2003a). The NASB Table 1 notes are the same as in the NAB Table 1, again with the exception of the added general note defining the meaning of asterisked standard scores. A similarly organized narrative interpretation of NASB Table 1 should immediately ensue, although with special remarks regarding indeterminate results.

Table 2 summarizes decisions for further full-module testing based upon Table 1 results. It is incumbent upon the testing psychologist to inform referring clinicians, patients, pertinent family members, and, in anticipation of requesting supplemental testing hours, third-party payors of the necessity of additional testing for purposes of accurate differential diagnosis and treatment planning. Because this is the essence of Table 2, it should always accompany Table 1 in the final report. This principle also applies to referrals explicitly asking for a limited neuropsychological screening. Table 2 educates referring clinicians as to the tentative nature of borderline screening results, and espouses the ethical practice of eschewing excessively ambitious and unwarranted interpretations.

In columnar order of presentation, Table 2 provides the following: (a) screening domain name, (b) dichotomous affirmative or negative recommendation on whether or not to administer the respective complete NAB module, and (c) the rationale for the recommendation enumerated in column two. Regarding the latter, I have entered two standardized statements. The first reads "Significant No evidence of impairment; further testing unlikely to provide additional diagnostic information." If the recommendation is "Negative," delete either the word "Significant" or the word "No," whichever alternative applies, then delete the entire second statement indicating that further testing is needed. On the other hand, if the recommendation is "Affirmative," the latter statement applies verbatim, "Further testing needed for differential diagnosis," and the entire former statement is now dropped as being inapplicable. In this manner, Table 2 can be completed rapidly and efficiently by the testing psychologist. A simple narrative summary of Table 2 highlighting recommendations for further testing should suffice.

Table 3 is fundamentally a replication of the NAB Full Battery Table 1 (see Form 6.5). If the case has been limited to neuropsychological screening, Table 3 may be deleted as being inapplicable. However, if follow-up complete module testing was done, in full or in part, Table 3 is pertinent. The single difference in this Table 1, in contrast to

Table 1 in Form 6.5, is the need to name which complete modules were subsequently administered in the title of the table, which should supplant the pending numerical symbols ##. The module names inserted within the title portion quickly identifies for the reader which specific complete modules were administered if less than the full battery. In this case, the Total NAB and all nonadministered modules should be deleted for purposes of brevity. Alternatively, Table 3 simply remains intact if the Full Battery was administered according to the screening results, and the supplemental portion of the title deleted. A narrative summary of Table 3 parallels that for Table 1 of the NAB Full Battery (see Form 6.5).

NAB Attention Module only. The last NAB Attention Module results and interpretation tables (Form 6.7) is for the narrowly defined purpose of attempting to rule out ADHD in adulthood. In practice, I have found consistent evidence that the complete NAB Attention Module and its subtests are remarkably useful in making or ruling out such diagnosis. Therefore, Form 6.7 includes two tables, the first devoted to the Attention Module Index and the second to its subtests.

Table 1 presents the Attention Module Index results utilizing the same organization as in Table 1 for the full module (Form 6.5), with a single specific table note defining the pertinent construct of working memory. Again, Box 6.1 assists in inserting the proper interpretive category. A simple narrative summary statement regarding whether or not the measured functioning is consistent with ADHD is all that is needed. The title default is set at Form 2 because I use it in these cases for the utilitarian purpose of inventory convenience. That is, if the Form 1 Attention Module Record Form and Response Booklet are used for ADHD evaluations, you will have an increasingly discrepant lower supply of these materials compared to the other four module Form 1 booklets when administering the full battery.

Table 2 is devoted to the Attention Module subtests and is comparably designed to the Table 2 NAB Daily Living subtests in Form 6.5. As an administrative note, the first Attention Module "Orientation" subtest is not necessary for computing the Table 1 index score. It is also of little assistance in making an ADHD diagnosis considering that orientation to time, place, and person items will usually be easily passed by those with such disorder. Therefore, I do not administer this subtest in these cases, which explains why it does not appear in Table 2.

This Table 2 should be used and interpreted as was advised for the aforementioned Table 2 Daily Living Skills (Form 6.5). A narrative summary of the subtest results pattern, its relationship to the Attention Module index score result, and its application to whether or not an ADHD diagnosis is supported should be succinctly addressed.

Wechsler Memory Scale, Fourth Edition

The Wechsler Memory Scale, Fourth Edition (WMS–IV) primarily measures the ability to consciously learn and remember novel information that is bound by the testing situation; that is, *declarative episodic memory* (Wechsler, 2009a, 2009b). To the extent that all information must first be processed through *semantic memory* prior to being encoded into episodic memory, the WMS–IV may also be considered an indirect measure of the former (Wechsler, 2009b). Briefly, semantic memory involves general knowledge, such as language and information learned through formal education. Furthermore, the WMS–IV measures both *immediate memory*, which involves short-term or temporary storage (i.e., seconds), and *delayed memory*, which involves longer term or more stable storage and retrieval (i.e., 20–30 minutes), consistent with empirically buttressed theoretical concepts (Atkinson & Shiffrin, 1968).

Therefore, the WMS–IV provides one of the most comprehensive standardized measures of memory functioning available, beginning in middle adolescence and extending through older adulthood. The norm-reference sample ranges from age 16 years 0 months to 90 years 11 months. In terms of Bennet's 1988 model of neuropsychological abilities, this instrument focuses on learning and memory. Thus, I have used this instrument most frequently when a referring clinician or other referral source, for various reasons, specifically requests a thorough measure of memory functioning.

For example, I have received several high-school referrals requesting a comprehensive memory evaluation of adolescent soccer players who failed a routine annual memory screening test. This usually occurs after years of using the head to redirect the trajectory of the soccer ball traveling at considerable velocity. It is also useful in the following instances: (a) ruling out Amnestic Disorder with its focal criterion of impairment in learning and memory, (b) measuring the progression of memory decline in a previously diagnosed case of Dementia, and (c) measuring the effects on memory of brain damage or trauma, another medical condition, or a chronic Substance-Related Disorder.

The WMS–IV has two forms, Ages 16 to 69 and Ages 65 to 90, and provides index scores ($M = 100$, $SD = 15$) for the following general abilities: (a) Auditory Memory, (b) Visual Memory, (c) Visual Working Memory (Ages 16 to 69 only), (d) Immediate Memory, and (e) Delayed Memory. Subtest scale scores ($M = 10$, $SD = 3$), once again referred to as primary scores, contribute in varying combinations to the index scores. Thus, the standard score transformations parallel those of the familiar Wechsler intelligence tests.

Two other WMS–IV features are noteworthy. First, by virtue of it being conormed with the WAIS–IV, ability–memory discrepancy analyses are possible for the index memory scores, thus analogous to the ability–achievement comparisons discussed in Chapter 5. Secondly, an optional Brief Cognitive Status Exam (BCSE) is available, which may be administered separately or as part of the full battery at the testing psychologist's discretion.

The WMS–IV Scoring Assistant (2009) provides rapid scoring and data analysis consistent with the Wechsler intelligence and achievement tests. This software includes all possible ability–memory discrepancy analyses between the WAIS–IV composite scores, including the General Ability Index (GAI) and all of the WMS–IV index scores at both the .05 and .01 alpha (α) probability levels. Lastly, a useful WMS–IV Training CD (2009) is available for new users.

Results and Interpretation Tables

I have prepared four WMS–IV results and interpretation tables. I shall first discuss those designed to report and interpret the index and primary subtest scores for the two WMS–IV forms: Ages 16 to 69 and Ages 65 to 90. The remaining two present the ability–memory discrepancy analyses for these forms. The organization of this section parallels that of the WIAT–III in Chapter 5.

WMS–IV. I have dichotomized the results and interpretation tables according to the two available forms: WMS–IV, Form Ages 16 to 69 (Form 6.8) and WMS–IV, Form Ages 65 to 90 (Form 6.9). Because they are similarly designed and organized, I discuss them contemporaneously as was done with the Wechsler intelligence and achievement tests. Important variances between the two are made explicit when indicated.

Table 1 of Forms 6.8 and 6.9 is circumscribed to the Brief Cognitive Status Exam (BCSE) results. It is sequestered from the index and subtest score summary tables because it is optional and I rarely administer it as part of the WMS–IV battery. Almost invariably, I administer one of the three MMSE–2 versions (Folstein, Folstein, White, & Messer, 2010) during the initial diagnostic interview to justify the WMS–IV testing, thus rendering the

BCSE superfluous. The only exception occurs when the patient's chronological age falls between 16 years 0 months and 17 years 11 months at the point of initial referral, thus falling below the MMSE–2 norms. In this event, I administer the BCSE during the initial interview and insert Table 1 results into the "Initial Psychological Assessment Report" (see Form 2.2). In any case, I seldom administer the BCSE as part of the WMS–IV battery and it is most easily deleted when designed as a separate table.

The BCSE raw score, weighted by chronological age and educational level, determines both the base rate and classification level (Wechsler, 2009a). Thus, in order of appearance, Table 1 lists the following: (a) chronological age in years and months, (b) years of formal education, (c) raw score, (d) base rate, (e) classification level, and (f) measured abilities. The latter was derived by its description in the administrative and scoring manual (Wechsler, 2009a). Classification levels include average, low average, borderline, low, and very low, and can be easily determined by reference to the scoring manual (Wechsler, 2009a, p. 47). Base rate data tables are also available in the scoring manual.[6]

General table notes define a "--" symbol for data not computed or reported and indicate the directional significance of lower raw scores. Two specific table notes define the meaning of base rate, and indicate that the classification level is additionally adjusted for age and education. An ensuing brief narrative interpretation should reference the patient's global cognitive functioning as indicated by Table 1 data.

Table 2 presents the essential index score summary results. It will typically be converted as "Table 1" in the likely event that the BCSE is not administered. The following information is included in columnar order of presentation: (a) index name, with abbreviation for ease of identification within a narrative interpretation; (b) index standard score ($M = 100$, $SD = 15$); (c) percentile rank; (d) 90% confidence interval; (e) index score qualitative description; and (f) measured memory abilities associated with each index, including a temporal descriptor (i.e., 20–30 minute delay) for the Delayed Memory Index. The measured abilities were culled from Table 1.2 in the administrative and scoring manual, which unlike many testing manuals, provides succinct and extremely useful descriptions of the various memory abilities that corresponds with each index (Wechsler, 2009a, Table 1.2, p. 5).

Note that the older adult battery does not contain a Visual Working Memory Index due to exclusion of the Spatial Addition Subtest (cf. Table 5 in Forms 6.8 and 6.9). I have prepared a succinct guideline for rapidly inserting the accurate qualitative descriptions for various index score ranges (Box 6.3), which is a condensed adaptation of Table 5.1 in the technical and interpretative manual (Wechsler, 2009b, Table 5.1, p. 151).

General table notes indicate the transformed index score mean, standard deviation, meaning of lower scores, and define tabular abbreviations, including the optional "--" symbol for data not computed or reported. Table 2 results should be ensued by a narrative interpretation of the index score pattern. Note that there is no WMS–IV total memory score which typically initiates narrative interpretation as in the NAB and other Wechsler-designed tests.

To facilitate the interpretation of Table 2, I have prepared and inserted a standardized narrative defining key psychological terms. First, an information processing model definition of memory is offered (Atkinson & Shiffrin, 1968). This is ensued by a more particular description of declarative episodic memory, which is the essential type of memory purported to be measured by the WMS–IV (Wechsler, 2009b). Finally, a diagnostic distinction is made between immediate and delayed memory, which provides the framework for discussing any significant differences in these abilities manifested by a particular patient.

Three subtest score summary tables follow the Table 2 Index Score Summary, including: (a) Auditory Memory (Table 3), (b) Visual Memory (Table 4), and (c) Visual Working Memory (Table 5). The table numbers should be amended accordingly if the BCSE has

[6] *The WMS–IV Scoring Assistant conveniently and rapidly provides both the proper classification levels and base rates.*

not been administered. There are no discrete tables summarizing the subtests loading on the Immediate and Delayed Memory Indices. This is because they are the same subtests loading on the Auditory and Visual Memory Indices in differing combinations. Hence, their presentation within Immediate and Delayed subtest score summary tables would be unnecessarily redundant and superfluous. As will become apparent, the subtests in Tables 3 and 4, which load on the Immediate and Delayed Memory Indices, are designated by general tabular symbols and notes.

All subtest score summary tables are organized by column order as follows: (a) subtest name, including abbreviation for easy reference within a narrative interpretation of table results, (b) subtest scaled score (*M* = 10, *SD* = 3), (c) percentile rank, (d) qualitative description, and (e) abilities measured by each subtest. Once again, the last were based upon my scrutiny of the more elaborate subtest descriptions presented within the two test manuals (Wechsler, 2009a, 2009b). As mentioned prior, because subtests of Tables 3 and 4 also load on the Immediate and Delayed Memory Indices, general table notes are added with "*" indicating contribution to the former, and "**" denoting contribution to the latter. Box 6.3 also assists in applying the correct qualitative description for varying subtest-scaled score ranges. Although not shown in Box 6.3 for the pragmatic purpose of brevity, they are based upon the same standard deviation ranges as the index scores (Wechsler, 2009b, p. 151).

Regarding subtest content, there exist two fundamental differences between the WMS–IV, Form Ages 16 to 69 (Form 6.8) and the WMS–IV, Form Ages 65 to 90 (Form 6.9). Regarding the latter, Table 4 does not include Designs I and II subtests, and Table 5 does not include Spatial Addition. These subtests are not part of the older adult battery.

Pertinent table notes are added, including scaled score mean and standard deviation, directional interpretation of lower scores, definition of asterisked table names as indicated above (Tables 3 and 4 only), the optional "--" symbol for data not computed or reported, and the specific duration of delayed memory; that is, 20 to 30 minutes (Tables 3 and 4 only). A specific note defines the paramount construct of working memory as measured and reported in Table 5.

Lastly, I advise including all subtest score summary tables in the final report. This is because a comprehensive analysis of a patient's memory functioning is most routinely the principal basis for selecting the WMS–IV for inclusion within a test battery. Each subtest table should be followed by a succinct narrative interpretation addressing the results profile, along with implications for diagnosis and intervention.

Ability–memory discrepancy analyses. Prior to presenting the results and interpretation tables for ability–memory discrepancy comparisons, some prelusory comments regarding their diagnostic usefulness are needed. Practically speaking, including such analyses within a battery will add an estimated 2 to 3 hours of testing time. Thus, there must exist compelling reasons for gathering such extended data.

First, and most obvious, such analyses are indicated if directly requested by diagnostically savvy referring clinicians. Second, and not so apparent, such analyses are advised if there is evidence from the initial report that the patient manifests remarkably high (i.e., superior or above) or low (i.e., borderline or below) intellectual functioning. In the former case, a patient may score within average limits regarding memory functioning and appear normal, belying the fact that such memory performance would be significantly lower than what would be expected had a standardized intelligence test been administered and scored. In such case, a disorder is likely to be missed, or at least early detection of such disorder. At the lower end of the intellectual ability spectrum, commensurately lower memory scores may appear "abnormal" although expected, thus risking excessive and inaccurate diagnosis; for example, fallaciously adding comorbid Axis I Dementia to an Axis II Borderline Intellectual Functioning or Mild Mental Retardation diagnosis.

Thus, when the initial assessment provides reasonable evidence that the patient's intellectual ability falls within either remarkably high or low ranges as previously defined, then ability–discrepancy comparisons are justified on diagnostic grounds. Alternatively, when the initial assessment indicates intellectual functioning falling somewhere within average limits (i.e., low average to high average or a composite score range of 80–119), which will effectively capture approximately 82% of the population according to the theoretical normal curve (see e.g., Gravetter & Wallnau, 2013), then ability–memory discrepancy analyses are unnecessary and unwarranted.

The following four results and interpretation tables are reviewed here in detail: (a) WAIS–IV/WMS–IV, Form Ages 16 to 69 Ability–Memory Discrepancy Analysis Simple Difference Method (Form 6.10); (b) WAIS–IV/WMS–IV, Form Ages 65 to 90 Ability–Memory Discrepancy Analysis Simple Difference Method (Form 6.11); (c) WAIS–IV/WMS–IV, Form Ages 16 to 69 Ability–Memory Discrepancy Analysis Predicted Difference Method (Form 6.12); and (d) WAIS–IV/WMS–IV, Form Ages 65 to 90 Ability–Memory Discrepancy Analysis Predicted Difference Method (Form 6.13). Note that because the WMS–IV norm-reference group age range is identical to that of the WAIS–IV, and because these tests are conormed, only the latter Wechsler version is applicable as a measure of intellectual competence. Due to their similar organization, I discuss these four results and interpretation tables simultaneously, while highlighting noteworthy differences when justified.

Prior to presenting the tables (Table 1 to Table 7) in earnest, some general comments will be constructive. These results and interpretation tables include the entire complement of tests, composites, index scores, and subtests necessary to fully describe memory functioning and execute the ability–memory discrepancy analyses. Again, this obviates the need to search for and insert the necessary tables from separate hard copy or electronic file locations into the analysis. Some of the memory subtest data may be edited out for purposes of brevity, although I do not recommend doing this using the same rationale above when I discussed the frequent need to provide a comprehensive analysis regarding a patient's memory functioning. Finally, tabular results should be immediately ensued by narrative interpretations where needed.

The analysis begins by selecting the intelligence test composite score that most accurately measures an examinee's cognitive competence. This score is used to quantitatively compute an examinee's expected level of memory functioning. In contrast to ability–achievement comparisons (see Chapter 5), the Full Scale is not utilized here as it incorporates the memory-related Processing Speed Index (PSI) and Working Memory Index (WMI). Thus, in practice, the most diagnostically useful options, in order of prominence, include the General Ability Index (GAI), Verbal Comprehension Index (VCI), and the Perceptual Reasoning Index (PRI).

Table 1 initiates the analysis of selecting the index that will afford the most diagnostically meaningful ability–memory comparisons. It is virtually identical to Table 1 presented within the WAIS–IV results and interpretation tables (Form 4.4), although with the irrelevant PSI, WMI, and Full Scale deleted. The GAI information appears in boldface, symbolizing its prominence both within the analysis and as a construct. Furthermore, a specific table note explicitly indicates the manner in which it is quantitatively derived, and states its consequence of reducing the effects of working memory and processing speed when measuring a patient's overall intellectual functioning.

Table 2 completes the process of selecting the WAIS–IV composite score, which shall be used for all ensuing ability–memory comparisons. In order of presentation, Table 2 reports the VCI, PRI, VCI–PRI difference, the critical value at the .05 probability level, an accompanying asterisk if statistically significant ($p < .05$), Cohen's *d* effect size computation, effect size result, and finally, the percentage of the normative sample who obtained the listed

VCI–PRI difference (i.e., base rate). Again, effect size is quickly computed by the absolute VCI–PRI difference, divided by the composite standard deviation of 15 (see Warner, 2008). The base rate is reported to provide practical ancillary evidence of any noted abnormality. Table 2 notes define statistical significance, effect size computation and interpretation, and base rate. Taken together, these notes facilitate test interpretation and feedback.

In terms of ability composite score selection, I advise using the GAI unless a cogent exception exists in the form of a grossly anomalous VCI–PRI variance. This is why the GAI is inserted as the default selection in Table 7, which presents the specific ability–memory discrepancy analyses. If a magnitude of variance exists such that the GAI's meaning is commensurately distorted, then I recommend using the VCI for the following reasons: (a) language and verbal ability tend to be less affected by brain dysfunction and trauma (i.e., what has been referred to as the dichotomous *hold* versus *don't hold* subtests) (Kaufman & Lichtenberger, 1999), (b) VCI manifesting generally higher correlations with general intelligence (e.g., Wechsler, 2008), and (c) capability of measuring memory deficits over and above verbal intelligence. The PRI may be selected if (a) it is remarkably higher versus the VCI and (b) the priority is to obtain a true positive diagnosis.

Immediately subsequent to Table 2 notes, I have inserted the above-listed potential interpretations in narrative form for convenience, beginning with the rationale for selecting the GAI. Of course, this is not meant to be an exhaustive list, and testing psychologists may delete and craft their own most frequent interpretations.

Table 3 reports the WMS–IV index score results, and Tables 4 to 6 report the WMS–IV subtest score results classified by Auditory, Visual, and Visual Working Memory domains, respectively. Note that they are virtually identical to the results and interpretation tables when reporting the WMS–IV results alone for Form Ages 16 to 69 (Form 6.8) and Form Ages 65 to 90 (Form 6.9). The one exception is the removal of the BCSE, which I have not administered when conducting such in-depth ability–memory statistical comparisons.

Unless there are further compelling reasons for prioritizing brevity, however, I advise retaining subtest score summary Tables 4 through 6 in the final report. They provide a complete profile analysis of both absolute (i.e., normative) and relative (i.e., ipsative) particular memory strengths and deficits. This is all the more significant considering that the ability–memory discrepancy analyses are circumscribed to the selected WAIS–IV composite score and WMS–IV index scores.

The WMS–IV ability–memory discrepancy analyses may be conducted by the same two statistical methods used in the Wechsler ability–achievement comparisons, including (a) simple difference (Forms 6.10 and 6.11) and (b) predicted difference (Forms 6.12 and 6.13). Next, I discuss the results and interpretation tables organized by these two statistical methods beginning with simple difference and ensued by predicted difference. The younger and older adult forms are reviewed together due to their similarity, with important differences highlighted when deemed necessary.

First, the simple difference discrepancies are obtained by subtracting the selected WAIS–IV composite score from each WMS–IV index score obtained. As mentioned in Chapter 5, this direct comparison is more easily comprehended by those unfamiliar with psychometrics and statistical analyses.

Also, as previously mentioned in this chapter, ability–memory discrepancy analyses are available only for the WMS–IV index scores that are presented within a single table (Table 7, Forms 6.10 and 6.11). Immediately preceding Table 7 are notations identifying which ability composite score was selected according to the results of Tables 1 and 2, with the GAI as the default, followed by the actual score obtained by the examinee. If either the VCI or PRI supplants the GAI, appropriate amendments must be made here, within the table body, and within the tabular notes.

The first column of Table 7 presents a list of the WMS–IV index score names, including abbreviations for ease of reference within a follow-up narrative interpretation of table results. Again, the older adult Table 7 does not include a Visual Working Memory Index for reasons stated prior (Form 6.11). This first column is followed by (a) the obtained WMS–IV index score, (b) ability composite score, (c) memory score minus ability score difference, (d) statistical significance results, and (e) base rate of the measured difference found in the norm-reference group.

Negative difference scores indicate that memory is lower than ability and thus potential dysfunction, whereas zero and positive differences palpably show no evidence of a memory-related Cognitive Disorder. Thus, if the WMS–IV memory score is equal to or exceeds the ability score, further analysis is obviated in terms of diagnosing disorder and a simple *N/A* notation is placed within the critical value and base rate columns for that particular index. Again, this renders the table more comprehensible in terms of identifying pathology.

Regarding statistical significance, the conventional $p < .05$ α level is the default. I chose this to be consistent with the precept of prioritizing the detection of neuropsychological disorder when it is actually present. As with the ability–achievement discrepancy tables (Chapter 5), Table 7 notes define the meaning of statistical significance and the N/A notation, the manner in which the difference score was computed, and the meaning of base rate.

Second, the predicted difference discrepancies are derived by subtracting each WMS–IV index score *predicted* by the selected intelligence test composite score from the *actual* or obtained WMS–IV standard score. Once again, this prediction-oriented method may be more compelling for those familiar with statistics and psychometrics, although should not alter the ultimate results (Wechsler, 2009a, 2009b).

Table 7 (Forms 6.12 and 6.13) comprises the predicted difference ability–memory discrepancy analyses. Prior to Table 7 is information regarding which ability score was selected for prediction purposes, along with the obtained ability score. Column 2 presents the examinee's *actual* or obtained WMS–IV index score, while the adjacent column 3 presents the WMS–IV index score *predicted* by the chosen intelligence test composite score. The subtraction is made such that negative scores again show potential disorder, and zero differences or positive scores are not in need of further analyses (i.e., N/A). Lastly, the only amendment in the predicted difference tabular notes is the alternative manner in which the difference scores were computed.

Conners' Continuous Performance Tests

There are two Conners' Continuous Performance Tests (CPT) in my recommended inventory. They include the following: (a) Conners' Kiddie Continuous Performance Test, Version 5 (K–CPT) (Conners, 2001), normed on individuals aged 4 years 0 months to 5 years 11 months and (b) Conners' Continuous Performance Test, Second Edition, Version 5 (CPT–II) (Conners, 2004), normed on individuals aged 6 years 0 months to 55 years 0 months and above. They are virtually identical in terms of administration and the data yield. Furthermore, they are completely automated regarding computer administration and scoring. The primary differences include (a) shorter administration time for the K–CPT (i.e., 7.5 minutes versus 14 minutes) and (b) stimuli presented by the K–CPT (i.e., pictures versus letters).

Essentially, examinees are to continuously respond, or to not respond, by computer mouse click (or key board space bar press) to random presentations of target and nontarget stimuli, respectively. Its principal clinical use is in determining the likelihood that an individual manifests a disorder of attention (Conners, 2001, 2004). Hence, I use the Conners CPT exclusively for ADHD evaluations; that is, to corroborate the results of standardized behavioral ratings and selected neuropsychological subtests, the latter measuring a broader range of abilities, including attention, executive functioning, memory, and learning (see the NEPSY–II and NAB).

The Conners CPT data yield comprises the following: (a) overall profile classification (i.e., nonclinical or clinical), (b) confidence index regarding the aforementioned classification, and (c) standardized *T*-scores (*M* = 50, *SD* = 10) on specific measures of attention, including sustained attention (i.e., vigilance) and impulse control. I will elaborate on the first two types of data such that their presence in the CPT results and interpretation tables are more comprehensible.

In order to explicate the manner in which the CPT overall profile classification works, I must briefly reference the groups comprising the norm-reference sample. Specifically, the norm-reference samples of both the K–CPT and the CPT–II include both a nonclinical group and clinical group (i.e., ADHD and neurological impairment). The profile classification is performed by *discriminant function analysis*. Briefly, discriminant analysis (DA) predicts group membership on a *Y* outcome variable (e.g., nonclinical and clinical) from a combination of numerical scores on several *X* predictor variables (e.g., CPT specific measure *T*-scores) (Warner, 2008). As employed by the CPT, the DA determines whether an examinee's *T*-score profile better predicts (i.e., is more correlated or associated with) the nonclinical profile norms or clinical profile norms (Conners, 2001, 2004).

Also, part of the overall assessment is a *confidence index*. The CPT confidence index measures the degree of fit with the classification indicated by the DA. The accompanying test manuals recommend interpreting confidence indices between 40 and 60 as inconclusive, with higher and lower values being conclusive (Conners, 2001, 2004). However, I have found such dichotomous interpretation to be rather unrefined in terms of precision. I advise that, in practice, the DA classification and its accompanying confidence index be interpreted with diligent consideration of the *T*-score specific measure results. As you shall see, this is the manner in which I have designed the CPT results and interpretation tables.

Lastly, the CPT specific measures are based upon signal detection theory (McNicole, 1972). *T*-scores above 60 indicate impairment on a specific measure. It is recommended that 0 or 1 *T*-score elevations above 60 indicate normal functioning, whereas two or more such elevations indicate the presence of an attention disorder (Conners, 2001, 2004).

Results and Interpretation Tables

I have prepared two CPT results and interpretation tables, one for the K–CPT (Form 6.14) and one for the CPT–II (Form 6.15). They are identical except for the acronyms. Thus, I shall discuss them together.

Validity of administration. Table 1 includes four CPT response patterns, which, if present, indicate that the examinee may not have followed test instructions due to intractability. The CPT computer scoring will effectively identify if any of these measures are positive. The first two rows of Table 1 identify the validity measure names. The third row indicates whether or not the invalid response pattern was present. If so, simply delete the "No" option and retain the "Yes." For the "Excessive Omissions" measure, I recommend inserting the raw score number of omission errors as a useful descriptive supplement. Omission errors occur when the examinee fails to respond to target stimuli. Excessive errors of omission indicate either (a) the examinee simply stopped responding due to test resistance or (b) the examinee manifested severe attention problems.

Row 4 provides the interpretations for each measure's result noted in row 3. If affirmative, type "Invalid." If negative, retain the more common "Valid," which is the default.

In practice, these CPT measures are most frequently valid, especially for middle childhood and older. To prevent invalid results on the K–CPT (i.e., ages 4 and 5 years), observing the child continuously throughout the rather brief test administration process is most efficacious. Lastly, the measure that most frequently produces invalid results is "Excessive Omissions." This is due to the fact that detection of true attention problems is a viable alternative interpretation.

That is, in the presence of excessive omissions, if the examinee successfully passed the practice administration and was observed to continue responding throughout the test administration procedure, I enter "Invalid" in the tabular interpretation, then qualify the overall interpretation of Table 1 validity results by indicating that despite some indications of invalidity, the overall results may be considered valid. For convenience, I have placed standardized narrative interpretations immediately following Table 1 covering valid, the aforementioned qualified valid, and invalid alternatives.

Confidence index assessment. Table 2 succinctly integrates the DA profile classification and its associated confidence index. In columnar order of presentation, Table 2 includes the following: (a) identification of the DA statistical analysis, (b) the DA profile classification, (c) the quantified confidence index by percentage, and (d) a pragmatic interpretation of the confidence index score.

Concerning the DA classification, the alternatives are clinical and nonclinical, which are nebulous and not well understood by nonprofessionals. Thus, I advise that these be supplanted with *ADHD* and *normal*, respectively. A third viable alternative that does not appear in the table due to space limitations is *Borderline*, to be applied for confidence index results at or proximate to 50%. Regarding the bottom row of columns 3 and 4, simply insert the confidence index score and repeat that number in the interpretation, replacing the "--" and selecting the proper *a/no* option. Table 2 is designed to be interpreted with Table 3 specific measure results. Thus, I advise that you defer narrative interpretation at this juncture.

Lastly, and most diagnostically relevant, Table 3 provides information regarding the examinee's specific profile. Proceeding from left to right, Table 3 includes the following: (a) specific measure name; (b) specific measure *T*-scores, including an asterisk symbol indicating a statistically significant clinical elevation; (c) percentile rank; (d) interpretive guideline; and (e) the meaning of a statistically significant result. The succinct entries in the latter column were derived from the narrative descriptions of each specific measure given in the CPT–II manual (Conners, 2004, pp. 29–32).

The computer software scoring automatically applies the appropriate guidelines. These guidelines are phrased somewhat differently within the computer report, depending on whether they are being reported in the *summary of overall measures* table, or supplemental tables classified by measure type, including *inattention, vigilance,* and *impulsivity.* Table 3 lists a combination of these guidelines that I believe communicate the results most effectively. Most pertinent, the guidelines provide distinctions between "marked" and "mild" abnormal elevations, which you may or may not decide to use. Similarly, there are discriminations of effective performance, including *very good performance, good performance,* and *within average range.* The testing psychologist may insert those that are most diagnostically descriptive in a particular case.

Note that I do not report the Response Style Beta Statistic (β) among the specific measures. It is listed within the summary of overall measures table of the computer report. In particular, this statistic measures an examinee's stylistic preference to either (a) avoid commission errors (i.e., responding incorrectly to nontargets) or, in the alternative, (b) maximize correct hits (i.e., responding correctly to targets). As such, Response Style (β) is more accurately conceptualized and interpreted either as (a) a validity indicator (Conners, 2004, p. 26), or, in my opinion, more cogently as (b) a motivational style in which one prefers to maximize correct responses (i.e., a *promotion focus*) or minimize incorrect responses (i.e., a *prevention focus*) (see e.g., Higgins et al., 2001). Therefore, to maintain brevity and the reporting of the most essential results, Response Style (β) is neither reported nor interpreted within the CPT–II and K–CPT validity and specific measures tables.

General table notes indicate the *T*-score mean and standard deviation, the directional meaning of high scores, and definitions of table symbols and abbreviations, once again including the optional "--" score not computed or available for completely invalid results. Lastly, an integrated summary narrative interpretation of the results of Tables 2 and 3 immediately follows the latter.

I have inserted the most frequent narrative interpretations of the results for convenience. At a minimum, results should be interpreted as either positive or negative of attention problems. I have inserted ADHD because this is my exclusive use of the CPT test. For positive results, I commonly identify the measured general areas of impairment (i.e., inattention and impulsivity) as this information assists in differentiating the three diagnosable types of ADHD (American Psychiatric Association, 2000).

Finally, as with all tests, there exists the possibility of false positive and false negative results due to measurement error. For example, in practice, it is not uncommon for an examinee to appear perfectly normal on the CPT, while patently failing relevant neuropsychological measures and being rated on standardized checklists as unequivocally ADHD. For these cases, I have inserted interpretative statements describing such false negative and positive results.

SUMMARY

This concludes a sequence of three chapters generally covering standardized tests of cognitive functioning for purposes of *DSM-IV-TR* differential diagnosis and addressing related referral questions. This particular chapter focused on neuropsychological testing as applied to a majority of the lifespan, ranging in age from 3 years 0 months to 97 years 11 months.

Neuropsychological functioning was initially defined so as to distinguish its measurement from that of intelligence and achievement. This was ensued by a discussion covering diagnostic reasons substantiating such testing, along with related insurance coverage issues. The majority of Chapter 6, however, was devoted to describing the selected neuropsychological tests and test batteries, with special attention to their results and interpretation tables, and the manner in which they are intended to be used in practice.

The ensuing chapters in Section II cover standardized testing primarily for the non-cognitive *DSM-IV-TR* Axis I and II Psychological and Personality Disorders. They also address the measurement of developmental milestones and adaptive behavior when these domains of functioning are diagnostically pertinent.

REFERENCES

American Psychiatric Association. (1987). *Diagnostic and statistical manual of mental disorders* (3rd ed. rev.). Washington, DC: Author.

American Psychiatric Association. (2000). *Diagnostic and statistical manual of mental disorders* (4th ed., text rev.). Washington, DC: Author.

American Psychological Association. (2010). *Publication manual of the American Psychological Association* (6th ed.). Washington, DC: Author.

Atkinson, R. C., & Shiffrin, R. M. (1968). A proposed system and its control processes. In K. W. Spence & J. T. Spence (Eds.), *The psychology of learning and motivation: Advances in research and theory* (Vol. 2, pp. 82–90). New York, NY: Academic Press.

Barlow, David H., & Durand, Mark V. (2012). *Abnormal psychology: An integrative approach* (6th ed.). Belmont, CA: Wadsworth, Cengage Learning.

Bennet, T. (1988). Use of the Halstead–Reitan neuropsychological test battery in the assessment of head injury. *Cognitive Rehabilitation*, 6, 18–25.

Conners, C. K. (2004). *Conners' Continuous Performance Test II, Version 5 for Windows (CPT–II): Technical guide and software manual*. North Tonawanda, NY: Multi-Health Systems.

Conners, C. K. (2001). *Conners' Kiddie Continuous Performance, Version 5 for Windows (K–CPT): Technical guide and software manual.* North Tonawanda, NY: Multi-Health Systems.

Folstein, M. F., Folstein, S. E., White, T., & Messer, M. A. (2010). *Mini–Mental State Examination, Second Edition: Users manual.* Lutz, FL: Psychological Assessment Resources.

Gravetter, F. J., & Wallnau, L. B. (2013). *Statistics for the behavioral sciences* (9th ed.). Belmont, CA: Wadsworth, Cengage Learning.

Gregory, R. J. (2011). *Psychological testing: History, principles, applications.* Boston, MA: Pearson Education.

Higgins, E. T., Friedman, R. S., Harlow, R. E., Idson, L. C., Ayduk, O. N., & Taylor, A. (2001). Achievement orientations from subjective histories of success: Promotion pride versus prevention pride. *European Journal of Social Psychology, 31,* 2–23.

Kaufman, A. S., & Lichtenberger, E. O. (1999). *Essentials of WAIS–III assessment.* New York, NY: John Wiley.

Korkman, M., Kirk, U., & Kemp, S. (2007a). *NEPSY–II: Administrative manual.* San Antonio, TX: The Psychological Corporation-Pearson.

Korkman, M., Kirk, U., & Kemp, S. (2007b). *NEPSY–II: Clinical and interpretative manual.* San Antonio, TX: The Psychological Corporation-Pearson.

Mcintosh, D. N., Reichmann-Decker, A., Winkielman, P., & Wilbarger, J. L. (2006). When the social mirror breaks: Deficits in automatic, but not voluntary, mimicry of emotional facial expressions in autism. *Developmental Science, 9,* 295–302.

McNicole, D. (1972). *A primer on signal detection theory.* London: George Allen & Unwin.

NAB Screening Module, Training Disk 1. (2004a). [DVD Computer software]. Lutz, FL: Psychological Assessment Resources (PAR).

NAB Attention Module, Training Disk 2. (2004b). [DVD Computer software]. Lutz, FL: Psychological Assessment Resources (PAR).

NAB Language Module, Training Disk 3. (2004c). [DVD Computer software]. Lutz, FL: Psychological Assessment Resources (PAR).

NAB Memory Module, Training Disk 4. (2004d). [DVD Computer software]. Lutz, FL: Psychological Assessment Resources (PAR).

NAB Spatial Module, Training Disk 5. (2004e). [DVD Computer software]. Lutz, FL: Psychological Assessment Resources (PAR).

NAB Executive Functions Module, Training Disk 6. (2004f). [DVD Computer Software]. Lutz, FL: Psychological Assessment Resources (PAR).

NEPSY–II Scoring Assistant & Assessment Planner. (2007). [CD-ROM Computer Software]. San Antonio, TX: PsychCorp Center–I, Pearson.

NEPSY–II Training CD Version 1.0. (2007). [CD-ROM Computer Software]. San Antonio, TX: Pearson (PsychCorp).

Neuropsychological Assessment Battery Software Portfolio (NAB–SP). (2008). [CD-ROM Computer Software]. Lutz, FL: Psychological Assessment Resources (PAR).

Oberman, L. M., & Ramachandran, V. S. (2007). The simulating social mind: The role of the mirror neuron system and simulation in the social and communicative deficits of autism spectrum disorders. *Psychological Bulletin, 133,* 310–327.

Pearson (PsychCorp). (2009). *Wechsler Individual Achievement Test, Third Edition (WIAT–III): Examiner's manual.* San Antonio, Texas: Author.

Peterson, B. S., Potenza, M. N., Wang, Z., Zhu, H., Martin, A., Marsh, R., & Yu, S. (2009). An fMRI study of the effects of psychostimulants on default-mode processing during Stroop task performance in youths with ADHD. *American Journal of Psychiatry, 166,* 1286–1294.

Shaw, P., Lalonde, F., Lepage, C., Rabin, C., Eckstrand, K., Sharp, W.,…Rapoport, J. (2009). Development of cortical asymmetry in typically developing children and its disruption in attention-deficit/hyperactivity disorder. *Archives of General Psychiatry, 66,* 888–896.

Sigelman, C. K., & Rider, E. A. (2012). *Life-span human development* (7th ed.). Belmont, CA: Thomson Wadsworth.

Stern, R. A., & White, T. (2003a). *Neuropsychological Assessment Battery (NAB): Administrative, scoring, and interpretation manual.* Lutz, FL: Psychological Assessment Resources.

Stern, R. A., & White, T. (2003b). *Neuropsychological Assessment Battery (NAB): Psychometric and technical manual.* Lutz, FL: Psychological Assessment Resources.

Warner, R. M. (2008). *Applied statistics.* Thousand Oaks, CA: Sage Publications.

Wechsler, D. (2008). *Wechsler Adult Intelligence Scale, Fourth Edition (WAIS–IV): Technical and interpretive manual.* San Antonio, TX: The Psychological Corporation-Pearson.

Wechsler, D. (2009a). *Wechsler Memory Scale, Fourth Edition (WMS–IV): Administration and scoring manual.* San Antonio, TX: The Psychological Corporation-Pearson.

Wechsler, D. (2009b). *Wechsler Memory Scale, Fourth Edition (WMS–IV): Technical and interpretive manual.* San Antonio, TX: The Psychological Corporation-Pearson.

White, T., & Stern, R. A. (2003a). *NAB demographically corrected norms manual.* Lutz, FL: Psychological Assessment Resources.

White, T., & Stern, R. A. (2003b). *NAB U.S. census-matched norms manual.* Lutz, FL: Psychological Assessment Resources.

WMS–IV Scoring Assistant. (2009). [CD-ROM Computer Software]. San Antonio, TX: PsychCorp Center–II, Pearson.

WMS–IV Training CD Version 1.0. (2009). [CD-ROM Computer Software]. San Antonio, TX: Pearson (PsychCorp).

BOX 6.1

NAB INTERPRETATIVE CATEGORY GUIDE

Index scores	Subtest scores	Interpretive category
130–155	Not applicable	Very superior
115–129	Not applicable	Superior
107–114	55–81	Above average
92–106	45–54	Average
85–91	40–44	Below average
77–84	35–39	Mildly impaired
70–76	30–34	Mildly-to-moderately impaired
62–69	25–29	Moderately impaired
55–61	20–24	Moderately-to-severely impaired
45–54	19	Severely impaired

Source: Adapted from Stern, R. A., & White, T. (2003). *Neuropsychological Assessment Battery (NAB): Administrative, scoring, and interpretation manual.* Lutz, FL: Psychological Assessment Resources, Tables 6.8 and 6.9, pp. 124 and 128, respectively.

BOX 6.2

NASB SCREENING BATTERY DECISION GUIDE FOR ADDITIONAL FULL MODULE TESTING

Screening domain	Impairment—no further administration	Borderline—further administration	Nonimpairment—no further administration
Attention	45–74	75–113	114–155
Language	45–75	76–125	126–155
Memory	45–75	76–118	119–155
Spatial	45–74	75–119	120–155
Executive functions	45–73	74–114	115–155

Source: Adapted from Stern, R. A., & White, T. (2003). *Neuropsychological Assessment Battery (NAB): Administrative, scoring, and interpretation manual.* Lutz, FL: Psychological Assessment Resources, Tables 6.3–6.7, pp. 122–124.

BOX 6.3

WMS–IV QUALITATIVE DESCRIPTOR GUIDE

Index scores	Subtest scaled scores	Qualitative descriptor
130–160	16–19	Very superior
120–129	14–15	Superior
110–119	12–13	High average
90–109	8–11	Average
80–89	6–7	Low average
70–79	4–5	Borderline
40–69	1–3	Extremely low

Source: Adapted from Wechsler, D. (2009). Wechsler Memory Scale, Fourth Edition (WMS–IV): Technical and interpretative manual. San Antonio, TX: The Psychological Corporation-Pearson, Table 5.1, p. 151.

FORM 6.1

NEPSY–II, FORM AGES 3 TO 4, FULL BATTERY RESULTS AND INTERPRETATION TABLES

NEPSY–II, Form Ages 3 to 4, Full Battery

TABLE 1 ■ ATTENTION AND EXECUTIVE FUNCTIONING

Score name	Scaled score	PR	Classification	Measured abilities
Statue Total	00	0.00	At expected level	General inhibitory ability

Note. Scaled score mean = 10, standard deviation = 3. Lower scores indicate greater neuropsychological impairment. Age range is for that particular score in years. PR, percentile rank.

Attention is the ability to focus on specific activities and suppress irrelevant stimuli. This includes *inhibition,* which is the ability to (a) resist urges and (b) stop oneself from engaging in automatic behaviors.

Executive functioning involves the ability to (a) engage in activities necessary for achieving objectives and (b) regulate one's actions based on environmental feedback.

TABLE 2 ■ LANGUAGE

Score name	Scaled score	PR	Classification	Measured abilities
Body Part Naming Total	00	0.00	Above expected level	Word finding; expressive language; vocabulary
Body Part Identification Total	--	--	At expected level	Semantic knowledge (general and specific to body parts)
Comprehension Of Instructions Total	--	--	Borderline	Linguistic and syntactic knowledge; ability to follow multistep commands
Oromotor Sequences Total	--	--	Below expected level	Muscle movements of the mouth, jaw, tongue, lips, and cheeks for speech production
Phonological Processing Total	--	--	Well below expected level	Phonological awareness and processing
Speeded Naming Combined	--	--	At expected level	Automaticity of lexical analysis; processing speed; naming ability
Word Generation Semantic Total	--	--	At expected level	Executive control of language production; initiative; ideation

Note. Scaled score mean = 10, standard deviation = 3. Lower scores indicate greater neuropsychological impairment. Age range is for that particular score in years. PR, percentile rank. -- denotes not administered, or score type not available or computed.

Language is the ability to express and understand verbal communication effectively. This consists of (a) receptive speech involving the comprehension and decoding of speech and (b) expressive speech or language production.

TABLE 3 ■ MEMORY AND LEARNING

Score name	Scaled score	PR	Classification	Measured abilities
Memory for Designs Total	00	0.00	At expected level	Visuospatial memory
Narrative Memory Total[a]	--	--	Well below expected level	Verbal expression and comprehension; verbal learning and memory
Sentence Repetition Total	--	--	At expected level	Verbal short-term memory

Note: Scaled score mean = 10, standard deviation = 3. Lower scores indicate greater neuropsychological impairment. Age range is for that particular score in years. PR, percentile rank. -- denotes not administered, or score type not available or computed.

[a]Includes free recall (i.e., no hints given) and cued recall (i.e., hints given).

Memory and *learning* include the ability to acquire, retain, and access new information. Learning includes the ability to acquire new information. Memory involves retaining and retrieving information.

(Cont.)

FORM 6.1

NEPSY–II, FORM AGES 3 TO 4, FULL BATTERY RESULTS AND INTERPRETATION TABLES (*Cont.*)

TABLE 4 ■ **SENSORIMOTOR**

Score name	Scaled score	PR	Classification	Measured abilities
Imitating Hand Positions Total[a]	00	0.00	At expected level	Fine-motor programming and differentiation; visuospatial skills
Manual Motor Sequences Total	--	--	Borderline	Manual motor programming
Visuomotor Precision Combined	--	--	Below expected level	Fine-motor coordination and speed

Note: Scaled score mean = 10, standard deviation = 3. Lower scores indicate greater neuropsychological impairment. Age range is for that particular score in years. PR, percentile rank. -- denotes not administered, or score type not available or computed.

[a]Includes both dominant and nondominant hands.

Sensorimotor abilities involve neural circuits, which integrate motor guidance with sensory (i.e., kinesthetic, tactile, visual) feedback.

TABLE 5 ■ **SOCIAL PERCEPTION**

Score name	Scaled score	PR	Classification	Measured abilities
Affect Recognition Total	00	0.00	Well below expected level	Facial affect recognition
Theory of Mind Total	--	--	At expected level	Comprehension of others' perspectives, experiences, and beliefs; matching appropriate affect to contextual cues

Note: Scaled score mean = 10, standard deviation = 3. Lower scores indicate greater neuropsychological impairment. Age range is for that particular score in years. PR, percentile rank. -- denotes not administered, or score type not available or computed.

Social perception involves intellectual processes that facilitate social interaction.

TABLE 6 ■ **VISUOSPATIAL PROCESSING**

Score name	Scaled score	PR	Classification	Measured abilities
Block Construction Total	00	0.00	At expected level	Visuoconstructional skills in three-dimensional tasks
Design Copying General Total	--	--	Borderline	Visuoconstructional skills in two-dimensional tasks
Geometric Puzzles Total	--	--	Below expected level	Visuospatial perception including mental rotation

Note: Scaled score mean = 10, standard deviation = 3. Lower scores indicate greater neuropsychological impairment. Age range is for that particular score in years. PR, percentile rank. -- denotes not administered, or score type not available or computed.

Visuospatial processing is the capacity to understand the orientation of visual information in two- and three-dimensional space.

FORM 6.2

NEPSY–II, FORM AGES 5 TO 16, FULL BATTERY RESULTS AND INTERPRETATION TABLES

NEPSY–II, Form Ages 5 to 16, Full Battery

TABLE 1 ■ ATTENTION AND EXECUTIVE FUNCTIONING

Score name	Age range	Scaled score	PR	Classification	Measured abilities
Animal Sorting Combined	7–16	00	0.00	Above expected level	Initiation, cognitive flexibility, and self-monitoring; conceptual reasoning; semantic knowledge
Auditory Attention Combined	5–16	--	--	At expected level	Selective and sustained attention; response speed; inhibitory control
Response Set Combined	7–16	--	--	Borderline	Selective and sustained attention; inhibitory control; working memory; response speed
Clocks Total	7–16	--	--	Below expected level	Planning and organization; clock drawing; clock-reading ability
Design Fluency Total	5–12	--	--	Well below expected level	Initiation and productivity; cognitive flexibility
Inhibition–Inhibition Combined	5–16	--	--	At expected level	Inhibitory control
Inhibition–Switching Combined	7–16	--	--	At expected level	Inhibitory control; cognitive flexibility
Statue Total	5–6	--	--	At expected level	General inhibitory ability

Note: Scaled score mean = 10, standard deviation = 3. Lower scores indicate greater neuropsychological impairment. Age range is for that particular score in years. PR, percentile rank. -- denotes not administered, or score type not available or computed.

Attention is the ability to focus on specific activities and suppress irrelevant stimuli. This includes *inhibition,* which is the ability to (a) resist urges and (b) stop oneself from engaging in automatic behaviors.

Executive functioning involves the ability to (a) engage in activities necessary for achieving objectives and (b) regulate one's actions based on environmental feedback.

TABLE 2 ■ LANGUAGE

Score name	Age range	Scaled score	PR	Classification	Measured abilities
Comprehension of Instructions Total	5–16	00	0.00	Borderline	Linguistic and syntactic knowledge; ability to follow multistep commands
Oromotor Sequences Total	5–12	--	--	Below expected level	Muscle movements of the mouth, jaw, tongue, lips, and cheeks for speech production
Phonological Processing Total	5–16	--	--	Well below expected level	Phonological awareness and processing
Repetition of Nonsense Words Total	5–12	--	--	At expected level	Phonological analysis and production of words; articulation of novel words
Speeded Naming Combined	5–16	--	--	At expected level	Automaticity of lexical analysis; processing speed; naming ability
Word Generation Semantic Total	5–16	--	--	At expected level	Executive control of language production; initiative; ideation

Note: Scaled score mean = 10, standard deviation = 3. Lower scores indicate greater neuropsychological impairment. Age range is for that particular score in years. PR, percentile rank. -- denotes not administered, or score type not available or computed.

Language is the ability to express and understand verbal communication effectively. This consists of (a) receptive speech involving the comprehension and decoding of speech and (b) expressive speech or language production.

(Cont.)

FORM 6.2

NEPSY–II, FORM AGES 5 TO 16, FULL BATTERY RESULTS AND INTERPRETATION TABLES (*Cont.*)

TABLE 3 ■ MEMORY AND LEARNING

Score name	Age range	Scaled score	PR	Classification	Measured abilities
List Memory Total[a]	7–12	00	0.00	Above expected level	Rote memory; supraspan learning skills for verbal material
Memory for Designs Total	5–16	--	--	At expected level	Visuospatial memory
Memory for Faces Total	5–16	--	--	Borderline	Visuospatial memory for human faces; face discrimination and recognition
Memory for Names Total	5–16	--	--	Below expected level	Learning and retrieval of verbal labels for visual material
Narrative Memory Total[b]	5–16	--	--	Well below expected level	Verbal expression and comprehension; verbal learning and memory
Sentence Repetition Total	5–6	--	--	At expected level	Verbal short-term memory
Word List Interference Recall Total	7–16	--	--	At expected level	Verbal working memory

Note: Scaled score mean = 10, standard deviation = 3. Lower scores indicate greater neuropsychological impairment. Age range is for that particular score in units of years. PR, percentile rank. -- denotes not administered, or score type not available or computed.

[a]Includes immediate and delayed (i.e., 25–35 minutes) memory.

[b]Includes free recall (i.e., no hints given) and cued recall (i.e., hints given).

Memory and *learning* include the ability to acquire, retain, and access new information. Learning includes the ability to acquire new information. Memory involves retaining and retrieving information. *Working memory* involves holding immediate memory traces, while executing cognitive tasks.

TABLE 4 ■ SENSORIMOTOR

Score name	Age range	Scaled score	PR	Classification	Measured abilities
Fingertip Tapping Dominant Hand Combined	5–16	00	0.00	Above expected level	Fine-motor control and programming in dominant hand
Fingertip Tapping Nondominant Hand Combined	5–16	--	--	Above expected level	Fine-motor control and programming in nondominant hand
Imitating Hand Positions Total[a]	5–12	--	--	At expected level	Fine-motor programming and differentiation; visuospatial skills
Manual Motor Sequences Total	5–12	--	--	Borderline	Manual motor programming
Visuomotor Precision Combined	5–12	--	--	Below expected level	Fine-motor coordination and speed

Note: Scaled score mean = 10, standard deviation = 3. Lower scores indicate greater neuropsychological impairment. Age range is for that particular score in units of years. PR, percentile rank. -- denotes not administered, or score type not available or computed.

[a]Includes both dominant and nondominant hands.

Sensorimotor abilities involve neural circuits, which integrate motor guidance with sensory (i.e., kinesthetic, tactile, visual) feedback.

(Cont.)

FORM 6.2

NEPSY–II, FORM AGES 5 TO 16, FULL BATTERY RESULTS AND INTERPRETATION TABLES (*Cont.*)

TABLE 5 ■ SOCIAL PERCEPTION

Score name	Age range	Scaled score	PR	Classification	Measured abilities
Affect Recognition Total	5–16	00	0.00	Well below expected level	Facial affect recognition
Theory of Mind Total	5–16	--	--	At expected level	Comprehension of others' perspectives, experiences, and beliefs; matching appropriate affect to contextual cues

Note: Scaled score mean = 10, standard deviation = 3. Lower scores indicate greater neuropsychological impairment. Age range is for that particular score in units of years. PR, percentile rank. -- denotes not administered, or score type not available or computed.

Social perception involves intellectual processes that facilitate social interaction.

TABLE 6 ■ VISUOSPATIAL PROCESSING

Score name	Age range	Scaled score	PR	Classification	Measured abilities
Arrows Total	5–16	00	0.00	Above expected level	Visuospatial skills in judging line orientation
Block Construction Total	5–16	--	--	At expected level	Visuoconstructional skills in three-dimensional tasks
Design Copying General Total	5–16	--	--	Borderline	Visuoconstructional skills in two-dimensional tasks
Geometric Puzzles Total	5–16	--	--	Below expected level	Visuospatial perception including mental rotation
Picture Puzzles Total	7–16	--	--	Well below expected level	Visual perception and scanning
Route Finding Total	5–12	--	--	At expected level	Visual-spatial relations and orientation

Note: Scaled score mean = 10, standard deviation = 3. Lower scores indicate greater neuropsychological impairment. Age range is for that particular score in units of years. PR, percentile rank. -- denotes not administered, or score type not available or computed.

Visuospatial processing is the capacity to understand the orientation of visual information in two- and three-dimensional space.

FORM 6.3

NEPSY–II, FORM AGES 3 TO 4, GENERAL BATTERY RESULTS AND INTERPRETATION TABLES

NEPSY–II, General Battery, Form Ages 3 to 4

TABLE 1 ■ **ATTENTION AND EXECUTIVE FUNCTIONING**

Score name	Scaled score	PR	Classification	Measured abilities
Statue total	00	0.00	At expected level	General inhibitory ability

Note: Scaled score mean = 10, standard deviation = 3. Lower scores indicate greater neuropsychological impairment. Age range is for that particular score in years. PR, percentile rank. -- denotes not administered, or score type not available or computed.

Attention is the ability to focus on specific activities and suppress irrelevant stimuli. This includes *inhibition,* which is the ability to (a) resist urges and (b) stop oneself from engaging in automatic behaviors.

Executive functioning involves the ability to (a) engage in activities necessary for achieving objectives and (b) regulate one's actions based on environmental feedback.

TABLE 2 ■ **LANGUAGE**

Score name	Scaled score	PR	Classification	Measured abilities
Comprehension of Instructions Total	--	--	Borderline	Linguistic and syntactic knowledge; ability to follow multistep commands
Speeded Naming Combined	--	--	At expected level	Automaticity of lexical analysis; processing speed; naming ability

Note: Scaled score mean = 10, standard deviation = 3. Lower scores indicate greater neuropsychological impairment. Age range is for that particular score in years. PR, percentile rank. -- denotes not administered, or score type not available or computed.

Language is the ability to express and understand verbal communication effectively. This consists of (a) receptive speech involving the comprehension and decoding of speech and (b) expressive speech or language production.

TABLE 3 ■ **MEMORY AND LEARNING**

Score name	Scaled score	PR	Classification	Measured abilities
Narrative Memory Total[a]	--	--	Well below expected level	Verbal expression and comprehension; verbal learning and memory

Note: Scaled score mean = 10, standard deviation = 3. Lower scores indicate greater neuropsychological impairment. Age range is for that particular score in years. PR, percentile rank. -- denotes not administered, or score type not available or computed.

[a]Includes free recall (i.e., no hints given) and cued recall (i.e., hints given).

Memory and *learning* include the ability to acquire, retain, and access new information. Learning includes the ability to acquire new information. Memory involves retaining and retrieving information.

TABLE 4 ■ **SENSORIMOTOR**

Score name	Scaled score	PR	Classification	Measured abilities
Visuomotor Precision Combined	--	--	Below expected level	Fine-motor coordination and speed

Note: Scaled score mean = 10, standard deviation = 3. Lower scores indicate greater neuropsychological impairment. Age range is for that particular score in years. PR, percentile rank. -- denotes not administered, or score type not available or computed.

[a]Includes both dominant and nondominant hands.

Sensorimotor abilities involve neural circuits, which integrate motor guidance with sensory (i.e., kinesthetic, tactile, visual) feedback.

(Cont.)

FORM 6.3

NEPSY–II, FORM AGES 3 TO 4, GENERAL BATTERY RESULTS AND INTERPRETATION TABLES (*Cont.*)

TABLE 5 ■ **VISUOSPATIAL PROCESSING**

Score name	Scaled score	PR	Classification	Measured abilities
Design Copying General Total	--	--	Borderline	Visuoconstructional skills in two-dimensional tasks
Geometric Puzzles Total	--	--	Below expected level	Visuospatial perception including mental rotation

Note: Scaled score mean = 10, standard deviation = 3. Lower scores indicate greater neuropsychological impairment. Age range is for that particular score in years. PR, percentile rank. -- denotes not administered, or score type not available or computed.

Visuospatial processing is the capacity to understand the orientation of visual information in two- and three-dimensional space.

FORM 6.4

NEPSY–II, FORM AGES 5 TO 16, GENERAL BATTERY RESULTS AND INTERPRETATION TABLES

NEPSY–II, General Battery, Form Ages 5 to 16

TABLE 1 ■ **ATTENTION AND EXECUTIVE FUNCTIONING**

Score name	Age range	Scaled score	PR	Classification	Measured abilities
Auditory Attention Combined	5–16	--	--	At expected level	Selective and sustained attention; response speed; inhibitory control
Response Set Combined	5–16	--	--	Borderline	Selective and sustained attention; inhibitory control; working memory; response speed
Inhibition–Inhibition Combined	5–16	--	--	At expected level	Inhibitory control
Inhibition–Switching Combined	7–16	--	--	At expected level	Inhibitory control; cognitive flexibility
Statue Total	5–6	--	--	At expected level	General inhibitory ability

Note: Scaled score mean = 10, standard deviation = 3. Lower scores indicate greater neuropsychological impairment. Age range is for that particular score in years. PR, percentile rank. -- denotes not administered, or score type not available or computed.

Attention is the ability to focus on specific activities and suppress irrelevant stimuli. This includes *inhibition,* which is the ability to (a) resist urges and (b) stop oneself from engaging in automatic behaviors.

Executive functioning involves the ability to (a) engage in activities necessary for achieving objectives and (b) regulate one's actions based on environmental feedback.

TABLE 2 ■ **LANGUAGE**

Score name	Age range	Scaled score	PR	Classification	Measured abilities
Comprehension of Instructions Total	5–16	00	0.00	Borderline	Linguistic and syntactic knowledge; ability to follow multistep commands
Speeded Naming Combined	5–16	--	--	At expected level	Automaticity of lexical analysis; processing speed; naming ability

Note: Scaled score mean = 10, standard deviation = 3. Lower scores indicate greater neuropsychological impairment. Age range is for that particular score in years. PR, percentile rank. -- denotes not administered, or score type not available or computed.

Language is the ability to express and understand verbal communication effectively. This consists of (a) receptive speech involving the comprehension and decoding of speech and (b) expressive speech or language production.

(Cont.)

FORM 6.4

NEPSY–II, FORM AGES 5 TO 16, GENERAL BATTERY RESULTS AND INTERPRETATION TABLES (*Cont.*)

TABLE 3 ■ MEMORY AND LEARNING

Score name	Age range	Scaled score	PR	Classification	Measured abilities
Memory for Faces Total[a]	5–16	--	--	Borderline	Visuospatial memory for human faces; face discrimination and recognition
Memory for Faces Delayed Total[b]	5–16	--	--	Below expected level	Learning and retrieval of verbal labels for visual material
Narrative Memory Total[c]	5–16	--	--	Well below expected level	Verbal expression and comprehension; verbal learning and memory
Word List Interference Recall Total	7–16	--	--	At expected level	Verbal working memory

Note: Scaled score mean = 10, standard deviation = 3. Lower scores indicate greater neuropsychological impairment. Age range is for that particular score in units of years. PR, percentile rank. -- denotes not administered, or score type not available or computed.

[a]Includes immediate recognition memory.

[b]Includes recognition memory after a 15 to 25 minute delay.

[c]Includes free recall (i.e., no hints given) and cued recall (i.e., hints given).

Memory and *learning* include the ability to acquire, retain, and access new information. Learning includes the ability to acquire new information. Memory involves retaining and retrieving information. *Working memory* involves holding immediate memory traces, while executing cognitive tasks.

TABLE 4 ■ SENSORIMOTOR

Score name	Age range	Scaled score	PR	Classification	Measured abilities
Visuomotor Precision Combined	5–12	--	--	Below expected level	Fine-motor coordination and speed

Note: Scaled score mean = 10, standard deviation = 3. Lower scores indicate greater neuropsychological impairment. Age range is for that particular score in units of years. PR, percentile rank. -- denotes not administered, or score type not available or computed.

Sensorimotor abilities involve neural circuits, which integrate motor guidance with sensory (i.e., kinesthetic, tactile, visual) feedback.

TABLE 5 ■ VISUOSPATIAL PROCESSING

Score name	Age range	Scaled score	PR	Classification	Measured abilities
Design Copying General Total	5–16	--	--	Borderline	Visuoconstructional skills in two-dimensional tasks
Geometric Puzzles Total	5–16	--	--	Below expected level	Visuospatial perception including mental rotation

Note: Scaled score mean = 10, standard deviation = 3. Lower scores indicate greater neuropsychological impairment. Age range is for that particular score in units of years. PR, percentile rank. -- denotes not administered, or score type not available or computed.

Visuospatial processing is the capacity to understand the orientation of visual information in two- and three-dimensional space.

FORM 6.5

NAB FULL BATTERY RESULTS AND INTERPRETATION TABLES

NAB, Form 1

TABLE 1 ■ **NAB MODULE INDEX SCORE SUMMARY**

Module index	Index score	PR	90% CI	Interpretive category	Measured abilities
Attention	--	--	[00, 00]	Average Below average	Working memory[a]; selective, divided, and sustained attention; attention to detail; information processing speed
Language	--	--	[00, 00]	Mildly-to-moderately impaired	Language production and comprehension; word finding; graphomotor skills
Memory[b]	--	--	[00, 00]	Moderately impaired	Verbal explicit learning[c] and visual learning; verbal and visual free recall memory[d]; and recognition memory[e]
Spatial	--	--	[00, 00]	Moderately-to-severely impaired	Attention to visual detail; visual–motor construction; right–left orientation; topographical orientation; visual scanning
Executive Functions[f]	--	--	[00, 00]	Severely impaired	Planning; foresight; judgment; concept formation; mental flexibility; self-monitoring; verbal fluency and generativity
Total NAB	**000**	**0.00**	**[000, 000]**	**Very superior**	**Overall neuropsychological functioning; omnibus measure of attention, language, memory, spatial, and executive functions**

Note: Index score mean = 100, standard deviation = 15. Index scores are derived by use of demographically corrected norms based on chronological age, educational attainment, and sex. Lower index scores indicate greater neuropsychological impairment. PR, percentile rank; CI, confidence interval. -- denotes not administered, or score type not available or computed. General neuropsychological functioning data are in boldface.

[a]Working memory is the ability to hold immediate memory traces, while executing cognitive tasks.

[b]Includes immediate and delayed (i.e., 6–15 minutes) memory.

[c]Includes the learning of discrete pieces of information and logically organized information.

[d]Examined by open-ended questions with no hints given.

[e]Examined by forced-choice item format (i.e., multiple-choice; yes/no).

[f]Ability to engage in activities necessary for achieving objectives and for regulating one's actions based upon environmental feedback.

(Cont.)

FORM 6.5

NAB FULL BATTERY RESULTS AND INTERPRETATION TABLES (Cont.)

TABLE 2 ■ **NAB DAILY LIVING SKILLS SCORE SUMMARY**

Subtest	T-score	PR	Interpretive category	Measured daily living skills
Driving Scenes	00	0.00	Average Below average	Attention to modifications in a two-lane road within the context of a small business town, viewed from behind the steering wheel of a car
Bill Payment	--	--	Mildly-to-moderately impaired	Understanding a household utility billing statement; writing a blank check; entering a check ledger; addressing a payment envelope
Memory—Immediate Recall[a]	--	--	Above average	Immediate recall of medication instructions; immediate recall of a person's name, address, and phone number
Memory—Delayed Recall[b]	--	--	Moderately impaired	Delayed recall of medication instructions; delayed recall of a person's name, address, and phone number
Map Reading	--	--	Moderately-to-severely impaired	Ability to follow verbal directions from start points to specified destinations using a street map, including a directional compass and legend in miles
Judgment	--	--	Severely impaired	Knowledge of, and decisional capacity within, important aspects of home safety and health/medical issues

Note: T-score mean = 50, standard deviation = 10. Lower T-scores indicate greater neuropsychological impairment. T-scores are derived by use of demographically corrected norms based on chronological age, educational attainment, and sex. PR, percentile rank. -- denotes not administered, or score type not available or computed.

[a]Memory examined using open-ended questions with no hints given.

[b]Duration of delay is approximately 6 to 7 minutes.

FORM 6.6

NASB SCREENING BATTERY RESULTS AND INTERPRETATION TABLES

NASB, Form 1

TABLE 1 ■ **NASB SCREENING DOMAIN SCORE SUMMARY**

Screening domain score	Standard score*	PR	90% CI	Interpretive category	Measured abilities
Screening Attention Domain	--	--	[00, 00]	Average Below average	Marker of attentional capacity; working memory;[a] psychomotor speed; selective attention; information processing speed
Screening Language Domain	--	--	[00, 00]	Mildly-to-moderately impaired	Marker of auditory comprehension; confrontation naming (possible aphasia)
Screening Memory Domain[b]	--	--	[00, 00]	Not yet determined	Marker of verbal explicit learning[c] and visual learning; verbal and visual free recall memory,[d] recognition memory[e]
Screening Spatial Domain	--	--	[00, 00]	Moderately-to-severely impaired	Marker of visuoperception; attention to visual detail; visuoconstruction
Screening Executive Functions Domain[f]	--	--	[00, 00]	Severely impaired	Marker of planning; verbal fluency; verbal generativity
Total Screening Index	**000**	**0.00**	**[000, 000]**	**Very superior**	**Screening of overall neuropsychological functioning**

Note: Standard score mean = 100, standard deviation = 15. Lower standard scores indicate greater likelihood of neuropsychological impairment. *denotes that administration of the complete NAB module is necessitated for reliable and valid interpretation of functioning within that domain. PR, percentile rank; CI, confidence interval. -- denotes not administered, or score type not available or computed. Overall neuropsychological screening data are in boldface.

[a]Working memory is the ability to hold immediate memory traces while executing cognitive tasks.

[b]Includes immediate and delayed (i.e., 6–15 minutes) memory.

[c]Includes learning discrete pieces of information and logically organized information.

[d]Examined by open-ended questions with no hints given.

[e]Examined by forced-choice item format (i.e., multiple-choice; yes/no).

[f]Ability to engage in activities necessary for achieving objectives and for regulating one's actions based upon environmental feedback.

TABLE 2 ■ **RECOMMENDATIONS FOR ADMINISTERING COMPLETE NAB MODULE**

Screening domain score	Administer complete NAB module?	Rationale
Screening Attention Domain	Negative Affirmative	Significant No evidence of impairment; further testing unlikely to provide additional diagnostic information. Further testing needed for differential diagnosis.
Screening Language Domain	Negative Affirmative	Significant No evidence of impairment; further testing unlikely to provide additional diagnostic information. Further testing needed for differential diagnosis.
Screening Memory Domain	Negative Affirmative	Significant No evidence of impairment; further testing unlikely to provide additional diagnostic information. Further testing needed for differential diagnosis.
Screening Spatial Domain	Negative Affirmative	Significant No evidence of impairment; further testing unlikely to provide additional diagnostic information. Further testing needed for differential diagnosis.
Screening Executive Functions Domain	Negative Affirmative	Significant No evidence of impairment; further testing unlikely to provide additional diagnostic information. Further testing needed for differential diagnosis.

Note: NAB, Neuropsychological Assessment Battery.

(Cont.)

FORM 6.6

NASB SCREENING BATTERY RESULTS AND INTERPRETATION TABLES (*Cont.*)

NAB, ##, and ## Modules, Form 1

TABLE 3 ■ NAB MODULE INDEX SCORE SUMMARY

Module index	Index score	PR	90% CI	Interpretive category	Measured abilities
Attention	--	--	[00, 00]	Average Below average	Working memory;[a] selective, divided, and sustained attention; attention to detail; information processing speed
Language	--	--	[00, 00]	Mildly-to-moderately impaired	Language production and comprehension; word finding
Memory[b]	--	--	[00, 00]	Moderately impaired	Verbal explicit learning[c] and visual learning; verbal and visual free recall memory;[d] and recognition memory[e]
Spatial	--	--	[00, 00]	Moderately-to-severely impaired	Attention to visual detail; visuoconstruction; right–left orientation; topographical orientation; visual scanning
Executive Functions[f]	--	--	[00, 00]	Severely impaired	Planning; judgment; conceptualization; cognitive response set; mental flexibility; verbal fluency and generativity
Total NAB	**000**	**0.00**	**[000, 000]**	**Very superior**	**General neuropsychological functioning; omnibus measure of attention, language, memory, spatial, and executive functions**

Note: Index score mean = 100, standard deviation = 15. Index scores are derived by use of demographically corrected norms based on chronological age, educational attainment, and sex. Lower index scores indicate greater neuropsychological impairment. PR, percentile rank; CI, confidence interval. -- denotes not administered, or score type not available or computed. General neuropsychological functioning data are in boldface.

[a]Working memory is the ability to hold immediate memory traces while executing cognitive tasks.

[b]Includes immediate and delayed (i.e., 6–15 minutes) memory.

[c]Includes the learning of discrete pieces of information and logically organized information.

[d]Examined by open-ended questions with no hints given.

[e]Examined by forced-choice item format (i.e., multiple-choice; yes/no).

[f]Ability to engage in activities necessary for achieving objectives and for regulating one's actions based upon environmental feedback.

FORM 6.7

NAB ATTENTION MODULE RESULTS AND INTERPRETATION TABLES

NAB, Attention Module, Form 2

TABLE 1 ■ **NAB ATTENTION MODULE INDEX SCORE**

Module index	Index score	PR	90% CI	Interpretive category	Measured abilities
Attention	--	--	[00, 00]	Average Below average	Working memory;[a] selective, divided, and sustained attention; attention to detail; information processing speed

Note: Index score mean = 100, standard deviation = 15. Index scores are derived by use of demographically corrected norms based on chronological age, educational attainment, and sex. Lower index scores indicate greater neuropsychological impairment. PR, percentile rank; CI, confidence interval. -- denotes not administered, or score type not available or computed.

[a]Working memory is the ability to hold immediate memory traces while executing cognitive tasks.

TABLE 2 ■ **NAB ATTENTION MODULE SUBTEST SCORE SUMMARY**

Subtest	T-score	PR	Interpretive category	Measured abilities
Digits Forward	00	0.00	Average Below average	Auditory attentional capacity
Digits Backward	--	--	Mildly-to-moderately impaired	Working memory[a] for orally presented information
Dots	--	--	Above average	Visuospatial working memory; visual scanning
Numbers and Letters Part A Speed	--	--	Moderately-to-severely impaired	Psychomotor and information processing speed
Numbers and Letters Part A Errors	--	--	Severely impaired	Sustained, focused, divided, and selective attention; concentration
Numbers and Letters Part A Efficiency	--	--	Severely impaired	Sustained, focused, divided, and selective attention; concentration; psychomotor and information processing speed
Numbers and Letters Part B Efficiency	--	--	Severely impaired	Sustained, focused, divided, and selective attention; concentration; psychomotor and information processing speed
Numbers and Letters Part C Efficiency	--	--	Severely impaired	Sustained, focused, divided, and selective attention; concentration; psychomotor and information processing speed
Numbers and Letters Part D Efficiency	--	--	Severely impaired	Sustained, focused, divided, and selective attention; concentration; psychomotor and information processing speed
Numbers and Letters Part D Disruption	--	--	Severely impaired	Sustained, focused, divided, and selective attention; concentration; psychomotor and information processing speed
Driving Scenes	--	--	Average Below average	Attention to modifications in a two-lane road within the context of a small business town, viewed from behind a car's steering wheel

Note: T-score mean = 50, standard deviation = 10. Lower T-scores indicate greater impairment. T-scores are derived by use of demographically corrected norms based on chronological age, educational attainment, and sex. PR, percentile rank. -- denotes not administered, or score type not available or computed.

[a]Working memory involves holding immediate memory traces, while executing cognitive tasks.

FORM 6.8

WMS–IV, FORM AGES 16 TO 69 RESULTS AND INTERPRETATION TABLES

WMS–IV, Form Ages 16 to 69

TABLE 1 ■ BRIEF COGNITIVE STATUS EXAM (BCSE)

Chronological age	Years of education	Raw score	Base rate[a]	Classification level[b]	Measured abilities
000 Years, 00 Months	00	000	0.0	Low average	Orientation to time; mental and inhibitory control; planning; visual-perceptual processing; incidental recall; verbal productivity

Note: Lower scores indicate greater cognitive impairment.

[a]Percentage of healthy normal controls who obtain the listed raw score.

[b]Adjusted for chronological age and educational level.

TABLE 2 ■ INDEX SCORE SUMMARY

Index	Index score	PR	90% CI	Qualitative description	Measured abilities
Auditory Memory Index (AMI)	000	00.0	[000, 000]	Very superior	Ability to remember orally presented information
Visual Memory Index (VMI)	--	--	[00, 00]	Superior	Ability to remember visually presented information
Immediate Memory Index (IMI)	--	--	[00, 00]	Average Borderline	Ability to remember both visually and orally presented information immediately after it is presented
Delayed Memory Index (DMI)	--	--	[00, 00]	Extremely low	Ability to remember both visually and orally presented information after a 20–30 minute delay

Note: Index score mean = 100, standard deviation = 15. Lower scores indicate greater memory impairment. PR, percentile rank; CI, confidence interval. -- denotes not administered, or score type not available or computed.

Memory involves (a) receiving information from the senses, (b) organizing and storing information, and (c) retrieving information from storage. The WMS–IV measures the ability to consciously learn and remember novel information that is bound by the testing situation (i.e., declarative episodic memory). *Immediate memory* refers to short-term or temporary storage (i.e., seconds), while *delayed memory* refers to long-term or more stable storage and retrieval (i.e., 20–30 minutes).

(Cont.)

FORM 6.8

WMS–IV, FORM AGES 16 TO 69 RESULTS AND INTERPRETATION TABLES (*Cont.*)

TABLE 3 ■ **AUDITORY MEMORY SUBTEST SCORE SUMMARY**

Subtest	Scaled score	PR	Qualitative description	Measured abilities
Logical Memory I (LM I)*	00	0.00	Very superior	Immediate free recall of conceptually organized and semantically related verbal information; immediate narrative memory
Logical Memory II (LM II)**	--	--	Superior High average	Delayed free recall and recognition of conceptually organized and semantically related verbal information; long-term narrative memory[a]
Verbal Paired Associates I (VPA I)*	--	--	Average Low average	Immediate cued recall of novel and semantically related word associations
Verbal Paired Associates II (VPA II)**	--	--	Borderline Extremely low	Delayed cued recall and recognition of novel and semantically related word associations[a]

Note: Scale score mean = 10, standard deviation = 3. Lower scores indicate greater memory impairment. PR, percentile rank. *denotes that this subtest also contributed to the Immediate Memory Index. **denotes that this subtest also contributed to the Delayed Memory Index. -- denotes not administered, or score type not available or computed.

[a]Duration of delay is 20 to 30 minutes.

TABLE 4 ■ **VISUAL MEMORY SUBTEST SCORE SUMMARY**

Subtest	Scaled score	PR	Qualitative description	Measured abilities
Designs I (DE I)*	00	0.00	Very superior	Immediate free recall of visual–spatial material; immediate spatial memory for novel visual material
Designs II (DE II)**	--	--	Superior High average	Delayed free recall and recognition of visual–spatial material; long-term spatial memory for novel visual material[a]
Visual Reproduction I (VR I)*	--	--	Average Low average	Ability to immediately recall and draw designs; immediate memory for nonverbal visual stimuli
Visual Reproduction II (VR II)**	--	--	Borderline Extremely low	Delayed ability to recall and draw designs; long-term memory for nonverbal visual stimuli[a]

Note: Scale score mean = 10, standard deviation = 3. Lower scores indicate greater memory impairment. PR, percentile rank. *denotes that this subtest also contributed to the Immediate Memory Index. **denotes that this subtest also contributed to the Delayed Memory Index. -- denotes not administered, or score type not available or computed.

[a]Duration of delay is 20 to 30 minutes.

TABLE 5 ■ **VISUAL WORKING MEMORYA SUBTEST SCORE SUMMARY**

Subtest	Scaled score	PR	Qualitative description	Measured abilities
Spatial Addition (SA)	00	0.00	Superior High average Average	Visual–spatial working memory[a] requiring storage (visual sketchpad), manipulation and ability to ignore competing stimuli (central executive)
Symbol Span (SSP)	--	--	Low average Borderline Extremely low	Visual working memory using novel visual stimuli; ability to retain (a) a mental image of a design and (b) the relative spatial position of the design on the page

Note: Scale score mean = 10, standard deviation = 3. Lower scores indicate greater memory impairment. PR, percentile rank. -- denotes not administered, or score type not available or computed.

[a]Working memory involves holding immediate memory traces while executing cognitive tasks.

FORM 6.9

WMS–IV, FORM AGES 65 TO 90 RESULTS AND INTERPRETATION TABLES

WMS–IV, Form Ages 16 to 69

TABLE 1 ■ BRIEF COGNITIVE STATUS EXAM (BCSE)

Chronological age	Years of education	Raw score	Base rate[a]	Classification level[b]	Measured abilities
000 Years, 00 Months	00	000	0.0	Low average	Orientation to time; mental and inhibitory control; planning; visual-perceptual processing; incidental recall; verbal productivity

Note: Lower scores indicate greater cognitive impairment.

[a]Percentage of healthy normal controls who obtain the listed raw score.

[b]Adjusted for chronological age and educational level.

TABLE 2 ■ INDEX SCORE SUMMARY

Index	Index score	PR	90% CI	Qualitative description	Measured abilities
Auditory Memory Index (AMI)	000	00.0	[000, 000]	Very superior	Ability to remember orally presented information
Visual Memory Index (VMI)	--	--	[00, 00]	Superior	Ability to remember visually presented information
Immediate Memory Index (IMI)	--	--	[00, 00]	Average Borderline	Ability to remember both visually and orally presented information immediately after it is presented
Delayed Memory Index (DMI)	--	--	[00, 00]	Extremely low	Ability to remember both visually and orally presented information after a 20–30 minute delay

Note: Index score mean = 100, standard deviation = 15. Lower scores indicate greater memory impairment. PR, percentile rank; CI, confidence interval. -- denotes not administered, or score type not available or computed.

Memory involves (a) receiving information from the senses, (b) organizing and storing information, and (c) retrieving information from storage. The WMS–IV measures the ability to consciously learn and remember novel information that is bound by the testing situation (i.e., declarative episodic memory). Immediate memory refers to short-term or temporary storage (i.e., seconds), while delayed memory refers to long-term or more stable storage and retrieval (i.e., 20 to 30 minutes).

TABLE 3 ■ AUDITORY MEMORY SUBTEST SCORE SUMMARY

Subtest	Scaled score	PR	Qualitative description	Measured abilities
Logical Memory I (LM I)*	00	0.00	Very superior	Immediate free recall of conceptually organized and semantically related verbal information; immediate narrative memory
Logical Memory II (LM II)**	--	--	Superior High average	Delayed free recall and recognition of conceptually organized and semantically related verbal information; long-term narrative memory[a]
Verbal Paired Associates I (VPA I)*	--	--	Average Low average	Immediate cued recall of novel and semantically related word associations
Verbal Paired Associates II (VPA II)**	--	--	Borderline Extremely low	Delayed cued recall and recognition of novel and semantically related word associations[a]

Note: Scale score mean = 10, standard deviation = 3. Lower scores indicate greater memory impairment. PR, percentile rank. *denotes that this subtest also contributed to the Immediate Memory Index. **denotes that this subtest also contributed to the Delayed Memory Index. -- denotes not administered, or score type not available or computed.

[a]Duration of delay is 20 to 30 minutes.

(Cont.)

FORM 6.9

WMS–IV, FORM AGES 65 TO 90 RESULTS AND INTERPRETATION TABLES (*Cont.*)

TABLE 4 ■ **VISUAL MEMORY SUBTEST SCORE SUMMARY**

Subtest	Scaled score	PR	Qualitative description	Measured abilities
Visual Reproduction I (VR I)*	--	--	Superior Low average	Ability to immediately recall and draw designs; immediate memory for nonverbal visual stimuli
Visual Reproduction II (VR II)**	--	--	Borderline Extremely low	Delayed ability to recall and draw designs; long-term memory for nonverbal visual stimuli[a]

Note: Scale score mean = 10, standard deviation = 3. Lower scores indicate greater memory impairment. PR, percentile rank. *denotes that this subtest also contributed to the Immediate Memory Index. **denotes that this subtest also contributed to the Delayed Memory Index. -- denotes not administered, or score type not available or computed.

[a]Duration of delay is 20 to 30 minutes.

TABLE 5 ■ **VISUAL WORKING MEMORY[a] SUBTEST**

Subtest	Scaled score	PR	Qualitative description	Measured abilities
Symbol Span (SSP)	--	--	Low average Borderline Extremely low	Visual working memory[b] using novel visual stimuli; ability to retain (a) a mental image of a design, and (b) the relative spatial position of the design on the page

Note: Scale score mean = 10, standard deviation = 3. Lower scores indicate greater memory impairment. PR, percentile rank. -- denotes not administered, or score type not available or computed.

[a]The Visual Working Memory Index is not available on the ages 65 to 90 older adult battery.

[b]Working memory involves holding immediate memory traces while executing cognitive tasks.

FORM 6.10

WAIS–IV/WMS–IV, FORM AGES 16 TO 69 ABILITY–MEMORY DISCREPANCY ANALYSIS SIMPLE DIFFERENCE METHOD RESULTS AND INTERPRETATION TABLES

WAIS–IV

TABLE 1 ■ COMPOSITE SCORE SUMMARY

Index/scale	Composite score	PR	90% CI	Qualitative description	Measured abilities
Verbal Comprehension Index (VCI)	000	00	[00, 00]	Very superior	Verbal reasoning, comprehension, and conceptualization
Perceptual Reasoning Index (PRI)	--	--	[00, 00]	Superior	Visual–spatial (nonverbal) reasoning, organization, and conceptualization
General Ability Index (GAI)[a]	**--**	**--**	**[000, 000]**	**Extremely low**	**General intelligence: the ability to learn from experience, acquire knowledge, and use resources effectively in adapting to new situations or solving problems**[b]

Note: Composite score mean = 100, standard deviation = 15. Lower scores indicate greater intellectual impairment. PR, percentile rank; CI: confidence interval. -- denotes not administered, or score type not available or computed. General intellectual ability data are in boldface.

[a]The General Ability Index includes only the Verbal Comprehension and Perceptual Reasoning composite scores; it thus minimizes the effects of working memory and processing speed in the measurement of general intelligence.

[b]Ciccarelli, S. K., & White, J. N. (2012). *Psychology* (3rd ed.). Upper Saddle River, NJ: Pearson Education; Wechsler, D. (1975). *The collected papers of David Wechsler*. New York, NY: Academic Press.

TABLE 2 ■ VCI–PRI INDEX LEVEL DISCREPANCY COMPARISON

VCI composite score	PRI composite score	Difference	Critical value .05*	Cohen's *d* effect size[a]	Effect size results[b]	Base rate[c]
000	000	±00	0.00	0.0	Large Medium	00.0%

Note: *denotes that the VCI–PRI difference occurs by chance less than 5 times in 100 and is therefore statistically significant.

[a]Computed as the absolute value of VCI–PRI/standard deviation (15).

[b]Effect size score ranges: 0.0 to 0.2 (small effect); 0.3 to 0.7 (medium effect); 0.8 and higher (large effect).

[c]Percentage of the normative sample who obtained the listed VCI–PRI difference.

The VCI–PRI difference was not statistically significant, manifested a small effect size, and yielded an acceptably high base rate in the normative sample. Thus, the GAI was deemed an acceptable measure of general intelligence and was used in the ability–memory discrepancy analysis.

The VCI–PRI difference was statistically significant and favored the former/latter. The difference also yielded both a large effect size and remarkably low base rate in the normative sample. Thus, the GAI was deemed an unacceptable measure of general intelligence and was dropped from further analysis. The ensuing ability–memory discrepancy analysis was completed using the VCI for the following reasons: (a) to determine if any measured memory deficits exist beyond the impact of language ability, (b) evidence that the VCI is the least of the WAIS–IV indices to be deleteriously affected by brain trauma, and (c) evidence that the VCI tends to yield higher correlations with general intelligence as compared to other WAIS–IV indices. The ensuing ability–memory discrepancy analysis was completed using the higher PRI to maximize true positive results.

(Cont.)

FORM 6.10

WAIS–IV/WMS–IV, FORM AGES 16 TO 69 ABILITY–MEMORY DISCREPANCY ANALYSIS SIMPLE DIFFERENCE METHOD RESULTS AND INTERPRETATION TABLES (*Cont.*)

WMS–IV, Form Ages 16 to 69

TABLE 3 ■ **INDEX SCORE SUMMARY**

Index	Index score	PR	90% CI	Qualitative description	Measured abilities
Auditory Memory Index (AMI)	000	00.0	[000, 000]	Very superior	Ability to remember orally presented information
Visual Memory Index (VMI)	--	--	[00, 00]	Superior	Ability to remember visually presented information
Visual Working Memory Index (VWMI)	--	--	[00, 00]	High average	Ability to remember and manipulate visually presented information in short-term memory storage
Immediate Memory Index (IMI)	--	--	[00, 00]	Average Borderline	Ability to remember both visually and orally presented information immediately after it is presented
Delayed Memory Index (DMI)	--	--	[00, 00]	Extremely low	Ability to remember both visually and orally presented information after a 20–30 minute delay

Note: Index score mean = 100, standard deviation = 15. Lower scores indicate greater memory impairment. PR, percentile rank; CI, confidence interval. -- denotes not administered, or score type not available or computed.

Memory involves (a) receiving information from the senses, (b) organizing and storing information, and (c) retrieving information from storage. The WMS–IV measures the ability to consciously learn and remember novel information that is bound by the testing situation (i.e., declarative episodic memory). *Immediate memory* refers to short-term or temporary storage (i.e., seconds), while *delayed memory* refers to long-term or more stable storage and retrieval (i.e., 20–30 minutes).

TABLE 4 ■ **AUDITORY MEMORY SUBTEST SCORE SUMMARY**

Subtest	Scaled score	PR	Qualitative description	Measured abilities
Logical Memory I (LM I)*	00	0.00	Very superior	Immediate free recall of conceptually organized and semantically related verbal information; immediate narrative memory
Logical Memory II (LM II)**	--	--	Superior High average	Delayed free recall and recognition of conceptually organized and semantically related verbal information; long-term narrative memory[a]
Verbal Paired Associates I (VPA I)*	--	--	Average Low average	Immediate cued recall of novel and semantically related word associations
Verbal Paired Associates II (VPA II)**	--	--	Borderline Extremely low	Delayed cued recall and recognition of novel and semantically related word associations[a]

Note: Scale score mean = 10, standard deviation = 3. Lower scores indicate greater memory impairment. PR, percentile rank. *denotes that this subtest also contributed to the Immediate Memory Index. **denotes that this subtest also contributed to the Delayed Memory Index. -- denotes not administered, or score type not available or computed.

[a]Duration of delay is 20 to 30 minutes.

(*Cont.*)

FORM 6.10

WAIS–IV/WMS–IV, FORM AGES 16 TO 69 ABILITY–MEMORY DISCREPANCY ANALYSIS SIMPLE DIFFERENCE METHOD RESULTS AND INTERPRETATION TABLES (*Cont.*)

TABLE 5 ■ VISUAL MEMORY SUBTEST SCORE SUMMARY

Subtest	Scaled score	PR	Qualitative description	Measured abilities
Designs I (DE I)*	00	0.00	Very superior	Immediate free recall of visual–spatial material; immediate spatial memory for novel visual material
Designs II (DE II)**	--	--	Superior High average	Delayed free recall and recognition of visual–spatial material; long-term spatial memory for novel visual material[a]
Visual Reproduction I (VR I)*	--	--	Average Low average	Ability to immediately recall and draw designs; immediate memory for nonverbal visual stimuli
Visual Reproduction II (VR II)**	--	--	Borderline Extremely low	Delayed ability to recall and draw designs; long-term memory for nonverbal visual stimuli[a]

Note: Scale score mean = 10, standard deviation = 3. Lower scores indicate greater memory impairment. PR, percentile rank. *denotes that this subtest also contributed to the Immediate Memory Index. **denotes that this subtest also contributed to the Delayed Memory Index. -- denotes not administered, or score type not available or computed.

[a]Duration of delay is 20 to 30 minutes.

TABLE 6 ■ VISUAL WORKING MEMORY SUBTEST SCORE SUMMARY

Subtest	Scaled score	PR	Qualitative description	Measured abilities
Spatial Addition (SA)	00	0.00	Superior High average Average	Visual–spatial working memory[a] requiring storage (visual sketchpad), manipulation, and ability to ignore competing stimuli (central executive)
Symbol Span (SSP)	--	--	Low average Borderline Extremely low	Visual working memory[a] using novel visual stimuli; ability to retain (a) a mental image of a design and (b) the relative spatial position of the design on the page

Note: Scale score mean = 10, standard deviation = 3. Lower scores indicate greater memory impairment. PR, percentile rank. -- denotes not administered, or score type not available or computed.

[a]Working memory involves holding immediate memory traces while executing cognitive tasks.

(*Cont.*)

FORM 6.10

WAIS–IV/WMS–IV, FORM AGES 16 TO 69 ABILITY–MEMORY DISCREPANCY ANALYSIS SIMPLE DIFFERENCE METHOD RESULTS AND INTERPRETATION TABLES (*Cont.*)

ABILITY–MEMORY DISCREPANCY ANALYSIS

ABILITY SCORE TYPE: WAIS–IV GENERAL ABILITY INDEX (GAI)

ABILITY SCORE: **000**

TABLE 7 ■ **SIMPLE DIFFERENCE METHOD**[a]

Index	WMS–IV index score	WAIS–IV GAI	Difference	Critical value .05*	Base rate[b]
Auditory Memory Index (AMI)	000	000	00	0.00	00.0%
Visual Memory Index (VMI)	000	000	00	N/A	N/A
Visual Working Memory Index (VWMI)	000	000	00	0.00	00.0%
Immediate Memory Index (IMI)	000	000	00	0.00	00.0%
Delayed Memory Index (DMI)	000	000	00	0.00	00.0%

Note: *denotes that the WMS–IV index score – WAIS–IV GAI difference occurs by chance less than five times in 100 and is therefore statistically significant. N/A, not applicable; the WMS–IV index score was equal to or exceeded the WAIS–IV GAI.

[a]The differences are obtained by subtracting each selected WAIS–IV composite score from the WMS–IV index score.

[b]Percentage of the healthy normative sample who obtained the listed WMS–IV index score – WAIS–IV GAI score difference.

FORM 6.11

WAIS–IV/WMS–IV, FORM AGES 65 TO 90 ABILITY–MEMORY DISCREPANCY ANALYSIS SIMPLE DIFFERENCE METHOD RESULTS AND INTERPRETATION TABLES

WAIS–IV

TABLE 1 ■ COMPOSITE SCORE SUMMARY

Index/Scale	Composite score	PR	90% CI	Qualitative description	Measured abilities
Verbal Comprehension Index (VCI)	000	00	[00, 00]	Very superior	Verbal reasoning, comprehension, and conceptualization
Perceptual Reasoning Index (PRI)	--	--	[00, 00]	Superior	Visual–spatial (nonverbal) reasoning, organization, and conceptualization
General Ability Index (GAI)[a]	--	--	**[000, 000]**	**Extremely low**	**General intelligence: the ability to learn from experience, acquire knowledge, and use resources effectively in adapting to new situations or solving problems**[b]

Note: Composite score mean = 100, standard deviation = 15. Lower scores indicate greater intellectual impairment. PR, percentile rank; CI: confidence interval. -- denotes not administered, or score type not available or computed. General intellectual ability data are in boldface.

[a]The General Ability Index includes only the Verbal Comprehension and Perceptual Reasoning composite scores; it thus minimizes the effects of working memory and processing speed in the measurement of general intelligence.

[b]Ciccarelli, S. K., & White, J. N. (2012). *Psychology* (3rd ed.). Upper Saddle River, NJ: Pearson Education; Wechsler, D. (1975). *The collected papers of David Wechsler.* New York, NY: Academic Press.

TABLE 2 ■ VCI–PRI INDEX LEVEL DISCREPANCY COMPARISON

VCI composite score	PRI composite score	Difference	Critical value .05*	Cohen's d effect size[a]	Effect size results[b]	Base rate[c]
000	000	±00	0.00	0.0	Large Medium	00.0%

Note: *denotes that the VCI–PRI difference occurs by chance less than five times in 100 and is therefore statistically significant.

[a]Computed as the absolute value of VCI–PRI/standard deviation (15).

[b]Effect size score ranges: 0.0 to 0.2 (small effect); 0.3 to 0.7 (medium effect); 0.8 and higher (large effect).

[c]Percentage of the normative sample who obtained the listed VCI–PRI difference.

The VCI–PRI difference was not statistically significant, manifested a small effect size, and yielded an acceptably high base rate in the normative sample. Thus, the GAI was deemed an acceptable measure of general intelligence and was used in the ability–memory discrepancy analysis.

The VCI–PRI difference was statistically significant and favored the former/latter. The difference also yielded both a large effect size and remarkably low base rate in the normative sample. Thus, the GAI was deemed an unacceptable measure of general intelligence and was dropped from further analysis. The ensuing ability–memory discrepancy analysis was completed using the VCI for the following reasons: (a) to determine if any measured memory deficits exist beyond the impact of language ability, (b) evidence that the VCI is the least of the WAIS–IV indices to be deleteriously affected by brain trauma, and (c) evidence that the VCI tends to yield higher correlations with general intelligence as compared to other WAIS–IV indices. The ensuing ability–memory discrepancy analysis was completed using the higher PRI to maximize true positive results.

(Cont.)

FORM 6.11

WAIS–IV/WMS–IV, FORM AGES 65 TO 90 ABILITY–MEMORY DISCREPANCY ANALYSIS SIMPLE DIFFERENCE METHOD RESULTS AND INTERPRETATION TABLES (*Cont.*)

WMS–IV, Form Ages 65 to 90

TABLE 3 ■ **INDEX SCORE SUMMARY**

Index	Index score	PR	90% CI	Qualitative description	Measured abilities
Auditory Memory Index (AMI)	000	00.0	[000, 000]	Very superior	Ability to remember orally presented information
Visual Memory Index (VMI)	--	--	[00, 00]	Superior	Ability to remember visually presented information
Immediate Memory Index (IMI)	--	--	[00, 00]	Average Borderline	Ability to remember both visually and orally presented information immediately after it is presented
Delayed Memory Index (DMI)	--	--	[00, 00]	Extremely low	Ability to remember both visually and orally presented information after a 20–30 minute delay

Note: Index score mean = 100, standard deviation = 15. Lower scores indicate greater memory impairment. PR, percentile rank; CI, confidence interval. -- denotes not administered, or score type not available or computed.

Memory involves (a) receiving information from the senses, (b) organizing and storing information, and (c) retrieving information from storage. The WMS–IV measures the ability to consciously learn and remember novel information that is bound by the testing situation (i.e., declarative episodic memory). *Immediate memory* refers to short-term or temporary storage (i.e., seconds), while *delayed memory* refers to long-term or more stable storage and retrieval (i.e., 20–30 minutes).

TABLE 4 ■ **AUDITORY MEMORY SUBTEST SCORE SUMMARY**

Subtest	Scaled score	PR	Qualitative description	Measured abilities
Logical Memory I (LM I)*	00	0.00	Very superior	Immediate free recall of conceptually organized and semantically related verbal information; immediate narrative memory
Logical Memory II (LM II)**	--	--	Superior High average	Delayed free recall and recognition of conceptually organized and semantically related verbal information; long-term narrative memory[a]
Verbal Paired Associates I (VPA I)*	--	--	Average Low average	Immediate cued recall of novel and semantically related word associations
Verbal Paired Associates II (VPA II)**	--	--	Borderline Extremely low	Delayed cued recall and recognition of novel and semantically related word associations[a]

Note: Scale score mean = 10, standard deviation = 3. Lower scores indicate greater memory impairment. PR, percentile rank. *denotes that this subtest also contributed to the Immediate Memory Index. **denotes that this subtest also contributed to the Delayed Memory Index. -- denotes not administered, or score type not available or computed.

[a]Duration of delay is 20 to 30 minutes.

(Cont.)

FORM 6.11

WAIS–IV/WMS–IV, FORM AGES 65 TO 90 ABILITY–MEMORY DISCREPANCY ANALYSIS SIMPLE DIFFERENCE METHOD RESULTS AND INTERPRETATION TABLES (*Cont.*)

TABLE 5 ■ VISUAL MEMORY SUBTEST SCORE SUMMARY

Subtest	Scaled score	PR	Qualitative description	Measured abilities
Visual Reproduction I (VR I)*	--	--	Superior Low average	Ability to immediately recall and draw designs; immediate memory for nonverbal visual stimuli
Visual Reproduction II (VR II)**	--	--	Borderline Extremely low	Delayed ability to recall and draw designs; long-term memory for nonverbal visual stimuli[a]

Note: Scale score mean = 10, standard deviation = 3. Lower scores indicate greater memory impairment. PR, percentile rank. *denotes that this subtest also contributed to the Immediate Memory Index. **denotes that this subtest also contributed to the Delayed Memory Index. -- denotes not administered, or score type not available or computed.

[a]Duration of delay is 20 to 30 minutes.

TABLE 6 ■ VISUAL WORKING MEMORY[a] SUBTEST

Subtest	Scaled score	PR	Qualitative description	Measured abilities
Symbol Span (SSP)	--	--	Low average Borderline Extremely low	Visual working memory[b] using novel visual stimuli; ability to retain (a) a mental image of a design and (b) the relative spatial position of the design on the page

Note: Scale score mean = 10, standard deviation = 3. Lower scores indicate greater memory impairment. PR, percentile rank. -- denotes not administered, or score type not available or computed.

[a]The Visual Working Memory Index is not available on the ages 65 to 90 older adult battery.

[b]Working memory involves holding immediate memory traces while executing cognitive tasks.

ABILITY–MEMORY DISCREPANCY ANALYSIS

ABILITY SCORE TYPE: WAIS–IV GENERAL ABILITY INDEX (GAI)

ABILITY SCORE: 000

TABLE 7 ■ SIMPLE DIFFERENCE METHOD[a]

Index	WMS–IV index score	WAIS–IV GAI	Difference	Critical value .05*	Base rate[b]
Auditory Memory Index (AMI)	000	000	00	0.00	00.0%
Visual Memory Index (VMI)	000	000	00	N/A	N/A
Immediate Memory Index (IMI)	000	000	00	0.00	00.0%
Delayed Memory Index (DMI)	000	000	00	0.00	00.0%

Note: *denotes that the WMS–IV index score – WAIS–IV GAI difference occurs by chance less than five times in 100 and is therefore statistically significant. N/A, not applicable; the WMS–IV index score was equal to or exceeded the WAIS–IV GAI.

[a]The differences are obtained by subtracting each selected WAIS–IV composite score from the WMS–IV index score.

[b]Percentage of the healthy normative sample who obtained the listed WMS–IV index score – WAIS–IV GAI score difference.

FORM 6.12

WAIS–IV/WMS–IV, FORM AGES 16 TO 69 ABILITY–MEMORY DISCREPANCY ANALYSIS PREDICTED DIFFERENCE METHOD RESULTS AND INTERPRETATION TABLES

WAIS–IV

TABLE 1 ■ COMPOSITE SCORE SUMMARY

Index/Scale	Composite score	PR	90% CI	Qualitative description	Measured abilities
Verbal Comprehension Index (VCI)	000	00	[00, 00]	Very superior	Verbal reasoning, comprehension, and conceptualization
Perceptual Reasoning Index (PRI)	--	--	[00, 00]	Superior	Visual–spatial (nonverbal) reasoning, organization, and conceptualization
General Ability Index (GAI)[a]	**--**	**--**	**[000, 000]**	**Extremely low**	**General intelligence: the ability to learn from experience, acquire knowledge, and use resources effectively in adapting to new situations or solving problems**[b]

Note: Composite score mean = 100, standard deviation = 15. Lower scores indicate greater intellectual impairment. PR, percentile rank; CI, confidence interval. -- denotes not administered, or score type not available or computed. General intellectual ability data are in boldface.

[a]The General Ability Index includes only the Verbal Comprehension and Perceptual Reasoning composite scores; it thus minimizes the effects of working memory and processing speed in the measurement of general intelligence.

[b]Ciccarelli, S. K., & White, J. N. (2012). *Psychology* (3rd ed.). Upper Saddle River, NJ: Pearson Education; Wechsler, D. (1975). *The collected papers of David Wechsler*. New York, NY: Academic Press.

TABLE 2 ■ VCI–PRI INDEX LEVEL DISCREPANCY COMPARISON

VCI composite score	PRI composite score	Difference	Critical value .05*	Cohen's *d* effect size[a]	Effect size results[b]	Base rate[c]
000	000	±00	0.00	0.0	Large Medium	00.0%

Note: *denotes that the VCI–PRI difference occurs by chance less than five times in 100 and is therefore statistically significant.

[a]Computed as the absolute value of VCI–PRI/standard deviation (15).

[b]Effect size score ranges: 0.0 to 0.2 (small effect); 0.3 to 0.7 (medium effect); 0.8 and higher (large effect).

[c]Percentage of the normative sample who obtained the listed VCI–PRI difference.

The VCI–PRI difference was not statistically significant, manifested a small effect size, and yielded an acceptably high base rate in the normative sample. Thus, the GAI was deemed an acceptable measure of general intelligence and was used in the ability–memory discrepancy analysis.

The VCI–PRI difference was statistically significant and favored the former/latter. The difference also yielded both a large effect size and remarkably low base rate in the normative sample. Thus, the GAI was deemed an unacceptable measure of general intelligence and was dropped from further analysis. The ensuing ability–memory discrepancy analysis was completed using the VCI for the following reasons: (a) to determine if any measured memory deficits exist beyond the impact of language ability, (b) evidence that the VCI is the least of the WAIS–IV indices to be deleteriously affected by brain trauma, and (c) evidence that the VCI tends to yield higher correlations with general intelligence as compared to other WAIS–IV indices. The ensuing ability–memory discrepancy analysis was completed using the higher PRI to maximize true positive results.

(Cont.)

FORM 6.12

WAIS–IV/WMS–IV, FORM AGES 16 TO 69 ABILITY–MEMORY DISCREPANCY ANALYSIS PREDICTED DIFFERENCE METHOD RESULTS AND INTERPRETATION TABLES (*Cont.*)

WMS–IV, Form Ages 16 to 69

TABLE 3 ■ INDEX SCORE SUMMARY

Index	Index score	PR	90% CI	Qualitative description	Measured abilities
Auditory Memory Index (AMI)	000	00.0	[000, 000]	Very superior	Ability to remember orally presented information
Visual Memory Index (VMI)	--	--	[00, 00]	Superior	Ability to remember visually presented information
Immediate Memory Index (IMI)	--	--	[00, 00]	Average Borderline	Ability to remember both visually and orally presented information immediately after it is presented
Delayed Memory Index (DMI)	--	--	[00, 00]	Extremely low	Ability to remember both visually and orally presented information after a 20–30 minute delay

Note: Index score mean = 100, standard deviation = 15. Lower scores indicate greater memory impairment. PR, percentile rank; CI, confidence interval. -- denotes not administered, or score type not available or computed.

Memory involves (a) receiving information from the senses, (b) organizing and storing information, and (c) retrieving information from storage. The WMS–IV measures the ability to consciously learn and remember novel information that is bound by the testing situation (i.e., declarative episodic memory). *Immediate memory* refers to short-term or temporary storage (i.e., seconds), while *delayed memory* refers to long-term or more stable storage and retrieval (i.e., 20–30 minutes).

TABLE 4 ■ AUDITORY MEMORY SUBTEST SCORE SUMMARY

Subtest	Scaled score	PR	Qualitative description	Measured abilities
Logical Memory I (LM I)*	00	0.00	Very superior	Immediate free recall of conceptually organized and semantically related verbal information; immediate narrative memory
Logical Memory II (LM II)**	--	--	Superior High average	Delayed free recall and recognition of conceptually organized and semantically related verbal information; long-term narrative memory[a]
Verbal Paired Associates I (VPA I)*	--	--	Average Low average	Immediate cued recall of novel and semantically related word associations
Verbal Paired Associates II (VPA II)**	--	--	Borderline Extremely low	Delayed cued recall and recognition of novel and semantically related word associations[a]

Note: Scale score mean = 10, standard deviation = 3. Lower scores indicate greater memory impairment. PR, percentile rank. *denotes that this subtest also contributed to the Immediate Memory Index. **denotes that this subtest also contributed to the Delayed Memory Index. -- denotes not administered, or score type not available or computed.

[a]Duration of delay is 20 to 30 minutes.

(Cont.)

FORM 6.12

WAIS–IV/WMS–IV, FORM AGES 16 TO 69 ABILITY–MEMORY DISCREPANCY ANALYSIS PREDICTED DIFFERENCE METHOD RESULTS AND INTERPRETATION TABLES (*Cont.*)

TABLE 5 ■ VISUAL MEMORY SUBTEST SCORE SUMMARY

Subtest	Scaled score	PR	Qualitative description	Measured abilities
Designs I (DE I)*	00	0.00	Very superior	Immediate free recall of visual-spatial material; immediate spatial memory for novel visual material
Designs II (DE II)**	--	--	Superior High average	Delayed free recall and recognition of visual–spatial material; long-term spatial memory for novel visual material[a]
Visual Reproduction I (VR I)*	--	--	Average Low average	Ability to immediately recall and draw designs; immediate memory for nonverbal visual stimuli
Visual Reproduction II (VR II)**	--	--	Borderline Extremely low	Delayed ability to recall and draw designs; long-term memory for nonverbal visual stimuli[a]

Note: Scale score mean = 10, standard deviation = 3. Lower scores indicate greater memory impairment. PR, percentile rank. *denotes that this subtest also contributed to the Immediate Memory Index. **denotes that this subtest also contributed to the Delayed Memory Index. -- denotes not administered, or score type not available or computed.

[a]Duration of delay is 20 to 30 minutes.

TABLE 6 ■ VISUAL WORKING MEMORY SUBTEST SCORE SUMMARY

Subtest	Scaled score	PR	Qualitative description	Measured abilities
Spatial Addition (SA)	00	0.00	Superior High average Average	Visual–spatial working memory[a] requiring storage (visual sketchpad), manipulation and ability to ignore competing stimuli (central executive)
Symbol Span (SSP)	--	--	Low average Borderline Extremely low	Visual working memorya using novel visual stimuli; ability to retain (a) a mental image of a design and (b) the relative spatial position of the design on the page

Note: Scale score mean = 10, standard deviation = 3. Lower scores indicate greater memory impairment. PR, percentile rank. -- denotes not administered, or score type not available or computed.

[a]Working memory involves holding immediate memory traces while executing cognitive tasks.

(*Cont.*)

FORM 6.12

WAIS–IV/WMS–IV, FORM AGES 16 TO 69 ABILITY–MEMORY DISCREPANCY ANALYSIS PREDICTED DIFFERENCE METHOD RESULTS AND INTERPRETATION TABLES (*Cont.*)

ABILITY–MEMORY DISCREPANCY ANALYSIS

ABILITY SCORE TYPE: WAIS–IV GENERAL ABILITY INDEX (GAI)

ABILITY SCORE: 000

TABLE 7 ■ **PREDICTED DIFFERENCE METHOD**[a]

Index	Actual WMS–IV index score	Predicted WAIS–IV GAI	Difference	Critical value .05*	Base rate[b]
Auditory Memory Index (AMI)	000	000	00	0.00	00.0%
Visual Memory Index (VMI)	000	000	00	N/A	N/A
Visual Working Memory Index (VWMI)	000	000	00	0.00	00.0%
Immediate Memory Index (IMI)	000	000	00	0.00	00.0%
Delayed Memory Index (DMI)	000	000	00	0.00	00.0%

Note: *denotes that the Actual WMS–IV index score – Predicted WMS–IV index score difference occurs by chance less than five times in 100 and is therefore statistically significant. N/A, not applicable; the Actual WMS–IV index score was equal to or exceeded the Predicted WMS–IV index score.

[a]The differences are obtained by subtracting each WMS–IV index score predicted by the employed WAIS–IV composite score from the actual WMS–IV index score.

[b]Percentage of the healthy normative sample who obtained the listed Actual WMS–IV index score – Predicted WMS–IV index score difference.

FORM 6.13

WAIS–IV/WMS–IV, FORM AGES 65 TO 90 ABILITY–MEMORY DISCREPANCY ANALYSIS PREDICTED DIFFERENCE METHOD RESULTS AND INTERPRETATION TABLES

WAIS–IV

TABLE 1 ■ **COMPOSITE SCORE SUMMARY**

Index/Scale	Composite score	PR	90% CI	Qualitative description	Measured abilities
Verbal Comprehension Index (VCI)	000	00	[00, 00]	Very superior	Verbal reasoning, comprehension, and conceptualization
Perceptual Reasoning Index (PRI)	--	--	[00, 00]	Superior	Visual–spatial (nonverbal) reasoning, organization, and conceptualization
General Ability Index (GAI)[a]	**--**	**--**	**[000, 000]**	**Extremely low**	**General intelligence: the ability to learn from experience, acquire knowledge, and use resources effectively in adapting to new situations or solving problems**[b]

Note: Composite score mean = 100, standard deviation = 15. Lower scores indicate greater intellectual impairment. PR, percentile rank; CI, confidence interval. -- denotes not administered, or score type not available or computed. General intellectual ability data are in boldface.

[a]The General Ability Index includes only the Verbal Comprehension and Perceptual Reasoning composite scores; it thus minimizes the effects of working memory and processing speed in the measurement of general intelligence.

[b]Ciccarelli, S. K., & White, J. N. (2012). *Psychology* (3rd ed.). Upper Saddle River, NJ: Pearson Education; Wechsler, D. (1975). *The collected papers of David Wechsler*. New York, NY: Academic Press.

TABLE 2 ■ **VCI–PRI INDEX LEVEL DISCREPANCY COMPARISON**

VCI composite score	PRI composite score	Difference	Critical value .05*	Cohen's *d* effect size[a]	Effect size results[b]	Base rate[c]
000	000	±00	0.00	0.0	Large Medium	00.0%

Note: *denotes that the VCI–PRI difference occurs by chance less than five times in 100 and is therefore statistically significant.

[a]Computed as the absolute value of VCI–PRI/standard deviation (15).

[b]Effect size score ranges: 0.0 to 0.2 (small effect); 0.3 to 0.7 (medium effect); 0.8 and higher (large effect).

[c]Percentage of the normative sample who obtained the listed VCI–PRI difference.

The VCI–PRI difference was not statistically significant, manifested a small effect size, and yielded an acceptably high base rate in the normative sample. Thus, the GAI was deemed an acceptable measure of general intelligence and was used in the ability–memory discrepancy analysis.

The VCI–PRI difference was statistically significant and favored the former/latter. The difference also yielded both a large effect size and remarkably low base rate in the normative sample. Thus, the GAI was deemed an unacceptable measure of general intelligence and was dropped from further analysis. The ensuing ability–memory discrepancy analysis was completed using the VCI for the following reasons: (a) to determine if any measured memory deficits exist beyond the impact of language ability, (b) evidence that the VCI is the least of the WAIS–IV indices to be deleteriously affected by brain trauma, and (c) evidence that the VCI tends to yield higher correlations with general intelligence as compared to other WAIS–IV indices. The ensuing ability–memory discrepancy analysis was completed using the higher PRI to maximize true positive results.

(Cont.)

FORM 6.13

WAIS–IV/WMS–IV, FORM AGES 65 TO 90 ABILITY–MEMORY DISCREPANCY ANALYSIS PREDICTED DIFFERENCE METHOD RESULTS AND INTERPRETATION TABLES (*Cont.*)

WMS–IV, Form Ages 65 to 90

TABLE 3 ■ INDEX SCORE SUMMARY

Index	Index score	PR	90% CI	Qualitative description	Measured abilities
Auditory Memory Index (AMI)	000	00.0	[000, 000]	Very superior	Ability to remember orally presented information
Visual Memory Index (VMI)	--	--	[00, 00]	Superior	Ability to remember visually presented information
Immediate Memory Index (IMI)	--	--	[00, 00]	Average Borderline	Ability to remember both visually and orally presented information immediately after it is presented
Delayed Memory Index (DMI)	--	--	[00, 00]	Extremely low	Ability to remember both visually and orally presented information after a 20–30 minute delay

Note: Index score mean = 100, standard deviation = 15. Lower scores indicate greater memory impairment. PR, percentile rank; CI, confidence interval. -- denotes not administered, or score type not available or computed.

Memory involves (a) receiving information from the senses, (b) organizing and storing information, and (c) retrieving information from storage. The WMS–IV measures the ability to consciously learn and remember novel information that is bound by the testing situation (i.e., declarative episodic memory). *Immediate memory* refers to short-term or temporary storage (i.e., seconds), while *delayed memory* refers to long-term or more stable storage and retrieval (i.e., 20 to 30 minutes).

TABLE 4 ■ AUDITORY MEMORY SUBTEST SCORE SUMMARY

Subtest	Scaled score	PR	Qualitative description	Measured abilities
Logical Memory I (LM I)*	00	0.00	Very superior	Immediate free recall of conceptually organized and semantically related verbal information; immediate narrative memory
Logical Memory II (LM II)**	--	--	Superior High average	Delayed free recall and recognition of conceptually organized and semantically related verbal information; long-term narrative memory[a]
Verbal Paired Associates I (VPA I)*	--	--	Average Low average	Immediate cued recall of novel and semantically related word associations
Verbal Paired Associates II (VPA II)**	--	--	Borderline Extremely low	Delayed cued recall and recognition of novel and semantically related word associations[a]

Note: Scale score mean = 10, standard deviation = 3. Lower scores indicate greater memory impairment. PR, percentile rank. *denotes that this subtest also contributed to the Immediate Memory Index. **denotes that this subtest also contributed to the Delayed Memory Index. -- denotes not administered, or score type not available or computed.

[a]Duration of delay is 20 to 30 minutes.

(*Cont.*)

FORM 6.13

WAIS–IV/WMS–IV, FORM AGES 65 TO 90 ABILITY–MEMORY DISCREPANCY ANALYSIS PREDICTED DIFFERENCE METHOD RESULTS AND INTERPRETATION TABLES (*Cont.*)

TABLE 5 ■ **VISUAL MEMORY SUBTEST SCORE SUMMARY**

Subtest	Scaled score	PR	Qualitative description	Measured abilities
Visual Reproduction I (VR I)*	--	--	Superior Low average	Ability to immediately recall and draw designs; immediate memory for nonverbal visual stimuli
Visual Reproduction II (VR II)**	--	--	Borderline Extremely low	Delayed ability to recall and draw designs; long-term memory for nonverbal visual stimuli[a]

Note: Scale score mean = 10, standard deviation = 3. Lower scores indicate greater memory impairment. PR, percentile rank. *denotes that this subtest also contributed to the Immediate Memory Index. **denotes that this subtest also contributed to the Delayed Memory Index. -- denotes not administered, or score type not available or computed.

[a]Duration of delay is 20 to 30 minutes.

TABLE 6 ■ **VISUAL WORKING MEMORY[a] SUBTEST**

Subtest	Scaled score	PR	Qualitative description	Measured abilities
Symbol Span (SSP)	--	--	Low average Borderline Extremely low	Visual working memory[b] using novel visual stimuli; ability to retain (a) a mental image of a design and (b) the relative spatial position of the design on the page

Note: Scale score mean = 10, standard deviation = 3. Lower scores indicate greater memory impairment. PR, percentile rank. -- denotes not administered, or score type not available or computed.

[a]The Visual Working Memory Index is not available on the ages 65 to 90 older adult battery.

[b]Working memory involves holding immediate memory traces while executing cognitive tasks.

ABILITY–MEMORY DISCREPANCY ANALYSIS

ABILITY SCORE TYPE: WAIS–IV GENERAL ABILITY INDEX (GAI)

ABILITY SCORE: **000**

TABLE 7 ■ **PREDICTED DIFFERENCE METHOD[a]**

Index	Actual WMS–IV index score	Predicted WMS–IV index score	Difference	Critical value .05*	Base rate[b]
Auditory Memory Index (AMI)	000	000	00	0.00	00.0%
Visual Memory Index (VMI)	000	000	00	N/A	N/A
Immediate Memory Index (IMI)	000	000	00	0.00	00.0%
Delayed Memory Index (DMI)	000	000	00	0.00	00.0%

Note: *denotes that the Actual WMS–IV index score – Predicted WMS–IV index score difference occurs by chance less than five times in 100 and is therefore statistically significant. N/A, not applicable; the Actual WMS–IV index score was equal to or exceeded the Predicted WMS–IV index score.

[a]The differences are obtained by subtracting each WMS–IV index score predicted by the employed WAIS–IV composite score from the actual WMS–IV index score.

[b]Percentage of the healthy normative sample who obtained the listed Actual WMS–IV index score – Predicted WMS–IV index score difference.

FORM 6.14

K–CPT RESULTS AND INTERPRETATION TABLES

K–CPT

TABLE 1 ■ VALIDITY OF ADMINISTRATION

	Validity measures			
	Timing difficulties	Noncompliance	Excessive omissions	Absence of hits per test block
Result	No Yes	No Yes	No Yes (X = --)	No Yes
Interpretation	Valid	Valid	Valid	Valid

The K–CPT administration is valid. Despite some indications of invalidity, the respondent successfully passed the practice administration and was observed to continue responding throughout the ensuing test administration procedure. Thus, the K–CPT administration is considered valid and the results interpretable. The K–CPT administration is invalid. The results are therefore not interpretable.

TABLE 2 ■ CONFIDENCE INDEX ASSESSMENT

Statistical analysis	Profile classification	Confidence index	Interpretation
Discriminant Function	Normal ADHD	--%	The chances are -- out of 100 that a/no clinical attention problem exists

TABLE 3 ■ SPECIFIC MEASURES

Measure	T-score*	PR	Guideline	Interpretation of statistically significant result
Omissions %	00	0.00	Normal inattention	Failure to respond to target letters (i.e., non-Xs)
Commissions %	--	--	Marked impulsivity	Responses given to nontargets (i.e., Xs)
Hit RT	--	--	Inattention and impulsivity	Atypical speed of correct responses for the entire test
Hit RT SE	--	--	Normal inattention	Inconsistency in response speed
Variability of SE	--	--	Normal inattention	Excessive within-respondent variability in 18 test segments compared to SE
Detectability (d')	--	--	Normal inattention	Inability to distinguish and detect X and non-X stimuli
Perseverations %	--	--	Normal impulsivity	RT < 100 milliseconds; that is, slow, random, or anticipatory responses
Hit RT by Block Change	--	--	Normal inattention	Substantial slowing of reaction time as the test progressed
Hit SE by Block Change	--	--	Normal inattention	Substantial loss of consistency as the test progressed
Hit RT by ISI Change	--	--	Normal inattention	Atypical changes in response speed across different ISIs
Hit SE by ISI Change	--	--	Normal inattention	Atypical changes in response consistency across different ISIs

Note: T-score mean = 50, standard deviation = 10. Higher T-scores indicate greater presence of significant result. *denotes that the T-score is statistically significant; specific measure supportive of an ADHD diagnosis. PR, percentile rank; RT, reaction time; SE, standard error; ISI, interstimulus interval. -- denotes not administered, or score type not available or computed.

K–CPT Interpretation: Positive Negative for ADHD, including measured impairments in general and sustained attention, and impulse control. False positive due to the majority of negative results for ADHD among the other reliable and valid test data. False negative due to the majority of positive results for ADHD among the other reliable and valid test data.

FORM 6.15

CPT–II RESULTS AND INTERPRETATION TABLES

CPT–II

TABLE 1 ■ VALIDITY OF ADMINISTRATION

	Validity measures			
	Timing difficulties	**Noncompliance**	**Excessive omissions**	**Absence of hits per test block**
Result	No Yes	No Yes	No Yes (X = --)	No Yes
Interpretation	Valid	Valid	Valid	Valid

The CPT–II administration is valid. Despite some indications of invalidity, the respondent successfully passed the practice administration and was observed to continue responding throughout the ensuing test administration procedure. Thus, the CPT–II administration is considered valid and the results interpretable. The CPT–II administration is invalid. The results are therefore not interpretable.

TABLE 2 ■ CONFIDENCE INDEX ASSESSMENT

Statistical analysis	Profile classification	Confidence index	Interpretation
Discriminant Function	Normal ADHD	--%	The chances are -- out of 100 that a/no clinical attention problem exists

TABLE 3 ■ SPECIFIC MEASURES

Measure	T-score*	PR	Guideline	Interpretation of statistically significant result
Omissions %	00	0.00	Normal inattention	Failure to respond to target letters (i.e., non-Xs)
Commissions %	--	--	Marked impulsivity	Responses given to nontargets (i.e., Xs)
Hit RT	--	--	Inattention and impulsivity	Atypical speed of correct responses for the entire test
Hit RT SE	--	--	Marked inattention	Inconsistency in response speed
Variability of SE	--	--	Normal inattention	Excessive within-respondent variability in 18 test segments compared to SE
Detectability (d')	--	--	Normal inattention	Inability to distinguish and detect X and non-X stimuli
Perseverations %	--	--	Normal impulsivity	RT < 100 milliseconds; that is, slow, random, or anticipatory responses
Hit RT by Block Change	--	--	Normal inattention	Substantial slowing of reaction time as the test progressed
Hit SE by Block Change	--	--	Normal inattention	Substantial loss of consistency as the test progressed
Hit RT by ISI Change	--	--	Normal inattention	Atypical changes in response speed across different ISIs
Hit SE by ISI Change	--	--	Normal inattention	Atypical changes in response consistency across different ISIs

Note: T-score mean = 50, standard deviation = 10. Higher T-scores indicate greater presence of significant result. *denotes that the T-score is statistically significant; specific measure supportive of an ADHD diagnosis. PR, percentile rank; RT, reaction time; SE, standard error; ISI, interstimulus interval. -- denotes not administered, or score type not available or computed.

CPT–II Interpretation: Positive Negative for ADHD, including measured impairments in general and sustained attention, and impulse control. False positive due to the majority of negative results for ADHD among the other reliable and valid test data. False negative due to the majority of positive results for ADHD among the other reliable and valid test data.

Symptom Rating Scales

This chapter is comprised of standardized symptom-focused rating scales, which are designed for diagnosing noncognitive and nonpsychotic Axis I Disorders as delineated in the *Diagnostic and Statistical Manual of Mental Disorders, Fourth Edition, Text Revision* (*DSM-IV-TR*) (American Psychiatric Association, 2000). More specifically, these include Mood Disorders, Anxiety Disorders, Disruptive Behavior Disorders, and Pervasive Developmental Disorders (PDD). Such disorders were previously conceptualized as Nonorganic Mental Disorders (American Psychiatric Association, 1987). Therefore, the rather expansive construct being measured here, and which will be defined next, is the *Axis I Clinical Disorder* (also known as the *Clinical Syndrome*).

THE CONSTRUCT OF CLINICAL DISORDER AND ITS MEASUREMENT

An Axis I Clinical Disorder is a clustering or covariance of psychological symptoms which cause dysfunction, and typically exhibit the following characteristics: (a) identifiable onset; (b) acute presentation; (c) precipitant of intervention; and (d) amenability to treatment (American Psychiatric Association, 2000). As it is currently designed, the *DSM-IV-TR* classifies disorders according to a categorical system, which adopts a *prototypical* approach (Barlow & Durand, 2012). That is, each disorder is defined by essential symptoms, which are accompanied by nonessential variations. To meet the criteria for a particular disorder, an individual must manifest the essential symptoms, in addition to a minimum number of nonessential variations. For selected disorders, additional essential criteria include age of onset and symptom duration. Furthermore, certain disorders contain particular characteristics deemed relevant to prognosis and treatment planning and intervention, including symptom course and degree of severity (e.g., mild, moderate, severe). These are referred to as *specifiers*.

Because the Axis I Disorders are categorical in nature, there is a considerable amount of symptom overlap. For example, impaired attention and concentration may be associated with Attention-Deficit/Hyperactivity Disorder (ADHD), Dysthymic Disorder, Bipolar Disorder, and Generalized Anxiety Disorder (GAD). Thus, comorbidity is not uncommon which renders precise differential diagnosis a complicated and arduous task (Krueger & Markon, 2006).

The symptom rating scales included in my selected inventory (see Form 2.7) contain many features that render them remarkably useful in making accurate Axis I differential diagnoses, including the detection of comorbidity. First, they possess exceptional content validity concerning the aforementioned *DSM-IV-TR* Axis I Clinical Disorders symptom criteria. Second, they are standardized in terms of item content, age, and gender. Third, parallel forms are typically available for observer ratings and self-ratings. Thus, interrater comparisons are routinely available. However, the self-ratings do exclude children younger than age 8 years for want of adequately developed psychological mindedness. Fourth, they are invariably self-administered by the respondent and the majority of symptom rating scales possess unlimited use of computer software scoring capability. Hence, they are extremely efficient and cost-effective regarding administration, scoring, and interpretation.

Finally, with two exceptions, validity scales are available, which are crucial considering that such ratings rely on both the veracity and accuracy of observer and self-report data.

DIAGNOSTIC REASONS FOR INCLUSION WITHIN A TEST BATTERY

Symptom rating scales are most typically ordered to rule out the presence of one or more *DSM-IV-TR* Axis I Clinical Disorders as defined prior. Although less frequently in practice, they may also be utilized to measure response to treatment intervention. Their efficiency permits the latter use. Compared to that of a diagnostic interview, they are remarkably useful in making much more refined and accurate Axis I differential diagnoses and in identifying comorbidity.

Symptom rating scales are most frequently indicated under the following conditions: (a) diagnostic uncertainty due to mixed symptom presentation or ambiguity in reporting symptoms, (b) poor response to treatment for equivocal or unidentifiable reasons, and/ or (c) the likely presence of comorbidity. In general, the symptom rating scales discussed subsequently provide the greatest differential diagnostic assistance for patients 18 years and younger for the following Axis I Clinical Disorders: (a) Oppositional-Defiant Disorder (ODD), (b) Conduct Disorder (CD), (c) Depressive Disorder, (d) Bipolar Disorder, (e) GAD, (f) Separation Anxiety Disorder, (g) Social Phobia, (h) Obsessive-Compulsive Disorder (OCD), (i) ADHD, (j) Autistic Disorder, (k) Asperger's Disorder, and (l) PDD *Not Otherwise Specified* (NOS) (also known as Atypical Autistic Disorder). Testing for the latter three should be supplemented with social perception neuropsychological testing as previously discussed (see Chapter 6).

For the youngest age range of 2 to 5 years, supplemental Developmental Milestone scales are extremely valuable in identifying areas of delay associated with Axis I psychopathology. Finally, for school-aged children and adolescents, some supplemental Academic scales assist in screening for Learning Disorders. As will be seen, the latter are not part of the core analyses and are best reported as ancillary results in the narrative portion of the final report.

Regarding adulthood, their use is more circumscribed to diagnosing ADHD. This is because the vast majority of *DSM-IV-TR* Axis I Clinical Disorders, along with the Axis II Personality Disorders, are most efficaciously measured by the self-report clinical and personality inventories and Rorschach Inkblot Test, Comprehensive System (Exner, 2003), properly normed for this large age group (see Form 2.7, and Chapters 8 and 9, respectively).

INSURANCE COVERAGE ISSUES

Concerning children and adolescents, testing referrals asking for Axis I *DSM-IV-TR* diagnostic clarification are extremely common in mental health practice. Consequently, such referrals are made by the largest variety of external and internal sources including (a) nonmental health medical practitioners (e.g., family physicians, pediatricians), (b) medical and nonmedical mental health clinicians (e.g., psychiatrists, psychologists, clinical social workers), (c) patients and family members, and (d) community service organizations (e.g., academic institutions). This also applies to testing referrals regarding ADHD in adulthood.

Because effective psychiatric and psychotherapeutic intervention is contingent upon the reliable and valid differential diagnosis of *DSM-IV-TR* disorders as defined by the American Psychiatric Association (2000), establishing medical necessity is typically viable. Diligent documentation of the following during the initial psychological assessment should effectuate insurance authorization of a reasonable number of testing hours: (a) the presence of diagnostic ambiguity subsequent to clinical interview, examination, and ongoing observation; (b) the manifestation of either poor or no response to treatment intervention for undetermined reasons; and/or (c) the need for objective standardized testing that will significantly impact treatment planning and outcome (see also the Introduction and Chapter 2).

This information is to be ensued by an enumeration of the current working diagnosis or diagnoses, those in need of ruling out, and any related referral questions. Use of the "Psychological Test Referral Form" (Form 2.1) and the "Initial Psychological Assessment Report" templates (Forms 2.2 and 2.3) shall ensure the inclusion of such requisite information.

THE SYMPTOM RATING SCALES

The following symptom rating scales are included in my recommended psychological test inventory: (a) Conners Early Childhood (EC) (Conners, 2009), (b) Conners Comprehensive Behavior Rating Scales (Conners, 2008), (c) Gilliam Autism Rating Scale, Second Edition (Gilliam, 2006), (d) Gilliam Asperger's Disorder Scale (Gilliam, 2001), and (e) Conners' Adult ADHD Rating Scales, Long Version (Conners, Erhardt, & Sparrow, 1999). I will discuss these instruments largely in this sequence, collapsing the two similar Gilliam measures for the Autistic Spectrum Disorders into one subsection. Each discussion begins with the instrument's essential characteristics, including the various available observer and self-report forms, ensued by the associated results and interpretation tables and their intended implementation.

Conners EC

The Conners EC is a standardized symptom rating scale normed on young children aged 2 years 0 months to 5 years 11 months. It includes two forms based upon the type of observer respondent, including parent ratings and teacher/childcare ratings. As stated prior, this age range precludes self-report ratings due to insufficiently developed psychological mindedness. Average time to complete the Conners EC is an efficient 25 minutes and requires a more than manageable fifth-grade reading level. Both forms yield virtually the same data on a child. The quantitative information I find most diagnostically useful include the (a) Validity scales, (b) Behavior and Global Index scales, and (c) Developmental Milestones scales.

The Validity scales are reported directly in raw score units, while the last two are transformed into standardized T-scores ($M = 50$, $SD = 10$). Although the Behavior scales are intended to measure more specifically defined problems versus the Global Index scales, I have found both to be equivalent in their effectiveness in *DSM-IV-TR* differential diagnosis. The Developmental Milestone scales are particularly useful in detecting PDDs (e.g., Play, Adaptive Skills, Communication), and screening for Learning Disorders (e.g., Preacademic Cognitive Skills).

Similar to the standardized tests discussed prior, the Conners EC affords a variety of optional supplementary data, including item analyses, standard errors of measurement (SEM), and percentiles. Again, these are best reported only when they provide diagnostically germane information not otherwise available by the core data and should be stated within the narrative portion of the final report.

The Conners EC Scoring Software (2009) is available for prompt and efficient data entry and scoring. The analyses include optional test–retest statistical comparisons to measure changes in symptom course and response to treatment, along with interrater comparisons.

Results and Interpretation Tables
The Conners EC results and interpretation tables appear in Form 7.1. Note that the parent ratings and teacher/childcare ratings are juxtaposed to facilitate interrater comparisons, in addition to maximizing the efficiency of data presentation. In order of appearance, three

tables (Table 1 to Table 3) report the following core data: (a) Validity scales, (b) Behavioral scales (which include Global Index scales), and (c) Developmental Milestone scales. I shall discuss these tables in this sequence.

Validity of ratings. Data within Table 1 identify test-taking response styles that may compromise the veracity of the subsequent behavioral and developmental milestones ratings. Thus, Table 1 should always be included first in the analysis. There are three such response styles, including (a) overly favorable ratings, (b) overly harsh ratings, and (c) contradictory ratings. As indicated prior, these data are presented in raw score units.

The top row apportions the table equally into parent ratings (left half) and teacher/caregiver ratings (right half). This order prioritizes the parent ratings for the following reasons: (a) such ratings are based upon a greater sampling of behavior across time and situations and (b) such data are more frequently available to the testing psychologist. Each half of Table 1 is further subdivided into three identical columns. In sequence, they include (a) Validity scale name, (b) Validity scale raw score, and (c) Validity scale dichotomous result (i.e., valid or invalid). The raw scores should be inserted first and the corresponding results retained.

General tabular notes define the directional meaning of lower raw scores and the "--" symbol for identifying unavailable data. Three specific notes succinctly delineate the test-taking response styles measured by the Conners EC. These response style notes were based upon the more elaborate narrative descriptions provided in the accompanying manual (Conners, 2009, pp. 37–38).

For convenience, I have drafted two of the most frequently occurring narrative interpretations of Table 1 results. Fortunately, both parent and teacher/childcare ratings typically show valid results. Hence, this is the first available narrative interpretation. However, occasionally one of the raters manifests evidence of invalidity. In practice, I have found negative impressions to be most common followed by inconsistency. The second narrative interpretation addresses such instances wherein one rater shows consistent validity, whereas the second evidences invalid response tendencies. It argues that the latter's subsequent scores should be deemed as accurate only when consistent with the valid ratings, and/or other test data or diagnostic information deemed reliable and valid. That is, sufficient corroboration is required before validity is assumed.

The particular narrative language describes parent ratings showing invalidity and the teacher/childcare ratings showing consistent validity. This is not to imply that this pattern is the most frequently occurring in practice. It is simply more efficient to describe one of the two potential interpretations, and simply reverse some of the wording for antithetical results. In the unusual event that both raters manifest invalid tendencies, the second narrative should be amended such that both raters' subsequent scores are in need of corroboration from other available test or assessment data. Finally, be wary to delete the inapplicable narrative interpretations before proceeding to Table 2.

Behavioral scales. Table 2 provides the standard *T*-scores for selected Conners EC Behavioral scales. Those listed in the table are those I have found most useful in rendering *DSM-IV-TR* differential diagnoses within this young age group. They have been enumerated within the table based upon two criteria, including (a) their measuring the same or similar *DSM-IV-TR* disorder and (b) the frequency with which that particular disorder is tested for in clinical practice among this age group. Therefore, those that measure the most frequently suspected disorders appear first or toward the top of the listing.

Prior to reviewing the specific organization of Table 2, I will list the Behavior scale names and *DSM-IV-TR* disorders most germane to those scales. This is necessary because there is not as direct correspondence between the two as there is with the older age Conners Comprehensive Behavior Rating Scales (Conners, 2008) discussed next.

Using the same row sequence as presented in Table 2, the Behavior scales and their respective *DSM-IV-TR* disorders are as follows: (a) Inattention–Hyperactivity—ADHD, (b) Restless–Impulsive—ADHD, (c) Defiance–Temper—ODD, (d) Aggression—ODD (risk for CD in later childhood and adolescence), (e) Social Functioning—PDD, (f) Atypical Behaviors—PDD, (g) Anxiety—GAD or Anxiety Disorder NOS (also known as Mild Anxiety Disorder), (h) Mood and Affect—Dysthymic Disorder or Depressive Disorder NOS (also known as Minor Depressive Disorder), and (i) Emotional Lability—Cyclothymic Disorder or Bipolar Disorder NOS. Being cognizant that the bipolar diagnosis in children is controversial among many clinicians, I will briefly address this issue and my related opinion here.

Data indicate that children and young adolescents can and do develop Bipolar Disorder, although usually with a varying symptom presentation as compared to older adolescents and adults (Geller & Luby, 1997). In particular, symptoms more commonly manifest as a mixed episode including depression, irritability, and temper tantrums (versus euphoria), and cycling is significantly more rapid and ongoing, thus rendering differential diagnosis from that of ADHD and ODD extremely challenging (National Institute of Mental Health, 2001; Weller, Weller, & Fristad, 1995).

Furthermore, early detection is crucial, considering the accumulating evidence that such early onset may indicate a more virulent form of Bipolar psychopathology, compared to the more typical onset in older adolescence and young adulthood (Carlson & Kashani, 1988; Geller & Luby, 1997). Also, relevant 2003 survey data revealed that as many as 1% of children and adolescents were diagnosed with Bipolar Disorder, which represents an increase of 40% over the previous 10 years (Holden, 2008). I believe that such a remarkable increase, at least in part, may be attributed to our enhanced ability to measure and diagnose true cases of this disorder using such symptom rating scales as the Conners EC. Finally, it is anticipated that the *DSM-V* will amend the diagnostic criteria for Bipolar Disorder as applied to children such that it is more correspondent with evidence of its idiosyncratic symptom presentation (Nevid, Rathus, & Greene, 2011).

Table 2 maintains the juxtaposition of parent and teacher/childcare ratings for purposes of interrater comparisons. This is reflected in the first abbreviated row, which labels only columns two and three as parent and teacher/childcare ratings. In columnar order of presentation, the body of Table 2 includes the following: (a) Behavior scale name, (b) parent and teacher/childcare standardized *T*-scores, including potential asterisk denoting statistical significance, (c) diagnostic result (i.e., negative, positive, or atypical presentation), and (d) the symptoms measured by each scale. The latter are based upon the behavior scale and global index descriptions available in the manual (Conners, 2009, Tables 4.4 and 4.6, pp. 40–41). I paraphrased and emended them to enhance test interpretation and reader comprehension, while maintaining accuracy. I also emphasized certain symptom descriptors that had evidence of validity (Conners, 2009, pp. 137–142).

Because *T*-score ranges 65 to 69, and 70 and higher, are designated as statistically *elevated* and *very elevated*, respectively (Conners, 2009, p. 34), the testing psychologist has discretion in applying the statistical significance asterisk to either of these ranges depending on (a) the relative desire to avoid false positive or negative results and (b) other comparable data within the test battery.

Regarding the contiguous results column, the following should routinely be entered for each scale assuming both raters yield valid scores: (a) *positive*—both raters' *T*-scores are statistically significant, (b) *negative*—both raters' *T*-scores are statistically nonsignificant, and (c) *atypical*—only one rater's *T*-score is statistically significant. *Atypical* indicates one of the following diagnostic possibilities: (a) an unusual symptom presentation that does not meet the full *DSM-IV-TR* disorder criteria, (b) the symptoms are associated with situational factors such as stress, and/or (c) the symptoms are part of a more inclusive *DSM-IV-TR* disorder.

As indicated before, in cases where one of the rater's scores manifest invalid tendencies, credence is afforded only when they are accordant with the valid ratings. Otherwise, the valid ratings are given priority in determining the results. Favoring one rater's scores over the other when both are valid and yield contradictory diagnostic results must be elucidated in the ensuing narrative interpretation of Table 2. For example, the parent ratings may be given priority because they are based upon a larger and more varied sampling of behavior. As a second example, teacher/childcare ratings may be given priority because they are more accordant with other reliable and valid test data.

I have found the application of this trichotomy in the results column (i.e., *positive*, *negative*, and *atypical*) to be remarkably useful and efficient in the process of score interpretation and diagnosis. Of course, testing psychologists who do not desire to employ this scheme may simply delete this column, along with the applicable specific tabular notes discussed subsequently, and interpret the results within a narrative summary immediately following Table 2.

General tabular notes denote the following: (a) *T*-score score mean and standard deviation, (b) directional meaning of higher scores, (c) import of the statistically significant asterisk, and (d) the "--" not administered, available, or computed symbol. Specific tabular notes define the meaning of positive, negative, and atypical results as inserted within the results column. Table 2 is designed to be immediately ensued by a pithy narrative interpretation of the core results.

For purposes of brevity, I advise deleting the Behavior scales that are not pertinent to that particular case's differential diagnostic issues and related referral questions. The exception to this guideline occurs when a significant result suggests the potential presence of a disorder not previously detected by either the referral source and/or testing psychologist. For instance, an ADHD testing case may show positive results on the Social Functioning and Atypical Behaviors Scales, and thus suggest the presence of Asperger's Disorder or high-functioning PPD. The testing psychologist may want to retain and report these results within Table 2 for purposes of consequently requesting supplementary testing for such disorders.

Developmental Milestones scales. Table 3 provides the Developmental Milestones scale data. In contrast to Tables 1 and 2, which are requisite to the analysis, Table 3 is discretionary and most pertinent in cases presenting suspected developmental delays. These involve testing for PDD, Mental Retardation, early screening for a potential Learning Disorder, and Neurocognitive Disorder.

Table 3 is designed as was Table 2, with the two exceptions being the five Developmental Milestones scales and their measured skills, and a self-explanatory dichotomous results column (*normal* versus *delay*). The measured skills were culled from Table 4.7 in the manual (Conners, 2009, Table 4.7, p. 42). The same *T*-score ranges 65 to 69 (i.e., elevated) and 70 and higher (i.e., very elevated) are employed in interpreting abnormal elevations (Conners, 2009, p. 34). Once again, this permits the same discretionary application of the statistical significance asterisk in Table 3 as in Table 2. Lastly, general table notes are analogous to those of Table 2.

Conners CBRS

Although the Conners CBRS is similar in design to that of the Conners EC, there are sufficient differences such that an independent discussion of this instrument is warranted.

The Conners CBRS is also a standardized symptom rating scale. However, it is comprised of three respondent forms including parent, teacher, and self-report. The first two observer respondent forms are based upon norm-referenced samples ranging in age from 6 years 0 months to 18 years 11 months, while the last self-report form is normed on individuals aged 8 years 0 months to 18 years 11 months. Analogous to the Conners EC, average time to complete the two observer respondent forms is an expeditious 25 minutes and requires a fifth-grade reading level. The self-report form average administration time is also 25 minutes, although with a more appropriate lower third-grade reading level. With some minor exceptions, especially regarding the self-report ratings, the three forms yield similar data. The core quantitative data I find most diagnostically useful include the (a) Validity scales and (b) Clinical scales.

The Conners CBRS contains the same three Validity scales as the Conners EC, although there is an additional datum on the Inconsistency Index (discussed subsequent). In contrast, the Clinical scales are significantly different as compared to the Conners EC Behavior scales. First, they have direct correspondence to the following *DSM-IV-TR* Axis I Clinical Disorders: (a) ADHD (including all subtypes), (b) ODD, (c) CD, (d) Major Depressive Episode (Disorder), (e) Manic Episode (Bipolar Disorder), (f) GAD, (g) Separation Anxiety Disorder, (h) Social Phobia, (i) OCD, (j) Autistic Disorder, and (k) Asperger's Disorder. Second, these disorders are measured by both the dimensional *T*-score metric ($M = 50$, $SD = 10$) and by the *DSM-IV-TR* categorical metric referred to as *symptom count*.

Symptom counts are unique to the Conners CBRS and augment test validity regarding *DSM-IV-TR* differential diagnosis, especially including the detection of comorbidity. Briefly, selected Conners CBRS items correspond directly to *DSM-IV-TR* criteria for the above-listed disorders. When a respondent rates an item on the Likert-type scale sufficiently high to be classified as either *indicated* or *may be indicated*, which varies somewhat from item to item, it is in effect marked as a symptom count. If ample essential and nonessential *DSM-IV-TR* symptom items are so classified, that diagnosis is identified as *probably met* (versus *probably not met*).

Specific guidelines are provided for interpreting the integration of *T*-score and symptom count results (Conners, 2008, p. 50). Briefly, a *T*-score at or above 60 coexisting with a positive symptom count indicates a *DSM-IV-TR* diagnosis; whereas, a lower *T*-score and negative symptom count indicates that such diagnosis is not supported. Guidelines are also provided in resolving discrepancies between these two measures (Conners, 2008, p. 49). I have developed supplemental guidelines consistent with the design of Table 2, which I have found to be reliable in practice (discussed subsequently).

In addition to the same optional ancillary data available in the Conners EC, the Conners CBRS provides a number of Content scales. Again, such data are most efficaciously reported when they provide unique diagnostically related information. In particular, the Content scales that I have most often inserted into the narrative interpretation of the final report include the following: (a) violence potential, (b) academic difficulties, (c) language, and (d) math. The first is useful when testing for CD and addressing referral questions regarding risk for aggression. The last three are relevant when screening for Learning Disorders. The Conners CBRS Scoring Software (2008) provides rapid computer scoring. The same optional test–retest and interrater statistical comparisons are available as on the Conners EC.

Results and Interpretation Tables

I have created three Conners CBRS results and interpretation tables based upon inclusion of the different available respondent ratings and their respective forms. The one I use most frequently includes the combined parent and teacher ratings (Form 7.2) much like the Conners EC. The second most common version includes the combined parent and self-report ratings (Form 7.3). This version is most useful when teacher ratings are unavailable, occurring frequently when the minor is being home schooled or when the evaluation is being completed during a major school recess or break. Recall, however, that this does not apply to children aged 6 to 7 years due to the more circumscribed self-report form norm-referenced sample.

The third of the Conners CBRS results and interpretation tables comprises only self-report ratings, again excluding ages 6 and 7 years (Form 7.4). I use this most typically when I desire all three respondent ratings. In such case, I use the parent and teacher observer-based version (Form 7.2) in sequence with the self-report version (Form 7.3) within the final report. The former is usually afforded priority in terms of test-reporting order, as it provides approximately twice the data in addition to direct interrater comparisons.

The three results and interpretation tables are designed in similar fashion such that I shall review them simultaneously. Pertinent differences are specifically highlighted when necessary. Furthermore, areas of overlap with the Conners EC are afforded more cursory attention, whereas differences are explicated in more detail.

Validity of ratings. Again, the analysis begins with determining if any of the same three test-taking response patterns reported in the Conners EC are present, which may qualify interpretation of the ensuing Conners CBRS Clinical scales. The Table 1 dual ratings (Forms 7.2 and 7.3) are designed as in the Conners EC to facilitate interrater comparisons. The fundamental difference regards the Inconsistency Index, which now includes the following two metrics: (a) raw score (i.e., sum of the discrepancies in ratings on comparable items) and the added (b) *differentials* (i.e., absolute frequency of occurrence of discrepant ratings on similar items of two or more points). Therefore, the differentials column is only pertinent to the Inconsistency Index scale; that is, the "--" symbol should invariably be retained in the differentials column for the Positive and Negative Impression scales as being inapplicable.

The Table 1 results column and alternative narrative validity interpretations are identical to the Conners EC Table 1. Regarding the separate self-report ratings (Form 7.4), the invalid narrative wording tendencies assume that the parent and teacher ratings were administered, scored, and interpreted as being valid. This paragraph may be easily amended for somewhat varying validity results. Table 1 general and specific notes are unmodified from the Conners EC (see Conners, 2008, pp. 45–46, for comparison of Validity scale descriptions). Thus, further commentary is obviated here.

Clinical scales. Table 2 for all three Conners CBRS versions presents the core results regarding *DSM-IV-TR* disorders. The dual rater versions (Forms 7.2 and 7.3) employ the juxtaposed design for interrater analyses. From left to right, the following information is provided: (a) Clinical scale name, (b) *T*-score and *DSM* symptom count dichotomous result (*met* or *not met*) per rater, (c) trichotomous diagnostic result (*positive*, *negative*, or *atypical* symptoms), and (d) measured symptoms. The measured symptoms are succinct descriptions of each scale and indicated as *DSM-IV-TR* disorder. They are essentially diagnostic summaries of each disorder as described more elaborately within the manual (Conners, 2008, pp. 14–17). For purposes of maintaining both brevity and precision, essential diagnostic summary words were occasionally inserted based upon *DSM-IV-TR* standards (e.g., *qualitative impairment* as associated with Autistic and Asperger's Disorder) (American Psychiatric Association, 2000).

The Clinical scale names are listed in terms of their testing frequency and diagnostic similarity. In particular, the initial four scales represent Disruptive Behavior Disorders, beginning with the most commonly tested for ADHD diagnosis and its subtypes. Next are the Mood Disorders, followed by the Anxiety Disorders and PDDs.

Note that the last are not included within the self-report ratings due to impaired social perception as being an essential etiological symptom (Oberman & Ramachandran, 2007). The *T*-score statistically significant asterisk should be applied for scores 60 and above due to its integrated interpretation with *DSM* symptom count criteria. The *T*-score/*DSM* symptom criteria integrated interpretation guidelines were reviewed in sufficient detail above and shall not be repeated here for purposes of expediency. Rather, the focus here is on the application of the *diagnostic result* column.

I want to first cover the Table 2 dual-form design (Forms 7.2 and 7.3) assuming valid results for both raters. First, *T*-scores of 60 and above coexistent with *DSM* symptom counts being *met* for both raters should receive the *positive* result option. Second, *T*-scores of 59 and below coexistent with *DSM* symptom counts being *not met* for both raters should receive the *negative* result alternative. Mixed results within and between raters should receive the *atypical symptoms* alternative unless an exception applies, such as favoring a negative result due to an absence of supporting data among the other tests within the battery. Again, exceptions should be explicated within the narrative summary interpretation of Table 2 results. Invalid response tendencies among one or both raters must be qualified as discussed before in the Conners EC.

When the individual self-report form results (Form 7.4) are reported along with the separate dual parent and teacher results (Form 7.2), the most logical strategy is to insert the result alternative based upon only the self-reported *T*-score and *DSM* symptom count data pattern. This is based on the principle that empirical results should be circumscribed to the table within which they appear (see e.g., American Psychological Association, 2010). Otherwise, the results column loses both logical integrity and coherence. Discrepancies between the self-report and observer-based ratings can be effectively interpreted in the narrative text of the report; for example, prioritizing the observer-based ratings due to evidence of a lack of introspection on the part of the child or adolescent. Within-rater consistency between the *T*-score and *DSM* symptom count data is the rule when only Conners CBRS self-report data appear within the test battery. Lastly, as in the Conners EC, I advise reporting only those Clinical scales pertinent to the particular case.

Tabular notes are the same as those for the Conners EC Table 2 (Form 7.1), with two differences reflecting the added symptom count metric and amended *atypical symptoms* result definition. First, the *DSM* symptom counts dichotomous alternatives (viz., *met* and *not met*) are explicitly defined to facilitate data interpretation and feedback. Second, the *atypical symptoms* result was given the more pithy meaning of indicating an alternative *DSM-IV-TR* diagnosis. This also explains the added word *symptoms* following *atypical* due to its more direct correspondence with such taxonomy as compared to the Conners EC. I have found this analysis extremely useful in making precise differential diagnostic decisions within this older child and adolescent age range. It also facilitates explanation of my logic during test feedback (see Chapter 3).

For instance, it is not usual to find consistent positive results for Bipolar Disorder, and an atypical result on ODD; that is, perhaps the ODD *T*-scores were significant, although the *DSM* symptom counts were not met. It is logically sound to interpret the significant ODD *T*-scores as being associated with the irritability component of the positive Bipolar Disorder. Again, this would be consistent on both empirical and logical grounds.

Finally, a narrative summary interpretation should follow Table 2 results. It is to be noted that supplementary data may include exactly which and how many *DSM-IV-TR* criteria were met. Noting this in the narrative interpretation of Table 2 results can be valuable in terms of determining severity specifiers when applicable (e.g., Major Depressive Disorder, *Mild Severity*).

Gilliam PDD Symptom Rating Scales

My recommended test inventory consists of the following two symptom rating scales designed specifically to measure the most commonly occurring PDDs: (a) Gilliam Autism Rating Scale, Second Edition (GARS–2) and (b) Gilliam Asperger's Disorder Scale (GADS). Because their test format, administration, scoring, and interpretation are similarly constructed, I discuss both of them here while identifying important differences when indicated.

Both the (GARS–2) and GADS include norm-referenced samples ranging in age from 3 years 0 months to 22 years 11 months with documented Autistic Disorder and Asperger's Disorder, respectively. This means that near-average or higher standard scores (SSs) are indicative of PDD symptoms of a clinical nature (discussed below). Why do I include these PDD symptom rating scales when the Conners EC and Conners CBRS (discussed before) also include Autistic and Asperger's Disorder data?

First, because of the (GARS–2) and GADS one-dimensional or single-construct design, their item content includes a much larger, and hence, more thorough, representative sample of *DSM-IV-TR* PDD symptom criteria in contrast with the aforementioned multidimensional instruments. Second, a relevant psychometric precept is that larger numbers of items enhance test reliability (Miller, McIntire, & Lovler, 2011; Warner, 2008). Third, these more thorough measures provide subscales on germane PDD symptom clusters, thus permitting more precise profile analyses, autistic spectrum differential diagnoses, and severity estimates. Fourth, average administration time for each Gilliam instrument is an extremely efficient 5 to 10 minutes. Although particular required reading level information is not reported (Gilliam, 2001, 2006), informal item analysis indicates comparability with the Conners observer respondent forms (i.e., approximately fifth grade). Fifth, my own case study analyses demonstrate a distinct risk of false-positive results on the Conners EC and CBRS PDD relevant scales, especially regarding the latter. Consequently, I circumscribe my use of these scales on the Conners EC and CBRS to the following: (a) corroborating GARS–2, GADS, neuropsychological social perception, and/or pertinent personality test data or (b) merely screening for such disorders.

A sixth reason for selecting these more comprehensive PDD measures for my test inventory is the increasing prevalence of Autistic Disorder, Asperger's Disorder, and PDD NOS. In particular, the aforementioned autistic spectrum disorders were estimated in 2006 to occur at a rate of 1 in 110 or an approximate 1% base rate within the general population, a remarkable increase from 2002 (Autism and Developmental Disabilities, 2009). Many researchers attribute this increase to improved recognition and detection of these disorders, especially concerning milder or higher functioning cases (Benaron, 2009; Grinker, 2007).

The implication of this increased prevalence is a concomitant increase in testing referrals for PDD diagnoses, especially for the more difficult to discern higher functioning or mild cases and atypical cases. Thus, it behooves the contemporary testing psychologist to possess standardized instruments that are both specifically and efficiently constructed to measure the presence, type, and severity of autistic spectrum disorders. The GARS–2 and GADS adequately serve these purposes.

The quantitative yield I find most diagnostically useful from these two measures include the (a) overall index or quotient ($M = 100$, $SD = 15$), (b) subscale SSs ($M = 10$, $SD = 3$), (c) confidence intervals based upon the associated standard error of measurement (SEM), and (d) percentile ranks. The three (GARS–2) subscales are directly correspondent with the *DSM-IV-TR* symptom clusters, including Stereotyped Behaviors, Communication, and Social Interaction (American Psychiatric Association, 2000). The GADS comprises four subscales including Restricted Patterns of Behavior, Social Interaction, Cognitive Patterns, and Pragmatic Skills. The last three provide a remarkably comprehensive measurement of the nature, extent, and severity of qualitative impairments within the social interaction cluster of both Asperger's Disorder and PDD NOS (American Psychiatric Association, 2000).

One limitation of both the GARS–2 and GADS is a lack of validity scales. This drawback may be effectively circumvented, however, by including the Conners EC or CBRS within the same test battery and extrapolating the Validity scale results to the same respondent on the applicable Gilliam measures. Supplementary data may be gathered by use of the GARS–2 and GADS structured interview, which appears on the response sheet/scoring forms. This information primarily regards developmental symptom onset and course. I do not typically spend additional time gathering such information because it is frequently redundant with the presenting symptoms information of the initial report (see Forms 2.2 and 2.3).

Finally, the GARS–2 Software Scoring and Reporting System (2009) affords computer-assisted data entry and scoring capability. Although the GADS does not yet offer such computer software, duration of manual scoring for both these instruments is comparable to the computer scoring if limited to obtaining the core index/quotient and subscale SSs, which I recommend.

Results and Interpretation Tables

Separate results and interpretation tables are available for the GARS–2 (Form 7.5) and GADS (Form 7.6). They both comprise the following two data tables: (a) overall index/quotient results (Table 1) and (b) subscale SS results (Table 2). Tables 1 and 2 for each measure are designed to be interpreted simultaneously rather than independently in the interests of expediency. This order of presentation is consistent with the general to specific analytic process I espoused in discussing the cognitive ability tests (see Chapters 4–6). I review the GARS–2 and GADS tables contemporaneously and in the above sequence, while highlighting significant differences.

Index scores/quotients. Table 1 presents the overall PDD results. Although the verbiage is somewhat different (i.e., Autistic Disorder Index versus Asperger's Disorder Quotient), the transformed score metric is identical ($M = 100$, $SD = 15$). In columnar order of appearance, Table 1 reports the (a) obtained index/quotient, (b) 95% confidence interval, (c) percentile rank, and (d) measured probability of the particular PDD. The confidence interval is based upon an SEM of 4. I chose the 95% confidence interval (i.e., $\pm 1.96 \times 4$ rounded to the nearest whole number), as opposed to the 68% and 99% confidence intervals, because I believe it possesses and communicates the most reasonable balance between confidence and precision. Thus, simply add and subtract 8 from the index/quotient to insert the proper numbers into column 2.

The final column trichotomous probability alternatives, along with their associated index/quotient score ranges, vary somewhat between the two measures. Concerning the GARS–2, they are as follows: (a) *very unlikely* (≤ 69), *possibly* (70–84), and (c) *very likely* (≥ 85). The GADS includes the following: (a) *low/not probable* (≤ 69), *borderline* (70–79), and (c) *high/probable* (≥ 80). Note that I have retained the different score ranges because they are predicated upon empirical data. In contrast, I have adopted an abbreviated form of the GADS probability designations for both measures. This is because (a) they are conceptually the same and (b) their consistency minimizes confusion when both instruments are included within the same test battery and final report. Furthermore, the *low–borderline–high* nomenclature is more consistent with those utilized by the cognitive tests included in my recommended battery (see Chapters 4–6).

General Table 1 notes communicate the following information: (a) index/quotient mean and standard deviation, (b) meaning of higher scores worded in the pathological direction, (c) clarification of pertinent abbreviations, and (d) optional "--" as denoting the lack of score availability. The latter may be due to missing ratings. It is to be noted that the GARS–2 allows the computation of the Autistic Disorder Index based upon the summation of two of the three subscale SSs (Gilliam, 2006, pp. 73–76). Finally, specific tabular notes delineate (a) the SEM upon which the 95% confidence interval is based and (b) the probability designations and related index/quotient score ranges.

Subscales. Table 2 presents the more specific subscale results. From left to right, they include (a) subscale score names, (b) subscale SSs, (c) 95% confidence intervals, (d) symptom severity categorical designations, and (e) the particular clusters of measured symptoms. The SEM for the subscales is 1. Thus, adding and subtracting 2 (i.e., 1 × 1.96 rounded to the nearest whole number) from each SS provides the 95% confidence interval. As in Table 1, this information is provided with a specific tabular note.

The symptom severity classifications and their associated SS ranges were developed by me through the use of psychometric principles (i.e., standard deviations from the mean), practical application, and experience. They include the following: (a) *absent* (SS = 1–4), (b) *mild* (SS = 5–7), (c) *moderate* (SS = 8–12), and (d) *severe* (SS = 13 and above). The latter three labels are frequently employed by the *DSM-IV-TR* disorders which permit severity specifiers (American Psychiatric Association, 2000), and are therefore readily understood by referring mental health clinicians. They are also quite easily comprehensible to lay-people which ultimately facilitates feedback.

As alluded to above, these severity designations are psychometrically accordant with their theoretical normal curve standard deviation ranges and percentile ranks. For example, the designation of absent is associated with -2 to -3 standard deviations from the mean, or a percentile rank range of about 2 and less. From these data, one may reasonably conclude that PDD symptoms on a particular subscale are virtually absent; that is, an effective descriptor for a true negative case. Similarly, the severe designation is applied to +1 to +3 standard deviations from the mean or about the 84th percentile and above. This effectively distinguishes the typical PDD cases from those remarkably more pathological and impaired.

Lastly, the four designations contribute to a well-differentiated subscale profile analysis for purposes of estimating relative degrees of impairment, therefore clarifying the overall PDD index/quotient obtained in Table 1. Thus, for example, GARS–2 subscale results showing severe impairment in Social Interaction, mild impairment in Communication, and absent Stereotyped Behaviors, occurring within the context of an overall Borderline Autistic Disorder Index, may warrant a PDD NOS diagnosis (American Psychiatric Association, 2000).

As indicated above, to facilitate the interpretation and communication process, the final column of Table 2 provides summary descriptions of the measured symptoms captured by each subscale. Regarding the GARS–2, these were based upon the general descriptions of the subscales provided in the manual, which included a listing of items loading on each subscale (Gilliam, 2006, pp. 10–11). The specific wording was selected so as to represent accurately both the item content and more general subscale description. The GADS summary descriptions were based upon a rather extensive discussion of Asperger's Disorder, including a literature review of empirical studies, *DSM-IV-TR* standards, and standards enumerated in the *International Statistical Classification of Diseases and Related Health Problems*, 10th Revision (*ICD-10*) (World Health Organisation, 1992), along with a description of the subscales and their associated items, all of which are presented within the manual (Gilliam, 2001, pp. 2–7).

General Table 2 notes are analogous to those reported in Table 1 and will not be further expounded here. As previously mentioned, Table 2 specific notes elucidate the means by which the 95% confidence intervals are computed, and define the aforementioned severity designations by their SS ranges.

Again, Tables 1 and 2 are designed to be interpreted together immediately ensuing the latter. To facilitate the process, I have worded some of the most frequently applicable narrative interpretations for the testing psychologist to select from, hence permitting rapid deletion of the alternatives that are not supported by the data. First, I have identified the default respondent to be the patient's mother, which can be quickly amended to identify another observer or observers working in collaboration who provided the ratings.[1] This is followed by a pithy statement of whether or not the results are positive or negative for the particular PDD. This statement may be used alone or accompanied by a succinct explanation for such conclusion, especially when the results are borderline or there exists an unusual data pattern.

There is one unique GADS narrative interpretation that applies only within the context of unequivocally positive GARS–2 results. According the *DSM-IV-TR* differential diagnostic guidelines, Asperger's Disorder is precluded when the criteria for Autistic Disorder are met (American Psychiatric Association, 2000). This is part of a more general diagnostic tenet that more inclusive diagnoses (e.g., Major Depressive Disorder) supersede less inclusive diagnoses (e.g., Primary Insomnia). Therefore, consistent with this principle, this narrative interprets positive GADS results as affording further support for the similarly positive GARS–2 results. The final two narratives address false positive and negative interpretations by integrating them with pertinent Conners EC or CBRS invalidity patterns (see above), and/or the preponderance of contrary data within the test battery.

[1] *For obvious reasons, the GARS–2 and GADS are designed to be exclusively observer-based as opposed to self-report.*

Conners' Adult ADHD Rating Scales, Long Version

The last of the symptom-rating scales in my recommended inventory pertains exclusively to adult testing referrals for ADHD. ADHD diagnosis in adulthood has previously been controversial (Smith, Waschbusch, Willoughby, & Evans, 2000). However, there is currently convincing evidence that such disorder exists within this age group (see, e.g., Biederman, 2005). In particular, approximately 50% of adults aged 30 to 40 years who were diagnosed with ADHD in childhood continue to manifest clinically significant symptoms associated with dysfunction (Biederman & Faraone, 2005). Therefore, such testing referrals are both valid and medically justified. Pursuant to *DSM-IV-TR* criteria, however, it is crucial during the initial diagnostic assessment to document the suspected presence of at least some of these symptoms prior to the age of 7 years (American Psychiatric Association, 2000).

There are three Conners' Adult ADHD Rating Scales (CAARS) versions, including Long, Short, and Screening (Conners, Erhardt, & Sparrow, 1999). I utilize the *Long Version* for several reasons. First, it possesses approximately twice the number of items (i.e., 9 and 12) on pertinent *DSM-IV-TR* subscales compared to the Short Form (i.e., 5 and 5). Second, because of the greater item coverage, the Long Version contains two subscales that measure both ADHD symptom cluster criteria as defined by the *DSM-IV* (American Psychiatric Association, 1994), whereas the Short Form lacks such subscale discrimination due to item brevity. The *DSM-IV* and *DSM-IV-TR* ADHD symptom criteria are identical (cf. American Psychiatric Association, 1994, 2000), and hence the content validity of the Long Version remains intact. Third, the Long Version possesses some supplementary subscales that are useful in screening for possible mood problems and self-confidence personality issues (discussed subsequently). Lastly, average time to complete the Long Form is a relatively swift 25 minutes. Incidentally, all versions of the CAARS require a practicable fifth grade reading level.

The CAARS–L comprises Self-Report and Observer Forms for interrater comparisons, analogous to the Conners CBRS. The norm-reference sample ranges in age from 18 years 0 months to 50 years and older. The norms are apportioned by gender and mostly 10-year age groups, including 18 to 29, 30 to 39, 40 to 49, and 50 and older. The final group is more open-ended, including individuals as old as 72 years. The core subscales I find most useful for making ADHD diagnoses in adulthood include the (a) single Inconsistency Index Validity scale, (b) *DSM-IV* based Inattentive Symptoms and Hyperactive–Impulsive Symptoms Clinical scales, and (c) ADHD Index Clinical scale.

The Validity scale measures random or careless responding using a raw score as in the Conners EC and CBRS. The *DSM-IV*-based Clinical scales provide a measure of each ADHD symptom cluster, thus providing evidence as to the predominant type of ADHD present (i.e., Inattentive, Hyperactive–Impulsive, or Combined). The ADHD Index contains the 12 items that best discriminate between adults with and without ADHD. I find it remarkably useful in providing further corroborating evidence of ADHD, especially if comorbidity is suspected (e.g., Dysthymic Disorder or Anxiety Disorder). The diagnostic subscales employ standardized *T*-score data ($M = 50$, $SD = 10$). *T*-scores above 65 are to be interpreted as clinically elevated (Conners et al., 1999).

There are a number of additional diagnostic subscales derived by factor analysis that measure ADHD-type symptoms and behaviors. Although the majority of these subscales are redundant and less diagnostically accurate in making *DSM* differential diagnoses, there are two worthwhile subscales to consider in supplementary analyses, including (a) Impulsivity/ Emotional Lability and (b) Self-Concept. The former screens for a hitherto unsuspected Mood Disorder, especially Bipolar Disorder. The latter may be useful to consider and interpret when ADHD results are negative. In particular, I have had several adult referrals for suspected ADHD that reliably indicated an absence of such disorder, coexisting with a statistically significant Self-Concept subscale (i.e., low self-esteem). This may be effectively interpreted as the patient manifesting self-confidence issues, perhaps associated with perfectionistic proclivities, which logically explains (a) the request for testing, (b) the subjectively reported presenting symptoms, and (c) the ultimate negative empirical results for ADHD.

At this juncture, I wish to reiterate a vital ADHD age-of-onset diagnostic standard. At least some ADHD symptoms and associated dysfunction must be present prior to the age of 7 years, hence the *DSM-IV-TR* superordinate classification, *Disorders Usually First Diagnosed in Infancy, Childhood, or Adolescence* (American Psychiatric Association, 2000). The CAARS–L instructions request that the respondent's ratings be based upon the frequency with which the item describes the patient *recently*. Because neither the CAARS–L standardized data, nor any concurrent neuropsychological testing data that may have been gathered within the battery, sufficiently address the ADHD onset criterion, such information must be explicitly documented within the presenting symptoms portion of both the initial and final reports.

Unlimited use of on-site computerized scoring software is currently not available for the CAARS–L as it is with the majority of tests covered heretofore. Although CAARS–L electronic forms may be purchased and downloaded for computer administration and scoring, I find it more efficient and cost effective to purchase the hard copy response sheet/ scoring forms. The efficiency and convenience pertain to permitting the patient and significant other to complete the forms off-site, and to submit them when the patient attends the ADHD neuropsychological testing session.[2] In practice, I have found manual scoring of both the self-report and observer ratings to be approximately 10 to 15 minutes. Therefore, the decision not to purchase the available computer-assisted software does not obviate use of the CAARS-L as it would with more intricate and complex instruments such as the Neuropsychological Assessment Battery (NAB) (see Chapter 6).

[2] *I have found an effective and efficient ADHD test battery for adults to include the Neuropsychological Assessment Battery (NAB) attention module and its subtests (with the exception of the orientation subtest), the Conners' Continuous Performance Test, Second Edition, Version 5 (CPT-II), and the CAARS-L self-report and observer forms. Please refer to Chapter 6 concerning the two neuropsychological measures. See also Chapter 13, Case 5, for an example of an adult ADHD testing case.*

Results and Interpretation Tables

Conners CAARS–L Self-Report and Observer Form results and interpretation tables appear in Form 7.7. Again, the self-report and observer ratings are contiguous for direct interrater comparisons. There are two relatively brief tables (Table 1 and Table 2), the first presenting the sole Inconsistency Index Validity scale, the second comprising the two *DSM-IV*-derived symptom cluster subscales, followed by the discriminating clinical/ normal ADHD Index. Because their design mirrors those of the Conners EC and CBRS, I will review them more succinctly.

Validity of ratings. Table 1 is apportioned for self-report data (left) and observer data (right), again prioritizing the former as typically being more frequently available. Each half presents identical information including scale name, scale raw score, and the dichotomous valid/invalid interpretations. The invalid interpretation is briefly elaborated regarding its alternative meanings. It is based upon the interpretive possibilities of an invalid pattern described in the manual (Conners et al., 1999, pp. 51–52). General table notes indicate the directional meaning of high raw scores and provide the "--" unavailable score option. Finally, similarly worded valid and invalid narrative interpretations immediately ensue Table 1 (cf. Table 1 narrative interpretations for the Conners EC and CBRS).

Clinical scales. Table 2 presents the core Clinical scale results. The left half presents the self-report data vis-à-vis the observer data. The right half is devoted to a more thorough delineation of measured symptoms or what that scale generally indicates. These were based upon the scale descriptions and recommended interpretations provided within the manual (Conners et al., 1999, pp. 22–44), supplemented by the insertion of key *DSM-IV* diagnostic indicators (e.g., *distractible, inattentive, restless*) (American Psychiatric Association, 1994). The particular wording is designed to be more applicable to adults. In the event of positive results, the symptom descriptions are intended to clarify for adult patients their particular symptom presentation for purposes of planning intervention. Because there are no *DSM* symptom count data, general table notes are the same as for the Conners EC Table 2 (see Form 7.1). True and false positive and negative result alternatives are addressed in the preworded narratives following Table 2.

SUMMARY

This chapter discussed measures employing the symptom rating scale format, principally designed for rendering accurate *DSM-IV-TR* Axis I noncognitive (previously known as nonorganic) and nonpsychotic Clinical Disorders. Although the major focus was on children and adolescents, one measure pertained exclusively to ADHD in adulthood. Thus, the chapter began with a conceptual definition of the *DSM-IV-TR* Clinical Disorder, along with the applicability of standardized symptom rating scales for accurate differential diagnosis and related insurance coverage issues. The vast majority of Chapter 7 was devoted to a detailed review of the particular instruments, beginning with the remarkably multidimensional Conners EC and CBRS forms, and ensued by the two Gilliam PDD measures and the CAARS–L, the latter used primarily for adult ADHD differential diagnoses.

Chapter 8 introduces key standardized self-report clinical and personality inventories. In addition to assisting in *DSM-IV-TR* Axis I differentials, these measures add the capability of rendering Axis I and II distinctions, including the identification of malingering and voluntary or involuntary defensiveness. They are therefore an integral part of contemporary psychological testing practice.

REFERENCES

American Psychiatric Association. (1987). *Diagnostic and statistical manual of mental disorders* (3rd ed. rev.). Washington, DC: Author.

American Psychiatric Association. (1994). *Diagnostic and statistical manual of mental disorders* (4th ed.). Washington, DC: Author.

American Psychiatric Association. (2000). *Diagnostic and statistical manual of mental disorders* (4th ed., text rev.). Washington, DC: Author.

American Psychological Association. (2010). *Publication manual of the American Psychological Association* (6th ed.). Washington, DC: Author.

Autism and Developmental Disabilities Monitoring Network Surveillance Year 2006 Principal Investigators. (2009, December 18). Prevalence of autism spectrum disorders–autism and developmental disabilities monitoring network, United States, 2006. *MMWR Surveillance Summaries, 58*(SS10), 1–20. Retrieved from www.cdc.gov/mmwr/preview/mmwrhtml/ss5810a1.htm

Barlow, David H., & Durand, Mark V. (2012). *Abnormal psychology: An integrative approach* (6th ed.). Belmont, CA: Wadsworth, Cengage Learning.

Benaron, L. D. (2009). *Autism*. Westport, CT: Greenwood Press.

Biederman, J. (2005). Attention-deficit/hyperactivity disorder: A selective overview. *Biological Psychiatry, 57*, 1215–1220.

Biederman, J., & Faraone, S. V. (2005). Attention-deficit/hyperactivity disorder. *The Lancet, 366*, 237–248.

Carlson, G. A., & Kashani, J. H. (1988). Phenomenology of major depression from childhood through adulthood: Analysis of three studies. *American Journal of Psychiatry, 145*, 1222–1225.

Conners CBRS Scoring Software. (2008). [USB key computer software]. North Tonawanda, NY: Multi-Health Systems.

Conners, C. K. (2008). *Conners Comprehensive Behavior Rating Scales (Conners CBRS): Manual and interpretive update*. North Tonawanda, NY: Multi-Health Systems.

Conners, C. K. (2009). *Conners Early Childhood (Conners EC): Manual*. North Tonawanda, NY: Multi-Health Systems.

Conners, C. K., Erhardt, D., & Sparrow, E. (1999). *Conners' Adult ADHD Rating Scales (CAARS): Technical manual*. North Tonawanda, NY: Multi-Health Systems.

Conners EC Scoring Software. (2009). [USB key computer software]. North Tonawanda, NY: Multi-Health Systems.

Exner, J. E. (2003). *The Rorschach a comprehensive system: Basic foundations and principles of interpretation* (4th ed., Vol. 1). Hoboken, NJ: John Wiley.

GARS–2 Software Scoring and Reporting System. (2009). [CD-ROM computer software]. Austin, TX: PRO–ED.

Geller, B., & Luby, J. (1997). Child and adolescent bipolar disorder: A review of the past 10 years. *Journal of the American Academy of Child and Adolescent Psychiatry, 36*, 1168–1176.

Gilliam, J. E. (2001). *Gilliam Asperger's Disorder Scale (GADS) examiner's manual*. Austin, TX: PRO–ED.

Gilliam, J. E. (2006). *Gilliam Autism Rating Scale (GARS–2) examiner's manual* (2nd ed.). Austin, TX: PRO–ED.

Grinker, R. R. (2007). *Unstrange minds: Remapping the world of autism*. New York, NY: Basic Books.

Holden, C. (2008). Bipolar disorder: Poles apart. *Science, 321*, 193–195.

Krueger, R. F., & Markon, K. E. (2006). Reinterpreting comorbidity: A model-based approach to understanding and classifying psychopathology. *Annual Review of Clinical Psychology, 2*, 111–133.

Miller, L. A., McIntire, S. A., & Lovler, R. L. (2011). *Foundations of psychological testing* (3rd ed.). Thousand Oaks, CA: Sage Publications.

National Institute of Mental Health. (2001). *Bipolar disorder*. Bethesda, MD: Author. Retrieved from http://www.nimh.nih.gov./publicat/bipolar.cfm

Nevid, J. S., Rathus, S. A., & Greene, B. (2011). *Abnormal psychology in a changing world* (8th ed.). Upper Saddle River, NJ: Prentice Hall.

Oberman, L. M., & Ramachandran, V. S. (2007). The simulating social mind: The role of the mirror neuron system and simulation in the social and communicative deficits of autism spectrum disorders. *Psychological Bulletin, 133*, 310–327.

Smith, B. H., Waschbusch, D. A., Willoughby, M. T., & Evans, S. (2000). The efficacy, safety, and practicality of treatments for adolescents with attention-deficit/hyperactivity disorder (ADHD). *Clinical Child and Family Psychology Review, 3*, 243–267.

Warner, R. M. (2008). *Applied statistics*. Thousand Oaks, CA: Sage Publications.

Weller, E., Weller, R., & Fristad, M. (1995). Bipolar diagnosis in children: Misdiagnosis, underdiagnosis, and future directions. *Journal of the American Academy of Child and Adolescent Psychiatry, 34*, 709–714.

World Health Organisation. (1992). *ICD-10 classifications of mental and behavioural disorder: Clinical descriptions and diagnostic guidelines*. Geneva, Switzerland: World Health Organisation.

FORM 7.1

CONNERS EC, PARENT AND TEACHER/CHILDCARE FORMS RESULTS AND INTERPRETATION TABLES

Conners EC, Parent and Teacher/Childcare Forms

TABLE 1 ■ VALIDITY OF RATINGS

Parent ratings			Teacher/childcare ratings		
Scale	Raw score	Result	Scale	Raw score	Result
Positive Impression[a]	--	Valid Invalid	Positive Impression[a]	--	Valid Invalid
Negative Impression[b]	--	Valid Invalid	Negative Impression[b]	--	Valid Invalid
Inconsistency Index[c]	--	Valid Invalid	Inconsistency Index[c]	--	Valid Invalid

Note: Lower raw scores indicate that the ratings are increasingly valid. -- denotes not administered, or score type not available or computed.

[a]Invalid indicates that the rater produced an overly positive description of the youth's behavior.

[b]Invalid indicates that the rater produced an overly negative description of the youth's behavior.

[c]Invalid indicates either variable attention or comprehension difficulties on the part of the rater.

Both parent and teacher/childcare ratings were valid.

The parent ratings manifested invalid response tendencies. The teacher/childcare ratings were valid. Therefore, the parent ratings were considered valid under the following conditions: (a) when consistent with the valid teacher/childcare ratings and (b) when reasonably supportive of other test data deemed reliable and valid, including data gathered from the diagnostic interview.

(Cont.)

FORM 7.1

CONNERS EC, PARENT AND TEACHER/CHILDCARE FORMS RESULTS AND INTERPRETATION TABLES (*Cont.*)

TABLE 2 ■ BEHAVIOR SCALE

Scale	Parent ratings T-score*	Teacher/ childcare ratings T-score*	Result[a]	Measured symptoms
Inattention-Hyperactivity	--	--	Negative	Poor concentration; easily distracted; quickly loses interest; overactive; difficultly remaining seated; impulsive; fidgety
Restless-Impulsive	--	--	Atypical	Easily distracted; restless; fidgety; impulsive; difficulty completing tasks; distracting others
Defiance-Temper	--	--	Positive	Argumentative; stubborn; defiant; manipulative; moody; whiny; poor anger control
Aggression	--	--	Negative	Fighting; bullying; rude; destructive; dishonest
Social Functioning	--	--	Negative	Poor social skills; difficulty with body language, social cues, and emotions; no friends; disliked or ignored by peers
Atypical Behaviors	--	--	Negative	Unusual interests and language; repetitive movements; inflexible; uninterested in relationships; limited emotional expression
Anxiety	--	--	Negative	Fearful; apprehensive; clingy; cries easily; easily hurt feelings; bodily complaints; sleep difficulties; nightmares
Mood and Affect	--	--	Negative	Irritability; sadness; negativity; lack of interests; tearful; sad themes during play
Emotional Liability	--	--	Negative	Mood swings; emotionally reactive; frequent crying; easily frustrated; frequent temper outbursts

*Note: T-*score mean = 50, standard deviation = 10. Higher *T*-scores indicate greater presence of symptoms. *denotes that the *T*-score is statistically significant; measured symptoms on that clinical scale are sufficiently severe to indicate a *DSM-IV-TR* diagnosis. -- denotes not administered, or score type not available or computed.

[a]Atypical indicates any of the following alternative interpretations: (a) symptoms due to situation-specific environmental variables, (b) an unusual mixture of *DSM-IV-TR* symptoms, or (c) symptoms secondary to another more inclusive *DSM-IV-TR* disorder.

TABLE 3 ■ DEVELOPMENTAL MILESTONES SCALE

Scale	Parent ratings T-score*	Teacher/ childcare ratings T-score*	Result	Measured skills
Adaptive Skills	--	--	Normal	Dressing; eating and drinking; toileting; personal hygiene; helping others
Communication Skills	--	--	Delay	Expressive and receptive language; verbal, facial, and gestural communication
Motor Skills	--	--	Normal	Fine and gross motor skills
Play	--	--	Delay	Imaginative and pretend play
Preacademic Cognitive Skills	--	--	Normal	Knowledge of colors, letters, numbers, body parts; prereading; memory and reasoning

*Note: T-*score mean = 50, standard deviation = 10. Higher *T*-scores indicate greater delays. *denotes that the *T*-score is statistically significant; measured skills are sufficiently delayed to indicate a *DSM-IV-TR* developmental disorder diagnosis. -- denotes not administered, or score type not available or computed.

FORM 7.2

CONNERS CBRS, PARENT AND TEACHER FORMS RESULTS AND INTERPRETATION TABLES

Conners CBRS, Parent and Teacher Forms

TABLE 1 ■ VALIDITY OF RATINGS

Parent ratings				Teacher ratings			
Scale	Raw score	Differentials	Result	Scale	Raw score	Differentials	Result
Positive Impression[a]	--	--	Valid Invalid	Positive Impression[a]	--	--	Valid Invalid
Negative Impression[b]	--	--	Valid Invalid	Negative Impression[b]	--	--	Valid Invalid
Inconsistency Index[c]	--	--	Valid Invalid	Inconsistency Index[c]	--	--	Valid Invalid

Note: Lower raw scores indicate that the ratings are increasingly valid. -- denotes not administered, or score type not available or computed.

[a]Invalid interpretation indicates that the rater produced an overly positive description of the youth's behavior.

[b]Invalid indicates that the rater produced an overly negative description of the youth's behavior.

[c]Invalid indicates either variable attention or comprehension difficulties on the part of the rater.

Both parent and teacher ratings were valid.

The parent ratings manifested invalid response tendencies. The teacher ratings were valid. Therefore, the parent ratings were considered valid under the following conditions: (a) when consistent with the valid teacher ratings and (b) when reasonably supportive of other test data deemed reliable and valid, including data gathered from the diagnostic interview.

(Cont.)

FORM 7.2

CONNERS CBRS, PARENT AND TEACHER FORMS RESULTS AND INTERPRETATION TABLES (*Cont.*)

TABLE 2 ■ **CLINICAL SCALE**

Scale	Parent ratings		Teacher ratings		Diagnostic result[a]	Measured symptoms
	T-score*	DSM symptom counts	T-score*	DSM symptom counts		
ADHD Inattentive	--	Not met	--	Not met	Negative	Impaired immediate and sustained attention; forgetful; distractible; disorganized
ADHD Hyperactive-Impulsive	--	Not met	--	Not met	Atypical symptoms	Overactive; fidgets; restless; loud; acts without thinking of consequences
Conduct Disorder	--	Not met	--	Not met	Positive	Repetitive and persistent violations of the basic rights of others and major societal norms or rules
Oppositional Defiant Disorder	--	Not met	--	Not met	Negative	Pattern of negativistic, hostile, and defiant behavior of minimum 6 months
Major Depressive Episode	--	Not met	--	Not met	Negative	Persistent sadness or irritability; lack of interest, pleasure, energy, self-worth, concentration
Manic Episode	--	Not met	--	Not met	Negative	Persistently elevated, expansive, or irritable mood; racing thoughts; distractible; impulsive
Generalized Anxiety Disorder	--	Not met	--	Not met	Negative	Excessive worry; feeling on edge; tense; irritable; difficulty concentrating; fatigued
Separation Anxiety Disorder	--	Not met	--	Not met	Negative	Recurrent excessive distress associated with separation from major attachment figures
Social Phobia	--	Not met	--	Not met	Negative	Persistent fear of social or performance situations; fear of humiliation
Obsessive-Compulsive Disorder	--	Not met	--	Not met	Negative	Persistent, intrusive, distressing thoughts; repetitive behaviors to reduce distress
Autistic Disorder	--	Not met	--	Not met	Negative	Qualitative impairments in social interaction and communication; stereotyped behaviors
Asperger's Disorder	--	Not met	--	Not met	Negative	Qualitative impairments in social interaction, stereotyped behaviors

Note: T-score mean = 50, standard deviation = 10. Higher T-scores indicate greater presence of symptoms. *denotes that the T-score is statistically significant; measured symptoms on that clinical scale are sufficiently severe to indicate a clinical diagnosis. Symptom counts "Met" when at or above the *DSM-IV-TR* cut-off score; symptom counts "Not met" when below the *DSM-IV-TR* cut-off score. -- denotes not administered, or score type not available or computed.

[a]Atypical symptoms indicate the presence of clinical symptoms due to an alternate *DSM-IV-TR* diagnosis.

FORM 7.3

CONNERS CBRS, PARENT AND SELF-REPORT FORMS RESULTS AND INTERPRETATION TABLES

Conners CBRS, Parent and Self-Report Forms

TABLE 1 ■ VALIDITY OF RATINGS

Parent ratings				Self-report ratings			
Scale	Raw score	Differentials	Result	Scale	Raw score	Differentials	Result
Positive Impression[a]	--	--	Valid Invalid	Positive Impression[a]	--	--	Valid Invalid
Negative Impression[b]	--	--	Valid invalid	Negative Impression[b]	--	--	Valid Invalid
Inconsistency Index[c]	--	--	Valid Invalid	Inconsistency Index[c]	--	--	Valid Invalid

Note: Lower raw scores indicate that the ratings are increasingly valid. -- denotes not administered, or score type not available or computed.

[a]Invalid interpretation indicates that the rater produced an overly positive description of the youth's behavior.

[b]Invalid indicates that the rater produced an overly negative description of the youth's behavior.

[c]Invalid indicates either variable attention or comprehension difficulties on the part of the rater.

Both parent and self-report ratings were valid.

The self-report ratings manifested invalid response tendencies. The parent ratings were valid. Therefore, the self-report ratings were considered valid under the following conditions: (a) when consistent with the valid parent ratings and (b) when reasonably supportive of other test data deemed reliable and valid, including data gathered from the diagnostic interview.   *(Cont.)*

FORM 7.3

CONNERS CBRS, PARENT AND SELF-REPORT FORMS RESULTS AND INTERPRETATION TABLES (*Cont.*)

TABLE 2 ■ **CLINICAL SCALE**

Scale	Parent ratings		Self-report rating		Diagnostic result[a]	Measured symptoms
	T-score*	*DSM* symptom counts	*T*-score*	*DSM* symptom counts		
ADHD Inattentive	--	Not met	--	Not met	Negative	Impaired immediate and sustained attention; forgetful; distractible; disorganized
ADHD Hyperactive-Impulsive	--	Not met	--	Not met	Atypical symptoms	Overactive; fidgets; restless; loud; acts without thinking of consequences
Conduct Disorder	--	Not met	--	Not met	Positive	Repetitive and persistent violations of the basic rights of others and major societal norms or rules
Oppositional Defiant Disorder	--	Not met	--	Not met	Negative	Pattern of negativistic, hostile, and defiant behavior of minimum 6 months
Major Depressive Episode	--	Not met	--	Not met	Negative	Persistent sadness or irritability; lack of interest, pleasure, energy, self-worth, concentration
Manic Episode	--	Not met	--	Not met	Negative	Persistently elevated, expansive, or irritable mood; racing thoughts; distractible; impulsive
Generalized Anxiety Disorder	--	Not met	--	Not met	Negative	Excessive worry; feeling on edge; tense; irritable; difficulty concentrating; fatigued
Separation Anxiety Disorder	--	Not met	--	Not met	Negative	Recurrent excessive distress associated with separation from major attachment figures
Social Phobia	--	Not met	--	Not met	Negative	Persistent fear of social or performance situations; fear of humiliation
Obsessive-Compulsive Disorder	--	Not met	--	Not met	Negative	Persistent, intrusive, distressing thoughts; repetitive behaviors to reduce distress
Autistic Disorder	--	Not met	--	--	Negative	Qualitative impairments in social interaction and communication; stereotyped behaviors
Asperger's Disorder	--	Not met	--	--	Negative	Qualitative impairments in social interaction, stereotyped behaviors

Note: T-score mean = 50, standard deviation = 10. Higher *T*-scores indicate greater presence of symptoms. *denotes that the *T*-score is statistically significant; measured symptoms on that clinical scale are sufficiently severe to indicate a clinical diagnosis. Symptom counts "Met" when at or above the *DSM-IV-TR* cut-off score; symptom counts "Not met" when below the *DSM-IV-TR* cut-off score. -- denotes not administered, or score type not available or computed.

[a]Atypical symptoms indicate the presence of clinical symptoms due to an alternate *DSM-IV-TR* diagnosis.

FORM 7.4

CONNERS CBRS, SELF-REPORT FORM RESULTS AND INTERPRETATION TABLES

Conners CBRS, Self-Report Form

TABLE 1 ■ **VALIDITY OF RATINGS**

Scale	Self-report ratings		Result
	Raw score	Differentials	
Positive Impression[a]	--	--	Valid
			Invalid
Negative Impression[b]	--	--	Valid
			Invalid
Inconsistency Index[c]	--	--	Valid
			Invalid

Note: Lower raw scores indicate that the ratings are increasingly valid. -- denotes not administered, or score type not available or computed.

[a]Invalid interpretation indicates that the rater produced an overly positive description of the youth's behavior.

[b]Invalid indicates that the rater produced an overly negative description of the youth's behavior.

[c]Invalid indicates either variable attention or comprehension difficulties on the part of the rater.

The self-report ratings were valid.

The self-report ratings manifested invalid response tendencies. The analogous Conners CBRS parent and teacher ratings were valid. Therefore, the self-report ratings were considered valid under the following conditions: (a) when consistent with the valid parent and teacher ratings and (b) when reasonably supportive of other test data deemed reliable and valid, including data gathered from the diagnostic interview.

TABLE 2 ■ **CLINICAL SCALE**

Scale	T-score*	DSM symptom counts	Diagnostic result[a]	Measured symptoms
ADHD Inattentive	--	Not met	Negative	Impaired immediate and sustained attention; forgetful; distractible; disorganized
ADHD Hyperactive-Impulsive	--	Not met	Atypical symptoms	Overactive; fidgets; restless; loud; acts without thinking of consequences
Conduct Disorder	--	Not met	Positive	Repetitive and persistent violations of the basic rights of others and major societal norms or rules
Oppositional Defiant Disorder	--	Not met	Negative	Pattern of negativistic, hostile, and defiant behavior of minimum 6 months
Major Depressive Episode	--	Not met	Negative	Persistent sadness or irritability; lack of interest, pleasure, energy, self-worth, concentration
Manic Episode	--	Not met	Negative	Persistently elevated, expansive, or irritable mood; racing thoughts; distractible; impulsive
Generalized Anxiety Disorder	--	Not met	Negative	Excessive worry; feeling on edge; tense; irritable; difficulty concentrating; fatigued
Separation Anxiety Disorder	--	Not met	Negative	Recurrent excessive distress associated with separation from major attachment figures
Social Phobia	--	Not met	Negative	Persistent fear of social or performance situations; fear of humiliation
Obsessive-Compulsive Disorder	--	Not met	Negative	Persistent, intrusive, distressing thoughts; repetitive behaviors to reduce distress

Note: T-score mean = 50, standard deviation = 10. Higher T-scores indicate greater presence of symptoms. *denotes that the T-score is statistically significant; measured symptoms on that clinical scale are sufficiently severe to indicate a clinical diagnosis. Symptom counts "Met" when at or above the *DSM-IV-TR* cut-off score; symptom counts "Not met" when below the *DSM-IV-TR* cut-off score. -- denotes not administered, or score type not available or computed.

[a]Atypical symptoms indicate the presence of clinical symptoms due to an alternate *DSM-IV-TR* diagnosis.

FORM 7.5

GARS–2 RESULTS AND INTERPRETATION TABLES

GARS–2

TABLE 1 ■ **AUTISTIC DISORDER INDEX**

Autistic Disorder index	95% CI[a]	PR	Probability of Autistic Disorder[b]
000	[000, 000]	0.00	Low; Borderline; High

Note: Autistic Disorder index mean = 100, standard deviation = 15. Higher scores indicate Autistic Disorder is more likely. CI, confidence interval; PR, percentile rank.

[a]CI is based upon a standard error of measurement = 4.

[b]*Low* is an index of 69 and below; *Borderline* is an index of 70 to 84; *High* is an index of 85 and above.

TABLE 2 ■ **SUBSCALES**

Subscale	SS	95% CI[a]	PR	Symptom severity[b]	Measured symptoms
Stereotyped Behaviors	00	[00, 00]	0.00	Absent Mild Moderate Severe	Restricted interests of abnormal intensity or focus; inflexible and specific nonfunctional routines or rituals; repetitive motor mannerisms; preoccupation with object parts
Communication	00	[00, 00]	0.00	Absent Mild Moderate Severe	Impaired spoken language; inability to have conversations; stereotyped, repetitive, idiosyncratic language; lack of make-believe or imitative play
Social Interaction	00	[00, 00]	0.00	Absent Mild Moderate Severe	Impaired nonverbal behaviors (e.g., gestures to regulate social interaction); lack of peer relationships; lack of spontaneous seeking of mutual shared enjoyment, interests, achievements; lack of reciprocity

Note: Standard score mean = 10, standard deviation = 3. Higher scores indicate increasing symptom severity. SS, standard score; CI, confidence interval; PR, percentile rank.

[a]CI is based upon a standard error of measurement = 1.

[b]*Absent* is a SS of 1 to 4; *Mild* is a SS of 5 to 7; *Moderate* is a SS of 8 to 12; *Severe* is a SS of 13 and above.

Respondent: Mother.

GARS–2 data are negative positive for autistic disorder.

GARS–2 data are interpreted as a false positive for the following reasons: (a) respondent's Conners CBRS EC validity scale scores indicated an overly negative description of the youth's behavior and (b) negative results for Autistic Disorder among the majority of other reliable and valid test data.

GARS–2 data are interpreted as a false negative for the following reasons: (a) respondent's Conners CBRS EC validity scale scores indicated an overly positive description of the youth's behavior and (b) positive results for Autistic Disorder among the majority of other reliable and valid test data.

FORM 7.6

GADS RESULTS AND INTERPRETATION TABLES

GADS

TABLE 1 ■ ASPERGER'S DISORDER QUOTIENT

Asperger's Disorder quotient	95% CI[a]	PR	Probability of Asperger's Disorder[b]
--	[000, 000]	0.00	Low; Borderline; High

Note: Asperger's Disorder quotient mean = 100, standard deviation = 15. Higher scores indicate Asperger's Disorder is more likely. CI, confidence interval; PR, percentile rank. -- denotes not administered, or score type not available or computed.

[a]CI is based upon a standard error of measurement = 4.

[b]*Low* is a quotient of 69 and below; *Borderline* is a quotient of 70 to 79; *High* is a quotient of 80 and above.

TABLE 2 ■ SUBSCALES

Subscale	SS	95% CI[a]	PR	Symptom severity[b]	Measured symptoms
Social Interaction	00	[00, 00]	0.00	Absent Mild Moderate Severe	Impaired nonverbal behaviors (e.g., gestures to regulate social interaction); lack of peer relationships; lack of spontaneous seeking of mutual shared enjoyment, interests, or achievements; lack of social reciprocity
Restricted Patterns of Behavior	00	[00, 00]	0.00	Absent Mild Moderate Severe	Stereotyped and restricted interests of abnormal intensity or focus; inflexible, specific, nonfunctional routines or rituals; stereotyped and repetitive motor mannerisms; preoccupation with object parts
Cognitive Patterns	00	[00, 00]	0.00	Absent Mild Moderate Severe	Lack of ability to initiate or sustain interpersonal conversations; idiosyncratic language and interests; lack of varied, spontaneous make–believe, or imitative play
Pragmatic Skills	00	[00, 00]	0.00	Absent Mild Moderate Severe	Impaired social perception; impaired understanding of others' perspectives, experiences, and beliefs (i.e., theory of mind); impaired affect recognition

Note: Standard score mean = 10, standard deviation = 3. Higher scores indicate increasing symptom severity. SS, standard score; CI, confidence interval; PR, percentile rank.

[a]CI is based upon a standard error of measurement = 1.

[b]*Absent* is a SS of 1 to 4; *Mild* is a SS of 5 to 7; *Moderate* is a SS of 8 to 12; *Severe* is a SS of 13 and above.

Respondent: Mother.

GADS data are negative positive for Asperger's Disorder.

Considering the positive GARS–2 results, these positive GADS data are interpreted as further support for the more severe and inclusive Autistic Disorder.

GADS data are interpreted as a false positive for the following reasons: (a) respondent's Conners CBRS EC validity scale scores indicated an overly negative description of the youth's behavior and (b) negative results for Asperger's Disorder among the majority of other reliable and valid test data.

GADS data are interpreted as a false negative for the following reasons: (a) respondent's Conners CBRS EC validity scale scores indicated an overly positive description of the youth's behavior and (b) positive results for Asperger's Disorder among the majority of other reliable and valid test data.

FORM 7.7

CONNERS' CAARS–L, SELF-REPORT AND OBSERVER FORMS RESULTS AND INTERPRETATION TABLES

Conners' CAARS–L, Self-Report and Observer Forms

TABLE 1 ■ VALIDITY OF RATINGS

Self-report ratings			Observer ratings		
Scale	Raw score	Interpretation	Scale	Raw score	Interpretation
Inconsistency Index	--	Valid. Invalid due to variable attention or comprehension difficulties	Inconsistency Index	--	Valid. Invalid due to variable attention or comprehension difficulties

Note: Lower raw scores indicate that the ratings are increasingly valid. -- denotes not administered, or score type not available or computed.

Both self-report and observer ratings were valid.

The observer ratings manifested invalid response tendencies. The self-report ratings were valid. Therefore, observer ratings were considered valid under the following conditions: (a) when consistent with the valid self-report ratings and (b) when reasonably supportive of other test data deemed reliable and valid, including data gathered from the diagnostic interview.

TABLE 2 ■ CLINICAL SCALES

Self-report ratings		Observer ratings		Measured symptoms
Clinical scale	T-score*	Clinical scale	T-score*	
DSM-IV-TR Inattentive Symptoms	--	*DSM-IV-TR* Inattentive Symptoms	--	Careless mistakes; inattentive; does not listen; fails to complete tasks; disorganized; avoids task requiring sustained mental effort; loses necessary things; distractible; forgetful
DSM-IV-TR Hyperactive-Impulsive Symptoms	--	*DSM-IV-TR* Hyperactive-Impulsive Symptoms	--	Fidgets; difficulty remaining seated; restless; loud; driven; talks excessively; blurts out answers before questions have been completed; difficulty waiting turn; interrupts or intrudes on others
ADHD Index	--	ADHD Index	--	Clinically significant levels of ADHD symptoms

Note: T-score mean = 50, standard deviation = 10. Higher T-scores indicate greater presence of measured symptoms. *denotes that the T-score is statistically significant; measured symptoms on that clinical scale are sufficiently severe to indicate an ADHD diagnosis. -- denotes not administered, or score type not available or computed.

Conners' CAARS–L data are negative positive for ADHD, Combined Type Predominantly Hyperactive-Impulsive Type Predominantly Inattentive type.

Conners' CAARS–L data are interpreted as a false positive for the following reasons: (a) negative results for ADHD among the majority of other reliable and valid test data and (b) results indicating the presence of an alternate *DSM-IV-TR* disorder which better accounts for the above-referenced measured symptoms.

Conners' CAARS–L data are interpreted as a false negative for the following reasons: (a) positive results for ADHD among the majority of other reliable and valid test data and (b) results indicating an absence of an alternate *DSM-IV-TR* disorder which better accounts for the above-referenced measured symptoms.

Self-Report Clinical and Personality Inventories

The genre of tests in this chapter comprises self-report inventories designed to measure Axis I Clinical Disorders and Axis II Personality Disorders as defined by the *Diagnostic and Statistical Manual of Mental Disorders, Fourth Edition, Text Revision* (*DSM-IV-TR*) (American Psychiatric Association, 2000). The categories of disorders of particular focus include Mood Disorders, Anxiety Disorders, Psychotic Disorders, Somatoform Disorders, Eating Disorders, Disruptive Behavior Disorders, and Personality Disorders. They also provide supporting evidence of Substance-Related Disorders, especially Alcohol Abuse and Dependence, along with Malingering and the related Factitious Disorder. The latter two are measured by means of an impressive array of sophisticated validity scales, which are capable of detecting symptom magnification and over-reporting test-taking response patterns. Alternatively, cognitive and developmentally based Axis I and II Disorders that are first evident during infancy and childhood are largely excluded among the data yield, including Pervasive Developmental Disorders, Learning Disorders, Communication Disorders, and Mental Retardation.

As such, the two paramount constructs being measured here are the Axis I Clinical Disorder and the newly considered *Axis II Personality Disorder* (American Psychiatric Association, 2000). The latter adds a second and vital dimension of diagnosable psychopathology. It also expands the complex issue of comorbidity both within and between two cardinal dimensions of psychological functioning. Hence, in the ensuing section, I shall initially recapitulate the Axis I Clinical Disorder, then compare and contrast it with an expanded discussion of the Axis II Personality Disorder, including an explication of the latter's unique diagnostic issues.

THE CONSTRUCTS OF CLINICAL DISORDER AND PERSONALITY DISORDER AND THEIR MEASUREMENT

The more traditional Axis I Clinical Disorder was previously defined as a cluster of essential and nonessential symptoms causing dysfunction, with an identifiable and acute onset, frequently precipitating intervention, and tending to be responsive to treatment (American Psychiatric Association, 2000; see also Chapter 7). To reiterate, all Axis I Clinical Disorders are classified by a categorical system, which assumes a prototypical approach.

In contrast, the Axis II Personality Disorder is conceptualized as a continuing pattern of aberrant thinking, feeling, and behavior, which is *inflexible* and *pervasive*, thus manifesting both cross-situational and temporal consistency, and which causes dysfunction (American Psychiatric Association, 2000, p. 686). In essence, it represents a chronic lifestyle problem. Although *DSM-IV-TR* Personality Disorder classifications are currently also based upon the prototypical approach, they possess distinct and more diagnostically complex issues and features frequently not encountered, or encountered to a much lesser extent, by the Axis I Clinical Disorder.[1]

For instance, analogous to Bipolar Disorder in the younger patient, Personality Disorder diagnoses in older childhood and adolescence have the potential for controversy due to enhanced concerns for the negative effects of labeling (Hinshaw & Stier, 2008).

[1] *The DSM-IV-TR actually permits clinicians to diagnose psychological disorders using an optional nonaxial format (American Psychiatric Association, 2000, p. 37). In employing such a format, the axes are dropped and all pertinent coexisting diagnoses are listed beginning with the principal disorder. I do not advise using this practice because the Axis I and II distinction, although not perfect, fosters more precision by requiring finer diagnostic discriminations. In particular, it facilitates case conceptualization and obviates missing a crucial latent disorder, most especially, the all too frequent underlying Personality Disorder.*

After all, the diagnosis refers to a disturbance in the younger individual's inherent character or at least developing character.

As an additional example, there currently exists considerable debate as to whether or not the Personality Disorder represents a disturbance in *type* or *degree* (Widiger & Trull, 2007). Those who advocate the latter position espouse a dimensional versus categorical system of diagnosis (Shedler & Westen, 2004). The remarkably high rate of Axis II comorbidity, even exceeding that for Axis I disorders, bolsters the argument for a dimensional approach (Zimmerman, Rothschild, & Chelminski, 2005). However, current dimensional diagnostic frameworks are remarkably more complex and therefore more cumbersome to employ in clinical practice, thus hindering consensus regarding the most useful standardized system (Larsen & Buss, 2010).

These issues notwithstanding, I believe that the current Axis II *DSM-IV-TR* system offers the most efficacious balance between diagnostic accuracy and utility in clinical practice. Furthermore, assessing personality by typology dates back to Hippocrates (460–370 BC) and Galen (130–200 AD), and has endured within contemporary personality psychology, especially concerning practical applications (see e.g., Block, 1971, 1977; Friedman & Rosenman, 1974; Myers, 1998; Myers, McCaulley, Quenk, & Hammer, 1998). Finally, some have cogently argued that the categorical (i.e., nominal) and dimensional (i.e., ordinal/interval/ratio) dichotomy is false and represents an artificial outcome of varying statistical assessment methods (see e.g., Chamorro-Premuzic, 2011). This shall become evident when I review the unique Base Rate (*BR*) standard scores of the Millon series of tests subsequent, which are a unique combination of nominal and ordinal data. These will be contrasted with traditional standardized *T*-scores most typically considered to be interval data (Graziano & Raulin, 2010; Warner, 2008), and hence singularly dimensional in nature.[2]

Therefore, I next review the Axis II *DSM-IV-TR* system standards in detail as it shall be the framework within which the standardized tests in this chapter are discussed, including their associated scoring and interpretation tables.

Evidence indicates that the Personality Disorder originates in childhood, has an insidious onset, and continues on a chronic course through adulthood (Barlow & Durand, 2012). This renders onset difficult to discern. Thus, a vital issue to clarify is at what particular point in development can and should an Axis II Personality Disorder be diagnosed?

Although Personality Disorders are usually diagnosed sometime in adulthood, during which time the maladaptive traits have most often become flagrantly rigid and ingrained, the *DSM-IV-TR* advises that such disorders may be legitimately diagnosed in children and adolescents if such characteristics are "pervasive, persistent, and unlikely to be limited to a developmental stage or an episode of an Axis I disorder," including a minimum duration of 1 year (American Psychiatric Association, 2000, p. 687). A pertinent *DSM-IV-TR* qualifier is that a childhood-onset Personality Disorder "will often not persist unchanged into adult life" (American Psychiatric Association, 2000, p. 687). This suggests that the maladaptive traits may diminish, exacerbate, and/or manifest differently with age and is consonant with evidence of the malleability of child and adolescent personality (Caspi & Roberts, 2001; McCrae & Costa, 2003). Interestingly, it is also accordant with the concept of *personality coherence* in which rank-order stability in a trait is maintained longitudinally, although the particular behavioral manifestations change predictably with chronological age (Larsen & Buss, 2010). For example, explosive temper tantrums in childhood were shown to be reliable predictors of poor occupational performance and marital dissolution 30 years later (Caspi, Elder, & Bem, 1987).

The single exception to permitting child and adolescent Axis II diagnoses is the Antisocial Personality Disorder (APD), which includes the proscribing criterion of a minimum of 18 years of age (American Psychiatric Association, 2000, p. 706). The critical implication of these *DSM-IV-TR* guidelines is that justifiable child and adolescent Axis

[2] *In retrospect, the Conners Comprehensive Behavior Rating Scales (CBRS) (Conners, 2008) employs a similar novel combined dimensional (i.e., interval T-scores) and categorical (i.e., DSM-IV-TR symptom counts) measurement approach in the diagnosis of Axis I Clinical Disorders among children and adolescents (see Chapter 7). The increasing use of this combined measurement approach in contemporary psychological testing and psychodiagnosis is testament to the increasingly apparent false dichotomy between dimensional and categorical variables. At a minimum, this indicates that the two approaches are complementary and thus not mutually exclusive. After all, scrutiny of specific DSM-IV-TR Axis I and II disorders reveals frequent references to dimensional aspects of its prototypically classified symptoms including, for example, some of the following intensity and frequency descriptors: (a) often, (b) easily, (c) severely, (d) in excess, (e) markedly, (f) persistent, (g) excessive, (h) repeated, and (i) almost always (American Psychiatric Association, 2000). Furthermore, severity and course specifiers, along with the Axis V Global Assessment of Functioning (GAF) scale, are unambiguously ordinal/interval or dimensional in nature.*

Finally, later in this chapter when I discuss the two selected Minnesota Multiphasic Personality Inventory (MMPI) tests, you shall become cognizant of my diagnostic use of the interval-based T-scores which integrates the categorical and dimensional approaches. Therefore, it is my opinion that psychodiagnosis is substantively an integration of both type and degree.

II diagnoses are necessary to promote effective early treatment intervention, analogous to Axis I diagnoses.

The particular self-report clinical and personality inventories included in my selected test inventory are the Millon and Minnesota Multiphasic Personality Inventory (MMPI) series (see Form 2.7). Together, they cover an age range of 9 years 0 months to 89 years 0 months; that is, preadolescence through older adulthood. Therefore, they are consonant with the aforementioned *DSM-IV-TR* age guidelines concerning the diagnosis of Personality Disorder and are exceptionally useful in making rapid and accurate both within and between Axis I and II differential diagnoses. As I stated prior, they also contain many of the most sophisticated validity scales available in contemporary standardized psychological testing. Lastly, they all may be computer self-administered and scored, and are thus remarkably efficient and cost-effective.

DIAGNOSTIC REASONS FOR INCLUSION WITHIN A TEST BATTERY

Concerning individuals who have obtained the age of majority (i.e., 18 years and older), mental health testing referrals frequently present both within and between Axis I and II *DSM-IV-TR* differential diagnostic issues. An excellent example of a diagnostically complex Axis I/II testing referral is the following: "Mood Disorder NOS, Provisional, rule out Major Depressive Disorder, Bipolar Disorder, Psychotic Disorder, and Borderline Personality Disorder." The potential Axis II Borderline psychopathology may present intense affective instability and transient psychotic symptoms (Kernberg, 1967; McWilliams, 2011) or extremely severe dissociative symptoms (American Psychiatric Association, 2000) suggestive of Axis I Bipolar and Psychotic Disorders, respectively. In the absence of objective, standardized clinical and personality testing, even the most sagacious mental health clinician would be taxed to render such precise differential diagnostic decisions using the clinical method of assessment. In such cases, excessive comorbid diagnoses, along with imprecise, poorly designed, and protracted trial and error treatment interventions are likely.

Within and between Axis I and II differentials are also becoming remarkably common concerning adolescents (i.e., aged 13–17 years). For preadolescents (i.e., aged 9–12 years), it is more likely that testing issues will focus more exclusively on Axis I differential diagnosis. However, it is not infrequent that an assessment of emerging maladaptive personality traits and risk for later development of a particular Personality Disorder is indicated in preadolescent referrals. Therefore, it is judicious to have a testing practice concerning this youngest age group to measure whether or not a Personality Disorder is either in its incipient stages so as to identify risk, or in the alternative, sufficiently pervasive pursuant to *DSM-IV-TR* guidelines for legitimate diagnosis (discussed prior).

INSURANCE COVERAGE ISSUES

Again, because effective psychiatric and psychotherapeutic intervention is contingent upon accurate *DSM-IV-TR* diagnoses as defined by the American Psychiatric Association (2000), substantiating medical necessity for such testing is routinely feasible. This is especially the case for testing requests to rule out an Axis II Personality Disorder, as such diagnoses are readily recognized as being more difficult to make based solely on the clinical method. In fact, *DSM-IV-TR* guidelines advise that Axis II Personality Disorder diagnoses frequently require multiple interviews interspersed over time, and supplemented by interviews with significant others who are most familiar with the patient (American Psychiatric Association, 2000, p. 686).

Insurance companies are cognizant of the cost-effectiveness of standardized personality testing for Axis II differential diagnosis. Scrupulous use of the "Psychological Test Referral Form" (see Form 2.1) and the "Initial Psychological Assessment Report" (see Forms 2.2 and 2.3) shall ensure inclusion of the requisite information for insurance authorization. This includes judicious selection of the most applicable self-report clinical and personality inventories, along with requesting a reasonable and viable number of testing hours.

THE SELF-REPORT CLINICAL AND PERSONALITY INVENTORIES

As indicated prior, my test inventory is comprised of the most recently published self-report clinical and personality inventories selected from the Millon and MMPI series. The Millon tests include the (a) Millon Pre-Adolescent Clinical Inventory (M–PACI) (Millon, Tringone, Millon, & Grossman, 2005), (b) Millon Adolescent Clinical Inventory (MACI) (Millon, 2006b), and (c) Millon Clinical Multiaxial Inventory–III (MCMI–III) (Millon, 2006a). The MMPI tests include the (a) Minnesota Multiphasic Personality Inventory–Adolescent (MMPI–A) (Butcher et al., 1992) and (b) Minnesota Multiphasic Personality Inventory–2–Restructured Form (MMPI–2–RF) (Ben-Porath &Tellegen, 2008).[3]

I simultaneously discuss the three Millon tests first because they are comparably and specifically designed for, and hence more directly pertinent to, Axis I and II differentials. I will highlight important differences where applicable. Next, I present the two MMPI tests. Because the adult test has undergone significant restructuring, I discuss each of them in separate sections beginning with the adolescent test.

The Millon Tests

The M–PACI is standardized on preadolescents aged 9 years 0 months to 12 years 11 months. It comprises 97 True/False statements and requires a minimum third-grade reading level. Average administration time is 15 to 20 minutes. The MACI is standardized on adolescents aged 13 years 0 months to 19 years 11 months. It contains 160 True/False items, may be completed in approximately 30 minutes, and requires a minimum fifth-grade reading level. Finally, the MCMI–III norm-reference sample ranges in age from 18 years 0 months to 88 years 11 months. It has 175 True/False items, takes an average 25 minutes to complete, and requires at least an eighth-grade reading level. Taken together, these instruments offer extremely efficient administration times, practicable reading levels, an extensive age range, and, as will become apparent, a wealth of Axis I and II diagnostic data. As such, I believe they are integral to contemporary psychological testing practice.

Prior to presenting the Millon results and interpretation tables, I succinctly review the theoretical model upon which these tests are predicated, along with their unique *BR* standard scores. As this book is not intended to focus on the minutiae of psychometric theory and principles, I shall discuss the *BR*-scores and their derivation chiefly for purposes of accurate test interpretation.

All three Millon inventories are based upon a biosocial evolutionary model, which posits that human personality is comprised of learned strategies to (a) secure reinforcement and (b) minimize punishment (Millon, 1990; Millon & Davis, 1996). This is accomplished through the following three polarities: (a) self–other (i.e., independent–ambivalent–dependent), (b) active–passive (i.e., initiate–accommodate), and (c) pleasure–pain (i.e., positive–negative reaction from others). Various types of personality disorders represent differing qualitative combinations of rigid, inflexible, and maladaptive positions on these polarities. Millon's conceptualization of Personality Disorders, along with their specific dysfunctional combinations, are directly correspondent with those of the *DSM-IV-TR*

[3] *You may notice that missing from the latter series is the Minnesota Multiphasic Personality Inventory–2 (MMPI–2) (Butcher et al., 1989). The immediate implications are that my psychological testing practice no longer includes (a) the traditional MMPI/MMPI–2 code-type interpretation strategy and (b) more than 50 years of research and development of the many MMPI–2 content and supplementary scales (Green, 2011).*

However, the MMPI–2–RF is (a) remarkably shorter in length and administration time, thus making it more amenable for patients to complete accurately (i.e., 338 items/35–50 minutes versus 567 items/60–90 minutes, respectively), (b) affords a greater number and variety of validity scales, (c) is comprised of scales that are more factorially pure (i.e., remarkably reduced between-scale item overlap), and (c) contains clinical and personality scales that are more DSM-IV-TR diagnostically pertinent. It is therefore also superior in terms of DSM-IV-TR differential diagnoses. I provide further details of the differences between the MMPI–2 and MMPI–2–RF, along with the diagnostic superiority of the latter later in the chapter.

(American Psychiatric Association, 2000), *DSM-IV* (American Psychiatric Association, 1994), and *DSM-III-R* (American Psychiatric Association, 1987), notwithstanding the *DSM*'s atheoretical design. Finally, Clinical Disorders or Syndromes are proposed to be extensions of the various Personality Disorders (McCann, 1999, 2008).

As stated prior, the Millon inventories employ *BR* standard scores as opposed to the more typical *T*-scores. *T*-scores (*M* = 50, *SD* = 10) are most frequently considered to be parametric interval data (Graziano & Raulin, 2010; Stevens, 1946; Warner, 2008), which assumes that all measured variables (in this instance, psychopathological symptoms, disorders, and traits), form a normal distribution in the population and occur at the same rate. In contrast, *BR*-scores account for the varying estimated prevalence of differing symptoms, disorders, and traits (Craig, 1999), and are considered to be nonparametric nominal/ordinal data (Kamp & Tringone, 2008; McCann, 1999, 2008; Strack, 2002). A succinct explanation of their derivation shall clarify their contrasting nature to those of *T*-scores.

For purposes of brevity and clarity, the following delineates the standardization procedure for the *diagnostic scales* of the M–PACI, MACI, and MCMI–III.[4] Diagnostic scales refer to those developed and used principally for differential diagnosis; namely, Clinical Syndromes, Personality Patterns, and Emerging Personality Patterns.

First, the selected norm-reference sample was administered the particular Millon inventory so as to obtain raw scores for all diagnostic scales. Second, expert clinicians rated each individual in the sample in terms of which single diagnostic scale represented (a) the *best-fit* diagnosis and (b) the *second best-fit* diagnosis. These ratings were then used as a basis for the Millon raw score to *BR*-score transformations for all diagnostic scales as follows.

Four *BR*-score *anchor* points or diagnostic thresholds were arbitrarily selected: 0 = minimum possible raw score (percentile = 0), 115 = maximum possible raw score (percentile = 100), 85 = raw score corresponding to the percentile of the norm-reference group rated as possessing that diagnostic scale as best fit (i.e., *prominence of a disorder*), and 75 = raw score corresponding to the percentile of the norm-reference group as possessing that disorder as second best fit (i.e., *presence of a disorder*). Intermediate *BR*-scores were estimated by statistical interpolation (e.g., see Gravetter & Wallnau, 2013, pp. 55–59).

A simple hypothetical example will suffice using the Dysthymic Disorder Clinical Syndrome scale on the MCMI–III. Suppose 5% of the norm group was rated as having this disorder as best fit or prominent, and an additional 10% as second best fit or present. A *BR*-score of 85 would correspond to the raw score falling at the 95th percentile (i.e., 100 – 5 = 95), and a *BR*-score of 75 would be assigned to the raw score falling at the 85th percentile (i.e., 100 – 5 – 10 = 85). Note that in contrast to *T*-scores, *BR*-scores account for differing measured prevalence rates among the diagnostic disorders. This is by virtue of *BR*-scores corresponding to varying percentiles across the diagnostic scales. This should also elucidate the nominal/ordinal nature of *BR*-scores as opposed to interval-based *T*-scores.

Thus, the Millon diagnostic scales are most accurately interpreted using a two-step process: (a) nominal interpretation that a particular disorder is either *prominent* (*BR* = 85 – 115), *present* (*BR* = 75 – 84), or *absent* (*BR* = 0 – 74); and (b) ordinal interpretation of the relative severity or nonseverity of a disorder (i.e., reference to the specific *BR*-score value). The latter is crucial when interpreting a Millon profile wherein multiple diagnostic scales are elevated within the prominent and/or present range (see, e.g., use of one- and two-point code types discussed by Craig, 1999). In such instances, the interpretation process is effectuated by further quantitative precision.

On the other hand, the various Millon validity and modifying indices scales were derived somewhat differently. Some are based, in whole or in part, on original raw scores (e.g., Inconsistency, Omissions). Those that rely on *BR*-scores were derived by norm-reference group raw score frequency distributions as follows: (a) *BR*-scores 85 to 115 capture

[4] *For a more detailed and technical discussion of the manner in which raw scores were transformed into BR-scores regarding the M–PACI, MACI, and MCMI–III, I refer the reader to the respective manuals (Millon, 2006a, 2006b; Millon et al., 2005).*

the top 10% (i.e., *extremely high*), (b) *BR*-scores 75 to 84 correspond to the next highest 15% (i.e., *moderately high*), (c) *BR*-scores 35 to 74 represent the next highest 60% (i.e., *average*), and (d) *BR*-scores 0 to 34 capture the lowest 15% (i.e., *low*). The italicized qualitative descriptors are my own and are logically derived by the test-taking style measured by these validity scales (see below).

One final pertinent note on Millon *BR*-scores regards what have been aptly referred to as *profile adjustments* (McCann, 1999, 2008) or *response bias corrections* (Strack, 2002), which are uniquely available on the MCMI–III and MACI. These are final statistical adjustments made for all or selected diagnostic scales, which may be distorted by various detectable response styles. The cardinal purpose of these statistical adjustments is to augment diagnostic accuracy. I next review two of the most common adjustments I have encountered in clinical testing practice so as to illustrate.

First, extremely high or low levels of disclosure (see Disclosure Modifying Index scale) result in a statistical decrease or increase in *BR*-scores among all diagnostic scales, respectively. Second, denial or complaint proclivities associated with various extreme personality patterns (e.g., Dramatizing and Inhibited) result in a respective statistical increase or decrease in *BR*-scores on selected diagnostic scales (e.g., Depressive Affect, Anxious Feelings). I refer the reader to Strack (2002) and McCann (1999, 2008) for more comprehensive and exemplary discussions of all such potential adjustments made on the MCMI–III and MACI.

The Millon scales I find most diagnostically useful to analyze and report are the (a) validity scales and (b) primary diagnostic scales most germane to Axis I and II disorders, along with addressing critical assessment questions or issues. Other available scales include the following: (a) Grossman Facet scales (MCMI–III and MACI), which are essentially more narrowly defined subscales of the primary diagnostic scales; and (b) Expressed Concerns scales, which are most relevant to Axis IV psychosocial stressors (MACI only). I find these data to be discretionary and most efficaciously reported as ancillary results within a narrative summary of the results and interpretation tables (see section on Results and Interpretation Tables below).

Computer self-administration and scoring for all three Millon tests is available through the Q Local Software (2011) application. Although there is a monetary charge for a predetermined number of administrations and score reports, the efficiency afforded by this modality is unequivocally cost-effective. I advise purchasing the *basic score reports*, as opposed to the more elaborate and expensive *interpretative summaries*, because the results and interpretation tables presented next serve this function. Furthermore, I reiterate my reticence about *blind*, computerized narrative reports and their likely distortion for want of clinical context and test data integration. Finally, I advise discontinuing Scantron booklet administration and hand scoring as being antiquated, prohibitively time consuming, and potentially contributing to unwanted measurement error.

Results and Interpretation Tables

Separate results and interpretation tables are available for the M–PACI (Form 8.1), MACI (Form 8.2), and MCMI–III (Form 8.3). In general, they consist of data tables that measure the following: (a) test validity, (b) Axis I Clinical Disorders, and (c) Axis II Personality Disorders and associated maladaptive traits. The tables are designed to be interpreted independently within the above-enumerated logical sequence. Because of their similar design, I will review the three Millon tests simultaneously following tabular order, once again highlighting important differences, most frequently occurring with the M–PACI.

Validity scales. Table 1 comprises what I have termed validity scales for purposes of uniformity, which are largely measured in raw score units and contribute to a trichotomous result and interpretation scheme; that is, test results are determined as being (a) *valid*,

(b) *questionably valid*, or (c) *invalid*. In columnar order of appearance, Table 1 includes the following: (a) scale name, (b) raw score, (c) percentile rank (M–PACI Response Negativity scale only), (d) trichotomous validity results, and (d) measured test-taking response style. The first two validity scales are identical across the three tests and measure whether (a) an adequate number of items were answered and (b) responses were made with sufficient honesty and/or accuracy (Millon 2006a, 2006b; Millon et al., 2005). The more sophisticated MCMI–III includes a third scale, which measures response consistency (Millon, 2006b).

The M–PACI includes a somewhat different third and final preliminary scale, which detects degrees of symptom minimization or magnification and is properly labeled Response Negativity (Millon et al., 2005). It is similar in design to the *Modifying Indices scales* of the MCMI–III and MACI (see Table 2), which contribute to the aforementioned *BR*-score statistical adjustments; hence the name. However, neither the M–PACI Response Negativity scale nor the initial two validity scales in Table 1 contribute to such adjustments. For this reason, and because this is the final M–PACI validity scale, I consolidated them all into one rather than two validity tables.

General Table 1 notes unique to the M–PACI include defining PR as percentile rank, and the "--" score not available symbol, both required due to the inclusion of the Response Negativity scale. Specific Table 1 notes common to all three tests include defining explicitly: (a) the number of omissions delineating valid and invalid profiles, which vary somewhat between tests[5] and (b) item content used in determining response honesty and/or accuracy. Note that the latter response style is measured directly by the M–PACI (e.g., "Are you answering honestly?") and indirectly by the MACI and MCMI–III (i.e., infrequently endorsed items). Also note that positive results on this response style may indicate either dishonesty or inaccuracy, the latter due to such causes as random responding, flagging attention, malingering, or sarcasm. They are reported together because discriminating precisely which occurred is immaterial from a validity standpoint and may be addressed within a narrative summary of the table.

Two different and final specific Table 1 notes are unique to the M–PACI and MCMI–III. First, the M–PACI Response Negativity scale's percentile rank ranges and results alternatives are enumerated. Second, the MCMI–III Inconsistency scale's meaning and significance is elaborated, ensued by the raw score ranges associated with validity and invalidity (Millon, 2006a). You shall find such pithy tabular notes invaluable for simultaneous interpretation and report-writing, and is beneficial for the reader's comprehension.

All of the Millon tables are designed to be interpreted independently and in their logical sequential order. Thus, to further expedite the report-writing process, I composed three alternative standardized narrative interpretations to Table 1 that will apply in the vast majority of cases. They include a valid interpretation, questionable validity interpretation, and invalid interpretation. The valid interpretation version limits validity of the profile to the results of Table 1 by the qualifying language *in these respects*. This is especially relevant for the more intricately designed MACI and MCMI–III, which comprise immediately ensuing Modifying Indices that also address test validity. The questionably valid version offers the cautious interpretation of requiring other corroborative data. The invalid interpretation properly terminates all further analysis on the test.[6]

Modifying indices. Modifying indices pertain only to the MACI and MCMI–III (Millon, 2006a, 2006b). Table 2 for these tests comprise scales that contribute to potential statistical adjustments to pertinent Clinical Syndrome and Personality Patterns scales, as discussed prior. Although other scales influence such *BR*-score corrections, the Modifying Indices are paramount and represent their essential purpose.

[5] *Note that the number of omissions can be rapidly counted by reference to the final Item Responses section of the basic score report if using the Q Local Software (2011) computer administration and scoring application.*

[6] *You shall find such emphasis on the reporting and interpreting of validity scales throughout this chapter on self-report clinical and personality inventories, and in the ensuing chapter when discussing the examiner-administered personality tests. I have perused many psychological reports wherein the psychologist will properly note the questionable validity of a profile, yet interpret the results without further reference to, or the cavalier minimization of, potential invalidity. I have always found such occurrences to be enigmatic. Diligent use of the validity scales incorporated into my results and interpretation tables will foster more disciplined analyses.*

In columnar order of appearance, Table 2 of the MACI and MCMI–III includes the following: (a) index name, (b) *BR*-score, (c) *BR*-score result (i.e., *low, average, moderately high, extremely high*), and (d) measured test-taking response style worded in the direction of high *BR*-scores. The particular response style descriptions appearing in the table were derived from the test manuals and supplementary interpretation references (Craig, 1999; McCann, 1999, 2008; Millon 2006a, 2006b; Strack, 2002). General table notes define the meaning of *BR* as Base Rate and explicitly report the numerical criteria for determining the *Result* column descriptive labels. The latter includes the respective *BR*-score ranges, percentile ranges, and result qualitative descriptors. Note that these data are accordant with the manner in which these validity scales were derived as I discussed prior. Incorporating such information with such proximity to the table is invaluable to the testing psychologist in terms of interpretation and is additionally informative to the reader.

As was done for Table 1, I composed three standardized narrative interpretations for Table 2 describing (a) completely valid results requiring no *BR*-score adjustments to the diagnostic scales, (b) valid results requiring *BR*-score adjustments, and (c) completely invalid results wherein *BR*-score adjustments would be ineffectual. The last two contain fill-in segments in which the testing psychologist is to type in the respondent's particular test-taking style.

If you are using the Q Local Software (2011) application for computer administration and scoring, which I again fervently advise, the basic score report will include a convenient summary indicating whether or not *BR*-score adjustments were necessitated, the reasons therefore, and if said adjustments would likely be ineffectual due to flagrant biases in the test-taking response styles measured within Table 2. Although some additional scales influence these adjustments, these Modifying Indices are paramount and it is most logical to report them here in the preliminary analyses. Again, invalid results preclude reporting and interpreting the Clinical Syndromes and Personality Patterns scales of the MACI and MCMI–III.

Clinical Syndromes scales. The diagnostic scales for all three Millon tests begin with the Axis I Clinical Syndromes scales (i.e., M–PACI, Table 2; MACI and MCMI–III, Table 3), hence mirroring the multiaxial system order (American Psychiatric Association, 2000). Three modifications to the original scales are noteworthy. First, I have relabeled the M–PACI scales from *Current Clinical Signs* (Millon et al., 2005) to *Clinical Syndromes* for purposes of uniformity with the two older age Millon versions, and due to what in my opinion is insufficient rationale for the former label's connoted diagnostic caution.[7] Second, I have moved the MACI Oppositional scale from its original listing as a Personality Patterns scale (Millon, 2006b) to the Clinical Syndromes scales due to its greater resemblance to *DSM-IV-TR* Axis I Disruptive Behavior Disorders (American Psychiatric Association, 2000).

Third, and lastly, I have made succinct parenthetical elaborations to selected original scale names for purposes of diagnostic clarity. These additions are more *DSM-IV-TR* diagnostically precise and accordant with the cluster of symptoms measured on a particular scale. Regarding the Axis I Clinical Syndrome scales, there is one such addition on the MCMI–III Table 3; that is, (Generalized) Anxiety. These diagnostic parentheticals appear more frequently concerning the Axis II (Emerging) Personality Patterns scales presented subsequently.

The Clinical Syndromes tables have the same organization for all three Millon tests. From left to right, the major columns include (a) scale name, (b) *BR*-score, and (c) essential symptoms measured by each scale. The scale order follows an approximate most-to-least severity sequence. Additionally, disorders falling under the same or similar *DSM-IV-TR* classification are listed proximately. Thus, for example, the MCMI–III

[7] *Note that I do retain the more diagnostically cautious M–PACI Axis II Emerging Personality Patterns (Millon et al., 2005), accordant with my previous discussion regarding Personality Disorder diagnoses in younger individuals.*

scale order includes the following sequence: (a) Psychotic Disorders, (b) Mood Disorders (severe), (c) Depressive Disorder (minor although chronic), (d) Anxiety Disorders, (e) Substance-Related Disorders, and (f) Somatoform Disorders. The measured symptoms listed in the final column of the Clinical Syndrome tables are key descriptors derived from the more detailed and elaborate scale descriptions provided in the respective test manuals (Millon, 2006a, 2006b; Millon et al., 2005), in addition to supplemental interpretative references largely authored by independent experts (Craig, 1999, Kamp & Tringone, 2008; McCann, 1999, 2008; Strack, 2002). These succinct symptom descriptions are designed to facilitate test interpretation and feedback.

General tabular notes to the Clinical Syndromes scales are identical for the three Millon tests and include the following: (a) defining *BR* as Base Rate; (b) minimum and maximum *BR*-score anchors so as to provide diagnostic context to measured variance and severity; and (c) directional significance of higher *BR*-scores as being more pathological. One vital specific note common to all three tests concerns the symbolic meaning of the presence or absence of asterisks when appended to the *BR*-scores. Specifically, no asterisk indicates an absence of disorder (i.e., *BR*-score 0–74), one asterisk indicates the presence of a secondary or a subthreshold disorder (i.e., *BR*-score 75–84), and two asterisks indicate the prominence of a disorder (i.e., *BR*-score 85–115). Note that these are the critical intermediate diagnostic thresholds upon which the three tests are standardized. Once again, their immediate availability facilitates test interpretation and report-writing, and provides valuable context for the reader.

Two unique Post-Traumatic Stress and Alcohol Dependence scales on the MCMI–III require additional diagnostic qualifiers astutely cited by Strack (2002), and highlights the necessity of an efficacious initial report (see Forms 2.2 and 2.3) for diagnostic context. Regarding the former, positive results in the absence of historically documented trauma generally indicates the presence of nontraumatic emotional turmoil (Strack, 2002, p. 34). This is a crucial distinction without which unnecessary and potentially damaging controversial accusations can arise. Regarding the latter, positive results for Alcohol Dependence in the absence of alcohol abuse is more indicative of Axis II personality psychopathology, including selfishness, impulsivity, rationalization, aggressiveness, and lack of adherence to societal standards (Strack, 2002, p. 32). Both diagnostic qualifiers are enumerated within two final specific MCMI–III Table 3 notes for easy and rapid reference. They may be quickly deleted if inapplicable.

Lastly, the Clinical Syndromes tables are designed to be interpreted independently within a narrative summary immediately ensuing the reported data and results. Scales not pertinent to the differential diagnostic issues may be deleted for purposes of brevity and focusing the analysis on the most germane scores.

(Emerging) Personality patterns scales. The final diagnostic scales for all three Millon tests pertain to Axis II personality psychopathology (i.e., M–PACI, Table 3; MACI and MCMI–III, Table 4). Because of their vital significance to Axis I and II differential diagnoses, I have prepared these tables with added diligence and organization. Several noteworthy comments are indicated prior to reviewing these scales in earnest.

First, regarding the M–PACI and MACI, I have appended to the original scale names the *DSM-IV-TR* and *DSM-III-R* (MACI only) Personality Disorder analogues (American Psychiatric Association, 1987, 2000). The purposes are to (a) facilitate the process of identifying a risk for later development of one or more bona fide personality disorders in order to encourage early intervention and (b) diagnose a Personality Disorder in those infrequent instances where *DSM-IV-TR* guidelines are met for such disorders prior to adulthood (see above). Regarding the M–PACI, note that I have retained the felicitous original title

Emerging Personality Patterns (Millon et al., 2005) so as to emphasize the greater malleability of personality in preadolescence.

Second, I have included all of the available Millon personality scales with the exception of those pertaining to Depressive Personality Disorder (i.e., MACI—Doleful; MCMI–III—Depressive). This is due to the remarkable resemblance in symptoms of this *DSM-IV-TR* Axis II experimental disorder to those of the Axis I Dysthymic Disorder, which is currently associated with significant controversy (American Psychiatric Association, 2000, p. 788) and risk for unnecessary and excessive psychodiagnosis. I am personally awaiting the completion of further research on whether or not Depressive Personality Disorder is a valid, independent, and useful Axis II diagnosis (e.g., see Orstavik, Kendler, Czajkowski, Tambs, & Reichborn-Kjennerud, 2007; Vachon, Sellbom, Ryder, Miller, & Bagby, 2009). Additionally, this Axis II diagnosis has shown little, if any, independent diagnostic utility in my clinical testing practice.

Pertaining to the MACI and MCMI–III, I do retain personality scales related to the diagnosis of other *DSM-III-R* and *DSM-IV-TR* experimental personality disorders (American Psychiatric Association, 1987, 2000), including Sadistic, Self-Defeating, and Passive–Aggressive (MCMI–III only). In my experience, these have shown sufficient diagnostic utility to justify their retention for the following three reasons. One, the presence of sadistic traits, usually coexisting with classic antisocial traits, is useful in predicting an enhanced risk of danger to others. Two, self-defeating patterns are helpful in predicting (a) the likelihood of subverting the treatment process and (b) the increased risk for becoming the target of abuse. Three, the presence of passive–aggressive traits is similarly useful in clarifying lack of progress in treatment that may have precipitated the testing referral, or predicting resistance to intervention if in the early stages of treatment.

The personality tables for all three Millon tests are organized in similar fashion, differing only with respect to their particular scales. In columnar order of appearance are the scale names, *BR*-scores, and measured maladaptive traits for each scale. Scale order was determined according to the following two factors: (a) frequency of appearance in referral questions and (b) general similarity of measured traits, including in order Cluster B dramatic, emotional, or erratic, Cluster C anxious or fearful, Cluster A odd or eccentric, and where applicable, experimental/Not Otherwise Specified (NOS) disorders (American Psychiatric Association, 2000, pp. 685–686). The particular sequence is as follows: (a) Borderline, (b) Narcissistic, (c) Antisocial, (d) Sadistic (MACI and MCMI–III only), (e) Histrionic, (f) Dependent, (g) Avoidant, (h) Obsessive-Compulsive, (i) Schizoid (MACI and MCMI–III only), (j) Schizotypal (MCMI–III only), (k) Paranoid (MCMI–III only), (l) Passive–Aggressive (MCMI–III only), and (M) Self-Defeating (MACI and MCMI–III only). The measured maladaptive traits appearing in the final column were derived from the same sources and in the same manner as the Clinical Syndrome tables (Craig, 1999; Kamp & Tringone, 2008; McCann, 1999, 2008; Millon, 2006a, 2006b; Millon et al., 2005; Strack, 2002). Once again, these summary descriptions are designed to facilitate test interpretation and feedback.

General tabular notes applicable to all three Millon tests include defining *BR* as Base Rate and the directional meaning of higher scores. The M–PACI and MACI include a note delineating scales that represent *DSM-IV-TR* Personality Disorder analogues. The MACI includes an added similar note identifying scales that represent *DSM-III-R* Personality Disorder analogues, with an addendum indicating the proper current *DSM-IV-TR* NOS designation with the listed maladaptive traits. The M–PACI and MACI general table notes end with a definition of OC as Obsessive-Compulsive.

The MCMI–III contains two final general notes, the first being unique to this test. Research has indicated that scores falling within the disordered range for Narcissistic and Obsessive-Compulsive may only reflect *normal* personality styles (see e.g., Strack,

2002). This attests to the person–environment fit as a vital mediating variable for certain traits, which can have a critical impact on ultimate psychological adjustment (e.g., see Chamorro-Premuzic, 2011; Larsen & Buss, 2010). That is, narcissism and obsessive-compulsive traits can be adaptive in various situations, and hence not associated with distress or dysfunction pursuant to *DSM-IV-TR* criteria (American Psychiatric Association, 2000, p. 686). Information gleaned during the initial assessment must be considered to determine whether or not elevated *BR*-scores on these scales constitute bona fide Personality Disorders. This general note is included to remind testing psychologists and readers of the report of this critical qualification. In the event that these scales are irrelevant to the differential diagnostic questions and therefore dropped from the analysis, this note may be deleted. The second and final general MCMI–III note indicates the proper current *DSM-IV-TR* NOS designation concerning scales pertaining to *DSM-III-R* and *DSM-IV* experimental disorders.

Lastly, all three tests contain the same specific note appearing in the Clinical Syndromes scales delineating the meaning of *BR*-score ranges and the presence or absence of asterisks; that is, 0 to 74, no disorder or asterisk; 75 to 84, presence of disorder with one asterisk; and 85 to 115, prominence of disorder with two asterisks. These are the identical intermediate diagnostic thresholds as in the Clinical Syndromes scales accordant with standardization procedures. A narrative summary of the results should immediately follow the table, with any irrelevant scales deleted from the analysis for purposes of maintaining focus and brevity.

The MMPI–A

The MMPI–A is standardized on individuals aged 14 years 0 months to 18 years 11 months. It is comprised of 478 True/False items, takes approximately 45 to 60 minutes to complete, and requires a minimum sixth-grade reading level. Although the data yield is considerable, it is also redundant due to the voluminous scales developed by various multivariate techniques using the same items. In total, there are 7 Validity scales, 10 Clinical scales, 15 Content scales, 31 Content Component scales, 11 Supplementary scales, 28 Harris-Lingoes subscales, and various special indices. In contrast to the Millon tests, these scales lack direct correspondence with *DSM-IV-TR* Axis I and II diagnoses. However, scrutiny of their particular measured symptoms reveals that they are to varying degrees useful in rendering such diagnoses (Archer, 1997; Butcher & Williams, 2000; Butcher et al., 1992). For this reason, and because of the aforementioned redundancy, I have selected what I believe are the most diagnostically pragmatic scales and organized them into tables based upon the degree of match between their measured symptoms and traits with those of *DSM-IV-TR* classifications. I do not use the traditional code-type interpretation approach because it (a) lacks *DSM-IV-TR* correspondence, (b) is limited to the basic Clinical scales 0 through 9, and (c) is associated with significantly large between-scale correlations due to excessive item overlap (see Butcher et al., 1992).

The MMPI–A is rather complex and sophisticated in terms of its seemingly illimitable number of validity and diagnostic scales. Therefore, I review the various scales, score types, and vital interpretive score ranges as a necessary prelude to reviewing my MMPI–A results and interpretation tables discussed subsequently. I begin with the Validity scales followed by the Clinical and personality relevant scales.

The CNS(?) is simply the number of item omissions or simultaneous True/False responses, the latter being effectively precluded when employing the computerized administration and scoring software discussed presently. CNS(?) raw scores are interpreted as follows: (a) 0 to 3 is *low*, (b) 4 to 10 is *moderate*, (c) 11 to 30 is *marked*, and (d) 31 to 478 is *invalid* (Archer, 1997). The first three represent varying degrees of test validity, while the last terminates consideration of the remaining MMPI–A scales due to insufficient data.

Although the True Response Inconsistency scale (TRIN) and Variable Response Inconsistency scale (VRIN) are reported using interval based *T*-scores (i.e., *M* = 50, *SD* = 10), they are similar to the CNS(?) in that they represent various forms of nonresponsiveness on the part of the respondent and will summarily terminate further interpretation should the scores fall within the invalid range; that is, indiscriminant and inconsistent responding, respectively. Their interpretation scheme is as follows: (a) 30 to 69 is *valid*, (b) 70 to 79 is *cautiously valid*, and (c) 80 to 120 is *invalid*. (Note that these are my personal validity labels, which are predicated upon the criteria reported in Archer [1997] and Butcher and Williams [2000].)

The traditional MMPI L, F, and K Validity scales also use standardized *T*-scores, which may be generally interpreted as such: (a) 30 to 40 is *low*, (b) 41 to 55 is *normal*, (c) 56 to 65 is *moderate*, and (d) 66 to 120 is *marked* (Archer, 1997). Regarding the latter, an extreme elevation on F (i.e., 90–120) may indicate a genuine psychotic process with severe thought disorganization (Archer, 1997; Butcher & Williams, 2000).

All of the MMPI–A diagnostic clinical and personality scales are measured using standard *T*-scores and interpreted as follows: (a) 30 to 59 is a *normal elevation*, (b) 60 to 64 is a *transitional elevation*, and (c) 65 to 120 is a *clinically significant elevation* (labels adapted from Archer, 1997 and Butcher & Williams, 2000). More specifically, I interpret a transitional elevation as indicative of a subthreshold or mild disorder, implying the need for coexisting corroborative data, whereas a clinically significant elevation may be interpreted as a genuine moderate to severe disorder. This interpretation scheme illustrates the integration of dimensional and categorical psychodiagnostic approaches discussed prior (viz., *disorder absent, subthreshold/mild disorder, moderate/severe disorder*). Of course, ultimate interpretation of the clinical and personality relevant score elevations should be qualified by any remarkable test-taking pattern identified by the validity scales. This is due to an absence of statistical adjustments that are available on the adolescent and adult Millon tests (see above).

Computer self-administration and scoring is available for the MMPI–A through the same Q Local Software (2011) application as for the Millon tests. Again, although there is a monetary charge for a predetermined number of administrations, I strongly advise this computerized testing as being cost-effective and as effectively reducing measurement error. More particularly, I recommend purchasing the *extended score report*, which shall instantly produce scores on all of the above-listed MMPI–A scales. Although I do not utilize all of these scales, the extended score report is needed to use my MMPI–A results and interpretation tables to their fullest extent. Alternatively, the *basic service report* provides insufficient data, whereas the available *interpretive report* may be supplanted by my MMPI–A results and interpretation tables discussed subsequently.

Results and Interpretation Tables

Form 8.4 presents the MMPI–A results and interpretation tables. There are nine tables in all. The initial three tables address test validity, while the remaining six measure various broad *DSM-IV-TR* categories, including (a) Mood Disorders, (b) Psychotic Disorders, (c) Anxiety Disorders, (d) Somatoform Disorders, (e) Substance-Related Disorders, and (f) Personality Disorders. Note that this order preserves the Axis I/Axis II interpretive sequence of both the *DSM-IV-TR* and Millon diagnostic scales.

Generally speaking, I have matched the cluster of symptoms measured by each MMPI–A diagnostic scale to those of the *DSM-IV-TR* disorders, then organized them into tables consistent with their general *DSM-IV-TR* classification. As mentioned previously, it should be immediately apparent that such a scheme precludes the traditional one- and two-point code-type interpretive approach, which is limited to the basic clinical scales 0 through 9 (e.g., see Archer, 1997). Rather, the general interpretation approach I am espousing here parallels that for the NEPSY–II (see Chapter 6). That is, the greater the number of statistically significant scales measuring a general category of disorder (e.g., Mood Disorder), the greater likelihood of a genuine *DSM-IV-TR* diagnosis within that broad classification. The particular pattern of remarkable scale elevations determines the more narrowly defined disorder present (e.g., Cyclothymic Disorder). This renders MMPI–A analysis much more conducive to *DSM-IV-TR* differential diagnosis, and hence, similar to the diagnostic expediency characteristic of the Millon tests (see above). As I review the various clinical and personality tables and their specific scales, I shall insert comments as to when the MMPI–A may be judiciously used to complement or supplant the MACI as both tests share the 14 to 18 year range.

Validity scales. Tables 1 through 3 present the six most efficacious MMPI–A Validity scales beginning with those indicative of nonresponding; that is, CNS(?), TRIN, and VRIN. These three nonresponsive scales logically initiate the analysis because invalid results summarily terminate all further score reporting and interpretation. From left to right, Table 1 columns include the scale name, *T*-score, descriptive result, and the particular measured test-taking response pattern. The latter was based upon interpretations of these scales provided in the test manual and supplementary interpretive references (Archer, 1997; Butcher & Williams, 2000; Butcher et al., 1992). Table 1 general notes clarify the *T*-score metric (*M* = 50, *SD* = 10) and the directional meaning of higher scores (i.e., generally referring to both raw and *T*-scores). Table 1 specific notes indicate (a) the CNS(?) unique raw score metric and (b) the particular score ranges and descriptive results for all three scales. The proximate availability of such information speeds interpretation and report-writing and renders table results more comprehensible to the reader. To further expedite the analysis, I have composed standard interpretations of Table 1 results. The testing psychologist merely retains or amends these as indicated by the data.

Table 2 presents the traditional L–K–F validity triad. The first two represent underreporting, and the last indicates over-reporting or possible psychosis if within the extreme score range. General table notes elucidate the meaning of the *T*-score, whereas specific table notes enumerate the score ranges and descriptive results similar to Table 1 (see Archer, 1997; Butcher & Williams, 2000; Butcher et al., 1992). Similar standard interpretive summaries of Table 2 are available.

Table 3 summarizes the results of Tables 1 and 2, and the consequent strategy employed in interpreting the ensuing diagnostic scales. Each row effectively covers all major permutations, including completely valid or invalid results, and varying combinations of cautiously valid results, with their indicated interpretation strategies regarding the ensuing diagnostic scales. The testing psychologist merely retains the applicable validity results listed in Table 3 and deletes the remaining alternatives by row. You will find that this approach efficaciously increases the speed of validity scale analysis and minimizes typing duration. Specifically, Table 3 includes the following information in columnar order of appearance: (a) overall validity result based upon Table 1 data (i.e., valid, four cautiously valid alternatives, and invalid), (b) reason for the overall result (e.g., moderate under- or over-reporting, extreme *F*-score potentially indicative of a disorder), and (c) the associated interpretation strategy employed on the ensuing diagnostic scales (e.g., standard, interpreted as valid only with corroborating evidence). The testing psychologist may add to or emend these table entries as necessary. Note that (a) Tables 1 to 3 are to be interpreted together, (b) MMPI–A Validity scale analysis is largely tabular, (c) narrative typing in paragraph form is significantly curtailed, and (d) Validity scale analysis is rapid, efficient, and more comprehensible to the reader.

Clinical and personality disorders scales. Tables 4 through 9 consist of the Clinical (i.e., Axis I) and Personality (i.e., Axis II) Disorders scales. A cursory glance at these tables should evince their *DSM-IV-TR* correspondence. With the exception of differing table title and varying scale content, they are identical in design. Note that each scale appears in only one table. Thus, the only covariance between table results lies within the inter-item overlap inherent in the MMPI–A factor structure (Butcher et al., 1992). I have ordered the tables in terms of (a) Axis I/II sequence, (b) frequency with which the disorders are included within the differential diagnostic questions for this age group, and (c) disorders most effectively tested for by the MMPI–A. These tables are designed to be interpreted independently within a succinct narrative. Therefore, those deemed irrelevant to the differential diagnostic questions may be deleted. However, note that results from diagnostically related tables may be effectively integrated as each one accumulates vital diagnostic information.

For instance, the sequence begins with Table 4 Mood Disorders scales that may show the presence of a mixed episode of Bipolar I Disorder and be interpreted as such within a narrative immediately following the table. This is ensued by Table 4 Psychotic Disorders scales, that may indicate the presence of psychotic symptoms, which although present, do not dominate the symptom picture. The narrative interpretation immediately subsequent to Table 4 may integrate these results with those of Table 3, for example, as indicating the presence of Bipolar I Disorder, Mixed Episode, Severe With Psychotic Features. Of course, ultimately all test results are integrated within the posttest diagnoses of the final report.

From left to right, columns included in these diagnostic tables consist of the following: (a) scale name identified by its alphabetic and/or numerical abbreviation for facile reference by the testing psychologist, (b) standardized *T*-score, and (c) symptoms measured by each scale. Once again, the latter represent essential symptoms culled from the extensive scale descriptions available in the test manual and supplementary interpretative references (Archer, 1997; Butcher & Williams, 2000; Butcher et al., 1992), and are fundamental to rapid and clear test reporting and interpretation. General table notes list the *T*-score metric (i.e., *M* = 50, *SD* = 10) and directional meaning of higher scores. The MMPI–A basic or core Clinical scales are identified primarily by their lettered abbreviations, ensued parenthetically by their numerical codes; for example, Pd (4). As in the MMPI–A validity tables and Millon tables, a specific note elucidates the meaning of the presence or absence of asterisks and associated *T*-score ranges.

I wish to complete discussion of the MMPI–A with commentary addressing (a) important aspects of two diagnostic tables and (b) judicious use of the MMPI–A. First, Table 4 Mood Disorders scales begin with those indicative of Depressive (i.e., Unipolar) Disorder, ensued by those pertinent to Bipolar Disorder. Second, I include the Harris-Lingoes Mental Dullness (D_4) scale among the former because it measures impairments in attention and concentration likely to be associated with depression (see e.g., Archer, 1997; Butcher & Williams, 2000). It is therefore efficacious in rendering an accurate differential diagnosis between a Depressive Mood Disorder versus Attention-Deficit/Hyperactivity Disorder (ADHD). Third, the MMPI–A personality scales are most thorough in measuring emerging antisocial personality traits. Hence, Table 8 Personality Disorders begin with these scales, followed by scales more pertinent to Paranoid, Avoidant, and Dependent Personality Disorders, respectively.

Finally, concerning shrewd use the MMPI–A, because the MACI does not include Clinical Syndromes scales for psychotic and manic symptoms, this is unequivocally the strength of the MMPI–A. Furthermore, although the Conners CBRS (see Chapter 7) does include the scale Manic Episode, it conspicuously lacks any scale that measures the presence of psychosis. Thus, at least for the 14 to 18 year age group, the MMPI–A simultaneously provides scales for Bipolar Disorder, Psychotic Disorder, and to some extent Axis II Personality Disorder, rendering it a pragmatic test if the differential diagnostic questions pertain to all three such disorders. Of course, if there is suspected Axis II psychopathology underlying Bipolar and Psychotic Disorders, using both the MMPI–A and MACI is indicated as effective complements.

The MMPI–2–RF

The MMPI–2–RF is an updated multivariate factor reanalysis of MMPI–2 items using essentially the same standardization sample; that is, ages 18 years 0 months to 89 years 11 months (Ben-Porath & Tellegen, 2008; Tellegen et al., 2003). The minor change in the MMPI–2–RF sample is the random elimination of 224 women such that the number of males and females were equalized at 1,138 each (Green, 2011). The cardinal purpose of this reanalysis was to improve both the discriminant and convergent validity of the scales by reducing scale intercorrelations, the latter being caused by remarkable item overlap characteristic of the MMPI–2 (see Butcher, Dahlstrom, Graham, Tellegen, & Kaemmer, 1989).

Succinctly, a *demoralization* factor was initially extracted that accounted for a significant degree of shared variance among the MMPI–2 scales (Ben-Porath & Tellegen, 2008; Tellegen et al., 2003). Subsequent factor analyses were efficacious in identifying distinctive core features of the remaining scales. The result was a series of new (i.e., *restructured*) scales, that generally possess the following more desirable psychometric features: (a) shorter in length (e.g., MMPI–2 scale 6 consists of 40 items versus the comparable MMPI–2–RF RC6 scale including 17 items); (b) reduced item overlap and concomitant reduction in scale intercorrelations; (c) equivalent or enhanced convergent and discriminative validity, while retaining reliability commensurate that of the MMPI–2; and (d) equivalent or enhanced ability to predict extra-test criteria (Ben-Porath & Tellegen, 2008; Green, 2011; Tellegen et al., 2003).

Hence, the MMPI–2–RF is both more efficient and effectual in terms of differential diagnosis. Furthermore, irrespective of the voluminous research completed in developing the MMPI–2 core Clinical scales and their code-types based upon empirical criterion keying, such test construction was directly responsible for the unacceptably large scale intercorrelations (Ben-Porath & Tellegen, 2008; Tellegen et al., 2003), hence rendering this interpretive approach ineffective in making precise *DSM-IV-TR* differential diagnoses. It is for these reasons I have supplanted the MMPI–2 with the diagnostically superior MMPI–2–RF in my testing practice. Those who continue to use the MMPI–2 may report the quantitative data using the MMPI–A results and interpretation tables (see Form 8.4) with some minor amendments due to the remarkable similarity between these tests.

In particular, the MMPI–2–RF contains 338 True/False items, may be completed within 35 to 50 minutes, and requires a minimum sixth-grade reading level (Ben-Porath & Tellegen, 2008; Green, 2011). Irrespective of its abbreviated length compared to the MMPI–2, the MMPI–2–RF data yield is impressive and includes the following: (a) 8 Validity scales; (b) 3 Higher Order (i.e., broadband) scales; (c) 9 Restructured Clinical (RC) scales; (d) 14 Somatic/Cognitive and Internalizing scales; (e) 11 Externalizing, Interpersonal, and Interest scales; and (f) 5 Personality Psychopathology Five (PSY–5) scales. Analogous to the MMPI–A, I utilize selected MMPI–2–RF scales that are diagnostically most relevant to *DSM-IV-TR* differential diagnosis based upon their measured symptoms (Ben-Porath & Tellegen, 2008; Green, 2011). Furthermore, I have similarly organized them into tables based upon broad *DSM-IV-TR* classifications. Again, because of the complexity and sophistication of the MMPI–2–RF, I shall review the various validity and diagnostic scale score types, ranges, and associated descriptive interpretations as a prelude to presenting the results and interpretation tables.

The MMPI–2–RF employs similarly designated although revised nonresponsive Validity scales as in MMPI–A. The CNS(?)–r raw score ranges and descriptive results include the following: (a) 0 is *low*, (b) 1 to 4 is *normal*, (c) 5 to 10 is *moderate*, and (d) 11 to 338 is *marked* (Green, 2011). Interpretation of the TRIN–r and VRIN–r inconsistency scales is complicated by the fact that they consist of significantly different item pairs as opposed to the MMPI–2. This is primarily due to remarkable changes in selection methodology. Despite such modifications in item content, however, there is as yet no evidence indicating that they function differently than their MMPI–2 counterparts (Green, 2011). For this reason, I employ comparable *T*-score ranges and descriptive results as reported for the MMPI–2, including the following: (a) 20 to 69 is *valid*, (b) 70 to 79 is *cautiously valid*, and (c) 80 to 120 is *invalid* (Butcher & Williams, 2000).

All remaining Validity scales are measured by the familiar *T*-score metric. The ones I utilize routinely in practice may be dichotomized as under-reporting and over-reporting, analogous to the MMPI–A. Key under-reporting scales (i.e., L–r and K–r) may be interpreted as follows: (a) 20 to 44 is *low*, (b) 45 to 57 is *normal*, (c) 58 to 64 is *moderate*, and 65 to 120 is *marked* (Green, 2011). Strategic over-reporting scales (i.e., F–r, Fp–r, Fs, and FBS–r) may be interpreted in the following manner: (a) 20 to 44 is *low*, (b) 45 to 57 is *normal*, (c) 58 to 80 is *moderate*, and (d) 81 to 120 is *marked* (Green, 2011). Although some specific scales further subdivide the extreme high or low score ranges for purposes of interpretation (e.g., *markedly low*, *extreme*), I have not found such additional discrimination to be pragmatically useful in clinical practice to justify the resulting increased complexity and duration of Validity scale interpretation.

More uniformly, all MMPI–2–RF Clinical and Personality (i.e., diagnostic) scales employ the same familiar *T*-score metric ($M = 50$, $SD = 10$). They are interpreted as follows: (a) 20 to 44 is *low*, (b) 45 to 64 is *normal*, (c) 65 to 79 is *moderate*, and (d) 80 to 120 is *marked* (Green, 2011). I interpret the first two score ranges to be within normal limits, while the last two are indicative of varying degrees of *DSM-IV-TR* psychopathology. Although *T*-scores represent a continuous interval scale of measurement (Gravetter & Wallnau, 2013; Warner, 2008), the latter two disordered ranges may be generally interpreted in the same manner as the two Millon disordered ranges (see above); that is, as categorically indicative as degrees of mild/moderate disorder and severe disorder, respectively. Again, this highlights the efficacious integration of dimensional and categorical approaches in psychodiagnosis. Again, in contrast to Millon test interpretation, which is facilitated by occasionally needed statistical diagnostic scale adjustments (see above), the MMPI–2–RF objective score elevations may require qualification within a narrative interpretation in the event one or more remarkable test-taking response patterns are detected by the Validity scales (Green, 2011).

Finally, MMPI–2–RF computer self-administration and scoring is available on the aforementioned Q Local Software (2011) application. A *score report* and *interpretive report* are available for purchase. The former functions as the MMPI–A extended score report by computing and reporting all available MMPI–2–RF scales. Thus, I advise purchase of the score report as this will suffice for use of my MMPI–2–RF results and interpretation tables discussed presently.

Results and Interpretation Tables

The MMPI–2–RF results and interpretation tables are displayed in Form 8.5. They consist of four validity tables and six diagnostic tables. The latter include five tables that are pertinent to Axis I Clinical Disorders, and one final table relevant to Axis II Personality Disorders. In general, they are similar in design and function as in the MMPI–A tables (Form 8.4).

Validity scales. The MMPI–2–RF offers a remarkably comprehensive analysis of a respondent's test-taking response pattern, including three nonresponsive scales (Table 1), two under-reporting scales (Table 2), and four over-reporting scales (Table 3). I have found the last to be extremely useful in detecting suspected Malingering or Factitious Disorder, especially concerning neuropsychological testing cases in which the patient has an ulterior motive for feigning neurocognitive dysfunction (e.g., obtaining or maintaining disability status).

Tables 1 through 3 are similar in design to the MMPI–A validity tables and include the following left to right columnar sequence: (a) scale name, (b) *T*-score (including a specific table note indicating the unique CNS(?)–r raw score metric), (c) descriptive result, and (d) test-taking response pattern measured by each scale. The test-taking descriptions entered were based upon those provided in the test manual and supplementary interpretive references (Ben-Porath & Tellegen, 2008; Green, 2011). Perusal of the diverse over-reporting scales measured in Table 3 elucidates their usefulness in providing objective quantitative measures of Malingering or the presence of a Factitious Disorder. Tables 1 to 3 all possess the following features: (a) general table note indicating the *T*-score mean, standard deviation, and directional meaning of higher scores; (b) specific note(s) delineating the pertinent score ranges and associated descriptive results; and (c) composed narrative interpretations covering the most frequent outcomes. Note that the score ranges and associated descriptive results are the same as I enumerated prior. Again, their proximity to each table assists the testing psychologist as they are immediately available for rapid reference, interpretation, and report-writing. They also clarify interpretation for the reader.

As in the MMPI–A, the validity analysis culminates in Table 4, which comprises all major interpretative permutations, including one valid, four cautiously valid, and one invalid. Therefore, the MMPI–2–RF Validity scale results are summarized in one final table that immediately lists the validity result, reason for the result, and the consequent interpretation strategy employed by the testing psychologist as applied to the diagnostic scale scores. You shall find that such approach hastens the validity analysis and, due to its brevity and clarity, facilitates actual use of that interpretation strategy when considering the meaning of the diagnostic scale elevations. Note that (a) the particular invalid result reason needs to be selected and (b) more than one validity result may apply (i.e., most frequently the over-reporting and extreme *F*-score[s] possibly indicative of disordered results).

Clinical and personality scales. Based upon the specified symptoms measured by each scale, I have selected what I believe are the most *DSM-IV-TR* diagnostically correspondent and organized them by general classification as follows: (a) Mood Disorders (Table 5), (b) Psychotic Disorders (Table 6), (c) Anxiety Disorders (Table 7), (d) Somatoform Disorders (Table 8), (e) Substance-Related Disorders (Table 9), and (f) Personality Disorders (Table 10). Note that I do not utilize the three Higher Order MMPI–2–RF scales, as they are diagnostically nebulous and possess divergent *T*-score interpretive elevations (see e.g., Green, 2011). As with the MMPI–A, tabular order again prioritizes the frequency of inclusion in testing referrals, diagnostic similarity and relationship, and Axis I/II sequence.

By column order, all diagnostic tables consist of (a) scale abbreviation, (b) *T*-score, and (c) measured symptoms/traits. Scale abbreviations versus names are used for rapid reference within the score report. A specific note symbol is affixed to the *T*-score referring the reader to a delineation of the diagnostic meaning of various quantitative ranges as reported by Green (2011) and discussed prior. Note that I have collapsed the low score range into the normal range, indicating an absence of disorder (i.e., no asterisk). Furthermore, I have interpreted a moderate elevation as indicative of a diagnosable disorder of mild to moderate severity (i.e., one asterisk), and a marked elevation as indicative of a severe diagnosable disorder (i.e., two asterisks). This asterisk scheme facilitates rapid and effective tabular profile analysis of the number, type, and degree of score elevations for purposes of psychodiagnosis. It is also similar to the MCMI–III interpretive scheme, which facilitates between-test comparisons with the MMPI–2–RF when both are included within the same battery and final report. As with previous results and interpretation tables, the measured symptoms appearing in summary form within the final column were based upon the extended and more detailed descriptions provided in the test manual and supplemental interpretive references (Ben-Porath & Tellegen, 2008; Green, 2011). Analogous to the MMPI–A, the tables are designed to be separately interpreted by a narrative summary of the results, and may be integrated with antecedent tabular results.

I wish to conclude discussion of the MMPI–2–RF diagnostic scales with some within table commentary. One, the Mood Disorders scales again begin with those that measure depressive symptoms, and ensued by those that measure manic symptoms. This allows diagnosis of Unipolar versus Bipolar Disorders. Two, the Mood Disorders table is immediately followed by the Psychotic Disorders table, which permits diagnosis of an existing Mood Disorder with Psychotic Features. Three, the Anxiety Disorders scale order is respectively pertinent to the following: (a) Obsessive-Compulsive Disorder (RC7); (b) Generalized Anxiety Disorder (AXY); (c) Type A Personality syndrome (Friedman & Rosenman, 1974) and risk for stress-related medical disorders, which would correspond most closely with either Adjustment Disorder With Anxiety or Psychological Factors Affecting a Medical Condition (STW, ANP); (d) possible Agoraphobia (BFR); and (e) Specific Phobia (MSF). Four, the Personality Disorders scales are again heavily loaded on APD relevant traits and risk for aggression or danger to others, including a pragmatic scale that measures the presence of conduct problems prior to the age of 18 years accordant with *DSM-IV-TR* criteria (American Psychiatric Association, 2000). As such, Table 10 begins with these scales. Other pertinent Personality Disorders addressed to a lesser extent by Table 10 scales, respectively, include the following: (a) Avoidant Personality Disorder (SAV, SHY), (b) Dependent Personality Disorder (IPP, SFD, NFC), and (c) Schizoid Personality Disorder (DSF).

SUMMARY

This chapter introduced the self-report clinical and personality inventories included in my recommended psychological test inventory, including three tests from the Millon series (i.e., M–PACI, MACI, and MCMI–III) and two from the MMPI series (i.e., MMPI–A and MMPI–2–RF). The Personality Disorder construct was similarly introduced, along with discussion of *DSM-IV-TR* within and between Axis I and II differential diagnoses. Vital related issues included (a) criteria for diagnosing Personality Disorders during older childhood and adolescence and (b) categorical versus dimensional approaches to Personality Disorder diagnosis. Regarding the latter, I have adopted the argument that the categorical approach is pragmatically superior and such dichotomy is fallacious because categorical criteria, along with psychological test data, in practice integrate both approaches.

The Millon tests were discussed simultaneously due to their similar design and correspondence with the *DSM-IV-TR* Axis I and II diagnostic classification system. Here, extended discussion was devoted to the unique and more esoteric *BR*-scores, including their development and integrated nominal/ordinal features for purposes of accurate test interpretation. This chapter concluded with separate presentations of the MMPI–A and MMPI–2–RF due to their greater divergence in test construction and factor structure. Here, I offered commentary regarding MMPI scale correspondence with *DSM-IV-TR* disorders, judicious use of the MMPI tests, and use of the traditional code-type approach as being antiquated and ineffective in terms of *DSM-IV-TR* differential diagnosis.

The next chapter continues with standardized examiner-administered personality tests relevant to Axis I and II disorders. The unique feature of these tests is that they represent direct quantitative measures of key personality abilities (e.g., reality testing, social cognition), and actuarial-based measures of personality traits, mechanisms, and symptoms, which are not contingent upon self-report.

REFERENCES

American Psychiatric Association. (1987). *Diagnostic and statistical manual of mental disorders* (3rd ed. rev.). Washington, DC: Author.

American Psychiatric Association. (1994). *Diagnostic and statistical manual of mental disorders* (4th ed.). Washington, DC: Author.

American Psychiatric Association. (2000). *Diagnostic and statistical manual of mental disorders* (4th ed., text rev.). Washington, DC: Author.

Archer, R. P. (1997). *MMPI–A: Assessing adolescent psychopathology* (2nd ed.). Mahwah, NJ: Lawrence Erlbaum.

Barlow, David H., & Durand, Mark V. (2012). *Abnormal psychology: An integrative approach* (6th ed.). Belmont, CA: Wadsworth, Cengage Learning.

Ben-Porath, Y. S., & Tellegen, A. (2008). *Minnesota Multiphasic Personality Inventory–2–RF (MMPI–2–RF): Manual for administration, scoring, and interpretation.* Minneapolis, MN: University of Minnesota Press.

Block, J. (1971). *Lives through time.* Berkeley, CA: Bancroft Books.

Block, J. (1977). Advancing the psychology of personality: Paradigmatic shift or improving the quality of research. In D. Magnusson & N. S. Endler (Eds.), *Personality at the crossroads* (pp. 37–63). Hillsdale, NJ: Erlbaum.

Butcher, J. N., Dahlstrom, W. G., Graham, J. R., Tellegen, A., & Kaemmer, B. (1989). *Minnesota Multiphasic Personality Inventory–2(MMPI–2): Manual for administration, and scoring.* Minneapolis, MN: NCS University of Minnesota Press.

Butcher, J. N., & Williams, C. L. (2000). *Essentials of MMPI–2 and MMPI–A interpretation* (2nd ed.). Minneapolis, MN: University of Minnesota Press.

Butcher, J. N., Williams, C. L., Graham, J. R., Archer, R. P., Tellegen, A., Ben-Porath, Y. S., & Kaemmer, B. (1992). *Minnesota Multiphasic Personality Inventory–Adolescent (MMPI–A): Manual for administration, scoring, and interpretation.* Minneapolis, MN: NCS University of Minnesota Press.

Caspi, A., Elder, G. H., Jr., & Bem, D. J. (1987). Moving against the world: Life-course patterns of explosive children. *Developmental Psychology, 23,* 308–313.

Caspi, A., & Roberts, B. W. (2001). Personality development across the life course: The argument for change and continuity. *Psychological Inquiry, 12,* 49–66.

Chamorro-Premuzic, T. (2011). *Personality and individual differences* (2nd ed.). Chichester, West Sussex, UK: British Psychological Society & Blackwell Publishing.

Conners, C. K. (2008). *Conners Comprehensive Behavior Rating Scales (Conners CBRS): Manual and interpretive update.* North Tonawanda, NY: Multi-Health Systems.

Craig, R. J. (1999). *Interpreting personality tests: A clinical manual for the MMPI–2, MCMI–III, CPI–R, and 16PF.* New York, NY: John Wiley.

Friedman, M., & Rosenman, R. H. (1974). *Type A behavior and your heart.* New York, NY: Alfred A. Knopf.

Gravetter, F. J., & Wallnau, L. B. (2013). *Statistics for the behavioral sciences* (9th ed.). Belmont, CA: Wadsworth, Cengage Learning.

Graziano, A. M., & Raulin, M. L. (2010). *Research methods: A process of inquiry* (7th ed.). Boston, MA: Allyn & Bacon.

Green, R. L. (2011). *The MMPI–2/MMPI–2–RF: An interpretative manual.* Boston, MA: Pearson.

Hinshaw, S. P., & Stier, A. (2008). Stigma as related to mental disorders. *Annual Review of Clinical Psychology, 4,* 367–393.

Kamp, J., & Tringone, R. F. (2008). Development and validation of the Millon Pre-Adolescent Clinical Inventory (M–PACI). In T. Millon & C. Bloom (Eds.), *The Millon inventories: A practitioner's guide to personalized clinical assessment* (2nd ed., pp. 528–547). New York, NY: The Guilford Press.

Kernberg, O. (1967). Borderline personality organization. *Journal of the American Psychoanalytic Association, 15,* 641–685.

Larsen, R. J., & Buss, D. M. (2010). *Personality psychology: Domains of knowledge about human nature* (4th ed.). New York, NY: McGraw-Hill.

McCann, J. T. (1999). *Assessing adolescents with the MACI; using the Millon Adolescent Clinical Inventory.* New York, NY: John Wiley.

McCann, J. T. (2008). Using the Millon Adolescent Clinical Inventory (MACI) and its facet scales. In T. Millon & C. Bloom (Eds.), *The Millon inventories: A practitioner's guide to personalized clinical assessment* (2nd ed., pp. 494–519). New York, NY: The Guilford Press.

McCrae, R. R., & Costa, P. T. (2003). *Personality in adulthood: A five-factor theory perspective* (2nd ed.). New York, NY: Guilford Press.

McWilliams, N. (2011). *Psychoanalytic diagnosis: Understanding personality structure in the clinical process* (2nd ed.). New York, NY: The Guilford Press.

Millon, T. (1990). *Toward a new personology: An evolutionary model.* New York, NY: John Wiley.

Millon, T. (with Millon, C., Davis, R. D., & Grossman, S. D.). (2006a). *Millon Clinical Multiaxial Inventory–III (MCMI–III) manual* (3rd ed.). Minneapolis, MN: NCS Pearson.

Millon, T. (with Millon, C., Davis, R. D., & Grossman, S. D.). (2006b). *Millon Adolescent Clinical Inventory (MACI) manual* (2nd ed.). Minneapolis, MN: NCS Pearson.

Millon, T., & Davis, R. D. (1996). *Disorders of personality: DSM-IV and beyond.* New York, NY: John Wiley.

Millon, T., Tringone, R., Millon, C., & Grossman, S. D. (2005). *Millon Pre–Adolescent Clinical Inventory (M–PACI) manual.* Minneapolis, MN: NCS Pearson.

Myers, I. B. (1998). *Introduction to type* (6th ed.). Palo Alto, CA: Consulting Psychologists Press.

Myers, I. B., McCaulley, M. H., Quenk, N. L., & Hammer, A. L. (1998). *MBTI manual: A guide to the development and use of the Myers–Briggs Type Indicator* (3rd ed.). Palo Alto, CA: Consulting Psychologists Press.

Orstavik, R. E., Kendler, K. S., Czajkowski, N., Tambs, K., & Reichborn-Kjennerud, T. (2007). The relationship between depressive personality disorder and major depressive disorder: A population-based twin study. *American Journal of Psychiatry, 164*(12), 1866–1872.

Q Local Software. (2011). [CD-ROM Computer Software]. San Antonio, TX: Pearson Assessments.

Shedler, J., & Westen, D. (2004). Dimensions of personality pathology: An alternative to the five-factor model. *American Journal of Psychiatry, 161*(10), 1743.

Stevens, S. S. (1946). On the theory of scales of measurement. *Science, 103*(2684), 677–680.

Strack, S. (2002). *Essentials of Millon inventories assessment* (2nd ed.). New York, NY: John Wiley.

Tellegen, A., Ben-Porath, Y. S., McNulty, J. L., Arbisi, P. A., Graham, J. R., & Kaemmer, B. (2003). *The MMPI–2 Restructured Clinical (RC) Scales: Development, validation, and interpretation.* Minneapolis, MN: University of Minnesota Press.

Vachon, D., Sellbom, M., Ryder, A., Miller, J., & Bagby, R. (2009). A five-factor model description of depressive personality disorder. *Journal of Personality Disorders, 23*(5), 447–465.

Warner, R. M. (2008). *Applied statistics.* Thousand Oaks, CA: Sage Publications.

Widiger, T., & Trull, T. J. (2007). Plate tectonics in the classification of personality disorder: Shifting to a dimensional model. *American Psychologist, 62*(2), 71.

Zimmerman, M., Rothschild, L., & Chelminski, I. (2005). The prevalence of *DSM-IV* personality disorders in psychiatric outpatients. *American Journal of Psychiatry, 162*, 1911–1918.

FORM 8.1

M–PACI RESULTS AND INTERPRETATION TABLES

M–PACI

TABLE 1 ■ VALIDITY SCALES

Scale	Raw score	PR	Result	Measured test-taking response style
Omissions[a]	0	--	Valid Invalid	Responding to a sufficient number of items according to test instructions
Invalidity[b]	0	--	Questionably valid	Honesty and accuracy in responding to item content
Response Negativity[c]	00	00	Low Average	Degree to which symptoms are minimized or magnified

Note: PR, percentile rank. -- denotes score type not available or computed.

[a]Omissions are items which remained unanswered; 0 to 4 = valid; 5 to 97 = invalid.

[b]Items on this scale directly ask if responses are being made truthfully; 0 = valid, 1 = questionably valid, 2 to 4 = invalid.

[c]PR range and result: (a) 0 to 10, extremely low; (b) 11 to 24, low ; (c) 25 to 75, average; (d) 76 to 89, high; and (e) 90 to 100, extremely high.

There is satisfactory evidence of sufficiency, honesty, and accuracy in responding. There is also ample evidence that symptoms are neither excessively minimized nor magnified. In these respects, the Current Clinical Signs and Emerging Personality Patterns diagnostic scales are deemed valid.

The Current Clinical Signs and Emerging Personality Patterns diagnostic scales are of questionable validity due to...possible dishonesty and/or inaccuracy in responding to item content...a measured tendency to minimize/magnify symptoms. Therefore, the M–PACI results shall be interpreted as valid only when corroborated by other available reliable and valid test data, including probative information gleaned from the diagnostic interview.

The Current Clinical Signs and Emerging Personality Patterns diagnostic scales are invalid due to insufficiency/dishonesty and/or inaccuracy in responding to item content...a marked test-taking response style reflecting a gross minimization/magnification of symptoms. Therefore, the M–PACI diagnostic results are neither interpreted nor reported.

(Cont.)

FORM 8.1

M–PACI RESULTS AND INTERPRETATION TABLES (*Cont.*)

TABLE 2 ■ CLINICAL SYNDROMES

Scale	BR-score[a]	Measured symptoms
Reality Distortions	000	Psychotic symptoms; auditory and/or visual hallucinations; paranoid ideation; mental confusion; secondary agitation
Depressive Moods	--	Sad mood; thoughts of death; loneliness; sense of despair; discouragement; presence of mood disorder
Anxiety/Fears	--	General apprehension, nervousness, and tension; associated physical complaints (e.g., headaches, stomachaches)
Obsessions/Compulsions	--	Intrusive thoughts; ritualistic behaviors; anxiety; social discomfort; emotionally overcontrolled
Conduct Problems	--	Protracted pattern of noncompliance; impaired judgment; poor frustration tolerance; intermittent aggression; hostility to authority
Disruptive Behaviors	--	Frequent lapses in impulse control; inability to delay a reaction; difficulty accepting limits; problems in relationships and authority
Attention Deficits	--	Difficulty sustaining attention and concentration; short attention span, distractibility; restlessness

Note: BR = Base Rate. 0 and 115 are minimum and maximum *BR*-scores, respectively. Higher *BR*-scores generally indicate greater presence of symptoms. -- denotes score type not available or computed.

[a]No asterisk = *BR*-score (0–74) is within normal limits, absence of a disorder; * = *BR*-score (75–84) indicates the presence of a disorder, disorder existent but secondary and/or subthreshold; ** = *BR*-score (85–115) indicates the prominence of a disorder, disorder considered best-fit and/or paramount.

TABLE 3 ■ EMERGING PERSONALITY PATTERNS

Scale	BR-score[a]	Measured maladaptive traits
Unstable (Borderline)[†]	00	Labile moods; unpredictable and impulsive behaviors; intense relationships; potential self-mutilation and suicidal symptoms
Confident (Narcissistic)[†]	--	Self-centered; exaggerated sense of self; exploitative; failing to reciprocate in relationships; takes others for granted
Unruly (Antisocial)[†]	--	Anger; disregard for others and rules; impulsive; need for immediate gratification; severe and repeated conduct problems
Outgoing (Histrionic)[†]	--	Sociable; desire to be the center of attention; emotionally expressive; lapses in impulse control and affective regulation
Submissive (Dependent)[†]	--	Intense dependency needs; excessively attached and reliant on others; clinging behavior; separation fears; low self-confidence
Inhibited (Avoidant)[†]	--	Fear of rejection and humiliation; socially apprehensive; desire to be close although mistrustful of others; low self-esteem
Conforming (OC)[†]	--	Excessively responsible, conscientious, and organized; rule-governed; strict morals; emotional constriction; tense

Note: BR = Base Rate. 0 and 115 are minimum and maximum *BR*-scores, respectively. Higher *BR*-scores generally indicate greater presence of symptoms. -- denotes score type not available or computed.
[†]denotes the *DSM-IV-TR* Personality Disorder analogue. OC, Obsessive-Compulsive.

[a]No asterisk = *BR*-score (0–74) is within normal limits, absence of a disorder; * = *BR*-score (75–84) indicates the presence of a disorder, disorder existent but secondary and/or subthreshold; ** = *BR*-score (85–115) indicates the prominence of a disorder, disorder considered best-fit and/or paramount.

FORM 8.2

MACI RESULTS AND INTERPRETATION TABLES

MACI

TABLE 1 ■ VALIDITY SCALES

Scale	Raw score	Result	Measured test-taking response style
Omissions[a]	0	Valid	Responding to a sufficient number of items according to test instructions
Reliability[b]	0	Questionably valid Invalid	Honesty and accuracy in responding to item content

[a]Omissions are items which remained unanswered; 0 to 9 = valid; 10 to 160 = invalid.

[b]Items on this scale indicate grossly bizarre symptoms infrequently endorsed by nonclinical and clinical samples; 0 = valid, 1 = questionably valid, 2 = invalid.

There is satisfactory evidence of sufficiency, honesty, and accuracy in responding. In these respects, the Clinical Syndromes and Personality Patterns diagnostic scales are deemed valid.

The Clinical Syndromes and Personality Patterns diagnostic scales are of questionable validity due to possible dishonesty and inaccuracy in responding to item content. Therefore, the MACI results shall be interpreted as valid only when corroborated by other available reliable and valid test data, including probative information gleaned from the diagnostic interview.

The Clinical Syndromes and Personality Patterns diagnostic scales are invalid due to lack of sufficiency/ honesty and accuracy in responding to item content. Therefore, the MACI diagnostic results are neither interpreted nor reported.

TABLE 2 ■ MODIFYING INDICES

Index	BR-score	Result	Measured test-taking response style
Disclosure	000	Low Average	Willingness to be forthcoming or open in reporting symptoms
Desirability	--	Moderately high	Wish to appear overly favorable, morally virtuous, and emotionally stable
Debasement	--	Extremely high	Degree to which symptoms are magnified

Note: BR = Base Rate. *BR*-score range, (percentile range), result: (a) 0 to 34, (0–15), low; (b) 35 to 74, (16–74), average; (c) 75 to 84, (75–89), moderately high; (d) 85 to 115, (90–100), extremely high. -- denotes score type not available or computed.

The Modifying Indices overall results indicate that the Clinical Syndromes and Personality Patterns scales are valid. No statistical adjustments to these diagnostic scales *BR*-scores were necessitated.

Test-taking response style indicated the presence of ... Statistical adjustments to the *BR*-scores of the Clinical Syndromes and Personality Patterns scales were necessitated to enhance diagnostic accuracy and for valid interpretation.

Test-taking response style indicated the presence of ... such that the MACI results are rendered invalid. Statistical adjustments to the *BR*-scores of the Clinical Syndromes and Personality Patterns scales would not enhance diagnostic accuracy sufficiently for valid interpretation. Therefore, the MACI diagnostic results are neither interpreted nor reported.

(Cont.)

FORM 8.2

MACI RESULTS AND INTERPRETATION TABLES (*Cont.*)

TABLE 3 ■ CLINICAL SYNDROMES

Scale	BR-score[a]	Measured symptoms
Depressive Affect	000	Sadness; lack of interests; pessimistic thoughts; hopelessness; helplessness; low self-confidence; social withdrawal
Suicidal Tendency	--	Suicidal thoughts and planning; risk for contemplating suicide as a viable option
Anxious Feelings	--	General apprehension and tension; associated physical complaints (e.g., headaches, stomachaches)
Delinquent Predisposition	--	Conduct disordered behavior; violation of major social norms and rules; lack of remorse and regard for others; self-centered
Substance Abuse Proneness	--	Admission of persistent alcohol and drug abuse; possible Substance-Related Disorder
Oppositional	--	Defiant, argumentative, and hostile; irritable temperament; stubborn; anger and resentment toward others
Impulsive Propensity	--	Difficulty controlling impulses; acting without considering behavioral consequences; behavioral and emotional dysregulation
Eating Dysfunctions	--	Preoccupation with food, caloric intake, and fear of gaining weight; body image disturbance; abnormal eating behaviors

Note: BR = Base Rate. 0 and 115 are minimum and maximum *BR*-scores, respectively. Higher *BR*-scores generally indicate greater presence of symptoms. -- denotes score type not available or computed.

[a]No asterisk = *BR*-score (0–74) is within normal limits, absence of a disorder; * = *BR*-score (75–84) indicates the presence of a disorder, disorder existent but secondary and/or subthreshold; ** = *BR*-score (85–115) indicates the prominence of a disorder, disorder considered best-fit and/or paramount.

TABLE 4 ■ PERSONALITY PATTERNS

Scale	BR-score[a]	Measured maladaptive traits
Borderline (Borderline)[†]	00	Intense inner conflicts; unstable moods and relationships; identity diffusion; unpredictable and self-destructive behaviors
Egotistic (Narcissistic)[†]	--	Self-centered; arrogant; difficulty empathizing with others; intense rage and dejection when needs are not met
Unruly (Antisocial)[†]	--	Need for immediate gratification; disregard of social rules and the rights of others; lack of remorse; need for power and control
Forceful (Sadistic)[††]	--	Striving to dominate, humiliate, and abuse others; hostile and combative; lack of empathy, compassion, and remorse
Dramatizing (Histrionic)[†]	--	Excessive need for attention and affection; exaggerated emotions; superficial relationships; impulsive; easily bored
Submissive (Dependent)[†]	--	Excessive need for support and guidance; lack of initiative and independence; indecision; lack of self-confidence
Inhibited (Avoidant)[†]	--	Fear of rejection and humiliation; shy; uncomfortable in social situations; mistrust in others; poor self-esteem
Conforming (OC)[†]	--	Excessively responsible and conscientious; rule-governed; serious-minded; emotionally constricted; repression of anger
Introversive (Schizoid)[†]	--	Socially and emotionally distant; lack of capacity to experience emotions; indifferent and aloof
Self-Demeaning (Self-Defeating)[††]	--	Allowing others to exploit oneself; undermining others' efforts to help; sabotaging one's own success; negative self-image

Note: BR = Base Rate. 0 and 115 are minimum and maximum *BR*-scores, respectively. Higher *BR*-scores generally indicate greater presence of symptoms. [†]denotes the *DSM-IV-TR* Personality Disorder analogue. [††]denotes the *DSM-III-R* Personality Disorder analogue; *DSM-IV-TR* diagnosis would be Personality Disorder NOS with the indicated maladaptive traits. OC, Obsessive-Compulsive.

[a]No asterisk = *BR*-score (0–74) is within normal limits, absence of a disorder; * = *BR*-score (75–84) indicates the presence of a disorder, disorder existent but secondary and/or subthreshold; ** = *BR*-score (85–115) indicates the prominence of a disorder, disorder considered best-fit and/or paramount.

FORM 8.3

MCMI–III RESULTS AND INTERPRETATION TABLES

MCMI–III

TABLE 1 ■ VALIDITY SCALES

Scale	Raw score	Result	Measured test-taking response style
Omissions[a]	0	Valid	Responding to a sufficient number of items according to test instructions
Invalidity[b]	0	Questionably valid	Honesty and accuracy in responding to item content
Inconsistency[c]	0	Invalid	Reliability in responding to item content

[a]Omissions are items which remained unanswered; 0 to 11 = valid; 12 to 175 = invalid.

[b]Items on this scale indicate grossly bizarre symptoms infrequently endorsed by nonclinical and clinical samples; 0 = valid, 1 = questionably valid, 2 to 3 = invalid.

[c]This scale measures the frequency with which items of similar content were answered in a contradictory fashion; 0 to 9 = valid; 10 and higher = invalid.

There is satisfactory evidence of sufficiency, honesty, accuracy, and consistency in responding. In these respects, the Clinical Syndromes and Personality Patterns diagnostic scales are deemed valid.

The Clinical Syndromes and Personality Patterns diagnostic scales are of questionable validity due to possible dishonesty and inaccuracy/inconsistency in responding to item content. Therefore, the MCMI–III results shall be interpreted as valid only when corroborated by other available reliable and valid test data, including probative information gleaned from the diagnostic interview.

The Clinical Syndromes and Personality Patterns diagnostic scales are invalid due to a lack of sufficiency/ honesty and accuracy/consistency in responding to item content. Therefore, the MCMI–III diagnostic results are neither interpreted nor reported.

TABLE 2 ■ MODIFYING INDICES

Index	BR-score	Result	Measured test-taking response style
Disclosure	000	Low Average	Willingness to be forthcoming or open in reporting symptoms
Desirability	--	Moderately high	Wish to appear overly favorable, morally virtuous, and emotionally stable
Debasement	--	Extremely high	Degree to which symptoms are magnified

Note: BR = Base Rate. BR-score range, (percentile range), result: (a) 0 to 34, (0–15), low; (b) 35 to 74, (16–74), average; (c) 75 to 84, (75–89), moderately high; (d) 85 to 115, (90–100), extremely high.

The Modifying Indices overall results indicate that the Clinical Syndromes and Personality Patterns scales are valid. No statistical adjustments to these diagnostic scales BR-scores were necessitated.

Test-taking response style indicated the presence of .... Statistical adjustments to the BR-scores of the Clinical Syndromes and Personality Patterns scales were necessitated to enhance diagnostic accuracy and for valid interpretation.

Test-taking response style indicated the presence of…such that the MCMI–III results are rendered invalid. Statistical adjustments to the BR-scores of the Clinical Syndromes and Personality Patterns scales would not enhance diagnostic accuracy sufficiently for valid interpretation. Therefore, the MCMI–III diagnostic results are neither interpreted nor reported.

(Cont.)

FORM 8.3

MCMI–III RESULTS AND INTERPRETATION TABLES (*Cont.*)

TABLE 3 ■ CLINICAL SYNDROMES

Scale	BR-score[a]	Measured symptoms
Thought Disorder	000	Disorganized, fragmented, confused, or bizarre thinking; hallucinations; delusions; inappropriate affect
Delusional Disorder	--	Delusional thinking, especially delusions of persecution and grandiosity; intense hypervigilance constituting paranoia
Bipolar Manic	--	Frequent mood swings; flight of ideas; pressured speech; excessive energy; unrealistic and expansive goals; impulsivity
Major Depression	--	Severe sadness; feeling worthless; fatigue; lack of interests; sleep and appetite disturbance; withdrawal; possible suicidal ideation
Dysthymia	--	Apathetic; pessimistic; socially withdrawn; preoccupied with feelings of inadequacy; can manage daily affairs
(Generalized) Anxiety	--	Chronic apprehension; inability to relax; restless; irritable; muscular tension; insomnia; headaches; palpitations; perspiration
Posttraumatic Stress	--	Distressing and intrusive thoughts; flashbacks; startle responses; emotional numbing; anger problems; concentration problems[b]
Alcohol Dependence	--	Pattern of alcohol abuse; problematic drinking[c]
Drug Dependence	--	Past or current problem with drug dependence; hedonism; self-indulgence; impulsivity; exploitiveness; narcissism
Somatoform	--	Chronic bodily complaints; persistent pursuit of medical care despite lack of evidence of physical disorder

Note: BR = Base Rate. 0 and 115 are minimum and maximum *BR*-scores, respectively. Higher *BR*-scores generally indicate greater presence of symptoms. -- denotes score type not available or computed.

[a]No asterisk = *BR*-score (0–74) is within normal limits, absence of a disorder; * = *BR*-score (75–84) indicates the presence of a disorder, disorder existent but secondary and/or subthreshold; ** = *BR*-score (85–115) indicates the prominence of a disorder, disorder considered best-fit and/or paramount.

[b]If there is no evidence of trauma in the patient's history, scores in the disordered range indicate nontraumatic emotional turmoil.

[c]If there is no evidence of alcohol abuse, scores in the disordered range indicate the presence of alcoholic personality traits including selfishness, impulsivity, rationalization, aggressiveness, and lack of adherence to societal standards.

(Cont.)

FORM 8.3

MCMI–III RESULTS AND INTERPRETATION TABLES (*Cont.*)

TABLE 4 ■ PERSONALITY PATTERNS

Scale	BR-score[a]	Measured maladaptive traits
Borderline	000	Intense and unstable relationships; labile emotions; impulsivity; strong dependency needs with fears of abandonment; diffuse identity; splitting (others/self all good or all bad); transient psychoses; self-mutilation
Narcissistic[†]	--	Extremely self-centered; expecting constant praise and recognition from others; feelings of entitlement; arrogant; conceited; boastful; may appear momentarily charming but exploiting others for self-gain
Antisocial	--	Intimidating; dominating; narcissistic; aggressive; argumentative; vengeful; provoking fear to control others; acting out as main defense; lack of remorse; warmth and intimacy viewed as weakness
Sadistic[††]	--	Flagrantly abusive of others; potential brutal force when angered; dominating; hostile; intimidating; fearless; aggressive; arrogant; touchy; irritable; disagreeable; frequent explosive outbursts
Histrionic	--	Emotionally dramatic; strong needs to be the center of attention; seductive; seeking constant stimulation; emotionally labile; easily excited; emotional outbursts; manipulative; superficial relationships
Dependent	--	Excessive needs for security, guidance, and direction from others; passive; submissive; conforming; constant need to be nurtured; pacifying and overly compliant to avoid conflict and ensure protection
Avoidant	--	Hypersensitive to rejection and depreciation; fearing and anticipating negative evaluations; conflict between desire to relate and expecting disapproval; cautious detachment; social withdrawal; use of fantasy
(Obsessive) Compulsive[†]	--	Behaviorally rigid; constricted; meticulous; overly conforming and organized; perfectionistic; formal; suppressing resentment toward authority figures; repetitive lifestyle; potential obsessive thoughts
Schizoid	--	Severe relationship deficits; aloofness; introverted; emotionally bland and detached; low need for social contact; requiring little affection; lack of warmth and emotional expression; solitary lifestyle
Schizotypal	--	Ideas of reference; odd beliefs or magical thinking (e.g., telepathy), illusions; vague or tangential speech; excessive social anxiety; paranoid ideation; inappropriate or restricted affect; socially isolated
Paranoid	--	Vigilantly mistrustful and suspicious; belief that people attempt to control and influence in malevolent ways; abrasive; irritable; hostile; belligerent if provoked; rigid and argumentative; accusatory
Passive–Aggressive[††]	--	Moody; irritable; hostile; grumbling; pessimistic; habitually complaining; disgruntled; feeling unappreciated; sulking; passively compliant followed by oppositional and self-defeating behavior
Self-Defeating[††]	--	Excessively self-sacrificing; martyr like; allowing oneself to be taken advantage of, dominated, and mistreated by others in exchange for security and affection; risk for being abused

Note: BR = Base Rate. 0 and 115 are minimum and maximum *BR*-scores, respectively. Higher *BR*-scores generally indicate greater presence of symptoms. -- denotes score type not available or computed. [†]denotes that the scale may measure a personality style versus disorder. [††]the proper *DSM-IV-TR* diagnosis would be Personality Disorder NOS with the indicated maladaptive traits.

[a]No asterisk = *BR*-score (0–74) is within normal limits, absence of a disorder; * = *BR*-score (75–84) indicates the presence of a disorder, disorder existent but secondary and/or subthreshold; ** = *BR*-score (85–115) indicates the prominence of a disorder, disorder considered best-fit and/or paramount.

FORM 8.4

MMPI–A RESULTS AND INTERPRETATION TABLES

MMPI–A

TABLE 1 ■ NONRESPONSIVE VALIDITY SCALES

Scale	T-score	Result	Measured test-taking response pattern
CNS(?)[a,b]	0	Low Moderate	Number of item omissions or improperly answered items
TRIN[c]	--	Cautiously valid	Fixed responding in either the "True" or "False" direction resulting in inconsistency
VRIN[c]	--	Valid Invalid	Indiscriminant and random responding

Note: T-score mean = 50, standard deviation = 10. Higher *T*-scores indicate greater presence of the measured response pattern by the respondent. -- denotes score type not available or computed.

[a]CNS(?) datum reported as a raw score.

[b]CNS(?) score range and result: (a) 0 to 3, low; (b) 4 to 10, moderate; (c) 11 to 30, marked; (d) 31 to 478, invalid.

[c]TRIN/VRIN score range and result: (a) 30 to 69, valid; (b) 70 to 79, cautiously valid; (c) 80 to 120, invalid.

The overall results are negative for a nonresponsive pattern. A remarkable nonresponsive pattern is detected, although it does not invalidate the results. An invalid nonresponsive pattern is detected.

TABLE 2 ■ UNDER-REPORTING AND OVER-REPORTING VALIDITY SCALES

Scale	T-score	Result[a]	Measured test-taking response pattern
L	000	Low Normal	Endorsement of rarely claimed moral attributes, activities, or virtues
K	--	Moderate	Endorsement of items in a manner that indicates noteworthy psychological well-adjustment
F[b]	--	Marked Extreme	Endorsement of infrequently reported symptoms

Note: T-score mean = 50, standard deviation = 10. Higher *T*-scores indicate greater presence of the measured response style by the respondent. -- denotes score type not available or computed.

[a]Score range and result: (a) 30 to 40, low; (b) 41 to 55, normal; (c) 56 to 65, moderate; (d) 66 to 120, marked.

[b]F extreme score 90 to 120 may indicate the genuine presence of severe thought disorganization reflective of a psychotic process.

The overall results are negative for under-reporting symptoms. A low/moderate/marked under-reporting response pattern is detected.

The overall results are negative for over-reporting symptoms. A low/moderate/marked over-reporting response pattern is detected.

(Cont.)

FORM 8.4

MMPI–A RESULTS AND INTERPRETATION TABLES *(Cont.)*

TABLE 3 ■ **MMPI–A VALIDITY RESULT**

Result	Reason	Interpretation strategy employed on the clinical and personality scale scores
Valid	Acceptable response pattern	Standard
Cautiously valid	Remarkably nonresponsive	Scores interpreted as valid only when corroborated by other test data
Cautiously valid	Moderate under-reporting	Elevated scores interpreted as valid, whereas low scores interpreted as invalid
Cautiously valid	Moderate over-reporting	Elevated scores interpreted as presence of disorder only when corroborated by other data
Cautiously valid	Extreme *F* score deemed as possibly indicative of disorder	Elevated scores interpreted as presence of disorder only when corroborated by other data
Invalid	Marked nonresponding/under-reporting/over-reporting	Scores neither reported nor interpreted

TABLE 4 ■ **CLINICAL: MOOD DISORDERS**

Scale	*T*-score[a]	Measured symptoms
D (2)	000	Severe depression; hopelessness; apathy; lack of interest in activities; excessive guilt; sense of inadequacy; social withdrawal and isolation
A–dep	--	Sadness; depression; despondency; fatigue; apathy; pervasive sense of hopelessness; possible suicidal ideation
D^4	--	Impairments in attention, concentration, and memory associated with depressive mood symptoms
Ma (9)	--	Mania; flight of ideas; euphoria; emotional lability; grandiosity in self-perceptions and aspirations; excessive activity; impulsivity; distractibility
Ma^2	--	Acceleration in thought and speech; racing thoughts; restlessness; hyperactivity; sensation-seeking and risk-taking behaviors
Ma^4	--	Excessive feelings of self-importance or grandiosity; resentfulness of perceived demands from, or interference by, others

Note: T-score mean = 50, standard deviation = 10. Higher *T*-scores indicate greater presence of measured symptoms. -- denotes score type not available or computed.

[a]No asterisk = *T*-score (30–59) is within normal limits and an absence of a disorder; * = *T*-score (60–64) is a transitional elevation and suggests the presence of a subthreshold or mild disorder in need of corroborating evidence; ** = *T*-score (65–120) indicates a clinically significant elevation indicative of a genuine moderate to severe disorder.

(Cont.)

FORM 8.4

MMPI–A RESULTS AND INTERPRETATION TABLES *(Cont.)*

TABLE 5 ■ CLINICAL: PSYCHOTIC DISORDERS

Scale	T-score[a]	Measured symptoms
Sc (8)	000	Delusions; hallucinations; mental confusion; disorganized thought process; disturbed reality testing
A–biz	--	Psychotic thought process; disturbed reality testing; hallucinations; delusions including paranoid symptoms
Sc[6]	--	Severe and bizarre sensory-perceptual disturbances; hallucinations
Pa (6)	--	Delusions of persecution and grandeur; ideas of reference; formal thought disorder; disturbed reality testing; secondary hostility and withdrawal
Pa[1]	--	Delusions of persecution; excessive use of projection; externalization of blame
PSYC	--	Psychosis; disconnection from consensual reality

Note: T-score mean = 50, standard deviation = 10. Higher T-scores indicate greater presence of measured symptoms. -- denotes score type not available or computed.

[a]No asterisk = T-score (30–59) is within normal limits and an absence of a disorder; * = T-score (60–64) is a transitional elevation and suggests the presence of a subthreshold or mild disorder in need of corroborating evidence; ** = T-score (65–120) indicates a clinically significant elevation indicative of a genuine moderate to severe disorder.

TABLE 6 ■ CLINICAL: ANXIETY DISORDERS

Scale	T-score[a]	Measured symptoms
Pt (7)	000	Obsessive thought patterns; compulsive behaviors; anxious; perfectionistic; emotionally over-controlled; ruminative; ambivalent in decision making
A–obs	--	Intrusive and obsessive thoughts; problems in concentration; difficulty making decisions
A–anx	--	Generally anxious, tense, nervous and ruminative; problems in concentration; fatigue

Note: T-score mean = 50, standard deviation = 10. Higher T-scores indicate greater presence of measured symptoms. -- denotes score type not available or computed.

[a]No asterisk = T-score (30–59) is within normal limits and an absence of a disorder; * = T-score (60–64) is a transitional elevation and suggests the presence of a subthreshold or mild disorder in need of corroborating evidence; ** = T-score (65–120) indicates a clinically significant elevation indicative of a genuine moderate to severe disorder.

TABLE 7 ■ CLINICAL: SOMATOFORM DISORDERS

Scale	T-score[a]	Measured symptoms
Hs (1)	000	Excessive somatic and bodily concerns that are likely vague in nature; somatic response to stress
A–hea	--	Multiple physical symptoms and complaints; fatigue; lack of energy
D[3]	--	Concern and preoccupation with physical health; multiple and wide-ranging physical complaints
Hy[4]	--	Multiple somatic complaints and concerns

Note: T-score mean = 50, standard deviation = 10. Higher T-scores indicate greater presence of measured symptoms. -- denotes score type not available or computed.

[a]No asterisk = T-score (30–59) is within normal limits and an absence of a disorder; * = T-score (60–64) is a transitional elevation and suggests the presence of a subthreshold or mild disorder in need of corroborating evidence; ** = T-score (65–120) indicates a clinically significant elevation indicative of a genuine moderate to severe disorder.

(Cont.)

FORM 8.4

MMPI–A RESULTS AND INTERPRETATION TABLES (*Cont.*)

TABLE 8 ■ CLINICAL: SUBSTANCE-RELATED DISORDERS

Scale	T-score[a]	Measured symptoms
ACK	000	Acknowledgment of alcohol and/or drug abuse problems
MAC–R	--	Increased likelihood of alcohol and drug abuse problems
PRO	--	Increased potential for the development of alcohol and drug problems

Note: T-score mean = 50, standard deviation = 10. Higher T-scores indicate greater presence of measured symptoms. -- denotes score type not available or computed.

[a]No asterisk = T-score (30–59) is within normal limits and an absence of a disorder; * = T-score (60–64) is a transitional elevation and suggests the presence of a subthreshold or mild disorder in need of corroborating evidence; ** = T-score (65–120) indicates a clinically significant elevation indicative of a genuine moderate to severe disorder.

TABLE 9 ■ PERSONALITY DISORDERS

Scale	T-score[a]	Measured symptoms
Pd (4)	000	Rebellious; hostile with authority; lack of remorse and distress; risk-taking; sensation-seeking; poor planning; impulsivity; cannot delay gratification
A–ang	--	Poor anger control; interpersonally hostile; irritable; impatient; potential episodes of physical aggression
A–con	--	Antisocial behaviors; attitudes and beliefs that conflict with societal norms and standards; poor impulse control; problems with authority
A–las	--	Poor academic achievement; persistent pattern of underachievement; low frustration tolerance
Pd²	--	History of legal violations; antisocial behavior; repeated conflicts with authority; resentful of societal norms and standards
A–cyn	--	Guarded and suspicious of the motives of others; unfriendly; hostile in relationships; paranoid tendencies
Si (0)	--	Social introversion and discomfort; interpersonally hypersensitive; underlying insecurity and lacking in self-confidence; timid
A–aln	--	Social withdrawal; sense of interpersonal isolation, alienation, and frustration
A–sod	--	Social discomfort and withdrawal; shyness; social introversion
A–lse	--	Poor self-esteem and self-confidence; feelings of inadequacy; interpersonally passive

Note: T-score mean = 50, standard deviation = 10. Higher T-scores indicate greater presence of measured symptoms. -- denotes score type not available or computed.

[a]No asterisk = T-score (30–59) is within normal limits and an absence of a disorder; * = T-score (60–64) is a transitional elevation and suggests the presence of a subthreshold or mild disorder in need of corroborating evidence; ** = T-score (65–120) indicates a clinically significant elevation indicative of a genuine moderate to severe disorder.

FORM 8.5

MMPI–2–RF RESULTS AND INTERPRETATION TABLES

MMPI–2–RF

TABLE 1 ■ NONRESPONSIVE VALIDITY SCALES

Scale	T-score	Result	Measured test-taking response pattern
CNS(?)–r[a,b]	0	Normal Moderate	Number of item omissions or improperly answered items
TRIN–r[c]	--	Cautiously valid	Fixed responding in either the "True" or "False" direction resulting in inconsistency
VRIN–r[c]	--	Valid Invalid	Indiscriminant and random responding

Note: T-score mean = 50, standard deviation = 10. Higher scores indicate greater presence of the measured response pattern by the respondent. -- denotes score type not available or computed.

[a]CNS(?) datum reported as a raw score.

[b]CNS(?) score range and result: (a) 0, low; (b) 1 to 4, normal; (c) 5 to 10, moderate; (d) 11 to 338, marked.

[c]TRIN–r/VRIN–r score range and result: (a) 20 to 69, valid; (b) 70 to 79, cautiously valid; (c) 80 to 120, invalid.

The overall results are negative for a nonresponsive pattern. A remarkable nonresponsive pattern is detected, although it does not invalidate the results. An invalid nonresponsive pattern is detected.

TABLE 2 ■ UNDER-REPORTING VALIDITY SCALES

Scale	T-score	Result[a]	Measured test-taking response pattern
L–r	000	Low Normal	Endorsement of rarely claimed moral attributes, activities, or virtues
K–r	--	Moderate Marked	Endorsement of items in a manner that indicates noteworthy psychological well-adjustment

Note: T-score mean = 50, standard deviation = 10. Higher T-scores indicate greater presence of the measured response style by the respondent. -- denotes score type not available or computed.

[a]Score range and result: (a) 20 to 44, low; (b) 45 to 57, normal; (c) 58 to 64, moderate; (d) 65 to 120, marked.

The overall results are negative for under-reporting symptoms. A low/moderate/marked under-reporting response pattern is detected.

TABLE 3 ■ OVER-REPORTING VALIDITY SCALES

Scale	T-score	Result[a]	Measured test-taking response pattern
F–r	000	Low Normal	Endorsement of infrequently reported symptoms in the general population
Fp–r	--	Moderate Marked	Endorsement of infrequently reported symptoms in psychiatric populations
Fs	--	Low Normal	Endorsement of infrequently reported somatic (physical) symptoms in medical populations
FBS–r	--	Moderate Marked	Endorsement of infrequently reported somatic (physical) and cognitive (mental) symptoms in medical populations

Note: T-score mean = 50, standard deviation = 10. Higher T-scores indicate greater presence of the measured response style by the respondent. -- denotes score type not available or computed.

[a]Score range and result: (a) 20 to 44, low; (b) 45 to 57, normal; (c) 58 to 80, moderate; (d) 81 to 120, marked.

The overall results are negative for over-reporting symptoms. A low/moderate/marked over-reporting response pattern is detected.

(Cont.)

FORM 8.5

MMPI–2–RF RESULTS AND INTERPRETATION TABLES (*Cont.*)

TABLE 4 ■ MMPI–2–RF VALIDITY RESULT

Result	Reason	Interpretation strategy employed on the clinical and personality scale scores
Valid	Acceptable response pattern	Standard
Cautiously valid	Remarkably nonresponsive	Scores interpreted as valid only when corroborated by other test data
Cautiously valid	Moderate under-reporting	Elevated scores interpreted as valid, whereas low scores interpreted as invalid
Cautiously valid	Moderate over-reporting	Elevated scores interpreted as presence of disorder only when corroborated by other data
Cautiously valid	Extreme *F* score(s) deemed as possibly indicative of disorder	Elevated scores interpreted as presence of disorder only when corroborated by other data
Invalid	Marked nonresponding/under-reporting/over-reporting	Scores neither reported nor interpreted

TABLE 5 ■ CLINICAL: MOOD DISORDERS

Scale	*T*-score[a]	Measured symptoms
RCd	000	Demoralization; general unhappiness and dissatisfaction; pessimism; depression
RC2	--	Low positive emotions; lack of positive emotional responsiveness; lack of pleasure (i.e., anhedonia)
HLP	--	Helplessness; hopelessness; pessimism; feeling useless
SUI	--	Ideas of suicide and death; direct report of suicidal ideas and/or past attempts
RC9	--	Hypomanic activation; hyperactivity; racing thoughts; aggression; impulsivity; grandiose ideas
ACT	--	Heightened activation, excitation, and energy level; unusually cheerful (i.e., euthymic)

Note: T-score mean = 50, standard deviation = 10. Higher *T*-scores indicate greater presence of symptoms. -- denotes score type not available or computed.

[a]No asterisk = *T*-score (0–64) is within normal limits, absence of a disorder; * = *T*-score (65–79) indicates the presence of a disorder of mild to moderate severity; ** = *T*-score (80–120) indicates the presence of a severe disorder.

TABLE 6 ■ CLINICAL: PSYCHOTIC DISORDERS

Scale	*T*-score[a]	Measured symptoms
RC6	000	Psychotic delusions, especially persecutory, grandiose, and reference types; suspicious, distrusting and socially alienated; feels mistreated
RC8	--	Psychotic symptoms; hallucinations and bizarre perceptual experiences; delusional beliefs
PSYC–r	--	Psychosis; disconnection from consensual reality

Note: T-score mean = 50, standard deviation = 10. Higher *T*-scores indicate greater presence of symptoms. -- denotes score type not available or computed.

[a]No asterisk = *T*-score (0–64) is within normal limits, absence of a disorder; * = *T*-score (65–79) indicates the presence of a disorder of mild to moderate severity; ** = *T*-score (80–120) indicates the presence of a severe disorder.

(*Cont.*)

FORM 8.5

MMPI–2–RF RESULTS AND INTERPRETATION TABLES (*Cont.*)

TABLE 7 ■ CLINICAL: ANXIETY DISORDERS

Scale	T-score[a]	Measured symptoms
RC7	000	Anxiety, fear, and irritability; worry (i.e., apprehension); intrusive and unwanted ideas (i.e., obsessions); rumination
AXY	--	Generalized (i.e., pervasive) anxiety; chronic worry (i.e., apprehension); difficulty concentrating
STW	--	Stress; worry (i.e., apprehension); preoccupation with potential misfortune; constant pressure to get things done
ANP	--	Easily angered and upset; impatient with people; irritable; may be hotheaded
BFR	--	Behavioral restrictions due to fears; multiple fears that restrict activities
MSF	--	Specific phobias (e.g., animal, nature); multiple specific fears

Note: T-score mean = 50, standard deviation = 10. Higher T-scores indicate greater presence of symptoms. -- denotes score type not available or computed.

[a]No asterisk = T-score (0–64) is within normal limits, absence of a disorder; * = T-score (65–79) indicates the presence of a disorder of mild to moderate severity; ** = T-score (80–120) indicates the presence of a severe disorder.

TABLE 8 ■ CLINICAL: SOMATOFORM DISORDERS

Scale	T-score[a]	Measured symptoms
RC1	000	Chronic and diffuse physical health complaints; excessive preoccupation with health; reports of fatigue, general weakness, and chronic pain
GIC	--	Gastrointestinal complaints including nausea, recurring upset stomach, and disturbed appetite
HPC	--	Complaints of chronic pain in the head and neck regions
NUC	--	Neurological complaints including dizziness, numbness, weakness, involuntary movement, and convulsions

Note: T-score mean = 50, standard deviation = 10. Higher T-scores indicate greater presence of symptoms. -- denotes score type not available or computed.

[a]No asterisk = T-score (0–64) is within normal limits, absence of a disorder; * = T-score (65–79) indicates the presence of a disorder of mild to moderate severity; ** = T-score (80–120) indicates the presence of a severe disorder.

TABLE 9 ■ CLINICAL: SUBSTANCE-RELATED DISORDERS

Scale	T-score[a]	Measured symptoms
SUB	000	Current and/or past substance abuse; report using alcohol excessively and marijuana on a daily basis

Note: T-score mean = 50, standard deviation = 10. Higher T-scores indicate greater presence of symptoms. -- denotes score type not available or computed.

[a]No asterisk = T-score (0–64) is within normal limits, absence of a disorder; * = T-score (65–79) indicates the presence of a disorder of mild to moderate severity; ** = T-score (80–120) indicates the presence of a severe disorder.

(*Cont.*)

FORM 8.5

MMPI–2–RF RESULTS AND INTERPRETATION TABLES (*Cont.*)

TABLE 10 ■ PERSONALITY DISORDERS

Scale	T-score[a]	Measured symptoms
RC4	000	Antisocial behavior; aggression towards others; irresponsible behavior; argumentative, angry, and antagonistic; poor achievement history
JCP	--	Court intervention as a juvenile; juvenile conduct problems, including poor school behavior and stealing
AGG	--	Direct physical aggression and violent behavior; destruction of inanimate objects; intimidation of others; belief in retaliation
AGGR–r	--	Instrumental (i.e., goal-oriented) aggression; desire to dominate, frighten, and control others; grandiose self-image
SAV	--	Social avoidance; avoiding social events; lack of enjoyment at social events
SHY	--	Shyness; easily embarrassed in front of others; discomfort when in the presence of others; may have effective social skills
IPP	--	Interpersonal passivity; unassertive; submissive and deferential; preference for others to make decisions to avoid conflict
SFD	--	Self-doubt; lack of self-confidence; feeling useless; preoccupation with self-inadequacy; unfavorable comparison with others
NFC	--	Indecisive; passive; belief that one is incapable of making decisions or coping effectively; giving up quickly when faced with obstacles
DSF	--	Disaffiliativeness; disliking people and their company; preference for solitude; possibly never having developed a meaningful relationship

Note: T-score mean = 50, standard deviation = 10. Higher T-scores indicate greater presence of maladaptive personality traits. -- denotes score type not available or computed.

[a]No asterisk = T-score (0–64) is within normal limits, absence of a disorder; * = T-score (65–79) indicates the presence of a disorder of mild to moderate severity; ** = T-score (80–120) indicates the presence of a severe disorder.

Examiner-Administered Personality Tests

Two tests are presented in this chapter and include (a) the Rorschach Inkblot Test, Comprehensive System (Rorschach–CS) (Exner, 2003) and (b) the Roberts–2 (Roberts & Gruber, 2005). Their test stimuli, administration, and scoring and interpretation procedures possess unique and complex features that have direct bearing on the psychological construct of *personality* for which they yield valuable quantitative data. Therefore, I shall initiate this chapter with an extended discussion on what I believe to be the most accurate way these tests may be conceptualized and employed in contemporary psychological testing practice.

The Rorschach–CS and Roberts–2 can be classified in two nonmutually exclusive ways. First, these tests are *implicit* measures in that they directly appraise (a) *perceptual sets and expectancies* and (b) *social–cognitive abilities*, both of which may be quantified and reliably associated with various psychological traits, emotional states, moods, beliefs, reality testing capability, thought process and content, and overall psychological adjustment. This is in contrast to *explicit* measures (McClelland, Koestner, & Weinberger, 1989), which involve self-attributed traits and symptoms characteristic of the self-report clinical and personality inventories discussed in Chapter 8. Let us scrutinize these two components.

Perceptual sets and expectancies represent automatic tendencies to perceive, interpret, and react to objects in certain ways based upon antecedent experiences and previously developed internalized beliefs (Ciccarelli & White, 2012). Perceptual sets are accordant with the concept of the *cognitive unconscious* in which it is assumed that (a) we may not be aware of information because it is at that particular moment simply not contained within our conscious working memory, (b) unconscious content is fundamentally the same as conscious content, and (c) knowledge and emotional memories can be encoded and stored without our explicit awareness and possess the capability of influencing behavior (Kihlstrom, 1999; Larsen & Buss, 2010). The latter include, but are certainly not limited to, classically conditioned reflexes and emotional reactions that are stored subcortically (Debiec, Diaz-Mataix, Bush, Doyere, & LeDoux, 2010), procedural memories (Squire, Knowlton, & Musen, 1993), prelinguistic experiences (Dollard & Miller, 1950), and subliminal perception of fearful and threatening stimuli (LeDoux & Phelps, 2008; Ohman, 2008). Again, this is contrasted with the psychoanalytic notion of the *motivated unconscious* in which it is believed that threatening memories, motivations, and beliefs are repressed as a defense against anxiety (Freud, 1936/1966).

On the other hand, social–cognitive abilities (i.e., *social intelligence* or *emotional intelligence*) may be defined as the level or degree of mastery of knowledge germane to interpersonal situations (Cantor & Kihlstrom, 1987; Friedman & Schustack, 2012). Several assumptions must be espoused in order to establish the connection between social–cognitive abilities and actual behavior and personality functioning. They include the following: (a) there are individual differences in social–cognitive abilities, (b) such differences can be reliably measured, and (c) greater social–cognitive abilities are related to, and therefore validly predict, more adaptive social behavior and personality functioning (see e.g., Bar-On, 2001; Goleman, 1995). Of course, the corollary is that impaired or deficient social–cognitive abilities should predict maladaptive behavior and, hence, can be diagnostic of psychological disorders or psychopathology.

Implicit measures have some distinct advantages over explicit self-report measures. The most salient and relevant is the remarkably enhanced difficulty examinees have in intentionally feigning or biasing the results (Huprich & Ganellen, 2006). A second and related advantage is that implicit measures do not rely upon the ability of respondents to introspect and accurately report their feelings, beliefs, traits, and psychological symptoms (Huprich & Ganellen, 2006). These advantages are due to (a) examinees being largely oblivious as to the psychological import of their responses and (b) various social–cognitive and perceptive abilities being directly measured akin to the cognitive ability tests discussed in Chapters 4 through 6. That is, they are performance-based as opposed to opinion-based.

In this sense, the second viable way to conceptualize these tests is in terms of their data source; that is, as providing *test data* or *T-data* (Larsen & Buss, 2010). *T*-data represent directly measured individual differences in behavior or responses elicited by uniform or standardized test stimuli, administration instructions, procedures, and tasks. These measured behavioral or response differences in turn serve as reliable and valid indicators of various personality and psychological variables (Block, 1977). This is contrasted with *self-report data* or *S-data* (see Chapters 7 and 8) and *observer-report data* or *O-data* (see Chapter 7).[1]

Although these performance-based tests may manifest less direct correspondence with disorders as defined by the *Diagnostic and Statistical Manual of Mental Disorders, Fourth Edition, Text Revision (DSM-IV-TR)* (American Psychiatric Association, 2000) as compared to previous measures (see e.g., Chapters 7 and 8), their variables can be cogently indicative of features inherent in particular Axis I and II Psychological Disorders (Huprich & Ganellen, 2006). For example, scores on key Rorschach–CS cognitive mediation variables (viz., XA+%, WDA+%, and X–%) represent direct quantitative and performance-based measures of reality testing ability that, if impaired, are diagnostic of *DSM-IV-TR* Psychotic Disorders. This proposition shall become increasingly incontrovertible when I present the Rorschach–CS and Roberts–2 results and interpretation tables subsequent. My point here is that, depending on the differential diagnostic issues and particular referral questions, these two tests can be employed as efficacious diagnostic complements when used judiciously in conjunction with selected symptom rating scales and/or self-report clinical and personality inventories (see Chapters 7 and 8).

To recapitulate, I have heretofore argued that the Rorschach–CS and Roberts–2, especially considering their standardized stimulus materials, administration procedures, and scoring and interpretation schemes, represent implicit and direct measures of perceptual sets, expectancies, and social–cognitive abilities, which yield quantitative *T*-data that are conceptually and actuarially associated with key personality variables indicative of *DSM-IV-TR* Psychological Disorders. I complete this discussion by delineating what I believe these tests do not represent, or at minimum, the manner in which they should not be used in contemporary mental health psychological testing.

First, neither test was originally designed as a *projective method* based upon the *projective hypothesis* (Exner, 2003; Roberts & Gruber, 2005; Weiner, 2003). Succinctly, the projective hypothesis proposes that the manner in which ambiguous stimuli are interpreted necessarily represents the examinee's unconscious needs, motives, and conflicts (Frank, 1939, 1948). That is, a projective test ostensibly measures the repressed contents of the motivated unconscious, which is a distinct psychoanalytic construct. In addition to the paucity of empirical support for the motivated unconscious (Holmes, 1990), and for that matter classic psychoanalytic theory in general (Stanovich, 2004), along with its internally inconsistent and nebulous constructs (Dawes, 2001), such personality constructs

[1] *For further explication of these data sources and the manner in which they are used to assess personality, see Larsen & Buss, 2010, pp. 24–31.*

are virtually *DSM-IV-TR* irrelevant. Therefore, it is fruitless to consume valuable psychological testing hours by employing these tests as projective instruments for purposes of contemporary psychodiagnosis. Perhaps projective tests have been chronically devoid of acceptable degrees of reliability and validity (Gittelman-Klein, 1978; Lilienfeld, 1999) simply because the projective hypothesis is fallacious.[2]

Second, referring to the standardized test stimuli of the Rorschach–CS (viz., inkblots) and Roberts–2 (viz., social scenes) as *ambiguous* is fraught with problems. In support of this proposition, I wish to make several points. One, Hermann Rorschach is reported to have diligently detailed all 10 inkblots with contours and colors in order to ensure that they would resemble both animate and inanimate real-world objects stored in examinees' memory (Exner, 2003, p. 8; Weiner, 2003). This report is corroborated by the publication of numerous books devoted entirely to measuring the form quality and frequency of content responses per location for the 10 inkblots (see e.g., Beck, Beck, Levitt, & Molish, 1961; Beizmann, 1966; Hertz, 1970). The original intent was to accurately discriminate "normals" from those with Schizophrenia by measuring individual differences in the ability to accurately perceive or translate a visual stimulus (i.e., cognitive mediation) in response to the pithy question, "What might this be?" (Rorschach, 1942).[3]

Two, the 16 stimulus cards that comprise the Roberts–2, "... reflect 'high press' or relatively structured social situations that are recognizable real-life events" (Roberts & Gruber, 2005, p. 4). That is, in requesting that the examinee make-up a complete story to each card by using the imagination, the stimulus cards are intentionally designed to elicit social–cognitive reasoning concerning a representative sample of well-defined social situations; for example, family interaction situations, peer interactions, and aggressive and fearful circumstances. Three, describing these test stimuli as ambiguous implies a categorical yes or no dichotomous quality, placing them in the former. In reality, I believe that these, and for that matter all psychological test stimuli, are more accurately described as possessing varying degrees of ambiguity. Therefore, such a discontinuous and discrete classification should be dropped as being both inaccurate and misleading.

To elaborate, even some of the most structured and objective test items possess potential degrees of ambiguity that permit idiosyncratic subjective responses on the part of examinees. Although I am not a great advocate of anecdotes, I wish to briefly share one here that is directly on point. While conducting a mental status examination during a competency to stand trial forensic case, I asked the defendant the following math word problem that required two sequential numerical operations: "If you had $12.00 and paid $3.00 for lunch, and your father later gave you $9.00 allowance, how much money would you have in total?" He replied rather abruptly, "$9.00." Now, at that point in the examination he was demonstrating at minimum average intelligence. His attentional capacity was also unequivocally normal and intact. Thus, I proposed a testing-the-limits follow-up question, "Tell me, how did you arrive at that figure?" His repartee, "You don't know my father."

Four, the term ambiguous connotes a mixed, nebulous, or obscure quality, which is antithetical to (a) the true nature of the Rorschach inkblots and Roberts–2 cards and (b) the manner in which they were created and designed. Five, I therefore prefer to portray these test stimuli as possessing the capability of measuring a continuum of quality and sophistication in perceptual and social cognitive abilities, and the response type as *open-ended*, all of which emphasizes the (a) item format and (b) nature of the task which must be resolved or mastered by the examinee. I believe that this depiction of the standardized set of 10 Rorschach inkblots and 16 Roberts–2 stimulus cards is more veritable and emphasizes the true performance-based feature of these standardized personality tests; that is, there are indeed responses of varying quality, accuracy, sophistication, and adaptability.

This completes my discussion concerning the nature of the Rorschach–CS and Roberts–2 as standardized tests of personality. Next, I define the construct of *personality*

[2] *I must admit that occasionally I do informally use sentence completion and family kinetic drawing measures with children and younger adolescents during the initial psychological assessment so as to (a) establish rapport and (b) acclimatize examinees to the anticipated standardized testing process.*

[3] *It is interesting to note that, analogous to the original purpose of developing intelligence tests for the purpose of predicting academic performance, which is still considered to be one of their most reliable and valid uses (see e.g., Ciccarelli & White, 2012; Larsen & Buss, 2010), the Rorschach–CS is, in my opinion, most effective in measuring the presence or absence of psychosis consistent with its original intent (Rorschach, 1942).*

and discuss the manner in which its measurement is relevant to contemporary *DSM-IV-TR* Axis I and II differential psychodiagnosis.

THE CONSTRUCT OF PERSONALITY AND ITS MEASUREMENT

For purposes of contemporary psychological testing and psychodiagnosis, I have found the most practicable definition of personality to be offered by two of the most prolific modern-day personality psychologists, Randy J Larsen and David M Buss. In particular, they conceptualize personality as comprising a collection of organized and relatively enduring internal *psychological traits* and *mechanisms* that influence behavioral interactions and *adaptation* to the environment (Larsen & Buss, 2010, p. 4).

Psychological traits are *average tendencies* that define the manner in which people are both different and the same, whereas psychological mechanisms refer to the *underlying processes* of personality (Larsen & Buss, 2010). Therefore, psychological traits include such variables as self-esteem, narcissism, and hypervigilance. In contrast, information processing, cognitive mediation, and social–cognitive ability would be classified as psychological mechanisms. Although both traits and mechanisms are directly pertinent to Axis II Personality Disorders, they are also accordant with, and hence relevant to, Axis I Clinical Disorders and their psychological symptoms, particularly performance-based measured variables that address the process aspects of personality (e.g., impaired cognitive mediation as measured by the Rorschach–CS representing a core symptom of Psychotic Disorder or Schizophrenia). Finally, the adaptation component is unequivocally and directly accordant with the dysfunction criterion inherent in virtually all Axis I and II *DSM-IV-TR* disorders. Thus, although the Rorschach–CS and Roberts–2 are herein classified as personality tests, their quantitative variables may be employed to effectively diagnose various Axis I Clinical Disorders *and* Axis II Personality Disorders as defined in Chapters 7 and 8. This argument is further buttressed if one adopts the assumption of Millon's personality theory (see Chapter 8) that Clinical Disorders are essentially extensions of the various Personality Disorders (McCann, 1999; Millon, 1990; Millon & Davis, 1996).

DIAGNOSTIC REASONS FOR INCLUSION WITHIN A TEST BATTERY

The corollary of the preceding discussion is that the Rorschach–CS and Roberts–2 may be generally used to resolve both Axis I and II differential diagnostic issues and related referral questions. However, as compared to the symptom rating scales and self-report clinical and personality inventories, they (a) are more labor intensive in terms of administration and scoring, (b) necessitate greater diagnostic inference, and hence, (c) require approximately twice the number of testing hours. Therefore, their inclusion within a test battery should be sufficiently justified. I shall next review three of the most frequent circumstances in which I have found these tests to be especially useful. They include (a) examinees who lack introspection, (b) examinees who are likely to attempt to manipulate test results, and (c) the presence of diagnostic issues that require the direct measurement of psychological mechanisms. I shall expound on these circumstances in this sequence.

First, they are imperative when testing for disorders in which the ability to introspect is deficient or likely to be severely impaired, thus precluding the use of the explicit self-report measures. Examples include Pervasive Developmental Disorders (PDDs), Obsessive-Compulsive Disorder With Poor Insight, Psychotic Disorders (especially involving disordered thought process), and severe Mood Disorders With Psychotic Features. This effectively exploits the *T*-data performance-based nature of these tests, which does not rely upon introspection.

Second, they may be effectively used when circumstances foster a distinct likelihood that the examinee will intentionally attempt to manipulate test results. Such instances include applications for disability, the presence of unresolved custody issues, personal injury plaintiffs, and testing for disorders, which by definition involve defensiveness in the form of intractable mistrust (e.g., Antisocial Personality Disorder, Conduct Disorder, Paranoid Personality Disorder) or proclivities toward symptom exaggeration (e.g., Histrionic Personality Disorder). This particular use capitalizes on the implicit nature of these tests wherein face validity is nebulous or obscure, hence, diminishing the examinee's ability to intentionally manipulate results.

Third, and finally, they are both informative and valuable when direct performance-based measures of information processing, reality testing, thought process, social perception, and social–cognitive abilities are pertinent to the *DSM-IV-TR* differential diagnostic issues and related referral questions. These largely involve the psychological mechanism component of personality as heretofore defined. Again, this is predicated upon the *T*-data characteristic of these tests.

INSURANCE COVERAGE ISSUES

As with the self-report clinical and personality inventories, obtaining insurance authorization for these standardized personality tests is typically viable, assuming the establishment of medical necessity as prior discussed (see Introduction). This assumes that the empirically based CS is explicitly identified by the testing psychologist when ordering the Rorschach test and the patient is within the age norms for both tests. Occasionally, the Rorschach–CS may be denied authorization when the differential diagnosis does not include ruling out a Psychotic Disorder, or a disorder with secondary psychotic symptoms; for example, Bipolar I Disorder, Severe With Psychotic Features; Borderline Personality Disorder With Transient Occurrences of Psychosis (see e.g., Kernberg, 1967; McWilliams, 2011).

The cardinal issue regards the number of test hours that insurance companies typically approve. In my experience, third-party payors will approve no more than 2 hours per test. Thus, if the testing psychologist does not employ an extremely efficient means of administering, scoring, and interpreting these tests, the outcome shall be virtually the same as an outright denial; that is, they will be rendered unviable and, hence, impracticable to order in the first place. Furthermore, the testing psychologist must remain cognizant of the fact that insurance companies are loath to exceed 3 to 5 hours of approved psychological testing for any individual case. If they were to approve 3 hours for the Rorschach–CS, they are likely to deny or circumscribe the time approved for other critical tests in the planned battery. The method delineated subsequently, including each test's results and interpretation tables, are specifically designed to procure the requisite efficiency of use, thus circumventing these potential difficulties.

THE EXAMINER-ADMINISTERED PERSONALITY TESTS

This section reviews the Rorschach–CS and Roberts–2 in this sequence, including their results and interpretation tables. This is accordant with the fact that I use the Rorschach–CS with much greater frequency in my testing practice. I review each test's administration process and tasks for the examinee, the data yield, and the diagnostic issues for which they are best utilized where pertinent.

The Rorschach Inkblot Test, Comprehensive System (Rorschach–CS)

In the summer of 1980, while matriculating within a terminal masters degree program in clinical psychology at Illinois State University, I was initially trained to use the Rorschach according to what my then professor Samuel Hutter, MS, referred to as a *modified Beck System* (Beck et al., 1961; Beizmann, 1966). At that time, it was considered to be one of the most empirically based and quantitatively sophisticated scoring and interpretation systems available. In the spring of 1985, I was retrained on the CS during my doctoral training in clinical psychology at Purdue University. I estimate using the Rorschach–CS in excess of 700 psychological testing cases, and double this figure when considering both systems combined. Therefore, I have had extensive use and experience with this test.

It would be accurate to delineate the manner in which I currently apply the Rorschach as a *modified CS system*, analogous to the way I was initially trained to use this test using a modified Beck System in psychodiagnosis. First, with one exception, I adhere strictly to the standardized administration and scoring instructions such that the norm-reference data and interpretation guidelines remain applicable (Exner, 2003; Weiner, 2003). The divergence lies in the manner in which I record responses. Specifically, the modifications include (a) recording only those verbalizations that contribute to scoring including the elimination of fillers (e.g., "the"), (b) not recording needed examiner prompts, and (c) maximizing the use personally developed short-hand which results from experience. In order to effectuate accurate scoring using such brevity, I routinely schedule sufficient additional testing time for scoring immediately ensuing administration while the responses remain readily accessible in my memory. Usually 2 hours is ample duration considering administration time is usually an hour or less (Exner, 2003).

Note that brevity is an especially emphasized leitmotif throughout my discussion of the use of the Rorschach–CS in contemporary psychological testing practice. This is because the CS is fraught with unnecessary and impractical redundancies, along with excessively detailed and numerous score discriminations and contingencies. In essence, the CS as designed is both ponderous and unwieldy. The harsh reality is, if you cannot complete the administration, scoring, and interpretation of the Rorschach–CS within 2 hours, which in my experience is the modal number of hours insurance companies will approve for this test and scoring system, it will be rendered impractical and therefore not feasible for purposes of mental health testing notwithstanding its diagnostic utility. Thus, I have made every effort to streamline the variable selection and interpretation process, while simultaneously improving *DSM-IV-TR* diagnostic correspondence and accuracy.

Upon the instruction, "What might this be?" the examinee rapidly proceeds through a perceptual–cognitive process involving (a) stimulus encoding and identification of potential responses; (b) paired comparison, discarding, and censorship; and (c) selecting and reporting the remaining responses (Exner, 2003, p. 167). These responses are coded using the CS standardized criteria and are summarized within a structural plot (i.e., a structural summary) that comprises approximately 100 initial variables, from which are derived 60 interpretively meaningful variables, ratios, percentages, and indices (Exner, 2002).

This is to be ensued by a thorough interpretive search strategy, which is determined by certain key variables and guides the order of review of variable clusters (Weiner, 2003). These variable clusters include the following: (a) Core, (b) Information Processing, (c) Cognitive Mediation, (d) Cognitive Ideation, (e) Affect, (f) Self-Perception, and (g) Interpersonal Perception. It is at this juncture that my interpretation strategy becomes distinctly disparate from CS guidelines.

Exner (2003, p. 68) adamantly believed that the neglect of any available Rorschach data represents, "…an abuse of the test and a disservice." I respectfully although patently disagree considering that my approach emphasizes brevity and circumspection in the selection of the most diagnostically useful data, thus being antithetic to Dr. Exner's CS interpretation guidelines. In particular, I have discarded data and analytic procedures that I have discovered in my clinical testing practice to be of insufficient diagnostic utility to justify the consequently increased complexity and time in interpretation and report-writing.

Among the most apparent, I have eliminated from consideration the Erlebnistypus style (i.e., EB, EBPer), including its ambient, extratensive, introversive, and pervasive versions, and its potential secondary interaction with a coexisting Lambda avoidant style. Succinctly, the EB is the degree to which an individual uses emotion or cognition during the process of coping (Exner, 2003). In my experience, this variable has little if any utility for clarifying *DSM-IV-TR* differential diagnostic issues and related referral questions. In fact, I do not recall ever using it in test interpretation in more than 700 administrations. Additionally, because there are separate norms for each of these EB versions, many of which are remarkably similar in value, the interpretation process rapidly becomes unwieldy and protracted. Furthermore, similar to the EB style itself, I have found that using the segregated norms to have insufficient diagnostic utility to justify the aforementioned escalation in interpretation duration and complexity. Finally, I have become increasingly incredulous regarding the employment of varying norms based upon the combination of only two variables. For instance, one may cogently argue that a high score on Morbid responses (e.g., MOR = 5) indicates the same degree of pessimism irrespective of EB style/lambda score. This approach is espoused by Weiner (2003) in his extensive discussion of Rorschach interpretation in which he consistently interprets CS variables using single score standards, and relates them more effectively to age or developmental trends as do my results and interpretation tables.

I have also discarded reanalysis of examinees' verbal responses for projective material, consistent with my previous argument that the projective hypothesis is (a) tenuous at best and (b) not useful in contemporary psychodiagnosis. Other single variables have been discarded due to either (a) lack of diagnostic usefulness (e.g., PER, Blends:R) or (b) unnecessary redundancy or incorporation with other more inclusive and effective variables (e.g., Sum Y, W:D:Dd).

So what norms do I use? This is a complicated issue because there are several problems regarding the available norm-reference samples of the CS that are not broken down by EB style. The initial adult sample (*N* = 600) ranged in age from 19 to 69 years, and included individuals who had received marital counseling and supportive psychotherapy (Exner, 2001, pp. 173–175; Exner, 2003, p. 190; Exner & Erdberg, 2005, pp. 467–468). Furthermore, these data were collected from 1973 through 1986, and were revised several times due to the inadvertent inclusion of duplicate and invalid records (i.e., *R* < 14), and repeated attempts to improve sample stratification (Exner, 2003, pp. 190–191; Exner & Erdberg, 2005, pp. 467–468). Thus, there are legitimate concerns regarding the representative nature of this initial sample, including questions regarding whether or not it accurately reflects scores for normal nonpatient adults.

Normative data on child and adolescent samples were also collected, including ages 5 through 16 years (Exner, 2003, pp. 639–662; Exner & Weiner, 1995, pp. 52–79). Major problems regarding these data include (a) small sample sizes (range 80–140) and (b) samples being overly representative of higher functioning children and adolescents (Exner, 2003, p. 638). Finally, considering all these data, ages 17, 18, and older than 69 years are not represented.

However, an unadulterated sample of normal nonpatient adults (*N* = 450) provided norms beginning in 1999 (Exner & Erdberg, 2005, pp. 471–473). This norm-reference sample includes a larger age range (i.e., 19–86 years) and is significantly more recent. In my testing practice, application of these more recent adult norms have demonstrated evidence of greater convergent validity with other tests used in the battery for adults and, with some modifications regarding developmental considerations, for children and adolescents as well.

Application of adult norms to younger age samples may be enigmatic. Thus, an illustration is in order. First, scrutiny of the child and adolescent normative data provided for each age by year (i.e., 5–16) paradoxically reveals more favorable means and restricted standard deviations compared to the adult norms. This is corroborative of the proposition that these data reflect a marked over-representation of higher than average functioning children and adolescents; that is, higher functioning even as compared to normal nonpatient adults. Therefore, if these data are utilized as norms for typical children and adolescents, it would unequivocally lead to an overestimation of psychopathology. For example, the Distorted Form (X–%) mean for adults is 0.10 (SD = 0.06, expected range = 0.00–0.22), compared to the Distorted Form (X–%) mean of 0.08 for 5-year-olds (SD = 0.04, expected range = 0.00–0.16).

Therefore, the expected ranges for the majority of variables in the results and interpretation tables presented subsequent were computed by using −1.00 to +1.00 standard deviations from the adult norm-reference sample mean. There are two primary exceptions. First, concerning Rorschach–CS variables most pertinent to diagnosing the presence of psychosis, I utilize −2.00 to +2.00 standard deviations to demarcate the expected ranges so as to be more conservative and minimize false positive severe psychotic diagnoses.

Second, necessary adjustments to the expected ranges were made for three variables that are impacted by psychological development. The ensuing adjustments were based upon CS empirical research and resulting special guidelines for various ages (Exner, 2003; Exner & Weiner, 1995) and are consistent with theory and research in developmental psychology (see e.g., Sigelman & Rider, 2012). First, the *EA* is a measure of the degree of psychological resources an individual has developed in order to cope with ordinary challenges and stressors (Exner, 2003). Because psychological resources represent a developmental variable, the expected range would be lower for younger ages (Grolnick, Bridges, & Connell, 1996; Malatesta, Culver, Tesman, & Shepard, 1989; Mangelsdorf, Shapiro, & Marzolf, 1995; Thompson, 1994). Therefore, relative to the adult norm, the expected range was extended downward one point for ages 11 to 17 years, two points for ages 8 to 10 years, and three points for ages 5 to 7 years (Exner & Weiner, 1995).

Second, the *WSum6* variable is a measure of ideational or cognitive control; that is, higher scores indicate the presence of cognitive slippage. Developmentally, children manifest less effective control over their logical thought process as compared to older individuals (see e.g., Bjorklund, 1995). Hence, the expected value of this variable was adjusted one point higher for ages 8 to 10 years and two points higher for ages 5 to 7 years (Exner & Weiner, 1995). Third, the variable $3r + (2)/R$ is a measure of self-esteem, with higher scores indicating greater self-esteem. Developmentally speaking, younger children typically demonstrate inflated self-esteem or confidence, thus manifesting a clear propensity to overestimate their skill and knowledge (Harter, 1999, 2006; Marsh, Craven, & Debus, 1999). To account for this developmental trend, the $3r + (2)/R$ expected range was increased by 0.10 points for 8- to 10-year-olds, and by 0.15 points for 5- to 7-year-olds (Exner & Weiner, 1995). Related to the $3r + (2)/R$, *Fr*, and *rF* responses are statistically associated with narcissism. Employing the same rationale, the expected range for those aged 11 years and older is 0, whereas one *Fr* or *rF* response is allowed or expected for 5- to 10-year-olds.

Therefore, as a final prelude to examining the Rorschach–CS results and interpretation tables, I wish to review their general nature and organization. First, only general adult norms without the EB style breakdowns are used, including of course the aforementioned adjustments for the developmentally influenced variables. These norms define the expected range based upon the deviation principle. However, falling outside the expected range is not necessarily psychopathological. Stated differently, an unexpected score may not be sufficiently extreme to be considered an indication of abnormality.

Second, the abnormal or *positive result* ranges are consequently derived in one of three ways contingent upon the variable's frequency distribution and empirical research that contributed to published CS interpretation guidelines. As you peruse the tables subsequent, you will note that the positive result ranges were determined by one of the following: (a) CS interpretation guidelines described in the manual, including the aforementioned developmental adjustments (Exner, 2003; Exner & Weiner, 1995); (b) the deviation principle (plus one or two standard deviations as indicated above) for variables showing evidence of at least an approximate normal distribution; and (c) the percentage base rate in the norm reference sample for variables manifesting skewness (usually in the positive direction or significantly fewer high scores). Interestingly, not infrequently more than one approach led to the same positive result range.

Third, the clinical and personality variables are organized by their correspondence to *DSM-IV-TR* general categories, analogous to the MMPI series (see Chapter 8). Fourth, they include validity scale variables. Fifth, they contain the following two classes of variables: (a) those actuarially associated with psychological traits and mechanisms (e.g., five positive criteria on the Depression Index [DEPI] being statistically associated with an Axis I Depressive Disorder) and (b) those that directly measure perceptual-cognitive ability (e.g., WSum6 directly measuring loosening of associations or formal thought disorder).

Lastly, Rorschach–CS responses can be rapidly computer scored using one of the following three software programs: (a) Rorschach Scoring Program (RIAP5:S) (2008), (b) Rorschach Interpretation Assistance Program: Version 5 (RIAP5) (2008), and (c) Rorschach Interpretation Assistance Program: Version 5 Forensic Edition (RIAP5 FE) (2008).[4] So as to remain within the targeted 2 hours duration for this test, this computer software is not merely recommended but mandatory. All of these are unlimited use programs, which render them extremely cost effective.

In particular, the former computes and presents the Sequence of Scores and Structural Summary, including an expanded Index Score Results page. The last two add an extended Interpretive Report following the CS Interpretive Search Strategy, with the RIAP5 FE offering supplemental statements addressing common legal issues (e.g., competency). I advise purchasing the RIAP5:S because it provides all the data needed for my results and interpretation tables and saves several hundred dollars in cost. I do not recommend using the last two as their automated interpretive statements have distinct inclinations to be redundant, contrived, and contradictory. This is principally due to an absence of requisite diagnostic context and consideration of other available test data (i.e., internal consistency reliability). Furthermore, they are not cross-referenced with the particular scores or combinations of scores from which they were derived, thus obviating a convenient check on their veracity.

[4] *Note that the Rorschach scoring software uses a more restrictive norm-reference age range of 5 to 70 years. However, this does not pose a serious problem for two reasons, First, the norms mainly influence interpretation and not scoring or the computation of the structural summary; the latter with the minor exception of developmental adjustments on two of the special indices (Exner, 2001, 2003). Second, I do not believe I have ever found it necessary to administer the Rorschach test to an individual older than 70 years. Tests of neuropsychological functioning are much more frequent in geriatric cases.*

Results and Interpretation Tables

The rather detailed description of the Rorschach–CS that preceded this section was necessary so as to render the results and interpretation tables more immediately comprehensible. There are five versions of these tables predicated upon the previously discussed age-related developmental adjustments in the expected and positive result ranges of specified variables, including such adjustments made on some of the special indices, in addition to the availability or nonavailability of the Suicide Constellation Index (S–CON) (Exner, 2003; Exner & Weiner, 1995). They include the following: (a) Rorschach–CS, Ages 5 to 7 (Form 9.1); (b) Rorschach–CS, Ages 8 to 10 (Form 9.2); (c) Rorschach–CS, Ages 11 to 14 (Form 9.3); (d) Rorschach–CS, Ages 15 to 17 (Form 9.4); and (e) Rorschach–CS, Ages 18 to 86 (Form 9.5). Because they share the same design, I will discuss them simultaneously according to table type while identifying noteworthy differences where indicated. First, some general prelusory comments are in order.

Analogous to the MMPI series, I have organized what I have found to be the most diagnostically useful Rorschach–CS variables into data tables according to the *DSM-IV-TR* general category to which they are most conceptually applicable. In order of presentation, they include the following classifications: (a) Psychotic Disorders, (b) Mood Disorders, (c) Anxiety and Stress-Related Disorders, (d) Attention-Deficit Disorders, and (e) Personality Disorders (American Psychiatric Association, 2000). Preceding these diagnostic clinical and personality variables are two validity tables that present response patterns that indicate defensiveness and volitional symptom exaggeration, respectively.

You will note that, unlike the MMPI series, several variables appear in more than one table. This is due to the fact that their measured personality traits or mechanisms may be equally pertinent to, or indicative of, more than one disorder or validity pattern, some of which straddle the *DSM-IV-TR* Axis I and II distinction. These include the following: (a) Obsessive Style Index (OBS) (viz., Axis I Obsessive Compulsive Disorder [OCD] and Axis II Obsessive Compulsive Personality Disorder [OCPD]), (b) Hypervigilance Index (viz., Posttraumatic Stress Disorder and Paranoid Personality Disorder), (c) EA Psychological Resources (viz., Adjustment Disorders involving an excessive reaction to psychosocial stressors, Pervasive Developmental Disorders, and Personality Disorders), (d) XA+% and X–% Form Quality (viz., Psychotic Disorders and intentional symptom exaggeration), and (e) SumC':WSumC Constriction Ratio (viz., excessive internalization of emotion indicating Anxiety Disorder [imbalanced left] and emotional unrestraint indicating Bipolar Disorder [imbalanced right]) (see Exner, 2003 for explication of these indices and variable definitions). The former may be due at least in part to a noted relationship between OCD and OCPD (American Psychiatric Association, 2000, p. 727; Eisen, Mancebo, Chiappone, Pinto, & Rasmussen, 2008; Oltmanns & Emery, 2004).

Also, in contrast to the MMPI series, the following variables occur twice within the same table: (a) EB Style (viz., emotional shutdown as a marker of Depressive Disorder [0 right side] and emotional flooding indicative of Bipolar Disorder [0 left side]), (b) FC:CF+C+Cn Form Color Ratio (viz., emotional constriction indicative of severe Depressive Disorder [imbalanced left] and emotional unrestraint indicative of Bipolar Disorder [imbalanced right]), (c) 3r + (2)/R Egocentricity Index (viz., low self-esteem [low scores] and inflated self-esteem [high scores]), and (d) SumT (viz., lack of empathic ability [low score] and recent object loss or chronic internal emptiness [high score]) (see Exner, 2003 for explication of these variable definitions). The bipolar nature of extreme scores inherent in these variables explains there dual appearance.

Several final notes are necessitated prior to reviewing the specific tables in earnest. First, the variables may be generally classified in two ways pursuant to the working definition of the construct of personality presented prior. First, many represent actuarial variables that have been shown to be statically related to clinical disorders or maladaptive personality traits. For instance, a DEPI score of 5 or greater is statistically associated with a clinical Depressive Disorder or at minimum a chronic vulnerability for such disorder (Exner, 2001, 2003, p. 312). Likewise, a positive OBS is statistically associated with a maladaptive disposition toward perfectionism (Exner, 2003; Exner & Erdberg, 2005). Second, other variables measure personality processes or mechanisms as defined prior that contribute to, and may be construed as, underlying causes of clinical and personality disorders. Some excellent examples include the (a) EB Style, which may indicate a massive containment or shutdown of emotion (Exner, 2003) and (b) FC:CF+C+Cn Form Color Ratio, which may indicate severe emotional constriction and internalization of affect (Exner, 2003). Although these are not per se *DSM-IV-TR* diagnostic criteria for a Depressive Disorder, they may logically be considered as causal or contributing factors and a vital target of psychotherapeutic intervention.

Third, if these CS norms are modified by more contemporary norm-reference samples, the changes may be easily inserted into these results and interpretation tables. Fourth, by discretion, testing psychologists may insert their personally developed norms that have proven diagnostically useful. Lastly, the testing psychologist also has discretion to move the variables to alternate or newly organized tables based upon their clinical experience and/or the particular nature of the case. Therefore, these tables are most accurately viewed and employed as a diagnostic framework and work in progress.

Validity tables. The Rorschach–CS variables are able to efficaciously detect two invalidity response patterns, including situational guardedness (Table 1) and the willful and intentional exaggeration of psychopathology (Table 2) (Exner, 2002, 2003; Exner & Erdberg, 2005; Weiner, 2003). The former represents a direct and objective measure of test defensiveness. It is indicated by an insufficient number of scorable responses (viz., less than 14), which precludes computation of a reliable and valid Structural Summary (Exner, 2001, 2003). The latter is more complex and subtle yet equally effective. It is measured in two ways. First, an excessive proportion of Distorted Form responses (i.e., $X-\% \geq 0.70$) would be indicative of an individual laboring under such severe psychological decompensation that test administration would have been precluded (Exner, 2003; Exner & Erdberg, 2005). The second is identified by a distinct paradoxical pattern of responses that (a) show evidence of adequate reality testing (i.e., $XA+\% \geq 0.75$) coexisting with (b) evidence of extremely distorted thinking (i.e., $X-\% \geq 0.26$) (Exner, 2003; Exner & Erdberg, 2005).

Both tables consist of the variable abbreviations, obtained scores, expected and positive result ranges, obtained results (i.e., positive or negative), and descriptive summaries of positive results (Exner, 2003; Exner & Erdberg, 2005). Note that CS variables in these and the vast majority of the remaining diagnostic tables are identified only by their score abbreviations (e.g., $X-\%$) rather than their narrative names (e.g., Distorted Form). This is to facilitate the insertion of scores reported on the Structural Summary to the data tables. Furthermore, adding the variables names would render the tables more cumbersome to read, while failing to foster test interpretation. General and specific table notes delineate the means by which the expected and positive result ranges were derived and provide useful ancillary information regarding the tabular descriptions of positive results, respectively.

These validity tables, as well as all subsequent diagnostic tables, are designed to be interpreted independently and in sequence. This explains why the validity tables begin with situational guardedness; that is, insufficient data, assuming unavailable time for retesting or continued recalcitrance on the part of the respondent, precludes all further test interpretation. Therefore, the most common narrative interpretations of each table immediately follow so as to expedite data integration and report-writing.

Clinical tables. Tables 3 through 8 comprise the diagnostic scales. By analyzing the measured psychological traits and mechanisms of each Rorschach–CS variable, I have organized them into those most conceptually and symptomatically pertinent to Axis I Clinical Disorders (viz., Tables 3 through 7), and Axis II Personality Disorders and functioning (viz., Table 8).

The Axis I sequence of tables begins with Rorschach–CS variables that generally measure disturbances reality testing and the presence of formal thought disorder; that is, Psychotic Disorders. Indeed, the initial purpose of the Rorschach test was to reliably distinguish between those with and without Schizophrenia (Rorschach, 1942; Weiner, 2003), and this continues to be one of its most frequent uses across several validated scoring systems (e.g., Beck et al., 1961; Exner & Erdberg, 2005; Holzman, Levy, & Johnston, 2005; Weiner, 2003).

In particular, Tables 3 and 4 comprise Rorschach–CS Cognitive Mediation and Cognitive Ideation variables, critical special scores contained therein, and the Perceptual Thinking Index (PTI), thus generally measuring reality testing, along with thought process and content (Exner, 2002, 2003; Exner & Erdberg, 2005; Exner & Weiner, 1995; Weiner, 2003). Table 3 presents the essential psychotic variables. Its title "Psychotic Disorders" can be modified to read "Reality Testing" and/or "Thought Disorders" in cases where such wording is more felicitous. Table 4 is an expanded breakdown of Table 3 WSum6 Critical Special Scores (Exner, 2001, 2002, 2003). The latter is intended to be reported only upon positive Table 3 results, as indicated in the first specific Table 4 note. It affords a more detailed analysis of the severity and type of disordered thought and disturbed reality testing present within a particular case. Note that these variables are reported by *both* their narrative names and abbreviations. This is because in these instances, the narrative names summarily and accurately describe the particular psychological mechanisms being measured as defined and reported by Exner (2002, 2003). Other Table 4 specific notes define the Level 1 and 2 Critical Special Score distinction applied to the majority of Critical Special Scores (Exner, 2001, 2002, 2003), and further specify that Inappropriate Logic (ALOG) and Contamination (CONTAM) responses are indicative of severe psychopathology (Exner, 2001), and hence circumscribed to the more bizarre Level 2 classification.

Table 5 presents the Rorschach–CS variables that most aptly address the major Mood Disorders. The initial four variables are indicative of Depressive Disorders, including (a) the DEPI, (b) pessimism (MOR), (c) emotional constriction (FC×3>CF+C+Cn), and (d) a massive containment or shutdown of emotion (EB 0–Right) (Exner, 2002, 2003; Exner & Erdberg, 2005; Weiner, 2003). The remaining three variables are indicative of manic or cyclic mood activity, including (a) problems in affective modulation (FC<CF+C+Cn), (b) emotional unrestraint (SumC' ≤ 3: WSumC ≥ 7.0), and (c) emotional flooding (EB 0–Left) (Exner, 2002, 2003; Exner & Erdberg, 2005; Exner & Weiner, 1995; Weiner, 2003).

Table 6 Rorschach–CS variables measure traits and mechanisms conceptually related to both Anxiety Disorders and the experience and management of stress. The first listed variable measures the presence of an excessive internalization of emotion (SumC' > WSumC), which contributes to irritability and chronic anxiety (Exner, 2002, 2003; Exner & Erdberg, 2005; Weiner, 2003). However, in my testing experience, this variable can also indicate irritability associated with a Depressive Disorder. In such cases, this variable can be moved to the Mood Disorders Table 5, and the words *chronic anxiety* deleted from the descriptive summary.

The ensuing three variables in Table 6 are all Rorschach–CS Indices and include the following: (a) OBS, which is indicative of Obsessive Compulsive Disorder (Exner, 2002, 2003; Exner & Erdberg, 2005; Weiner, 2003); (b) Hypervigilance Index (HVI), which can represent a principal symptom of Posttraumatic Stress Disorder (American Psychiatric Association, 2000; Barlow & Durand, 2012); and (c) Coping Deficit Index, which is a measured deficiency in the ability manage stressors, especially those that are interpersonal in nature (Exner, 2002, 2003; Exner & Erdberg, 2005; Exner & Weiner, 1995). The latter may be considered a psychological mechanism as previously defined, which contributes to an Anxiety or Adjustment Disorder.

The final three variables in Table 6 are Rorschach–CS core variables. First, D and Adjusted D (Adj D) measure the presence of current situationally related stress and chronic stress overload, respectively (Exner, 2002, 2003; Exner & Erdberg, 2005; Weiner, 2003). They are extremely useful in that they simultaneously provide (a) corroborating diagnostic evidence of an Anxiety or Adjustment Disorder (Acute or Chronic) and (b) the etiology or correlates of such disorders that can be noted on Axis IV and flagged as a target of psycho-therapeutic intervention (Exner & Erdberg, 2005; Weiner, 2003).

Table 7 Rorschach–CS variables are all from the Information Processing cluster (Exner, 2002, 2003). In general, they address psychological mechanisms related to the quality of scanning activity and attentional capacity (Exner, 2002, 2003; Exner & Erdberg, 2005). More specifically, the variables measure (a) the inability to shift attention (PSV $\geq$ 2), (b) poor quality processing (Zf $\leq$ 8), (c) underincorporation or hasty and haphazard scanning activity (Zd $\leq$ –3.0), (d) overly narrow focus of attention (L $\geq$ 1.00), (e) problems with sustained attention (DQv $\geq$ 3), and (f) inability to synthesize aspects of experience (DQ+ $\leq$ 4) (Exner, 2002, 2003; Exner & Erdberg, 2005). As applied to *DSM-IV-TR* disorders, they are most symptomatically relevant to Attention-Deficit/Hyperactivity Disorder (ADHD), hence the table name. However, if several of these variables yield positive results within the context of testing for a Mood or Anxiety Disorder, they can be shifted to the Mood Disorders (Table 5) and Anxiety and Stress-Related Disorders (Table 6) tables, respectively. To reiterate, as a general rule, the Rorschach–CS diagnostic variables may be rapidly and efficiently moved among the tables as dictated by a particular case.

Personality table. Although there is only one table devoted to variables that are most applicable to Axis II functioning based upon their measured traits and mechanisms (see Table 8), it is the lengthiest and most complex. Prior to beginning review of these particular variables, it is critical to emphasize that a one-to-one correspondence between any specific result and a single *DSM-IV-TR* Personality Disorder does not exist (Huprich & Ganellen, 2006). Rather, these Rorschach–CS variables may be more or less indicative of several Personality Disorders that may be efficaciously corroborated by other test data and assessment information from the diagnostic interview (Huprich & Ganellen, 2006). The review undertaken here shall first identify the particular personality trait or mechanism measured by each Rorschach–CS variable listed in Table 8, followed by the Personality Disorder *most indicative* of a positive result. It is certainly not meant to suggest that this is the only disorder present or possible. Most certainly, effective and judicious interpretation assiduously utilizes additional diagnostic and test data for maximum accuracy in psychodiagnosis.

The initial five variables measure some aspect of self-worth and self-concept and include (a) narcissism (Fr + rF) (Exner, 2002, 2003; Exner & Erdberg, 2005; Exner & Weiner, 1995; Handler & Hilsenroth, 2006; Weiner, 2003), (b) inflated self-esteem (3r + (2)/R High) (Exner, 2002, 2003; Exner & Erdberg, 2005; Exner & Weiner, 1995; Handler & Hilsenroth, 2006; Weiner, 2003), (c) low self-esteem (3r + (2)/R Low) (Bornstein, 2006; Exner, 2002, 2003; Exner & Erdberg, 2005; Exner & Weiner, 1995; Ganellen, 2006; Huprich, 2006; Weiner, 2003), (d) negative self-preoccupation (SumV) (Bornstein, 2006; Exner, 2002, 2003; Exner & Erdberg, 2005; Exner & Weiner, 1995; Ganellen, 2006; Huprich, 2006; Weiner, 2003), and (e) distortion in self-image (H < (H) + Hd + (Hd)) (Exner, 2002, 2003; Exner & Erdberg, 2005; Exner & Weiner, 1995; Foley, 2006; Kleiger & Huprich, 2006; Weiner, 2003).

The reader shall note that particular combinations of positive results are especially diagnostic, which are highlighted by specific table notes. The first listed in Table 8 is the presence of narcissism (Fr + rF) further exacerbated by inflated self-esteem (3r + (2)/R High), together indicating that a grandiose sense of self represents a core, rigid, and particularly ingrained aspect of personality structure (Exner, 2002, 2003; Handler & Hilsenroth, 2006). The second detects the paradoxical coexistence of narcissism (Fr + rF) with low self-esteem (3r + (2)/R High), indicating the presence of an extremely unstable sense of self or splitting inherent within *borderline* personality structure and organization (Kernberg, 1967; Lerner, 2006; Mihura, 2006). It is also consistent with empirical research in personality psychology that shows a predictable relationship between self-esteem variability and severe psychopathology (Butler, Hokanson, & Flynn, 1994; Kernis, Grannemann, & Barclay, 1992; Roberts & Monroe, 1992).

The ensuing two variables measure chronic loneliness or emptiness (Sum T High) and ambivalence towards self and others (Color-Shading Blends) (Exner, 2002, 2003; Exner & Erdberg, 2005; Weiner, 2003). Although they may be conceptually consistent with several personality disorders, they are particularly indicative of *borderline* personality psychopathology (see e.g., Mihura, 2006). The Sum T High possesses an alternative interpretation of recent object loss (Exner, 2002, 2003; Exner & Erdberg, 2005), which can be determined by reference to the developmental history. Thus, a third table note is inserted to that effect.

The next two variables measure the presence of chronic anger directed outward in the form of oppositional behavior (S) (Exner, 2002, 2003; Exner & Erdberg, 2005; Weiner, 2003) and hostile and negative attitudes toward people (AG) (Exner, 2002, 2003; Exner & Erdberg, 2005; Weiner, 2003), and represents corroborative evidence of Antisocial Personality Disorder (Loving & Lee, 2006) and possible Paranoid Personality Disorder (Kaser-Boyd, 2006). The Hypervigilance Index (HVI) follows and, although was listed in Table 6 as a possible symptom of Posttraumatic Stress Disorder (PTSD), may also indicate severe suspiciousness characteristic of Paranoid Personality Disorder (Exner, 2002, 2003; Exner & Erdberg, 2005; Kaser-Boyd, 2006; Weiner, 2003).

In a general sense, the next five variables measure social or emotional intelligence (Cantor & Kihlstrom, 1987; Friedman & Schustack, 2012). Positive results or impairments in these measured variables may be indicative of Personality Disorder or other psychopathology most associated with deficits in this ability. These include most especially Schizoid Personality Disorder (Kleiger & Huprich, 2006) and PDDs (Oberman & Ramachandran, 2007). My proposal that the same Rorschach–CS variables may be particularly indicative of these two disorders is bolstered by empirical data linking them to similar biological dysfunction (Constantino et al., 2009). The specific variables include the measurement of (a) inability to empathize (Sum T Low) (Exner, 2002, 2003; Exner & Erdberg, 2005; Exner & Weiner, 1995; Weiner, 2003), (b) inability to understand people (H < (H) + Hd + (Hd)) (Exner, 2002, 2003; Exner & Erdberg, 2005; Exner & Weiner, 1995; Weiner, 2003), (c) lack of introspection (FD = 0) (Exner, 2002, 2003; Exner & Erdberg, 2005; Exner & Weiner, 1995; Weiner, 2003), (d) lack of interest in people (Human Content ≤ 3) (Exner, 2002, 2003; Exner & Erdberg, 2005; Exner & Weiner, 1995; Weiner, 2003), and (e) general deficiency in psychological resources (EA Low) (Exner, 2002, 2003; Exner & Erdberg, 2005; Exner & Weiner, 1995; Weiner, 2003).

The following two variables may be generally useful in identifying both the presence and deleterious effects of manifesting a Personality Disorder. They include impaired social skills and likelihood of disordered personality (GHR < PHR) and the presence of interpersonal isolation (Isolate/R High) (Exner, 2002, 2003; Exner & Erdberg, 2005; Exner & Weiner, 1995; Weiner, 2003). The next dyad includes related variables that if positive, detect the presence of dependent traits (Fd High) and interpersonal passivity ($a + 1 < p$) (Exner, 2002, 2003; Exner & Erdberg, 2005; Exner & Weiner, 1995; Weiner, 2003). In circumstances where positive results are yielded on both, this indicates that *dependency* represents a core aspect of personality structure and organization (Exner, 2002, 2003). A specific table note has been inserted to this effect. Relatively speaking, these variables show the closest conceptual relationships to Dependent Personality Disorder (Bornstein, 2006), and to a lesser extent, Avoidant Personality Disorder (Ganellen, 2006).

The ensuing dyad consists of variables measuring the presence of an obsessive style (OBS Positive) and the use of cognition as a defense against negative affect (viz., intellectualization) (2AB + Art + Ay High) (Exner, 2002, 2003; Exner & Erdberg, 2005; Exner & Weiner, 1995; Weiner, 2003). The former most conspicuously represents a core aspect of

Obsessive-Compulsive Personality Disorder (OCPD) (Exner, 2002, 2003; Ganellen, 1996; Schneider, 2006). Furthermore, although the use of intellectualization is certainly not limited to OCPD, it does represent a rather salient indicator of such disorder (Gabbard, 2000; Schneider, 2006; Weiner, 2003).

The final two variables measure the presence of abusing fantasy to deny reality (Ma + 1 < Mp) and denying negative affect by improperly substituting positive affect (CP) (Exner, 2002, 2003; Exner & Erdberg, 2005). Assuming that excessive fantasy use for purposes of removing oneself from reality is accordant with the definition of *dissociation* as a disruption in normal consciousness (American Psychiatric Association, 2000), the former variable may be interpreted as a manifestation of such symptom. Once again, although not limited to any one disorder, this would be expected as a salient indicator of either Borderline Personality Disorder (American Psychiatric Association, 2000; Mihura, 2006) or Histrionic Personality Disorder (Blais & Baity, 2006; Fenichel, 1945). Although CP responses are infrequent, when present they more clearly detect the presence of a hysteroid process (Exner, 2002, 2003; Exner & Erdberg, 2005; Weiner, 2003), most conceptually consistent with Histrionic Personality Disorder (Blais & Baity, 2006).

The Roberts–2

The Roberts–2 is principally designed as a measure of social–cognitive ability as reflected in expressive language (Roberts & Gruber, 2005, p. 4). That is, its Developmental/Adaptive scales largely measure social or emotional intelligence; or the level of mastery of knowledge relevant to interpersonal and intrapersonal functioning and adjustment (Cantor & Kihlstrom, 1987; Goleman, 1995). As stated at the beginning of this chapter, in order to link such social–cognitive ability to actual personality and behavioral functioning, the following three assumptions must be made: (a) individual differences in this ability exist, (b) such differences can be reliably measured, and (c) those with greater ability will predictably exhibit more effective and adaptive interpersonal skills and personality functioning (Cantor & Kihlstrom, 1987; Friedman & Schustack, 2012; Goleman, 1995; Roberts & Gruber, 2005). In addition, however, the Roberts–2 consists of Emotion, Unusual, and Atypical Clinical scales that are statistically associated with personality maladjustment or psychological disorders (Roberts & Gruber, 2005).

The test stimuli consist of 16 stimulus cards, which together present a structured and representative sample of key intrapersonal and interpersonal scenes. Each scene involves specific emotions, behaviors, and/or problem situations that require sophisticated problem solving for purposes of effective resolution; for example, family and peer interaction scenes, fearful and aggressive situations. Respondents are instructed to make-up a complete story to each card using the *imagination*, including what led up to the scene, what occurs and how it ends, and in the process addressing the thoughts, feelings, and actions of the character(s) (Roberts & Gruber, 2005, p. 11).

The examiner's written record of each story represents the database that produces raw scores, which are thereafter transformed into standard scores on multiple scales classified as either Developmental/Adaptive or Clinical. The former primarily measures social–cognitive abilities and includes the following four scale clusters: (a) Theme Overview (i.e., general social–cognitive competence or ability), (b) Available Resources (i.e., ability to understand the effective use of various intrapersonal and interpersonal resources in order to resolve a problem feeling or situation), (c) Problem Identification (i.e., ability to comprehend interpersonal problems and feelings), and (d) Resolution (i.e., ability to resolve interpersonal problems and feelings) (Roberts & Gruber, 2005). The latter measures the presence of personality pathology or psychological disorders and includes the following three scale clusters: (a) Emotion (i.e., presence of maladaptive emotions and behaviors),

(b) Outcome (i.e., presence of various types of undesirable or ineffective outcomes), and (c) Unusual or Atypical Responses (i.e., presence of severe neurocognitive and psychological dysfunction) (Roberts & Gruber, 2005).

I have made some adjustments to this original organization of scales and the manner in which they are scored based upon my clinical testing experience and *DSM-IV-TR* applicability. First and most apparently, I report the Clinical Outcome scales immediately subsequent to the Developmental/Adaptive Resolution scales within the same data table (see Form 9.6) for two reasons. One, they are conceptually more similar and serve as effective complements; that is, together they measure the tendency to produce problematic results (or resolutions that exacerbate matters) and the related ability (or lack of ability) to resolve intrapersonal and interpersonal situations, respectively. Two, Outcome scales show evidence of an inverse or negative relationship with Resolution scales (Roberts & Gruber, 2005).

The second adjustment is more minor in that it involves moving the Limit Setting Available Resource scale to the same data table that combines the Resolution and Outcome scales (see Form 9.6). This is because a statistically high score on Limit Setting indicates that the respondent believes behavioral control requires external disciplinary consequences (e.g., scolding, spanking, time out, losing privileges, paying for damage) as opposed to utilizing internal coping resources such as emotional self-regulation (Roberts & Gruber, 2005). In this sense, it represents a developmentally immature, and hence maladaptive, strategy for problem resolution and story outcome (Fox & Calkins, 2003; Rothbart, Posner, & Kieras, 2006). Following this rational, I believe that from a diagnostic perspective, this Available Resource scale is more accordant with the Resolution and Outcome scales.

The third adjustment concerns the Unusual scale, which comprises of the following three separate scores: (a) Refusal (i.e., rejecting a card), (b) No Score (i.e., rote physical description of the card stimulus scene), and (c) Antisocial (i.e., violations of social norms and laws) (Roberts & Gruber, 2005). I do not score refusals and antisocial story content on this scale because the former is accounted for in measuring test validity (see Form 9.6), and the latter is largely redundant with the Aggressive Emotion Clinical scale. Excessive No Score responses (i.e., simple physical scene descriptions) (Roberts & Gruber, 2005) are analogous to mechanical perseverations on the Rorschach–CS, which are strongly suggestive of neurocognitive dysfunction (Exner, 2002, 2003). Hence, the modified Unusual–No Score Scale *T*-score represents a standardized quantitative measure of such impairment, and can effectively lead to a cogent argument that supplemental neuropsychological testing is indicated.

The fourth and final modification from the original Roberts–2 scale scheme and scoring rules concerns the Atypical Categories scale, which is an amalgamation of nine more specific aberrant score responses ranging from excessive violence (ATYP4) to sexual content (ATYP8) (Roberts & Gruber, 2005). The one I have found most useful regarding *DSM-IV-TR* diagnosis is *ATYP1—Illogical*, which measures the presence of cognitive distortions and loosening of associations (Roberts & Gruber, 2005, p. 125); that is, thought disorder or psychosis. Scoring the modified Atypical—Illogical scale in this manner, the resulting standard score will represent a quantitative measure of psychotic disturbance or formal thought disorder. Raw scores on the eight other atypical categories can be noted by the testing psychologist and interpreted qualitatively in the narrative, which is required in any case due to the integration of all these responses into one scale.

The Roberts–2 employs standardized *T*-scores ($M = 50$; $SD = 10$) for all of the Developmental/Adaptive and Clinical scales. Separate norms are available for the following age groups by year: (a) 6 to 7, (b) 8 to 9, (c) 10 to 13, and (d) 14 to 18 (Roberts & Gruber, 2005). Transforming raw scores into *T*-scores may be done directly on the Roberts–2 record form or by the available unlimited use Roberts–2 Computer Scoring

CD (2005) software. The *T*-score range on the form is from 30 to 80, although the scoring software may result in slightly higher or lower scores due to its greater precision. The results and interpretation tables follow the minimum and maximum scores reported on the record form. This permits greater uniformity in reporting results. Furthermore, such infinitesimal precision in the extremes is diagnostically unnecessary. In cases where the computer scoring results in slightly higher or lower scores than reported on the record form (e.g., *T* = 82), I simply round to the nearest maximum or minimum score (e.g., *T* = 80). In addition to expediting the transformation of raw to *T*-scores and minimizing error rate, another advantage of the Roberts–2 Computer Scoring CD (2005) software is that it assists in deriving the proper raw scores from the written recorded stories.

Using the Roberts–2 record form as a guide, the score ranges and associated qualitative descriptions concerning the Developmental/Adaptive scales are as follows: (a) 30 to 39, *low*; (b) 40 to 59, *average*; (c) 60 to 69, *high*; and (d) 70 to 80, *extremely high* (Roberts & Gruber, 2005, pp. 156–160). Using the record form in similar fashion, the score ranges and qualitative descriptions as applied to the Clinical scales are as follows: (a) 30 to 59, *within normal limits*; (b) 60 to 69, *mild to moderate disorder*; and (c) 70 to 80, *severe disorder*. Note that these are my recommended qualitative descriptors as the test manual does not provide such information. Next, I review the results and interpretation tables that I have prepared for the Roberts–2.

Results and Interpretation Tables

The Roberts–2 results and interpretation tables are presented in Form 9.6. There are seven tables in total. Included is one Validity table (Table 1), four Developmental/ Adaptive tables (Tables 2–5), and two Clinical tables (Tables 6 and 7). Because they are designed to be independently interpreted, the testing psychologist may selectively use any or all of the tables, depending upon the differential diagnostic issues and related referral questions.

Validity scales. Table 1 initiates the analysis with validity indicators analogous to the Rorschach–CS, particularly in terms of whether or not the respondent has provided sufficient data. In columnar order of appearance, the table presents the (a) validity result, (b) rationale for each result, and (c) interpretation strategy employed on the subsequent diagnostic scales. There are three potential validity results that I find most commonly in practice (i.e., *valid, qualified valid,* and *invalid*) from which the psychologist selects contingent on the data. Pursuant to test instructions, administration is to be summarily halted in cases where the examinee manifests a card refusal to one of the first two cards (Roberts & Gruber, 2005, p. 12). This represents the invalid version in the third and last row of Table 1 as it is not a common result, especially if the examinee has been properly prepared for the testing procedure.

I inserted the qualified valid version in the second row because I have had cases, especially with younger children, wherein the examinee becomes progressively fatigued somewhere in the process of creating 16 stories and consequently begins providing cursory and hence nonscorable stories. Because the test instructions do not stipulate precisely how many nonscorable stories should prompt a cautious interpretation (Roberts & Gruber, 2005), the testing psychologist must employ clinical judgment in the use of this version. The actual number of nonscorable stories, which includes card refusals, should be recorded in the reason for result section. The testing psychologist may insert a unique and less typical validity result into one of the rows. Usually this will be the qualified result row. Because the retained result within Table 1 is self-explanatory, there is no need for table notes or standardized narrative summaries.

Developmental/adaptive scales. Tables 2 through 5 include the Roberts–2 Developmental/Adaptive scales and hence together provide a measure of the examinee's social–cognitive abilities. Table titles identify the general category or combination of categories from which the specific scales come. The table bodies are similarly designed and include the following columns: (a) scale name, (b) *T*-score, (c) qualitative result associated with each *T*-score, and (d) a succinct description of the social–cognitive ability being measured, and in some cases, the type and/or degree of sophistication of response captured by that particular scale. The last were carefully composed based upon their more elaborate descriptions and numerous examples provided within the test manual (Roberts & Gruber, 2005, pp. 25–41, 50–53).

All of these tables also include general and specific notes listing the *T*-score metric and the directional meaning of higher scores, along with standard score ranges and their associated qualitative descriptors, respectively. These are afforded for purposes of facilitating test interpretation and reader comprehension. Finally, a narrative statement or statements immediately follow the tabular notes, which succinctly define the measurement focus of the Roberts–2 category or categories included in each table (Roberts & Gruber, 2005, pp. 25–41, 50–53).

More particularly, Table 2 consists of the two *Theme Overview scales*, which measure the most general abilities. They include (a) *Popular Pull*, which measures the ability to understand emotion, behavior, and problem situations of an interpersonal nature and (b) *Complete Meaning*, which measures the ability to understand and effectively resolve a sequence of problematic interpersonal interactions and feelings (Roberts & Gruber, 2005, pp. 25–27). Not infrequently, these two general measures of social intelligence suffice in addressing *DSM-IV-TR* differential diagnostic issues; namely, ruling out a PDD. More commonly, however, providing a more detailed analysis of the examinee's social cognitive deficits is indicated, especially for the purposes of targeting specific treatment goals.

Table 3 enumerates the four *Available Resources scales*, which generally measure the examinee's ability to understand the effective use of various intrapersonal and interpersonal resources in order to resolve a problem feeling or situation (Roberts & Gruber, 2005). They include the following specific scales and measured abilities: (a) *Support Self-Feeling*— ability to understand the effective use of one's own positive emotions (e.g., happiness), (b) *Support Self-Advocacy*—ability to understand the effective use of one's own resources (e.g., problem solving, perseverance), (c) *Support Other–Feeling*—ability to understand the effective use of others' emotional responsiveness (e.g., caring, affection), (d) *Support Other–Help*—ability to understand the effective use of others' unsolicited instrumental assistance (e.g., accepting another's offer of help on a task), and (e) *Reliance on Other*— ability to understand the effective use of proactively seeking assistance from appropriate others (e.g., parents, teachers) (Roberts & Gruber, 2005, pp. 27–34).

Table 4 includes the Roberts–2 *Problem Identification scales*. These scales measure a continuum of social–cognitive abilities directly related to comprehending interpersonal problems and feelings, ranging in degree of sophistication from vague and simplistic to elaborate and differentiated. Greater degrees of elaboration and differentiation are associated with a greater likelihood of developing more effective resolutions or outcomes. They specifically include the following scales and their associated level of social–cognitive problem identification abilities: (a) *Recognition*—simple detection of a current problem feeling or situation expressed in vague terms and without explanation of preceding factors; (b) *Description*—description of a specific problem with associated feelings, although with poorly defined preceding factors and lack of an internal cognitive process (e.g., wondering about); (c) *Clarification*—elaborated description of a problem situation, with identification of an internal cognitive state (e.g., cannot understand), but limited description of preceding factors; (d) *Definition*—description of a problem and its cause, including reasons for feelings and behavior, some mention of prior circumstances, and elaboration of an internal process; and (e) *Explanation*—complete description of the problem situation, including full identification and elaboration of feelings, with clear reference to, and processing of, preceding causal factors (Roberts & Gruber, 2005, pp. 35–38). The latter two rarely occur and are therefore not scored for the two youngest age groups (viz., 6–7 years and 8–9 years) (Roberts & Gruber, 2005). This necessitated an additional "--" general table note symbol denoting that the score type is not available or computed for the respondent's age.

Table 5 is the final, longest, and most elaborate of the Developmental/Adaptive tables. In order of appearance, it includes the *Resolution scales*, the *Outcome scales*, which as stated prior were shifted from their original Clinical scale designation, and finally, one Available Resource scale (viz., *Limit Setting*). Analogous to the Problem Identification scales, the Resolution scales generally measure a continuum of social–cognitive abilities, although in this case those directly related to resolving interpersonal problems and feelings. Greater degrees of sophistication are associated with the development of more effective outcomes. Hence, the inversely related Outcome scales measure the degree of presence of various types of undesirable or ineffective outcomes, which are associated with lesser degrees of social–cognitive sophistication. As argued prior, Limit Setting similarly represents an immature resolution strategy and hence its placement immediately subsequent to the Outcome scales.

The particular Resolution scales and their associated social–cognitive problem-solving abilities include the following: (a) *Simple Closure*—easy ending, consisting of an abrupt and poorly defined outcome, along with a lack of problem-solving process or mediating steps; (b) *Easy Positive Outcome*—ending is related to the present situation with a positive outcome, although there is no description of process or how the solution was achieved; (c) *Constructive Resolution*—elaborated description of a problem situation, with identification of an internal cognitive state (e.g., cannot understand), and limited description of preceding factors; (d) *Constructive Resolution of Feelings and Situation*—description of a problem and its cause, including reasons for feelings and behavior, some mention of prior circumstances, and elaboration of an internal process; and (e) *Elaborated Process With Insight*—complete description of the problem situation, including full identification and elaboration of feelings, with clear reference to, and processing of, preceding causal factors (Roberts & Gruber, 2005, pp. 38–41). Again, the latter two are not scored for 6- to 9-year-olds and a score not available symbol has been added to the general table notes.

The Outcome scales and their associated undesirable result type are as follows: (a) *Unresolved Outcome*—no ending or resolution such that the problem feelings and situation remain completely unprocessed and unresolved; (b) *Nonadaptive Outcome*—problem feelings and situation processed, however, coping strategy does not resolve the problem adequately; (c) *Maladaptive Outcome*—coping strategy makes the situation worse and often includes acting-out behavior; and (d) *Unrealistic Outcome*—coping strategy is unrealistic and represents fantasy and wishful thinking, thus rendering it ineffectual despite its apparent positive quality (Roberts & Gruber, 2005, pp. 50–53).

Table 5 ends with the Limit Setting scale, which indicates that coping and adjustment are dependent upon external disciplinary consequences and control (e.g., scolding, spanking, time out, losing privileges, paying for damage) (Roberts & Gruber, 2005, pp. 34–35). Finally, specific table notes have been added which identify each scale as Resolution, Outcome, or Available Resource.

Clinical scales. The final two tables consist entirely of Clinical scales which measure the presence of psychopathology. The Table 6 title elaborates on the original Roberts–2 label of Emotion scales and reads, "Emotional and Behavioral Disorders" so as to be more applicable to the *DSM-IV-TR* nosology. The table bodies are designed the same and include the following columns: (a) scale name; (b) *T*-score; and (c) measured maladaptive emotions, problematic behaviors, or social–cognitive disturbance. The *T*-score has an affixed specific table note symbol referring the reader to information regarding the *within normal limits range* (i.e., no asterisk), presence of a *mild to moderate disorder range* (i.e., one asterisk), and presence of a *severe disorder range* (i.e., two asterisks). Entries in the final column are again based upon the more detailed narrative descriptions provided in the test manual (Roberts & Gruber, 2005, pp. 41–56). General table notes indicate the *T*-score metric and directional meaning of higher scores.

First, Table 6 scales generally measure the presence of maladaptive emotions and behaviors as reflected in Roberts–2 story content. *T*-score elevations falling within the disordered range are interpreted as representing a social–cognitive perceptual set within the respondent making it likely that such disorder is actually present. More specifically, Table 6 includes the following Emotional and Behavioral Disorders Clinical scales and their associated symptoms: (a) *Anxiety*—anxious state and fear, including worry, guilt, embarrassment, and apprehension about environmental demands; (b) *Depression*—depressive feelings, sadness, unhappiness, sorrow, crying, disappointment, apathy, fatigue, and inability to cope with situational factors or problems; (c) *Rejection*—jealousy, being ostracized, unloved or disliked, and including major disruptions in attachment (e.g., abandonment, loss of primary object-relations), separation or distancing; and (d) *Aggression*—angry feelings (e.g., madness, rage, frustration), along with verbal aggression (e.g., arguing, teasing, belittling) and physical aggression (e.g., bullying, destroying property) (Roberts & Gruber, 2005, pp. 41–50).

The concluding Table 7 is titled "Severe Disorders" to reflect its content and distinguish it from Table 6. They consist of the two modified scales discussed prior and include (a) *Unusual—No Score*, which represents concrete, mechanical, rigid, and inflexible descriptions of card stimuli scenes indicative of neurocognitive dysfunction and (b) *Atypical—Illogical*, which represents the presence of formal thought disorder or psychosis (Roberts & Gruber, 2005, pp. 53–56).

I wish to conclude with one general note regarding the judicious use of these tables. Reference to the final column descriptions of each scale by the testing psychologist during actual scoring of the recorded stories will expedite the process. This is because they essentially represent a succinct description of the type of response that would qualify as scorable on each respective scale.

SUMMARY

This chapter discussed two major standardized examiner-administered personality tests, including the Rorschach–CS and Roberts–2, both of which are performance-based and actuarial in design. They were more particularly defined as implicit measures that directly assess perceptual sets and expectancies, along with social–cognitive abilities, both of which are empirically associated with personality traits, mechanisms, emotional states, adaptation, and psychological symptoms, therefore rendering them useful in *DSM-IV-TR* Axis I and II differential diagnosis.

Next, the diagnostic reasons for selecting these tests as part of a battery were reviewed, including their advantages over explicit self-report inventories, along with insurance coverage issues. The body of the chapter described in detail the particular nature of both tests within the context of their associated results and interpretation tables. Chapter 10 is the last of Section II and presents the final category and its test within my recommended inventory; namely, the Vineland Adaptive Behavior Scales, Second Edition.

REFERENCES

American Psychiatric Association. (2000). *Diagnostic and statistical manual of mental disorders* (4th ed., text rev.). Washington, DC: Author.

Barlow, David H., & Durand, Mark V. (2012). *Abnormal psychology: An integrative approach* (6th ed.). Belmont, CA: Wadsworth, Cengage Learning.

Bar-On, R. (2001). Emotional intelligence and self-actualization. In J. Ciarrochi & J. P. Forgas (Eds.), *Emotional intelligence in everyday life: A scientific inquiry* (pp. 82–97). Philadelphia, PA: Psychology Press.

Beck, S. J., Beck, A. G., Levitt, E. E., & Molish, H. B. (1961). *Rorschach's test: Basic processes* (3rd ed.). New York, NY: Grune & Stratton.

Beizmann, C. (1966). *Handbook for scoring Rorschach responses* (Trans. Samuel J. Beck). Appliquee, Paris: Centre de Psychologie.

Bjorklund, D. F. (1995). *Children's thinking: Developmental function and individual differences.* Pacific Grove, CA: Brooks/Cole.

Blais, M. A., & Baity, M. R. (2006). Rorschach assessment of histrionic personality disorder. In S. K. Huprich (Ed.), *Rorschach assessment of the personality disorders* (pp. 205–221). Mahwah, NJ: Lawrence Erlbaum.

Block, J. (1977). Advancing the psychology of personality: Paradigmatic shift or improving the quality of research. In D. Magnusson & N. S. Endler (Eds.), *Personality at the crossroads* (pp. 37–63). Hillsdale, NJ: Erlbaum.

Bornstein, R. F. (2006). Rorschach assessment of dependent personality disorder. In S. K. Huprich (Ed.), *Rorschach assessment of the personality disorders* (pp. 289–310). Mahwah, NJ: Lawrence Erlbaum.

Butler, A. C., Hokanson, J. E., & Flynn, H. A. (1994). A comparison of self-esteem lability and low trait self-esteem as vulnerability factors for depression. *Journal of Personality and Social Psychology, 66,* 166–177.

Cantor, N., & Kihlstrom, J. F. (1987). *Personality and social intelligence.* Englewood Cliffs, NJ: Prentice-Hall.

Ciccarelli, S. K., & White, J. N. (2012). *Psychology* (3rd ed.). Upper Saddle River, NJ: Pearson Education.

Constantino, J., Abbacchi, A., Lavesser, P., Reed, H., Givens, L., Chiang, L., . . . Todd, R. D. (2009). Developmental course of autistic social impairment in males. *Development and Psychopathology, 21,* 127–138.

Dawes, R. M. (2001). *Everyday irrationality: How pseudo-scientists, lunatics, and the rest of us fail to think rationally.* Boulder, CO: Westview Press.

Debiec, J., Diaz-Mataix, L., Bush, D. E., Doyere, V., & LeDoux, J. E. (2010). The amygdala encodes specific sensory features of an aversive reinforce. *Nature Neuroscience, 13,* 536–537.

Dollard, J., & Miller, N. E. (1950). *Personality and psychotherapy: An analysis in terms of learning, thinking and culture.* New York, NY: McGraw-Hill.

Eisen, J., Mancebo, M., Chiappone, K., Pinto, A., & Rasmussen, S. (2008). Obsessive-compulsive personality disorder. In J. S. Abramowitz, D. McKay, & S. Taylor (Eds.), *Clinical handbook of obsessive-compulsive disorder and related problems* (pp. 316–334). Baltimore, MD: John Hopkins University Press.

Exner, J. E. (2001). *A Rorschach workbook for the comprehensive system* (5th ed.). Asheville, NC: Rorschach Workshops.

Exner, J. E. (2002). *A primer for Rorschach interpretation.* Asheville, NC: Rorschach Workshops.

Exner, J. E. (2003). *The Rorschach a comprehensive system: Basic foundations and principles of interpretation* (4th ed., Vol. 1). Hoboken, NJ: John Wiley.

Exner, J. E., & Erdberg, P. (2005). *The Rorschach a comprehensive system: Advanced interpretation* (3th ed., Vol. 2). Hoboken, NJ: John Wiley.

Exner, J. E., & Weiner, I. B. (1995). *The Rorschach a comprehensive system: Assessment of children and adolescents* (2nd ed., Vol. 3). New York, NY: John Wiley.

Fenichel, O. (1945). *The psychoanalytic theory of neurosis.* New York, NY: W. W. Norton.

Foley, D. D. (2006). Rorschach assessment of schizotypal personality disorder. In S. K. Huprich (Ed.), *Rorschach assessment of the personality disorders* (pp. 113–135). Mahwah, NJ: Lawrence Erlbaum.

Fox, N. A., & Calkins, S. D. (2003). The development of self-control of emotion: Intrinsic and extrinsic influences. *Motivation and Emotion, 27,* 7–26.

Frank, L. K. (1939). Projective methods for the study of personality. *Journal of Psychology, 8,* 389–413.

Frank, L. K. (1948). *Projective methods.* Springfield, IL: Thomas.

Freud, A. (1936/1966). *The ego and the mechanisms of defense* (Rev. ed.). New York, NY: International Universities Press.

Friedman, H. S., & Schustack, M. W. (2012). *Personality: Classic theories and modern research.* Boston, MA: Pearson.

Gabbard, G. O. (2000). *Psychodynamic psychiatry in clinical practice* (3rd ed.). Washington, DC: American Psychiatric Press.

Ganellen, R. J. (1996). Comparing the diagnostic efficiency of the MMPI, MCMI–II, and Rorschach: A review. *Journal of Personality Assessment, 67,* 219–247.

Ganellen, R. J. (2006). Rorschach assessment of avoidant personality disorder. In S. K. Huprich (Ed.), *Rorschach assessment of the personality disorders* (pp. 265–288). Mahwah, NJ: Lawrence Erlbaum.

Gittelman-Klein, R. (1978). Validity in projective tests for psychodiagnosis in children. In R. L. Spitzer & D. F. Klein (Eds.), *Critical issues in psychiatric diagnosis* (pp. 141–166). New York, NY: Raven Press.

Goleman, D. (1995). *Emotional intelligence: Why it can matter more than IQ.* New York, NY: Bantam.

Grolnick, W. S., Bridges, L. J., & Connell, J. P. (1996). Emotion regulation in two-year-olds: Strategies and emotional expression in four contexts. *Child Development, 67,* 928–941.

Handler, L., & Hilsenroth, M. J. (2006). Rorschach assessment of narcissistic personality disorder. In S. K. Huprich (Ed.), *Rorschach assessment of the personality disorders* (pp. 223–253). Mahwah, NJ: Lawrence Erlbaum.

Harter, S. (1999). *The construction of the self: A developmental perspective.* New York, NY: Guilford.

Harter, S. (2006). The self. In N. Eisenberg (Ed.) & W. Damon & R. M. Lerner (Series Eds.), *Handbook of child psychology: Social, emotional, and personality development* (Vol. 3, 6th ed., pp. 571–645). Hoboken, NJ: John Wiley.

Hertz, M. R. (1970). *Frequency tables for scoring Rorschach responses* (5th ed. rev. & enlarged). Los Angeles, CA: Western Psychological Services (WPS).

Holmes, D. (1990). The evidence for repression: An examination of sixty years of research. In J. Singer (Ed.), *Repression and dissociation: Implications for personality, theory, psychopathology, and health* (pp. 85–102). Chicago, IL: University of Chicago Press.

Holzman, P. S., Levy, D. L., & Johnston, M. H. (2005). The use of the Rorschach technique for assessing formal thought disorder. In R. F. Bornstein & J. M. Masling (Eds.), *Scoring the Rorschach: Seven validated systems* (pp. 55–95). Mahwah, NJ: Lawrence Erlbaum.

Huprich, S. K. (2006). Rorschach assessment of depressive personality disorder. In S. K. Huprich (Ed.), *Rorschach assessment of the personality disorders* (pp. 371–393). Mahwah, NJ: Lawrence Erlbaum.

Huprich, S. K., & Ganellen, R. J. (2006). The advantages of assessing personality disorders with the Rorschach. In S. K. Huprich (Eds.), *Rorschach assessment of the personality disorders* (pp. 27–53). Mahwah, NJ: Lawrence Erlbaum.

Kaser-Boyd, N. (2006). Rorschach assessment of paranoid personality disorder. In S. K. Huprich (Ed.), *Rorschach assessment of the personality disorders* (pp. 139–169). Mahwah, NJ: Lawrence Erlbaum.

Kernberg, O. (1967). Borderline personality organization. *Journal of the American Psychoanalytic Association, 15,* 641–685.

Kernis, M. H., Grannemann, B. D., & Barclay, L. C. (1992). Stability of self-esteem: Assessment, correlates, and excuse making. *Journal of Personality, 60,* 621–643.

Kihlstrom, J. F. (1999). The psychological unconscious. In L. A. Pervin & O. P. John (Eds.), *Handbook of personality: Theory and research* (pp. 424–442). New York, NY: Guilford Press.

Kleiger, J. H., & Huprich, S. K. (2006). Rorschach assessment of schizoid personality disorder. In S. K. Huprich (Ed.), *Rorschach assessment of the personality disorders* (pp. 85–112). Mahwah, NJ: Lawrence Erlbaum.

Larsen, R. J., & Buss, D. M. (2010). *Personality psychology: Domains of knowledge about human nature* (4th ed.). New York, NY: McGraw-Hill.

LeDoux, J. E., & Phelps, E. A. (2008). Emotional networks in the brain. In M. Lewis, J. M. Haviland-Jones, & L. F. Barret (Eds.), *Handbook of emotions* (3rd ed., pp. 159–179). New York, NY: Guilford Press.

Lerner, P. M. (2006). Rorschach assessment of object relations: The personality disorders. In S. K. Huprich (Ed.), *Rorschach assessment of the personality disorders* (pp. 397–422). Mahwah, NJ: Lawrence Erlbaum.

Lilienfeld, S. O. (1999). Projective measures of personality and psychopathology: How well do they work? *Skeptical Inquirer, 23*(5), 32–39.

Loving, J. L., & Lee, A. J. (2006). Rorschach assessment of antisocial personality disorder and psychopathy. In S. K. Huprich (Ed.), *Rorschach assessment of the personality disorders* (pp. 139–169). Mahwah, NJ: Lawrence Erlbaum.

Malatesta, C. Z., Culver, C., Tesman, J. R., & Shepard, B. (1989). The development of emotion expression during the first two years of life. *Monographs of the Society for Research in Child Development, 54* (1–2, Serial No. 219).

Mangelsdorf, S. C., Shapiro, J. R., & Marzolf, D. (1995). Developmental and temperamental differences in emotion regulation in infancy. *Child Development, 66,* 1817–1828.

Marsh, H. W., Craven, R., & Debus, R. (1999). Separation of competency and affect components of multiple dimensions of academic self-concept: A developmental perspective. *Merrill-Palmer Quarterly, 45,* 567–701.

McCann, J. T. (1999). *Assessing adolescents with the MACI; using the Millon Adolescent Clinical Inventory.* New York, NY: John Wiley.

McClelland, D. C., Koestner, R., & Weinberger, J. (1989). How do self-attributed and implicit motives differ? *Psychological Review, 96,* 690–702.

McWilliams, N. (2011). *Psychoanalytic diagnosis: Understanding personality structure in the clinical process* (2nd ed.). New York, NY: The Guilford Press.

Mihura, J. L. (2006). Rorschach assessment of borderline personality disorder. In S. K. Huprich (Ed.), *Rorschach assessment of the personality disorders* (pp. 171–203). Mahwah, NJ: Lawrence Erlbaum.

Millon, T. (1990). *Toward a new personology: An evolutionary model.* New York, NY: John Wiley.

Millon, T., & Davis, R. D. (1996). *Disorders of personality: DSM-IV and beyond.* New York, NY: John Wiley.

Oberman, L. M., & Ramachandran, V. S. (2007). The simulating social mind: The role of the mirror neuron system and simulation in the social and communicative deficits of autism spectrum disorders. *Psychological Bulletin, 133,* 310–327.

Ohman, A. (2008). Fear and anxiety. In M. Lewis, J. M. Haviland-Jones, & L. F. Barret (Eds.), *Handbook of emotion* (3rd ed., pp. 709–729). New York, NY: Guilford Press.

Oltmanns, T. F., & Emery, R. E. (2004). *Abnormal psychology* (4th ed.). Upper Saddle River, NJ: Prentice Hall.

Roberts, G. E., & Gruber, C. (2005). *Roberts–2: Manual.* Los Angeles, CA: Western Psychological Services.

Roberts, J. E., & Monroe, S. M. (1992). Vulnerable self-esteem and depressive symptoms: Prospective findings comparing three alternative conceptualizations. *Journal of Personality and Social Psychology, 62,* 804–812.

Roberts–2 Computer Scoring CD [CD-ROM & USB Key Computer software]. (2005). Torrance, CA: Western Psychological Services (WPS).

Rorschach, H. (1942). *Psychdiagnostik* (Trans. Hans Huber). Bern, Switzerland: Rorschach Archives.

Rorschach Interpretation Assistance Program: Version 5. [CD-ROM Computer software]. (2008). Lutz, FL: Exner, Weiner, & Psychological Assessment Resources (PAR).

Rorschach Interpretation Assistance Program: Version 5 Forensic Edition. [CD-ROM Computer software]. (2008). Lutz, FL: Weiner & Psychological Assessment Resources (PAR).

Rorschach Scoring Program. [CD-ROM Computer software]. (2008). Lutz, FL: Exner, Weiner, & Psychological Assessment Resources (PAR).

Rothbart, M. K., Posner, M. I., & Kieras, J. (2006). Temperament, attention, and the development of self-regulation. In K. McCartney & D. Phillips (Eds.), *Blackwell handbook of early childhood development* (pp. 338–357). Malden, MA: Blackwell.

Schneider, R. B. (2006). Rorschach assessment of obsessive-compulsive personality disorder. In S. K. Huprich (Ed.), *Rorschach assessment of the personality disorders* (pp. 311–333). Mahwah, NJ: Lawrence Erlbaum.

Sigelman, C. K., & Rider, E. A. (2012). *Life-span human development* (7th ed.). Belmont, CA: Thomson Wadsworth.

Squire, L. R., Knowlton, B., & Musen, G. (1993). The structure and organization of memory. *Annual Review of Psychology, 44,* 453–495.

Stanovich, K. E. (2004). *How to think straight about psychology* (7th ed.). Boston, MA: Allyn and Bacon.

Thompson, R. A. (1994). Emotion regulation: A theme in search of definition. *Monographs of the Society for Research in Child Development, 59* (2–3, Serial No. 240), The development of emotion regulation: Biological and behavioral considerations, 25–52.

Weiner, I. B. (2003). *Principles of Rorschach interpretation* (2nd ed.). Mahwah, NJ: Lawrence Erlbaum.

FORM 9.1

RORSCHACH–CS, AGES 5 TO 7 RESULTS AND INTERPRETATION TABLES

RORSCHACH–CS, Ages 5 to 7

TABLE 1 ■ **TEST VALIDITY: SITUATIONAL GUARDEDNESS**

Variable	Score	Expected range	Positive result range	Result[a]	Meaning of positive result
R	00	18–29*	≤13[†]	Negative	Excessively nonproductive; defensive

Note: *denotes that the listed range is based on –1.00 to +1.00 standard deviations from the normative mean including rounding for ease of interpretation. [†]denotes that the listed range is determined by Comprehensive System interpretation guidelines.

[a]When R < 14, the entire Rorschach protocol is per se invalid. There is insufficient test data for meaningful scoring and interpretation.

There is no evidence of situational guardedness. In this regard, the clinical and personality variables are deemed valid.

There is remarkable situational guardedness. Therefore, this test is deemed invalid. The remaining scores are neither interpreted nor reported.

TABLE 2 ■ **TEST VALIDITY: SYMPTOM EXAGGERATION**

Variable	Score	Expected range	Positive result range	Result[a]	Meaning of positive result
X–%[b]	0.00	0.00–0.18*	≥0.70[†]	Negative	Exaggerating or malingering symptoms
XA+%	0.00	0.80–0.95*	≥0.75[††]	Positive	Indications of adequate reality testing
X–%	0.00	0.00–0.18*	≥0.26[†]	Negative	Extremely distorted thinking

Note: *denotes that the listed range is based on –1.00 to +1.00 standard deviations from the normative mean including rounding for ease of interpretation. [†]denotes that the listed range is determined by Comprehensive System interpretation guidelines. [††]denotes that the listed range is determined by the percentage base rate in the norm-reference sample due to skewness in that variable's frequency distribution.

[a]When the first row variable is X–% < 0.70, and hence negative, both remaining variables must yield positive results to indicate an invalid response pattern.

[b]X–% ≥ 0.70 indicates such gross psychological impairment that testing would have been precluded; therefore the entire Rorschach protocol is deemed per se invalid irrespective of the remaining variables.

There is no evidence of exaggeration of symptoms or malingering. In this regard, the clinical and personality variables are deemed valid.

There is remarkable evidence of an intentional exaggeration of symptoms or malingering. Therefore, the clinical and personality variables are deemed invalid. The remaining scores are neither interpreted nor reported.

The paradoxical data of adequate reality testing and extremely distorted thinking is evidence of an intentional exaggeration of symptoms or malingering. Therefore, the clinical and personality variables are deemed invalid. The remaining scores are neither interpreted nor reported.

There exists evidence of a tendency toward magnifying symptoms. Therefore, ensuing Rorschach variables are considered credible when reasonably supportive of other reliable and valid test data, including information gathered during the diagnostic interview.

(Cont.)

FORM 9.1

RORSCHACH–CS, AGES 5 TO 7 RESULTS AND INTERPRETATION TABLES (*Cont.*)

TABLE 3 ■ **CLINICAL VARIABLES: PSYCHOTIC DISORDERS**

Variable	Score	Expected range	Positive result range	Result	Meaning of positive result
WSum6	0	0–20[†]	≥21[†]	Negative	Ideational or cognitive slippage; disordered thought process
Level 2	0	0[††]	≥1[††]	Positive	Manifestly bizarre responses
PTI	0	0–2[††]	3–5[††]	Negative	Disturbance in formal thinking and reality testing; psychosis
XA+%	0.00	0.74–1.00**	≤0.73[†σ]	Negative	Disturbed mediation or reality testing
WDA+%	0.00	0.79–1.00**	≤0.78[†σ]	Negative	Pervasively disturbed mediation or reality testing
X–%	0.00	0.00–0.25**	≥0.26[†σ]	Positive	Extremely distorted thinking

Note: PTI, Perceptual Thinking Index. **denotes that the listed range is based on –2.00 to +2.00 standard deviations from the normative mean including rounding for ease of interpretation. [†]denotes that the listed range is determined by Comprehensive System interpretation guidelines. [††]denotes that the listed range is determined by the percentage base rate in the norm-reference sample due to skewness in that variable's frequency distribution. [σ]denotes that the listed positive result range is based on the deviation principle.

TABLE 4 ■ **CLINICAL VARIABLES: WSUM6 THOUGHT DISORDER SCORES**[a]

Variable	Level 1 score[b]	Level 2 score[c]	Meaning of variable presence
Deviant Verbalization (DV)	0	0	Neologisms; odd redundancies
Incongruous Combination (INCOM)	0	0	Implausible or impossible integration of elements within a single object
Deviant Response (DR)	0	0	Inappropriate or irrelevant phrases; circumstantial (fluid or rambling) responses
Fabulized Combination (FABCOM)	0	0	Implausible or impossible relationship between objects
Inappropriate Logic (ALOG)[d]	--	0	Loose and simplistic reasoning that leads to flawed judgment
Contamination (CONTAM)[e]	--	0	Fusion of impressions into a single object that clearly violates reality

Note: -- denotes score type not available.

[a]This table is reported only upon a positive WSum6 result for purposes of further scrutinizing the examinee's cognitive slippage and disordered thought process.

[b]Modest instances of illogical, fluid, peculiar, or circumstantial thinking.

[c]Severe instances of illogical, fluid, peculiar, or circumstantial thinking.

[d]ALOG scored only as Level 2.

[e]CONTAM scored only as Level 2.

(*Cont.*)

FORM 9.1

RORSCHACH–CS, AGES 5 TO 7 RESULTS AND INTERPRETATION TABLES (*Cont.*)

TABLE 5 ■ **CLINICAL VARIABLES: MOOD DISORDERS**

Variable	Score	Expected range	Positive result range	Result	Meaning of positive result
DEPI	0	0–4[†]	5–7[†]	Negative	Affective disruption; emotional disarray; depression
MOR	0	0–2[††]	≥3[††]	Negative	Pessimism; low self-worth
FC:CF+C+Cn	0:0	FC×2 > CF+C+Cn[†]	FC×3 > CF+C+Cn[†]	Positive	Emotional constriction
EB 0–Right	0:0.0	3–7:2.5–6.5*	≥3:0.0[†]	Negative	Massive containment or shutdown of emotion
FC:CF+C+Cn	0:0	FC×2 > CF+C+Cn[†]	FC < CF+C+Cn[†]	Negative	Problems in affective modulation; affective instability; mood swings
SumC′:WSumC	0:0.0	0–3:2.5–6.5*	≤3:≥7.0[†]	Negative	Emotional unrestraint; mood swings
EB 0–Left	0:0.0	3–7:2.5–6.5*	0:≥4.0[†]	Negative	Emotional flooding; mood swings and impulsiveness

Note: DEPI, Depression Index. *denotes that the listed range is based on –1.00 to +1.00 standard deviations from the normative mean including rounding for ease of interpretation. [†]denotes that the listed range is determined by Comprehensive System interpretation guidelines. [††]denotes that the listed range is determined by the percentage base rate in the norm-reference sample due to skewness in that variable's frequency distribution.

TABLE 6 ■ **CLINICAL VARIABLES: ANXIETY AND STRESS-RELATED DISORDERS**

Variable	Score	Expected range	Positive result range	Result	Meaning of positive result
SumC′:WSumC	0:0.0	0–3:2.5–6.5*	SumC′ > WSumC[†]	Negative	Excessive internalization of emotion; irritability; chronic anxiety
OBS	--	--	--	Negative[†]	Compulsive behaviors; obsessive thoughts, especially perfectionism
HVI	--	--	--	Negative[†]	Excessive chronic alertness and preparedness for danger
CDI	0	0–3[†]	4–5[†]	Negative	Coping deficiencies in dealing with stress
D	±0	0[†]	≤–1[†]	Negative	Current situationally related or acute stress
Adj D	±0	0[†]	≤–1[†]	Negative	Chronic stress overload
EA	00.0	4.0–9.0[†]	≤3.5[†]	Positive	Deficiency in psychological resources for dealing with stress

Note: OBS, Obsessive Style Index (scored as either positive or negative result). HVI, Hypervigilance Index (scored as either positive or negative result). CDI, Coping Deficit Index. *denotes that the listed range is based on –1.00 to +1.00 standard deviations from the normative mean including rounding for ease of interpretation. [†]denotes that the listed range and/or result is determined by Comprehensive System interpretation guidelines. -- denotes score type not reported.

(*Cont.*)

FORM 9.1

RORSCHACH–CS, AGES 5 TO 7 RESULTS AND INTERPRETATION TABLES (*Cont.*)

TABLE 7 ■ CLINICAL VARIABLES: ATTENTION-DEFICIT DISORDERS

Variable	Score	Expected range	Positive result range	Result	Meaning of positive result
PSV	0	0–1[†]	≥2[†]	Positive	Impaired ability to shift attention
Zf	0	9–18*	≤8[σ]	Negative	Poor-quality processing
Zd	–0.00	–3.5–+4.5*	≤–3.0[σ]	Negative	Underincorporation; hasty and haphazard scanning activity
L	0.00	0.23–0.99*	≥1.00[†σ]	Negative	Overly narrow focus of attention
DQv	0	0–2[†]	≥3[†]	Negative	Problems maintaining focus of attention
DQ+	0	5–11*	≤4[†σ]	Positive	Impaired ability to analyze and synthesize aspects of experience

Note: PSV, Perseveration. *denotes that the listed range is based on –1.00 to +1.00 standard deviations from the normative mean including rounding for ease of interpretation. [†]denotes that the listed range is determined by Comprehensive System interpretation guidelines. [σ]denotes that the listed positive result range is based on the deviation principle.

(*Cont.*)

FORM 9.1

RORSCHACH–CS, AGES 5 TO 7 RESULTS AND INTERPRETATION TABLES (*Cont.*)

TABLE 8 ■ **PERSONALITY VARIABLES**

Variable	Score	Expected range	Positive result range	Result	Meaning of positive result
Fr + rF	0	0–1[†]	≥2[†]	Positive	Narcissism; inflated sense of self-worth
3r + (2)/R High[a]	0.00	0.52–0.83[†]	≥0.84[†]	Negative	Inflated self-esteem
3r + (2)/R Low[b]	0.00	0.52–0.83[†]	≤0.51[†]	Negative	Low self-esteem
SumV	0	0–1*	≥2[σ]	Negative	Preoccupation with negative features of the self
H:(H)+Hd+(Hd)	00:00	2–5:0–6*	H < (H)+Hd+(Hd)[†]	Negative	Distorted self-image
Sum T High	0	0–2[††]	≥3[††]	Negative	Either (a) recent object loss or (b) chronic loneliness or emptiness[c]
Blends: Color-Shading	0	0	≥1[†]	Negative	Confused and ambivalent feelings toward self and/or others
S	0	0–3[†]	≥4[†]	Negative	Oppositional; chronic anger toward people and environment
AG	0	0–3[†]	≥4[†]	Negative	Hostile and negative attitudes toward people
HVI	--	--	--	Negative[†]	Irrationally and chronically suspicious of others; paranoid
Sum T Low	0	1–2[†]	0[†]	Negative	Impaired ability to empathize with other people
H:(H)+Hd+(Hd)	0:0	H ≥ (H)+Hd+(Hd)[†]	H < (H)+Hd+(Hd)[†]	Negative	Poor understanding of people
FD	0	1–2[†]	0[†]	Negative	Lack of introspection
Human Content	0	4–9*	≤3[σ]	Negative	Lack of interest in people
EA	00.0	4.0–9.0[†]	≤3.5[†]	Positive	General deficiency in psychological resources
GHR:PHR	0:0	GHR ≥ PHR[†]	GHR < PHR[†]	Negative	Social ineptness; risk of rejection; probable personality disorder
Isolate/R	0.00	0.11–0.31*	≥0.32[†σ]	Negative	Interpersonally isolated
Fd	0	0–1*	≥2[σ]	Negative	Dependent traits
a:p[d]	0:0	4–10:2–6*	a + 1 < p[†]	Negative	Passivity in interpersonal relations
OBS	--	--	--	Negative[†]	Preoccupation with correctness; perfectionism, and precision
2AB + Art + Ay	0	0–5*	≥6[σ]	Negative	Intellectualization; use of ideation to minimize impact of emotions
Ma:Mp	0:0	2–5:1–3*	Ma + 1 < Mp[†σ]	Positive	Excessive abuse of fantasy to deny reality; dissociation
CP	0	0[†]	≥1[†]	Negative	Improper substitution of positive for negative emotions; histrionic

Note: HVI, Hypervigilance Index (scored as either positive or negative result). OBS, Obsessive Style Index (scored as either positive or negative result). *denotes that the listed range is based on –1.00 to +1.00 standard deviations from the normative mean including rounding for ease of interpretation. [†]denotes that the listed range is determined by Comprehensive System interpretation guidelines. [††]denotes that the listed range is determined by the percentage base rate in the norm-reference sample due to skewness in that variable's frequency distribution. [σ]denotes that the listed positive result range is based on the deviation principle. -- denotes score type not reported.

[a]When both 3r + (2)/R High and Fr + rF are positive, this indicates that narcissism is a core aspect of personality structure and organization.

[b]When both 3r + (2)/R Low and Fr + rF are positive, this indicates extreme fluctuations in sense of self or splitting object-relations consistent with borderline personality structure and organization.

[c]Requires the use of information from the diagnostic interview to determine the most accurate positive result alternative.

[d]When both Fd and a:p are positive, this indicates that dependency is a core aspect of personality structure and organization.

FORM 9.2

RORSCHACH–CS, AGES 8 TO 10 RESULTS AND INTERPRETATION TABLES

RORSCHACH–CS, Ages 8 to 10

TABLE 1 ■ TEST VALIDITY: SITUATIONAL GUARDEDNESS

Variable	Score	Expected range	Positive result range	Result[a]	Meaning of positive result
R	00	18–29*	≤13[†]	Negative	Excessively nonproductive; defensive

Note: *denotes that the listed range is based on −1.00 to +1.00 standard deviations from the normative mean including rounding for ease of interpretation. [†]denotes that the listed range is determined by Comprehensive System interpretation guidelines.

[a]When R < 14, the entire Rorschach protocol is per se invalid. There is insufficient test data for meaningful scoring and interpretation.

There is no evidence of situational guardedness. In this regard, the clinical and personality variables are deemed valid.

There is remarkable situational guardedness. Therefore, this test is deemed invalid. The remaining scores are neither interpreted nor reported.

TABLE 2 ■ TEST VALIDITY: SYMPTOM EXAGGERATION

Variable	Score	Expected range	Positive result range	Result[a]	Meaning of positive result
X–%[b]	0.00	0.00–0.18*	≥ 0.70[†]	Negative	Exaggerating or malingering symptoms
XA+%	0.00	0.80–0.95*	≥0.75[††]	Positive	Indications of adequate reality testing
X–%	0.00	0.00–0.18*	≥0.26[†]	Negative	Extremely distorted thinking

Note: *denotes that the listed range is based on −1.00 to +1.00 standard deviations from the normative mean including rounding for ease of interpretation. [†]denotes that the listed range is determined by Comprehensive System interpretation guidelines. [††]denotes that the listed range is determined by the percentage base rate in the norm-reference sample due to skewness in that variable's frequency distribution.

[a]When the first row variable is X–% < 0.70, and hence negative, both remaining variables must yield positive results to indicate an invalid response pattern.

[b]X–% ≥ 0.70 indicates such gross psychological impairment that testing would have been precluded; therefore the entire Rorschach protocol is deemed per se invalid irrespective of the remaining variables.

There is no evidence of exaggeration of symptoms or malingering. In this regard, the clinical and personality variables are deemed valid.

There is remarkable evidence of an intentional exaggeration of symptoms or malingering. Therefore, the clinical and personality variables are deemed invalid. The remaining scores are neither interpreted nor reported.

The paradoxical data of adequate reality testing and extremely distorted thinking is evidence of an intentional exaggeration of symptoms or malingering. Therefore, the clinical and personality variables are deemed invalid. The remaining scores are neither interpreted nor reported.

There exists evidence of a tendency toward magnifying symptoms. Therefore, ensuing Rorschach variables are considered credible when reasonably supportive of other reliable and valid test data, including information gathered during the diagnostic interview.

(Cont.)

FORM 9.2

RORSCHACH–CS, AGES 8 TO 10 RESULTS AND INTERPRETATION TABLES (*Cont.*)

TABLE 3 ■ **CLINICAL VARIABLES: PSYCHOTIC DISORDERS**

Variable	Score	Expected range	Positive result range	Result	Meaning of positive result
WSum6	0	0–19[†]	≥20[†]	Negative	Ideational or cognitive slippage; disordered thought process
Level 2	0	0[††]	≥1[††]	Positive	Manifestly bizarre responses
PTI	0	0–2[††]	3–5[††]	Negative	Disturbance in formal thinking and reality testing; psychosis
XA+%	0.00	0.74–1.00**	≤0.73[†σ]	Negative	Disturbed mediation or reality testing
WDA+%	0.00	0.79–1.00**	≤0.78[†σ]	Negative	Pervasively disturbed mediation or reality testing
X–%	0.00	0.00–0.25**	≥0.26[†σ]	Positive	Extremely distorted thinking

Note: PTI, Perceptual Thinking Index. **denotes that the listed range is based on –2.00 to +2.00 standard deviations from the normative mean including rounding for ease of interpretation. [†]denotes that the listed range is determined by Comprehensive System interpretation guidelines. [††]denotes that the listed range is determined by the percentage base rate in the norm-reference sample due to skewness in that variable's frequency distribution. [σ]denotes that the listed positive result range is based on the deviation principle.

TABLE 4 ■ **CLINICAL VARIABLES: WSUM6 THOUGHT DISORDER SCORES[a]**

Variable	Level 1 score[b]	Level 2 score[c]	Meaning of variable presence
Deviant Verbalization (DV)	0	0	Neologisms; odd redundancies
Incongruous Combination (INCOM)	0	0	Implausible or impossible integration of elements within a single object
Deviant Response (DR)	0	0	Inappropriate or irrelevant phrases; circumstantial (fluid or rambling) responses
Fabulized Combination (FABCOM)	0	0	Implausible or impossible relationship between objects
Inappropriate Logic (ALOG)[d]	--	0	Loose and simplistic reasoning that leads to flawed judgment
Contamination (CONTAM)[e]	--	0	Fusion of impressions into a single object that clearly violates reality

Note: -- denotes score type not available.

[a]This table is reported only upon a positive WSum6 result for purposes of further scrutinizing the examinee's cognitive slippage and disordered thought process.

[b]Modest instances of illogical, fluid, peculiar, or circumstantial thinking.

[c]Severe instances of illogical, fluid, peculiar, or circumstantial thinking.

[d]ALOG scored only as Level 2.

[e]CONTAM scored only as Level 2.

(*Cont.*)

FORM 9.2

RORSCHACH–CS, AGES 8 TO 10 RESULTS AND INTERPRETATION TABLES (*Cont.*)

TABLE 5 ■ CLINICAL VARIABLES: MOOD DISORDERS

Variable	Score	Expected range	Positive result range	Result	Meaning of positive result
DEPI	0	0–4[†]	5–7[†]	Negative	Affective disruption; emotional disarray; depression
MOR	0	0–2[††]	≥3[††]	Negative	Pessimism; low self-worth
FC:CF+C+Cn	0:0	FCx2 > CF+C+Cn[†]	FCx3 > CF+C+Cn[†]	Positive	Emotional constriction
EB 0–Right	0:0.0	3–7:2.5–6.5*	≥3:0.0[†]	Negative	Massive containment or shutdown of emotion
FC:CF+C+Cn	0:0	FCx2 > CF+C+Cn[†]	FC < CF+C+Cn[†]	Negative	Problems in affective modulation; affective instability; mood swings
SumC':WSumC	0:0.0	0–3:2.5–6.5*	≤3:≥7.0[†]	Negative	Emotional unrestraint; mood swings
EB 0–Left	0:0.0	3–7:2.5–6.5*	0:≥4.0[†]	Negative	Emotional flooding; mood swings and impulsiveness

Note: DEPI, Depression Index. *denotes that the listed range is based on –1.00 to +1.00 standard deviations from the normative mean including rounding for ease of interpretation. [†]denotes that the listed range is determined by Comprehensive System interpretation guidelines. [††]denotes that the listed range is determined by the percentage base rate in the norm reference sample due to skewness in that variable's frequency distribution.

TABLE 6 ■ CLINICAL VARIABLES: ANXIETY AND STRESS-RELATED DISORDERS

Variable	Score	Expected range	Positive result range	Result	Meaning of positive result
SumC':WSumC	0:0.0	0–3:2.5–6.5*	SumC' > WSumC[†]	Negative	Excessive internalization of emotion; irritability; chronic anxiety
OBS	--	--	--	Negative[†]	Compulsive behaviors; obsessive thoughts, especially perfectionism
HVI	--	--	--	Negative[†]	Excessive chronic alertness and preparedness for danger
CDI	0	0–3[†]	4–5[†]	Negative	Coping deficiencies in dealing with stress
D	±0	0[†]	≤–1[†]	Negative	Current situationally related or acute stress
Adj D	±0	0[†]	≤–1[†]	Negative	Chronic stress overload
EA	00.0	5.0–10.0[†]	≤4.5[†]	Positive	Deficiency in psychological resources for dealing with stress

Note: OBS, Obsessive Style Index (scored as either positive or negative result). HVI, Hypervigilance Index (scored as either positive or negative result). CDI, Coping Deficit Index. *denotes that the listed range is based on –1.00 to +1.00 standard deviations from the normative mean including rounding for ease of interpretation. [†]denotes that the listed range and/or result is determined by Comprehensive System interpretation guidelines. -- denotes score type not reported.

(*Cont.*)

FORM 9.2

RORSCHACH–CS, AGES 8 TO 10 RESULTS AND INTERPRETATION TABLES (*Cont.*)

TABLE 7 ■ **CLINICAL VARIABLES: ATTENTION-DEFICIT DISORDERS**

Variable	Score	Expected range	Positive result range	Result	Meaning of positive result
PSV	0	0–1[†]	≥2[†]	Positive	Impaired ability to shift attention
Zf	0	9–18*	≤8[σ]	Negative	Poor-quality processing
Zd	−0.00	−3.5–+4.5*	≤−3.0[σ]	Negative	Underincorporation; hasty and haphazard scanning activity
L	0.00	0.23–0.99*	≥1.00[†σ]	Negative	Overly narrow focus of attention
DQv	0	0–2[†]	≥3[†]	Negative	Problems maintaining focus of attention
DQ+	0	5–11*	≤4[†σ]	Positive	Impaired ability to analyze and synthesize aspects of experience

Note: PSV, Perseveration. *denotes that the listed range is based on −1.00 to +1.00 standard deviations from the normative mean including rounding for ease of interpretation. [†]denotes that the listed range is determined by Comprehensive System interpretation guidelines. [σ]denotes that the listed positive result range is based on the deviation principle.

(*Cont.*)

FORM 9.2

RORSCHACH–CS, AGES 8 TO 10 RESULTS AND INTERPRETATION TABLES (*Cont.*)

TABLE 8 ■ **PERSONALITY VARIABLES**

Variable	Score	Expected range	Positive result range	Result	Meaning of positive result
Fr + rF	0	0–1[†]	≥2[†]	Positive	Narcissism; inflated sense of self-worth
3r + (2)/R High[a]	0.00	0.47–0.74[†]	≥0.75[†]	Negative	Inflated self-esteem
3r + (2)/R Low[b]	0.00	0.47–0.74[†]	≤0.46[†]	Negative	Low self-esteem
SumV	0	0–1[*]	≥2[σ]	Negative	Preoccupation with negative features of the self
H:(H)+Hd+(Hd)	00:00	2–5:0–6[*]	H < (H)+Hd+(Hd)[†]	Negative	Distorted self-image
Sum T High	0	0–2[††]	≥3[††]	Negative	Either (a) recent object loss or (b) chronic loneliness or emptiness[c]
Blends:Color-Shading	0	0	≥1[†]	Negative	Confused and ambivalent feelings toward self and/or others
S	0	0–3[†]	≥4[†]	Negative	Oppositional; chronic anger toward people and environment
AG	0	0–3[†]	≥4[†]	Negative	Hostile and negative attitudes toward people
HVI	--	--	--	Negative[†]	Irrationally and chronically suspicious of others; paranoid
Sum T Low	0	1–2[†]	0[†]	Negative	Impaired ability to empathize with other people
H:(H)+Hd+(Hd)	0:0	H ≥ (H)+Hd+(Hd)[†]	H < (H)+Hd+(Hd)[†]	Negative	Poor understanding of people
FD	0	1–2[†]	0[†]	Negative	Lack of introspection
Human Content	0	4–9[*]	≤3[σ]	Negative	Lack of interest in people
EA	00.0	5.0–10.0[†]	≤4.5[†]	Positive	General deficiency in psychological resources
GHR:PHR	0:0	GHR ≥ PHR[†]	GHR < PHR[†]	Negative	Social ineptness; risk of rejection; probable personality disorder
Isolate/R	0.00	0.11–0.31[*]	≥0.32[†σ]	Negative	Interpersonally isolated
Fd	0	0–1[*]	≥2[σ]	Negative	Dependent traits
a:p[d]	0:0	4–10:2–6[*]	a+1 < p[†]	Negative	Passivity in interpersonal relations
OBS	--	--	--	Negative[†]	Preoccupation with correctness, perfectionism, and precision
2AB + Art + Ay	0	0–5[*]	≥6[σ]	Negative	Intellectualization; use of ideation to minimize impact of emotions
Ma:Mp	0:0	2–5:1–3[*]	Ma+1 < Mp[†σ]	Positive	Excessive abuse of fantasy to deny reality; dissociation
CP	0	0[†]	≥1[†]	Negative	Improper substitution of positive for negative emotions; histrionic

Note: HVI, Hypervigilance Index (scored as either positive or negative result). OBS, Obsessive Style Index (scored as either positive or negative result). *denotes that the listed range is based on –1.00 to +1.00 standard deviations from the normative mean including rounding for ease of interpretation. [†]denotes that the listed range is determined by Comprehensive System interpretation guidelines. [††]denotes that the listed range is determined by the percentage base rate in the norm reference sample due to skewness in that variable's frequency distribution. [σ]denotes that the listed positive result range is based on the deviation principle. -- denotes score type not reported.

[a]When both 3r + (2)/R High and Fr + rF are positive, this indicates that narcissism is a core aspect of personality structure and organization.

[b]When both 3r + (2)/R Low and Fr + rF are positive, this indicates extreme fluctuations in sense of self or splitting object-relations consistent with borderline personality structure and organization.

[c]Requires the use of information from the diagnostic interview to determine the most accurate positive result alternative.

[d]When both Fd and a:p are positive, this indicates that dependency is a core aspect of personality structure and organization.

FORM 9.3

RORSCHACH–CS, AGES 11 TO 14 RESULTS AND INTERPRETATION TABLES

RORSCHACH–CS, Ages 11 to 14

TABLE 1 ■ **TEST VALIDITY: SITUATIONAL GUARDEDNESS**

Variable	Score	Expected range	Positive result range	Result[a]	Meaning of positive result
R	00	18–29*	≤13[†]	Negative	Excessively nonproductive; defensive

Note: *denotes that the listed range is based on –1.00 to +1.00 standard deviations from the normative mean including rounding for ease of interpretation. [†]denotes that the listed range is determined by Comprehensive System interpretation guidelines.

[a]When R < 14, the entire Rorschach protocol is per se invalid. There is insufficient test data for meaningful scoring and interpretation.

There is no evidence of situational guardedness. In this regard, the clinical and personality variables are deemed valid.

There is remarkable situational guardedness. Therefore, this test is deemed invalid. The remaining scores are neither interpreted nor reported.

TABLE 2 ■ **TEST VALIDITY: SYMPTOM EXAGGERATION**

Variable	Score	Expected range	Positive result range	Result[a]	Meaning of positive result
X–%[b]	0.00	0.00–0.18*	≥0.70[†]	Negative	Exaggerating or malingering symptoms
XA+%	0.00	0.80–0.95*	≥0.75[††]	Positive	Indications of adequate reality testing
X–%	0.00	0.00–0.18*	≥0.26[†]	Negative	Extremely distorted thinking

Note: *denotes that the listed range is based on –1.00 to +1.00 standard deviations from the normative mean including rounding for ease of interpretation. [†]denotes that the listed range is determined by Comprehensive System interpretation guidelines. [††]denotes that the listed range is determined by the percentage base rate in the norm-reference sample due to skewness in that variable's frequency distribution.

[a]When the first row variable is X–% < 0.70 and hence negative, both remaining variables must yield positive results to indicate an invalid response pattern.

[b]X–% ≥ 0.70 indicates such gross psychological impairment that testing would have been precluded; therefore the entire Rorschach protocol is deemed per se invalid irrespective of the remaining variables.

There is no evidence of exaggeration of symptoms or malingering. In this regard, the clinical and personality variables are deemed valid.

There is remarkable evidence of an intentional exaggeration of symptoms or malingering. Therefore, the clinical and personality variables are deemed invalid. The remaining scores are neither interpreted nor reported.

The paradoxical data of adequate reality testing and extremely distorted thinking is evidence of an intentional exaggeration of symptoms or malingering. Therefore, the clinical and personality variables are deemed invalid. The remaining scores are neither interpreted nor reported.

There exists evidence of a tendency toward magnifying symptoms. Therefore, ensuing Rorschach variables are considered credible when reasonably supportive of other reliable and valid test data, including information gathered during the diagnostic interview.

(Cont.)

FORM 9.3

RORSCHACH–CS, AGES 11 TO 14 RESULTS AND INTERPRETATION TABLES *(Cont.)*

TABLE 3 ■ CLINICAL VARIABLES: PSYCHOTIC DISORDERS

Variable	Score	Expected range	Positive result range	Result	Meaning of positive result
WSum6	0	0–18**	≥19[†σ]	Negative	Ideational or cognitive slippage; disordered thought process
Level 2	0	0[††]	≥1[††]	Positive	Manifestly bizarre responses
PTI	0	0–2[††]	3–5[††]	Negative	Disturbance in formal thinking and reality testing; psychosis
XA+%	0.00	0.74–1.00**	≤0.73[†σ]	Negative	Disturbed mediation or reality testing
WDA+%	0.00	0.79–1.00**	≤0.78[†σ]	Negative	Pervasively disturbed mediation or reality testing
X–%	0.00	0.00–0.25**	≥0.26[†σ]	Positive	Extremely distorted thinking

Note: PTI, Perceptual Thinking Index. **denotes that the listed range is based on –2.00 to +2.00 standard deviations from the normative mean including rounding for ease of interpretation. [†]denotes that the listed range is determined by Comprehensive System interpretation guidelines. [††]denotes that the listed range is determined by the percentage base rate in the norm reference sample due to skewness in that variable's frequency distribution. [σ]denotes that the listed positive result range is based on the deviation principle.

TABLE 4 ■ CLINICAL VARIABLES: WSUM6 THOUGHT DISORDER SCORES[a]

Variable	Level 1 score[b]	Level 2 score[c]	Meaning of variable presence
Deviant Verbalization (DV)	0	0	Neologisms; odd redundancies
Incongruous Combination (INCOM)	0	0	Implausible or impossible integration of elements within a single object
Deviant Response (DR)	0	0	Inappropriate or irrelevant phrases; circumstantial (fluid or rambling) responses
Fabulized Combination (FABCOM)	0	0	Implausible or impossible relationship between objects
Inappropriate Logic (ALOG)[d]	--	0	Loose and simplistic reasoning that leads to flawed judgment
Contamination (CONTAM)[e]	--	0	Fusion of impressions into a single object that clearly violates reality

Note: -- denotes score type not available.

[a]This table is reported only upon a positive WSum6 result for purposes of further scrutinizing the examinee's cognitive slippage and disordered thought process.

[b]Modest instances of illogical, fluid, peculiar, or circumstantial thinking.

[c]Severe instances of illogical, fluid, peculiar, or circumstantial thinking.

[d]ALOG scored only as Level 2.

[e]CONTAM scored only as Level 2.

(Cont.)

FORM 9.3

RORSCHACH–CS, AGES 11 TO 14 RESULTS AND INTERPRETATION TABLES (*Cont.*)

TABLE 5 ■ **CLINICAL VARIABLES: MOOD DISORDERS**

Variable	Score	Expected range	Positive result range	Result	Meaning of positive result
DEPI	0	0–4[†]	5–7[†]	Negative	Affective disruption; emotional disarray; depression
MOR	0	0–2[††]	≥3[††]	Negative	Pessimism; low self-worth
FC:CF+C+Cn	0:0	FC×2 > CF+C+Cn[†]	FC×3 > CF+C+Cn[†]	Positive	Emotional constriction
EB 0–Right	0:0.0	3–7:2.5–6.5*	≥3:0.0[†]	Negative	Massive containment or shutdown of emotion
FC:CF+C+Cn	0:0	FC×2 > CF+C+Cn[†]	FC < CF+C+Cn[†]	Negative	Problems in affective modulation; affective instability; mood swings
SumC':WSumC	0:0.0	0–3:2.5–6.5*	≤3:≥7.0[†]	Negative	Emotional unrestraint; mood swings
EB 0–Left	0:0.0	3–7:2.5–6.5*	0:≥4.0[†]	Negative	Emotional flooding; mood swings and impulsiveness

Note: DEPI, Depression Index. *denotes that the listed range is based on –1.00 to +1.00 standard deviations from the normative mean including rounding for ease of interpretation. [†]denotes that the listed range is determined by Comprehensive System interpretation guidelines. [††]denotes that the listed range is determined by the percentage base rate in the norm reference sample due to skewness in that variable's frequency distribution.

TABLE 6 ■ **CLINICAL VARIABLES: ANXIETY AND STRESS-RELATED DISORDERS**

Variable	Score	Expected range	Positive result range	Result	Meaning of positive result
SumC':WSumC	0:0.0	0–3:2.5–6.5*	SumC' > WSumC[†]	Negative	Excessive internalization of emotion; irritability; chronic anxiety
OBS	--	--	--	Negative[†]	Compulsive behaviors; obsessive thoughts, especially perfectionism
HVI	--	--	--	Negative[†]	Excessive chronic alertness and preparedness for danger
CDI	0	0–3[†]	4–5[†]	Negative	Coping deficiencies in dealing with stress
D	±0	0[†]	≤–1[†]	Negative	Current situationally related or acute stress
Adj D	±0	0[†]	≤–1[†]	Negative	Chronic stress overload
EA	00.0	7.0–11.0[†]	≤6.5[†]	Positive	Deficiency in psychological resources for dealing with stress

Note: OBS, Obsessive Style Index (scored as either positive or negative result). HVI, Hypervigilance Index (scored as either positive or negative result). CDI, Coping Deficit Index. *denotes that the listed range is based on –1.00 to +1.00 standard deviations from the normative mean including rounding for ease of interpretation. [†]denotes that the listed range and/or result is determined by Comprehensive System interpretation guidelines. -- denotes score type not reported.

(*Cont.*)

FORM 9.3

RORSCHACH–CS, AGES 11 TO 14 RESULTS AND INTERPRETATION TABLES (*Cont.*)

TABLE 7 ■ **CLINICAL VARIABLES: ATTENTION-DEFICIT DISORDERS**

Variable	Score	Expected range	Positive result range	Result	Meaning of positive result
PSV	0	0–1[†]	≥2[†]	Positive	Impaired ability to shift attention
Zf	0	9–18*	≤8[σ]	Negative	Poor-quality processing
Zd	–0.00	–3.5–+4.5*	≤–3.0[σ]	Negative	Underincorporation; hasty and haphazard scanning activity
L	0.00	0.23–0.99*	≥1.00[†σ]	Negative	Overly narrow focus of attention
DQv	0	0–2[†]	≥3[†]	Negative	Problems maintaining focus of attention
DQ+	0	5–11*	≤4[†σ]	Positive	Impaired ability to analyze and synthesize aspects of experience

Note: PSV, Perseveration. *denotes that the listed range is based on –1.00 to +1.00 standard deviations from the normative mean including rounding for ease of interpretation. [†]denotes that the listed range is determined by Comprehensive System interpretation guidelines. [σ]denotes that the listed positive result range is based on the deviation principle.

(Cont.)

FORM 9.3

RORSCHACH–CS, AGES 11 TO 14 RESULTS AND INTERPRETATION TABLES (*Cont.*)

TABLE 8 ■ **PERSONALITY DISORDERS VARIABLES**

Variable	Score	Expected range	Positive result range	Result	Meaning of positive result
Fr + rF	0	0[†]	≥1[†]	Positive	Narcissism; inflated sense of self-worth
3r + (2)/R High[a]	0.00	0.37–0.58[†]	≥0.59[†]	Negative	Inflated self-esteem
3r + (2)/R Low[b]	0.00	0.37–0.58[†]	≤0.36[†]	Negative	Low self-esteem
SumV	0	0–1*	≥2[σ]	Negative	Preoccupation with negative features of the self
H:(H)+Hd+(Hd)	00:00	2–5:0–6*	H < (H)+Hd+(Hd)[†]	Negative	Distorted self-image
Sum T High	0	0–2[††]	≥3[††]	Negative	Either (a) recent object loss, or (b) chronic loneliness or emptiness[c]
Blends:Color-Shading	0	0	≥1[†]	Negative	Confused and ambivalent feelings toward self and/or others
S	0	0–3[†]	≥4[†]	Negative	Oppositional; chronic anger toward people and environment.
AG	0	0–3[†]	≥4[†]	Negative	Hostile and negative attitudes toward people
HVI	--	--	--	Negative[†]	Irrationally and chronically suspicious of others; paranoid
Sum T Low	0	1–2[†]	0[†]	Negative	Impaired ability to empathize with other people
H:(H)+Hd+(Hd)	0:0	H ≥ (H)+Hd+(Hd)[†]	H < (H)+Hd+(Hd)[†]	Negative	Poor understanding of people
FD	0	1–2[†]	0[†]	Negative	Lack of introspection
Human Content	0	4–9*	≤3[σ]	Negative	Lack of interest in people
EA	00.0	6.0–10.0[†]	≤5.5[†]	Positive	General deficiency in psychological resources
GHR:PHR	0:0	GHR ≥ PHR[†]	GHR < PHR[†]	Negative	Social ineptness; risk of rejection; probable personality disorder
Isolate/R	0.00	0.11–0.31*	≥0.32[†σ]	Negative	Interpersonally isolated
Fd	0	0–1*	≥2[σ]	Negative	Dependent traits
a:p[d]	0:0	4–10:2–6*	a + 1 < p[†]	Negative	Passivity in interpersonal relations
OBS	--	--	--	Negative[†]	Preoccupation with correctness, perfectionism, and precision
2AB + Art + Ay	0	0–5*	≥6[σ]	Negative	Intellectualization; use of ideation to minimize impact of emotions
Ma:Mp	0:0	2–5:1–3*	Ma + 1 < Mp[†σ]	Positive	Excessive abuse of fantasy to deny reality; dissociation
CP	0	0[†]	≥1[†]	Negative	Improper substitution of positive for negative emotions; histrionic

Note: HVI, Hypervigilance Index (scored as either positive or negative result). OBS, Obsessive Style Index (scored as either positive or negative result). *denotes that the listed range is based on −1.00 to +1.00 standard deviations from the normative mean including rounding for ease of interpretation. [†]denotes that the listed range is determined by Comprehensive System interpretation guidelines. [††]denotes that the listed range is determined by the percentage base rate in the norm reference sample due to skewness in that variable's frequency distribution. [σ]Denotes that the listed positive result range is based on the deviation principle. -- denotes score type not reported.

[a]When both 3r + (2)/R High and Fr + rF are positive, this indicates that narcissism is a core aspect of personality structure and organization.

[b]When both 3r + (2)/R Low and Fr + rF are positive, this indicates extreme fluctuations in sense of self or splitting object-relations consistent with borderline personality structure and organization.

[c]Requires the use of information from the diagnostic interview to determine the most accurate positive result alternative.

[d]When both Fd and a:p are positive, this indicates that dependency is a core aspect of personality structure and organization.

FORM 9.4

RORSCHACH–CS, AGES 15 TO 17 RESULTS AND INTERPRETATION TABLES

RORSCHACH–CS, Ages 15 to 17

TABLE 1 ■ TEST VALIDITY: SITUATIONAL GUARDEDNESS

Variable	Score	Expected range	Positive result range	Result[a]	Meaning of positive result
R	00	18–29*	≤13[†]	Negative	Excessively nonproductive; defensive

Note: *denotes that the listed range is based on –1.00 to +1.00 standard deviations from the normative mean including rounding for ease of interpretation. [†]denotes that the listed range is determined by Comprehensive System interpretation guidelines.

[a]When R < 14, the entire Rorschach protocol is per se invalid. There is insufficient test data for meaningful scoring and interpretation.

There is no evidence of situational guardedness. In this regard, the clinical and personality variables are deemed valid.

There is remarkable situational guardedness. Therefore, this test is deemed invalid. The remaining scores are neither interpreted nor reported.

TABLE 2 ■ TEST VALIDITY: SYMPTOM EXAGGERATION

Variable	Score	Expected range	Positive result range	Result[a]	Meaning of positive result
X–%[b]	0.00	0.00–0.18*	≥0.70[†]	Negative	Exaggerating or malingering symptoms
XA+%	0.00	0.80–0.95*	≥0.75[††]	Positive	Indications of adequate reality testing
X–%	0.00	0.00–0.18*	≥0.26[†]	Negative	Extremely distorted thinking

Note: *denotes that the listed range is based on –1.00 to +1.00 standard deviations from the normative mean including rounding for ease of interpretation. [†]denotes that the listed range is determined by Comprehensive System interpretation guidelines. [††]denotes that the listed range is determined by the percentage base rate in the norm-reference sample due to skewness in that variable's frequency distribution.

[a]When the first row variable is X–% < 0.70 and hence negative, both remaining variables must yield positive results to indicate an invalid response pattern.

[b]X–% ≥ 0.70 indicates such gross psychological impairment that testing would have been precluded; therefore the entire Rorschach protocol is deemed per se invalid irrespective of the remaining variables.

There is no evidence of exaggeration of symptoms or malingering. In this regard, the clinical and personality variables are deemed valid.

There is remarkable evidence of an intentional exaggeration of symptoms or malingering. Therefore, the clinical and personality variables are deemed invalid. The remaining scores are neither interpreted nor reported.

The paradoxical data of adequate reality testing and extremely distorted thinking is evidence of an intentional exaggeration of symptoms or malingering. Therefore, the clinical and personality variables are deemed invalid. The remaining scores are neither interpreted nor reported.

There exists evidence of a tendency toward magnifying symptoms. Therefore, ensuing Rorschach variables are considered credible when reasonably supportive of other reliable and valid test data, including information gathered during the diagnostic interview.

(Cont.)

FORM 9.4

RORSCHACH–CS, AGES 15 TO 17 RESULTS AND INTERPRETATION TABLES (*Cont.*)

TABLE 3 ■ **CLINICAL VARIABLES: PSYCHOTIC DISORDERS**

Variable	Score	Expected range	Positive result range	Result	Meaning of positive result
WSum6	0	0–18**	≥19[t][σ]	Negative	Ideational or cognitive slippage; disordered thought process
Level 2	0	0[tt]	≥1[tt]	Positive	Manifestly bizarre responses
PTI	0	0–2[tt]	3–5[tt]	Negative	Disturbance in formal thinking and reality testing; psychosis
XA+%	0.00	0.74–1.00**	≤0.73[t][σ]	Negative	Disturbed mediation or reality testing
WDA+%	0.00	0.79–1.00**	≤0.78[t][σ]	Negative	Pervasively disturbed mediation or reality testing
X–%	0.00	0.00–0.25**	≥0.26[t][σ]	Positive	Extremely distorted thinking

Note: PTI, Perceptual Thinking Index. **denotes that the listed range is based on –2.00 to +2.00 standard deviations from the normative mean including rounding for ease of interpretation. [t]denotes that the listed range is determined by Comprehensive System interpretation guidelines. [tt]denotes that the listed range is determined by the percentage base rate in the norm-reference sample due to skewness in that variable's frequency distribution. [σ]denotes that the listed positive result range is based on the deviation principle.

TABLE 4 ■ **CLINICAL VARIABLES: WSUM6 THOUGHT DISORDER SCORES**[a]

Variable	Level 1 score[b]	Level 2 score[c]	Meaning of variable presence
Deviant Verbalization (DV)	0	0	Neologisms; odd redundancies
Incongruous Combination (INCOM)	0	0	Implausible or impossible integration of elements within a single object
Deviant Response (DR)	0	0	Inappropriate or irrelevant phrases; circumstantial (fluid or rambling) responses
Fabulized Combination (FABCOM)	0	0	Implausible or impossible relationship between objects
Inappropriate Logic (ALOG)[d]	--	0	Loose and simplistic reasoning that leads to flawed judgment
Contamination (CONTAM)[e]	--	0	Fusion of impressions into a single object that clearly violates reality

Note: -- denotes score type not available.

[a]This table is reported only upon a positive WSum6 result for purposes of further scrutinizing the examinee's cognitive slippage and disordered thought process.

[b]Modest instances of illogical, fluid, peculiar, or circumstantial thinking.

[c]Severe instances of illogical, fluid, peculiar, or circumstantial thinking.

[d]ALOG scored only as Level 2.

[e]CONTAM scored only as Level 2.

(*Cont.*)

FORM 9.4

RORSCHACH–CS, AGES 15 TO 17 RESULTS AND INTERPRETATION TABLES (*Cont.*)

TABLE 5 ■ CLINICAL VARIABLES: MOOD DISORDERS

Variable	Score	Expected range	Positive result range	Result	Meaning of positive result
DEPI	0	0–4[†]	5–7[†]	Negative	Affective disruption; emotional disarray; depression
S–CON	0	0–7[†]	≥8[†]	Negative	Risk for effecting one's own suicide
MOR	0	0–2[††]	≥3[††]	Negative	Pessimism; low self-worth
FC:CF+C+Cn	0:0	FC×2 > CF+C+Cn[†]	FC×3 > CF+C+Cn[†]	Positive	Emotional constriction
EB 0–Right	0:0.0	3–7:2.5–6.5*	≥3:0.0[†]	Negative	Massive containment or shutdown of emotion
FC:CF+C+Cn	0:0	FC×2 > CF+C+Cn[†]	FC < CF+C+Cn[†]	Negative	Problems in affective modulation; affective instability; mood swings
SumC':WSumC	0:0.0	0–3:2.5–6.5*	≤3:≥7.0[†]	Negative	Emotional unrestraint; mood swings
EB 0–Left	0:0.0	3–7:2.5–6.5*	0:≥4.0[†]	Negative	Emotional flooding; mood swings and impulsiveness

Note: DEPI, Depression Index. S–CON, Suicide Constellation Index. *denotes that the listed range is based on –1.00 to +1.00 standard deviations from the normative mean including rounding for ease of interpretation. [†]denotes that the listed range is determined by Comprehensive System interpretation guidelines. [††]denotes that the listed range is determined by the percentage base rate in the norm-reference sample due to skewness in that variable's frequency distribution.

TABLE 6 ■ CLINICAL VARIABLES: ANXIETY AND STRESS-RELATED DISORDERS

Variable	Score	Expected range	Positive result range	Result	Meaning of positive result
SumC':WSumC	0:0.0	0–3:2.5–6.5*	SumC' > WSumC[†]	Negative	Excessive internalization of emotion; irritability; chronic anxiety
OBS	--	--	--	Negative[†]	Compulsive behaviors; obsessive thoughts, especially perfectionism
HVI	--	--	--	Negative[†]	Excessive chronic alertness and preparedness for danger
CDI	0	0–3[†]	4–5[†]	Negative	Coping deficiencies in dealing with stress
D	±0	0[†]	≤–1[†]	Negative	Current situationally related or acute stress
Adj D	±0	0[†]	≤–1[†]	Negative	Chronic stress overload
EA	00.0	6.0–10.0[†]	≤5.5[†]	Positive	Deficiency in psychological resources for dealing with stress

Note: OBS, Obsessive Style Index (scored as either positive or negative result). HVI, Hypervigilance Index (scored as either positive or negative result). CDI, Coping Deficit Index. *denotes that the listed range is based on –1.00 to +1.00 standard deviations from the normative mean including rounding for ease of interpretation. [†]denotes that the listed range and/or result is determined by Comprehensive System interpretation guidelines. -- denotes score type not reported.

TABLE 7 ■ CLINICAL VARIABLES: ATTENTION-DEFICIT DISORDERS

Variable	Score	Expected range	Positive result range	Result	Meaning of positive result
PSV	0	0–1[†]	≥2[†]	Positive	Impaired ability to shift attention
Zf	0	9–18*	≤8[σ]	Negative	Poor-quality processing
Zd	–0.00	–3.5–+4.5*	≤–3.0[σ]	Negative	Underincorporation; hasty and haphazard scanning activity
L	0.00	0.23–0.99*	≥1.00[†σ]	Negative	Overly narrow focus of attention
DQv	0	0–2[†]	≥3[†]	Negative	Problems maintaining focus of attention
DQ+	0	5–11*	≤4[†σ]	Positive	Impaired ability to analyze and synthesize aspects of experience

Note: PSV, Perseveration. *denotes that the listed range is based on –1.00 to +1.00 standard deviations from the normative mean including rounding for ease of interpretation. [†]denotes that the listed range is determined by Comprehensive System interpretation guidelines. [σ]denotes that the listed positive result range is based on the deviation principle.

(Cont.)

FORM 9.4

RORSCHACH–CS, AGES 15 TO 17 RESULTS AND INTERPRETATION TABLES (*Cont.*)

TABLE 8 ■ PERSONALITY DISORDERS VARIABLES

Variable	Score	Expected range	Positive result range	Result	Meaning of positive result
Fr + rF	0	0[†]	≥1[†]	Positive	Narcissism; inflated sense of self-worth
3r + (2)/R High[a]	0.00	0.37–0.58[†]	≥0.59[†]	Negative	Inflated self-esteem
3r + (2)/R Low[b]	0.00	0.37–0.58[†]	≤0.36[†]	Negative	Low self-esteem
SumV	0	0–1[*]	≥2[σ]	Negative	Preoccupation with negative features of the self
H:(H)+Hd+(Hd)	00:00	2–5:0–6[*]	H < (H)+Hd+(Hd)[†]	Negative	Distorted self-image
Sum T High	0	0–2[††]	≥3[††]	Negative	Either (a) recent object loss or (b) chronic loneliness or emptiness[c]
Blends:Color-Shading	0	0	≥1[†]	Negative	Confused and ambivalent feelings toward self and/or others
S	0	0–3[†]	≥4[†]	Negative	Oppositional; chronic anger toward people and environment
AG	0	0–3[†]	≥4[†]	Negative	Hostile and negative attitudes toward people
HVI	--	--	--	Negative[†]	Irrationally and chronically suspicious of others; paranoid
Sum T Low	0	1–2[†]	0[†]	Negative	Impaired ability to empathize with other people
H:(H)+Hd+(Hd)	0:0	H ≥ (H)+Hd+(Hd)[†]	H < (H)+Hd+(Hd)[†]	Negative	Poor understanding of people
FD	0	1–2[†]	0[†]	Negative	Lack of introspection
Human content	0	4–9[*]	≤3[σ]	Negative	Lack of interest in people
EA	00.0	6.0–10.0[†]	≤5.5[†]	Positive	General deficiency in psychological resources
GHR:PHR	0:0	GHR ≥ PHR[†]	GHR < PHR[†]	Negative	Social ineptness; risk of rejection; probable personality disorder
Isolate/R	0.00	0.11–0.31[*]	≥0.32[†σ]	Negative	Interpersonally isolated
Fd	0	0–1[*]	≥2[σ]	Negative	Dependent traits
a:p[d]	0:0	4–10:2–6[*]	a + 1 < p[†]	Negative	Passivity in interpersonal relations
OBS	--	--	--	Negative[†]	Preoccupation with correctness, perfectionism, and precision
2AB + Art + Ay	0	0–5[*]	≥6[σ]	Negative	Intellectualization; use of ideation to minimize impact of emotions
Ma:Mp	0:0	2–5:1–3[*]	Ma + 1 < Mp[†σ]	Positive	Excessive abuse of fantasy to deny reality; dissociation
CP	0	0[†]	≥1[†]	Negative	Improper substitution of positive for negative emotions; histrionic

Note: HVI, Hypervigilance Index (scored as either positive or negative result). OBS, Obsessive Style Index (scored as either positive or negative result). [*]denotes that the listed range is based on −1.00 to +1.00 standard deviations from the normative mean including rounding for ease of interpretation. [†]denotes that the listed range is determined by Comprehensive System interpretation guidelines. [††]denotes that the listed range is determined by the percentage base rate in the norm reference sample due to skewness in that variable's frequency distribution. [σ]denotes that the listed positive result range is based on the deviation principle. -- denotes score type not reported.

[a]When both 3r + (2)/R High and Fr + rF are positive, this indicates that narcissism is a core aspect of personality structure and organization.

[b]When both 3r + (2)/R Low and Fr + rF are positive, this indicates extreme fluctuations in sense of self or splitting object-relations consistent with borderline personality structure and organization.

[c]Requires the use of information from the diagnostic interview to determine the most accurate positive result alternative.

[d]When both Fd and a:p are positive, this indicates that dependency is a core aspect of personality structure and organization.

FORM 9.5

RORSCHACH–CS, AGES 18 TO 86 RESULTS AND INTERPRETATION TABLES

RORSCHACH–CS, Ages 18 to 86

TABLE 1 ■ TEST VALIDITY: SITUATIONAL GUARDEDNESS

Variable	Score	Expected range	Positive result range	Result[a]	Meaning of positive result
R	00	18–29*	≤13[†]	Negative	Excessively nonproductive; defensive

Note: *denotes that the listed range is based on −1.00 to +1.00 standard deviations from the normative mean including rounding for ease of interpretation. [†]denotes that the listed range is determined by Comprehensive System interpretation guidelines.

[a]When R < 14, the entire Rorschach protocol is per se invalid. There is insufficient test data for meaningful scoring and interpretation.

There is no evidence of situational guardedness. In this regard, the clinical and personality variables are deemed valid.

There is remarkable situational guardedness. Therefore, this test is deemed invalid. The remaining scores are neither interpreted nor reported.

TABLE 2 ■ TEST VALIDITY: SYMPTOM EXAGGERATION

Variable	Score	Expected range	Positive result range	Result[a]	Meaning of positive result
X–%[b]	0.00	0.00–0.18*	≥0.70[†]	Negative	Exaggerating or malingering symptoms
XA+%	0.00	0.80–0.95*	≥0.75[††]	Positive	Indications of adequate reality testing
X–%	0.00	0.00–0.18*	≥0.26[†]	Negative	Extremely distorted thinking

Note: *denotes that the listed range is based on −1.00 to +1.00 standard deviations from the normative mean including rounding for ease of interpretation. [†]denotes that the listed range is determined by Comprehensive System interpretation guidelines. [††]denotes that the listed range is determined by the percentage base rate in the norm-reference sample due to skewness in that variable's frequency distribution.

[a]When the first row variable is X–% < 0.70 and hence negative, both remaining variables must yield positive results to indicate an invalid response pattern.

[b]X–% ≥ 0.70 indicates such gross psychological impairment that testing would have been precluded; therefore the entire Rorschach protocol is deemed per se invalid irrespective of the remaining variables.

There is no evidence of exaggeration of symptoms or malingering. In this regard, the clinical and personality variables are deemed valid.

There is remarkable evidence of an intentional exaggeration of symptoms or malingering. Therefore, the clinical and personality variables are deemed invalid. The remaining scores are neither interpreted nor reported.

The paradoxical data of adequate reality testing and extremely distorted thinking is evidence of an intentional exaggeration of symptoms or malingering. Therefore, the clinical and personality variables are deemed invalid. The remaining scores are neither interpreted nor reported.

There exists evidence of a tendency toward magnifying symptoms. Therefore, ensuing Rorschach variables are considered credible when reasonably supportive of other reliable and valid test data, including information gathered during the diagnostic interview.

(Cont.)

FORM 9.5

RORSCHACH–CS, AGES 18 TO 86 RESULTS AND INTERPRETATION TABLES (*Cont.*)

TABLE 3 ■ CLINICAL VARIABLES: PSYCHOTIC DISORDERS

Variable	Score	Expected range	Positive result range	Result	Meaning of positive result
WSum6	0	0–18**	≥19[tσ]	Negative	Ideational or cognitive slippage; disordered thought process
Level 2	0	0[tt]	≥1[tt]	Positive	Manifestly bizarre responses
PTI	0	0–2[tt]	3–5[tt]	Negative	Disturbance in formal thinking and reality testing; psychosis
XA+%	0.00	0.74–1.00**	≤0.73[tσ]	Negative	Disturbed mediation or reality testing
WDA+%	0.00	0.79–1.00**	≤0.78[tσ]	Negative	Pervasively disturbed mediation or reality testing
X–%	0.00	0.00–0.25**	≥0.26[tσ]	Positive	Extremely distorted thinking

Note: PTI, Perceptual Thinking Index. **denotes that the listed range is based on –2.00 to +2.00 standard deviations from the normative mean including rounding for ease of interpretation. [t]denotes that the listed range is determined by Comprehensive System interpretation guidelines. [tt]denotes that the listed range is determined by the percentage base rate in the norm reference sample due to skewness in that variable's frequency distribution. [σ]denotes that the listed positive result range is based on the deviation principle.

TABLE 4 ■ CLINICAL VARIABLES: WSUM6 THOUGHT DISORDER SCORES[a]

Variable	Level 1 score[b]	Level 2 score[c]	Meaning of variable presence
Deviant Verbalization (DV)	0	0	Neologisms; odd redundancies
Incongruous Combination (INCOM)	0	0	Implausible or impossible integration of elements within a single object
Deviant Response (DR)	0	0	Inappropriate or irrelevant phrases; circumstantial (fluid or rambling) responses
Fabulized Combination (FABCOM)	0	0	Implausible or impossible relationship between objects
Inappropriate Logic (ALOG)[d]	--	0	Loose and simplistic reasoning that leads to flawed judgment
Contamination (CONTAM)[e]	--	0	Fusion of impressions into a single object that clearly violates reality

Note: -- denotes score type not available.

[a]This table is reported only upon a positive WSum6 result for purposes of further scrutinizing the examinee's cognitive slippage and disordered thought process.

[b]Modest instances of illogical, fluid, peculiar, or circumstantial thinking.

[c]Severe instances of illogical, fluid, peculiar, or circumstantial thinking.

[d]ALOG scored only as Level 2.

[e]CONTAM scored only as Level 2.

(*Cont.*)

FORM 9.5

RORSCHACH–CS, AGES 18 TO 86 RESULTS AND INTERPRETATION TABLES (*Cont.*)

TABLE 5 ■ **CLINICAL VARIABLES: MOOD DISORDERS**

Variable	Score	Expected range	Positive result range	Result	Meaning of positive result
DEPI	0	0–4[†]	5–7[†]	Negative	Affective disruption; emotional disarray; depression
S–CON	0	0–7[†]	≥8[†]	Negative	Risk for effecting one's own suicide
MOR	0	0–2[††]	≥3[††]	Negative	Pessimism; low self-worth
FC:CF+C+Cn	0:0	FCx2 > CF+C+Cn[†]	FCx3 > CF+C+Cn[†]	Positive	Emotional constriction
EB 0–Right	0:0.0	3–7:2.5–6.5*	≥3:0.0[†]	Negative	Massive containment or shutdown of emotion
FC:CF+C+Cn	0:0	FCx2 > CF+C+Cn[†]	FC < CF+C+Cn[†]	Negative	Problems in affective modulation; affective instability; mood swings
SumC':WSumC	0:0.0	0–3:2.5–6.5*	≤3:≥7.0[†]	Negative	Emotional unrestraint; mood swings
EB 0–Left	0:0.0	3–7:2.5–6.5*	0:≥4.0[†]	Negative	Emotional flooding; mood swings and impulsiveness

Note: DEPI, Depression Index. S–CON, Suicide Constellation Index. *denotes that the listed range is based on –1.00 to +1.00 standard deviations from the normative mean including rounding for ease of interpretation. [†]denotes that the listed range is determined by Comprehensive System interpretation guidelines. [††]denotes that the listed range is determined by the percentage base rate in the norm reference sample due to skewness in that variable's frequency distribution.

TABLE 6 ■ **CLINICAL VARIABLES: ANXIETY AND STRESS-RELATED DISORDERS**

Variable	Score	Expected range	Positive result range	Result	Meaning of positive result
SumC':WSumC	0:0.0	0–3:2.5–6.5*	SumC' > WSumC[†]	Negative	Excessive internalization of emotion; irritability; chronic anxiety
OBS	--	--	--	Negative[†]	Compulsive behaviors; obsessive thoughts, especially perfectionism
HVI	--	--	--	Negative[†]	Excessive chronic alertness and preparedness for danger
CDI	0	0–3[†]	4–5[†]	Negative	Coping deficiencies in dealing with stress
D	±0	0[†]	≤–1[†]	Negative	Current situationally related or acute stress
Adj D	±0	0[†]	≤–1[†]	Negative	Chronic stress overload
EA	00.0	7.0–11.0[†]	≤6.5[†]	Positive	Deficiency in psychological resources for dealing with stress

Note: OBS, Obsessive Style Index (scored as either positive or negative result). HVI, Hypervigilance Index (scored as either positive or negative result). CDI, Coping Deficit Index. *denotes that the listed range is based on –1.00 to +1.00 standard deviations from the normative mean including rounding for ease of interpretation. [†]denotes that the listed range and/or result is determined by Comprehensive System interpretation guidelines. -- denotes score type not reported.

TABLE 7 ■ **CLINICAL VARIABLES: ATTENTION-DEFICIT DISORDERS**

Variable	Score	Expected range	Positive result range	Result	Meaning of positive result
PSV	0	0–1[†]	≥2[†]	Positive	Impaired ability to shift attention
Zf	0	9–18*	≤8[σ]	Negative	Poor quality processing
Zd	–0.00	–3.5–+4.5*	≤–3.0[σ]	Negative	Underincorporation; hasty and haphazard scanning activity
L	0.00	0.23–0.99*	≥1.00[†σ]	Negative	Overly narrow focus of attention
DQv	0	0–2[†]	≥3[†]	Negative	Problems maintaining focus of attention
DQ+	0	5–11*	≤4[†σ]	Positive	Impaired ability to analyze and synthesize aspects of experience

Note: PSV, Perseveration. *denotes that the listed range is based on –1.00 to +1.00 standard deviations from the normative mean including rounding for ease of interpretation. [†]denotes that the listed range is determined by Comprehensive System interpretation guidelines. [σ]denotes that the listed positive result range is based on the deviation principle.

(Cont.)

FORM 9.5

RORSCHACH–CS, AGES 18 TO 86 RESULTS AND INTERPRETATION TABLES (*Cont.*)

TABLE 8 ■ **PERSONALITY DISORDERS VARIABLES**

Variable	Score	Expected range	Positive result range	Result	Meaning of positive result
Fr + rF	0	0[†]	≥1[†]	Positive	Narcissism; inflated sense of self-worth
3r + (2)/R High[a]	0.00	0.37–0.58[†]	≥0.59[†]	Negative	Inflated self-esteem
3r + (2)/R Low[b]	0.00	0.37–0.58[†]	≤0.36[†]	Negative	Low self-esteem
SumV	0	0–1*	≥2[σ]	Negative	Preoccupation with negative features of the self
H:(H)+Hd+(Hd)	00:00	2–5:0–6*	H < (H)+Hd+(Hd)[†]	Negative	Distorted self-image
Sum T High	0	0–2[††]	≥3[††]	Negative	Either (a) recent object loss or (b) chronic loneliness or emptiness[c]
Blends:Color-Shading	0	0	≥1[†]	Negative	Confused and ambivalent feelings toward self and/or others
S	0	0–3[†]	≥4[†]	Negative	Oppositional; chronic anger toward people and environment
AG	0	0–3[†]	≥4[†]	Negative	Hostile and negative attitudes toward people
HVI	--	--	--	Negative[†]	Irrationally and chronically suspicious of others; paranoid
Sum T Low	0	1–2[†]	0[†]	Negative	Impaired ability to empathize with other people
H:(H)+Hd+(Hd)	0:0	H ≥ (H)+Hd+(Hd)[†]	H < (H)+Hd+(Hd)[†]	Negative	Poor understanding of people
FD	0	1–2[†]	0[†]	Negative	Lack of introspection
Human Content	0	4–9*	≤3[σ]	Negative	Lack of interest in people
EA	00.0	7.0–11.0[†]	≤6.5[†]	Positive	General deficiency in psychological resources
GHR:PHR	0:0	GHR ≥ PHR[†]	GHR < PHR[†]	Negative	Social ineptness; risk of rejection; probable personality disorder
Isolate/R	0.00	0.11–0.31*	≥0.32[†σ]	Negative	Interpersonally isolated
Fd	0	0–1*	≥2[σ]	Negative	Dependent traits
a:p[d]	0:0	4–10:2–6*	a + 1 < p[†]	Negative	Passivity in interpersonal relations
OBS	--	--	--	Negative[†]	Preoccupation with correctness, perfectionism, and precision
2AB + Art + Ay	0	0–5*	≥6[σ]	Negative	Intellectualization; use of ideation to minimize impact of emotions
Ma:Mp	0:0	2–5:1–3*	Ma + 1 < Mp[†σ]	Positive	Excessive abuse of fantasy to deny reality; dissociation
CP	0	0[†]	≥1[†]	Negative	Improper substitution of positive for negative emotions; histrionic

Note: HVI, Hypervigilance Index (scored as either positive or negative result). OBS, Obsessive Style Index (scored as either positive or negative result). *denotes that the listed range is based on –1.00 to +1.00 standard deviations from the normative mean including rounding for ease of interpretation. [†]denotes that the listed range is determined by Comprehensive System interpretation guidelines. [††]denotes that the listed range is determined by the percentage base rate in the norm-reference sample due to skewness in that variable's frequency distribution. [σ]denotes that the listed positive result range is based on the deviation principle. -- denotes score type not reported.

[a]When both 3r + (2)/R High and Fr + rF are positive, this indicates that narcissism is a core aspect of personality structure and organization.

[b]When both 3r + (2)/R Low and Fr + rF are positive, this indicates extreme fluctuations in sense of self or splitting object-relations consistent with borderline personality structure and organization.

[c]Requires the use of information from the diagnostic interview to determine the most accurate positive result alternative.

[d]When both Fd and a:p are positive, this indicates that dependency is a core aspect of personality structure and organization.

FORM 9.6

ROBERTS–2 RESULTS AND INTERPRETATION TABLES

ROBERTS–2

TABLE 1 ■ TEST VALIDITY

Result	Reason for result	Interpretation strategy employed on the Developmental/ Adaptive and Clinical Scales
Valid	Scorable stories were provided for the 1st two cards, and were ensued by a sufficient number of scorable stories to the remaining 14 cards	Standard
Valid— Qualified	Scorable stories were provided for the first two cards, although were ensued by a remarkable number of nonscorable stories (N = ##)	High scores interpreted as valid, whereas low scores interpreted as invalid due to a lack of data
Invalid	One of the first two cards was refused despite prompting; test administration was therefore discontinued according to test guidelines	Test neither scored nor interpreted

TABLE 2 ■ DEVELOPMENTAL/ADAPTIVE: THEME OVERVIEW

Scale	T-score	Result[a]	Measured social–cognitive ability
Popular Pull	00	Low Average High	Ability to understand emotion, behavior, and problem situations of an interpersonal nature
Complete Meaning	00	Extremely high	Ability to understand and effectively resolve a sequence of problematic interpersonal interactions and feelings

Note: T-score mean = 50, standard deviation = 10. Higher *T*-scores indicate greater presence of the measured social–cognitive ability.

[a]Score range and result: (a) 30 to 39, low; (b) 40 to 59, average; (c) 60 to 69 high; and (d) 70 to 80, extremely high.

Theme Overview scales measure general social–cognitive competence or ability.

(Cont.)

FORM 9.6

ROBERTS–2 RESULTS AND INTERPRETATION TABLES (*Cont.*)

TABLE 3 ■ DEVELOPMENTAL/ADAPTIVE: AVAILABLE RESOURCES

Scale	T-score	Result[a]	Measured social–cognitive ability and available resource
Support Self-Feeling	00	Extremely high	Ability to understand the effective use of one's own positive emotions in resolving a problem feeling or situation, including happiness, pride, love, admiration, and pleasure
Support Self-Advocacy	00	High	Ability to understand the effective use of one's own resources in resolving a problem feeling or situation, including insight, problem solving, and task persistence
Support Other-Feeling	00	Average	Ability to understand the effective use of others' emotional responsiveness in resolving a problem feeling or situation (e.g., hugging, caring, mirroring, empathy, and affection)
Support Other-Help	00	Low	Ability to understand the effective use of others' unsolicited instrumental assistance in resolving a problem feeling or situation (e.g., accepting another's offer of help on a task)
Reliance On Other	00	Average	Ability to understand the effective use of proactively seeking assistance from appropriate others within a social support system (e.g., actively asking for help to resolve a problem)

Note: *T*-score mean = 50, standard deviation = 10. Higher *T*-scores indicate greater presence of the measured social–cognitive ability and available resource.

[a]Score range and result: (a) 30 to 39, low; (b) 40 to 59, average; (c) 60 to 69 high; and (d) 70 to 80, extremely high.

Available Resources scales measure the social–cognitive ability to understand the effective use of various intrapersonal and interpersonal resources in order to resolve a problem feeling or situation.

TABLE 4 ■ DEVELOPMENTAL/ADAPTIVE: PROBLEM IDENTIFICATION

Scale	T-score	Result[a]	Measured level of social–cognitive problem identification ability
Recognition	00	Extremely high	Simple detection of a current problem feeling or situation expressed in vague terms, without explanation of preceding factors
Description	00	High	Description of a specific problem with associated feelings, although with poorly defined preceding factors and lack of an internal cognitive process (e.g., wondering about)
Clarification	00	Average	Elaborated description of a problem situation, with identification of an internal cognitive state (e.g., cannot understand), but limited description of preceding factors
Definition	--	Low	Description of a problem and its cause, including reasons for feelings and behavior, some mention of prior circumstances, and elaboration of an internal process
Explanation	--	Average	Complete description of the problem situation, including full identification and elaboration of feelings, with clear reference to, and processing of, preceding causal factors

Note: *T*-score mean = 50, standard deviation = 10. Higher *T*-scores indicate a greater prominence of the measured level of problem identification ability. -- denotes score type not available or computed for the respondent's age.

[a]Score range and result: (a) 30 to 39, low; (b) 40 to 59, average; (c) 60 to 69 high; and (d) 70 to 80, extremely high.

Problem Identification scales measure a continuum of social–cognitive abilities directly related to comprehending interpersonal problems and feelings, ranging in degree of sophistication from vague and simplistic to elaborate and differentiated. Greater degrees of elaboration and differentiation are associated with a greater likelihood of developing more effective resolutions or outcomes.

(*Cont.*)

FORM 9.6

ROBERTS–2 RESULTS AND INTERPRETATION TABLES (*Cont.*)

TABLE 5 ■ **DEVELOPMENTAL/ADAPTIVE: RESOLUTION AND OUTCOME**

Scale	*T*-score	Result[a]	Measured degree of sophistication of social–cognitive problem-solving ability (i.e., resolution); measured degree and type of undesirable result (i.e., outcome)
Simple Closure*	00	Extremely high	Easy ending, including an abrupt and poorly defined outcome, and lack of problem-solving process or mediating steps
Easy Positive Outcome*	00	High	Ending is related to the present situation with a positive outcome; however, there is no description of process or how the solution was achieved
Constructive Resolution (CR)*	00	Average	Elaborated description of a problem situation, with identification of an internal cognitive state (e.g., cannot understand), and limited description of preceding factors
CR of Feelings and Situation*	--	Low	Description of a problem and its cause, including reasons for feelings and behavior, some mention of prior circumstances, and elaboration of an internal process
Elaborated Process With Insight*	--	Extremely high	Complete description of the problem situation, including full identification and elaboration of feelings, with clear reference to, and processing of, preceding causal factors
Unresolved Outcome[†]	00	High	No ending or resolution; problem feelings and situation remain unprocessed and unresolved
Nonadaptive Outcome[†]	00	Average	Problem feelings and situation processed, however, coping strategy does not resolve the problem adequately
Maladaptive Outcome[†]	00	Low	Coping strategy makes the situation worse or more problematic, and often includes acting-out behavior
Unrealistic Outcome[†]	00	Average	Coping strategy is unrealistic and represents fantasy and wishful thinking; outcome is positive although conspicuously beyond a reasonable possibility
Limit Setting[††]	00	Average	Coping and adjustment are dependent upon external disciplinary consequences and control (e.g., scolding, spanking, time out, losing privileges, paying for damage)

Note: *T*-score mean = 50, standard deviation = 10. Higher *T*-scores indicate greater presence of the measured social–cognitive problem resolution ability or type of undesirable outcome. *denotes Resolution scale. [†]denotes Outcome scale. [††]Available Resource scale; higher *T*-scores associated with greater likelihood of undesirable resolution and outcome. -- denotes score type not available or computed for the respondent's age.

[a]Score range and result: (a) 30 to 39, low; (b) 40 to 59, average; (c) 60 to 69 high; and (d) 70 to 80, extremely high.

Resolution scales generally measure a continuum of social–cognitive abilities directly related to resolving interpersonal problems and feelings. Greater degrees of sophistication are associated with the development of more effective outcomes. The related *Outcome* scales measure the degree of presence of various types of undesirable or ineffective outcomes, which are associated with lesser degrees of social–cognitive sophistication.

(Cont.)

FORM 9.6

ROBERTS–2 RESULTS AND INTERPRETATION TABLES (*Cont.*)

TABLE 6 ■ **CLINICAL: EMOTIONAL AND BEHAVIORAL DISORDERS**

Scale	T-score[a]	Measured maladaptive emotions and/or problematic behaviors
Anxiety	00	Anxious state and fear, including worry, guilt, embarrassment, apprehension about environmental demands
Depression	00	Depressive feelings; sadness; unhappiness; sorrow; crying, disappointment; apathy; fatigue; inability to cope with situational factors or problems
Rejection	00	Jealousy; being ostracized; being unloved or disliked; major disruptions in attachment (e.g., abandonment, loss of primary object-relations); separation or distancing
Aggression	00	Angry feelings (e.g., madness, rage, frustration); verbal aggression (e.g., arguing, teasing, belittling); physical aggression (e.g., bullying, destroying property)

Note: T-score mean = 50, standard deviation = 10. Higher *T*-scores indicate greater presence of the measured maladaptive emotion and/or behaviors.

[a]No asterisk = *T*-score (30–59) is within normal limits, absence of a disorder; * = *T*-score (60–69) indicates the presence of a disorder of mild to moderate severity; ** = *T*-score (70–80) indicates the presence of a severe disorder.

Emotional and *Behavioral Disorders* scales generally measure the presence of maladaptive emotions and behaviors as reflected in the Roberts–2 story content. *T*-score elevations falling within the disordered range are interpreted as representing a social–cognitive perceptual set within the respondent making it likely that such disorder is actually present.

TABLE 7 ■ **CLINICAL: SEVERE DISORDERS**

Scale	T-score[a]	Measured severe disturbance in social–cognitive reasoning and ability
Unusual—No Score	00	Rote physical description of the card stimulus scene; indication of severe impairment in reasoning ability; rule out neurocognitive dysfunction
Atypical—Illogical	00	Severe cognitive distortions; looseness of thought; indication of formal thought disorder; rule out psychotic disorder

Note: T-score mean = 50, standard deviation = 10. Higher *T*-scores indicate greater presence of the measured severe disturbance in social–cognitive reasoning and ability.

[a]No asterisk = *T*-score (30–59) is within normal limits, absence of a disorder; * = *T*-score (60–69) indicates the presence of a disorder of mild to moderate severity; ** = *T*-score (70–80) indicates the presence of a severe disorder.

These *Unusual* and *Atypical* scales measure the likely presence of severe neurocognitive and psychological dysfunction, respectively.

THE CONSTRUCT OF ADAPTIVE BEHAVIOR AND ITS MEASUREMENT

Adaptive behavior is defined as "... the performance of daily activities required for personal and social sufficiency" (Sparrow, Cicchetti, & Balla, 2005, p. 6). It consists of the following three domains: (a) conceptual (e.g., language, reading, number concepts), (b) practical (e.g., daily living skills, occupational skills), and (c) social (e.g., interpersonal relationships, responsibility, conforming to rules and laws) (American Association on Mental Retardation [AAMR], 2002).

The aforementioned definition assumes that adaptive behavior: (a) is age related or developmental in nature, (b) is determined by the expectations of other people through the internalization of societal standards, (c) is plastic or modifiable, and (d) represents typical behavior. A significant implication of the latter is that adaptive behavior is more akin to a stylistic personality trait versus a more ingrained ability trait, such as intelligence (see Chapter 4). Stated differently, determining if an individual demonstrates the behavior *when* it is required is paramount, thus rendering subordinate the issue of whether or not the individual per se possesses such ability (Sparrow et al., 2005). Defined and measured in this way, the construct of adaptive behavior involves amenability to change through efficacious intervention, and thus should be interpreted as such barring the coexistence of more enduring and chronic cognitive or neuropsychological impairments or disabilities.

Historically, the construct of adaptive behavior has been conceptually associated with independent or autonomous functioning and social responsibility (Heber, 1961). As such, it has long been an integral part of diagnosing Mental Retardation (American Psychiatric Association, 2000; Grossman, 1983). In more recent years, the measurement of adaptive behavior has become increasingly implemented as evidenced by it being required by state statutes in diagnosing other developmental disabilities (e.g., children classified by the school system as Behavior Disordered or Emotionally Handicapped) (Jacobson & Mulick, 1996; Patrick & Reschly, 1982).

DIAGNOSTIC REASONS FOR INCLUSION WITHIN A TEST BATTERY

From the aforementioned discussion, it follows logically that the most evident reason for measuring adaptive behavior in the field of mental health is to rule out the presence of Mental Retardation (although as discussed subsequent, there are distinct potential problems in obtaining insurance authorization for such testing). It is not uncommon for referring mental health clinicians to request psychological testing in order to determine the suspected presence of some degree of Mental Retardation. This assists them in (a) designing interventions commensurate with their patients' cognitive abilities and behavioral skills and/or (b) referring their patients to more appropriate rudimentary level, comprehensive, and longer term case management services, including potential supplemental referrals to such social agencies as vocational rehabilitation. In particular, the Full Scale IQ score or General Ability Index (GAI) obtained on a Wechsler intelligence test determines the severity level (see Chapter 4), while the adaptive behavior measure confirms the diagnosis (i.e., assuming that onset prior to the age of 18 years has been established) (American Psychiatric Association, 2000, p. 49). Additionally, both of these measures contribute to the Axis V Global Assessment of Functioning (GAF) dimensional rating as employed by the *Diagnostic and Statistical Manual of Mental Disorders, Fourth Edition, Text Revision (DSM-IV-TR)* (American Psychiatric Association, 2000, p. 34).

Although somewhat less frequent, measures of adaptive behavior can assist in the diagnosis of Pervasive Developmental Disorders (PPDs). That is, in addition to an intelligence test score if available, knowing a patient's degree and profile of adaptive behavior skills (a) provides developmental data corroborating a PDD diagnosis, (b) contributes to an informed estimate of prognosis, and (c) facilitates a more effectively designed and targeted treatment plan. Thus, for example, when diagnosing an autistic spectrum disorder, identifying the presence of intact language ability, communication skills, and intellectual functioning indicates a significantly more favorable prognosis, which is vital to identify for any particular case (Ben Itzchak, Lahat, Burgin, & Zachor, 2008).

In cases of suspected Dementia, it may be diagnostically useful to supplement a neuropsychological test battery with a measure of adaptive behavior so as to (a) quantify severity level that will more thoroughly identify needed living and health care accommodations and/or (b) make an accurate differential diagnosis on the Dementia specifier *With* or *Without Behavioral Disturbance* (American Psychiatric Association, 2000, p. 155). Analogously, measuring adaptive behavior in patients with confirmed Cognitive Disorders, such as Dementia, can be invaluable in identifying the associated degree of behavioral limitations and/or providing evidence relevant to progression. Although there are many other potential diagnostic reasons for measuring adaptive behavior, I have found these to be the most commonly encountered in contemporary mental health testing practice.

INSURANCE COVERAGE ISSUES

In outpatient mental health, the most frequent insurance precertification denials concerning testing requests to measure adaptive behavior occur within the context of attempting to rule out Mental Retardation, especially as applied to patients who are of school age. This is ironic considering that this represents a remarkably frequent diagnostic use of adaptive behavior tests (American Psychiatric Association, 2000; Grossman, 1983; Heber, 1961). The typical rationale for denial is the same as that encountered when requesting intelligence and achievement testing to rule out the presence of Learning Disorders (see Chapter 5). That is, medical necessity is routinely determined to be lacking because such testing is considered to be educational in nature and more appropriately conducted by school psychologists.

Therefore, if attempting to obtain insurance authorization to measure adaptive behavior for the specific purpose of ruling out Mental Retardation, the testing psychologist must convincingly address the manner in which being cognizant of a patient's intellectual and adaptive behavior functioning will significantly impact treatment planning and intervention. This serves the following two related goals: (a) it evinces the presence of medical necessity and (b) it demonstrates that such testing will be cost-effective by facilitating more accurately designed interventions, and thus effectuating greater and more rapid treatment gains. In contrast, insurance approval for measuring adaptive behavior is more likely when attempting to rule out a PDD. This is most likely due to the diagnostically pertinent developmental aspect of the adaptive behavior construct as heretofore defined.

Similarly, there is a greater probability of insurance authorization when ordering an adaptive behavior test to either assist in the diagnosis of, or measure the degree of behavioral impairment associated with, a *DSM-IV-TR* Cognitive Disorder, especially Dementia. Medical necessity is more immediately apparent when requesting a neuropsychological test battery for the Cognitive Disorders, particularly when the patient is referred by a medical practitioner (see Chapter 6). Furthermore, measuring the degree of behavioral deterioration is directly relevant to both diagnosis and planning the degree of medical and social intervention indicated. One caveat is applicable here. Requesting complete neuropsychological test batteries can quickly accumulate a substantial number of required testing hours. In general, the more hours requested, the greater likelihood the number of authorized hours will be circumscribed. Therefore, ordering additional hours for measuring adaptive behavior should be done with due diligence and be well substantiated.

THE VINELAND TEST

I have selected the *Vineland Adaptive Behavior Scales, Second Edition (Vineland–II)*, which is normed on individuals 0 years 1 month to 90 years 11 months (Sparrow et al., 2005). Although there are various test formats, including Teacher and Parent/Caregiver Rating Forms analogous to the Conners EC, along with an Expanded Interview Form, the *Survey Interview* affords the most ideal combination of thoroughness, efficiency, and rater reliability due to the interactive nature of administration. Regarding the latter, this form is completed by means of a semistructured interview involving the clinician and a respondent who is sufficiently familiar with the examinee (e.g., family member, case manager). The items are clearly stated with pertinent examples to facilitate the respondent's ratings. Furthermore, the manual consists of an appendix within which more detailed scoring criteria for each item are provided in the event the rater continues to manifest some uncertainty (Sparrow et al., 2005, Appendix E, pp. 301–325).

Typical administration time is estimated to be 20 to 60 minutes (Sparrow et al., 2005), which is consistent with my clinical experience using the Survey Interview. Computer software is available that allows the testing psychologist to directly enter the respondent's ratings given orally during the course of the semistructured interview. Once administration is completed, the computer software immediately computes and reports all available standard scores (Vineland–II ASSIST Scoring and Reporting System for Survey Forms, 2008). This speeds administration time, minimizes scoring errors, and is cost-effective in that the same Survey Interview Form can be used repeatedly by virtue of the fact that the ratings can be made orally rather than in writing.

The Vineland–II principally consists of a three-domain structure, which contributes to an overall Adaptive Behavior Composite. Each domain includes three subdomains and consists of the following: (a) *Communication*—Expressive, Receptive, Written; (b) *Daily Living Skills*—Personal, Domestic, Community; and (c) *Socialization*—Interpersonal Relationships, Play and Leisure Time, Coping Skills. These correspond to the areas of adaptive behavior espoused by the AAMR (2002). More pertinently, these domains and their subdomains are also consistent with the adaptive behavior criteria specified in the *DSM-IV-TR* in defining Mental Retardation, including, "... communication, self-care, home living, social/interpersonal skills, use of community resources, self-direction, functional academic skills, work, leisure, health, and safety" (American Psychiatric Association, 2000, p. 49).

Additionally, the Vineland–II contains a fourth Motor Skills domain intended for ages 1 month through 6 years, which includes both Gross and Fine Motor Skills subdomains. For this youngest age range, all four domains contribute to the overall Adaptive Behavior Composite. However, because the Motor Skills domain is optional for those 7 years and above, it does not contribute to the composite for this older age group.

Of interpretive convenience, the composite and domain standard scores include a mean of 100 and standard deviation of 15, which is the same familiar metric used by the Wechsler Full Scale IQ and Index/IQ Scores (see Chapter 4). The maximum standard scores are 20 to 160, including an impressive range extending 5 standard deviations below and 4 standard deviations above the mean. This is vital as it affords greater levels of diagnostic discrimination, especially at the lower end. Using similar logic, the subdomain-derived scores (termed *v-scale scores*) have a mean of 15 and standard deviation of 3. Its mean is intentionally designed to be higher than the more customary T-score ($M = 10$) because this affords an extended lower range of diagnostic discrimination consisting of $4\frac{2}{3}$ standard deviations (versus 3) from the mean. Again, this is critical when testing lower functioning individuals so as to obviate floor effects. Other useful data I utilize in test reporting and interpretation include confidence intervals and percentile ranks. Note that these statistics are similar to those reported in the results and interpretation tables of the cognitive tests (Chapters 4–6).

Additional available scores that I do not typically report include the optional Maladaptive Behavior Index, stanine scores, and age equivalents. The former is extremely brief and hence does not provide sufficient *DSM-IV-TR* diagnostic discrimination to be of utility; namely, *Externalizing, Internalizing*, and *Other*. Stanines are uncommon and thus esoteric. Age equivalents can be misleading due to their representing unequal units (i.e., ordinal data) (Miller, McIntire, & Lovler, 2011; Sparrow et al., 2005). However, the latter can be occasionally reported within the narrative text of a report so as to emphasize a diagnostic or therapeutic point. This is because age equivalents are better understood by those not versed in psychometrics (Miller et al., 2011).

Results and Interpretation Tables

The Vineland–II Survey Interview Form results and interpretation tables are presented in Form 10.1. Table 1 consists of the domain and composite data, while Tables 2 through 5 include the subdomain data. The design and structure of these tables are by intent analogous to the Wechsler intelligence tables (see Chapter 4) and neuropsychological test tables (see Chapter 6) because they are frequently part of the same test battery. This similarity in tabular design (a) facilitates test interpretation and (b) improves comprehension on the part of readers as they more rapidly accommodate to searching for key data in similar locations.

Domain Score Profile

Table 1 presents the domain and composite scores. It includes the following columns and specific information: (a) scale name, (b) standard score, (c) percentile rank, (d) 90% confidence interval, (e) adaptive level, and (f) summary of skills measured by each scale. The latter is simply a listing of the subdomains contributing to each domain. I inserted them because of their descriptive nature and to facilitate cross-referencing with subdomain Tables 2 through 5 (see below). The Adaptive Behavior Composite information is presented in bold font to highlight the overall results. Additionally, the adaptive behavior construct is defined consistent with that of the test authors and as espoused in this chapter (Sparrow et al., 2005, p. 6; also see above). General table notes define the standard score metric, the directional meaning of lower scores (i.e., in the impaired direction), and clarify table abbreviations and pertinent symbols. The latter includes the "--" symbol denoting that the score was not administered, which is necessary due to the optional Motor Skills domain for ages 7 years and older. Specific table notes clarify which domains contributed to the Adaptive Behavior Composite, contingent on the examinee's age, and provide a citation for the provided definition of adaptive behavior.

As with the cognitive-based tests, the Vineland–II table results are designed to be summarized in the narrative, independently, and in sequence, hence following a deductive logical analysis of the results. Immediately subsequent to the Table 1 notes appears an identification of the respondent or respondents who provided the ratings, after which the narrative summary should be inserted by the testing psychologist.

Subdomain Score Profile

Tables 2 through 5 provide the subdomain data in the same domain sequence as enumerated in Table 1 to further facilitate cross-referencing. As with the intelligence and achievement tests, the testing psychologist can easily use discretion regarding whether or not the report necessitates inclusion of all or selected subdomain scores. The subdomain tables are designed similar to that of Table 1 and include the scale name, *v*-scale score, 90% confidence interval, adaptive level, and particular measured skills. The listed measured skills are adapted from the subdomain content descriptions provided in the manual (Sparrow et al., 2005, Table 1.1, p. 3).

To facilitate the insertion of the correct adaptive level for all of the Vineland–II tables (i.e., Tables 1–5), I have designed one succinct interpretation table that lists the domain/composite score ranges, *v*-scale score ranges, and corresponding level descriptors (Sparrow et al., 2005, Tables 4.1 and C.4, pp. 65 and 253, respectively), with the *low* adaptive level partitioned into *deficit level* descriptors based on Grossman (1983) (cited in Sparrow et al., 2005, p. 253) (see Box 10.1). Because the Vineland–II manual only applies the Grossman (1983) deficit level descriptors to the standard score ranges (Sparrow et al., 2005, p. 253), my adapted Box 10.1 also associates these deficit levels to the *v*-scale score ranges by reference to the same standard score standard deviation ranges. Thus, quick reference to this single adapted table will effectively circumvent a more protracted and time-consuming scrutiny of three separate and more detailed tables provided by the test manual. It also permits application of the deficit levels to the *v*-scale scores, which is not available in the test manual.[1]

Finally, each subdomain table lists the following general table notes: (a) *v*-scale score metric, (b) directional meaning of lower scores as indicative of greater degrees of impairment, and (c) table abbreviations and symbols. To reiterate, the results of each table are designed to be independently summarized in the narrative so as to supplement and clarify the more general domain and composite data.

SUMMARY

This concluding chapter of Section II first defined the construct of adaptive behavior and the manner in which it is measured and applied. This was ensued by a discussion of the most common reasons for which adaptive behavior testing is employed for purposes of psychodiagnosis within the mental health field today. Insurance coverage issues, potential difficulties in obtaining insurance authorization, and strategies to circumvent such difficulties were reviewed. Lastly, the body of the chapter presented the Vineland–II as the single adaptive behavior test that I utilize, including its most advantageous Survey Interview Form, data, and results and interpretation tables.

The final section of the book is devoted to case examples. The purpose is to explicitly demonstrate the manner in which the testing process, forms, report templates, and results and interpretation tables are designed to be employed in actual practice by the testing clinician. Two cases will be presented within each of three major developmental stages, including childhood, adolescence, and adulthood. They are *prototypical* cases selected from my own testing practice with identifying data sufficiently modified for anonymity. By

---

[1] *The Vineland–II computer scoring software automatically applies the corresponding level descriptors to all of the domain and subdomain scores, although it does not report the Grossman (1983) deficit-level descriptors (Vineland–II ASSIST Scoring and Reporting System for Survey Forms, 2008). Therefore, reference to my adapted Box 10.1 will continue to be necessary so to apply the proper deficit-level descriptors to low domain, and particularly, subdomain scores with celerity.*

prototype, I mean cases that (a) are typical in terms of diagnostic issues and referral questions for that developmental age group and (b) yield clear and reliable test results. More atypical cases and complex data patterns are more appropriate for separate volumes on advanced interpretation for these age groups using this system. The book ends with a special chapter on the manner in which this system can be extended to competency to stand trial criminal forensic examinations. A modified competency examination report template is provided with a case example for illustration purposes.

REFERENCES

American Association on Mental Retardation (AAMR). (2002). *Mental retardation definition, classification, and systems of supports* (10th ed.). Washington, DC: Author.

American Psychiatric Association. (2000). *Diagnostic and statistical manual of mental disorders* (4th ed., text rev.). Washington, DC: Author.

Ben Itzchak, E., Lahat, E., Burgin, R., & Zachor, A. D. (2008). Cognitive, behavior, and intervention outcome in young children with autism. *Research in Developmental Disabilities, 29*(5), 447–458.

Grossman, H. J. (Ed.). (1983). *Classification in mental retardation* (rev. ed.). Washington DC: American Association on Mental Deficiency. (Cited in Sparrow, S. S., Cicchetti, D. V., & Balla, D. A. (2005). *Vineland Adaptive Behavior Scales, 2nd edition (Vineland–II): Survey forms manual.* Minneapolis, MN: Pearson, p. 253.).

Heber, R. F. (1961). A manual on terminology and classification in mental retardation (2nd ed.). [Monograph supplement]. *American Journal of Mental Deficiency, 64.*

Jacobson, J. W., & Mulick, J. A. (1996). *Manual of diagnosis and professional practice in mental retardation.* Washington, DC: American Psychological Association.

Miller, L. A., McIntire, S. A., & Lovler, R. L. (2011). *Foundations of psychological testing* (3rd ed.). Thousand Oaks, CA: Sage Publications.

Patrick, J. L., & Reschly, D. J. (1982). Relationship of state educational criteria and demographic variables to school-system prevalence of mental retardation. *American Journal of Mental Deficiency, 86,* 351–360.

Sparrow, S. S., Cicchetti, D. V., & Balla, D. A. (2005). *Vineland Adaptive Behavior Scales, 2nd edition (Vineland–II): Survey forms manual.* Minneapolis, MN: Pearson.

Vineland–II ASSIST Scoring and Reporting System for Survey Forms. [CD-ROM Computer Software]. (2008). San Antonio, TX: Pearson.

Box 10.1 Vineland–II Adaptive Level Guide **277**

BOX 10.1

VINELAND–II ADAPTIVE LEVEL GUIDE

Standard scores	v-Scale scores	Adaptive level
130 to 160	21 to 24	High
115 to 129	18 to 20	Moderately high
86 to 114	13 to 17	Adequate
71 to 85	10 to 12	Moderately low
50–55 to 70	8 to 10	Mild deficit
35–40 to 50–55	5 to 7	Moderate deficit
25 to 35–40	4 to 6	Severe deficit
20 to 25	1 to 3	Profound deficit

Source: Adapted from Sparrow, S. S., Cicchetti, D. V., & Balla, D. A. (2005). *Vineland Adaptive Behavior Scales, 2nd edition (Vineland–II): Survey forms manual*. Minneapolis, MN: Pearson, Tables 4.1 and C.4, pp. 65 and 253. Adapted from Grossman, H. J. (Ed.). (1983). *Classification in mental retardation* (rev. ed.). Washington, DC: American Association on Mental Deficiency, p. 13. (Cited in Sparrow, S. S., Cicchetti, D. V., & Balla, D. A. (2005). *Vineland Adaptive Behavior Scales, 2nd edition (Vineland–II): Survey forms manual*. Minneapolis, MN: Pearson, p. 253.)

FORM 10.1

VINELAND–II, SURVEY INTERVIEW FORM RESULTS AND INTERPRETATION TABLES

VINELAND–II, Survey Interview Form

TABLE 1 ■ DOMAIN SCORE PROFILE

Domain	Standard score	PR	90% CI	Adaptive level	Measured skills
Communication	--	--	[00, 00]	Moderately low	Receptive, expressive, and written communication
Daily Living Skills	--	--	[00, 00]	Mild deficit	Personal, domestic, and community skills
Socialization	--	--	[00, 00]	Moderate deficit	Interpersonal relationships, play and leisure time, and coping skills
Motor Skills	--	--	[00, 00]	Severe deficit	Gross and fine motor skills
Adaptive Behavior Composite[a]	**000**	**0.00**	**[00, 00]**	**Adequate**	**General adaptive behavior: "… the performance of daily activities required for personal and social sufficiency."**[b]

Note: Standard score mean = 100, standard deviation = 15. Lower scores indicate greater adaptive behavior impairment. PR, percentile rank; CI, confidence interval. -- denotes not administered, or score type not available or computed. General adaptive behavior data are in boldface.

[a]The Adaptive Behavior Composite includes: (a) Communication, Daily Living Skills, Socialization, and Motor Skills domains (ages birth–6 years) and (b) Communication, Daily Living Skills, and Socialization domains (ages 7–90 years).

[b]Sparrow, S. S., Cicchetti, D. V., & Balla, D. A. (2005). *Vineland Adaptive Behavior Scales, Second Edition (Vineland–II): Survey forms manual.* Minneapolis, MN: Pearson Assessments, p. 6.

Respondent: Mother.

TABLE 2 ■ COMMUNICATION SUBDOMAIN SCORE PROFILE

Subdomain	*v*-Scale score	90% CI	Adaptive level	Measured skills
Receptive	00	[00, 00]	Adequate	Listening; paying attention; comprehending others' speech
Expressive	--	[00, 00]	Moderately low	Speaking to others; use of words and sentences to gather and provide information
Written	--	[00, 00]	Moderately high	Understanding how letters make words; comprehending what one reads and writes

Note: v-Scale score mean = 15, standard deviation = 3. Lower scores indicate greater impairment. CI, confidence interval. -- denotes not administered, or score type not available or computed.

TABLE 3 ■ DAILY LIVING SKILLS SUBDOMAIN SCORE PROFILE

Subdomain	*v*-Scale score	90% CI	Adaptive level	Measured skills
Personal	00	[00, 00]	Adequate	Eating; dressing; personal hygiene
Domestic	--	[00, 00]	Moderately low	Performing household tasks
Community	--	[00, 00]	Mild deficit	Using time, money, telephone, and computer; job skills

Note: v-Scale score mean = 15, standard deviation = 3. Lower scores indicate greater impairment. CI, confidence interval. -- denotes not administered, or score type not available or computed.

(Cont.)

FORM 10.1

VINELAND–II, SURVEY INTERVIEW FORM RESULTS AND INTERPRETATION TABLES (*Cont.*)

TABLE 4 ■ SOCIALIZATION SUBDOMAIN SCORE PROFILE

Subdomain	v-Scale score	90% CI	Adaptive level	Measured skills
Interpersonal Relationships	00	[00, 00]	Adequate	Interacting with others
Play and Leisure Time	--	[00, 00]	Moderately low	Playing; using leisure time
Coping Skills	--	[00, 00]	Moderate deficit	Demonstrating responsibility and sensitivity to others

Note: v-Scale score mean = 15, standard deviation = 3. Lower scores indicate greater impairment. CI, confidence interval. -- denotes not administered, or score type not available or computed.

TABLE 5 ■ MOTOR SKILLS SUBDOMAIN SCORE PROFILE

Subdomain	v-Scale score	90% CI	Adaptive level	Measured skills
Gross	00	[00, 00]	Severe deficit	Using arms and legs for movement and coordination
Fine	--	[00, 00]	Profound deficit	Using hands and fingers to manipulate objects

Note: v-Scale score mean = 15, standard deviation = 3. Lower scores indicate greater impairment. CI, confidence interval. -- denotes not administered, or score type not available or computed.

Child Cases 11

Chapter 11 begins the final section of this book, which consists of a sequence of chapters devoted to demonstrating the assessment and testing system delineated prior. The cases were culled from my extensive caseload on the basis of their ability to illustrate the most typical issues encountered during the assessment and testing process. Data gathered during the diagnostic interview were modified in a fastidious manner in order to ensure anonymity, although the alterations affect neither test scoring nor interpretation.

Regarding child cases, I searched within an age range extending from 3 to 12 years inclusive. Case 1 concerns diagnostic questions regarding the possible presence of Attention-Deficit/Hyperactivity Disorder (ADHD) comorbid with Communication and Reading Disorders. Such differential diagnostic questions frequently precipitate testing referrals for young individuals who are in the incipient stages of formal schooling, and who are manifesting both academic and behavioral problems. Case 2 presents differential diagnostic issues that are developmental in nature, again frequently encountered in this youngest age range. This latter case was referred subsequent to previously established valid and reliable diagnoses as set out in the *Diagnostic and Statistical Manual of Mental Disorders, Fourth Edition, Text Revision* (*DSM-IV-TR*) (American Psychiatric Association, 2000). It illustrates the manner in which psychological testing can effectively measure and detect developmental disorders that were previously masked by more acute Axis I diagnoses that tend to dominate the symptom picture.

CASE 1: RULE OUT ADHD AND PHONOLOGICAL DISORDER, SCREEN FOR READING DISORDER

Referral for Testing

Zachary was a 7-year-old male referred by his parents. They explicitly asked that Zachary be tested for ADHD and to determine whether or not he was manifesting significant reading problems. In this technological information age, direct requests from parents to test for specific *DSM-IV-TR* diagnoses is becoming increasingly common as they are educating themselves regarding such disorders as ADHD, Autistic Disorder, Asperger's Disorder, and Learning Disorders. Similarly, they are becoming more cognizant of the availability of formal psychological testing and its effectiveness in deriving valid and reliable differential diagnoses.

At the time of the initial referral, Zachary was nearing the completion of his second quarter period of Grade 1 (i.e., early November). This is a common point of referral because the presenting symptoms are usually of sufficient duration and severity so as to be evident within the school progress report, and therefore precipitate the request for formal psychological evaluation and testing. Because this was a parent referral, use of the "Psychological Test Referral Form" (Form 2.1) was not applicable.

Initial Psychological Assessment Report

The complete Initial Psychological Assessment Report is presented in Form 11.1. The ensuing sections highlight essential psychological assessment information gleaned by use of the clinical method.

Clinical Interview Information

The referral information section emphasized prototypic presenting symptoms of ADHD, with the requisite documentation of onset prior to 7 years of age. The possibility of ADHD was also indicated by the following: (a) mental status examination and behavioral observations (e.g., fidgeting, difficulty focusing), (b) positive family psychiatric history of ADHD, and (c) association of the presenting symptoms with academic underachievement (see "Referral Information" and "Education" sections). The last explicitly provided evidence of dysfunction, which is a vital criterion of virtually all *DSM-IV-TR* disorders.

Potential symptoms of a Reading Disorder were listed secondarily because testing for Learning Disorders is routinely considered outside the purview of outpatient mental health testing (see Chapter 5). A likely Phonological Disorder was documented within both the "Mental Status Examination and Behavioral Observation" and the "Developmental" sections, the latter reporting a mild delay in speech production. Note that the "Family" section was deliberately deemphasized and thus succinct because family relationship issues regarding these diagnoses lack etiological relevance. If significant psychosocial stressors were present, they would have been generally noted in the "Referral Information" section and pertinent ensuing sections (e.g., "Family," "Social," "Vocational"). In addition, a need to rule out a stress-related disorder (e.g., Adjustment Disorder With Mixed Anxiety and Depressed Mood) would have been added to the differential diagnostic issues to be resolved by testing.

Maintaining brevity, pertinence, and continuity is essential to establishing medical necessity for testing. As a general precept, information that lacks immediate and direct diagnostic utility should be excluded from the report.

DSM-IV-TR Diagnoses to Be Ruled Out

From the initial assessment information, it was evident that ruling out ADHD was most prominent in this case and would direct the ensuing testing process. However, there were potential Phonological and Reading Disorders that, if present and remained undetected, would likely deleteriously affect this child's development. As a rule, selective and precisely targeted neuropsychological testing can contribute to definitively ruling out both ADHD and Phonological Disorder, while simultaneously screening for a possible Reading Disorder. Therefore, the provisional diagnosis for this child was Disruptive Behavior Disorder Not Otherwise Specified (NOS), with the need to rule out all types of ADHD, Phonological Disorder, and Reading Disorder. The latter was planned to be screened for by adding several neuropsychological language subtests, which, if positive, could provide invaluable empirical data that would serve as an impetus for the school system to initiate its own more comprehensive evaluation for a Reading Disorder.

Test Selection and Requested Number of Hours

Examination of the "Psychological Test Listing Form" (Form 2.7) and germane NEPSY–II full battery results and interpretation tables (Form 6.2) facilitated the selection of tests and subtests. Children with ADHD can be expected to perform poorly on tasks measuring selective and sustained attention, and inhibitory control. Furthermore, deficiencies in the abilities to focus and concentrate should predictably be associated with measured impairments in learning and memory.

Hence, NEPSY–II, Form Ages 5 to 16 (NEPSY–II) (Korkman, Kirk, &Kemp, 2007a, 2007b) subtests that directly measure attention and executive functioning, and memory and learning, were requested so as to directly evaluate neurocognitive abilities relevant to ADHD. These neuropsychological subtests were supplemented by the efficient, fully automated, Conners' Continuous Performance Test, Second Edition, Version 5 (CPT–II) (Conners, 2004) for purposes of establishing intertest reliability and convergent validity of the diagnosis, if present. Finally, the Conners Comprehensive Behavior Rating Scales (Conners CBRS) (Conners, 2008) standardized symptom checklists for parent and teacher were ordered to measure the presence of ADHD symptoms as they may be manifesting in the real world, and to facilitate determination of the ADHD predominant type (i.e., Hyperactive-Impulsive, Inattentive, or Combined). Although the ADHD diagnosis is categorical in nature, these tests are capable of elucidating the severity of these symptoms if *DSM-IV-TR* criteria are met (see Chapter 8 for an explication on integrating categorical and dimensional approaches to psychodiagnosis).

Secondarily, NEPSY–II language subtests were ordered, particularly those that measure abilities of phonetic awareness and analysis, and speech articulation ability. Regarding the former, a child who cannot decode the English sound–symbol system effectively is at significant risk for Reading Disorder (see e.g., Sigelman & Rider, 2012).

In order to remain within the advised 3- to 5-hour test request range, 2 hours were estimated for the NEPSY–II subtests, along with 1 hour each for the CPT–II and Conners CBRS symptom rating scales, totaling four test hours. This was a viable estimate made possible by a devised test battery, which included the following characteristics: (a) computer administration (CPT–II), (b) self-administration (Conners CBRS), and (c) computer-assisted scoring software (CPT–II; Conners CBRS Scoring Software, 2008; NEPSY–II Scoring Assistant & Assessment Planner, 2002). Use of the corresponding results and interpretation tables prepared for these tests and subtests (Forms 6.4, 6.15, and 7.2) also contributed to the feasibility of this time estimate. Note that no time was requested for data integration and report-writing because this is frequently denied unless precertification for testing is not required pursuant to insurance policy. Finally, the selected billing code was neuropsychological testing (96118). This is consistent with the following guidelines: (a) if any test in the battery is neuropsychological in nature, the entire test request should be coded as such and (b) the test request should be coded according to the majority of tests comprising the battery (see Chapter 2).

Test Instructions

Patients and/or family members. The "Patient Test Instruction Form" (Form 2.8) was completed and reviewed with Zachary's parents. Item 5 was inapplicable and thus stricken. They were particularly informed that the total maximum test hours was estimated to be four, including administration, scoring, interpretation, and report-writing. Additional instructions to Zachary's parents were to (a) complete the parent and teacher Conners CBRS forms at first opportunity, and (b) wait for me to obtain insurance approval by submission of the initial report whereupon support staff would contact them to schedule a two-hour appointment. It was explained that test administration would consume between one and two hours, and the estimated additional time would be devoted to scoring, interpretation, and report writing. It is imperative that patients and their family members be continuously reminded of the billable testing hours that are not face-to-face, in contrast to other mental health services, such as psychotherapy, so as to obviate misunderstandings. Advising that symptom rating scales be completed prior to insurance authorization is prudent because (a) they are self-administered and therefore extremely efficient, and (b) doing so expedites the testing process.

Support staff. The "Psychological Test Request and Log Form" (Form 2.9) was completed for purposes of recording testing progress, along with scheduling instructions to support staff once insurance authorization was obtained. The "Initial Psychological Assessment Report" (Form 11.1) was completed by the end of the standard 50 minute hour and thus immediately forwarded to the department that was responsible for obtaining insurance authorization.

Test Administration Process

All 4 requested neuropsychological test hours were approved. Authorization was obtained within 24 hours. Zachary's parents were immediately contacted and the planned two-hour test administration appointment was scheduled. They were reminded to bring the completed Conners CBRS forms to this appointment. Note that test administration was scheduled to be completed within about three weeks of the initial assessment due principally to my heavy testing caseload. A viable goal is to have the entire testing process completed within three to five weeks of the initial assessment. Meeting this criterion reliably ensures that testing results are completed and communicated to patients, family members, and referral sources in a timely fashion.

Zachary's parents submitted the completed Conners CBRS forms at the initiation of the test administration appointment. A cursory review of both forms indicated that they were completed in their entirety without missing data. Test administration began with the NESPY–II. The selected subtests were administered in the order they appeared in the administrative manual and associated record form (Korkman et al., 2007a). This was immediately ensued by CPT–II computer administration and scoring. Total administration time was approximately 90 minutes. This relatively brief administration time effectively minimized fatigue, deleterious effects on motivation, and other sources of systematic error variance that can occur within the test measurement process. It additionally left a manageable 2½ hours for computer scoring, and simultaneous interpretation and report writing.

Final Psychological Evaluation Report

The complete final "Neuropyschological Evaluation Report" is presented in Form 11.2. The ensuing sections highlight essential modifications from the initial report, with a particular focus on the inserted data tables and interpretation process.

Modifications to the Initial Report

The report writing process virtually began with the initial assessment report. The essential alterations included the following: (a) title change to "Neuropsychological Evaluation Report"; (b) insertion of the assessment and test battery in the order presented in the report with parenthetical dates of completion; and (c) deleting the now irrelevant testing request information. As a general rule, any diagnostically pertinent clinical assessment facts gathered subsequent to completion of the initial report should also be inserted. In most cases, this will include additional mental status and behavioral observations noted during the testing process (e.g., low frustration tolerance, irritable mood, impulsivity, fragmented thinking).

While these minor modifications were being made, all clinical assessment information was being reviewed and refreshed within my immediate memory, which is an important prelude to the scoring and interpretation process. The disorders being ruled out were also afforded cursory review prior to test interpretation. In general, the latter guides the decision of which scales to report on the comprehensive symptom checklists, self-report clinical and personality inventories, personality tests, and the adaptive behavior test (Chapters 7–10). In the case of Zachary, there was no need to add clinical assessment facts and thus the initial report review and alterations were done within ten minutes.

Test Scoring and Interpretation Process

The body and focus of the final report is contained within the "Test Results and Interpretation" section.

Initial test order. Direct ability measures of the most pertinent psychological constructs were afforded priority. Therefore, the initial test order included the following: (a) NEPSY–II subtests (ADHD, Language), (b) CPT–II (ADHD), and (c) Conners CBRS (ADHD).

Scoring and interpretation sequence. Considering that ADHD was the prominent disorder being ruled out, NEPSY–II subtests measuring attention, inhibitory control, and memory and learning were analyzed and reported first, ensued by the language subtests.

In Table 1, it was immediately evident that Zachary's attention and executive functioning abilities were consistently below expectations. Thus, one sentence in the narrative to that effect and its consistency with ADHD symptoms sufficed. Similar impairments in memory and learning were noted in Table 2, which was ensued by a second and independent narrative interpretation of consistency with ADHD.

The Language subtest results in Table 3 confirmed the Phonological Disorder diagnosis. They were also screen positive for a Reading Disorder with empirical evidence of remarkable delays in phonetic analysis and awareness. A succinct narrative paragraph interpreting the empirical data in Table 3 communicated these most vital diagnostic results.

The most logical test to report next was the CPT–II because it is performance-based and provided additional data relevant to the ADHD diagnosis. In general, the CPT–II tables (Table 4 to Table 6) are extremely data driven and require a minimum of narrative interpretation. Zachary's performance was valid, indicated an ADHD classification, and yielded multiple clinical elevations among the specific measures. Thus, the positive result option was selected, and a supplemental narrative sentence was added indicating that these results were consistent with those of the NEPSY–II.

Finally, the Conners CBRS data were presented beginning with the validity scales (Table 7). Note that the parent ratings yielded an inconsistent pattern. Hence, the cautionary narrative interpretation was selected (see Chapter 7). Table 8 presented the germane clinical scales. In particular, the two ADHD scales were the only Conners CBRS data that were pertinent to the differential diagnostic issues in Zachary's case and therefore were the only two retained in the final report. It should be noted that it is effective testing practice to quickly examine the other diagnostic scales so as to identify any unexpected, although potentially vital, scale elevations. In Zachary's case, analysis of the other Conners CBRS Clinical scales (Form 7.2) revealed no consistent signs of other potential disorders (e.g., depression or anxiety), and were thus not reported. The standard scores and *DSM* symptom counts were consistently positive for both raters and the presence of ADHD, Combined Type, was confirmed in the narrative following Table 8. This succinct narrative text concluded with a statement indicating the presence of intertest reliability.

Final test order. In Zachary's case, there was no reason to modify the initial order of test scoring, interpretation, and report-writing. Thus was due to the consistency of results obtained.

Final diagnoses and treatment recommendations. The Axis I corroborated diagnoses followed logically and predictably from the sequence of test data and their narrative interpretations. In particular, the comorbid diagnoses of ADHD, Combined Type, and Phonological Disorder were listed in order of prominence. Secondarily, although no less critical to Zachary's ongoing psychological adjustment, appeared the notation of the need to rule out a possible Reading Disorder, with appended neuropsychological test results supporting such recommendation. It is prudent to note such information conveniently and in summary form within the *DSM-IV-TR* multiaxial format. Not to do so risks that the reader will consider such recommendation to be unreliable and simply based upon clinical judgment as opposed to objective empirical data. It also permits the reader to quickly cross-reference this statement with the empirical results reported within the body of the report.

Lastly, the treatment recommendations addressed systematically, although again succinctly, all of the indicated diagnoses. They were presented within a pithy list beginning with the corroborated diagnosis of ADHD, which drove the analysis, and ensued by Phonological Disorder, which represented a secondary diagnosis. The latter two recommendations advised further inquiry regarding whether or not a Reading Disorder was present in Zachary's case, including a need to share these results with the school system.

Billing

All 4 test hours were billed on the date of service corresponding to that of test administration, scoring, interpretation, and report-writing (i.e., November 29, 2011). This was feasible because time during the latter part of the business day was set aside to complete the final report on the same date as test administration. Insurance companies may occasionally deny remuneration for hours that are billed on a date of service that does not involve face-to-face contact. This practice effectively obviates this risk.

Communication of Results

A follow-up feedback appointment with Zachary's parents was competed several weeks later. A hard copy was presented to them and the results were reviewed, with special emphasis on the data tables and consistency of results. Treatment options were discussed along with psychiatric referral. Supportive psychotherapeutic interventions were employed during the feedback process, including assisting the parents to process their feelings and concerns, providing empathy, and most especially psychoeducation. The parents signed a release of information to themselves so as to obtain a copy for their own records. Soon thereafter, they presented the report to school officials who utilized the results to initiate school psychological test for a Learning Disorder. Subsequent school psychological testing showed that he indeed had a Learning Disorder in Reading and proper educational intervention was afforded. He was also provided with speech therapy. Although not all cases yield such salutary results, without efficient and well-targeted mental health neuropsychological testing, such outcome would have been reduced to a very low order of probability.

CASE 2: RULE OUT PERVASIVE DEVELOPMENTAL DISORDER AND MENTAL RETARDATION

Referral for Testing

Joey was a case internally referred by a treating psychiatrist, Candice Jackson, DO. Joey had been in outpatient psychiatric treatment for approximately 7 months, with established working diagnoses of ADHD, Combined Type, comorbid with Posttraumatic Stress Disorder (PTSD), Chronic. Although Dr. Jackson did not complete the "Psychological Test Referral Form" (Form 2.1) due to her being new to the agency, her case file progress notes indicated a lack of satisfactory therapeutic progress due to potentially undiagnosed Pervasive Developmental Disorder (PDD) and some degree of coexisting Mental Retardation (MR).

Joey was initially referred to Dr. Jackson by his foster parents, with concurrence by the state welfare system caseworker for psychiatric evaluation. More particularly, he was declared a *child in need of services* (i.e., CHINS) due to a documented history of maltreatment, and thus he was a ward of the state. Joey's pretest diagnoses were made by Dr. Jackson using the clinical method (i.e., ADHD, PTSD) and supported by a favorable, although partial, response to his prescribed psychotropic medication and social intervention by the welfare system. The precipitants for testing referral were increasingly apparent delays in both social and intellectual functioning. Many clinicians are cognizant of the need for standardized testing when attempting to diagnose psychological disorders with inherent delays in development, including PDD and MR diagnoses. Furthermore, referrals within the foster care system are notorious for providing a paucity of vital developmental information, which exacerbates the imprecision of the clinical method considering its heavy reliance on such assessment information.

Hence, such testing referrals are relatively common within outpatient mental health practice. For the testing psychologist, the challenge is to establish medical necessity so that such testing is approved, in whole or in part, and therefore permitting this child to be more thoroughly diagnosed and provided with effective early intervention.

Initial Psychological Assessment Report

The complete "Initial Psychological Assessment Report" is presented in Form 11.3. Once again, the ensuing sections highlight vital assessment information gathered through use of the clinical method, along with testing issues that were particular to this case.

Clinical Interview Information

In contrast to Case 1, Joey was referred with established working diagnoses for which treatment was previously initiated. There was no evidence that such diagnoses were either inaccurate or being questioned. In fact, the assessment information indicated that the symptoms associated with these incoming disorders were responding favorably to treatment. Therefore, the presenting symptoms began with the key word *pertinent*, and included only those that suggested the presence of PDD and MR, which formed the basis of the referral. Onset was difficult to establish in Joey's case because he was placed with his foster parents just several years prior to this assessment, and such information was not otherwise available. However, it is reasonable to infer that such symptoms significantly predated his foster care placement, especially due to the developmental nature of these symptoms and their apparent chronicity.

The "Mental Status Examination and Behavioral Observations" section included supporting evidence of possible PDD and MR through careful, although targeted, observation. Concerning the former, documenting such things as flat emotional expression and deficits in interpersonal skills (e.g., lack of reciprocity and meaningful communication) was important and provided continuity to the problems listed in the presenting symptoms. Similarly, limitations in verbal and reasoning abilities, and other cognitive skills, such as short- and long-term memory, were important to establish the need for intelligence testing. Note that Joey was on his ADHD medication during the initial assessment. When this occurs, it should be clearly stated when discussing behavioral observations so that apparently *normal* behavior (e.g., activity level) can be accurately interpreted as likely being due to the therapeutic effects of his medication.

The "Developmental" section highlighted observed delays in adaptive behavior and communication immediately upon his foster care placement. Likewise, the "Interpersonal" section indicated an association between deficits in peer relationships and the presenting symptoms, while the "Education" section documented general delays in achievement that would be expected if intellectual deficits were present. Taken together, the referenced sections showed consistent evidence of pervasive delays or impairments in socialization, functional behavior, communication, and cognitive abilities, in addition to associating such symptoms with dysfunction. The latter particularly justified a sufficiently low Axis V Global Assessment of Functioning (GAF) score so as to quantitatively support the need for testing. Note that such vital information can be presented rather succinctly in approximately two pages. Also note that the diagnoses to be ruled out and the tests ordered (see below) followed logically and coherently from the documented information gathered through the clinical method.

DSM-IV-TR Diagnoses to Be Ruled Out

The initial assessment information did not suggest the need to rule out diagnoses in addition to those mentioned by Dr. Jackson. Therefore, Joey's incoming Axis I diagnoses were listed first with *historical diagnosis* parentheticals, and ensued by the special 995 Code (American Psychiatric Association, 2000), which acknowledged the documented history of child maltreatment. The provisional qualifier on Axis I followed, with all major types of PDD enumerated as needing to be ruled out. Axis II diagnosis was deferred with the need to rule out the most probable degrees of MR, including Mild and Moderate. Note the Axis V GAF score of 45, serious symptoms, which was both logically consistent with the tenor of the report and provided further evidence of medical necessity for testing. It is prudent not to underestimate the importance of establishing an accurate, justified, and sufficiently low GAF score in obtaining insurance approval for testing. Of course, an MD referral in this case further buttressed the presence of medical necessity.

Test Selection and Requested Number of Hours

Requesting a viable although limited number of testing hours to rule out PDD and MR is extremely challenging, which is one of the reasons I chose this case to present. The probability that intelligence testing would be approved in this case was low (see Chapter 4). Adaptive behavior testing was more viable due to the need to rule out PDD. Hence, the strategy I adopted was to request 2 hours for the Wechsler Intelligence Scale for Children, Fourth Edition (WISC–IV) (Wechsler, 2003a, 2003b) and to compute the estimated hours for the remaining tests in the battery to total no more than 4 hours. To accomplish this, note that the estimated time for the Conners Comprehensive Behavior Rating Scales (Conners CBRS) (Conners, 2008), Gilliam Asperger's Disorder Scale (GADS) (Gilliam, 2001), and Gilliam Autism Rating Scale, Second Edition (GARS–2) (Gilliam, 2006) was consolidated into 1 hour, leaving a manageable 2 hours for the Vineland Adaptive Behavior Scales, Second Edition (Vineland–II) (Sparrow, Cicchetti, & Balla, 2005) and 1 hour for the NEPSY–II, Form Ages 5 to 16, Social Perception Subtests (NEPSY–II) (Korkman et al., 2007a, 2007b).

Finally, I requested all six test hours to be coded standard psychological testing (i.e., 96101). This followed the rule to code all testing according to the vast majority of tests in the battery (see Chapter 2). The only unequivocal neuropsychological tests included the two NEPSY–II Social Perception Subtests, which represented an almost imperceptible minority. To portray such a battery as neuropsychological testing (i.e., 96118) would, in my opinion, risk denial or more likely modification of approval.

Test Instructions

Patients and/or family members. Having completed the initial report during the waning minutes of the diagnostic interview hour, I quickly entered the pertinent information on the "Patient Test Instruction Form" (Form 2.8). In particular, I recorded the estimated testing hours at six and indicated that testing would be completed in two sessions. The first session would consist of a 2-hour appointment to administer tests to Joey, and a follow-up 2-hour appointment for administration of the Vineland–II to Joey's foster mother. The second hour within the latter appointment would permit me to continue scoring, interpretation, and report-writing, while that data were still well within my memory. In these cases, it is important to mention to patients and/or family members the purpose of that second hour such that they do not mistakenly expect a 2-hour test administration. Joey's foster mother was also instructed to bring the completed rating scales to his first 2-hour appointment so that scoring them could be initiated, if time permitted. Item 5 on the form was stricken as not applicable to Joey's case.

Finally, Joey's foster mother was instructed to have Joey remain on his Concerta medication as prescribed for his test administration appointment because the goal was to measure *maximum performance* on his intelligence test and social perception subtests. If Joey's psychiatrist had referred him for the single purpose of confirming his ADHD diagnosis, which is not uncommon, his foster mother would have instead been instructed to consult with his psychiatrist to determine how long he would need to be off his medication for purposes of his testing appointment. Of course, this is to avoid confounding test performance with treatment effectiveness.

Support staff. Next, I completed the "Psychological Test Request and Log Form" (Form 2.9) indicating the need for two testing appointments, the first to be Joey's 2-hour appointment, the second the planed 2-hour appointment for his foster mother for purposes of Vineland–II administration.

Test Administration Process

Not surprisingly, four of the six requested test hours were approved, the two for intelligence testing being denied. Thus, in this case, the insurance company acknowledged the general attempt to target and minimize the testing hours and was consequently amenable to approving those deemed medically necessary for ruling out PDD. However, I made the decision to include the entire battery as planned for the following reasons: (a) inclusion of the intelligence test was clearly in this child's best interests, (b) 4 hours was still deemed viable for this test battery by employing my system (see Sections I and II), and (c) Joey's psychiatrist was ultimately provided with a thorough and valuable service that would prompt more testing referrals.

Joey attended the first 2-hour appointment as planned. He was properly on his Concerta medication. Additionally, his foster mother returned all of the standardized rating scales, which upon inspection were properly and fully completed.

Joey was first administered the WISC–IV. However, it quickly became apparent that floor effects were likely. Therefore, the Wechsler Preschool and Primary Scale of Intelligence–Third Edition (WPPSI–III) (Wechsler, 2002a, 2002b) was used in its stead. In hindsight, I should have ordered the WPPSI–III in the first place. However, this does serve as an effective illustration of how similarly designed tests can be used interchangeably as testing circumstances arise. Briefly, other examples of circumstances and acceptable test substitutions include the following: (a) change of age (e.g., the child has just turned 6 years of age, thus replacing the Conners Kiddie Continuous Performance Test, Version 5 (K–CPT) (Conners, 2001) with the Conners Continuous Performance Test, Second Edition, Version 5 (CPT–II) (Conners, 2004) and (b) patient's degree of impairment precludes administering an entire battery (e.g., replacing the 3½ to 4 hour Neuropsychological Assessment Battery [NAB] full battery with the 45 minute Neuropsychological Assessment Screening Battery [NASB]) (Stern & White, 2003a, 2003b). Of course, such substitutions and their rationale should always be explicitly noted in the final report (see Form 11.4).

Duration of the WPPSI–III administration was about 1 hour. Administration of the NEPSY–II Social Perception subtests immediately ensued and was completed in approximately 20 minutes. In consequence, Joey did not manifest any observable fatigue effects and his motivation remained more than satisfactory. During the remaining 40 minutes, all administered tests, including the completed symptoms rating scales, were scored and ready for interpretation. This was possible by virtue of all tests, with the single exception of the GADS, being rapidly computer scored (Conners CBRS Scoring Software, 2008; GARS–2 Software Scoring and Reporting System, 2009; NEPSY–II Scoring Assistant & Assessment Planner, 2002; Vineland–II ASSIST Scoring and Reporting System for Survey Forms, 2008; WPPSI–III Scoring Assistant, 2002).

Joey's foster mother attended her 2-hour appointment 2 days later within the same week. Because her oral ratings were entered by me directly into the Vineland–II scoring software (Vineland–II ASSIST Scoring and Reporting System for Survey Forms, 2008), test administration and scoring was done within 40 minutes, thus leaving 80 minutes for simultaneous interpretation and report-writing.

Final Psychological Evaluation Report

Joey's final "Psychological Evaluation Report" is presented in Form 11.4. The sections that follow emphasize important aspects of his final results and diagnoses.

Modifications to the Initial Report

No new relevant information was obtained subsequent to the initial report. Thus, with the exception of necessary cosmetic changes, such as report title and date (see Chapter 3 and Form 3.1), no substantive modifications were needed. Review of the initial report was essentially for proofreading and reviewing the case for purposes of providing context for test interpretation.

Test Scoring and Interpretation Process

The test data and their interpretative sequence are all reported in the "Test Result and Interpretation" section of the final report.

Initial test order. The initial test order reported data most pertinent to the MR diagnosis, followed by those for PDD. Thus, the initial test order was as such: (a) WPPSI–III (MR), (b) Vineland–II (MR/PDD), (c) GARS–2 (PDD), (d) GADS (PDD), (e) NEPSY–II Social Perception Subtests (PDD), and (f) Conners CBRS (PDD).

Scoring and interpretation sequence. The WPPSI–III intelligence test results were reported first (Table 1) as this was deemed integral to the MR diagnosis; that is, such data can immediately rule out such diagnosis or indicate both the likely presence and severity level of MR. However, a testing note immediately preceded the tabular results indicating the substitution of the WPPSI–III for the WISC–IV due to evidence of floor effects, and the intended goal of permitting Joey to demonstrate his maximum intellectual competence. To maintain brevity and focus, only the composite scores were reported. The narrative summary to Table 1 highlighted the extremely low Full Scale IQ score, the statistical (although not abnormal) difference between his Verbal IQ and Performance IQ, the extremely low Processing Speed Quotient being consistent with his ADHD historical diagnosis, and the highest General Language Composite representing a favorable prognostic sign.

Vineland–II results of Table 2 logically followed the IQ test scores so as to immediately determine if MR was confirmed, and as ancillary to the PDD diagnosis. Once again for purposes of brevity, the reported data were limited to the most diagnostically pertinent domain score profile. Two brief interpretative paragraphs followed Table 2, the first confirming the MR diagnosis with the Adaptive Behavior Composite showing a mild deficit, while the second paragraph summarized the largely mild deficit domain score profile as consistent with PDD.

The most logical tests interpreted next were the two PDD Gilliam rating scales. This was because (a) these data flowed consistently from the last interpretive paragraph of the Vineland–II and (b) the test format was similar in that it involved the foster mother's self-report. The GARS–2 was reported first because Autistic Disorder is considered as more inclusive than Asperger's Disorder (American Psychiatric Association, 2000; see also Chapter 7). Tables 3 and 4 immediately and unequivocally showed evidence of Autistic Disorder, with all three requisite symptom clusters manifesting statistically remarkable symptoms. Therefore, the succinct *data are positive for Autistic Disorder* interpretive statement was retained (Form 7.5). Parallel results were obtained for GADS data presented in Tables 5 and 6. However, note that these positive results were specifically interpreted as further support for the more inclusive Autistic Disorder. Note also the consistency of results for PDD beginning with the Vineland–II data.

A direct measure of social perception followed naturally, both regarding test interpretation and report-writing. Hence, the NEPSY–II subtests (Table 7) were reported immediately subsequent. Note the consistency and severity of impairment, both regarding Affect Recognition and the most diagnostic Theory of Mind. Such consistency in the data required little interpretative elaboration and speeds report-writing.

The "Test Results and Interpretation" section ended with the Conners CBRS data. Although these scores may appear redundant and unnecessary, they were instead vital to confirm with confidence the PDD diagnosis. First, they provided validity scales as a check on the foster mother's accuracy in all of her previous self-report data. Second, they provided corroboration from an independent observer; namely, Joey's teacher. Thus, Table 8 data confirmed test validity, while Table 9 results rendered the Autistic Disorder diagnosis virtually incontrovertible. Note that the ADHD scales were not reported, as this diagnosis was not in question. Furthermore, the ratings would have been based upon Joey's behavior while being medicated and would therefore not have assisted in directly confirming such diagnosis.

Final test order. Nothing in the test scoring and interpretation sequence indicated a need to alter the initial test order. This was essentially due to the reliability and integrity of the results. Should the foster parent's Conners CBRS validity scales been suspect within the context of ambiguous PDD data provided by Joey and his teacher, the test order would have been modified by placing the Conners CBRS data earlier in the list so as to most effectively qualify the foster parent's subsequent ratings.

Final diagnoses and treatment recommendations. The final diagnoses followed directly and logically from the results. Autistic Disorder was intentionally listed first on Axis I so as to highlight this new diagnosis. All other Axis I historical diagnoses remained as listed from the initial report. Mild MR was added to Axis II with the Full Scale IQ score and Adaptive Behavior Composite listed below. Supplementing the multiaxial diagnoses with selected and vital test data is of remarkable usefulness to mental health clinicians who frequently find their time limited with unwieldy caseloads, especially psychiatrists who see patient's at 15-minute intervals for medication follow-up appointments. Allowing them to rapidly identify the bottom line, with proximate evidence pertinent to severity, is not only useful but also courteous and respectful of their time. More referrals will likely follow.

The tenor of the treatment recommendations was to communicate the need to construct and implement a more comprehensive treatment intervention plan. This was due to the fact that both developmental disorders were confirmed by the data. This included any palliative medical intervention for PDD, cognitive behavioral therapy to improve social intelligence and interpersonal abilities, child case management services for behavior modification strategies, and communication of the results with Joey's school for continuity of care.

Billing

Test administration, interpretation, and report-writing of the entire planned battery was accomplished using the 4 approved hours. All four hours were billed on the final date of service and completion of the report with a note to that effect, along with a parenthetical note that the WPPSI–III and NEPSY–II were administered 2 days prior. I have not encountered problems billing all testing hours on the final date of face-to-face contact once service has been fully completed. It is a more efficient practice, minimizes errors due to miscounting previously billed hours, and communicates that remuneration will not be requested until the agreed upon and approved service has been completed in its entirety. All four hours were reimbursed without complication.

Communication of Results

The final report was immediately forwarded to Dr. Jackson, who upon follow-up with Joey ordered child case management services, along with group therapy for children diagnosed with PDD, with the focus of improving both social skills and social intelligence. The results were also reviewed with Joey's foster mother who retained a copy for her records. Psychoeducation and treatment implications for Joey's new diagnoses were discussed, along with supportive interventions that facilitated the feedback process. An emphasis was made on the need for more comprehensive intervention. A copy of the report was also released to Child Welfare such that they could pursue additional services for Joey. Finally, Joey's foster mother shared the results with Joey's school, which was efficacious in serving to initiate supplemental school psychological testing.

SUMMARY

This chapter reviewed two typical child cases. The first involved an external parent referral to rule out ADHD and screen for a Learning Disorder. This case illustrated the increasing sophistication of lay people regarding testing for the various *DSM–IV-TR* diagnoses, and the manner in which a well-targeted test battery could effectively resolve such diagnostic issues. Case 2 was more intricate in the sense that significant comorbidity was present upon referral, and testing was requested in order to detect more chronic underlying developmental disorders that were significantly inhibiting progress. The next chapter presents two adolescent testing cases with diagnostic issues more typical of this age group.

REFERENCES

American Psychiatric Association. (2000). *Diagnostic and statistical manual of mental disorders* (4th ed., text rev.). Washington, DC: Author.

Conners, C. K. (2001). *Conners' Kiddie Continuous Performance, Version 5 for Windows (K–CPT): Technical guide and software manual*. North Tonawanda, NY: Multi-Health Systems.

Conners, C. K. (2004). *Conners' Continuous Performance Test II, Version 5 for Windows (CPT–II): Technical guide and software manual*. North Tonawanda, NY: Multi-Health Systems.

Conners, C. K. (2008). *Conners Comprehensive Behavior Rating Scales (Conners CBRS): Manual and interpretive update*. North Tonawanda, NY: Multi-Health Systems.

Conners CBRS Scoring Software [USB Key Computer software]. (2008). North Tonawanda, NY: Multi-Health Systems.

GARS–2 Software Scoring and Reporting System [CD-ROM Computer software]. (2009). Austin, TX: PRO–ED.

Gilliam, J. E. (2001). *Gilliam Asperger's Disorder Scale examiner's manual (GADS)*. Austin, TX: PRO–ED.

Gilliam, J. E. (2006). *Gilliam Autism Rating Scale examiner's manual* (2nd ed.) *(GARS–2)*. Austin, TX: PRO–ED.

Korkman, M., Kirk, U., & Kemp, S. (2007a). *NEPSY–II: Administrative manual*. San Antonio, TX: The Psychological Corporation-Pearson.

Korkman, M., Kirk, U., & Kemp, S. (2007b). *NEPSY–II: Clinical and interpretative manual*. San Antonio, TX: The Psychological Corporation-Pearson.

NEPSY–II Scoring Assistant & Assessment Planner [CD-ROM Computer software]. (2002). San Antonio, TX: PsychCorp Center–I, Pearson.

Sigelman, C. K., & Rider, E. A. (2012). *Life-span human development* (7th ed.). Belmont, CA: Thomson Wadsworth.

Sparrow, S. S., Cicchetti, D. V., & Balla, D. A. (2005). *Vineland Adaptive Behavior Scales, 2nd edition (Vineland–II): Survey forms manual*. Minneapolis, MN: Pearson.

Stern, R. A., & White, T. (2003a). *Neuropsychological Assessment Battery (NAB): Administrative, scoring, and interpretation manual*. Lutz, FL: Psychological Assessment Resources.

Stern, R. A., & White, T. (2003b). *Neuropsychological Assessment Battery (NAB): Psychometric and technical manual*. Lutz, FL: Psychological Assessment Resources.

Vineland–II ASSIST Scoring and Reporting System for Survey Forms [CD-ROM Computer software]. (2008). San Antonio, TX: Pearson.

Wechsler, D. (2002a). *Wechsler Preschool and Primary Scale of Intelligence–Third Edition (WPPSI–III): Administration and scoring manual*. San Antonio, TX: The Psychological Corporation-Pearson.

Wechsler, D. (2002b). *Wechsler Preschool and Primary Scale of Intelligence–Third Edition (WPPSI–III): Technical and interpretive manual*. San Antonio, TX: The Psychological Corporation-Pearson.

Wechsler, D. (2003a). *Wechsler Intelligence Scale for Children–Fourth Edition (WISC–IV): Administration and scoring manual*. San Antonio, TX: The Psychological Corporation-Pearson.

Wechsler, D. (2003b). *Wechsler Intelligence Scale for Children–Fourth Edition (WISC–IV): Technical and interpretive manual*. San Antonio, TX: The Psychological Corporation-Pearson.

WPPSI–III Scoring Assistant [CD-ROM Computer software]. (2002). San Antonio, TX: PsychCorp Center–I, Pearson.

FORM 11.1

CASE 1: INITIAL PSYCHOLOGICAL ASSESSMENT REPORT

COMMUNITY MENTAL HEALTH CENTER

Outpatient Department

INITIAL PSYCHOLOGICAL ASSESSMENT REPORT

Patient Name: Anderson, Zachary
Account Number: 111111
Date: November 7, 2011

Patient Identifying Information: Chronological age is 7 years1 month. Gender is male. DOB: 10/1/2004.

Referral Information: The referral sources are Zachary's mother and father.

The specific *DSM-IV-TR* referral questions include the need to rule out Attention-Deficit/Hyperactivity Disorder (ADHD), and a Reading Disorder.

Presenting symptoms included difficulty concentrating, impairments in immediate and sustained attention, difficulty focusing, distractibility, disorganization, mind-wandering, acting without considering consequences, fidgeting, low frustration tolerance, and difficulty remaining seated. Additional symptoms included difficulties with reading, phonics, and printing letters. School officials estimate that he is at a kindergarten reading level.

Onset was estimated to be at the initiation of formal schooling, approximately 1 year ago when he was age 6 years. These symptoms have been chronic and associated with academic underachievement.

Clinical Psychologist: John M. Spores, PhD, JD, HSPP
                              Psychologist – Indiana #20040638A
                              Attorney at Law – Indiana #21404–64

Mental Status Examination and Behavioral Observations: Affect was broad. Mood was normal. Thought process was logical, sequential, relevant, and coherent. Thought content was reality-based and normal. He did have significant difficulty with speech articulation such that it was occasionally difficult to understand his responses to interview questions. Short-term memory function was moderately impaired as evidenced by his difficulty maintaining sufficient attention and concentration on a sentence completion activity given to him during the interview process. He had similar difficulty remaining focused on a family kinetic drawing activity. Long-term memory function was normal and intact as he was able to provide some key historical dates consistent with his young age. He was oriented to time and person. Activity level was somewhat above normal. He showed evidence of fidgeting and was somewhat impulsive. Social skills were normal, including effective eye contact and reciprocity. Estimated intellectual function based on verbal skills and reasoning abilities is average. Psychotic symptoms were not evident. There was no evidence of suicidal thoughts, intentions, or plans. There was no evidence of self-mutilation or self-harm.

Psychiatric/Medical/Psychological: No previous Behavioral Health Evaluation (i.e., 90801) has been previously done. Psychiatric history is unremarkable. Family psychiatric history is positive for ADHD, Anxiety Disorder, and Bipolar Disorder. Medical functioning is unremarkable. Zachary is not taking any current medications. There is a negative history

(Cont.)

FORM 11.1

CASE 1: INITIAL PSYCHOLOGICAL ASSESSMENT REPORT (*Cont.*)

of prolonged high fevers, severe head injuries, seizure disorder, and major surgeries. Vision is normal. Hearing is normal. Previous neuropsychological testing has not been done.

Developmental: There were no pre-, peri-, or post-natal complications reported. Gestation was full-term. Birth weight was 7 pounds 1 ounce. Birth length was 20 inches. Developmental milestones were reported as falling within the normal range, with the exception of a mild delay in speech production.

Family: Zachary lives with his mother, father, and three older sisters.

Interpersonal: Interpersonal relationships were described as satisfactory in both quality and quantity.

Educational: Zachary is in Grade 1. Academic performance has typically been low average to failing, hence distinctly underachieving, associated with the presenting symptoms. There has been no grade retention. Zachary is receiving general education services.

Vocational: None.

Substance Abuse: Unremarkable.

Legal: Unremarkable.

Initial Assessment Summary: Based upon the initial psychological assessment evidence, pretest working diagnosis and disorders needed to be ruled out are listed below in the ensuing *Pretest DSM-IV-TR Diagnosis* section. Of note, neuropsychological subtests that measure language functioning are being added to the battery in order to screen for a possible Reading Disorder.

The following tests and estimated hours are requested:

1. NEPSY–II, Form Ages 5 – 16, Attention and Executive Functioning, Memory and Learning, and Language Subtests (2 hours)
2. Conners' Continuous Performance Test, Second Edition, Version 5 (CPT–II) (1 hour)
3. Conners Comprehensive Behavior Rating Scales (Conners CBRS), Parent and Teacher Forms (1 hour)

Total requested neuropsychological testing hours is 4 (Billing Code 96118).

Finally, one (1) individual hour (Billing Code 90806) is requested for follow-up test feedback session and treatment planning.

All of the above-enumerated tests have sufficient empirically derived reliability and validity, and are age-appropriate. Furthermore, these tests are the most recently published editions.

Pretest *DSM-IV-TR* Diagnoses:

Axis I:
❏ 312.9 Disruptive Behavior Disorder NOS
Provisional, Rule Out:
❏ 314.01 Attention-Deficit/Hyperactivity Disorder, Combined Type

(*Cont.*)

FORM 11.1

CASE 1: INITIAL PSYCHOLOGICAL ASSESSMENT REPORT (*Cont.*)

❏ 314.01 Attention-Deficit/Hyperactivity Disorder, Predominantly Hyperactive-Impulsive Type
❏ 314.00 Attention-Deficit/Hyperactivity Disorder, Predominantly Inattentive Type
❏ 315.39 Phonological Disorder
❏ 315.00 Reading Disorder

Axis II:
❏ V71.09 No Diagnosis

Axis III:
❏ No major medical problems noted

Axis IV:
❏ Psychosocial Stressors – Educational

Axis V:
❏ Global Assessment of Functioning (GAF): 55 Moderate symptoms

Prognosis: Deferred pending neuropsychological assessment and test results.

John M. Spores, PhD, JD, HSPP
Psychologist – Indiana #20040638A
Attorney at Law – Indiana #21404–64

FORM 11.2

CASE 1: NEUROPSYCHOLOGICAL EVALUATION REPORT

COMMUNITY MENTAL HEALTH CENTER

Outpatient Department

NEUROPSYCHOLOGICAL EVALUATION REPORT

Patient Name: Anderson, Zachary
Account Number: 111111
Date: November 29, 2011

Patient Identifying Information: Chronological age is 7 years 1 month. Gender is male. DOB: 10/1/2004.

Referral Information: The referral sources are Zachary's mother and father.

The specific *DSM-IV-TR* referral questions include the need to rule out Attention-Deficit/Hyperactivity Disorder (ADHD), and a Reading Disorder.

Presenting symptoms included difficulty concentrating, impairments in immediate and sustained attention, difficulty focusing, distractibility, disorganization, mind-wandering, acting without considering consequences, fidgeting, low frustration tolerance, and difficulty remaining seated. Additional symptoms included difficulties with reading, phonics, and printing letters. School officials estimate that he is at a kindergarten reading level.

Onset was estimated to be at the initiation of formal schooling, approximately 1 year ago when he was age 6 years. These symptoms have been chronic and associated with academic underachievement.

Assessment and Test Battery

1. Diagnostic Interview (11/07/2011)
2. Mental Status Examination and Behavioral Observations (11/07/2011)
3. NEPSY–II, Form Ages 5 to 16, Attention and Executive Functioning, Memory and Learning, Language Subtests (11/29/2011)
4. Conners' Continuous Performance Test, Second Edition, Version 5 (CPT–II) (11/29/2011)
5. Conners Comprehensive Behavior Rating Scales (Conners CBRS), Parent and Teacher Forms (11/14/2011; 11/16/2011)

Clinical Psychologist: John M. Spores, PhD, JD, HSPP
                                    Psychologist – Indiana #20040638A
                                    Attorney at Law – Indiana #21404–64

Mental Status Examination and Behavioral Observations: Affect was broad. Mood was normal. Thought process was logical, sequential, relevant, and coherent. Thought content was reality-based and normal. He did have significant difficulty with speech articulation such that it was occasionally difficult to understand his responses to interview questions. Short-term memory function was moderately impaired as evidenced by his difficulty maintaining sufficient attention and concentration on a sentence completion activity given to him during the interview process. He had similar difficulty remaining focused on a family kinetic drawing activity. Long-term memory function was normal and intact as he was able to provide some key historical dates consistent with his young age. He was oriented to time

(Cont.)

FORM 11.2

CASE 1: NEUROPSYCHOLOGICAL EVALUATION REPORT *(Cont.)*

and person. Activity level was somewhat above normal. He showed evidence of fidgeting and was somewhat impulsive. Social skills were normal, including effective eye contact and reciprocity. Estimated intellectual function based on verbal skills and reasoning abilities is average. Psychotic symptoms were not evident. There was no evidence of suicidal thoughts, intentions, or plans. There was no evidence of self-mutilation or self-harm.

Psychiatric/Medical/Psychological: No previous Behavioral Health Evaluation (i.e., 90801) has been previously done. Psychiatric history is unremarkable. Family psychiatric history is positive for ADHD, Anxiety Disorder, and Bipolar Disorder. Medical functioning is unremarkable. Zachary is not taking any current medications. There is a negative history of prolonged high fevers, severe head injuries, seizure disorder, and major surgeries. Vision is normal. Hearing is normal. Previous neuropsychological testing has not been done.

Developmental: There were no pre-, peri-, or post-natal complications reported. Gestation was full-term. Birth weight was 7 pounds 1 ounce. Birth length was 20 inches. Developmental milestones were reported as falling within the normal range, with the exception of a mild delay in speech production.

Family: Zachary lives with his mother, father, and three older sisters.

Interpersonal: Interpersonal relationships were described as satisfactory in both quality and quantity.

Educational: Zachary is in Grade 1. Academic performance has typically been low average to failing, hence distinctly underachieving. There has been no grade retention. Zachary is receiving general education services.

Vocational: None

Substance Abuse: Unremarkable

Legal: Unremarkable

TEST RESULTS AND INTERPRETATION

NEPSY–II, Form Ages 5 to 16, Attention and Executive Functioning, Memory and Learning, Language Subtests

TABLE 1 ■ **ATTENTION AND EXECUTIVE FUNCTIONING**

Score name	Age range	Scaled score	PR	Classification	Measured abilities
Auditory Attention Combined	5–16	4	2	Below expected level	Selective and sustained attention; response speed; inhibitory control
Response Set Combined	5–16	4	2	Below expected level	Selective and sustained attention; inhibitory control; working memory; response speed
Inhibition-Inhibition Combined	5–16	5	5	Below expected level	Inhibitory control
Inhibition-Switching Combined	7–16	3	1	Well below expected level	Inhibitory control; cognitive flexibility

Note: Scaled score mean = 10, standard deviation = 3. Lower scores indicate greater neuropsychological impairment. Age range is for that particular score in years. PR, percentile rank.

Attention is the ability to focus on specific activities and suppress irrelevant stimuli. This includes *inhibition,* which is the ability to (a) resist urges, and (b) stop oneself from engaging in automatic behaviors.

Executive functioning involves the ability to (a) engage in activities necessary for achieving objectives, and (b) regulate one's actions based on environmental feedback.

All Attention and Executive Functioning subtests show evidence of impairment consistent with ADHD symptoms.

(Cont.)

TABLE 2 ■ **MEMORY AND LEARNING**

Score name	Age range	Scaled score	PR	Classification	Measured abilities
List Memory Total	7–12	4	2	Below expected level	Rote memory; supraspan learning skills for verbal material
Narrative Memory Total[a]	5–16	5	5	Below expected level	Verbal expression and comprehension; verbal learning and memory
Word List Interference Recall Total[b]	7–16	6	9	Borderline	Verbal working memory

Note: Scaled score mean = 10, standard deviation = 3. Lower scores indicate greater neuropsychological impairment. Age range is for that particular score in units of years. PR, percentile rank.

[a]Includes immediate and delayed (i.e., 25–35 minutes) memory.

[b]Includes free recall (i.e., no hints given) and cued recall (i.e., hints given).

Memory and *learning* include the ability to acquire, retain, and access new information. Learning includes the ability to acquire new information. Memory involves retaining and retrieving information. *Working memory* involves holding immediate memory traces while executing cognitive tasks.

Two of three Memory and Learning subtests show clear evidence impairment, once again consistent with ADHD symptoms.

TABLE 3 ■ **LANGUAGE**

Score name	Age range	Scaled score	PR	Classification	Measured abilities
Comprehension of Instructions Total	5–16	5	5	Below expected level	Linguistic and syntactic knowledge; ability to follow multistep commands
Oromotor Sequences Total	5–12	--	<2	Well below expected level	Muscle movements of the mouth, jaw, tongue, lips, and cheeks for speech production
Phonological Processing Total	5–16	5	5	Below expected level	Phonological awareness and processing
Repetition of Nonsense Words Total	5–12	3	1	Well below expected level	Phonological analysis and production of words; articulation of novel words
Speeded Naming Combined	5–16	2	0.4	Well below expected level	Automaticity of lexical analysis; processing speed; naming ability
Word Generation Semantic Total	5–16	5	5	Below expected level	Executive control of language production; initiative; ideation

Note: Scaled score mean = 10, standard deviation = 3. Lower scores indicate greater neuropsychological impairment. Age range is for that particular score in years. PR, percentile rank. -- denotes not administered, or score type not available or computed.

Language is the ability to express and understand verbal communication effectively. This consists of (a) receptive speech involving the comprehension and decoding of speech, and (b) expressive speech or language production.

All Language subtests show evidence of impairment. This is consistent with a Phonological Disorder, and also screen positive for a learning disorder in Reading, including remarkable impairment in phonetics.

CPT–II

TABLE 4 ■ **VALIDITY OF ADMINISTRATION**

	Validity measures			
	Timing difficulties	Noncompliance	Excessive omissions	Absence of hits per test block
Result	No	No	No	No
Interpretation	Valid	Valid	Valid	Valid

The CPT–II administration is valid.

(Cont.)

FORM 11.2

CASE 1: NEUROPSYCHOLOGICAL EVALUATION REPORT (*Cont.*)

TABLE 5 ■ CONFIDENCE INDEX ASSESSMENT

Statistical analysis	Profile classification	Confidence index	Interpretation
Discriminant Function	ADHD	62%	The chances are 62 out of 100 that a clinical attention problem exists

TABLE 6 ■ SPECIFIC MEASURES

Measure	T-score*	PR	Guideline	Interpretation of statistically significant result
Omissions %	56	75	Normal	Failure to respond to target letters (i.e., non-Xs).
Commissions %	62*	89	Impulsivity	Responses given to nontargets (i.e., Xs)
Hit RT	36	8	Normal	Atypical speed of correct responses for the entire test
Hit RT SE	61*	88	Inattention	Inconsistency in response speed
Variability of SE	61*	88	Inattention	Excessive within-respondent variability in 18 test segments compared to SE
Detectability (d')	47	40	Normal	Inability to distinguish and detect X and non-X stimuli
Perseverations %	123*	99	Marked impulsivity	RT < 100 milliseconds; that is, slow, random, or anticipatory responses
Hit RT by Block Change	67*	96	Marked inattention	Substantial slowing of reaction time as the test progressed
Hit SE by Block Change	61*	88	Inattention	Substantial loss of consistency as the test progressed
Hit RT by ISI Change	50	51	Normal	Atypical changes in response speed across different ISIs
Hit SE by ISI Change	55	71	Normal	Atypical changes in response consistency across different ISIs

Note: T-score mean = 50, standard deviation = 10. Higher T-scores indicate greater presence of significant result. *denotes that the T-score is statistically significant; specific measure supportive of an ADHD diagnosis. PR, percentile rank; RT, reaction time; SE, standard error; ISI interstimulus-interval.

CPT–II Interpretation: Positive for ADHD, including measured impairments in attention and impulse control. These data are consistent with the NEPSY–II results.

Conners CBRS, Parent and Teacher Forms

TABLE 7 ■ VALIDITY OF RATINGS

Parent ratings				Teacher ratings			
Scale	Raw score	Differentials	Result	Scale	Raw score	Differentials	Result
Positive Impression[a]	0	--	Valid	Positive Impression[a]	0	--	Valid
Negative Impression[b]	3	--	Valid	Negative Impression[b]	1	--	Valid
Inconsistency Index[c]	7	3	Invalid	Inconsistency Index[c]	4	2	Valid

Note: Lower raw scores indicate that the ratings are increasingly valid. -- denotes not administered, or score type not available or computed.

[a]Invalid interpretation indicates that the rater produced an overly positive description of the youth's behavior.

[b]Invalid indicates that the rater produced an overly negative description of the youth's behavior.

[c]Invalid indicates either variable attention or comprehension difficulties on the part of the rater.

The parent ratings manifested some invalid response tendencies. The teacher ratings were valid. Therefore, the parent ratings were considered valid under the following conditions: (a) when consistent with the valid teacher ratings and (b) when reasonably supportive of other test data deemed reliable and valid, including data gathered from the diagnostic interview.

(Cont.)

FORM 11.2

CASE 1: NEUROPSYCHOLOGICAL EVALUATION REPORT (*Cont.*)

TABLE 8 ■ CLINICAL SCALE

Scale	Parent ratings		Teacher ratings		Diagnostic result[a]	Measured symptoms
	T-score*	*DSM* symptom counts	*T*-score*	*DSM* symptom counts		
ADHD Inattentive	83*	Met	80*	Met	Positive	Impaired immediate and sustained attention; forgetful; distractible; disorganized
ADHD Hyperactive-Impulsive	90*	Met	83*	Met	Positive	Overactive; fidgets; restless; loud; acts without thinking of consequences

Note: *T*-score mean = 50, standard deviation = 10. Higher *T*-scores indicate greater presence of symptoms. *denotes that the *T*-score is statistically significant; measured symptoms on that clinical scale are sufficiently severe to indicate a clinical diagnosis. Symptom counts "Met" when at or above the *DSM-IV-TR* cut-off score; symptom counts "Not met" when below the *DSM-IV-TR* cut-off score.

[a]Atypical symptoms indicate the presence of clinical symptoms due to an alternate *DSM-IV-TR* diagnosis.

The Conners CBRS results are positive for ADHD, Combined Type. These results are consistent with both the CPT–II and NEPSY–II data.

Posttest *DSM-IV-TR* Diagnoses

Axis I:

❏ 314.01 Attention-Deficit/Hyperactivity Disorder, Combined Type
❏ 315.39 Phonological Disorder

Rule out: Reading Disorder; neuropsychological screening results positive for possible Reading Disorder, including measured impairment in phonetics.

Axis II:

❏ V71.09 No Diagnosis

Axis III:

❏ No major medical problems noted

Axis IV:

❏ Psychosocial Stressors – Educational

Axis V:

❏ Global Assessment of Functioning (GAF): 55 Moderate symptoms

Prognosis: Good with intervention and remediation

TREATMENT RECOMMENDATIONS

1. Psychiatric biological intervention for ADHD, Combined Type.
2. Supplemental testing for Learning Disorder in Reading.
3. Speech therapy.
4. It is advised that these assessment and test results be shared with Zachary's school for coordination of mental health treatment intervention with academic assessment and intervention, for continuity of care, and to assist in determining eligibility for special services.

John M. Spores, PhD, JD, HSPP
Psychologist – Indiana #20040638A
Attorney at Law – Indiana #21404–64

FORM 11.3

CASE 2: INITIAL PSYCHOLOGICAL ASSESSMENT REPORT

COMMUNITY MENTAL HEALTH CENTER

Outpatient Department

INITIAL PSYCHOLOGICAL ASSESSMENT REPORT

Patient Name: Smith, Joey
Account Number: 222222
Date: February 24, 2011

Patient Identifying Information: Chronological age is 6 years 5 months. Gender is male. DOB: 09/21/2004.

Referral Information: The referral source is Joey's outpatient psychiatrist Candice Jackson, D.O. The stated *DSM-IV-TR* diagnoses needed to be ruled out include a Pervasive Developmental Disorder (PDD) and Mental Retardation (MR). Her working diagnoses for Joey are Attention-Deficit/Hyperactivity Disorder, Combined Type (ADHD–C), comorbid with Posttraumatic Stress Disorder, Chronic (PTSD), the latter associated with a reported history of child maltreatment. These working diagnoses are not being questioned.

Pertinent presenting symptoms included chronic deficits in the ability to bond emotionally with others, lack of interest in forming relationships with others, ineffectual interpersonal skills, lack of eye contact and reciprocity, lack of empathy, isolative play, social isolation, repetitive and stereotyped behavior patterns, and impaired ability to communicate effectively with others. Additional symptoms included difficulties with mental tasks, including limitations in both verbal and reasoning abilities relative to his age.

Onset was estimated to be at least July 2009 when he was placed with his foster parents, although it is likely that symptom onset was much earlier prior to his placement.

Clinical Psychologist: John M. Spores, PhD, JD, HSPP
                             Psychologist – Indiana #20040638A
                             Attorney at Law – Indiana #21404–64

Mental Status Examination and Behavioral Observations: Affect was flat. Mood was mildly anxious. Thought process was somewhat alogical, although relevant and coherent. Thought content was reality-based and normal. Short-term memory functioning was mildly impaired as evidenced by his difficulty focusing on my interview questions and similar difficulty completing his kinetic family drawing activity. Long-term memory functioning was also mildly impaired as he manifested difficulty recalling some major family events that occurred during the past month and year. Sensorium was clear. Activity level was normal, although it should be noted that he was on his ADHD medication. Social skills were awkward and ineffectual as he had remarkable difficulty with turn-taking skills, reciprocity, coordinated eye contact, and modulation of voice tone. He also had difficulty maintaining a meaningful conversation. Estimated intellectual function based on limited verbal skills and reasoning abilities is borderline to extremely low. Psychotic symptoms were not evident. There was no evidence of suicidal thoughts, intentions, or plans. There was evidence of a history of self-harm that specifically included biting himself and self-inflicted head banging, although no such episodes occured within the past year.

(Cont.)

FORM 11.3

CASE 2: INITIAL PSYCHOLOGICAL ASSESSMENT REPORT *(Cont.)*

Psychiatric/Medical/Psychological: The referring clinician completed a Behavioral Health Evaluation (i.e., 90801) in or about July 2010. Psychiatric history includes outpatient treatment by Dr. Jackson. Family psychiatric history is positive for Bipolar Disorder. Medical functioning is unremarkable. Current medication includes Concerta. There is a positive history of severe head injuries from reported physical abuse. There is a negative history of seizure disorder and major surgeries. Vision is normal. Hearing is normal. Previous psychological testing has not been done.

Developmental: Prenatal development is unknown. Upon his placement with his foster parents July 2009, he manifested general delays in adaptive behavior and communication. He has made some progress since then.

Family: Joey lives with his foster parents and two other children.

Interpersonal: Social skills were described as ineffectual with deficits in friendships of adequate intimacy, associated with the presenting symptoms.

Educational: Joey is in Grade K. Academic performance has thus far been unsatisfactory and significantly below expected level. Joey is currently in general education.

Vocational: None.

Substance Abuse: Unremarkable.

Legal: Unremarkable.

Initial Assessment Summary: Based upon the initial psychological assessment evidence, pretest working diagnosis and disorders needed to be ruled out are listed below in the ensuing *Pretest DSM-IV-TR Diagnosis* section.

The following tests and estimated hours are requested:

1. Wechsler Intelligence Scale for Children, Fourth Edition (WISC–IV) (2 hours)
2. Vineland Adaptive Behavior Scales, Second Edition (Vineland–II) (2 hours)
3. NEPSY–II, Form Ages 5 to 16, Social Perception Subtests (1 hour)
4. Conners Comprehensive Behavior Rating Scales (Conners CBRS), Parent and Teacher Forms (1 hour)
5. Gilliam Asperger's Disorder Scale (GADS) (time included in the Conners CBRS symptom rating scales)
6. Gilliam Autism Rating Scale, Second Edition (GARS–2) (time included in the Conners CBRS symptom rating scales)

Total requested psychological testing hours is 6 (Billing Code 96101).

Finally, one (1) individual hour (Billing Code 90806) is requested for follow-up test feedback session and treatment planning.

All of the above-enumerated tests have sufficient empirically derived reliability and validity, and are age-appropriate. Furthermore, these tests are the most recently published editions.

(Cont.)

FORM 11.3

CASE 2: INITIAL PSYCHOLOGICAL ASSESSMENT REPORT (*Cont.*)

Pretest *DSM-IV-TR* Diagnoses

Axis I:

❏ 314.01 Attention-Deficit/Hyperactivity Disorder, Combined Type (historical diagnosis)

❏ 309.81 Posttraumatic Stress Disorder, Chronic (historical diagnosis)

❏ 995.54 Physical Abuse of Child (historical diagnosis)

Provisional, Rule Out:

❏ 299.00 Autistic Disorder

❏ 299.80 Asperger's Disorder

❏ 299.80 Pervasive Developmental Disorder NOS (Atypical Autistic Disorder)

Axis II:

❏ 799.9 Diagnosis Deferred

Rule Out:

❏ 317 Mild Mental Retardation

❏ 318.0 Moderate Mental Retardation

Axis III:

❏ No Contributory or Pertinent Medical Disorders Noted

Axis IV:

❏ Psychosocial Stressors – Social, Educational

Axis V:

❏ Global Assessment of Functioning (GAF): 45 Serious symptoms

Prognosis: Deferred pending psychological assessment and test results

John M. Spores, PhD, JD, HSPP
Psychologist – Indiana #20040638A
Attorney at Law – Indiana #21404–64

FORM 11.4

CASE 2: PSYCHOLOGICAL EVALUATION REPORT

COMMUNITY MENTAL HEALTH CENTER

Outpatient Department

PSYCHOLOGICAL EVALUATION REPORT

Patient Name: Smith, Joey
Account Number: 222222
Date: March 19, 2011

Patient Identifying Information: Chronological age is 6 years 5 months. Gender is male. DOB: 09/21/2004.

Referral Information: The referral source is Joey's outpatient psychiatrist Candice Jackson, D.O. The stated *DSM-IV-TR* diagnoses needed to be ruled out include a Pervasive Developmental Disorder (PDD) and Mental Retardation (MR). Her working diagnoses for Joey are Attention-Deficit/Hyperactivity Disorder, Combined Type (ADHD–C), comorbid with Posttraumatic Stress Disorder, Chronic (PTSD), the latter associated with a reported history of child maltreatment. These working diagnoses are not being questioned.

Pertinent presenting symptoms included chronic deficits in the ability to bond emotionally with others, lack of interest in forming relationships with others, ineffectual interpersonal skills, lack of eye contact and reciprocity, lack of empathy, isolative play, social isolation, repetitive and stereotyped behavior patterns, and impaired ability to communicate effectively with others. Additional symptoms included difficulties with mental tasks, including limitations in both verbal and reasoning abilities relative to his age.

Onset was estimated to be at least July 2009 when he was placed with his foster parents, although it is likely that symptom onset was much earlier prior to his placement.

Assessment and Test Battery

1. Diagnostic Interview (02/24/2011)
2. Mental Status Examination and Behavioral Observations (02/24/2011)
3. Wechsler Preschool and Primary Scale of Intelligence, Third Edition, Form Ages 4:0 to 7:3 (WPPSI–III, Form Ages 4:0 to 7:3) (03/19/2011)
4. Vineland Adaptive Behavior Scales, Second Edition (Vineland–II) (03/21/2011)
5. Gilliam Autism Rating Scale, Second Edition (GARS–2) (02/24/2011)
6. Gilliam Asperger's Disorder Scale (GADS) (02/24/2011)
7. NEPSY–II, Form Ages 5 to 16, Social Perception Subtests (03/19/2011)
8. Conners Comprehensive Behavior Rating Scales (Conners CBRS), Parent and Teacher Forms (02/24/2011; 03/01/2011)

Clinical Psychologist: John M. Spores, PhD, JD, HSPP
Psychologist – Indiana #20040638A
Attorney at Law – Indiana #21404–64

Mental Status Examination and Behavioral Observations: Affect was flat. Mood was mildly anxious. Thought process was somewhat alogical, although relevant and coherent. Thought content was reality-based and normal. Short-term memory functioning was

(Cont.)

FORM 11.4

CASE 2: PSYCHOLOGICAL EVALUATION REPORT (*Cont.*)

mildly impaired as evidenced by his difficulty focusing on my interview questions and similar difficulty completing his kinetic family drawing activity. Long-term memory functioning was also mildly impaired as he manifested difficulty recalling some major family events that occurred during the past month and year. Sensorium was clear. Activity level was normal, although it should be noted that he was on his ADHD medication. Social skills were awkward and ineffectual as he had remarkable difficulty with turn-taking skills, reciprocity, coordinated eye contact, and modulation of voice tone. He also had difficulty maintaining a meaningful conversation. Estimated intellectual function based on limited verbal skills and reasoning abilities is borderline to extremely low. Psychotic symptoms were not evident. There was no evidence of suicidal thoughts, intentions, or plans. There was evidence of a history of self-harm that specifically included biting himself and self-inflicted head banging, although no such episodes occurring within the past year.

Psychiatric/Medical/Psychological: The referring clinician completed a Behavioral Health Evaluation (i.e., 90801) in or about July 2010. Psychiatric history includes outpatient treatment by Dr. Jackson. Family psychiatric history is positive for Bipolar Disorder. Medical functioning is unremarkable. Current medication includes Concerta. There is a positive history of severe head injuries from reported physical abuse. There is a negative history of seizure disorder and major surgeries. Vision is normal. Hearing is normal. Previous psychological testing has not been done.

Developmental: Prenatal development is unknown. Upon his placement with his foster parents July 2009, he manifested general delays in adaptive behavior and communication. He has made some progress since then.

Family: Joey lives with his foster parents and two other children.

Interpersonal: Social skills were described as ineffectual with deficits in friendships of adequate intimacy, associated with the presenting symptoms.

Educational: Joey is in Grade K. Academic performance has thus far been unsatisfactory and significantly below expected level. Joey is currently in general education.

Vocational: None.

Substance Abuse: Unremarkable.

Legal: Unremarkable.

TEST RESULTS AND INTERPRETATION

Testing note: The Wechsler Intelligence Scale for Children, Fourth Edition (WISC–IV) was initially ordered, although replaced with the WPPSI–III due to evidence of floor effects when the former administration was initiated. Thus, the WPPSI–III being based upon a younger norm reference sample allowed Joey to demonstrate his cognitive abilities to a greater extent.

(*Cont.*)

FORM 11.4

CASE 2: PSYCHOLOGICAL EVALUATION REPORT (*Cont.*)

WPPSI–III, Form Ages 4:0 to 7:3

TABLE 1 ■ COMPOSITE SCORE SUMMARY

Scale	Composite score	PR	90% CI	Qualitative description	Measured abilities
Verbal Intelligence Quotient (VIQ)	72	3	[68, 79]	Borderline	Verbal reasoning, comprehension, and conceptualization
Performance Intelligence Quotient (PIQ)	61	0.5	[58, 69]	Extremely low	Visual-spatial (non-verbal) reasoning, organization, and conceptualization
Processing Speed Quotient (PSQ)	68	2	[64, 79]	Extremely low	Mental processing speed; graphomotor processing; attention and concentration
Full Scale Intelligence Quotient (FSIQ)[a]	**64**	**1**	**[61, 69]**	**Extremely low**	**General intelligence: ability to learn from experience, acquire knowledge, and use resources effectively in adapting or solving problems[b]**
General Language Composite (GLC)[c]	83	13	[78, 91]	Low Average	Receptive and expressive language; word retrieval from memory; association of visual stimuli with language

Note: Composite score mean = 100, standard deviation = 15. Lower scores indicate greater intellectual impairment. PR, percentile rank; CI, confidence interval. General intellectual ability data are in boldface.

[a]The Full Scale Intelligence Quotient includes the Verbal and Performance Intelligence Quotient composite scores, and the Processing Speed Coding subtest score.

[b]Ciccarelli, S. K., & White, J. N. (2012). *Psychology* (3rd ed.). Upper Saddle River, NJ: Pearson Education; Wechsler, D. (1975). *The collected papers of David Wechsler.* New York, NY: Academic Press.

[c]Optional composite not included in the Full Scale Intelligence Quotient.

Overall intellectual functioning is measured to be extremely low. Joey's verbal intelligence is statistically higher than his performance or nonverbal abilities (p < .05). Mental processing speed is extremely low consistent with his ADHD diagnosis. His strongest abilities are demonstrated on the optional GLC, which falls within the low average range, hence within normal limits.

(*Cont.*)

FORM 11.4

CASE 2: PSYCHOLOGICAL EVALUATION REPORT (*Cont.*)

Vineland–II, Survey Interview Form

TABLE 2 ■ DOMAIN SCORE PROFILE

Domain	Standard score	PR	90% CI	Adaptive level	Measured skills
Communication	87	19	[80, 94]	Adequate	Receptive, expressive, and written communication
Daily Living Skills	60	<1	[53, 67]	Mild deficit	Personal, domestic, and community skills.
Socialization	65	1	[59, 71]	Mild deficit	Interpersonal relationships, play and leisure time, and coping skills.
Motor Skills	67	1	[58, 76]	Mild deficit	Gross and fine motor skills.
Adaptive Behavior Composite[a]	**66**	**1**	**[62, 70]**	**Mild deficit**	**General adaptive behavior: "… the performance of daily activities required for personal and social sufficiency."**[b]

Note: Standard score mean = 100, standard deviation = 15. Lower scores indicate greater adaptive behavior impairment. PR, percentile rank; CI, confidence interval. General adaptive behavior data are in boldface.

[a]The Adaptive Behavior Composite includes: (a) Communication, Daily Living Skills, Socialization, and Motor Skills domains (ages birth–6 years) and (b) Communication, Daily Living Skills, and Socialization domains (ages 7–90 years).

[b]Sparrow, S. S., Cicchetti, D. V., & Balla, D. A. (2005). *Vineland Adaptive Behavior Scales, Second Edition (Vineland–II): Survey forms manual.* Minneapolis, MN: Pearson Assessments, p. 6.

Respondent: Foster mother.

The Adaptive Behavior Composite is measured to be within the mild deficit range of functioning. Integrating this datum with empirical evidence of extremely low general intellectual functioning and onset prior to the age of 18 years, the criteria for Mild Mental Retardation are met.

All domains showed similar deficits, with the exception of Communication. These results are also consistent with a PDD, especially regarding the mild deficit in Socialization.

GARS–2

TABLE 3 ■ AUTISTIC DISORDER INDEX

Autistic Disorder index	95% CI[a]	PR	Probability of Autistic Disorder[b]
119	[111, 127]	90	High

Note: Autistic Disorder index mean = 100, standard deviation = 15. Higher scores indicate Autistic Disorder is more likely. CI, confidence interval; PR, percentile rank.

[a]CI is based upon a standard error of measurement = 4.

[b]*Low* is an index of 69 and below, *Borderline* is an index of 70 to 84, and *High* is an index of 85 and above.

(*Cont.*)

FORM 11.4

CASE 2: PSYCHOLOGICAL EVALUATION REPORT (*Cont.*)

TABLE 4 ■ SUBSCALES

Subscale	SS	95% CI[a]	PR	Symptom severity[b]	Measured symptoms
Stereotyped Behaviors	7	[5, 9]	16	Mild	Restricted interests of abnormal intensity or focus; inflexible and specific nonfunctional routines or rituals; repetitive motor mannerisms; preoccupation with object parts
Communication	17	[15, 19]	99	Severe	Impaired spoken language; inability to have conversations; stereotyped, repetitive, idiosyncratic language; lack of make-believe or imitative play
Social Interaction	15	[13, 17]	95	Severe	Impaired nonverbal behaviors (e.g., gestures to regulate social interaction); lack of peer relationships; lack of spontaneous seeking of mutual shared enjoyment, interests, achievements; lack of reciprocity

Note: Standard score mean = 10, standard deviation = 3. Higher scores indicate increasing symptom severity. SS, standard score; CI, confidence interval; PR, percentile rank.

[a]CI is based upon a standard error of measurement = 1.

[b]*Absent* is a SS of 1 to 4, *Mild* is a SS of 5 to 7, *Moderate* is a SS of 8 to 12, and *Severe* is a SS of 13 and above.

Respondent: Foster mother.

GARS–2 data are positive for Autistic Disorder.

GADS

TABLE 5 ■ ASPERGER'S DISORDER QUOTIENT

Asperger's Disorder quotient	95% CI[a]	PR	Probability of Asperger's Disorder[b]
118	[110, 126]	89	High

Note: Asperger's Disorder quotient mean = 100, standard deviation = 15. Higher scores indicate Asperger's Disorder is more likely. CI, confidence interval; PR, percentile rank.

[a]CI is based upon a standard error of measurement = 4.

[b]*Low* is a quotient of 69 and below, *Borderline* is a quotient of 70 to 79, and *High* is a quotient of 80 and above.

(*Cont.*)

FORM 11.4

CASE 2: PSYCHOLOGICAL EVALUATION REPORT *(Cont.)*

TABLE 6 ■ SUBSCALES

Subscale	SS	95% CI[a]	PR	Symptom severity[b]	Measured symptoms
Social Interaction	11	[9, 13]	63	Moderate	Impaired nonverbal behaviors (e.g., gestures to regulate social interaction); lack of peer relationships; lack of spontaneous seeking of mutual shared enjoyment, interests, or achievements; lack of social reciprocity
Restricted Patterns of Behavior	15	[13, 17]	95	Severe	Stereotyped and restricted interests of abnormal intensity or focus; inflexible, specific, nonfunctional routines or rituals; stereotyped and repetitive motor mannerisms; preoccupation with object parts
Cognitive Patterns	12	[10, 14]	75	Moderate	Lack of ability to initiate or sustain interpersonal conversations; idiosyncratic language and interests; lack of varied, spontaneous make-believe, or imitative play
Pragmatic Skills	13	[11, 15]	84	Severe	Impaired social perception; impaired understanding of others' perspectives, experiences, and beliefs (i.e. theory of mind); impaired affect recognition

Note: Standard score mean = 10, standard deviation = 3. Higher scores indicate increasing symptom severity. SS, standard score; CI, confidence interval; PR, percentile rank.

[a]CI is based upon a standard error of measurement = 1.

[b]*Absent* is a SS of 1 to 4, *Mild* is a SS of 5 to 7, *Moderate* is a SS of 8 to 12, and *Severe* is a SS of 13 and above.

Respondent: Foster mother.

Considering the positive GARS–2 results, these positive GADS data are interpreted as further support for the more severe and inclusive Autistic Disorder.

NEPSY–II, Form Ages 5 to 16, Social Perception Subtests

TABLE 7 ■ SOCIAL PERCEPTION

Score name	Age range	Scaled score	PR	Classification	Measured abilities
Affect Recognition Total	5–16	1	0.1	Well below expected level	Facial affect recognition
Theory of Mind Total	5–16	1	0.1	Well below expected level	Comprehension of others' perspectives, experiences, and beliefs; matching appropriate affect to contextual cues

Note: Scaled score mean = 10, standard deviation = 3. Lower scores indicate greater neuropsychological impairment. Age range is for that particular score in units of years. PR, percentile rank.

Social perception involves intellectual processes that facilitate social interaction.

Social perception was measured as being remarkably impaired, including a severe impairment in theory of mind abilities. This is corroborative evidence of Autistic Disorder.

(Cont.)

FORM 11.4

CASE 2: PSYCHOLOGICAL EVALUATION REPORT (*Cont.*)

Conners CBRS, Parent and Teacher Forms

TABLE 8 ■ VALIDITY OF RATINGS

	Parent ratings			Teacher ratings			
Scale	Raw score	Differentials	Result	Scale	Raw score	Differentials	Result
Positive Impression[a]	2	--	Valid	Positive Impression[a]	2	--	Valid
Negative Impression[b]	1	--	Valid	Negative Impression[b]	1	--	Valid
Inconsistency Index[c]	4	1	Valid	Inconsistency Index[c]	5	0	Valid

Note: Lower raw scores indicate that the ratings are increasingly valid. -- denotes not administered, or score type not available or computed.

[a]Invalid interpretation indicates that the rater produced an overly positive description of the youth's behavior.

[b]Invalid indicates that the rater produced an overly negative description of the youth's behavior.

[c]Invalid indicates either variable attention or comprehension difficulties on the part of the rater.

Both parent and teacher ratings are valid.

TABLE 9 ■ CLINICAL SCALE

	Parent ratings		Teacher ratings			
Scale	T-score*	DSM symptom counts	T-score*	DSM symptom counts	Diagnostic result[a]	Measured symptoms
Autistic Disorder	90*	Met	90*	Met	Positive	Qualitative impairments in social interaction and communication; stereotyped behaviors
Asperger's Disorder	90*	Met	90*	Met	Positive	Qualitative impairments in social interaction, stereotyped behaviors

Note: T-score mean = 50, standard deviation = 10. Higher *T*-scores indicate greater presence of symptoms. *denotes that the *T*-score is statistically significant; measured symptoms on that clinical scale are sufficiently severe to indicate a clinical diagnosis. Symptom counts "Met" when at or above the *DSM-IV-TR* cut-off score; symptom counts "Not met" when below the *DSM-IV-TR* cut-off score.

[a]Atypical symptoms indicate the presence of clinical symptoms due to an alternate *DSM-IV-TR* diagnosis.

The Conners CBRS data provide additional support for Autistic Disorder, with additional corroboration from Joey's teacher.

Posttest *DSM-IV-TR* Diagnoses

Axis I:
❐ 299.00 Autistic Disorder
❐ 314.01 Attention-Deficit/Hyperactivity Disorder, Combined Type (historical diagnosis)
❐ 309.81 Posttraumatic Stress Disorder, Chronic (historical diagnosis)
❐ 995.54 Physical Abuse of Child (historical diagnosis)

Axis II:
❐ 317 Mild Mental Retardation
    Full Scale IQ = 64
    Adaptive Behavior Composite = 66

Axis III:
❐ No Contributory or Pertinent Medical Disorders Noted

(*Cont.*)

FORM 11.4

CASE 2: PSYCHOLOGICAL EVALUATION REPORT (*Cont.*)

Axis IV:

❏ Psychosocial Stressors – Social, Educational

Axis V:

❏ Global Assessment of Functioning (GAF): 40 Serious symptoms

Prognosis: Guarded due to comorbidity on Axes I and II

TREATMENT RECOMMENDATIONS

1. Continued psychiatric biological intervention for ADHD–C and PTSD, Chronic, and palliative for Autistic Disorder.
2. Cognitive behavioral therapy to improve executive functioning skills, emotional self-regulation, emotional intelligence, social and interpersonal skills, and for symptom reduction.
3. Child case management services are advised for more comprehensive behavioral intervention.
4. It is advised that these assessment and test results be shared with Joey's school for coordination of mental health treatment intervention with academic intervention, for continuity of care, and to assist in determining any modification in special education services, the latter based upon school officials' discretion.

John M. Spores, PhD, JD, HSPP
Psychologist – Indiana #20040638A
Attorney at Law – Indiana #21404–64

Adolescent Cases

The two cases presented in this chapter were culled from an age range extending from 13 years to 17 years inclusive. The first is a neuropsychological test referral requiring a diagnostic differential between a Disruptive Behavior Disorder and Cognitive Disorder with associated personality changes and mood symptoms; that is, Nonorganic versus Organic Mental Disorders (American Psychiatric Association, 1987). It is a felicitous example of how a well-targeted and efficient test battery can effectively assist in distinguishing between such disorders. The second case is a psychological test referral asking for a differential between a Mood Disorder with or without psychosis. Although such question appears to regard Axis I only, this case was more intricate in that Axis II psychopathology was a distinct possibility. Therefore, an Axis I versus II differential diagnosis was also required which made this case an intriguing one to include in this book.

CASE 3: RULE OUT CONDUCT DISORDER, NEUROCOGNITIVE DISORDER, AND PERSONALITY CHANGE DUE TO HEAD TRAUMA

Referral for Testing

Robert was a 15-year-old who was in outpatient psychiatric treatment with Tammy Sperry, MD, for 6 months at the time of referral. He was being treated for Attention-Deficit/Hyperactivity Disorder, Combined Type (ADHD–C), a diagnosis that was not in question. Precipitants for the referral included severe, repeated, and escalating conduct-disordered behavior, including episodes of explosive behavior involving physical aggression toward people and other illegal acts (e.g., assault and battery, burglary). The latter led to legal system intervention, including felony charges.

The completed referral form (Form 2.1) specifically asked for neuropsychological testing due to a closed head injury Robert sustained at the age of 8 months, which consequently caused significant internal bleeding and required neurosurgery. Dr. Sperry noted that the right frontal lobe was most deleteriously affected. Diagnoses to be ruled out as requested by Dr. Sperry included Conduct Disorder, Personality Change Due to Head Trauma, and a Cognitive Disorder.

Initial Psychological Assessment Report

Robert's initial report is presented in Form 12.1. In the sections that follow, I highlight vital assessment information and unique diagnostic issues that were an integral part of Robert's case.

Clinical Interview Information

Several issues rendered Robert's case particularly complex. First, he came in with the premorbid condition of ADHD–C. Thus, using the clinical method, it was necessary to diligently document symptoms clearly in excess of ADHD–C, including onset and subsequent course. In the "Referral Information" section, the most acute conduct-disordered symptoms were enumerated first, hence immediately showing evidence of severe dysfunction exceeding that of ADHD–C and substantiating the reason for the testing referral. Onset of at least some of these symptoms in the form of anger outbursts was documented to be at the age of 7 years, with significant exacerbation noted when Robert was approximately 10 years of age; that is, 5 years prior to this testing referral.

Age, severity, and location (i.e., frontal lobe potentially influencing personality functioning) of the traumatic brain injury (TBI) were also crucial to document, along with the referral source being identified as a medical practitioner (i.e., MD). Therefore, the initial import of the report was that of establishing medical necessity as defined prior (see Introduction, which sets forth medical necessity criteria). The likelihood of neurocognitive dysfunction was also buttressed in the "Developmental" section, including the reference to the use of forceps during delivery and subsequent general developmental delays. Finally, the positive family history of Dementia in the absence of other psychiatric disorders (e.g., Bipolar Disorder) was crucial to note. In particular, such information strongly suggested that Robert's behavioral and mood symptoms had neurocognitive implications which were potentially progressive. Lastly, the documenting of abrupt and severe mood swings in the presenting symptoms was necessitated, as head trauma can be an etiological factor in Mood Disorder (American Psychiatric Association, 2000).

DSM-IV-TR Diagnoses to Be Ruled Out

The pertinent presenting symptoms were largely consistent with Dr. Sperry's differential diagnostic request. Therefore, in accordance with her request, the rule outs included Conduct Disorder and Personality Change Due to Head Trauma. As indicated prior, an additional rule out indicated by the presenting symptoms was Mood Disorder Due to Head Trauma. As a general principle, I do list other related potential disorders not detected or stated by the referring clinician. In retrospect, in Robert's case I should have also added Dementia Due to Head Trauma as a fourth rule out. Although listing the Dementia rule out was not necessary for establishing medical necessity and the ordering of proper tests (discussed next), it would have facilitated subsequent test interpretation to a greater extent as it would have more immediately focused my analysis on the possibility of such disorder. Lastly, note that in the "Initial Assessment Summary" section, the goal of measuring the nature and extent of neuropsychological deficits language was retained in the differential diagnostic objectives of testing; that is, the disorders to be ruled out as defined by the *Diagnostic and Statistical Manual of Mental Disorders, Fourth Edition, Text Revision (DSM-IV-TR)*. The latter was important to note because it was directly relevant to treatment planning and intervention.

Test Selection and Requested Number of Hours

Clearly, a comprehensive neuropsychological test battery was required in Robert's case. Therefore, I ordered the NEPSY–II Full Battery, Form Ages 5 to 16 (Korkman, Kirk, & Kemp, 2007a, 2007b). However, the differential diagnostic questions also required a standardized measurement of behavioral and mood symptoms. Therefore, I additionally ordered the efficient Conners CBRS, Parents and Teacher Forms (Conners, 2008). Self-report tests were not included because patients with severe Cognitive Disorders frequently lack the psychological mindedness and introspection required of such measurement devices. So as to remain within the 3 to 5 hour guideline for ordering test batteries (see Chapter 2), I requested 4 hours for the NEPSY–II Full Battery, and 1 hour for the Conners CBRS forms, therefore totaling 5 in all. The 96118 neuropsychological test billing code was chosen for all five test hours, consistent with both the principal purpose of testing and the majority of tests and subtests within the requested battery (see Chapter 2).

Test Instructions

Patients and/or family members. The "Patient Test Instruction Form" (Form 2.8) was completed by entering (a) the estimated 5 testing hours into the blank on Item 2, (b) two 2-hour appointments for NEPSY–II administration on Item 3, and (c) striking out Item 5 as not applicable (i.e., N/A) to Robert's case. Robert's parents were specifically advised to continue his Vyvanse ADHD medication throughout the test administration procedures because the objectives of testing were to (a) obtain a measure of Robert's maximum performance and (b) distinguish his symptoms and any measured neurocognitive deficits from that of ADHD.

Support staff. The "Psychological Test Request and Log Form" (Form 2.9) was rapidly completed by entering the scheduling of two 2-hour testing appointments once insurance authorization was obtained and the requesting of 5 neuropsychological test hours. No independent self-administered tests were being ordered for Robert to complete. Therefore, this portion of the form was stricken as not applicable (i.e., N/A).

Test Administration Process

Four of the five testing hours were ultimately authorized under billing code 96118 neuropsychological testing. In particular, 1 of the 4 NEPSY–II hours was denied as exceeding published administration time for the Full Battery; namely, 3 hours (see Korkman et al., 2007a). Not infrequently, some insurance companies will circumscribe authorization to published estimated face-to-face administrative time for specified tests. This is especially likely when consulting psychologists, who are intimately familiar with administrative test manual information, are hired by insurance companies to review and determine the number of hours to be approved. This insurance standard underscores the need for extremely rapid and efficient scoring, interpretation, and report-writing, which I have repeatedly emphasized is an inherent part of contemporary psychological testing practice.

Two 2-hour testing appointments were scheduled as planned. At the initiation of the first session, Robert's parents submitted the Conners CBRS forms as requested, which upon cursory inspection were properly completed. Approximately two-thirds of the NEPSY–II battery was completed during appointment one, although we ended somewhat early at 1 hour and 45 minutes as Robert was beginning to show evidence of fatigue. This is not uncommon among those manifesting Cognitive Disorders or brain dysfunction. The remaining 15 minutes were used to computer score the Conners CBRS Parent and Teacher Forms (Conners CBRS Scoring Software, 2008).

Robert completed the remaining NEPSY–II subtests in the first hour of session two, leaving 1 hour for scoring, interpretation, and report-writing. Interestingly, the total 3-hour administrative time in Robert's case was precisely accordant with the time estimated for the Full Battery for ages 5 to 16 cited within the administrative manual (Korkman et al., 2007a). Because the NEPSY–II has computer scoring capability (NEPSY–II Scoring Assistant & Assessment Planner, 2007), and the Conners CBRS forms were previously computer scored during the latter portion of session one, the entire final report was completed within 75 minutes, thus exceeding insurance authorized time by only 15 minutes. This is manageable from a pecuniary business perspective. Of greater import, however, the patient and his family were provided with the complete complement of testing services needed to effectively resolve the complex differential diagnostic issues presented in this particular case (see Form 12.2).

Final Psychological Evaluation Report

The entire "Neuropsychological Evaluation Report" is presented in Form 12.2. Once again, the ensuing sections highlight the unique and vital issues evinced in Robert's testing case.

Modifications to the Initial Report

As designed by my system (see Chapters 1–3), Robert's initial report (Form 12.1) served as the beginning template for the final report. Except for needed minor changes in the date, title, insertion of the assessment and test battery (i.e., use of Box 3.1), deletion of test ordering information, and titling the "Test Results and Interpretation" section (see Form 3.1 and compare to Form 12.2), no other substantive changes were necessary. Simultaneously, the assessment information was both proofread and reviewed for interpretative context, including a cursory review of the listed rule out diagnoses prior to beginning the scoring and interpretation process. Again, this was all completed within a brief 10 minutes.

Test Scoring and Interpretation Process

As in previous case presentations (see Chapter 11), the focus and body of the final report is contained within the "Test Results and Interpretation" section (Form 12.2).

Initial test order. Measuring the potential presence of neurocognitive dysfunction was the principal objective of the testing. Therefore, the NESPY–II Full Battery was clearly priority and was listed first (Table 1 to Table 6), ensued by the Conners CBRS forms (Table 7 and Table 8).

Scoring and interpretation sequence. The NEPSY–II Full Battery, Form Ages 5 to 16 scoring and interpretation tables (Form 6.2) were inserted into the "Test Results and Interpretation" section. Those subtests falling outside Robert's age range were deleted from the tables for the dual purpose of maintaining brevity and focus. In sequential order, the data and subtest classifications were entered into the table body, and the results interpretively summarized in narrative text prior to proceeding to the next table. Note that the narrative interpretations of each table focused on evidence of measured impairment. Where there existed more narrowly defined or specific types of impairment, this was so indicated (see e.g., Table 1, Attention and Executive Functioning narrative). Alternatively, where there evinced more extensive impairment (see e.g., Table 3, Memory and Learning narrative), the overall trend was noted including the measured range of dysfunction (e.g., borderline to well below expected level). In the latter case, the reader has the immediate opportunity to review the proximate tabular results for a more detailed analysis of the extent and range of measured deficits. Of course, this also includes the capability of perusing the tables for areas of nonimpairment or normal functioning (see e.g., Table 6, Visuospatial Processing). Again, this writing style is consistent with APA publishing guidelines that sagely advise that data tables should stand on their own in terms of comprehension, and specific tabular results should not be redundantly presented in the narrative text but rather effectively summarized (American Psychological Association, 2010). This maintains both concision and focus during the test interpretation and report-writing process, and furthermore enhances its quality.

Note that as you proceed through the NEPSY–II tabular data and interpretive summaries (Tables 1–6), it becomes increasingly evident that Robert manifested significant neurocognitive dysfunction, thus confirming the presence of Cognitive Disorder or organicity (American Psychiatric Association, 1987). Furthermore, the succinctness of the tabular narrative interpretations facilitated the cross-referencing of Robert's measured neurocognitive deficits with the *DSM-IV-TR* criteria for Dementia. In particular, the data showed impairments in memory (i.e., an essential criterion), language dysfunction (viz., aphasia), and (visual)-motor impairment (viz., apraxia). Hence, as suggested in the initial assessment, the data pattern was consistent with the presence of Dementia. At this juncture in the report, two diagnoses were yet to be determined. They included Personality Change Due to Head Trauma and Mood Disorder Due to Head Trauma. To resolve these differentials, analysis moved to the Conners CBRS forms.

Table 7 indicated that while the Conners CBRS teacher ratings were valid, the parallel parent ratings manifested some inconsistency. Therefore, the cautionary interpretation version concerning the parent ratings was retained (see Form 7.2). Table 8 reported the diagnostically pertinent Conners CBRS Clinical scales, including Conduct Disorder, Major Depressive Episode, and Manic Episode. The remaining Clinical scales were deleted as not being applicable to the differential diagnostic issues. The results were remarkably positive for severe mood disturbance involving bipolar-type symptoms and severe conduct disturbance, both consistent with the presenting symptoms.

The narrative interpretation of Table 8 data addressed three diagnostic issues in sequence, the first two of which required integration of the NESPY–II results, along with onset and course information gleaned by use of the clinical method. First, the positive result for Conduct Disorder was interpreted as supporting a Dementia *With Behavioral Disturbance* and Personality Change Due to Head Trauma, the latter due to its being associated with measured evidence of neurocognitive impairment temporally associated with TBI, and representing a marked divergence from what would be considered normal development (American Psychiatric Association, 2000). Second, the positive results for severe mood disturbance were similarly interpreted as being indicative of a Mood Disorder Due to Head Trauma, again with its relationship to his documented TBI and measured neurocognitive impairment. Finally, the Conners CBRS Violence Potential Content scale (see Chapter 7) was immediately relevant in Robert's case because of his documented history of physical aggression toward people. Its positive result was vital to report in the narrative text as indicating (a) an Aggressive Type of Personality Change Due to Head Trauma and (b) a risk for future violence and aggression. This is a felicitous example of the manner in which supplemental data available in these test instruments can be used judiciously in narrative tabular interpretations to enhance diagnostic precision.

Final test order. As alluded to above, the initial test order was retained due to the neuropsychological focus of Robert's testing case. Furthermore, there was not a diagnostic need to modify the order of the NEPSY–II tables within the initial results and interpretation sequence.

Final diagnoses and treatment recommendations. Concerning posttest diagnoses, there was significant comorbidity on Axis I and thus decisions to make in terms of order. Dementia was listed first because it is potentially the most severe and disabling compared to the other diagnoses. It was also important to prioritize because it was not particularly specified by the referring psychiatrist Dr Sperry. This fact does not necessarily indicate that Dr. Sperry never considered such diagnosis. Frequently, referring clinicians will list only the most suspected diagnoses to be ruled out by testing due to time constraints. Note that for convenience, the specific Dementia criteria indicated by the neuropsychological testing were enumerated immediately subsequent to the diagnosis. This was ensued by a need to rule out the presence of progression. On this issue, the data were equivocal. Dementia due to a single occurrence of TBI is most likely to be nonprogressive (American Psychiatric Association, 2000). However, there were suggestions of brain trauma during perinatal delivery with the use of forceps and subsequent developmental delays, along with a documented history of significant symptom exacerbation within the 5 years prior to testing and a positive family history of Dementia. These were indicators of a progressive form of Dementia notwithstanding his young age. Hence, whether or not this was a progressive form of Dementia could only be determined by subsequent clinical observation of symptom course and response to treatment.

Personality Change Due to Head Trauma and Mood Disorder Due to Head Trauma were listed next, both of which superseded the premorbid and historical ADHD–C diagnosis. Regarding the former, and as indicated previously, the test data were able to identify more precisely an *Aggressive Type* of personality change, which was increasingly dominating the symptom picture. The Mood Disorder diagnosis was necessitated because the other listed diagnoses did not adequately capture and report the severe mood instability also present in Robert's case. Immediately thereafter was the noted risk of future violence and aggression evinced by the presenting symptoms, test data, and diagnoses. *DSM-IV-TR* requires an Axis III diagnosis when etiological or aggravating medical conditions are noted as being related to the listed Axis I disorder(s); hence, the Axis III Head Injury listing (American Psychiatric Association, 2000).

The final "Treatment Recommendations" section began with noting the need for psychiatric medical intervention to address the newly added diagnoses. However, they went on to emphasize the following: (a) need for neurological consultation and follow-up intervention as indicated, (b) need for more comprehensive mental health intervention due to the extent and severity of his symptoms, and finally, (c) neuropsychological retesting should clinical observations suggest the presence of progression.

Billing

All 4 used test hours previously approved by insurance were billed on the last date of face-to-face administration (i.e., June 16, 2011), which corresponded to the date the report was completed. The date of first test administration with the NEPSY–II was also noted in the progress note associated with billing.

Communication of Results

The final report was forwarded to Dr Sperry immediate subsequent to its completion (i.e., June 16, 2011). She consequently ordered the addition of neurological consultation, cognitive behavioral treatment, and child case management services in Robert's case.

The report was reviewed with Robert and his parents, with special emphasis on psychoeducational intervention regarding psychological disorders caused by head trauma and their treatment. Providing such feedback to patients and their families, especially regarding the presence of Dementia that may be progressive, can be remarkably distressing to them. In addition to psychoeducation, interventions such as reframing, empathy, cognitive restructuring of negative and unrealistic beliefs, and support are essential, along with assisting them in remaining realistically optimistic. They understandably obtained a copy of the final report for their records, especially in the event of retesting. Immediate availability of this first report and its data would permit a quantitative and objective measure of any change from baseline functioning.

CASE 4: RULE OUT MAJOR DEPRESSIVE DISORDER WITH OR WITHOUT PSYCHOTIC FEATURES, AND PREVIOUSLY UNSUSPECTED BORDERLINE PERSONALITY PSYCHOPATHOLOGY

Referral for Testing

Penny was a 16-year-old female who had been receiving outpatient psychotherapeutic services for a Depressive Disorder Not Otherwise Specified (NOS) about 13 months at the point of her testing referral. Her therapist James Brown, MA, LMHC, noted both a lack of response to treatment intervention and symptom exacerbation within the most recent 6 months. Regarding the latter, he reported the more palpable psychotic-like symptoms, which included occasional sensory–perceptual disturbances, although he was not cognizant of her two episodes of self-mutilation and escalating urges to repeat such aberrant behavior.

Therefore, he indicated on the "Psychological Test Referral Form" (Form 2.1) the need to make an Axis I differential diagnosis between a Major Depressive Disorder either With or Without Psychotic Features. The possible presence of Axis II psychopathology was not mentioned either within the "Disorders needed to be ruled out" or "Additional referral question(s)" items available on this form. This was in part due to reluctance on Mr. Brown's part to consider a Personality Disorder in a 16-year-old case. However, I believe it was also due to the continuing difficulty clinicians encounter when attempting to discriminate between Axis I and II disorders through the sole use of the clinical method (see Chapter 8 for an extended discussion of the difficulties in rendering Axis II diagnoses).

Initial Psychological Assessment Report

The complete initial report is presented in Form 12.3. Key assessment information and assessment issues are presented subsequent.

Clinical Interview Information

The "Referral Information" section began with highlighting symptom onset and course of her depressive symptoms, including exacerbation within the past 2 years and association with a significant drop in her academic performance. More noteworthy was the documentation of her periodic visual and auditory sensory–perceptual disturbances, which precipitated the testing referral, along with the newly introduced evidence of self-mutilation that eluded detection by her therapist. This does not necessarily indicate that Mr. Brown did not attempt to examine this issue with Penny. Not infrequently, patients are reticent to inform their therapists of seemingly ignominious behavior subsequent to establishing longer term intimacy and rapport within the psychotherapeutic process. Her revealing this information at the initiation of the testing process was crucial to adding the need to rule out emerging Axis II Borderline personality traits or a fully developed disorder.

Further evidence of potential Borderline Personality Disorder was noted in the following sections: (a) "Mental Status Examination and Behavioral Observations" (viz., ineffectual social skills and self-harm); (b) "Family" (viz., strained relationship with her mother); and particularly, (c) "Interpersonal" (viz., relationship pattern of mistrust, instability, intensity, and conflict). Note that the latter was effectively phrased in succinct form and portrayed as average tendencies (Larsen & Buss, 2010), thus indicating the presence of maladaptive personality traits in need of further standardized testing.

The "Education" section reiterated the temporal decline in grades so as to emphasize dysfunction and further contribute to a justifiably low Global Assessment of Functioning (GAF) score. The "Substance Abuse" section was elaborated somewhat due to the presence of sensory–perceptual disturbances, with corroboration from Penny's mother of no such evidence of drug use or abuse. Here, corroboration from a third party was deemed necessary due to the potential for Axis II Borderline Personality Disorder. Finally, documented evidence of potential psychotic symptoms substantiated the low GAF score of 35, indicating some degree of impairment in reality testing abilities (American Psychiatric Association, 2000). All of the aforementioned initial assessment information contributed to the establishment of medical necessity for subsequent psychological testing (see Form 12.3).

DSM-IV-TR Diagnoses to Be Ruled Out

First, I added a provisional *Psychotic Disorder NOS* to Mr. Brown's working diagnosis for Penny of Depressive Disorder NOS. This was accordant with the presenting symptoms and GAF score of 35. The differentials were those of Mr. Brown's, including Major Depressive Disorder With or Without Psychotic Features, along with an additional deferral on Axis II with the need to rule out Borderline Personality Disorder or at minimum the presence of such maladaptive traits. Such apparent reality testing aberrations were deemed to be potentially transient psychotic symptoms (Kernberg, 1967; McWilliams, 2011) or severe dissociative symptoms (American Psychiatric Association, 2000) as part of the Borderline syndrome (see also Chapter 8).

Test Selection and Requested Number of Hours

The test battery consisted of one personality test and two self-report clinical and personality inventories, hence all consisting of standard psychological testing (i.e., billing code 96101). More specifically, the Rorschach Inkblot Test, Comprehensive System, RIAP Fifth Edition (Rorschach–CS) (Exner, 2003) was chosen as (a) a direct measure of reality testing ability, (b) an implicit measure of depression and suicide risk, and (c) a measure of personality traits and mechanisms that possess the capability of detecting the presence of Borderline Personality organization and structure. The Minnesota Multiphasic Personality Inventory–Adolescent (MMPI–A) (Butcher et al., 1992) was also selected because of its strength in symptomatically diagnosing the presence and severity of Major Depressive Disorder and Psychotic Disorder. Finally, and perhaps most importantly, the Millon Adolescent Clinical Inventory (MACI) (Millon, 2006) was included essentially due to its *DSM-IV-TR* correspondent Axis I and II differential diagnostic design and capability. Total test hours were four and hence viable for purposes of insurance authorization.

Lastly, as a billing note, although this was an *internal* referral, the initial psychological assessment was precertified and billed as a *behavioral health evaluation* (i.e., billing code 90801). This was approved because such evaluation had not been done for 13 months (see Form 12.3, "Psychiatric/Medical/Psychological" section).

Test Instructions

Patients and/or family members. The "Patient Test Instruction" form (Form 2.8) was completed such that the family was cognizant of the following: (a) 4 test hours were being requested, (b) one 2-hour appointment would be scheduled for Rorschach–CS administration subsequent to insurance authorization, and (c) Penny was to complete the MACI and MMPI–A on her own ensuing insurance authorization and prior to her scheduled Rorschach–CS appointment (Form 2.8; Items 2, 3, and 5, respectively). Item 4 on the form was stricken as not applicable (i.e., N/A) because the test battery did not include symptom rating scales.

Support staff. Next, the "Psychological Test Request and Log Form" (Form 2.9) was completed and recorded the following: (a) date of initial assessment, (b) number of hours being requested, all of which were coded psychological testing, (c) one 2-hour testing appointment for Penny to be scheduled by staff, and (d) reminder for staff to request that Penny complete the two self-report clinical and personality inventories on her own at the office prior to her testing appointment.

Test Administration Process

All four psychological test hours were approved as requested (billing code 96101). Penny duly completed the MACI and MMPI–A on the same day approximately 2½ weeks prior to her scheduled Rorschach–CS appointment. They were both immediately computer scored and the results printed out through the Q Local Software (2011). Rorschach–CS administration consumed about 45 minutes, with an additional 45 minutes for (a) manual coding of her 23 responses and (b) subsequent computer scoring of her sequence of scores for rapid computation of her Structural Summary and statistical indices (Rorschach Scoring Program, 2008). The remaining time (i.e., 2½ hours) was used for test interpretation and report-writing, thus remaining within the four approved hours.

Final Psychological Evaluation Report

Penny's final report is presented in Form 12.4. Highlights from this report ensue within the succeeding sections.

Modifications to the Initial Report

As frequently occurs, no new relevant assessment information was obtained following the initial report. Therefore, I reviewed the previous assessment sections for accuracy, made the necessary preliminary changes (e.g., insertion of the "Assessment and Test Battery" section, Box 3.1), reviewed the provisional and rule out diagnoses, and, most importantly, added the "Test Results and Interpretation" section within which the pertinent results and interpretation tables served as the basis for data analysis and the final report.

Test Scoring and Interpretation Process

Initial test order. From Mr. Brown's perspective, the determination of the presence or absence of genuine Axis I psychotic symptoms was essential to his testing referral. Furthermore, and accordant with the referring clinician's concerns, determining the Axis I or II nature of Penny's aberrant visual and auditory presenting symptoms was diagnostically critical. For these reasons, I began the analysis with the Rorschach–CS (Table 1 to Table 5) and its unique capability of providing direct measures of Penny's reality testing and formal thinking. I selected the MMPI–A (Table 6 to Table 10) next as an explicit-measure counterpart to the Rorschach–CS. Together these tests would ultimately determine the severity of her Axis I Depressive Disorder, and whether or not psychotic symptoms were an inherent part of such disorder. Additionally, the Rorschach–CS would also begin to shed light on her underlying Axis II personality organization and structure. Finally, the MACI (Table 11 to Table 14) was the final test in the initial sequence. In the event there was insufficient evidence of Axis I psychosis, the MACI would determine if such symptoms were more related to Axis II psychopathology.

Scoring and interpretation sequence. The Rorschach–CS two validity tables were unremarkable and therefore the data were thereafter interpreted as accurate and diagnostically meaningful. Most pertinently, all of the Table 3 Psychotic Disorders variables were negative. This indicated that her reality testing presenting symptoms were unlikely to be genuine Axis I psychotic features. This rendered the supplemental WSum6 Thought Disorder Scores supplementary table unnecessary to report (see Chapter 9; see also Form 9.4, Table 4). Interestingly, several pertinent Rorschach–CS Mood Disorders variables were positive, including a statistically significant Depression Index (viz., 6 of 7 criteria), and a remarkable degree of pessimism (MOR responses = 8). The latter was important to report and highlight as a necessary and useful target for psychotherapeutic intervention. Furthermore, the Suicide Constellation Index (S–CON) applied in Penny's case and was vital to report as being negative, especially considering her severe depressive symptoms and reported suicidal ideation. Note that not all available Mood Disorders variables were reported in the interest of maintaining brevity and focus (see Form 9.4, Table 5).

The most remarkable Rorschach data were yielded among the Personality Disorders Variables (Form 12.4, Table 5). More specifically, the first two variables measured the paradoxical coexistence of narcissism and low self-worth, indicating an extremely unstable sense of self or splitting (Kernberg, 1967). The specific Table 5 note highlighted this inference for me during the process of test interpretation and report-writing, and for any subsequent reader of the report. Note that because not all personality variables were reported, many of the otherwise available specific table notes were deleted and the remaining note identifying letter changed from *b* to *a* (see Form 9.4, Table 8). Penny's fragile sense of self-worth was further evidenced by the third positive variable in Table 5 (viz., Sum V = 3). Taken together, the positive results in Table 5 showed empirical evidence of the presence of psychological traits and mechanisms that were remarkably consistent with a Borderline Personality structure and organization. A succinct narrative summary to this effect followed Table 5, with the core result of self-instability highlighted.

Next, test interpretation moved to the MMPI–A results as initially planned. Test validity was obtained as evidenced by a *modal* or *acceptable* test-taking response pattern. Hence, a standard interpretation strategy was employed (see Form 12.4, Tables 6–8). The MMPI–A pertinent Mood Disorders scales yielded key clinically significant elevations evidencing the presence of severe Major Depressive Disorder (Form 12.4, Table 9). A succinct narrative summary to this effect ensued with a note indicating convergent validity with that of the Rorschach–CS data. The Psychotic Disorders scales were largely negative with two transitional elevations. This was evidence that Penny's psychotic-like presenting symptoms were more likely part of a Borderline syndrome with transient psychotic experiences precipitated by perceived stressors (Kernberg, 1967; McWilliams, 2011), as opposed to acute Axis I psychopathology. Of note, although not in Penny's case, an analogous data pattern and interpretation scheme can potentially arise among the Rorschach–CS Psychotic Disorders variables (see e.g., Chapter 13, Case 6). This type of interpretation was made in the narrative summary immediately following the MMPI–A Table 9, along with an added note of consistency with Rorschach–CS results. Note that the MMPI–A Personality Disorders scales (see Form 8.4, Table 9) were not reported as they were not of much assistance in further clarifying a Borderline diagnosis in Penny's case. That is, they would have unnecessarily protracted the report with a risk of obfuscating rather than clarifying the results.

Finally, the test reporting and interpretation process reached the MACI, which provided the most direct Axis I/II differential diagnostic data and ultimately corroborated the preliminary Axis II Personality Disorders Rorschach–CS data. Once again validity was largely obtained with MACI statistical adjustments being made for evidence of dejection and self-deprecating tendencies (Millon, 2006). Although not stated in the report, in hindsight, such data could have been interpreted as further evidence of a fragile sense of self as part of a Borderline Disorder. However, the data pattern was so clear and convincing in Penny's case that this would have been superfluous. I mention this use of validity results here because they may be extremely useful in clarifying more ambiguous and inconsistent results frequently encountered in psychological testing cases.

The MACI Axis I Clinical Syndrome scales were largely consistent with previous results. Note that only those scales measuring Depressive psychopathology were reported because they were most diagnostically pertinent. There are no psychotic scales on the MACI (see Chapter 8) which is why none appeared in Penny's case. Lastly, and most critically, the MACI Borderline Personality Patterns scale was unequivocally measured to be within the range of a *prominence* of a disorder, with Self-Defeating traits (American Psychiatric Association, 1987) being present or secondary. Although the construct validity of the latter diagnosis is questionable from a research perspective, clinically it was extremely important to detect and report the presence of such traits because they would present an added hindrance to treatment progress. That is, I believed that the potential benefits of reporting their presence significantly outweighed any identifiable risks (e.g., excessive pathologizing). This is why I include this scale in the MACI tables; see also Chapter 8 for an extended discussion of both the inclusion and exclusion of Millon personality scales not currently recognized by the *DSM-IV-TR* (American Psychiatric Association, 2000).

Final test order. Once again, because of the remarkable intertest reliability and integrity of the test data, no changes in test order were necessitated. As I stated prior to beginning Section III of this book on case studies, these are representative cases with prototypical diagnostic questions and test data patterns for purposes of illustration. In the event that the Rorschach–CS and/or the MMPI–A yielded completely invalid results, they would have been placed subsequent to the MACI which contained the statistical adjustments for preserving test validity (Millon, 2006).

Final diagnoses and treatment recommendations. Penny's posttest diagnoses were the logical outcomes of the empirical data reported in the "Test Results and Interpretation" section. The Axis I diagnosis most supported by the data was Major Depressive Disorder, Single Episode, Severe. The single-episode specifier was selected because there were no previously documented episodes of Major Depression in Penny's history. Occasionally, I have observed clinicians insert *First Diagnosed Episode* in lieu of Single Episode in cases where a previous episode is strongly suspected, although not confirmed. However, this is inconsistent with *DSM-IV-TR* nomenclature (American Psychiatric Association, 2000).

The Borderline diagnosis immediately followed. Note that I deemed it more accurate to diagnose the complete disorder in Penny's case. This was due to the consistency and severity of her scores on the Rorschach–CS and MACI, which I believed made the full diagnosis irrefutable. The Self-Defeating secondary traits detected by the MACI were also listed, along with a notation indicating that Penny's reality testing problems were attributable to her Axis II psychopathology.

Treatment recommendations first called for psychiatric biological intervention for Penny's Axis I and II disorders, with the qualifier *palliative* regarding the Borderline diagnosis. Next psychotherapy was recommended for her personality psychopathology, with an admonishment to not overlook her self-defeating proclivities as a likely contributing impediment to treatment progress.

Billing

The 4 approved psychological test hours were billed on the same day and date of her Rorschach–CS administration (i.e., June 16, 2010). Again, all 4 hours were reimbursed.

Communication of Results

The final report was immediately forwarded to the referring clinician Mr. Brown. Because this was an internal referral, we consulted personally regarding the results and treatment options. He met with Penny and her parents the very next week during her scheduled weekly therapy appointment and reviewed the final report with them. He was able to do this effectively as his MA degree was in clinical psychology and he was thus sufficiently familiar with both psychometrics and *DSM-IV-TR* nomenclature. Mr. Brown referred Penny for psychiatric evaluation and psychotropic medication as indicated. He also modified his treatment approach to include more object-relations psychotherapeutic interventions (see e.g., Kernberg, 1967), in addition to incorporating the principles and techniques of dialectical behavior therapy (Dimeff & Koerner, 2007). The family was satisfied with Mr. Brown's feedback and asked that their follow-up appointment with me be waived for purposes of expediency.

SUMMARY

Chapter 12 presented two adolescent cases, the first including largely neuropsychological testing and the second more standard psychological testing. The former primarily required a differential diagnosis between a Cognitive Disorder involving organicity and a Conduct Disorder. This case was complicated by the presence of premorbid ADHD. The case essentially demonstrated the manner in which a neuropsychological test battery may be utilized with standardized symptom checklists to effectuate such differential diagnosis.

The second case required an Axis I/II differential diagnosis. It was demonstrated how the Rorschach–CS may be effectively employed with self-report clinical and personality inventories to render such diagnoses. Chapter 13 continues such testing case presentations as applied to adults.

REFERENCES

American Psychiatric Association. (1987). *Diagnostic and statistical manual of mental disorders* (3rd ed. rev.). Washington, DC: Author.

American Psychiatric Association. (2000). *Diagnostic and statistical manual of mental disorders* (4th ed., text rev.). Washington, DC: Author.

American Psychological Association. (2010). *Publication manual of the American Psychological Association* (6th ed.). Washington, DC: Author.

Butcher, J. N., Williams, C. L., Graham, J. R., Archer, R. P., Tellegen, A., Ben-Porath, Y. S., & Kaemmer, B. (1992). *Minnesota Multiphasic Personality Inventory–Adolescent (MMPI–A): Manual for administration, scoring, and interpretation.* Minneapolis, MN: NCS University of Minnesota Press.

Conners, C. K. (2008). *Conners Comprehensive Behavior Rating Scales (Conners CBRS): Manual and interpretive update.* North Tonawanda, NY: Multi-Health Systems.

Conners CBRS Scoring Software [USB Key Computer software]. (2008). North Tonawanda, NY: Multi-Health Systems.

Dimeff, L. A., & Koerner, K. (Eds.). (2007). *Dialectical behavior therapy in clinical practice: Applications across disorders and settings.* New York, NY: The Guilford Press.

Exner, J. E. (2003). *The Rorschach a comprehensive system: Basic foundations and principles of interpretation* (4th ed., Vol. 1). Hoboken, NJ: John Wiley.

Kernberg, O. (1967). Borderline personality organization. *Journal of the American Psychoanalytic Association, 15,* 641–685.

Korkman, M., Kirk, U., & Kemp, S. (2007a). *NEPSY–II: Administrative manual.* San Antonio, TX: The Psychological Corporation-Pearson.

Korkman, M., Kirk, U., & Kemp, S. (2007b). *NEPSY–II: Clinical and interpretative manual.* San Antonio, TX: The Psychological Corporation-Pearson.

Larsen, R. J., & Buss, D. M. (2010). *Personality psychology: Domains of knowledge about human nature* (4th ed.). New York, NY: McGraw-Hill.

McWilliams, N. (2011). *Psychoanalytic diagnosis: Understanding personality structure in the clinical process* (2nd ed.). New York, NY: The Guilford Press.

Millon, T. (with Millon, C., Davis, R. D., & Grossman, S. D.). (2006). *Millon Adolescent Clinical Inventory (MACI) manual* (2nd ed.). Minneapolis, MN: NCS Pearson.

NEPSY–II Scoring Assistant & Assessment Planner [CD-ROM Computer software]. (2007). San Antonio, TX: PsychCorp Center–I, Pearson.

Q Local Software [CD-ROM Computer software]. (2011). San Antonio, TX: Pearson Assessments.

Rorschach Scoring Program [Computer software]. (2008). Lutz, FL: Exner, Weiner, & Psychological Assessment Resources (PAR).

FORM 12.1

CASE 3: INITIAL PSYCHOLOGICAL ASSESSMENT REPORT

COMMUNITY MENTAL HEALTH CENTER

Outpatient Department

INITIAL PSYCHOLOGICAL ASSESSMENT REPORT

Patient Name: Ashe, Robert
Account Number: 333333
Date: May 9, 2011

Patient Identifying Information: Chronological age is 15 years 7 months. Gender is male. DOB: 9/18/1995.

Referral Information: The referral source is Tammy Sperry, MD, who indicated that the diagnosis remains ambiguous subsequent to clinical interview and observations, and objective standardized testing will significantly impact treatment planning and outcome.

The specific *DSM-IV-TR* referral questions include the need to rule out Personality Change Due to Head Trauma, a Neurocognitive Disorder, and Conduct Disorder, Adolescent Onset Type. He has a working diagnosis of Attention-Deficit/Hyperactivity Disorder, Combined Type (ADHD–C). The latter was diagnosed when he was age 7 years and this diagnosis is not in question.

Pertinent presenting symptoms included severe anger outbursts and explosive behavior, including repeated episodes of assault and battery, and reports of recurring abrupt and severe mood swings. He has shown several episodes of burglary and theft, and thus major violations of the rights and property of others. Furthermore, he fractured his sister's collar bone by battery. Onset of the anger outbursts was estimated to be at age 7 years, although the severe conduct problems and mood instability have become increasingly apparent throughout his older childhood and into adolescence.

Of diagnostic note, Robert sustained a severe closed traumatic head injury (TBI) by falling down a flight of stairs at 8 months of age. This caused significant internal hemorrhaging in his right hemisphere, frontal lobe, which required neurosurgery.

Clinical Psychologist: John M. Spores, PhD, JD, HSPP
Psychologist – Indiana #20040638A
Attorney at Law – Indiana #21404–64

Mental Status Examination and Behavioral Observations: Affect was restricted. Mood was dysphoric and irritable. Thought process was logical, sequential, relevant, and coherent. Thought content was reality-based and normal. Short-term and long-term memory function was normal and intact. Activity level was normal. However, it should be noted that he was on his Vyvanse medication during the initial assessment. He was oriented to time, place, and person. Estimated intellectual function based on verbal skills and reasoning abilities is average. Psychotic symptoms were not evident. There was no evidence of suicidal thoughts, intentions, or plans. There was no evidence of self-mutilation or self-harm.

Psychiatric/Medical/Psychological: The referring clinician completed a Behavioral Health Evaluation (i.e., 90801) in or about September 2010. Robert has been psychiatrically

(Cont.)

FORM 12.1

CASE 3: INITIAL PSYCHOLOGICAL ASSESSMENT REPORT (*Cont.*)

hospitalized six times associated with the presenting complaints. Psychiatric history also includes ongoing outpatient treatment by several different psychiatrists. Family psychiatric history is remarkable for Dementia. Current medical functioning is unremarkable. Current medication includes Vyvanse 50 mg. There is a negative history of prolonged high fevers. Medical history is remarkable for the aforementioned TBI and subsequent neurosurgery. There was one medicine-induced seizure in 2004. Vision is normal. Hearing is normal. Previous neuropsychological testing has never been done.

Developmental: There were no pre- or post-natal complications reported. Peri-natal complication was the required use of forceps. Gestation was full-term. Birth weight was 8 pounds, 14 ounces. Birth length was 20 inches. Developmental milestones were generally delayed especially in productive and receptive language.

Family: Robert lives with his parents, older sister, and younger brother.

Interpersonal: Interpersonal relationships are negatively impacted by the presenting complaints.

Educational: Robert is in Grade 8. Academic performance has typically been average. Behavioral grades have typically been poor. There has been no grade retention. Robert is receiving special education instruction, has a continuing IEP, and is classified as Emotionally Handicapped (EH).

Vocational: None.

Substance Abuse: Denied. This was corroborated by his parents.

Legal: Robert is being charged with 2 felonies, for burglary and theft, and a misdemeanor for one of his alleged batteries.

Initial Assessment Summary: Based upon the initial psychological assessment evidence, pre-test working diagnosis and disorders needed to be ruled out are listed below in the ensuing *Pretest DSM-IV-TR Diagnosis* section. The test data shall also empirically measure the extent and severity of any neuropsychological deficits for purposes of treatment planning.

The following tests and estimated hours are requested:

1. Conners Comprehensive Behavior Rating Scales (Conners CBRS), Parent and Teacher Forms (1 hour)
2. NEPSY–II, Form Ages 5 to 16, Full Battery (4 hours)

Total requested neuropsychological testing hours is 5 (Billing Code 96118).

Finally, one (1) individual hour (Billing Code 90806) is requested for follow-up test feedback session and treatment planning.

All of the above-enumerated tests have sufficient empirically derived reliability and validity, and are age-appropriate. Furthermore, these tests are the most recently published editions.

(*Cont.*)

FORM 12.1

CASE 3: INITIAL PSYCHOLOGICAL ASSESSMENT REPORT *(Cont.)*

Pretest *DSM-IV-TR* Diagnoses

Axis I:

❏ 314.01 Attention-Deficit/Hyperactivity Disorder, Combined Type

Provisional, Rule Out:

❏ 312.82 Conduct Disorder, Adolescent-Onset Type
❏ 310.1 Personality Change Due to Head Trauma
❏ 293.83 Mood Disorder Due to Head Trauma

Axis II:

❏ V71.09 No Diagnosis

Axis III:

❏ 854.00 Head Injury

Axis IV:

❏ Psychosocial Stressors – Social, Educational, Legal

Axis V:

❏ Global Assessment of Functioning (GAF): 45 Serious symptoms
   Prognosis: Deferred pending neuropsychological assessment and test results

John M. Spores, PhD, JD, HSPP
Psychologist – Indiana #20040638A
Attorney at Law – Indiana #21404–64

FORM 12.2

CASE 3: NEUROPSYCHOLOGICAL EVALUATION REPORT

COMMUNITY MENTAL HEALTH CENTER

Outpatient Department

NEUROPSYCHOLOGICAL EVALUATION REPORT

Patient Name: Ashe, Robert
Account Number: 333333
Date: June 16, 2011

Patient Identifying Information: Chronological age is 15 years 8 months. Gender is male. DOB: 9/18/1995.

Referral Information: The referral source is Tammy Sperry, MD, who indicated that the diagnosis remains ambiguous subsequent to clinical interview and observations, and objective standardized testing will significantly impact treatment planning and outcome.

The specific *DSM-IV-TR* referral questions include the need to rule out Personality Change Due to Head Trauma, a Neurocognitive Disorder, and Conduct Disorder, Adolescent Onset Type. He has a working diagnosis of Attention-Deficit/Hyperactivity Disorder, Combined Type (ADHD–C). ADHC–C was diagnosed when he was age 7 years and this diagnosis is not in question.

Pertinent presenting symptoms included severe anger outbursts and explosive behavior, including repeated episodes of assault and battery, and reports of recurring abrupt and severe mood swings. He has shown several episodes of burglary and theft, and thus major violations of the rights and property of others. Furthermore, he fractured his sister's collar bone by battery. Onset of the anger outbursts was estimated to be at age 7 years, although the severe conduct problems and mood instability have become increasingly apparent throughout his older childhood and into adolescence.

Of diagnostic note, Robert sustained a severe closed traumatic head injury (TBI) by falling down a flight of stairs at 8 months of age. This caused significant internal hemorrhaging in his right hemisphere, frontal lobe, which required neurosurgery.

Assessment and Test Battery

1. Diagnostic Interview (05/09/2011)
2. Mental Status Examination and Behavioral Observations (05/09/2011)
3. NEPSY–II, Full Battery, Form Ages 5 to 16 (06/14/2011; 06/16/2011)
4. Conners Comprehensive Behavior Rating Scales (Conners CBRS), Parent and Teacher Forms (05/30/2011)

Clinical Psychologist: John M. Spores, PhD, JD, HSPP
                                  Psychologist – Indiana #20040638A
                                  Attorney at Law – Indiana #21404–64

Mental Status Examination and Behavioral Observations: Affect was restricted. Mood was dysphoric and irritable. Thought process was logical, sequential, relevant, and coherent. Thought content was reality-based and normal. Short-term and long-term

(Cont.)

FORM 12.2

CASE 3: NEUROPSYCHOLOGICAL EVALUATION REPORT (*Cont.*)

memory function was normal and intact. Activity level was normal. However, it should be noted that he was on his Vyvanse medication during the initial assessment. He was oriented to time, place, and person. Estimated intellectual function based on verbal skills and reasoning abilities is average. Psychotic symptoms were not evident. There was no evidence of suicidal thoughts, intentions, or plans. There was no evidence of self-mutilation or self-harm.

Psychiatric/Medical/Psychological: The referring clinician completed a Behavioral Health Evaluation (i.e., 90801) in or about September 2010. Robert has been psychiatrically hospitalized six times associated with the presenting complaints. Psychiatric history also includes ongoing outpatient treatment by several different psychiatrists. Family psychiatric history is remarkable for Dementia. Current medical functioning is unremarkable. Current medication includes Vyvanse 50 mg. There is a negative history of prolonged high fevers. Medical history is remarkable for the aforementioned TBI and subsequent neurosurgery. There was one medicine-induced seizure in 2004. Vision is normal. Hearing is normal. Previous neuropsychological testing has never been done.

Developmental: There were no pre- or post-natal complications reported. Peri-natal complication was the required use of forceps. Gestation was full-term. Birth weight was 8 pounds, 14 ounces. Birth length was 20 inches. Developmental milestones were generally delayed especially in productive and receptive language.

Family: Robert lives with his parents, older sister, and younger brother.

Interpersonal: Interpersonal relationships are negatively impacted by the presenting complaints.

Educational: Robert is in Grade 8. Academic performance has typically been average. Behavioral grades have typically been poor. There has been no grade retention. Robert is receiving special education instruction, has a continuing IEP, and is classified as Emotionally Handicapped (EH).

Vocational: None.

Substance Abuse: Denied. This was corroborated by his parents.

Legal: Robert is being charged with two felonies, for burglary and theft, and a misdemeanor for one of his alleged batteries.

(*Cont.*)

FORM 12.2

CASE 3: NEUROPSYCHOLOGICAL EVALUATION REPORT (*Cont.*)

TEST RESULTS AND INTERPRETATION

NEPSY–II, Form Ages 5 to 16, Full Battery

TABLE 1 ■ **ATTENTION AND EXECUTIVE FUNCTIONING**

Score name	Age range	Scaled score	PR	Classification	Measured abilities
Animal Sorting Combined	7–16	7	16	Borderline	Initiation, cognitive flexibility, and self-monitoring; conceptual reasoning; semantic knowledge
Auditory Attention Combined	5–16	12	75	At expected level	Selective and sustained attention; response speed; inhibitory control
Response Set Combined	7–16	6	9	Borderline	Selective and sustained attention; inhibitory control; working memory; response speed
Clocks Total	7–16	9	37	At expected level	Planning and organization; clock drawing; clock reading ability
Inhibition-Inhibition Combined	5–16	3	1	Well below expected level	Inhibitory control
Inhibition-Switching Combined	7–16	3	1	Well below expected level	Inhibitory control; cognitive flexibility

Note: Scaled score mean = 10, standard deviation = 3. Lower scores indicate greater neuropsychological impairment. Age range is for that particular score in years. PR, percentile rank.

Attention is the ability to focus on specific activities and suppress irrelevant stimuli. This includes *inhibition*, which is the ability to (a) resist urges and (b) stop oneself from engaging in automatic behaviors.

Executive functioning involves the ability to (a) engage in activities necessary for achieving objectives and (b) regulate one's actions based on environmental feedback.

Inhibitory control is measured to be remarkably impaired.

TABLE 2 ■ **LANGUAGE**

Score name	Age range	Scaled score	PR	Classification	Measured abilities
Comprehension of Instructions Total	5–16	3	1	Well below expected level	Linguistic and syntactic knowledge; ability to follow multistep commands
Phonological Processing Total	5–16	6	9	Borderline	Phonological awareness and processing
Speeded Naming Combined	5–16	5	5	Below expected level	Automaticity of lexical analysis; processing speed; naming ability
Word Generation Semantic Total	5–16	3	1	Well below expected level	Executive control of language production; initiative; ideation

Note: Scaled score mean = 10, standard deviation = 3. Lower scores indicate greater neuropsychological impairment. Age range is for that particular score in years. PR, percentile rank.

Language is the ability to express and understand verbal communication effectively. This consists of (a) receptive speech involving the comprehension and decoding of speech and (b) expressive speech or language production.

The majority of Language subtests are showing clear evidence of impairment. This indicates the presence of aphasia.

(*Cont.*)

FORM 12.2

CASE 3: NEUROPSYCHOLOGICAL EVALUATION REPORT (*Cont.*)

TABLE 3 ■ **MEMORY AND LEARNING**

Score name	Age range	Scaled score	PR	Classification	Measured abilities
Memory for Designs Total	5–16	1	0.1	Well below expected level	Visuospatial memory
Memory for Faces Total	5–16	7	16	Borderline	Visuospatial memory for human faces; face discrimination and recognition
Memory for Names Total	5–16	2	0.4	Well below expected level	Learning and retrieval of verbal labels for visual material
Narrative Memory Total[a]	5–16	4	2	Below expected level	Verbal expression and comprehension; verbal learning and memory
Word List Interference Recall Total[b]	7–16	6	9	Borderline	Verbal working memory

Note: Scaled score mean = 10, standard deviation = 3. Lower scores indicate greater neuropsychological impairment. Age range is for that particular score in units of years. PR, percentile rank.

[a]Includes immediate and delayed (i.e., 25–35 minutes) memory.

[b]Includes free recall (i.e., no hints given) and cued recall (i.e., hints given).

Memory and *learning* include the ability to acquire, retain, and access new information. Learning includes the ability to acquire new information. Memory involves retaining and retrieving information. *Working memory* involves holding immediate memory traces while executing cognitive tasks.

There is evidence of extensive memory impairment as all of the Memory and Learning subtests range from borderline to well below expected level.

TABLE 4 ■ **SENSORIMOTOR**

Score name[a]	Age range	Scaled score	PR	Classification	Measured abilities
Fingertip Tapping Dominant Hand Combined	5–16	2	0.4	Well below expected level	Fine-motor control and programming in dominant hand
Fingertip Tapping Nondominant Hand Combined	5–16	2	0.4	Well below expected level	Fine-motor control and programming in nondominant hand

Note: Scaled score mean = 10, standard deviation = 3. Lower scores indicate greater neuropsychological impairment. Age range is for that particular score in units of years. PR, percentile rank.

[a]Includes both dominant and nondominant hands.

Sensorimotor abilities involve neural circuits, which integrate motor guidance with sensory (i.e., kinesthetic, tactile, visual) feedback.

Both Sensorimotor subtests show impairment involving both dominant and nondominant hands. Thus, there is evidence of apraxia and bilateral neuropsychological impairment.

TABLE 5 ■ **SOCIAL PERCEPTION**

Score name	Age range	Scaled score	PR	Classification	Measured abilities
Affect Recognition Total	5–16	5	5	Below expected level	Facial affect recognition
Theory of Mind Total	5–16	--	2–5	Below expected level	Comprehension of others' perspectives, experiences, and beliefs; matching appropriate affect to contextual cues

Note: Scaled score mean = 10, standard deviation = 3. Lower scores indicate greater neuropsychological impairment. Age range is for that particular score in units of years. PR, percentile rank. -- denotes not administered, or score type not available or computed.

Social perception involves intellectual processes that facilitate social interaction.

Social perception is significantly impaired. This explains the presence of conduct problems of an interpersonal nature, which is associated with neuropsychological dysfunction.

(*Cont.*)

FORM 12.2

CASE 3: NEUROPSYCHOLOGICAL EVALUATION REPORT (*Cont.*)

TABLE 6 ■ **VISUOSPATIAL PROCESSING**

Score name	Age range	Scaled score	PR	Classification	Measured abilities
Arrows Total	5–16	12	75	At expected level	Visuospatial skills in judging line orientation
Block Construction Total	5–16	2	0.4	Well below expected level	Visuoconstructional skills in three-dimensional tasks
Design Copying General Total	5–16	--	51–75	At expected level	Visuoconstructional skills in two-dimensional tasks
Geometric Puzzles Total	5–16	6	9	Borderline	Visuospatial perception including mental rotation
Picture Puzzles Total	7–16	3	1	Well below expected level	Visual perception and scanning

Note: Scaled score mean = 10, standard deviation = 3. Lower scores indicate greater neuropsychological impairment. Age range is for that particular score in units of years. PR, percentile rank. -- denotes not administered, or score type not available or computed.

Visuospatial processing is the capacity to understand the orientation of visual information in two- and three-dimensional space.

There is some measured impairment in visuoconstructional skills on three-dimensional tasks and on mental rotation tasks, the former showing further evidence of apraxia.

Conners CBRS, Parent and Teacher Forms

TABLE 7 ■ **VALIDITY OF RATINGS**

	Parent ratings				Teacher ratings		
Scale	Raw score	Differentials	Result	Scale	Raw score	Differentials	Result
Positive Impression[a]	0	--	Valid	Positive Impression[a]	0	--	Valid
Negative Impression[b]	3	--	Valid	Negative Impression[b]	3	--	Valid
Inconsistency Index[c]	6	2	Invalid	Inconsistency Index[c]	2	0	Valid

Note: Lower raw scores indicate that the ratings are increasingly valid. -- denotes not administered, or score type not available or computed.

[a]Invalid interpretation indicates that the rater produced an overly positive description of the youth's behavior.

[b]Invalid indicates that the rater produced an overly negative description of the youth's behavior.

[c]Invalid indicates either variable attention or comprehension difficulties on the part of the rater.

The parent ratings manifested some invalid response tendencies. The teacher ratings were valid. Therefore, the parent ratings were considered valid under the following conditions: (a) when consistent with the valid teacher ratings and (b) when reasonably supportive of other test data deemed reliable and valid, including data gathered from the diagnostic interview.

(*Cont.*)

FORM 12.2

CASE 3: NEUROPSYCHOLOGICAL EVALUATION REPORT (*Cont.*)

TABLE 8 ■ **CLINICAL SCALE**

Scale	Parent ratings		Teacher ratings		Diagnostic result[a]	Measured symptoms
	T-score*	DSM symptom counts	T-score*	DSM symptom counts		
Conduct Disorder	90*	Met	90*	Met	Positive	Repetitive and persistent violations of the basic rights of others and major societal norms or rules
Major Depressive Episode	76*	Met	82*	Met	Positive	Persistent sadness or irritability; lack of interest, pleasure, energy, self-worth, concentration
Manic Episode	90*	Met	90*	Met	Positive	Persistently elevated, expansive, or irritable mood; racing thoughts; distractible; impulsive

Note: T-score mean = 50, standard deviation = 10. Higher *T*-scores indicate greater presence of symptoms. *denotes that the *T*-score is statistically significant; measured symptoms on that clinical scale are sufficiently severe to indicate a clinical diagnosis. Symptom counts "Met" when at or above the *DSM-IV-TR* cut-off score; symptom counts "Not met" when below the *DSM-IV-TR* cut-off score.

[a]Atypical symptoms indicate the presence of clinical symptoms due to an alternate *DSM-IV-TR* diagnosis.

The results are positive for severe conduct problems that, from the history, began developing subsequent to his TBI, along with current evidence of neuropsychological dysfunction and thus brain damage. This indicates the presence of Personality change Due to Head Trauma.

There is also evidence of severe mood disorder involving bipolar-type symptoms, again associated with his TBI and neuropsychological dysfunction. Hence, there is support for the presence of Mood Disorder Due to Head Trauma.

Of note, the Conners CBRS Violence Potential Content scales was statistically significant in both parent and teacher ratings (Ts = 90, 86, respectively). This indicates the risk for future violence and aggression toward others.

Posttest *DSM-IV-TR* Diagnoses

Axis I:
❑ 294.11 Dementia Due to Head Trauma, With Behavioral Disturbance
Noted: Neuropsychological Test Results:
      Memory Impairment
      Aphasia
      Apraxia
Rule out: Progressive due to evidence of exacerbation past five years
❑ 310.1 Personality Change Due to Head Trauma, Aggressive Type
❑ 293.83 Mood Disorder Due to Head Trauma, With Bipolar Symptoms
❑ 314.01 Attention-Deficit/Hyperactivity Disorder, Combined Type (Premorbid – historical diagnosis)
Noted: Risk for aggression and violence

Axis II:
❑ V71.09 No Diagnosis

Axis III:
❑ 854.00 Head Injury

Axis IV:
❑ Psychosocial Stressors – Social, Educational, Legal

(*Cont.*)

FORM 12.2

CASE 3: NEUROPSYCHOLOGICAL EVALUATION REPORT (*Cont.*)

Axis V:
❏ Global Assessment of Functioning (GAF): 40 Serious symptoms

Prognosis: Guarded due to neuropsychological dysfunction and comorbidity

TREATMENT RECOMMENDATIONS

1. Psychiatric intervention for the above-listed Axis I *DSM-IV-TR* diagnoses.
2. Neurological consultation and follow-up treatment as indicated.
3. Cognitive behavioral treatment to improve executive functioning skills, impulse control, anger management, and social and interpersonal perception and skills.
4. Case management services are advised for more comprehensive behavioral intervention.
5. Neuropsychological retesting in the event that clinical observations indicate the presence of Dementia progression.

John M. Spores, PhD, JD, HSPP
Psychologist – Indiana #20040638A
Attorney at Law – Indiana #21404–64

FORM 12.3

CASE 4: INITIAL PSYCHOLOGICAL ASSESSMENT REPORT

COMMUNITY MENTAL HEALTH CENTER

Outpatient Department

INITIAL PSYCHOLOGICAL ASSESSMENT REPORT

Patient Name: Mann, Penny
Account Number: 444444
Date: May 15, 2010

Patient Identifying Information: Chronological age is 16 years 4 months. Gender is female. DOB: 01/14/1994.

Referral Information: The referral source is James Brown, MA, LMHC, who indicated that the diagnosis remains ambiguous subsequent to clinical interview and observations, there has been poor or no response to treatment intervention for unknown reasons, and objective standardized testing will significantly impact treatment planning and outcome.

The stated *DSM-IV-TR* diagnosis needed to be ruled out includes a Major Depressive disorder With or Without Psychosis. Her current working diagnosis is Depressive Disorder NOS.

Presenting symptoms included dysphoria, irritability, sad mood, fatigue, lack of interest, social withdrawal, blunted affect, feelings of worthlessness, periodic vague suicidal thoughts, although without intent or plan, hypersomnia, and diminished attention and concentration. Onset was estimated to be at 12 years of age, although with remarkable exacerbation within the past 2 years. These symptoms are associated with declining academic grades from above average to low average and failing.

Additional symptoms included visual disturbances in the form of "black shadows" of people following her, along with periodic auditory disturbances of voices instructing her to harm herself. Furthermore, there have been two episodes of self-mutilation in the form of cutting, with escalating urges to repeat such behavior. These symptoms have a more recent onset within the past 6 months and largely precipitated this testing referral.

Clinical Psychologist: John M. Spores, PhD, JD, HSPP
Psychologist – Indiana #20040638A
Attorney at Law – Indiana #21404–64

Mental Status Examination and Behavioral Observations: Affect was blunted. Mood was depressed. Thought process was periodically alogical, although sequential, relevant, and coherent. Thought content included some ideas of persecution. Short-term and long-term memory functioning was normal and intact. She was oriented to time, place, and person. Activity level was normal. Social skills were somewhat ineffectual, marked by difficulty elaborating on her feelings and thoughts. Estimated intellectual function based on verbal skills and reasoning abilities is average. Psychotic symptoms were evident in the form of sensory-perceptual disturbances as previously documented in the presenting symptoms. There was evidence of vague suicidal thoughts, although without intentions or plans. There was some evidence of self-mutilation or self-harm in the form of cutting.

(Cont.)

FORM 12.3

CASE 4: INITIAL PSYCHOLOGICAL ASSESSMENT REPORT (*Cont.*)

Psychiatric/Medical/Psychological: The referring clinician completed a Behavioral Health Evaluation (i.e., 90801) in or about April 2009. Psychiatric history is unremarkable. Family psychiatric history is positive for Attention-Deficit/Hyperactivity Disorder (ADHD) and Depressive Disorder. Medical functioning is unremarkable. She is not taking any current psychotropic medications. There is a negative history of severe head injuries, seizure disorder, and major surgeries. Vision is corrected for astigmatism. Hearing is normal. Previous psychological testing has not been done.

Developmental: There were no pre-, peri-, or post-natal complications reported. Gestation was full-term. Birth weight was 9 pounds 5 ounces. Birth length was 20 inches. Developmental milestones were reported as falling within the normal range.

Family: Penny lives with her mother. Their relationship has become increasingly strained associated with the presenting symptoms.

Interpersonal: Penny's relationships have a history of being intense, unstable, and marked by issues of mistrust and conflict.

Educational: Penny is in Grade 11. Academic performance has typically been above average, although has declined to low average and failing associated with the presenting complaints.

Vocational: None.

Substance Abuse: Denied. This was corroborated by her mother.

Legal: Unremarkable.

Initial Assessment Summary: Based upon the initial psychological assessment evidence, pre-test working diagnosis and disorders needed to be ruled out are listed below in the ensuing *Pretest DSM-IV-TR Diagnosis* section.

The following tests and estimated hours are requested:

1. Millon Adolescent Clinical Inventory (MACI) (1 hour)
2. Minnesota Multiphasic Personality Inventory–Adolescent (MMPI–A) (1 hour)
3. Rorschach Inkblot Test, Comprehensive System, RIAP, Fifth Edition (2 hours)

Total requested psychological testing hours is 4 (Billing Code 96101).

Finally, one (1) individual hour (Billing Code 90806) is requested for follow-up test feedback session and treatment planning.

All of the above-enumerated tests have sufficient empirically derived reliability and validity, and are age-appropriate. Furthermore, these tests are the most recently published editions.

Pretest *DSM-IV-TR* Diagnoses

Axis I:
❑ 311 Depressive Disorder NOS
❑ 298.9 Psychotic Disorder NOS

(*Cont.*)

FORM 12.3

CASE 4: INITIAL PSYCHOLOGICAL ASSESSMENT REPORT *(Cont.)*

Provisional, Rule Out:
- ❒ 296.23 Major Depressive Disorder, Single Episode, Severe
- ❒ 296.24 Major Depressive Disorder, Single Episode, Severe With Psychotic Features

Axis II:
- ❒ 799.9 Diagnosis Deferred

Rule Out:
- ❒ 301.83 Borderline Personality Traits/Disorder

Axis III:
- ❒ No Contributory or Pertinent Medical Disorders Noted

Axis IV:
- ❒ Psychosocial Stressors – Social, Educational

Axis V:
- ❒ Global Assessment of Functioning (GAF): 35 Impaired reality testing

Prognosis: Deferred pending psychological assessment and test results

John M. Spores, PhD, JD, HSPP
Psychologist – Indiana #20040638A
Attorney at Law – Indiana #21404–64

FORM 12.4

CASE 4: PSYCHOLOGICAL EVALUATION REPORT

COMMUNITY MENTAL HEALTH CENTER

Outpatient Department

PSYCHOLOGICAL EVALUATION REPORT

Patient Name: Mann, Penny
Account Number: 444444
Date: June 16, 2010

Patient Identifying Information: Chronological age is 16 years 5 months. Gender is female. DOB: 01/14/1994.

Referral Information: The referral source is James Brown, MA, LMHC, who indicated that the diagnosis remains ambiguous subsequent to clinical interview and observations, there has been poor or no response to treatment intervention for unknown reasons, and objective standardized testing will significantly impact treatment planning and outcome.

The stated *DSM-IV-TR* diagnosis needed to be ruled out includes a Major Depressive disorder With or Without Psychosis. Her current working diagnosis is Depressive Disorder NOS.

Presenting symptoms included dysphoria, irritability, sad mood, fatigue, lack of interest, social withdrawal, blunted affect, feelings of worthlessness, periodic vague suicidal thoughts, although without intent or plan, hypersomnia, and diminished attention and concentration. Onset was estimated to be at 12 years of age, although with remarkable exacerbation within the past 2 years. These symptoms are associated with declining academic grades from above average to low average and failing.

Additional symptoms included visual disturbances in the form of "black shadows" of people following her, along with periodic auditory disturbances of voices instructing her to harm herself. Furthermore, there have been two episodes of self-mutilation in the form of cutting, with escalating urges to repeat such behavior. These symptoms have a more recent onset within the past 6 months and largely precipitated this testing referral.

Assessment and Test Battery

1. Diagnostic Interview (05/15/2010)
2. Mental Status Examination and Behavioral Observations (05/15/2010)
3. Rorschach Inkblot Test, Comprehensive System, RIAP Fifth Edition, Ages 15 to 17 (Rorschach–CS, Ages 15 to 17) (06/16/2010)
4. Minnesota Multiphasic Personality Inventory–Adolescent (MMPI–A) (05/27/2010)
5. Millon Adolescent Clinical Inventory (MACI) (05/27/2010)

Clinical Psychologist: John M. Spores, PhD, JD, HSPP
                                    Psychologist – Indiana #20040638A
                                    Attorney at Law – Indiana #21404–64

Mental Status Examination and Behavioral Observations: Affect was blunted. Mood was depressed. Thought process was periodically alogical, although sequential, relevant, and coherent. Thought content included some ideas of persecution. Short-term and long-term memory functioning was normal and intact. She was oriented to time, place, and

(Cont.)

FORM 12.4

CASE 4: PSYCHOLOGICAL EVALUATION REPORT (*Cont.*)

person. Activity level was normal. Social skills were somewhat ineffectual, marked by difficulty elaborating on her feelings and thoughts. Estimated intellectual function based on verbal skills and reasoning abilities is average. Psychotic symptoms were evident in the form of sensory-perceptual disturbances as previously documented in the presenting symptoms. There was evidence of vague suicidal thoughts, although without intentions or plans. There was some evidence of self-mutilation or self-harm in the form of cutting.

Psychiatric/Medical/Psychological: The referring clinician completed a Behavioral Health Evaluation (i.e., 90801) in or about April 2009. Psychiatric history is unremarkable. Family psychiatric history is positive for Attention-Deficit/Hyperactivity Disorder (ADHD) and Depressive Disorder. Medical functioning is unremarkable. She is not taking any current psychotropic medications. There is a negative history of severe head injuries, seizure disorder, and major surgeries. Vision is corrected for astigmatism. Hearing is normal. Previous psychological testing has not been done.

Developmental: There were no pre-, peri-, or post-natal complications reported. Gestation was full-term. Birth weight was 9 pounds 5 ounces. Birth length was 20 inches. Developmental milestones were reported as falling within the normal range.

Family: Penny lives with her mother. Their relationship has become increasingly strained associated with the presenting symptoms.

Interpersonal: Penny's relationships have a history of being intense, unstable, and marked by issues of mistrust and conflict.

Educational: Penny is in Grade 11. Academic performance has typically been above average, although has declined to low average and failing associated with the presenting complaints.

Vocational: None.

Substance Abuse: Denied. This was corroborated by her mother.

Legal: Unremarkable.

TEST RESULTS AND INTERPRETATION

Rorschach–CS, Ages 15 to 17

TABLE 1 ■ **TEST VALIDITY: SITUATIONAL GUARDEDNESS**

Variable	Score	Expected range	Positive result range	Result[a]	Meaning of positive result
R	23	18–29*	≤13[†]	Negative	Excessively nonproductive; defensive

Note: *denotes that the listed range is based on −1.00 to +1.00 standard deviations from the normative mean including rounding for ease of interpretation. [†]denotes that the listed range is determined by Comprehensive System interpretation guidelines.

[a]When R < 14, the entire Rorschach protocol is per se invalid. There is insufficient test data for meaningful interpretation.

There is no evidence of situational guardedness. In this regard, the clinical and personality variables are deemed valid.

(*Cont.*)

FORM 12.4

CASE 4: PSYCHOLOGICAL EVALUATION REPORT (*Cont.*)

TABLE 2 ■ TEST VALIDITY: SYMPTOM EXAGGERATION

Variable	Score	Expected range	Positive result range	Result[a]	Meaning of positive result
X–%[b]	0.13	0.00–0.18*	≥0.70[†]	Negative	Exaggerating or malingering symptoms
XA+%	0.87	0.80–0.95*	≥0.75[††]	Positive	Indications of adequate reality testing
X–%	0.13	0.00–0.18*	≥0.26[†]	Negative	Extremely distorted thinking

Note: *denotes that the listed range is based on –1.00 to +1.00 standard deviations from the normative mean including rounding for ease of interpretation. [†]denotes that the listed range is determined by Comprehensive System interpretation guidelines. [††]denotes that the listed range is determined by percentage base rate in the norm reference sample due to that variable's skewed distribution.

[a]When the first row variable is X–% < 0.70, and hence negative, both remaining variables must yield positive results to indicate an invalid response pattern.

[b]X–% ≥ 0.70 indicates such gross psychological impairment that testing would have been precluded; therefore the entire Rorschach protocol is deemed per se invalid irrespective of the remaining variables.

There is no evidence of exaggeration of symptoms or malingering. In this regard, the clinical and personality variables are deemed valid.

TABLE 3 ■ CLINICAL VARIABLES: PSYCHOTIC DISORDERS

Variable	Score	Expected range	Positive result range	Result	Meaning of positive result
WSum6	4	0–18[†]	≥19[†]	Negative	Ideational or cognitive slippage; formal thought disorder
Level 2	0	0[††]	≥1[††]	Negative	Manifestly bizarre responses
PTI	1	0–2[††]	3–5[††]	Negative	Psychotic index; psychotic disorder
XA+%	0.87	0.74–1.00**	≤0.73[†σ]	Negative	Disturbed mediation or reality testing
WDA+%	0.95	0.79–1.00**	≤0.78[†σ]	Negative	Pervasively disturbed mediation or reality testing
X–%	0.13	0.00–0.25**	≥0.26[†σ]	Negative	Extremely distorted thinking

Note: PTI, Perceptual Thinking Index. **denotes that the listed range is based on –2.00 to +2.00 standard deviations from the normative mean including rounding for ease of interpretation. [†]denotes that the listed range is determined by Comprehensive System interpretation guidelines. [††]denotes that the listed range is determined by percentage base rate in the norm reference sample due to that variable's skewed distribution. [σ]denotes that the listed positive result range is based on the deviation principle.

All the Psychotic Disorders variables are negative. There is no evidence of a Psychotic Disorder.

TABLE 4 ■ CLINICAL VARIABLES: MOOD DISORDERS

Variable	Score	Expected range	Positive result range	Result	Meaning of positive result
DEPI	6	0–4[†]	5–7[†]	Positive	Affective disruption; emotional disarray; depression
MOR	8	0–2[††]	≥3[††]	Positive	Pessimism; low self-worth
S–CON	5	0–7[†]	≥8[†]	Negative	Risk for effecting one's own suicide

Note: DEPI, Depression Index. S–CON, Suicide Constellation Index. *denotes that the listed range is based on –1.00 to +1.00 standard deviations from the normative mean including rounding for ease of interpretation. [†]denotes that the listed range is determined by Comprehensive System interpretation guidelines. [††]denotes that the listed range is determined by percentage base rate in the norm reference sample due to that variable's skewed distribution.

There is evidence of a severe depressive disorder, including six of seven positive criteria on the DEPI and remarkable pessimism. However, the S–CON is negative. Therefore, there is no evidence of an imminent risk for suicide.

(*Cont.*)

FORM 12.4

CASE 4: PSYCHOLOGICAL EVALUATION REPORT (*Cont.*)

TABLE 5 ■ PERSONALITY DISORDERS VARIABLES

Variable	Score	Expected range	Positive result range	Result	Meaning of positive result
Fr + rF	1	0[†]	≥1[†]	Positive	Narcissism; inflated sense of self-worth
3r + (2)/R Low[a]	0.35	0.37–0.58[†]	≤0.36[†]	Positive	Low self-esteem
Sum V	3	0–1[*]	≥2[σ]	Positive	Preoccupation with negative features of the self
H:(H)+Hd+(Hd)	2:4	2–5:0–6[*]	H < (H)+Hd+(Hd)[†]	Positive	Distorted self-image
Sum T High	3	0–2[††]	≥3[††]	Positive	Either (a) recent object loss or (b) chronic loneliness or emptiness
AG	4	0–3[†]	≥4[†]	Positive	Hostile and negative attitudes toward people
GHR:PHR	1:6	GHR ≥ PHR[†]	GHR < PHR[†]	Positive	Likelihood of personality disorder

Note: [*]denotes that the listed range is based on –1.00 to +1.00 standard deviations from the normative mean including rounding for ease of interpretation. [†]denotes that the listed range is determined by Comprehensive System interpretation guidelines. [††]denotes that the listed range and/or result is determined by percentage base rate in the norm-reference sample due to that variable's skewed distribution. [σ]denotes that the listed positive result range is based on the deviation principle.

[a]When both 3r + (2)/R Low and Fr + rF are positive, this indicates extreme fluctuations in sense of self or splitting object-relations consistent with *borderline* personality structure and organization.

The positive results on the Personality Disorders variables are consistent with Borderline Personality, including most especially evidence of extreme fluctuations in Penny's sense of self.

MMPI–A

TABLE 6 ■ NONRESPONSIVE VALIDITY SCALES

Scale	T-score	Result	Measured test-taking response pattern
CNS(?)[a,b]	0	Low	Number of item omissions or improperly answered items
TRIN[c]	59	Valid	Fixed responding in either the "True" or "False" direction resulting in inconsistency
VRIN[c]	40	Valid	Indiscriminant and random responding

Note: T-score mean = 50, standard deviation = 10. Higher T-scores indicate greater presence of the measured response pattern by the respondent.

[a]CNS(?) datum reported as a raw score.

[b]CNS(?) score ranges and result: (a) 0 to 3, low; (b) 4 to 10, moderate; (c) 11 to 30, marked; and (d) 31 to 478, invalid.

[c]TRIN/VRIN score ranges and result: (a) 30 to 69, valid; (b) 70 to 79, cautiously valid; and (c) 80 to 120, invalid.

The overall results are negative for a non-responsive pattern.

TABLE 7 ■ UNDER-REPORTING AND OVER-REPORTING VALIDITY SCALES

Scale	T-score	Result[a]	Measured test-taking response pattern
L	43	Normal	Endorsement of rarely claimed moral attributes, activities, or virtues
K	37	Low	Endorsement of items in a manner that indicates noteworthy psychological well adjustment
F[b]	54	Normal	Endorsement of infrequently reported symptoms

Note: T-score mean = 50, standard deviation = 10. Higher T-scores indicate greater presence of the measured response style by the respondent.

[a]Score ranges and result: (a) 30 to 40, low; (b) 41 to 55, normal; (c) 56 to 65 moderate; and (d) 66 to 120, marked.

[b]F extreme score 90 to 120 may indicate the genuine presence of severe thought disorganization reflective of a psychotic process.

The overall results are negative for both under-reporting and over-reporting symptoms.

(*Cont.*)

FORM 12.4

CASE 4: PSYCHOLOGICAL EVALUATION REPORT *(Cont.)*

TABLE 8 ■ MMPI–A VALIDITY RESULT

Result	Reason	Interpretation strategy employed on the clinical and personality scale scores
Valid	Acceptable response pattern	Standard

TABLE 9 ■ CLINICAL: MOOD DISORDERS

Scale	T-score[a]	Measured symptoms
2	89**	Severe depression; hopelessness; apathy; lack of interest in activities; excessive guilt; sense of inadequacy; social withdrawal and isolation
A–dep$_1$	71**	Sadness; depression; despondency; fatigue; apathy; pervasive sense of hopelessness; possible suicidal ideation
D$_4$	79**	Impairments in attention, concentration, and memory associated with depressive mood symptoms

Note: T-score mean = 50, standard deviation = 10. Higher T-scores indicate greater presence of measured symptoms.

[a]No asterisk = T-score (30–59) is within normal limits and an absence of a disorder; * = T-score (60–64) is a moderate elevation and indicates the possible presence of a disorder in need of corroborating evidence; ** = T-score (65–120) indicates a clinically significant elevation indicative of an Axis I *DSM-IV-TR* diagnosis.

There is further evidence of severe depressive disorder, consistent with Rorschach results (see Table 4 above).

TABLE 10 ■ CLINICAL: PSYCHOTIC DISORDERS

Scale	T-score*[a]	Measured symptoms
Sc (8)	57	Delusions; hallucinations; mental confusion; disorganized thought process; disturbed reality testing
A–biz	55	Psychotic thought process; disturbed reality testing; hallucinations; delusions including paranoid symptoms
Sc$_6$	62*	Severe and bizarre sensory-perceptual disturbances; hallucinations
Pa (6)	64*	Delusions of persecution and grandeur; ideas of reference; formal thought disorder; disturbed reality testing; secondary hostility and withdrawal
Pa$_1$	59	Delusions of persecution; excessive use of projection; externalization of blame
PSYC	51	Psychosis; disconnection from consensual reality

Note: T-score mean = 50, standard deviation = 10. Higher T-scores indicate greater presence of measured symptoms.

[a]No asterisk = T-score (30–59) is within normal limits and an absence of a disorder; * = T-score (60–64) is a transitional elevation and suggests the presence of a sub-threshold or mild disorder in need of corroborating evidence; ** = T-score (65–120) indicates a clinically significant elevation indicative of a genuine moderate to severe disorder.

None of the Psychotic Disorders Scales fall within the range of a clinically significant elevation. Hence, there is no evidence of a Psychotic Disorder. These results are consistent with those of the Rorschach Inkblot Test (see Table 3 above). The two subthreshold elevations are consistent with severe personality disturbance, including Borderline psychopathology, once again consistent with Rorschach data (see Table 5 above).

(Cont.)

FORM 12.4

CASE 4: PSYCHOLOGICAL EVALUATION REPORT (*Cont.*)

MACI

TABLE 11 ■ VALIDITY SCALES

Scale	Raw score	Result	Measured test-taking response style
Omissions[a]	0	Valid	Responding to a sufficient number of items according to test instructions
Reliability[b]	0	Valid	Honesty and accuracy in responding to item content

[a]Omissions are items that remained unanswered; 0 to 9 = valid; 10 to 160 = invalid.

[b]Items on this scale indicate grossly bizarre symptoms infrequently endorsed by nonclinical and clinical samples; 0 = valid, 1 = questionably valid, and 2 = invalid.

There is satisfactory evidence of sufficiency, honesty, and accuracy responding. In these respects, the Clinical Syndromes and Personality Patterns diagnostic scales are deemed valid.

TABLE 12 ■ MODIFYING INDICES

Index	BR-score	Result	Measured test-taking response style
Disclosure	74	Average	Willingness to be forthcoming or open in reporting symptoms
Desirability	35	Average	Wish to appear overly favorable, morally virtuous, and emotionally stable
Debasement	83	Moderately high	Degree to which symptoms are magnified

Note: BR = Base Rate. BR-score ranges (percentile ranges) result: (a) 0 to 34 (0–15), low; (b) 35 to 74 (16–74), average; (c) 75 to 84 (75–89), moderately high; and (d) 85 to 115 (90–100), extremely high.

Test-taking response style indicated the presence of dejection and self-deprecating tendencies. Statistical adjustments to the *BR*-scores of the Clinical Syndromes and Personality Patterns scales were necessitated to enhance diagnostic accuracy and for valid interpretation.

TABLE 13 ■ CLINICAL SYNDROMES

Scale	BR-score[a]	Measured symptoms
Depressive Affect	105**	Sadness; lack of interests; pessimistic thoughts; hopelessness; helplessness; low self-confidence; social withdrawal
Suicidal Tendency	94**	Suicidal thoughts and planning; risk for contemplating suicide as a viable option

Note: BR = Base Rate. 0 and 115 are minimum and maximum *BR*-scores, respectively. Higher *BR*-scores generally indicate greater presence of symptoms.

[a]No asterisk = BR-score (0–74) is within normal limits, absence of a disorder; * = BR-score (75–84) indicates the presence of a disorder, disorder existent but secondary and/or subthreshold; ** = BR-score (85–115) indicates the prominence of a disorder, disorder considered best-fit and/or paramount.

MACI data provide further support for a severe depressive disorder. There is also evidence of suicidal ideation consistent with data from the initial assessment.

(Cont.)

FORM 12.4

CASE 4: PSYCHOLOGICAL EVALUATION REPORT (*Cont.*)

TABLE 14 ■ **PERSONALITY PATTERNS**

Scale	BR-score[a]	Measured maladaptive traits
Borderline (Borderline)[†]	86**	Intense inner conflicts; unstable moods and relationships; identity diffusion; unpredictable and self-destructive behaviors
Self-Demeaning (Self-Defeating)[††]	80*	Allowing others to exploit oneself; undermining others' efforts to help; sabotaging one's own success; negative self-image

Note: BR = Base Rate. 0 and 115 are minimum and maximum *BR*-scores, respectively. Higher *BR*-scores generally indicate greater presence of symptoms. [†]denotes the *DSM-IV-TR* Personality Disorder analogue. [††]denotes the *DSM-III-R* Personality Disorder analogue; *DSM-IV-TR* diagnosis would be Personality Disorder NOS with the indicated maladaptive traits.

[a]No asterisk = *BR*-score (0–74) is within normal limits, absence of a disorder; * = *BR*-score (75–84) indicates the presence of a disorder, disorder existent but secondary and/or subthreshold; ** = *BR*-score (85–115) indicates the prominence of a disorder, disorder considered best-fit and/or paramount.

Results are positive for Borderline Personality Disorder, with secondary mixed Self-Defeating traits. The former is consistent with the Rorschach data (see Table 5 above).

Posttest *DSM-IV-TR* Diagnoses

Axis I:

❏ 296.33 Major Depressive Disorder, Recurrent, Severe

Axis II:

❏ 301.83 Borderline Personality Disorder, With Mixed Self-Defeating Traits

Noted: Transient disturbances in reality testing

Axis III:

❏ No Contributory or Pertinent Medical Disorders Noted

Axis IV:

❏ Psychosocial Stressors – Social, Educational

Axis V:

❏ Global Assessment of Functioning (GAF): 45 Serious symptoms

Prognosis: Fair due to comorbidity including Axis II psychopathology

TREATMENT RECOMMENDATIONS

1. Psychiatric biological intervention for Major Depressive Disorder, Severe, and palliative for Borderline Personality Disorder.
2. Psychotherapy to treat Borderline Personality Disorder and supplementary for Depressive Disorder. Self-defeating traits need also be addressed as they will likely further impede treatment progress.

John M. Spores, PhD, JD, HSPP
Psychologist – Indiana #20040638A
Attorney at Law – Indiana #21404–64

The two adult cases presented in this chapter were selected from my caseload extending from 18 years to 92 years. The first case involved a referral in which Attention-Deficit/Hyperactivity Disorder (ADHD) in adulthood was suspected. This case serves as a counterpart to that of Zachary Anderson (Case 1, Chapter 11) in which I illustrated an effective and efficient test battery for ADHD in childhood. The second case diverted from the typical referral process in that a Rorschach Inkblot Test was ordered on an urgent basis by an inpatient psychiatrist. I chose this case in order to demonstrate the flexibility of testing process delineated in Sections I and II of this book.

CASE 5: RULE OUT ATTENTION-DEFICIT/HYPERACTIVITY DISORDER IN ADULTHOOD

Referral for Testing

Roger was a 47-year-old married male referred internally by Daniel Taylor, MD. Roger was being treated for Bipolar Disorder Not Otherwise Specified (NOS) at the point of referral. Because Roger continued to manifest difficulties with attention and concentration, significant disorganization, distractibility, and other symptoms suggestive of ADHD, despite his mood symptoms being efficaciously treated with Depakote, Dr. Taylor referred him for ADHD testing. Dr. Taylor completed the test referral form (Form 2.1) rather succinctly, simply indicating Bipolar Disorder NOS for his working diagnosis and ADHD for the single rule out diagnosis.

Initial Psychological Assessment Report

Roger's initial report is presented in Form 13.1. The ensuing sections highlight diagnostic issues and assessment information particular to his case.

Clinical Interview Information

The "Referring Information" section documented current key presenting symptoms indicative of ADHD, along with the presence of at least some of these symptoms prior to the age of 7 years (American Psychiatric Association, 2000). Furthermore, noting the chronic course of his symptoms through childhood and adulthood was vital, especially concerning the temporal association between such symptoms and both poor academic achievement and work productivity. The former was elaborated upon in the "Educational" section. Here, evidence of chronic academic underachievement with consequential grade retention and school dropout was documented in summary form. The latter was expounded upon within the "Vocational" section, which duly recorded his erratic and continuing poor-quality work performance and associated job terminations.

Due to some historical controversy regarding the adult ADHD diagnosis (see e.g., Smith, Waschbusch, Willoughby, & Evans, 2000), I chose to administer the Mini-Mental State Examination, Second Edition, Expanded Version, Blue Form (MMSE–2–EV–BF) (Folstein, Folstein, White, & Messer, 2010) to Roger during the initial assessment. My rationale was that the additional empirical evidence of likely cognitive impairments in short-term memory, and thus attention and concentration, would further buttress the presence of medical necessity for ordering a more formal and thorough test battery for purposes of ruling out ADHD in this adult case. In particular, I administered the *Extended Version*, which included the valuable *Story Memory* and *Processing Speed* multiple-point items. In effect, this maximized the probability of a true positive screening result; that is, minimizing the odds of an undesirable false negative outcome or Type II error (Gravetter & Wallnau, 2013; Warner, 2008; see also Chapter 2). In statistical terms, I was essentially increasing the power of my test (Gravetter & Wallnau, 2013).

As can be seen (Table 1), Roger predictably obtained only 6 of 25 points on Story Memory and 12 of 35 points on Processing Speed, together being largely responsible for the positive screening result; that is, 45 total points, which is less than the 50-point threshold. Although more subtle than Story Memory, low scores on Processing Speed ability have also been reliably associated with problems in attention and concentration (see e.g., Weiss, Saklofske, Coalson, & Raiford, 2010). Lastly, the absence of family and relationship stressors was briefly documented so as to rule out the presence of a stress-related disorder that could otherwise account for his presenting symptoms.

DSM-IV-TR Diagnoses to Be Ruled Out

The Bipolar NOS diagnosis was retained by history with a provisional qualifier, and ADHD with all of its threes subtypes (American Psychiatric Association, 2000) were listed as rule out diagnoses. In contrast to the two adolescent cases presented prior (see Chapter 12, Cases 3 and 4), the initial assessment evidence did not suggest any additional diagnoses in need of testing that were not listed by the referring clinician. Finally, it was my opinion that a Global Assessment of Functioning (GAF) score of *45 Serious symptoms* was justified due to both the chronic deleterious effects of the presenting symptoms on his historical academic record and vocational functioning, in conjunction with a positive MMSE–2–EV–BF screening result for neuropsychological dysfunction.

Test Selection and Requested Number of Hours

As stated prior (see Chapter 6), ADHD is considered to be associated with focal neuropsychological impairment (see e.g., Peterson et al., 2009; Shaw et al., 2009). Thus, it may be logically assumed that if this disorder continues into adulthood, such neuropsychological dysfunction would also remain and be amenable to both psychological measurement and detection. Employing this rationale, I ordered the Neuropsychological Assessment Battery (NAB) Attention Module and its subtests (Stern & White, 2003a, 2003b) (with the exception of *Orientation*—see Chapter 6) and the Conners' Continuous Performance Test, Second Edition, Version 5 (CPT–II) (Conners, 2004). In addition, the Conners' Adult ADHD Rating Scales, Long Version (CAARS–L) Self-Report and Observer Forms (Conners, Erhardt, & Sparrow, 1999) were ordered as a symptom-focused standardized measure of ADHD symptoms according to those set out by the *Diagnostic and Statistical Manual of Mental Disorders, Fourth Edition, Text Revision (DSM-IV-TR)* (American Psychiatric Association, 2000). Total estimated time was 4 hours, thus falling within the targeted 3- to 5-hour range. Finally, all 4 hours were requested under the neuropsychological test billing code (i.e., 96118), as they represented the majority of the tests and subtests comprising the battery (see Chapter 2).

Test Instructions

Patients and/or family members. The "Patient Test Instruction Form" (see Form 2.8) was completed for Roger. In particular, the 4 estimated testing hours was recorded (Item 2) and ensued by the written instruction that a one 2-hour appointment would be scheduled for purposes of test administration subsequent to insurance authorization (Item 3). Referencing Item 4, he was then given one copy each of the CAARS–L Self-Report and Observer Forms to take home to complete and return when he arrived for his test administration appointment. He stated that his wife would complete the latter form. Item 5 was stricken as not applicable (i.e., N/A). Finally, it was emphasized that he remain medication compliant with his Depakote. This was because the purpose of testing was to measure and detect attention and impulse control symptoms independent of his Bipolar Disorder.

Support staff. Next, the "Psychological Request and Log Form" (Form 2.9) was completed, with the instruction for support staff to schedule the one 2-hour appointment as planned once test authorization was obtained. A special note was placed in the "Additional Information" section of the form advising staff to remind Roger to bring to his testing appointment the CAARS–L symptom rating scales. After all, not recalling these forms without an additional reminder was a distinct risk considering his presenting symptoms, along with his educational and vocational histories (see Form 13.1).

Test Administration Process

All four requested test hours were approved under the 96118 neuropsychological testing billing code. Roger arrived at his 2-hour testing appointment with the completed CAARS–L forms, although he confessed that he would have forgotten them had it not been for his wife. In general, however, this does show evidence of the remarkable degree of motivation spouses possess when the goal is to accurately diagnose and successfully treat their partners.

Test administration began with the NAB Attention Module subtests, which consumed about 40 minutes. CPT–II administration ensued and was completed within 20 minutes. Because both of these tests were computer scored (Conners, 2004; Neuropsychological Assessment Battery Software Portfolio, 2008), the CPT–II automatically so, both tests were scored within 15 minutes. Manual scoring for the two CAARS–L forms was done within 20 minutes. This left just under 2½ hours for test interpretation and report-writing.

Final Psychological Evaluation Report

Roger's final report is presented in Form 13.2. The subsequent sections discuss important facets of the data pattern and interpretation sequence leading to his final diagnoses and treatment recommendations.

Modifications to the Initial Report

As most typically occurs, there was no diagnostically relevant assessment information gleaned subsequent to the initial interview. Hence, the report was reviewed for accuracy, the standard modifications were made (see Form 3.1 and compare with Form 13.2), and the diagnoses to be ruled out were reviewed.

Test Scoring and Interpretation Process

The test reporting and interpretation sequence is located in the "Test Results and Interpretation" section (Form 13.2). The process is discussed in more detail immediately subsequent.

Initial test order. Because the analysis focused exclusively on the presence or absence of ADHD, the initial test sequence began with the neuropsychological performance-based tests. The NAB Attention subtests provided a more extensive and varied measurement of his attentional neurocognitive abilities, and hence preceded the CPT–II (Table 4 to Table 6). The CAARS–L standardized symptom rating scales (Table 7 and Table 8) completed the analysis.

Scoring and interpretation sequence. Table 2 provided an overall empirical measure of Roger's attention ability. This was immediately ensued by Table 3, which provided the NAB attention subtest profile. Once again, this followed the general to specific deductive logic of data analysis espoused throughout this book. His Attention Module standard score was unequivocally within the severely impaired range of functioning and was succinctly interpreted as being consistent with ADHD. Furthermore, the Table 3 subtest score pattern showed clear and convincing empirical evidence of impaired functioning ranging from mild to severe. Such data made it immediately apparent as to why Roger's Attention Module Index in the preceding table was severely deficient. The ensuing Table 3 narrative summarily referenced this subtest profile pattern and reiterated its consistency with ADHD.

The CPT–II tables followed the NAB results with their data-driven statistical emphases. In particular, Tables 4 shows unambiguous evidence of test validity. The discriminant function analysis in Table 5 yielded a rather confident ADHD classification, which was deductively followed by the multiple statistical elevations revealed within the Table 6 specific measures. Note that the abnormal standard scores can be easily identified by the reader due to the affixed asterisks. The single *positive for ADHD* interpretation was retained, including the important diagnostic remarks indicating impairments in both attention and impulse control. This was deemed useful in suggesting the presence of ADHD, Combined Type. Note that within the Table 5 Guideline column, I chose to identify *marked* elevations in order to emphasize the presence of dysfunction.

Lastly, the analysis moved to the CAARS–L, wherein the ratings would (a) corroborate the ADHD diagnosis pursuant to *DSM-IV-TR* behavioral criteria and (b) assist in determining the type of ADHD present. First, Table 7 confirmed test validity for both raters, at least in terms of consistency. This was especially important to establish as applied to Roger's self-report data considering his measured impairment in attention on both the NAB and CPT–II. Second, Table 8 data corroborated the presence of ADHD, Combined Type, particularly noting the remarkable interrater reliability for positive results on all scales.

Final test order. As can be seen, the data flowed logically and coherently from the two performance-based neuropsychological tests to the behavioral ratings. Because no other test sequence would improve upon the clarity of the results, the original test sequence was retained in the final report.

Final diagnoses and treatment recommendations. The singular diagnostic question and the integrity of the results rendered the posttest diagnoses both simple and straightforward. That is, the ADHD, Combined Type diagnosis was added below that of the historical Bipolar Disorder NOS. The GAF score of 45 was retained because (a) the serious dysfunction manifested in his real-world behavior was previously established during the initial assessment and (b) the subsequent test data were commensurate with and corroborative of such dysfunction. Lastly, the added ADHD diagnosis was germane to his prognosis. In particular, I listed it as fair due to the presence of comorbid disorders, at least one of which had shown remarkable chronicity (i.e., ADHD).

Billing

As indicated above, about 2½ hours were available for test interpretation and report-writing. Both were completed in 90 minutes. This was due to (a) the ADHD rule out focus, (b) the use of the prepared data tables, (c) the minimal narrative interpretations without the need for qualification, and (d) the reliability and integrity of the results such that no modifications in test order were necessitated. Thus, only 3 of the 4 authorized test hours were billed on the same date as test administration, scoring, interpretation, and report composition (i.e., March 10, 2011). As expected, remuneration of all 3 hours was obtained. Furthermore, as a general rule, providers of testing services are afforded enhanced credibility by insurance carriers when they bill for less than the number of preauthorized hours. I adamantly believe that, in conjunction with making consistently reasonable testing requests (viz., 3 to 5 testing hours with the occasional exception of complete neuropsychological test batteries), genuinely billing for less than the authorized hours when that periodically occurs contributes to the ease with which future testing requests are approved.

Communication of Results

Attending the feedback session was both Roger and his wife. In this case, the positive results evoked both relief and hope of improvement in both individuals. Undiagnosed ADHD can easily lead to self-blame and misattributions by others that the presenting problems are due to recalcitrance or indolence. This was especially important in Roger's case as his Bipolar symptoms had largely remitted and there remained no other diagnostic explanation for his presenting symptoms and vocational difficulties. Thus, cognitive restructuring, empathy, and support were easily employed in light of the results. In response to receiving the final report, Dr. Taylor immediately initiated ADHD medication with positive results.

CASE 6: RULE OUT MAJOR DEPRESSIVE DISORDER WITH OR WITHOUT PSYCHOTIC FEATURES, AND PREVIOUSLY UNSUSPECTED BORDERLINE PERSONALITY PSYCHOPATHOLOGY

Referral for Testing

Denise was a 36-year-old divorced female who was being treated on an outpatient psychiatric basis for Generalized Anxiety Disorder (GAD). She had been in treatment for approximately 3 years at the point of testing referral. The precipitant for testing was a diagnostically unexpected and atypical suicide attempt in the form of cutting her wrists, which also involved failed attempts to overdose her two children with prescription medication. In consequence, she was psychiatrically hospitalized on an involuntary basis pursuant to what the State of Indiana refers to as a 72-hour emergency detention order. According to such order, the patient may be committed for 72 hours and must be released unless it is established by clear and convincing evidence that "… the individual is *mentally ill* and either dangerous or gravely disabled …" (Rights of Persons, 2 Indiana Code § IC 12–26–2-5(e)(1), 2000).[1] Briefly, the legal term mentally ill usually constitutes the most disabling psychological conditions such as the presence of psychosis.

The attending inpatient psychiatrist Lori Jennings, MD, wanted to rule out the presence of a Psychotic Disorder and specifically ordered Rorschach testing. I was initially consulted regarding this case and the number of hours that needed to be preauthorized for such urgent testing. In response, I asked for 2 hours. Staff on the inpatient unit obtained such authorization within the next several hours. Thereafter, I was scheduled to test her the following day due to the time sensitivity of this case.

As this is the final standard psychological testing example presented in this book, I wanted to include this atypical case for several reasons. First, I wanted an opportunity to demonstrate the flexibility of my proposed system. Although Section I details the testing

[1] *The listed year in this statutory citation represents the most recent date that such statute was either added to or amended.*

process in its entirety, in some instances you may omit rather significant steps, especially those comprising the initial stages. Denise's case illustrates this rather explicitly. Second, although there are many adequately designed standardized tests available, those comprising my recommended inventory are remarkably suitable for contemporary mental health practice. You will find them extremely useful both individually, as here in Denise's case (see Form 13.3), and more frequently, in innumerable combinations so as to answer most *DSM-IV-TR* differential diagnostic dilemmas and related referral questions. Third, as referring clinicians become increasingly cognizant of the effectiveness of psychological testing services as outlined here, their sophistication regarding the use of particular tests will grow in commensurate fashion, even to the point of accurately requesting the administration of particular tests. Denise's case also illustrates this point. Related to the latter, if clinicians realize more the potential usefulness of such psychological testing, the testing referrals shall increase in exponential fashion.

The ensuing sections present an abbreviated sequence symbolic of Denise's case. The focus is on her final report and the manner in which her Rorschach–CS data effectively addressed both the fundamental Axis I diagnostic question posed by Dr. Jennings, in addition to Axis II psychopathology.

Test Administration Process

The date of her testing represented the second of her 3-day emergency commitment. Hence, it was crucial to have the completed final report available for Dr. Jennings prior to her rounds on the unit later that same day. The Rorschach Inkblot Test, Comprehensive System, RIAP 5th Edition (Rorschach–CS) (Exner, 2003) had previously been ordered and approved. Thus, I simply arrived on the unit with the test administration materials and my laptop computer for computer scoring and report-writing.

I first reviewed her inpatient record for identifying information and her initial psychiatric assessment. She continued to carry the diagnosis of GAD, although with the need to rule out an Axis I Psychotic Disorder and a deferral on Axis II. Of particular note, the presenting symptoms in her initial psychiatric report revealed a chronic history of both anxiety and *loneliness*. Because this information was readily available, I was able to obtain this information in about 15 minutes.

Thereafter, I met with Denise for her Rorschach–CS test administration. I briefly stated that Dr. Jennings had ordered this testing so as to assist in an accurate diagnosis. She was initially hesitant although became amenable as evidenced by her following test instructions and providing an interpretable protocol (see Form 13.3). I believe that the implicit nature of this test was vital in preventing her from intentionally minimizing her psychopathology as would have likely occurred on a self-report clinical and personality inventory (see Chapter 9 for an explication of implicit versus explicit tests).

The duration of test administration was about 40 minutes. Manual coding of her responses consumed another 20 minutes. Finally, during the next 10 minutes, I entered her sequence of scores into the Rorschach computer software (Rorschach Scoring Program, 2008), and her Structural Summary and indices were immediately computed and available. Thus, 35 minutes remained for test interpretation and report-writing, which was viable due to the abbreviated nature of her final report.

Final Psychological Evaluation Report

Denise's final report is presented in Form 13.3. Highlights from this report ensue within the succeeding sections, with a clear emphasis on her Rorschach–CS data (Table 1 to Table 6) which represented the core aspect of her testing case.

Test Scoring and Interpretation Process

Note that the report first briefly reviewed identifying and referral information followed by the single Rorschach–CS test listing. In my opinion, it is crucial in such testing requests to proceed quickly to the test data. Dr. Jennings had already completed an initial psychiatric assessment using the clinical method and was thus intimately familiar with such information. As such, there was no need to be redundant in my testing report. Furthermore, the Rorschach–CS variables that I reported in my tables (a) represented direct empirical measures of her reality testing ability, formal thinking, and personality mechanisms and (b) measured key personality traits using actuarial data. Such data were able to effectively address her psychiatrist's request to rule out psychosis and also address Axis II psychopathology with less dependence on detailed assessment data. That is, her reality testing and formal thinking would either be measured as impaired or unimpaired irrespective of history. In addition, her personality structure would either contain an unstable self-image or not. As will become apparent, one Rorschach–CS variable was reliant upon assessment information for accurate interpretation. Although this clearly is not standard test interpretation practice, because Denise's case was unique such approach was effective.

Scoring and interpretation sequence. Due to the presence of involuntary commitment, analysis of the presence of situational-guardedness was vital (see Table 1). As evidenced by the data, Denise produced a sufficient number of responses for Rorschach–CS scoring. Although less likely in Denise's case, there was also insufficient evidence of symptom exaggeration or malingering (see Table 2). Thus, the remaining clinical and personality variables were deemed both valid and reliable for purposes of interpretation.

Table 3 presented the crucial Psychotic Disorders variables. Although the vast majority of these variables were negative, she produced two rather bizarre Level 2 responses that represented her single positive result. These are extremely unusual (see e.g., Exner, 2003) and indicated that occasionally her reality testing can become quite disturbed, thus accounting for her aberrant behavior precipitating her hospitalization. Although this profile pattern is only suggestive, it did reveal the distinct possibility of a severe Axis II disorder. This interpretation was succinctly inserted into the narrative text immediately subsequent to the Psychotic Disorders data table. The largely negative results in Table 3 rendered unnecessary the inclusion of the optional table titled *WSum6 Thought Disorder Scores*, which I designed as part of the Rorschach–CS results and interpretation tables (see Form 9.5, Table 4). That is, it would not have provided additional useful information regarding a psychotic process due to the single positive variable in Table 3.

Next, considering Denise's harmful behavior to herself and to her children, I included the Mood Disorders variables in order to rule out a severe Depressive or Bipolar Disorder previously unsuspected, and to report the Suicide Constellation Index result (see Table 4). In this case, I believed that reporting and briefly interpreting such negative empirical results was important to document and include in her inpatient mental health record. I also included a number of positive empirical results related to anxiety and stress (see Table 5), as it provided support for (a) her historical GAD diagnosis and (b) an Axis II Personality Disorder. Concerning the latter, the EA was remarkably low, indicating a dispositional deficiency in psychological resources; that is, character pathology (Exner, 2003).

Lastly, although as it turned out most importantly, the Table 6 Personality Disorders Variables were reported and interpreted in detail. Note particularly the measured paradoxical evidence of narcissism coexisting with low self-esteem, thus indicating splitting object-relations as a marker of Borderline Personality Disorder (Kernberg, 1967; McWilliams, 2011). Additional corroborating data included (a) distorted self-image (H < (H)+Hd +(Hd)), (b) likelihood of Axis II psychopathology (GHR < PHR), (c) dissociative ego defenses (Ma + 1 < Mp), and (d) chronic loneliness or emptiness (Sum T = 5). The latter was supported by (a) the presenting symptoms and (b) the statistical presence of such an abnormally high Sum T score (Exner, 2003). There was also some evidence of dependent traits (Fd = 2). Note that all of these results were briefly interpreted in the narrative text immediately following Table 6, which ended the "Test Results and Interpretation" section.

Final diagnoses and treatment recommendations. The GAD historical diagnosis was retained, because it not only was the disorder of record, but also had empirical support in the her test data. Furthermore, an Axis I notation was added indicating no evidence for an acute Psychotic Disorder. This permitted Dr. Jennings to rapidly review the bottom line results with the option of perusing the empirical data at her discretion. Although I am generally wary of rendering a conclusive Axis II diagnosis using strictly Rorschach–CS data, in this case it was my opinion that Denise's remarkably aberrant behavior and unequivocal test data pattern for Borderline Personality rendered it more of a risk to be cautious, as it may have hindered or unnecessarily delayed needed psychotherapeutic intervention. Note also that I attached Dependent Traits to her Axis II psychopathology. The treatment recommendations emphasized the need to incorporate psychotherapy so as to adequately address her Borderline Personality Disorder.

Billing

Both testing hours were billed that same day and were duly covered by insurance.

Communication of Results

The final report was done and available for Dr. Jennings 2 hours prior to her rounds that same day. Due to the emergency nature of this case, Dr. Jennings and nursing staff provided the feedback. I was informed that Denise ultimately signed herself in voluntarily, thus precluding further legal proceedings, and began ongoing psychotherapy on an outpatient basis following her discharge. Of course, she also returned to her outpatient psychiatric treatment for follow-up medication management.

SUMMARY

Chapter 13 presented the final two cases illustrating the manner in which the testing system proposed in this book is to be utilized in mental health practice. In contrast to the previous two chapters, two adult cases were presented. The first illustrated an adult ADHD test battery that was largely neuropsychological in nature. The second demonstrated the general flexibility of this testing system and how it may be specifically adapted for emergency testing cases. The final chapter of this book is devoted to showing the manner in which this testing system may be adapted for forensic competence to stand trial criminal cases.

REFERENCES

American Psychiatric Association. (2000). *Diagnostic and statistical manual of mental disorders* (4th ed., text rev.). Washington, DC: Author.

Conners, C. K. (2004). *Conners' Continuous Performance Test II, Version 5 for Windows (CPT–II): Technical guide and software manual*. North Tonawanda, NY: Multi-Health Systems.

Conners, C. K., Erhardt, D., & Sparrow, E. (1999). *Conners' Adult ADHD Rating Scales (CAARS–L): Technical manual*. North Tonawanda, NY: Multi-Health Systems.

Exner, J. E. (2003). *The Rorschach a comprehensive system: Basic foundations and principles of interpretation* (4th ed., Vol. 1). Hoboken, NJ: John Wiley.

Folstein, M. F., Folstein, S. E., White, T., & Messer, M. A. (2010). *Mini–Mental State Examination, 2nd edition: Users manual.* Lutz, FL: Psychological Assessment Resources.

Gravetter, F. J., & Wallnau, L. B. (2013). *Statistics for the behavioral sciences* (9th ed.). Belmont, CA: Wadsworth, Cengage Learning.

Kernberg, O. (1967). Borderline personality organization. *Journal of the American Psychoanalytic Association, 15,* 641–685.

McWilliams, N. (2011). *Psychoanalytic diagnosis: Understanding personality structure in the clinical process* (2nd ed.). New York, NY: The Guilford Press.

Neuropsychological Assessment Battery Software Portfolio (NAB–SP) [CD-ROM Computer software]. (2008). Lutz, FL: Psychological Assessment Resources (PAR).

Peterson, B. S., Potenza, M. N., Wang, Z., Zhu, H., Martin, A., Marsh, R., & Yu, S. (2009). An fMRI study of the effects of psychostimulants on default-mode processing during Stroop task performance in youths with ADHD. *American Journal of Psychiatry, 166,* 1286–1294.

Rights of Persons, 2 Indiana Code § IC 12–26–2-5(e)(1). (2000).

Rorschach Scoring Program [Computer software]. (2008). Lutz, FL: Exner, Weiner, & Psychological Assessment Resources (PAR).

Shaw, P., Lalonde, F., Lepage, C., Rabin, C., Eckstrand, K., Sharp, W.,...Rapoport, J. (2009). Development of cortical asymmetry in typically developing children and its disruption in attention-deficit/hyperactivity disorder. *Archives of General Psychiatry, 66,* 888–896.

Stern, R. A., & White, T. (2003a). *Neuropsychological Assessment Battery (NAB): Administrative, scoring, and interpretation manual.* Lutz, FL: Psychological Assessment Resources.

Stern, R. A., & White, T. (2003b). *Neuropsychological Assessment Battery (NAB): Psychometric and technical manual.* Lutz, FL: Psychological Assessment Resources.

Warner, R. M. (2008). *Applied statistics.* Thousand Oaks, CA: Sage Publications.

Weiss, L. G., Saklofske, D. H., Coalson, D., & Raiford, S. E. (Eds.). (2010). *WAIS–IV clinical use and interpretation: Scientist-practitioner perspective.* San Diego, CA: Elsevier.

FORM 13.1

CASE 5: INITIAL PSYCHOLOGICAL ASSESSMENT REPORT

COMMUNITY MENTAL HEALTH CENTER

Outpatient Department

INITIAL PSYCHOLOGICAL ASSESSMENT REPORT

Patient Name: Gold, Roger
Account Number: 555555
Date: September 15, 2011

Patient Identifying Information: Chronological age is 47 years 9 months. Gender is male. DOB: 12/13/1963.

Referral Information: The referral source is Daniel Taylor, MD, who indicated that the diagnosis remains ambiguous subsequent to clinical interview, examination, and ongoing observation, there has been poor or no response to treatment intervention for unknown reasons, and objective standardized testing will significantly impact treatment planning and outcome.

The specific *DSM-IV-TR* referral question includes the need to rule out adult Attention-Deficit/Hyperactivity Disorder (ADHD). His current working diagnosis is Bipolar Disorder NOS, which is not in question.

Relevant presenting symptoms included difficulties concentrating, impairments in immediate and sustained attention, difficulties focusing, distractibility, disorganization, mind-wandering, acting without considering consequences, fidgeting, and difficulties remaining seated. At least some of these symptoms were present prior to the age of seven years. They have had a chronic course and have been associated with a history of academic underachievement as a child and adolescent, and during Roger's adulthood, poor work productivity.

Clinical Psychologist: John M. Spores, PhD, JD, HSPP
Psychologist – Indiana #20040638A
Attorney at Law – Indiana #21404–64

Mental Status Examination Including the Mini-Mental State Examination, Second Edition, Expanded Version, Blue Form (MMSE–2–EV–BF): Affect was restricted. Mood was mildly anxious. Thought process was logical, sequential, relevant, and coherent. Thought content was reality-based and normal. The MMSE–2–EV–BF results were as follows:

(Cont.)

FORM 13.1

CASE 5: INITIAL PSYCHOLOGICAL ASSESSMENT REPORT (*Cont.*)

TABLE 1 ■ **MMSE–2–EV–BF RESULTS**

Cognitive function	Patient's raw score	Maximum possible raw score
Registration	3	3
Orientation to Time	5	5
Orientation to Place	5	5
Recall	2	3
Attention and Calculation	3	5
Naming	2	2
Repetition	1	1
Comprehension	3	3
Reading	1	1
Writing	1	1
Drawing	1	1
Story Memory	6	25
Processing Speed	12	35
Total Raw Score[a]	**45**	**90**

Note: Lower raw scores indicate greater neurocognitive dysfunction. Overall neurocognitive function data are in boldface.

[a]Raw scores of 50 or less indicate the need for more comprehensive neuropsychological testing.[b]

[b]Using this cut-off, there is 97% confidence that a true case of neuropsychological disorder is recommended for further testing.

Screening Result: Positive for neuropsychological disorder.

Immediate and intermediate memory functions were remarkably impaired. Long-term memory functions were normal and intact, as evidenced by Roger's ability to provide a coherent developmental history with key historical dates. He was oriented to time, place, and person. Estimated intellectual function based on verbal skills, fund of general knowledge, and abstract reasoning abilities is average. Psychotic symptoms were not evident. There was no evidence of suicidal thoughts, intentions, or plans. There was no evidence of self-mutilation or self-harm.

Psychiatric/Medical/Psychological: A Behavioral Health Evaluation (i.e., 90801) was preauthorized for this initial psychological assessment. Inpatient psychiatric history is negative. Family psychiatric history is positive for Bipolar Disorder and Depressive Disorder. Medical functioning is remarkable for Type II Diabetes. Current psychotropic medication includes Depakote for his diagnosed Bipolar Disorder. There is a negative history of severe head injuries and seizure disorder. There is a history of one surgery for cataracts. Vision is corrected for both reading and a nearsighted condition. Hearing is normal. Previous neuropsychological testing has not been done.

Family: Roger lives with his wife. He has two young adult daughters who live independently. He denied the presence of stressors within the family.

Interpersonal: Interpersonal relationships were generally described as satisfactory in both quality and quantity.

Educational: Roger completed formal schooling through Grade 10. He was retained in Grade 4 due to unsatisfactory academic performance. He dropped out of formal schooling due to chronic low academic achievement, which he associated with his presenting symptoms. Roger subsequently earned his GED in or about 1981 when he was approximately 18 years of age.

(Cont.)

FORM 13.1

CASE 5: INITIAL PSYCHOLOGICAL ASSESSMENT REPORT (*Cont.*)

Vocational: Roger was recently hired as a sales clerk. His work history is erratic. His longest employment is three years. He has been terminated from several jobs due to poor work quality. The latter has involved incomplete and late work assignments, along with frequent tardiness.

Substance Abuse: Unremarkable.

Legal: Unremarkable.

Initial Assessment Summary: Based upon the initial psychological assessment evidence, pre-test working diagnosis and disorders needed to be ruled out are listed below in the ensuing *Pretest DSM-IV-TR Diagnosis* section.

The following tests and estimated hours are requested:

1. Neuropsychological Assessment Battery (NAB), Attention Module Subtests, Form 2 (2 hours)
2. Conners' Continuous Performance Test, Second Edition, Version 5 (CPT–II) (1 hour)
3. Conners' Adult ADHD Rating Scales, Long Version (CAARS–L), Self–Report and Observer Forms (1 hour)

Total requested neuropsychological testing hours is 4 (Billing Code 96118).

All of the above-enumerated tests have sufficient empirically derived reliability and validity, and are age-appropriate. Furthermore, these tests are the most recently published editions.

Pretest *DSM-IV-TR* Diagnoses

Axis I:
❑ 296.80 Bipolar Disorder NOS (by history)

Provisional, Rule Out:
❑ 314.01 Attention-Deficit/Hyperactivity Disorder, Combined Type
❑ 314.01 Attention-Deficit/Hyperactivity Disorder, Predominantly Hyperactive-Impulsive Type
❑ 314.00 Attention-Deficit/Hyperactivity Disorder, Predominantly Inattentive Type

Axis II:
❑ V71.09 No Diagnosis

Axis III:
❑ 250.00 Diabetes Mellitus, Type II

Axis IV:
❑ Psychosocial Stressors – Occupational

Axis V:
❑ Global Assessment of Functioning (GAF): 45 Serious symptoms
Prognosis: Deferred pending neuropsychological assessment and test results

John M. Spores, PhD, JD, HSPP
Psychologist – Indiana #20040638A
Attorney at Law – Indiana #21404–64

FORM 13.2

CASE 5: NEUROPSYCHOLOGICAL EVALUATION REPORT

COMMUNITY MENTAL HEALTH CENTER

Outpatient Department

NEUROPSYCHOLOGICAL EVALUATION REPORT

Patient Name: Gold, Roger
Account Number: 555555
Date: October 3, 2011

Patient Identifying Information: Chronological age is 47 years 9 months. Gender is male. DOB: 12/13/1963.

Referral Information: The referral source is Daniel Taylor, MD, who indicated that the diagnosis remains ambiguous subsequent to clinical interview, examination, and ongoing observation, there has been poor or no response to treatment intervention for unknown reasons, and objective standardized testing will significantly impact treatment planning and outcome.

The specific *DSM-IV-TR* referral question includes the need to rule out adult Attention-Deficit/Hyperactivity Disorder (ADHD). His current working diagnosis is Bipolar Disorder NOS, which is not in question.

Relevant presenting symptoms included difficulties concentrating, impairments in immediate and sustained attention, difficulties focusing, distractibility, disorganization, mind-wandering, acting without considering consequences, fidgeting, and difficulties remaining seated. At least some of these symptoms were present prior to the age of seven years. They have had a chronic course and have been associated with a history of academic underachievement as a child and adolescent, and during Roger's adulthood, poor work productivity.

Assessment and Test Battery

1. Diagnostic Interview (09/15/2011)
2. Mental Status Examination Including the Mini-Mental State Examination, Second Edition, Expanded Version, Blue Form (MMSE–2–EV–BF) (09/15/2011)
3. Neuropsychological Assessment Battery (NAB), Attention Module, Form 2 (10/03/2011)
4. Conners' Continuous Performance Test, Second Edition, Version 5 (CPT–II) (10/03/2011)
5. Conners' Adult ADHD Rating Scales, Long Version (CAARS–L), Self–Report and Observer Forms (Submitted 09/21/2011)

Clinical Psychologist: John M. Spores, PhD, JD, HSPP
                             Psychologist – Indiana #20040638A
                             Attorney at Law – Indiana #21404–64

(Cont.)

FORM 13.2

CASE 5: NEUROPSYCHOLOGICAL EVALUATION REPORT (*Cont.*)

Mental Status Examination Including the Mini-Mental State Examination, Second Edition, Expanded Version, Blue Form (MMSE–2–EV–BF): Affect was restricted. Mood was mildly anxious. Thought process was logical, sequential, relevant, and coherent. Thought content was reality-based and normal. The MMSE–2–EV–BF results were as follows:

TABLE 1 ■ **MMSE–2–EV–BF RESULTS**

Cognitive function	Patient's raw score	Maximum possible raw score
Registration	3	3
Orientation to Time	5	5
Orientation to Place	5	5
Recall	2	3
Attention and Calculation	3	5
Naming	2	2
Repetition	1	1
Comprehension	3	3
Reading	1	1
Writing	1	1
Drawing	1	1
Story Memory	6	25
Processing Speed	12	35
Total Raw Score[a]	**45**	**90**

Note: Lower raw scores indicate greater neurocognitive dysfunction. Overall neurocognitive function data are in boldface.

[a]Raw scores of 50 or less indicate the need for more comprehensive neuropsychological testing.[b]

[b]Using this cut-off, there is 97% confidence that a true case of neuropsychological disorder is recommended for further testing.

Screening Result: Positive for neuropsychological disorder.

Immediate and intermediate memory functions were remarkably impaired. Long-term memory functions were normal and intact, as evidenced by Roger's ability to provide a coherent developmental history with key historical dates. He was oriented to time, place, and person. Estimated intellectual function based on verbal skills, fund of general knowledge, and abstract reasoning abilities is average. Psychotic symptoms were not evident. There was no evidence of suicidal thoughts, intentions, or plans. There was no evidence of self-mutilation or self-harm.

Psychiatric/Medical/Psychological: A Behavioral Health Evaluation (i.e., 90801) was preauthorized for this initial psychological assessment. Inpatient psychiatric history is negative. Family psychiatric history is positive for Bipolar Disorder and Depressive Disorder. Medical functioning is remarkable for Type II Diabetes. Current psychotropic medication includes Depakote for his diagnosed Bipolar Disorder. There is a negative history of severe head injuries and seizure disorder. There is a history of one surgery for cataracts. Vision is corrected for both reading and a nearsighted condition. Hearing is normal. Previous neuropsychological testing has not been done.

Family: Roger lives with his wife. He has two young adult daughters who live independently. He denied the presence of stressors within the family.

(Cont.)

FORM 13.2

CASE 5: NEUROPSYCHOLOGICAL EVALUATION REPORT (*Cont.*)

Interpersonal: Interpersonal relationships were generally described as satisfactory in both quality and quantity.

Educational: Roger completed formal schooling through Grade 10. He was retained in Grade 4 due to unsatisfactory academic performance. He dropped out of formal schooling due to chronic low academic achievement, which he associated with his presenting symptoms. Roger subsequently earned his GED in or about 1981 when he was approximately 18 years of age.

Vocational: Roger was recently hired as a sales clerk. His work history is erratic. His longest employment is three years. He has been terminated from several jobs due to poor work quality. The latter has involved incomplete and late work assignments, along with frequent tardiness.

Substance Abuse: Unremarkable.

Legal: Unremarkable.

TEST RESULTS AND INTERPRETATION

NAB, Attention Module, Form 2

TABLE 2 ■ **NAB ATTENTION MODULE INDEX SCORE**

Module index	Index score	PR	90% CI	Interpretive category	Measured abilities
Attention	54	0.11	[47, 61]	Severely impaired	Working memory;[a] selective, divided, and sustained attention; attention to detail; information processing speed

Note: Index score mean = 100, standard deviation = 15. Index scores are derived by use of demographically corrected norms based on chronological age, educational attainment, and sex. Lower index scores indicate greater neuropsychological impairment. PR, percentile rank; CI, confidence interval.

[a]Working memory is the ability to hold immediate memory traces while executing cognitive tasks.

Overall attention is severely impaired, consistent with ADHD.

(*Cont.*)

FORM 13.2

CASE 5: NEUROPSYCHOLOGICAL EVALUATION REPORT (*Cont.*)

TABLE 3 ■ **NAB ATTENTION MODULE SUBTEST SCORE SUMMARY**

Subtest	*T*-score	PR	Interpretive category	Measured abilities
Digits Forward	44	27	Below average	Auditory attentional capacity.
Digits Backward	30	2	Mildly-to-moderately impaired	Working memory[a] for orally presented information
Dots	44	27	Below average	Visuospatial working memory; visual scanning
Numbers and Letters Part A Speed	19	<1	Severely impaired	Psychomotor and information processing speed
Numbers and Letters Part A Errors	58	79	Above average	Sustained, focused, divided, and selective attention; concentration
Numbers and Letters Part A Efficiency	19	<1	Severely impaired	Sustained, focused, divided, and selective attention; concentration; psychomotor and information processing speed
Numbers and Letters Part B Efficiency	36	8	Mildly impaired	Sustained, focused, divided, and selective attention; concentration; psychomotor and information processing speed
Numbers and Letters Part C Efficiency	33	4	Mildly-to-moderately impaired	Sustained, focused, divided, and selective attention; concentration; psychomotor and information processing speed
Numbers and Letters Part D Efficiency	19	<1	Severely impaired	Sustained, focused, divided, and selective attention; concentration; psychomotor and information processing speed
Numbers and Letters Part D Disruption	39	14	Mildly impaired	Sustained, focused, divided, and selective attention; concentration; psychomotor and information processing speed
Driving Scenes	29	2	Moderately impaired	Attention to modifications in a two-lane road within the context of a small business town, viewed from behind a car's steering wheel

Note: T-score mean = 50, standard deviation = 10. Lower *T*-scores indicate greater impairment. *T*-scores are derived by use of demographically corrected norms based on chronological age, educational attainment, and sex. PR, percentile rank.

[a]Working memory involves holding immediate memory traces while executing cognitive tasks.

The majority of NAB Attention subtests show varying degrees of impairment, consistent with ADHD.

CPT–II

TABLE 4 ■ **VALIDITY OF ADMINISTRATION**

	Validity measures			
	Timing difficulties	Noncompliance	Excessive omissions	Absence of hits per test block
Result	No	No	No	No
Interpretation	Valid	Valid	Valid	Valid

The CPT–II administration is valid.

(*Cont.*)

FORM 13.2

CASE 5: NEUROPSYCHOLOGICAL EVALUATION REPORT (*Cont.*)

TABLE 5 ■ **CONFIDENCE INDEX ASSESSMENT**

Statistical analysis	Profile classification	Confidence index	Interpretation
Discriminant Function	ADHD	73%	The chances are 73 out of 100 that a clinical attention problem exists

TABLE 6 ■ **SPECIFIC MEASURES**

Measure	T-score*	PR	Guideline	Interpretation of statistically significant result
Omissions %	52	58	Normal	Failure to respond to target letters (i.e., non-Xs)
Commissions %	63*	89	Impulsivity	Responses given to non-targets (i.e., Xs)
Hit RT	53	66	Normal	Atypical speed of correct responses for the entire test
Hit RT SE	68*	96	Marked inattention	Inconsistency in response speed
Variability of SE	75*	99	Marked inattention	Excessive within-respondent variability in 18 test segments compared to SE
Detectability (d')	63*	91	Inattention	Inability to distinguish and detect X and non-X stimuli
Perseverations %	67*	96	Marked impulsivity	RT < 100 milliseconds; that is, slow, random, or anticipatory responses
Hit RT by Block Change	47	41	Normal	Substantial slowing of reaction time as the test progressed
Hit SE by Block Change	45	35	Normal	Substantial loss of consistency as the test progressed
Hit RT by ISI Change	65*	94	Inattention	Atypical changes in response speed across different ISIs
Hit SE by ISI Change	48	46	Normal	Atypical changes in response consistency across different ISIs

Note: T-score mean = 50, standard deviation = 10. Higher *T*-scores indicate greater presence of significant result. *denotes that the *T*-score is statistically significant; specific measure supportive of an ADHD diagnosis. PR, percentile rank; RT, reaction time; SE, standard error; ISI, interstimulus-interval.

CPT–II Interpretation: Positive for ADHD, including measured impairments in general and sustained attention, and impulse control.

Conners' CAARS–L, Self–Report and Observer Forms

TABLE 7 ■ **VALIDITY OF RATINGS**

Self-report ratings			Observer ratings		
Scale	Raw score	Interpretation	Scale	Raw score	Interpretation
Inconsistency Index	4	Valid	Inconsistency Index	6	Valid

Note: Lower raw scores indicate that the ratings are increasingly valid.

Both self-report and observer ratings are valid.

(Cont.)

FORM 13.2

CASE 5: NEUROPSYCHOLOGICAL EVALUATION REPORT (*Cont.*)

TABLE 8 ■ **CLINICAL SCALES**

Self-report ratings		Observer ratings		Measured symptoms
Clinical scale	**T-score***	**Clinical scale**	**T-score***	
DSM-IV-TR Inattentive Symptoms	90*	*DSM-IV-TR* Inattentive Symptoms	83*	Careless mistakes; inattentive; does not listen; fails to complete tasks; disorganized; avoids task requiring sustained mental effort; loses necessary things; distractible; forgetful
DSM-IV-TR Hyperactive-Impulsive Symptoms	74*	*DSM-IV-TR* Hyperactive-Impulsive Symptoms	73*	Fidgets; difficulty remaining seated; restless; loud; driven; talks excessively; blurts out answers before questions have been completed; difficulty waiting turn; interrupts or intrudes on others
ADHD Index	82*	ADHD Index	73*	Clinically significant levels of ADHD symptoms

Note: T-score mean = 50, standard deviation = 10. Higher *T*-scores indicate greater presence of measured symptoms. *denotes that the *T*-score is statistically significant; measured symptoms on that clinical scale are sufficiently severe to indicate an ADHD diagnosis.

Conners' CAARS–L data are positive for ADHD, Combined Type.

Posttest *DSM-IV-TR* Diagnoses

Axis I:
❏ 296.80 Bipolar Disorder NOS (by history)
❏ 314.01 Attention-Deficit/Hyperactivity Disorder, Combined Type

Axis II:
❏ V71.09 No Diagnosis

Axis III:
❏ 250.00 Diabetes Mellitus, Type II

Axis IV:
❏ Psychosocial Stressors – Occupational

Axis V:
❏ Global Assessment of Functioning (GAF): 45 Serious symptoms

Prognosis: Fair due to co-morbidity

TREATMENT RECOMMENDATIONS:

1. Psychiatric biological intervention for the above-listed Axis I *DSM-IV-TR* diagnoses, including the need to treat the underlying comorbid ADHD, Combined Type.

John M. Spores, PhD, JD, HSPP
Psychologist – Indiana #20040638A
Attorney at Law – Indiana #21404–64

FORM 13.3

CASE 6: PSYCHOLOGICAL EVALUATION REPORT

COMMUNITY MENTAL HEALTH CENTER

Outpatient Department

PSYCHOLOGICAL EVALUATION REPORT

Patient Name: Stewart, Denise
Account Number: 666666
Date: November 15, 2011

Patient Identifying Information: Chronological age is 36 years 2 months. Gender is female. DOB: 09/12/1975.

Referral Information: The referral source is Lori Jennings, MD. She is requesting Rorschach testing to rule out a Psychotic Disorder, along with assessing Denise's personality functioning.

Denise was psychiatrically hospitalized on a 72-hour emergency commitment subsequent to cutting her wrists and attempting to overdose her two children with prescription medication.

Presenting symptoms included a long history of anxiety and chronic loneliness. Her working diagnosis is Generalized Anxiety Disorder (GAD). There was no evidence of Psychotic Disorder in her history or mental health record.

Test

1. Rorschach Inkblot Test, Comprehensive System, RIAP, Fifth Edition, Ages 18 to 86 (Rorschach–CS, Ages 18 to 86) **(11/15/2011)**

Clinical Psychologist: John M. Spores, PhD, JD, HSPP
Psychologist – Indiana #20040638A
Attorney at Law – Indiana #21404–64

TEST RESULTS AND INTERPRETATION

Rorschach–CS, Ages 18 to 86

TABLE 1 ■ TEST VALIDITY: SITUATIONAL GUARDEDNESS

Variable	Score	Expected range	Positive result range	Result[a]	Meaning of positive result
R	16	18–29*	≤13[†]	Negative	Excessively nonproductive; defensive

Note: *denotes that the listed range is based on −1.00 to +1.00 standard deviations from the normative mean including rounding for ease of interpretation. [†]denotes that the listed range is determined by Comprehensive System interpretation guidelines.

[a]When R < 14, the entire Rorschach protocol is per se invalid. There is insufficient test data for meaningful interpretation.

There is no evidence of situational guardedness. In this regard, the clinical and personality variables are deemed valid.

(Cont.)

FORM 13.3

CASE 6: PSYCHOLOGICAL EVALUATION REPORT (*Cont.*)

TABLE 2 ■ TEST VALIDITY: SYMPTOM EXAGGERATION

Variable	Score	Expected range	Positive result range	Result[a]	Meaning of positive result
X–%[b]	0.13	0.00–0.18*	≥0.70[†]	Negative	Exaggerating or malingering symptoms
XA+%	0.88	0.80–0.95*	≥0.75[††]	Positive	Indications of adequate reality testing
X–%	0.13	0.00–0.18*	≥0.26[†]	Negative	Extremely distorted thinking

Note: *denotes that the listed range is based on –1.00 to +1.00 standard deviations from the normative mean including rounding for ease of interpretation. [†]denotes that the listed range is determined by Comprehensive System interpretation guidelines. [††]denotes that the listed range is determined by percentage base rate in the norm reference sample due to that variable's skewed distribution.

[a]When the first row variable is X–% < 0.70, and hence negative, both remaining variables must yield positive results to indicate an invalid response pattern.

[b]X–% ≥ 0.70 indicates such gross psychological impairment that testing would have been precluded; therefore the entire Rorschach protocol is deemed per se invalid irrespective of the remaining variables.

There is no evidence of exaggeration of symptoms or malingering. In this regard, the clinical and personality variables are deemed valid.

TABLE 3 ■ CLINICAL VARIABLES: PSYCHOTIC DISORDERS

Variable	Score	Expected range	Positive result range	Result	Meaning of positive result
WSum6	11	0–18**	≥19[†σ]	Negative	Ideational or cognitive slippage; formal thought disorder
Level 2	2	0[††]	≥1[††]	Positive	Manifestly bizarre responses
PTI	0	0–2[††]	3–5[††]	Negative	Psychotic index; psychotic disorder
XA+%	0.88	0.74–1.00**	≤0.73[†σ]	Negative	Disturbed mediation or reality testing
WDA+%	0.87	0.79–1.00**	≤0.78[†σ]	Negative	Pervasively disturbed mediation or reality testing
X–%	0.13	0.00–0.25**	≥0.26[†σ]	Negative	Extremely distorted thinking

Note: PTI, Perceptual Thinking Index. **denotes that the listed range is based on –2.00 to +2.00 standard deviations from the normative mean including rounding for ease of interpretation. [†]denotes that the listed range is determined by Comprehensive System interpretation guidelines. [††]denotes that the listed range is determined by percentage base rate in the norm reference sample due to that variable's skewed distribution. [σ]denotes that the listed positive result range is based on the deviation principle.

With one exception, all of the Psychotic Disorders variables are negative, including the Perceptual Thinking Index. There are two Level 2 bizarre responses, indicating that there may be occasional lapses in mediation or reality testing, likely associated with severe Axis II personality psychopathology (see Table 6).

(*Cont.*)

FORM 13.3

CASE 6: PSYCHOLOGICAL EVALUATION REPORT (*Cont.*)

TABLE 4 ■ **CLINICAL VARIABLES: MOOD DISORDERS**

Variable	Score	Expected range	Positive result range	Result	Meaning of positive result
DEPI	3	0–4[†]	5–7[†]	Negative	Affective disruption; emotional disarray; depression
S-CON	6	0–7[†]	≥8[†]	Negative	Risk for effecting one's own suicide
MOR	2	0–2[††]	≥3[††]	Negative	Pessimism; low self-worth
FC:CF+C+Cn	2:2	FCx2 > CF+C+Cn[†]	FCx3 > CF+C+Cn[†]	Negative	Emotional constriction
EB 0–Right	3:3.0	3–7:2.5–6.5*	≥3:0.0[†]	Negative	Massive containment of emotion; extreme constriction of affect
FC:CF+C+Cn	2:2	FCx2 > CF+C+Cn[†]	FC < CF+C+Cn[†]	Negative	Problems in affective modulation; affective instability; mood swings
SumC':WSumC	1:3.0	0–3:2.5–6.5*	≤3:≥7.0[†]	Negative	Emotional unrestraint; mood swings
EB 0–Left	3:3.0	3–7:2.5–6.5*	0:≥4.0[†]	Negative	Emotional flooding; mood swings and impulsiveness

Note: DEPI, Depression Index. S-CON, Suicide Constellation Index. *denotes that the listed range is based on –1.00 to +1.00 standard deviations from the normative mean including rounding for ease of interpretation. [†]denotes that the listed range is determined by Comprehenesive System interpretation guidelines. [††]denotes that the listed range is determined by percentage base rate in the norm-reference sample due to that variable's skewed distribution.

None of the Mood Disorders variables are positive, including the Suicide Constellation Index.

TABLE 5 ■ **CLINICAL VARIABLES: ANXIETY AND STRESS-RELATED DISORDERS**

Variable	Score	Expected range	Positive result range	Result	Meaning of positive result
CDI	5	0–3[†]	4–5[†]	Positive	Coping deficiencies in dealing with stress
D	–1	0[†]	≤–1[†]	Positive	Current situationally related or acute stress
Adj D	–1	0[†]	≤–1[†]	Positive	Chronic stress overload
EA	6.0	7.0–11.0[†]	≤6.5[†]	Positive	Deficiency in psychological resources for dealing with stress

Note: CDI, Coping Deficit Index. [†]denotes that the listed range is determined by Comprehensive System interpretation guidelines.

All of the Anxiety and Stress Disorders variables are positive. There is evidence of severe current stress superimposed on a pre-existing chronic level of anxiety and stress. This supports her working diagnosis of Generalized Anxiety Disorder. It is also suggestive of Axis II psychopathology as she has a measured deficiency in psychological resources for coping with stressors.

(Cont.)

FORM 13.3

CASE 6: PSYCHOLOGICAL EVALUATION REPORT (*Cont.*)

TABLE 6 ■ **PERSONALITY DISORDERS VARIABLES**

Variable	Score	Expected range	Positive result range	Result	Meaning of positive result
Fr + rF	1	0[†]	≥1[†]	Positive	Narcissism; inflated sense of self-worth
3r + (2)/R Low[a]	0.28	0.30–0.50*	≤0.29[σ]	Positive	Low self-esteem
Sum V	0	0–1*	≥2[σ]	Negative	Preoccupation with negative features of the self
H:(H)+Hd+(Hd)	0:4	2–5:0–6*	H < (H)+Hd+(Hd)[†]	Positive	Distorted self-image
Sum T High	5	0–1[††]	≥2[††]	Positive	Either (a) recent object loss or (b) chronic loneliness or emptiness[b]
3r + (2)/R High[c]	0.38	0.30–0.50*	≥0.51[σ]	Negative	Inflated self-esteem
S	2	0–3[†]	≥4[†]	Negative	Oppositional; chronic anger toward people and environment
AG	1	0–3[†]	≥4[†]	Negative	Hostile and negative attitudes toward people
Sum T Low	2	1–2[†]	0[†]	Negative	Impaired ability to empathize with other people
FD	0	1–2[†]	0[†]	Negative	Lack of introspection
H+(H)+Hd+(Hd)	4	4–9*	≤3[σ]	Negative	Lack of interest in people
GHR:PHR	1:4	GHR ≥ PHR[†]	GHR < PHR[†]	Positive	Likelihood of personality disorder
Isolate/R	0.00	0.11–0.31*	≥0.32[†σ]	Negative	Interpersonally isolated
Fd	2	0–1*	≥2[σ]	Positive	Dependent traits
a:p[d]	0:0	4–10:2–6*	a + 1 < p[†]	Negative	Passivity in interpersonal relations
OBS	--	--	--	Negative[†]	Preoccupation with correctness, perfectionism, and precision
2AB + Art + Ay	2	0–5*	≥6[σ]	Negative	Intellectualization; use of ideation to minimize impact of emotions
Ma:Mp	1:2	2–5:1–3*	Ma + 1 < Mp[†σ]	Positive	Excessive abuse of fantasy to deny reality; dissociation
CP	0	0[†]	≥1[†]	Negative	Improper substitution of positive for negative emotions; hysteria

Note: OBS, Obsessive Style Index (scored as either positive or negative result). *denotes that the listed range is based on −1.00 to +1.00 standard deviations from the normative mean including rounding for ease of interpretation. [†]denotes that the listed range is determined by Comprehensive System interpretation guidelines. [††]denotes that the listed range and/or result is determined by percentage base rate in the norm-reference sample due to that variable's skewed distribution. [σ]denotes that the listed positive result range is based on the deviation principle. -- denotes score type not reported.

[a]When both 3r + (2)/R Low and Fr + rF are positive, this indicates extreme fluctuations in sense of self or splitting object-relations consistent with borderline traits.

[b]Requires the use of data from the developmental history to determine the correct meaning of a positive result.

[c]When both 3r + (2)/R High and Fr + rF are positive, this indicates pervasive narcissistic traits.

[d]When both Fd and a:p are positive, this indicates pervasive dependent traits.

There is evidence of Axis II Personality Disorder including the following: extremely unstable sense of self; distortion in self-image; chronic loneliness and internal emptiness; dissociative ego defenses; and dependent traits. This pattern of maladaptive traits and mechanisms is most consistent with Borderline Personality psychopathology, with secondary dependent traits.

(*Cont.*)

FORM 13.3

CASE 6: PSYCHOLOGICAL EVALUATION REPORT (*Cont.*)

Posttest *DSM-IV-TR* Diagnoses

Axis I:

❐ 300.02 Generalized Anxiety Disorder

Noted: No evidence of Psychosis

Axis II:

❐ 301.83 Borderline Personality Disorder, Mixed Dependent Traits

Axis III:

❐ No Contributory or Pertinent Medical Disorders Noted

Axis IV:

❐ Psychosocial Stressors – Legal System Intervention

Axis V:

❐ Global Assessment of Functioning (GAF): 45 Serious symptoms

Prognosis: Guarded due to severe Axis II psychopathology

TREATMENT RECOMMENDATIONS

1. Psychiatric biological intervention for Generalized Anxiety Disorder, and palliative for Borderline Personality Disorder.
2. Psychotherapy to treat Axis II psychopathology.

John M. Spores, PhD, JD, HSPP
Psychologist – Indiana #20040638A
Attorney at Law – Indiana #21404–64

Forensic Competence to Stand Trial Examinations

14

Forensic psychology is the application of psychological science for the resolution of legal issues. With modifications, use of the psychological assessment and testing system as delineated in this book (Sections I and II) is capable of assisting criminal courts in determining competency to stand trial issues. Therefore, the objective of this concluding chapter is to illustrate the manner in which the assessment and testing process and selected tests heretofore presented can be applied to the resolution of this legal issue. Antecedent to this is a primer on criminal law.

CRIMINAL LAW

The cardinal purpose of criminal law is to prevent harm to society. This area of the law has been conceptually partitioned into *substance* and *procedure* (see e.g., LaFave, 2010). I will briefly discuss each area because, as will become apparent below, competency applies only to the latter.

Substantive Criminal Law

First, *substantive criminal law* defines which acts and mental states, together with any attendant circumstances or consequences, are necessary elements of various crimes. It also prescribes sentencing and the punishments to be imposed. Principal justifications for punishment include the following: (a) specific deterrence (i.e., the perpetrator will be discouraged from committing additional illicit acts), (b) general deterrence (i.e., the population as a whole will be discouraged from engaging in illegal behavior), (c) retribution (i.e., the punishment is deserved, fair, and promotes justice), and (d) rehabilitation (i.e., the individual will learn a lesson and engage in beneficial reform).

Today, the majority of substantive criminal laws throughout the various state jurisdictions are statutory as opposed to common law (i.e., judge-made law). For example, in the State of Indiana wherein I practice, all crimes are defined pursuant to statute. For each crime, the statute sets out the following three fundamental elements: (a) the act or omission to act when there exists a duty (i.e., *actus reus* or voluntary conduct), (b) state of mind that accompanies the act or omission (i.e., *mens rea* or guilty mind), and (c) attendant circumstances and consequences. Affirmative defenses are a key part of substantive criminal law because they involve newly introduced facts or explanations that can justify or excuse a criminal charge. That is, a criminal charge can be defeated even if the facts supporting such charge are accurate and true. An infamous affirmative defense includes the *insanity* plea.[1] If successful, insanity operates to negate the second fundamental element of substantive criminal law; that is, the guilty mind.

[1] *The criteria for insanity have varied significantly over the years and currently among the various state and federal jurisdictions. In fact, the insanity defense is not available in several states including Kansas, Montana, Idaho, and Utah. Furthermore, in contrast to competency, what renders insanity examinations much more complex and difficult to conduct is that such psychological disturbance must be established at the time of the offense. Thus, in my opinion, my proposed assessment and testing system is not conducive to conducting such examinations. For interested readers, Melton et al. (1997, Chapter 8, pp. 186–248), present an excellent and rather thorough discussion regarding methods and techniques used to evaluate a defendant's mental state at the time of the offense (viz., MSO evaluations).*

Procedural Criminal Law

Second, and more pertinent to this chapter, criminal procedural law delineates all of the legal steps through which court proceedings must pass. This begins with the initial investigation through the termination of punishment. It is based upon fundamental rights contained within the Fourth, Fifth, Sixth, and Fourteenth Amendments to the U.S. Constitution, and further articulated in the Bill of Rights of U.S. state constitutions. General areas of criminal procedural law include search and seizure, confessions and interrogations, identifications and lineups, indictments and information, pretrial proceedings, pleadings and pleas, discovery, constitutional rights of a defendant during trial, privilege against self-incrimination, trial procedure, double jeopardy, appeals, postconviction relief, and writ of habeas corpus.

The determination of competency is a *pretrial* procedural issue. This is because a defendant must be competent in order for the trial to proceed (see below for specific criteria). If deemed incompetent, the defendant is typically committed to a state hospital and the trial process postponed or held in abeyance until such time competence is established.

COMPETENCY TO STAND TRIAL EXAMINATIONS

As stated prior, defendants must be competent in order to stand trial for alleged offenses as set out by substantive criminal laws. *Dusky v. United States* (1960) defined competency by stating that, "... the test must be whether he has sufficient present ability to consult with his attorney with a reasonable degree of rational understanding and a rational as well as factual understanding of the proceedings against him." Thus, to meet the legal standard of competence, defendants must be able to (a) understand the legal proceedings against them and (b) assist in their own defense. Because this standard was held by the U.S. Supreme Court, it is adopted and codified in analogous form by federal and state laws. For example, the Indiana statutory language reads as follows:

> ...whether the defendant has the ability to understand the proceedings and assist in the preparation of the defendant's defense...(Competence to Stand Trial, Indiana Code § 35–36–3-1(b), 2004).[2]

[2] The listed year in this statutory citation represents the most recent date that such statute was either added to or amended.

As defined, the defendant's *current* psychological status is at issue. The disorders defined in the *Diagnostic and Statistical Manual of Mental Disorders, Fourth Edition, Text Revision (DSM-IV-TR)* (American Psychiatric Association, 2000) that would most likely compromise competency include the following classifications: (a) Psychotic Disorders (e.g., Schizophrenia, Paranoid Type), (b) severe mood disorders with distinct psychotic features (e.g., Bipolar I Disorder, Severe With Psychotic Features), (c) Cognitive Disorders (e.g., Dementia), and (d) Axis II Mental Retardation. In my experience, the presence of psychosis is the most likely candidate among this listing, which also frequently has a measureable deleterious effect on cognitive functioning.

The Standard Competency Assessment and Test Battery

Considering the aforementioned legal criteria and disorders most likely to impair competency, the standard assessment and test battery I employ includes the following: (a) clinical interview including a general mental status examination, (b) Mini-Mental State Examination, Second Edition, Expanded Version, Blue Form (MMSE–2–EV–BF) (Folstein, Folstein, White, & Messer, 2010), (c) Rorschach Inkblot Test, Comprehensive System, RIAP Fifth Edition, Ages 18 to 86 (Rorschach–CS, Ages 18 to 86) (Exner, 2003), and (d) the Legal System Questionnaire (LSQ) (Spores, 2011). The interview provides initial factual information regarding such things as presenting symptoms, personal and family psychiatric histories, medical functioning and history, interpersonal history, medications, current legal and past criminal charges, and vocational and educational backgrounds. Simultaneously, an informal mental status examination can be completed by noting such things as longer term memory functioning (e.g., can the defendant provide a coherent developmental history with key dates), verbal and reasoning skills, thought process and content, affect, and mood.

Moving to the test battery, the MMSE–2–EV–BF provides an efficient quantitative measurement of cognitive functioning as a supplement to the aforementioned informal mental status information. As an effective complement, the Rorschach–CS variables possess the capability of detecting and directly measuring (a) defensiveness, (b) malingering, and (c) psychosis (i.e., disturbed reality testing and formal thought disorder). Lastly, the LSQ is my own recently developed measure and requires some explication.

Although atypical, defendants can manifest psychotic symptoms and/or cognitive dysfunction and still meet statutory criteria for competency as heretofore defined (Melton, Petrila, Poythress, & Slobogin, 1997). This is particularly possible when such symptoms are present, although either subclinical or not severely impairing. Therefore, it is crucial to have some assessment of defendants' (a) basic understanding of the legal system and (b) knowledge and awareness of key information pertinent to their case. While some examiners perform such evaluation solely by oral interview (see Melton et al., 1997), I prefer a written format, which can be supplemented by follow-up oral questioning for clarification or elaboration purposes. This provides written documentation of defendants' comprehension of the legal system and essential knowledge regarding their case.

For years I utilized the Competency Screening Test (CST) (Lipsitt, Lelos, & McGarry, 1971) to perform such assessment. The CST is essentially a brief sentence completion test (i.e., 22 items) that is designed in an open-ended projective format. Defendants' responses are scored from 0 to 2 with higher scores indicating greater knowledge of the legal system. Total scores below 20 suggest deficient understanding and the need for more comprehensive evaluation. Thus, it is a paradoxical integration of unreliable and questionably valid projective testing (Gittelman-Klein, 1978; Lilienfeld, 1999) and purportedly objective standardized scoring. I became particularly disenchanted with this instrument for the following evidentiary-based reasons: (a) extremely mixed results regarding reliability and validity, (b) scoring bias against defendants who have negative views of the legal system, and (c) unacceptably high false positive outcomes (i.e., competent defendants evaluated as being incompetent (see Melton et al., 1997, pp. 139–141). Furthermore, such research results were becoming increasingly apparent among the data in my own competency examinations. Finally, I was never enthusiastic about the indirect and tenuous projective nature of this test (e.g., "What concerns Fred most about his lawyer …").

Thus, early in 2011, I developed the Legal System Questionaire (LSQ) based upon my legal education and readings. The LSQ is presented in Form 14.1. Logically, I reasoned that perhaps the most effective way to examine a person's basic knowledge about a subject area is to directly ask them pertinent questions which cover its most rudimentary content (i.e., content validity). Admittedly, the self-report format and high face validity of the LSQ renders it vulnerable to faking deficiency (i.e., fake bad). However, the Rorschach–CS as part of the battery contains empirically based malingering indicators, which may be further supplemented by more informal behavioral observations obtained during the clinical interview process indicating the exaggeration of psychopathology.

More specifically, the LSQ is generally organized into two parts that mirror the legal elements of the competency rule of law. In part one (Items 1–6), defendants are asked the manner in which the basic facets of the criminal court system are *intended* to function. The word intended was inserted in the instructions so as to minimize the confounding nature of negative attitudes and cynicism defendants frequently possess regarding the criminal justice system. Content areas include the function of a judge and jury, defense attorney, and prosecuting attorney, along with the manner in which defendants can best assist their attorneys in case preparation. The next two items address defendants' understanding of a cardinal precept of criminal law (viz., *innocent until proven guilty*) and the frequently employed process of plea bargaining. The former addresses the elementary burden of proof standard employed in criminal trials. I added the latter because criminal cases are commonly resolved in this manner (see e.g., LaFave, 2010). Note that these items are most pertinent to determining whether or not the defendant can understand the legal proceedings (*Dusky v. United States*, 1960).

Part two (Items 7–10) examines defendants' knowledge of vital information more particular to their cases. Therefore, the preceding instructions prompt defendants to answer each item to the *best* of their knowledge. Content areas of coverage include (a) their attorney's identity, (b) the charges against them, (c) the potential penalties they face, and (d) the events that precipitated their arrest. Together, these assess key information defendants must possess in order to meaningfully assist their attorneys in developing a viable defense strategy. For example, defendants would not be able to aid their attorneys in devising an effective defense if they could not coherently communicate the events antecedent to and precipitating their arrest, including such things as identifying potential exculpatory facts or witnesses.

Note that the LSQ is designed to be direct and efficient, and cover essential aspects of the legal system and pertinent information regarding a defendant's particular case. The open-ended format also permits supplementary mental status analysis of thought content and process. Finally, as stated prior, examiners may follow-up incomplete or ambiguous answers through oral questioning. Of course, examiners may also insert additional items or substitute another measure of their preference. Next, I present the competency examination report template and the manner in which it is intended to be used.

The Competency Examination Report Template

The Competency Examination Report template is presented in Form 14.2. I want to initiate discussion of this report by noting general alterations in format as compared to the standard psychological evaluation report (see Forms 3.1 and 13.2 for comparison purposes). First, all major headings and subheadings are numbered and lettered. Additionally, the narrative text of each section is to begin on a separation line from the heading and subheading. Both of these features assist both the Court and attorneys in referencing relevant information (e.g., Section IV, A, 1, Presenting Symptoms...racing thoughts ...), especially when there is a need or desire to read pertinent sections of the report into the record. Second, special font is limited to major headings and the most vital information (e.g., the ultimate opinion). This is standard practice for effective legal writing (see e.g., Bouchoux, 2005, p. 215). The leading information includes essential legal case information that appears on all filed documents including (a) case name (i.e., *Plaintiff v. Defendant*) and (b) cause number(s).[3] This facilitates proper filing by the clerk of the court or judge's secretary, whomever the report is sent to, along with subsequent distribution to the Court and opposing parties in the case. Third, the defendant is referred to by Mr. or Ms. and last name befitting the legal formality of the examination.

Finally, the "Assessment and Test Battery" and "Assessment and Test Results" sections are already filled in with the respective names and data tables of the standard battery reviewed prior. However, the test portion of the battery may be easily modified according to the uniqueness of a particular case. For instance, the Wechsler Adult Intelligence Scale, Fourth Edition (WAIS–IV) (Wechsler, 2008a, 2008b) can be used in lieu of the Rorschach–CS, Ages 18 to 86, in cases where Mental Retardation is a distinct possibility and in which there is no evidence of psychotic disturbance. In such cases, the MMSE–2 Standard or Brief Form can be used or completely dropped as being superfluous. Next, I highlight sections of the report that are in need of explication.

[3] *Your jurisdiction may use an alternate term such as Case Number in lieu of Cause Number. Of course, in that event simply use the term of your jurisdiction.*

Initial Information

Prior to Section I appears case identifying information, including the defendant's name and date of report, legal case name and cause number (there can be more than one if the defendant is being charged with multiple counts), the judge and court name, and your office file number for cross-referencing. Immediately following the examiner's name and credentials is an informed consent notation for ethical purposes. It is in smaller font to distinguish it from examination data per se.

Court Required Information

Information in Sections I and II of the report must be provided by the referring court. Section II, in particular, requires a copy of the *court order* for competency examination. This order is typically brief although includes key information, including (a) case name, (b) cause number(s), (c) title of the order (e.g., "Order Appointing Psychiatrist and Psychologist"), (b) order date, (c) judge name, (d) court name, and usually, (e) names of the attorneys of record. The order will also typically include a citation to the pertinent competency statute or case law, which I routinely incorporate into my reports. In addition to the order, I also ask the Court to send me a legal document that the State of Indiana titles "Information." This court-filed document enumerates the crimes for which the defendant is being charged (e.g., Count I Child Molesting, Class B Felony, Count II …). These two legal documents provide the information needed to evaluate the accuracy of the defendant's responses on part two of the LSQ (viz., Items 7–10). Furthermore, considering the heavy caseloads of criminal courts, it is useful to both the judge and attorneys to have such legal information incorporated within your report, and hence readily available.

Assessment and Test Results

The "Assessment and Test Results" (Section IV) represent both the core analysis and body of the report. It begins with diagnostic interview information using the clinical method. Notice that a second notation again appears in smaller font immediately antecedent to the diagnostic interview subsections. In particular, it identifies the typical sources of such information and obviates the need to repeatedly say, "Mr. Smith stated that…." Subsections 1 through 8 provide a useful semistructured interview guideline for the initiation of your competency examination. Note that I have not provided standard narrative statements in the majority of these subsections simply because I am usually pithy in this portion of the report. Indeed, at times I omit the social and legal histories (viz., Subsections 2 and 8) because, as stated prior, the core analysis is on the defendant's *current* psychological functioning.

Within the "Mental Status Examination" section, I inserted the MMSE–2–EV–BF table (Table 1) with somewhat modified narratives (cf. Form 2.6) that can be tailored according to your particular observations. The Rorschach–CS, Ages 18 to 86 follows beginning with the two validity tables (Table 2 and Table 3) for measuring defensiveness and malingering, respectively, and ensued by the two Psychotic Disorders tables. The follow-up WSum6 Thought Disorder Scores table should be deleted when the preceding psychotic variables are negative. In the event the defendant is manifesting severe mood disturbance with psychosis, I advise that you insert the Rorschach–CS Mood Disorders table (see Form 9.5, Table 5). Of course, you have the discretion to add as much Rorschach–CS data as indicated by a particular case (see Form 9.5).

The LSQ is the last instrument to be reported. Because it is currently an unpublished and nonstandardized measure, the LSQ results begin with a succinct description of the format, item content, and objectives of this questionnaire. The "Assessment and Test Results" section ends with the *DSM-IV-TR* multiaxial diagnostic scheme, including *Legal System Intervention* as an invariable stressor on Avis IV, a deferral on Axis II regarding Personality Disorders, and a full reference to the *DSM-IV-TR* (American Psychiatric Association,

2000). The Axis II deferral is to notify the Court that the assessment of maladaptive traits was not germane to the competency analysis.

Opinion Regarding the Competency Issue

The ultimate section of the report includes the examiner's opinion regarding competency. It begins with the stated criteria for competency and legal citation. The latter will typically be a statutory citation that, as I stated prior, is usually noted in the court order. For convenience, I have entered language consistent with the *Dusky v. United States* (1960) standard. However, I advise that you replace this with the specific language adopted by the law of your jurisdiction, along with the legal citation. In addition to making your report both legally and psychologically inclusive, it will facilitate your analysis.

As in my state jurisdiction, it is likely that the burden of proof for incompetency is on the defendant and that the standard is *preponderance of the evidence*.[4] That is, the defendant is presumed competent unless incompetency is established by a preponderance of the evidence (see e.g., *Medina v. California*, 1992). Preponderance of the evidence is defined as, "... evidence that outweighs other evidence" (Mellinkoff, 1992, p. 498). Thus, if your jurisdiction employs this standard, the question for the examiner is "Is it more likely than not that the defendant is incompetent to stand trial?" In statistical terms, if $p > .50$, then conclude not competent to stand trial. Therefore, applying the assessment and test results to competency criteria is the same inductive logic used in arriving at a *DSM-TR-IV* diagnosis. It also mirrors the manner in which courts decide whether or not fact patterns meet the stated elements of particular crimes for purposes of adjudication. The report conveniently ends with the opinion in bold font with the capitalized words, "**NOT COMPETENT**." Simply delete the "**NOT**" if your opinion is that the defendant is competent to stand trial.

In my experience, completion of this standard competency assessment and test battery and associated report template will consistently require an efficient 2 to 3 hours. The precise duration is contingent upon a variety of variables, including some of the following: (a) cooperation of the defendant; (b) rate at which the defendant responds to interview questions, test instructions, and items; (c) number and complexity of responses on the Rorschach–CS; and (d) complexity of the data pattern. A prototypical "Competency Examination Report" is presented in Form 14.3. Pertinent portions of the report are reviewed subsequent in order to illustrate the application of the standard competency assessment and test battery and report template.

Case 7: Competence to Stand Trial

Referral Information

Mr. Bass was a 34-year-old male who was referred by the local county superior court to determine whether or not he was competent to stand trial. He was indicted for possession of a controlled substance. In this instance, I received only the court order, which is cited in § II B of the report. That is, the Court did not provide the "Information" listing the formal charges. This information was forwarded to me in paraphrased form by the local county jail staff, which was responsible for transporting Mr. Bass to my office for the examination. Hence, the legal charges were summarized more informally than typical of my forensic reports (see Form 14.3, § II, A). Date of birth and current medications were also provided by jail staff.

Assessment and Test Battery

The assessment and test battery included my standard techniques and measures as reviewed prior, which is one reason why I selected this case. Note that the diagnostic interview

[4] *Do not presume, however, that the law in your jurisdiction has the same burden of proof standard. For example, it may incorporate the higher clear and convincing evidence standard. Thus, always scrutinize the applicable burden of proof rules employed within your jurisdiction of practice.*

information is remarkably succinct. Clinical interview information emphasized the following: (a) psychotic and mood-related presenting symptoms with an early onset, chronic course, and episodes of acute exacerbation; (b) positive family psychiatric history of Schizophrenia and Bipolar Disorder; (c) personal history of long-term inpatient and outpatient psychiatric treatment; and (d) current prescription of antipsychotic medication. Cannabis Dependence was also noted, although he had been abstinent for the months of his incarceration awaiting trial.

Mr. Bass's MMSE–2–EV–BF performance was measured as impaired (Form 14.3, Table 1), which is quite common in the presence of psychosis. Informal mental status observations also indicated instances of bizarre thinking. His Rorschach data were measured as valid (Form 14.3, Tables 2 and 3). Rorschach–CS Psychotic Disorders variables (Form 14.3, Table 4) corroborated the presence of formal thought disorder and disturbed reality testing, including a positive Perceptual Thinking Index (PTI), extremely high WSum6 score, and seven bizarre Level 2 responses. The latter two were elaborated upon in the ensuing Table 5 (Form 14.3). Due to the unequivocal quantitative evidence of psychosis and in the interests of expediency, I did not believe it was necessary to report the Rorschach–CS Mood Disorders data. Rather, I thought it was sufficient to list Bipolar Disorder as a rule out diagnosis later in the report, which would be more relevant to treatment and the establishment of competency. Finally, the open-ended format of the LSQ provided supplementary evidence of his extremely disturbed thought process and content, and its deleterious effects on his cognitive functioning.

Regarding his *DSM-IV-TR* diagnostic profile, I found it sufficient to diagnose more generally (viz., Psychotic Disorder NOS), and mention more specific rule out diagnoses for purposes of guiding subsequent assessment and treatment intervention. Cannabis Dependence was also listed as being in early full remission, although this was primarily due to his incarceration, hence the *DSM-IV-TR* qualifier *within a controlled environment* (American Psychiatric Association, 2000).

Competency Opinion

The assessment and test data unequivocally weighed in favor of incompetency to stand trial. The facts included an acute psychotic condition, which was interfering with both cognitive functioning and Mr. Bass's knowledge of the legal proceedings and the particulars of his case.

Case Outcome

Mr. Bass's competency examination was completed in approximately 2½ hours, which included review of Court documents and jail information, diagnostic interview, test administration, scoring, interpretation, and report-writing using the competency template (Form 14.2). Hence, the county court was billed for this time of service. In determinations of competency, Indiana law requires two independent examiners and, in the event of contrary opinions, a third examination as a deciding factor (Competence to Stand Trial, Indiana Code § 35–36–3–1(a), 2004). In this case, a psychiatrist also determined Mr. Bass to be incompetent to stand trial. He was consequently referred to an Indiana State Hospital, whereupon he received effective psychiatric treatment and eventually proceeded to trial. The case was ultimately resolved through the frequently employed plea bargaining process for a lesser included offense, and incorporating a reduced sentence for time served.

SUMMARY

The objective of this concluding chapter was to demonstrate the manner in which the psychological assessment and testing scheme presented in this book can be generalized to conducting competency to stand trial forensic criminal examinations. The specialty area of forensic psychology was first defined. This was ensued by a primer on criminal law and procedure, with an emphasis on classifying competency within the latter as a pretrial issue. The legal standards for competency were delineated, followed by presentation of a standard assessment and test battery for rendering competency opinions. Next, a specially designed competency examination report template was presented and its intended use discussed. At this juncture, it was noted that the test battery portion of the competency examination could be easily modified according to the unique aspects of a particular case. Lastly, the chapter concluded by presenting a prototypical case example for demonstration purposes.

REFERENCES

American Psychiatric Association. (2000). *Diagnostic and statistical manual of mental disorders* (4th ed., text rev.). Washington, DC: Author.

Bouchoux, D. (2005). *Aspen handbook for legal writers: A practical reference.* New York, NY: Aspen.

Competence to Stand Trial, 3 Indiana Code §§ 35–36–3–1(a-b). (2004).

Dusky v. United States, 362 U.S. 402. (1960).

Exner, J. E. (2003). *The Rorschach a comprehensive system: Basic foundations and principles of interpretation* (4th ed., Vol. 1). Hoboken, NJ: John Wiley.

Folstein, M. F., Folstein, S. E., White, T., & Messer, M. A. (2010). *Mini–Mental State Examination, 2nd edition: Users manual.* Lutz, FL: Psychological Assessment Resources.

Gittelman-Klein, R. (1978). Validity in projective tests for psychodiagnosis in children. In R. L. Spitzer & D. F. Klein (Eds.), *Critical issues in psychiatric diagnosis* (pp. 141–166). New York, NY: Raven Press.

LaFave, W. R. (2010). *Criminal law* (5th ed.). St. Paul, MN: West Publishing.

Lilienfeld, S. O. (1999). Projective measures of personality and psychopathology: How well do they work? *Skeptical Inquirer, 23*(5), 32–39.

Lipsitt, P. D., Lelos, D., & McGarry, A. L. (1971). Competency for trial: A screening instrument. *American Journal of Psychiatry, 128*(1), 105–109.

Medina v. California 505 U.S. 437. (1992).

Mellinkoff, D. (1992). *Mellinkoff's dictionary of American legal usage.* St. Paul, MN: West Publishing.

Melton, G. B., Petrila, J., Poythress, N. G., & Slobogin, C. (1997). *Psychological evaluations for the courts: A handbook for mental health professionals and lawyers* (2nd ed.). New York, NY: The Guilford Press.

Spores, J. M. (2011). *Legal System Questionnaire.* Unpublished measure. Westville, IN: Social Sciences Department, Purdue University North Central.

Wechsler, D. (2008a). *Wechsler Adult Intelligence Scale, Fourth Edition (WAIS–IV): Administration and scoring manual.* San Antonio, TX: The Psychological Corporation-Pearson.

Wechsler, D. (2008b). *Wechsler Adult Intelligence Scale, Fourth Edition (WAIS–IV): Technical and interpretive manual.* San Antonio, TX: The Psychological Corporation-Pearson.

FORM 14.1

LEGAL SYSTEM QUESTIONNAIRE (LSQ)

Legal System Questionnaire

Instructions: Please answer items 1 through 6 according to how the legal system is *intended* to work so as to make fair and correct decisions. Write your answers clearly in the spaces provided.

1. What are the main duties and responsibilities of the judge and jury?_____
_____
_____.

2. What are the main duties and responsibilities of my defense attorney?_____
_____
_____.

3. What are the main duties and responsibilities of the prosecuting attorney?_____
_____
_____.

4. How can you best help your attorney prepare for court?_____
_____
_____.

5. How is this rule used in criminal cases, "Innocent until proven guilty?"_____
_____
_____.

6. How does *plea bargaining* work in criminal cases?_____
_____
_____.

Instructions: Please answer items 7 through 10 to the *best* of your knowledge. Once again, write your answers clearly in the spaces provided.

7. What is your attorney's name? _____.

8. What are you being charged with?
_____
_____.

9. What are the possible penalties for the charge(s) you face?
_____
_____.

10. Please describe the events that led to your arrest and current charge(s).
_____
_____
_____
_____
_____
_____.

FORM 14.2

COMPETENCY EXAMINATION REPORT TEMPLATE

COMMUNITY MENTAL HEALTH CENTER

Outpatient Department

COMPETENCY EXAMINATION

Defendant Name: Last, First: _____

Examination Date: November 4, 2012

Office File Number: _____

Legal Case Title: State of _____ vs._____

Cause Number: 64D45–5647-001

Judge: Name _____

Court: Name of Court_____

Examiner: _____

                           Psychologist Name, PhD, PsyD, HSPP

                           Psychologist – State License #_____

Note. Mr. _____ was initially informed that all data gathered during the course of this evaluation would be released to the above listed Court pursuant to court order, and subsequently to the attorneys of record in the above listed cause. He acknowledged that he understood and verbally consented.

I.   **Identifying Information:**

Mr. _____'s age is years months. Gender is male. DOB: (--/--/----)

II. **Presenting Legal Issue(s):**

A. Criminal Charges:

B. Court Order:

Judge _____ ordered that Mr. _____ be examined to determine his competency to stand trial. State Statute § __-__ -_-_(__) (_____)

III. **Assessment and Test Battery:**

A. Clinical Diagnostic Interview (--/--/----)

B. Mental Status Examination Including the Mini-Mental State Examination, Second Edition, Extended Version, Blue Form (MMSE–2–EV–BF) (--/--/----)

C. Rorschach Inkblot Test, Comprehensive System, RIAP, Fifth Edition, Ages 18 to 86 (Rorschach–CS, Ages 18 to 86) (--/--/----)

D. Legal System Questionnaire (LSQ) (--/--/----)

IV. **Assessment and Test Results:**

A. Clinical Diagnostic Interview:

Note. All information in this section was based on statements made by the defendant in response to interview questions, or by available archival records and reports.

1. Presenting Symptoms:

Mr. _____ complained of _____

(Cont.)

FORM 14.2

COMPETENCY EXAMINATION REPORT TEMPLATE (*Cont.*)

2. Family Psychiatric History: _____
3. Social History: _____
4. Educational History: _____
5. Vocational History: _____
6. Substance Abuse History: _____
7. Psychiatric/Medical History: _____
8. Legal History Prior to Current Charges: _____

B. Mental Status Examination including the Mini-Mental State Examination, Second Edition, Extended Version, Blue Form (MMSE–2–EV–BF):

TABLE 1 ■ **MMSE–2–EV–BF RESULTS**

Cognitive Function	Patient's raw score	Maximum possible raw score
Registration	3	3
Orientation to Time	5	5
Orientation to Place	5	5
Recall	3	3
Attention and Calculation	5	5
Naming	2	2
Repetition	1	1
Comprehension	3	3
Reading	1	1
Writing	1	1
Drawing	1	1
Story Memory	25	25
Processing Speed	35	35
Total Raw score[a]	**90**	**90**

Note: Lower raw scores indicate greater cognitive dysfunction. Overall cognitive function data are in boldface.

[a]Raw scores of 50 or less indicate cognitive impairment.

MMSE–2–EV–BF Result: Negative Positive for cognitive impairment.

Mr. _____ was oriented to person, stating and spelling his full name and providing his date of birth accurately, when compared to independent court and mental health records. He was oriented to time and place as evidenced by the MMSE–2–EV–BF results. Immediate and intermediate memory functions were normal and intact as evidenced by the MMSE–2–EV–BF results. Long-term memory was intact as evidenced by Mr. _____ providing a coherent developmental history. Mr. _____'s intellectual functioning was estimated to be average based upon his verbal skills, reasoning abilities, and the MMSE–2–EV–BF results. Thought process was logical, sequential, relevant, and coherent. Thought content was normal and reality based. Psychotic symptoms were not evident. Affect was mildly restricted. Mood was mildly dysphoric. Mr. _____ denied any current suicidal or homicidal thoughts, intentions, or plans. There was no current evidence of self-mutilation or self-harm.

(Cont.)

FORM 14.2

COMPETENCY EXAMINATION REPORT TEMPLATE (*Cont.*)

C. Rorschach Inkblot Test, Comprehensive System, RIAP, Fifth Edition, Ages 18 to 86 (Rorschach–CS, Ages 18 to 86):

TABLE 2 ■ TEST VALIDITY: SITUATIONAL GUARDEDNESS

Variable	Score	Expected range	Positive result range	Result[a]	Meaning of positive result
R	00	18–29*	≤13[†]	Negative	Excessively nonproductive; defensive

Note: *denotes that the listed range is based on –1.00 to +1.00 standard deviations from the normative mean including rounding for ease of interpretation. [†]denotes that the listed range is determined by Comprehensive System interpretation guidelines.

[a]When R < 14, the entire Rorschach protocol is per se invalid. There is insufficient test data for meaningful interpretation.

There was insufficient evidence of situational guardedness. In this regard, the clinical variables were deemed valid.

There was remarkable situational guardedness. Therefore, the clinical variables were deemed invalid. The remaining scores were neither interpreted nor reported.

TABLE 3 ■ TEST VALIDITY: SYMPTOM EXAGGERATION

Variable	Score	Expected range	Positive result range	Result[a]	Meaning of positive result
X–%[b]	0.00	0.00–0.18*	≥0.70[†]	Negative	Exaggerating or malingering symptoms
XA+%	0.00	0.80–0.95*	≥0.75[††]	Positive	Indications of adequate reality testing
X–%	0.00	0.00–0.18*	≥0.26[†]	Negative	Extremely distorted thinking

Note: *denotes that the listed range is based on –1.00 to +1.00 standard deviations from the normative mean including rounding for ease of interpretation. [†]denotes that the listed range is determined by Comprehensive System interpretation guidelines. [††]denotes that the listed range is determined by percentage base rate in the norm reference sample due to that variable's skewed distribution.

[a]When the first row variable is X–% < 0.70, and hence negative, both remaining variables must yield positive results to indicate an invalid response pattern.

[b]X–% ≥ 0.70 indicates such gross psychological impairment that testing would have been precluded; therefore the entire Rorschach protocol is deemed per se invalid irrespective of the remaining variables.

There was insufficient evidence of exaggeration of symptoms or malingering. In this regard, the clinical variables were deemed valid.

There was remarkable evidence of exaggeration of symptoms or malingering. Therefore, the clinical variables were deemed invalid. The remaining scores were neither interpreted nor reported.

TABLE 4 ■ CLINICAL VARIABLES: PSYCHOTIC DISORDERS

Variable	Score	Expected range	Positive result range	Result	Meaning of positive result
WSum6	00	0–18**	≥19[†σ]	Negative	Ideational or cognitive slippage; formal thought disorder
Level 2	00	0[††]	≥1[††]	Positive	Manifestly bizarre responses
PTI	0	0–2[††]	3–5[††]	Negative	Psychotic index; psychotic disorder
XA+%	0.00	0.74–1.00**	≤0.73[†σ]	Negative	Disturbed mediation or reality testing
WDA+%	0.00	0.79–1.00**	≤0.78[†σ]	Negative	Pervasively disturbed mediation or reality testing
X–%	0.00	0.00–0.25**	≥0.26[†σ]	Positive	Extremely distorted thinking

Note: PTI, Perceptual Thinking Index. **denotes that the listed range is based on –2.00 to +2.00 standard deviations from the normative mean including rounding for ease of interpretation. [†]denotes that the listed range is determined by Comprehensive System interpretation guidelines. [††]denotes that the listed range is determined by percentage base rate in the norm reference sample due to that variable's skewed distribution. [σ]denotes that the listed positive result range is based on the deviation principle.

The psychotic disorders variables _____.

(*Cont.*)

FORM 14.2

COMPETENCY EXAMINATION REPORT TEMPLATE (*Cont.*)

TABLE 5 ■ **CLINICAL VARIABLES: WSUM6 THOUGHT DISORDER SCORES**[a]

Variable	Level 1 score[b]	Level 2 score[c]	Meaning of variable presence
Deviant Verbalization (DV)	00	00	Neologisms; odd redundancies
Deviant Response (DR)	00	00	Inappropriate or irrelevant phrases; circumstantial (fluid or rambling) responses
Incongruous Combination (INCOM)	00	00	Implausible or impossible integration of elements within a single object
Fabulized Combination (FABCOM)	00	00	Implausible or impossible relationship between objects
Contamination (CONTAM)[d]	--	00	Fusion of impressions into a single object that clearly violates reality
Inappropriate Logic (ALOG)[d]	--	00	Loose and simplistic reasoning that leads to flawed judgment

Note: -- denotes score type not available.

[a]This table is reported only upon a positive WSum6 result for purposes of further scrutinizing the examinee's disordered thought process.

[b]Modest instances of illogical, fluid, peculiar, or circumstantial thinking.

[c]Severe instances of illogical, fluid, peculiar, or circumstantial thinking.

[d]Contamination and inappropriate logic responses are always considered Level 2 scores.

The specific thought disorder scores _____.

D. Legal System Questionnaire (LSQ):

This questionnaire is in short answer written format and examines the defendant's knowledge regarding (a) the manner in which fundamental components of the criminal legal system are intended to work so as render fair and impartial decisions, and (b) the specifics in the above-listed cause(s) of action (e.g., the defense attorney's identity, criminal charges, potential penalties). The open-ended response format also allows supplementary analysis of the defendant's thought process and content.

Mr. _____ responses indicated _____.

E. Current *DSM-IV-TR* Diagnoses:

Axis I: 000.00
Axis II: 799.9 Diagnosis Deferred Regarding Personality Disorders
Axis III: No Contributory Medical Problems Noted
Axis IV: Psychosocial Stressors: Legal System Intervention
Axis V: GAF: 70 Mild symptoms

American Psychiatric Association. (2000). *Diagnostic and statistical manual of mental disorders* (4th ed., text rev.) (*DSM-IV-TR*). Washington, DC: Author

V. **Opinion Regarding the Competency Issue:**

A. Statutory Criteria:

Competency. Whether or not the defendant can understand the proceedings and assist in the preparation of his or her defense. State Statute § __-__ -_-_(__) (_____)

B. Analysis of Facts as Applied to Statutory Criteria:

C. **Opinion:**

Mr. _____ is currently **NOT COMPETENT to stand trial in the above-listed cause(s).**

Psychologist Name, PhD, PsyD, HSPP
Psychologist – State License #_____

FORM 14.3

CASE 7: COMPETENCY EXAMINATION REPORT

COMMUNITY MENTAL HEALTH CENTER

Outpatient Department

COMPETENCY EXAMINATION

Defendant Name: Bass, Todd
Examination Date: March 15, 2011

Office File Number: 777777
Legal Case Title: State of Indiana vs. Todd Bass
Cause Number: 77D77–7777-FB-7777

Judge: Jill Dedrick
Court: County Superior Court

Examiner: John M. Spores, PhD, JD, HSPP
Psychologist – Indiana #20040638A
Attorney at Law – Indiana #21404–64

Note. Mr. Bass was initially informed that all data gathered during the course of this evaluation would be released to the above listed Court pursuant to court order, and subsequently to the attorneys of record in the above listed cause. He acknowledged that he understood and verbally consented.

I. **Identifying Information:**
Mr. Bass's age is 34 years 2 months. Gender is male. DOB: 01/11/1977.

II. **Presenting Legal Issue(s):**
A. Criminal Charges:
Mr. Bass is being charged with criminal possession of a controlled substance. He attempted to sell prescription medication to an undercover police officer.

B. Court Order:
Judge Dedrick ordered that Mr. Bass be examined to determine his competency to stand trial. Ind. Code § 35–36–3–1(a) (2004). Order Appointing Psychiatrist and Psychologist (February 24, 2011).

III. **Assessment and Test Battery:**
A. Clinical Diagnostic Interview (03/15/2011)
B. Mental Status Examination Including the Mini-Mental State Examination, Second Edition, Extended Version, Blue Form (MMSE–2–EV–BF) (03/15/2011)
C. Rorschach Inkblot Test, Comprehensive System, RIAP, Fifth Edition, Ages 18 to 86 (Rorschach–CS, Ages 18 to 86) (03/15/2011)
D. Legal System Questionnaire (LSQ) (03/15/2011)

(Cont.)

FORM 14.3

CASE 7: COMPETENCY EXAMINATION REPORT (*Cont.*)

IV. **Assessment and Test Results:**

A. Clinical Diagnostic Interview:

Note. All information in this section was based on statements made by the defendant in response to interview questions, or by available archival records and reports.

1. Presenting Symptoms:

Mr. Bass complained of auditory disturbances in the form of hearing voices conversing with him, racing thoughts, restlessness, anxiety, and depressed mood. Onset was estimated to be in early childhood with episodes of acute exacerbation during adulthood.

2. Family Psychiatric History:

There is a positive family psychiatric history of Schizophrenia and Bipolar Disorder.

3. Social History:

Mr. Bass's interpersonal relationships have been erratic and unstable.

4. Educational History:

Mr. Bass has an 11th grade education. Academic performance was variable.

5. Vocational History:

Work history is erratic and unstable. He has largely worked in manual labor jobs. His longest employment is nine months.

6. Substance Abuse History:

Substance abuse is positive for Cannabis Dependence for the past 8 years prior to incarceration. He has been abstinent since his incarceration in or about January 2011.

7. Psychiatric/Medical History:

Mr. Bass has a long history of both inpatient and outpatient psychiatric treatment. His current medications while incarcerated are Risperdal (oral and by injection) and Allegra.

8. Legal History Prior to Current Charges:

Denied.

(*Cont.*)

FORM 14.3

CASE 7: COMPETENCY EXAMINATION REPORT (*Cont.*)

B. Mental Status Examination including the Mini-Mental State Examination, Second Edition, Extended Version, Blue Form (MMSE–2–EV–BF):

Affect was labile. Mood was mixed euthymic and dysphoric. Thought process was alogical, tangential, and at times incoherent. Speech was pressured and rapid. He was agitated and restless. Thought content was delusional, believing for example that he "kissed the stars." The MMSE–2–EV–BF results were as follows:

TABLE 1 ■ **MMSE–2–EV–BF RESULTS**

Cognitive function	Patient's raw score	Maximum possible raw score
Registration	3	3
Orientation to Time	3	5
Orientation to Place	5	5
Recall	1	3
Attention and Calculation	3	5
Naming	2	2
Repetition	1	1
Comprehension	3	3
Reading	1	1
Writing	0	1
Drawing	0	1
Story Memory	3	25
Processing Speed	16	35
Total Raw Score[a]	**41**	**90**

Note: Lower raw scores indicate greater cognitive dysfunction. Overall cognitive function data are in boldface.

[a]Raw scores of 50 or less indicate the presence of cognitive impairment.

Screening Result: Positive for cognitive impairment.

Immediate, intermediate, and long-term memory functions were impaired. Although he was oriented to person and place, he was disoriented to time. Estimated intellectual function based on verbal skills, fund of general knowledge, and reasoning abilities is low average. Psychotic symptoms were evident in the form of bizarre mentation and auditory hallucinations. There was evidence of suicidal thoughts, although without immediate intent or plan.

C. Rorschach Inkblot Test, Comprehensive System, RIAP, Fifth Edition, Ages 18 to 86 (Rorschach–CS, Ages 18 to 86):

TABLE 2 ■ **TEST VALIDITY: SITUATIONAL GUARDEDNESS**

Variable	Score	Expected range	Positive result range	Result[a]	Meaning of positive result
R	15	18–29*	≤13[†]	Negative	Excessively nonproductive; defensive

Note: *denotes that the listed range is based on −1.00 to +1.00 standard deviations from the normative mean including rounding for ease of interpretation. [†]denotes that the listed range is determined by Comprehensive System interpretation guidelines.

[a]When R < 14, the entire Rorschach protocol is per se invalid; there is insufficient test data for meaningful interpretation.

There was no evidence of situational guardedness. In this regard, the clinical variables were deemed valid.

(Cont.)

FORM 14.3

CASE 7: COMPETENCY EXAMINATION REPORT (*Cont.*)

TABLE 3 ■ TEST VALIDITY: SYMPTOM EXAGGERATION

Variable	Score	Expected range	Positive result range	Result[a]	Meaning of positive result
X–%[b]	0.20	0.00–0.18*	≥0.70[†]	Negative	Exaggerating or malingering symptoms
XA+%	0.73	0.80–0.95*	≥0.75[††]	Negative	Indications of adequate reality testing
X–%	0.20	0.00–0.18*	≥0.26[†]	Negative	Extremely distorted thinking

Note: *denotes that the listed range is based on –1.00 to +1.00 standard deviations from the normative mean including rounding for ease of interpretation. [†]denotes that the listed range is determined by Comprehensive System interpretation guidelines. [††]denotes that the listed range is determined by percentage base rate in the norm reference sample due to that variable's skewed distribution.

[a]When the first row variable is X–% < 0.70, and hence negative, both remaining variables must yield positive results to indicate an invalid response pattern.

[b]X–% ≥ 0.70 indicates such gross psychological impairment that testing would have been precluded; therefore the entire Rorschach protocol is deemed per se invalid irrespective of the remaining variables.

There was no evidence of exaggeration of symptoms or malingering. In this regard, the clinical variables were deemed valid.

TABLE 4 ■ CLINICAL VARIABLES: PSYCHOTIC DISORDERS

Variable	Score	Expected range	Positive result range	Result	Meaning of positive result
WSum6	96	0–18**	≥19[†σ]	Positive	Ideational or cognitive slippage; formal thought disorder
Level 2	7	0[††]	≥1[††]	Positive	Manifestly bizarre responses
PTI	4	0–1[††]	3–5[††]	Positive	Psychotic index; psychotic disorder
XA+%	0.73	0.74–1.00**	≤0.73[†σ]	Positive	Disturbed mediation or reality testing
WDA+%	0.79	0.79–1.00**	≤0.78[†σ]	Negative	Pervasively disturbed mediation or reality testing
X–%	0.20	0.00–0.25**	≥0.26[†σ]	Negative	Extremely distorted thinking

Note: PTI, Perceptual Thinking Index. **denotes that the listed range is based on –2.00 to +2.00 standard deviations from the normative mean including rounding for ease of interpretation. [†]denotes that the listed range is determined by Comprehensive System interpretation guidelines. [††]denotes that the listed range is determined by percentage base rate in the norm-reference sample due to that variable's skewed distribution. [σ]denotes that the listed positive result range is based on the deviation principle.

The majority of Psychotic Disorders variables were positive. This is empirical evidence of psychosis.

(*Cont.*)

FORM 14.3

CASE 7: COMPETENCY EXAMINATION REPORT (*Cont.*)

TABLE 5 ■ **CLINICAL VARIABLES: WSUM6 THOUGHT DISORDER SCORES[a]**

Variable	Level 1 score[b]	Level 2 score[c]	Meaning of variable presence
Deviant Verbalization (DV)	0	0	Neologisms; odd redundancies
Deviant Response (DR)	3	5	Inappropriate or irrelevant phrases; circumstantial (fluid or rambling) responses
Incongruous Combination (INCOM)	0	0	Implausible or impossible integration of elements within a single object
Fabulized Combination (FABCOM)	0	4	Implausible or impossible relationship between objects
Contamination (CONTAM)[d]	--	4	Fusion of impressions into a single object that clearly violates reality
Inappropriate Logic (ALOG)[d]	--	3	Loose and simplistic reasoning that leads to flawed judgment

[a]This table is reported only upon a positive WSum6 result for purposes of further scrutinizing the examinee's disordered thought process.

[b]Modest instances of illogical, fluid, peculiar, or circumstantial thinking.

[c]Severe instances of illogical, fluid, peculiar, or circumstantial thinking.

[d]Contamination and inappropriate logic responses are always considered Level 2 scores.

The specific thought disorder scores showed clear evidence of formal thought disorder and severely disturbed reality testing.

D. Legal System Questionnaire (LSQ):

This questionnaire is in short answer written format and examines the defendant's knowledge regarding (a) the manner in which fundamental components of the criminal legal system are *intended* to work so as render fair and impartial decisions, and (b) the specifics in the above-listed cause(s) of action (e.g., the defense attorney's identity, criminal charges, potential penalties). The open-ended response format also allows supplementary analysis of the defendant's thought process and content.

Mr. Bass's written responses largely showed additional evidence of incoherence, which impaired his ability to demonstrate an adequate understanding of the legal system on this questionnaire. Responses were also concrete, brief, simplistic, and in many cases did not address the legal questions posed.

E. Current *DSM-IV-TR* Diagnoses:
   Axis I: 298.9 Psychotic Disorder NOS, Provisional, rule out Schizophrenia, Bipolar Disorder With Psychosis, Schizoaffective Disorder, Bipolar Type
            304.30 Cannabis Dependence, Early Full Remission Within a Controlled Environment
   Axis II: 799.9 Diagnosis Deferred Regarding Personality Disorders
   Axis III: No Contributory Medical Problems Noted
   Axis IV: Psychosocial Stressors: Legal System Intervention
   Axis V: GAF: 35 Impaired reality testing

American Psychiatric Association. (2000). *Diagnostic and statistical manual of mental disorders* (4th ed., text rev.) (*DSM-IV-TR*). Washington, DC: Author.

(Cont.)

FORM 14.3

CASE 7: COMPETENCY EXAMINATION REPORT (*Cont.*)

V. **Opinion Regarding the Competency Issue:**

A. Statutory Criteria:

Competency. ... whether the defendant has the ability to understand the proceedings and assist in the preparation of the defendant's defense ... Ind. Code § 35–36-3–1(b) (2004).

B. Analysis of Facts as Applied to Statutory Criteria:

Mr. Bass manifested clear and consistent evidence of acute psychosis, which was also associated with remarkable cognitive impairment. These symptoms are deemed to be interfering with Mr. Bass's ability to demonstrate an adequate understanding of the legal system, and will impair his ability to assist his attorney in his defense.

C. **Opinion:**

Mr. Bass is currently NOT COMPETENT to stand trial in the above-listed cause.

John M. Spores, PhD, JD, HSPP
Psychologist – Indiana #20040638A
Attorney at Law – Indiana #21404–64

Appendix A: Test Publishers and Distributors

Multi-Health Systems, Inc. (MHS), P.O. Box 950, North Tonawanda, NY, 14120-0950. Phone: 1-800456-3003. Fax: 1-888-540-4484. Available at www.mhs.com

PRO–ED, Inc., 8700 Shoal Creek Boulevard, Austin, TX, 78757-6897. Phone: 1-800-897-3202. Fax: 1-800-397-7633. Available at www.proedinc.com

Psychological Assessment Resources, Inc. (PAR, Inc.), 16201 North Florida Avenue, Lutz, FL, 33549-8119. Phone: 1-800-331-8378. Fax: 1-800-727-9329. Available at www.parinc.com

Psychological Corporation (PsychCorp), Pearson, 19500 Bulverde Road, San Antonio, TX, 78259-370. Phone: 1-800-627-7271. Fax: 1-800-232-1223. Available at www.pearsonassessments.com

Western Psychological Services (WPS), 625 Alaska Avenue, Torrance, CA, 90503-5124. Phone: 1-800-648-8857. Fax: 1-424-201-6950. Available at www.wpspublish.com

Glossary

ability–achievement discrepancy analysis. Statistically comparing measured intellectual competence with measured achievement, most frequently for diagnosing Learning Disorders. The simple difference method accomplishes this by subtracting the selected intelligence test composite score from each actual or obtained achievement standard score. The predicted difference method accomplishes this by subtracting each achievement standard score predicted by the selected intelligence test composite score from the actual or obtained achievement standard score. See also *Learning Disorder.*

ability–memory discrepancy analysis. Statistically comparing measured intellectual competence with measured memory ability, most frequently for diagnosing Dementia or Amnestic Disorder. The simple difference method accomplishes this by subtracting the selected intelligence test composite score from each actual or obtained memory standard score. The predicted difference method accomplishes this by subtracting each memory ability standard score predicted by the selected intelligence test composite score from the actual or obtained memory ability standard score. See also *Amnestic Disorder and Dementia.*

achievement. The degree of previous learning or accomplishment in various types of subject matter or specific academic areas. Standardized psychological tests of achievement typically measure mastery within fundamental academic subjects, including oral language, reading, writing, and mathematics.

achievement view of intelligence. Degree of educational attainment.

actus reus. In criminal law, the act or omission to act when there exists a duty; that is, voluntary conduct.

adaptive behavior. The execution of daily activities which are required for self-sufficiency or autonomous functioning consists of the following three domains: (a) conceptual (e.g., language, reading, number concepts); (b) practical (e.g., daily living skills, occupational skills); and (c) social (e.g., interpersonal relationships, responsibility, conforming to rules and laws).

affirmative defense. Newly introduced facts or explanations that can justify or excuse a criminal charge. That is, a criminal charge can be defeated even if the facts supporting such charge are accurate and true. An infamous affirmative defense includes the insanity plea.

age equivalent. Score that is based on the age that the average person earns a given score within the norm-reference sample. Although easily understood by laypeople, age equivalents can be misleading due to their representing unequal units (i.e., ordinal data). See also *ordinal data.*

agnosia. Failure to interpret objects accurately despite normal sensory function. A symptom of Dementia. See also *Dementia.*

ambiguous stimulus. Test stimuli which can be interpreted in more than one way. All test stimuli may potentially possess some degree of ambiguity.

Amnestic Disorder. *DSM-IV-TR* Axis I Cognitive Disorder, which includes memory impairment caused by disease, drugs, or toxins.

Anxiety Disorders. *DSM-IV-TR* Axis I disorders generally involving negative affect and apprehension regarding anticipated future danger.

aphasia. Language impairment caused by brain damage or dysfunction. A symptom of Dementia. See also *Dementia*.

apraxia. Motor disability in the presence of intact motor function. A symptom of Dementia. See also *Dementia*.

area transformations. Raw score conversions which tend to be easier to comprehend for laypeople, although which exaggerate deviation changes near the mean and minimize such changes in the extremes; for example, percentile ranks (PR). See also *percentile rank*.

Asperger's Disorder. *DSM-IV-TR* Pervasive Developmental Disorder, which includes repetitive behaviors and a severe and widespread inability to bond effectively with people. In contrast to Autistic Disorder, communication and cognitive functioning are intact. It is referred to as a spectrum disorder in the sense that it manifests in degrees of severity. See also *Autistic Disorder* and *Pervasive Developmental Disorder*.

Attention-Deficit/Hyperactivity Disorder (ADHD). *DSM-IV-TR* Disruptive Behavior Disorder involving fidgeting, restlessness, acting without thinking, distractibility, and poor concentration. Onset of at least some of these symptoms must be present prior to the age of 7 years. It has been associated with neuropsychological brain dysfunction within the prefrontal cortex.

Autistic Disorder. *DSM-IV-TR* Pervasive Developmental Disorder, which includes repetitive behaviors, and a severe and widespread inability to bond and communicate with people. It is referred to as a spectrum disorder in the sense that it manifests in degrees of severity.

base rate. Percentage of a test's norm-reference sample who obtained a particular standard score or result.

Base Rate standard score (*BR-score*). Standard test score on the Millon self-report clinical and personality inventories, which accounts for the varying estimated prevalence of differing symptoms, disorders, and traits, and are considered to be nonparametric nominal/ordinal data. On the Millon diagnostic scales, *BR*-scores are most accurately interpreted using the following two-step process: (a) nominal interpretation that a particular disorder is either *prominent* (*BR* = 85–115), *present* (*BR* = 75–84), or *absent* (*BR* = 0–74); and (b) ordinal interpretation of the relative severity or nonseverity of a disorder (i.e., reference to the specific *BR*-score value). Compare to *T-score*.

Bennet's (1988) model of brain–behavior relationships. Proposed sequence of neuropsychological processing in the brain which corresponds with many of the fundamental abilities measured by current neuropsychological test batteries. In successive order of brain processing, they include (a) sensory input, (b) attention and concentration, (c) memory and learning, (d) language and sequential processing (i.e., left hemisphere functions) occurring contemporaneously with spatial processing and manipulatory ability (i.e., right hemisphere functions), (e) executive functioning (i.e., logical analysis, concept formation, reasoning, planning, flexibility of thinking), and (f) motor output.

biosocial evolutionary model of personality. Posits that human personality is comprised of learned strategies to (a) secure reinforcement and (b) minimize punishment. This is accomplished through the following three polarities: (a) self–other (i.e., independent–ambivalent–dependent), (b) active–passive (i.e., initiate–accommodate), and (c) pleasure–pain (i.e., positive–negative reaction from others). Various types of Personality Disorders represent differing qualitative combinations of rigid, inflexible, and maladaptive positions on these polarities. In such model, Axis I Clinical Disorders are considered as extensions of the Axis II Personality Disorders. See also *Clinical Disorder and Personality Disorder.*

Bipolar Disorder in children and young adolescents. Symptoms more commonly manifest as a mixed episode including depression, irritability, and temper tantrums (versus euphoria), and cycling is significantly more rapid and continual.

Borderline Intellectual Functioning. *DSM-IV-TR* Axis II V Code defined as an IQ score of about 71 to 79 (*M* = 100, *SD* = 15).

Borderline Personality Disorder. *DSM-IV-TR* Axis II disorder involving extreme fear of abandonment, unstable and intense relationships, extreme vacillations between idealizing and devaluing others, unstable self-image, internal emptiness, mood instability, self-mutilation to relieve emotional distress, recurrent suicidal behavior, severe dissociation, and potential transient or brief psychotic episodes.

Character Disorder. See **Personality Disorder.**

Clinical Disorder. A clustering or covariance of psychological symptoms which cause dysfunction, and typically exhibit the following characteristics: (a) identifiable onset, (b) acute presentation, (c) precipitant of intervention, and (d) amenability to treatment. In the *DSM-IV-TR* multiaxial diagnostic scheme, these are noted on Axis I. See also *prototypical classification.*

clinical method. Method of psychological assessment in which the clinician typically employs a semistructured interview so as to gather detailed information regarding a patient's presenting symptoms, current mental status, and developmental history. The clinician essentially relies on experience and expert judgment in arriving at diagnostic impressions and treatment recommendations. It is most effectively used when integrated with the statistical method. See also *statistical method.*

code-type interpretation approach. On the MMPI–A and MMPI–2, interpreting the presence of various kinds of psychopathology based upon the particular basic Cinical scale profile or standard score configuration. The various code types were developed through a statistical technique called empirical criterion keying in which items are selected which best discriminate among various psychological symptoms and traits regardless of item content. Empirical criterion keying led to excessive item overlap among the basic Clinical scales and paradoxically reduced diagnostic discriminability.

Cognitive Disorders. *DSM-IV-TR* general class of Axis I disorders involving the following as their predominant symptoms: severe impairments in memory, attention, perception, thinking, and reasoning. They include Dementia, Delirium, and Amnestic Disorder. See also *Dementia, Delirium,* and *Amnestic Disorder.*

cognitive unconscious. Contemporary definition of the unconscious in which it is assumed that (a) we may not be aware of information because it is at that particular moment simply not contained within our conscious working memory, (b) unconscious content is fundamentally the same as conscious content, and (c) knowledge and emotional memories can be encoded and stored without our explicit awareness and possess the capability of influencing behavior. Examples include classically conditioned reflexes and emotional reactions which are stored subcortically. Compare with *motivated unconscious.*

Cohen's *d.* Standardized measure of effect size in which an obtained difference is measured in standard deviation units. Effect size score ranges are interpreted as follows: 0.0 to 0.2 (small effect), 0.30 to 0.70 (medium effect), 0.80 and higher (large effect). See also *effect size.*

common law. Judge-made law. Compare with *statutory law.*

comorbidity. The coexistence of two or more psychological disorders in the same case. Remarkable symptom overlap among the *DSM-IV-TR* diagnostic categories is considered one contributor, especially regarding the Axis II Personality Disorders.

Competency Screening Test (CST). Twenty-two-item brief sentence completion test designed to examine defendants' knowledge of the legal system. Total scores below 20 suggest deficient understanding and the need for more comprehensive evaluation.

competency to stand trial. Defendants must be competent in order to stand trial for alleged offenses as set out by substantive criminal laws. To meet the legal standard of competency, defendants must be able to (a) understand the legal proceedings against them and (b) assist in their own defense (*Dusky v. United States*, 1960).

conorming. Two tests employing the same standardization sample for the purpose of performing statistical comparisons; for example, ability–achievement discrepancy analyses.

confidence index assessment. Measures the degree of fit with the classification indicated by a discriminant function analysis (DA). See also *discriminant function analysis (DA).*

confidence interval. The range within which an examinee's true or actual score is estimated to fall. Confidence intervals account for and acknowledge the error rate of standardized tests. It has been argued that when reporting the results of test scores, 90% confidence intervals provide the most ideal balance between precision and certainty.

Conners' Adult ADHD Rating Scales, Long Version (CAARS–L). ADHD symptom rating scale including both Self-Report and Observer Forms normed on individuals ranging in age from 18 years 0 months to 50 years and older.

Conners Comprehensive Behavior Rating Scales (Conners CBRS). Standardized symptom rating scale including parent ratings and teacher ratings normed on individuals ranging in age from 6 years 0 months to 18 years 11 months, and self-report ratings normed on individuals aged 8 years 0 months to 18 years 11 months. It consists of Validity and Clinical scales which assist in *DSM-IV-TR* Axis I differential diagnosis. In addition to standardized *T*-scores, it includes *DSM* symptom count data to supplement diagnosis.

Conners' Continuous Performance Test, Second Edition, Version 5 (CPT–II). CPT test normed on individuals aged 6 years 0 months to 55 years 0 months and older. Examinees are to continuously respond, or to not respond, by computer mouse click (or key board space bar press) to random presentations of target and nontarget stimuli, respectively. Its principal clinical use is in determining the likelihood that an individual manifests a disorder of attention.

Conners Early Childhood (Conners EC). Standardized symptom rating scale normed on young children aged 2 years 0 months to 5 years 11 months. It includes two forms based upon the type of observer respondent, including parent ratings and teacher/childcare ratings. It consists of Validity scales, Behavior and Global Index scales, and Developmental Milestones scales, all of which assist in psychodiagnosis.

Conners' Kiddie Continuous Performance Test, Version 5 (K–CPT). CPT test normed on individuals aged 4 years 0 months to 5 years 11 months. Examinees are to continuously respond, or to not respond, by computer mouse click (or key board space bar press) to random presentations of target and nontarget stimuli, respectively. Its principal clinical use is in determining the likelihood that an individual manifests a disorder of attention.

construct. Rational abstract idea used to organize, interpret, and explain observed facts. Many psychological symptoms (e.g., anxiety) represent psychological constructs that must be logically inferred from historical behavior and subjective experience, thus rendering them difficult for patients to describe and report during the course of a diagnostic interview.

construct validity. Extent to which an instrument measures a particular psychological variable as theoretically defined.

criminal law. Area of the law primarily designed to prevent harm to society. It is further subdivided into substantive criminal law and procedural criminal law. See also *substantive criminal law* and *procedural criminal law.*

declarative episodic memory. The ability to consciously learn and remember novel information that is bound by the testing situation.

deductive reasoning. Reasoning from general to specific. The recommended approach to analyzing and reporting standardized test data.

Delirium. *DSM-IV-TR* Cognitive Disorder which includes mental confusion, clouded consciousness, disorientation, and agitation. It manifests a distinctive rapid onset. See also *Cognitive Disorders.*

Dementia. *DSM-IV-TR* Cognitive Disorder which includes the essential symptom of memory impairment, along with a minimum of one or more of the following: (a) language dysfunction, (b) motor disability in the presence of intact motor function, (c) failure to interpret objects accurately despite normal sensory function, and (d) impaired executive functioning. See also *agnosia, aphasia, apraxia, Cognitive Disorders,* and *executive functioning.*

demographically corrected norms. Compare an examinee's performance to normal individuals of the same age, sex, and education. Compare with *U.S. census-matched norms.*

Developmental Milestones scales. Observer-report ratings that assist in identifying areas of delay associated with Axis I psychopathology. See also Clinical Disorder.

differentials. The absolute frequency of occurrence of discrepant ratings on similar items. An indication of inconsistent responding.

dimensional approach. Approach to psychological diagnosis which defines disorders in terms of degree versus kind or type. Compare with *prototypical (categorical) classification.*

discriminant function analysis (DA). Statistical procedure that predicts group membership on a Y outcome variable (e.g., nonclinical and clinical) from a combination of numerical scores on several X predictor variables. See also *confidence index assessment.*

Disruptive Behavior Disorders. *DSM-IV-TR* Axis I disorders generally involving acting out or externalizing behavior problems.

dissociation. Any alteration or disruption in normal consciousness.

effect size. Statistical measure of the magnitude of a result. As applied to psychological testing, the difference between two standard scores as a ratio of their shared standard deviation. For example, the magnitude of the difference between an examinee's Verbal Comprehension Index and Perceptual Reasoning Index can be quantitatively measured by taking the difference between these two scores and dividing by their common standard deviation. See also *Cohen's d.*

emotional handicap (EH). Academic classification indicating that a child is eligible for special education services due to a severe emotional or behavioral disorder.

emotional intelligence. See social–cognitive ability.

emotion regulation. The ability to control and manage one's own feelings.

empirical criterion keying. See *code-type interpretation approach.*

executive functioning. The ability to (a) engage in activities necessary for achieving objectives and (b) regulate one's actions based on environmental feedback.

experimentwise error rate. Inflated chance of committing a Type I error due to repeated statistical tests of significance. See also *Type I error.*

explicit measures. Psychological tests which ask respondents to directly report the presence of traits or symptoms with respect to themselves or other individuals. Although they tend to be more *DSM-IV-TR* correspondent, they are vulnerable to faking, lack of introspection, or any other eccentric test-taking response approach that can deleteriously affect test validity.

external validity. Generalizability of a test's results to real-world functioning.

Factitious Disorder. *DSM-IV-TR* disorder involving an intentional exaggeration of symptoms without an identifiable ulterior motive.

factor analysis. Statistical technique for identifying interitem correlations defined as factors. Generally considered a data-reduction technique. As applied to the most recently published Wechsler intelligence tests, they are referred to as *indices* as opposed to quotients.

false negative result. Test data indicating an absence of disorder when in fact such disorder is present.

false positive result. Test data indicating the presence of disorder when in fact such disorder is absent.

forensic psychology. The application of psychological science for the resolution of legal issues.

Gilliam Asperger's Disorder Scale (GADS). Observer–report standardized rating scale for Asperger's Disorder including a norm-referenced sample ranging in age from 3 years 0 months to 22 years 11 months with documented Asperger's Disorder. It includes an Asperger's Disorder Quotient and subscale scores which measure the severity of stereotyped behaviors, and impairments in pragmatic skills, social interaction, and social–cognitive abilities.

Gilliam Autism Rating Scale–Second Edition (GARS–2). Observer–report standardized rating scale for Autistic Disorder including a norm-referenced sample ranging in age from 3 years 0 months to 22 years 11 months with documented Autistic Disorder. It includes an Autistic Disorder Index and subscale scores which measure the severity of stereotyped behaviors, communication impairment, and social impairment.

Global Assessment of Functioning (GAF). Dimensional rating of a patient's overall psychological adjustment in the real-world based upon clinical assessment information and any available standardized test data. Such rating is made on *DSM-IV-TR* Axis V and ranges from 0 to 100. Commonly used ratings in clinical practice include 55 (moderate symptoms), 45 (serious symptoms), and 35 (impaired reality testing).

Health Service Provider in Psychology (HSPP). In some state jurisdictions, designation that indicates an autonomously functioning psychologist without the need of formal peer supervision.

hypothesis confirmation bias. The potential for clinicians to gather only that kind of assessment information which corroborates their suspected diagnoses. This has the greatest likelihood of occurring when clinician's rely exclusively on the clinical method of assessment and contributes to misdiagnoses. See also *clinical method*.

implicit measures. Psychological tests which measure psychological traits, mechanisms, and symptoms indirectly. Advantages over explicit self-report measures include (a) enhanced difficulty examinees have in intentionally feigning or biasing the results and (b) lack of reliance upon the ability of respondents to introspect and accurately report their feelings, beliefs, traits, and psychological symptoms. Compare to *explicit measures*.

Inconsistency Index. The sum of the discrepancies in ratings on comparable items. One type of Validity scale.

individual session. Psychotherapeutic interventions provided to a patient for purposes of treating one or more *DSM-IV-TR* disorders (billing code 90806). See also *therapeutic assessment*.

initial behavioral health evaluation. The first psychological assessment session in an individual or group practice that typically involves a comprehensive diagnostic interview (billing code 90801). During such assessment, detailed information is gleaned regarding a patient's presenting symptoms, mental status, and developmental history so as to arrive at initial diagnostic impressions and recommendations for either (a) follow-up psychological testing for purposes of diagnostic clarification or (b) treatment interventions. Insurance companies will typically limit such evaluations to one per 12-month period within the same individual or group practice.

intellectualization. Coping or defense mechanism involving the use of ideation in order to minimize the impact of emotions.

intelligence. The ability to learn from experience, acquire knowledge, and use resources effectively in adapting to new situations or solving problems (Ciccarelli & White, 2012; Wechsler, 1975). This definition espouses the aptitude view of intelligence; that is, the ability to learn. Also referred to as general factor *g* or IQ. See also *achievement view of intelligence*.

interval data. Measurement scale indicating equal intervals along consecutive values. Includes the properties of identity, magnitude, and distance of the abstract number system. It lacks an absolute zero. Compare with *nominal, ordinal,* and *ratio data*.

introspection. The ability to examine and report accurately one's own thoughts and feelings. Lack of such self-awareness impairs patients' ability to accurately report their psychological symptoms during a clinical interview and contributes to misdiagnoses.

learning. The ability to acquire new information.

Learning Disability (LD). Academic classification indicating that a child is eligible for special education services due to the equivalent of one or more *DSM-IV-TR* Learning Disorders. See also *Learning Disorders*.

Learning Disorders. *DSM-IV-TR* Axis I Code defined as a significant discrepancy between measured intelligence and achievement which causes dysfunction. Such diagnosis requires an ability–achievement discrepancy analysis from a psychological testing perspective. The specific Learning Disorders listed in the *DSM–IV–TR* include Reading Disorder, Mathematics Disorder, Disorder of Written Expression, and Learning Disorder NOS. See also *ability–achievement discrepancy analysis*.

Legal System Questionnaire (LSQ). Written questionnaire in short answer format designed to examine criminal defendants' knowledge in the following two areas: (a) the manner in which the basic facets of the criminal court system are intended to function and (b) vital information more particular to their case. It is designed to be used in competency to stand trial examinations.

linear transformations. Raw score to standard score conversions which preserve the position of scores in the distribution, although tends to be more difficult for laypeople to comprehend; for example, *Z*-scores (*M* = 0, *SD* = 1.00), and *T*-scores (*M* = 50, *SD* = 10). Such transformations are generally performed by adding, subtracting, multiplying, or dividing by a constant and are analogous to converting units of measurement (e.g., inches to feet).

Malingering. *DSM-IV-TR* disorder involving an intentional feigning of psychological symptoms for an ulterior motive. Many standardized psychological tests consist of validity scales designed to detect symptom exaggeration and potential malingering (e.g., the MMPI–2–RF).

medical necessity. The need for more accurate *DSM-IV-TR* diagnoses, which will ultimately lead to one or more of the following: (a) symptom alleviation, (b) improvement in overall functioning, (c) prevention of deterioration, and/or (d) restoration of an expected level of development in children. It is based upon the medical model of disorder and is a fundamental criterion employed by insurance companies in determining psychological test approval or authorization.

memory. The ability to retain and retrieve information.

mens rea. State of mind that accompanies an act or omission; that is, guilty mind.

Mental Retardation. *DSM-IV-TR* Axis II Code defined as an IQ score of about 70 and below (*M* = 100, *SD* = 15), deficits in adaptive behavior, and onset before the age of 18 years. It is anticipated that *Intellectual Disability* will supplant the label of Mental Retardation in the *DSM–V* due to remarkable negative connotation associated with the latter. See also *adaptive behavior*.

mental status examination. Observation of the manner in which a patient thinks, feels, and behaves during a clinical interview which helps determine if a psychological disorder is present. Typical areas of focus include: (a) affect; (b) mood; (c) thought process and content; (d) short- and long-term memory functioning; (e) sensorium; (f) estimated intellectual functioning based upon verbal skills and reasoning ability; (g) sensory–perceptual functioning; (h) suicidal thoughts, intentions, and plans; and (i) evidence of self-mutilation and self-harm. See also *sensorium*.

Millon Adolescent Clinical Inventory (MACI). Self-report clinical and personality inventory normed on adolescents aged 13 years 0 months to 19 years 11 months. It consists of (a) Validity scales and (b) primary diagnostic scales most germane to *DSM-IV-TR* Axis I and II disorders. It is based upon the biosocial evolutionary model of personality which is accordant with the *DSM-IV-TR* Personality Disorders. Several Validity scales include profile adjustments or response bias corrections for aberrant test-taking response styles so as to enhance test validity. See also *biosocial evolutionary model of personality* and *profile adjustments*.

Millon Clinical Multiaxial Inventory–III (MCMI–III). Self-report clinical and personality inventory normed on individuals ranging in age from 18 years 0 months to 88 years 11 months. It consists of (a) Validity scales and (b) primary diagnostic scales most germane to *DSM-IV-TR* Axis I and II disorders. Several Validity scales include statistical adjustments for aberrant test-taking response styles so as to enhance test validity. It is based upon the biosocial evolutionary model of personality which is accordant with the *DSM-IV-TR* Personality Disorders. See also *biosocial evolutionary model of personality*.

Millon Pre-Adolescent Clinical Inventory (M–PACI). Self-report clinical and personality inventory normed on preadolescents aged 9 years 0 months to 12 years 11 months. It consists of (a) Validity scales and (b) primary diagnostic scales most germane to *DSM-IV-TR* Axis I and II disorders. It is based upon the biosocial evolutionary model of personality which is accordant with the *DSM-IV-TR* Personality Disorders. See also *biosocial evolutionary model of personality*.

Minnesota Multiphasic Personality Inventory–Adolescent (MMPI–A). Self-report clinical and personality inventory normed on individuals aged 14 years 0 months to 18 years 11 months. It consists of 7 Validity scales, 10 Clinical scales, 15 Content scales, 31 Content Component Scales, 11 Supplementary scales, 28 Harris-Lingoes subscales, and various special indices. Its greatest diagnostic strengths are in diagnosing Psychotic Disorders and Mood Disorders With or Without Psychotic Features within this age group. See also *code-type interpretation approach*.

Minnesota Multiphasic Personality Inventory–2 (MMPI–2). Self-report clinical and personality inventory normed on individuals aged 18 years 0 months to 89 years 11 months. Compared to the MMPI–2–RF, it is significantly longer in length (i.e., 567 items) and suffers from excessive interscale item overlap; hence, reducing its ability to discriminate among various *DSM-IV-TR* diagnoses. See also *code-type interpretation approach*.

Minnesota Multiphasic Personality Inventory–2–Restructured Form (MMPI–2–RF). Self-report clinical and personality inventory normed on individuals aged 18 years 0 months to 89 years 11 months. It was developed through a multivariate factor reanalysis of MMPI–2 items using largely the same standardization sample. As compared to the MMPI–2, it is significantly shorter in length (i.e., 338 items), and possesses superior discriminant and convergent validity due to a significant reduction in scale intercorrelations. It includes the following impressive data yield: (a) 8 Validity scales; (b) 3 Higher-Order (i.e., broad-band) scales; (c) 9 Restructured Clinical (RC) scales; (d) 14 Somatic/Cognitive and Internalizing scales; (e) 11 Externalizing, Interpersonal, and Interest scales; and (f) 5 Personality Psychopathology Five (PSY–5) scales. Compare with *Minnesota Multiphasic Personality Inventory–2 (MMPI–2)*.

Mini-Mental State Examination, Second Edition (MMSE–2). Standardized measure of neurocognitive functioning used primarily to screen for *DSM-IV-TR* Cognitive Disorders (e.g., Dementia) or disorders involving neuropsychological dysfunction (e.g., ADHD) in adults (Folstein, Folstein, White, & Messer, 2010).

mirror neurons. Brain cells that permit our comprehension of others' thoughts and feelings by reacting to them as if they were our own.

Mood Disorders. *DSM-IV-TR* Axis I disorders primarily of emotion or feeling, including Depressive and Bipolar Disorders.

motivated unconscious. Psychoanalytic notion in which it is believed that threatening memories, motivations, and beliefs are repressed as a defense against anxiety. Compare with *cognitive unconscious*.

negative impression. Observer-report test-taking response style in which ratings are excessively severe, thus exaggerating the measured degree of psychological disorder. Considered a contributor to test invalidity. Compare with *positive impression*.

NEPSY–II. Standardized comprehensive neuropsychological test battery normed on children and adolescents from 3 years 0 months to 16 years 11 months. This test measures the following domains of neuropsychological functioning: (a) attention and executive functioning, (b) language, (c) memory and learning, (d) sensorimotor, (e) social perception, and (e) visuospatial processing.

neurocognitive functioning. See *neuropsychological functioning.*

Neuropsychological Assessment Battery (NAB). Comprehensive neuropsychological test battery normed on individuals aged 18 years through 97 years. It yields an overall measure of neuropsychological functioning which is contributed to by the following module indices: Attention, Language, Memory, Spatial, and Executive Functions. It also contains Daily Living Subtests (e.g., Bill Payment) so as to enhance external validity. See also *external validity.*

Neuropsychological Assessment Screening Battery (NASB). Abbreviated measure of an examinee's neuropsychological functioning in each of the NAB domains or modules. This measure provides empirical data so as to determine whether or not follow-up testing with the respective complete NAB modules are necessitated. See also *Neuropsychological Assessment Battery (NAB).*

neuropsychological testing. Typically refers to the use of a neuropsychological test battery which measures brain–behavior relationships and/or a standardized comprehensive measure of memory functioning for the primary purpose of diagnosing *DSM-IV-TR* Cognitive Disorders (previously known as organic mental disorders). Billing code 96118 is used for such specialized testing services. See also *Cognitive Disorders* and *psychological testing.*

neuropsychology. The study of brain–behavior relationships.

995 codes. Special *DSM-IV-TR* Axis I child maltreatment victim-focused codes.

nominal data. Measurement scale indicating type or category. Includes the property of identity from the abstract number system. Compare with *ordinal, interval,* and *ratio data.*

nonaxial format. Optional *DSM-IV-TR* diagnostic approach in which the five axes are dropped and all pertinent coexisting diagnoses are listed beginning with the principal disorder.

nonorganic mental disorders. A now antiquated term which referred to psychological disorders that were not caused primarily by brain damage, disease, or dysfunction.

observer–report data (O–data). Facts regarding an individual's personality or psychological symptoms provided by one or more third parties. Compare to *self-report data (S–data)* and *test data (T–data).*

ordinal data. Measurement scale indicating rank or order. Includes the properties of identity and magnitude from the abstract number system. It does not include the property of distance. Compare with *nominal, interval,* and *ratio data.*

percentile rank. The percentage of the norm-reference sample that falls at or below a particular score. Considered an area transformation. Percentile ranks are reported on some tests in lieu of standard scores when skewness or a restricted range is present within the score distribution. See also *area transformations.*

perceptual sets and expectancies. Automatic tendencies to perceive, interpret, and react to objects in certain ways based upon antecedent experiences and previously developed internalized beliefs.

Personality Disorder. Class of *DSM-IV-TR* Axis II disorders involving a continuing pattern of aberrant thinking, feeling, and behavior, which is inflexible and pervasive, thus manifesting both cross-situational and temporal consistency, and which causes dysfunction. These disorders originate in childhood, have an insidious onset, and continue on a chronic course through adulthood. Therefore, onset is difficult to pinpoint.

Pervasive Developmental Disorder (PDD). Class of *DSM-IV-TR* Axis I disorders first evident in early childhood which consist of varying combinations of severe and widespread disruptions in socialization, communication, and adaptive behavior. They include Autistic Disorder, Asperger's Disorder, and PDD NOS or Atypical Autistic Disorder. It has been associated with deficits in theory of mind and dysfunction in mirror neurons. See also *Asperger's Disorder, Autistic Disorder, mirror neurons,* and *theory of mind.*

positive impression. Observer-report test-taking response style in which ratings are excessively favorable, thus exaggerating the measured degree of psychological well adjustment. Considered a contributor to test invalidity. Compare with *negative impression.*

predicted difference method. See *ability–achievement discrepancy analysis* and *ability–memory discrepancy analysis.*

preponderance of the evidence. Burden of proof standard in a court trial defined as "… evidence that outweighs other evidence" (Mellinkoff, 1992, p. 498).

prevention focus. Test-taking response or motivational style in which one prefers to minimize incorrect responses. Compare to *promotion focus.*

procedural criminal law. Delineates all of the legal steps through which court proceedings must pass, beginning with the initial investigation through the termination of punishment. Competency to stand trial is a procedural pretrial issue. See *competency to stand trial.*

profile adjustments. Final statistical adjustments made for all or selected diagnostic scales on the MCMI–III and MACI, which may be distorted by various detectable aberrant response styles. The cardinal purpose of these statistical adjustments is to augment test validity and hence diagnostic accuracy.

prognosis. Any evidence-based prediction or forecast. An expected outcome of a psychological disorder based upon scientific evidence.

projective hypothesis. Proposition that the manner in which ambiguous stimuli are interpreted necessarily represents the examinee's unconscious needs, motives, and conflicts. See also *projective method or test* and *motivated unconscious.*

projective method or test. Test designed to measure the repressed contents of the motivated unconscious. Such test is predicated upon the projective hypothesis. See also *motivated unconscious* and *projective hypothesis.*

promotion focus. Test-taking response or motivational style in which one prefers to maximize correct responses. Compare with *prevention focus.*

prototypical (categorical) classification. Approach to classification in which each disorder is defined by essential symptoms, which are accompanied by nonessential variations. The *DSM-IV-TR* Clinical and Personality Disorders adopt this approach. Compare with *dimensional approach.*

provisional diagnoses. See *rule out diagnoses.*

psychological mechanisms. Refer to the underlying process of personality.

psychological testing. Typically refers to the use of intelligence tests, achievement tests, symptoms rating scales, self-report clinical and personality inventories, examiner-administered personality tests, and adaptive behavior tests for diagnosing noncognitive (previously known as nonorganic) *DSM-IV-TR* disorders. Billing code 96101 is used for such testing services. Compare with *neuropsychological testing*.

psychological traits. Average tendencies that define the manner in which people are both different and the same.

Psychotic Disorders. *DSM-IV-TR* Axis I disorders generally involving impairments in reality testing and formal thought disorder.

qualitative descriptions. Summary interpretive labels associated with various standard score ranges to facilitate test interpretation.

ratio data. Measurement scale indicating equal intervals along consecutive values and an absolute zero indicating an absence of the variable being measured. Includes the properties of identity, magnitude, distance, and true zero from the abstract number system. Compare with *nominal, ordinal,* and *interval data*.

response bias corrections. See *profile adjustments*.

Roberts–2. Implicit measure of social-cognitive ability as reflected in expressive language normed on individuals ranging in age from 6 years 0 months to 18 years 11months. The test stimuli consist of 16 stimulus cards of key intrapersonal and interpersonal scenes from which the examinee is asked to formulate a complete story. In addition to measuring a variety of social-cognitive abilities, it also consists of clinical scales which measure the presence of psychological disorders (e.g., illogical thinking).

Rorschach Inkblot Test, Comprehensive System (Rorschach–CS). Examiner administered standardized personality test normed on individuals ranging in age from 5 years 0 months to 86 years 0 months. It is an implicit measure that directly appraises (a) perceptual sets and expectancies and (b) social–cognitive abilities, both of which may be quantified and reliably associated with various psychological traits, emotional states, moods, beliefs, reality testing capability, thought process and content, and overall psychological adjustment.

rule out diagnoses. Those disorders which are suspected based upon the clinical method of assessment, which are in need of formal psychological testing so as to confirm their presence or absence. Same as *provisional* diagnoses.

self–report data (S–data). Facts regarding personality or psychological symptoms provided by the people themselves. Compare to *test data (T–data)* and *observer–report data (O–data)*.

semantic memory. The ability to retain and retrieve general knowledge, such as language and information learned through formal education.

sensorium. Orientation to time, place, and person.

simple difference method. See *ability–achievement discrepancy analysis* and *ability–memory discrepancy analysis*.

social–cognitive ability. The level or degree of mastery of knowledge germane to interpersonal situations.

social intelligence. See *social–cognitive ability*.

Somatoform Disorders. *DSM-IV-TR* Axis I disorders generally involving physical symptoms or complaints in the absence of medical disease or injury.

specifier. Extensions to various *DSM-IV-TR* diagnoses that clarify their onset, course, or severity, and/or that identify any unique features (e.g., Childhood Onset, Severe With Psychotic Features).

standard scores. Uniform scores derived by the linear transformation of raw scores with a predetermined mean and standard deviation. Examples include Z-scores ($M = 0$, $SD = 1.00$) and T-scores ($M = 50$, $SD = 10$). See also linear transformations and T-score.

stanine score. Standard score based upon a nine-point scale. One to three is considered below average, four to six is average, and seven to nine is above average. Stanines are uncommon and thus esoteric.

statistical method. Method of assessment which relies on standardized test data and actuarial statistics (i.e., principles of probability) in arriving at psychological diagnoses. It is used most effectively when integrated with the clinical method. See also *clinical method*.

statistically significant score differences. A determination that the difference between two standardized test scores would occur by chance less than five times ($p < .05$) or one time ($p < .01$) in 100, thus indicating a meaningful systematic difference.

statutory law. Law passed through the legislative process. Compare with *common law*.

substantive criminal law. Area of criminal law that defines which acts and mental states, together with any attendant circumstances or consequences, are necessary elements of various crimes. It also prescribes sentencing and the punishments to be imposed. See also *criminal law* and *procedural criminal law*.

test data (*T*–data). Directly measured individual differences in behavior or responses elicited by uniform or standardized test stimuli, administration instructions, procedures, and tasks. These measured behavioral or response differences in turn serve as reliable and valid indicators of various personality and psychological variables. Compare to *self-report data (S–data)* and *observer–report data (O–data)*.

theory of mind. The ability to understand that people possess internal mental states, including feelings, desires, beliefs, and intentions, which direct and explain their behavior.

therapeutic assessment. Technique in which communication of psychological test results are utilized in order to promote positive behavior change. Such technique integrates psychological test feedback with psychotherapeutic intervention and justifies the use of the 90806 individual billing code for providing such service. See also *individual session*.

T-score. Standard score with a mean of 50 and standard deviation of 10. Considered to represent an interval scale of measurement. Compare to *Base Rate standard score (BR-score)*. See also *interval data*.

Type I error. Concluding an effect is present when in fact it is not. It is determined by the probability or alpha (α) level chosen in a statistical test of significance. For example, if a probability level of less than 5 times in 100 is chosen (i.e., $p < .05$) to rule out chance as an explanation for a result and conclude a real effect, the Type I error rate is 5%.

U.S. census-matched norms. Compare an examinee's performance to key U.S. demographic characteristics including geographic region by age group, education, sex, and ethnicity. Compare with *demographically corrected norms*.

USB flash drive. A portable flash memory card that plugs into the USB port of a computer. It operates as an external hard drive and is ideal for saving initial psychological assessment reports and final psychological evaluation reports.

validity scales. Scales that assist in determining the veracity and accuracy of observer-report and self-report data.

vigilance. A measure of sustained attention within the context of a continuous performance test (CPT).

Vineland Adaptive Behavior Scales, Second Edition (Vineland–II). Adaptive behavior test which is normed on individuals 0 years 1 month to 90 years 11 months. It principally consists of the following three-domain structure: (a) Communication–Expressive, Receptive, Written; (b) Daily Living Skills–Personal, Domestic, Community; and (c) Socialization–Interpersonal Relationships, Play and Leisure Time, Coping Skills. A Motor Skills Domain is also available for individuals younger than 7 years of age.

Wechsler Adult Intelligence Scale, Fourth Edition (WAIS–IV). Standardized test of intelligence normed on individuals 16 years 0 months to 90 years 11 months. The following indices contribute to the Full Scale IQ score: Verbal Comprehension Index (VCI), Perceptual Reasoning Index (PRI), Working Memory Index (WMI), and Processing Speed Index (PSI).

Wechsler Individual Achievement Test, Third Edition (WIAT–III). Standardized test of achievement normed on individuals 4 years 0 months to 50 years 11 months and with an academic coverage from preschool (i.e., Prekindergarten) through Grade 12. The preschool total achievement score measures general proficiency in basic prekindergarten subjects, including oral language, early reading, alphabet writing, and math problem solving. The school age total achievement score measures the degree of knowledge and proficiency in basic academic subjects, including oral language, reading, written expression, and mathematics It is conormed on both the WAIS–IV and WISC–IV for purposes of ability-achievement discrepancy analyses.

Wechsler Intelligence Scale for Children, Fourth Edition (WISC–IV). Standardized test of intelligence normed on children ages 6 years 0 months to 16 years 11 months. The following indices contribute to the Full Scale IQ score: Verbal Comprehension Index (VCI), Perceptual Reasoning Index (PRI), Working Memory Index (WMI), and Processing Speed Index (PSI).

Wechsler Memory Scale, Fourth Edition (WMS–IV). Standardized comprehensive test of memory functioning normed on individuals ranging in age from 16 years 0 months to 90 years 11 months. It has two forms, Ages 16 to 69 and Ages 65 to 90, and provides index scores for the following general abilities: (a) Auditory Memory, (b) Visual Memory, (c) Visual Working Memory (Ages 16 to 69 only), (d) Immediate Memory, and (e) Delayed

Memory. It is conormed with the WAIS–IV for the purpose of conducting ability–memory discrepancy analyses. See also *conorming* and *ability–memory discrepancy analysis*.

Wechsler Preschool and Primary Scale of Intelligence, Third Edition (WPPSI–III). Standardized test of intelligence normed on children aged 2 years 6 months to 7 years 3 months. There exist two forms based upon the following age ranges: (a) 2 years 6 months to 3 years 11 months and (b) 4 years 0 months to 7 years 3 months. For the younger version, the Full Scale Intelligence Quotient (FSIQ) includes a Verbal Intelligence Quotient (VIQ) and Performance Intelligence Quotient (PIQ). For the older version, the FSIQ consists of a VIQ, PIQ, and Processing Speed Quotient (PSQ). Both forms also possess an optional General Language Composite (GLC).

working memory. Holding immediate memory traces, while executing cognitive tasks.

Name Index

Subject Index